USING INTERNATIONAL LAW IN CANADIAN COURTS

Using International Law in Canadian Courts

THIRD EDITION

Gib van Ert

UNIVERSITY OF TORONTO PRESS
Toronto Buffalo London

Irwin Law
An imprint of University of Toronto Press
Toronto Buffalo London
utorontopress.com
Printed and bound by CPI Group (UK) Ltd, Croydon, CR0 4YY

ISBN 978-1-4875-6666-1 (paper)
ISBN 978-1-4875-6668-5 (EPUB)
ISBN 978-1-4875-6667-8 (PDF)

Library and Archives Canada Cataloguing in Publication

Title: Using international law in Canadian courts / Gib van Ert.
Names: Van Ert, Gib, 1973– author
Description: Third edition. | Includes bibliographical references and index.
Identifiers: Canadiana (print) 20240494210 | Canadiana (ebook) 20240494261 | ISBN 9781487566661 (paper) | ISBN 9781487566685 (EPUB) | ISBN 9781487566678 (PDF)
Subjects: LCSH: International law – Canada. | LCSH: Jurisdiction (International law) | LCSH: Jurisdiction – Canada. | LCSH: Conflict of laws – Canada. | LCSH: Indigenous peoples – Legal status, laws, etc. – Canada.
Classification: LCC KE4252 .V35 2025 | DDC 341.0971–dc23

Cover design: Ashley Bernicky
Cover image: Alison Mitchell

We wish to acknowledge the land on which the University of Toronto Press operates. This land is the traditional territory of the Wendat, the Anishnaabeg, the Haudenosaunee, the Métis, and the Mississaugas of the Credit First Nation.

University of Toronto Press acknowledges the financial support of the Government of Canada, the Canada Council for the Arts, and the Ontario Arts Council, an agency of the Government of Ontario, for its publishing activities.

Canada Council for the Arts | Conseil des Arts du Canada

ONTARIO ARTS COUNCIL
CONSEIL DES ARTS DE L'ONTARIO
an Ontario government agency
un organisme du gouvernement de l'Ontario

Funded by the Government of Canada | Financé par le gouvernement du Canada
Canada

It is obvious that the life of every state is, under the swift transformations of these days, becoming deeply implicated *with* that of the others in a *de facto* society of nations. If in 1767 Lord Mansfield, as in *Heathfield v. Chilton* . . . could say, "The law of nations will be carried as far in England, as any where," in this country, in the 20th century, in the presence of the United Nations and the multiplicity of impacts with which technical developments have entwined the entire globe, we cannot say anything less.

Rand J in *Saint John v Fraser-Brace Overseas*, [1958] SCR 263 at 268–9

The author is strongly of the opinion that the common law of the British Commonwealth and the United States can and must in the future make greater contributions both to the content and to the practical application of international law.

Lord McNair, *The Law of Treaties* (1961)

It is an oversimplification to say that treaties are of no legal effect unless implemented by legislation.

Pigeon J (dissenting) in *Capital Cities Communications Inc v CRTC*, [1978] 2 SCR 141 at 188

What is more, I do not think that the free and democratic society that is Canada, any more than any other modern society, should today confine itself to parochial and nationalistic concepts of community. Canadians today form part of an emerging world community from which not only benefits but responsibilities flow.

La Forest J in *United States of America v Cotroni; United States of America v El Zein*, [1989] 1 SCR 1469 at 1486

[T]he strictly dualistic view of the relationship between international law and municipal law is becoming less serviceable and the old well defined boundaries between public international law . . . and municipal law are no longer boundaries but grey areas.

R.Y. Jennings, "The Judiciary, International and National, and the Development of International Law" (1996) *International & Comparative Law Quarterly* 1 at 4

Summary table of contents

Detailed table of contents

Note on abbreviations

Standard legal abbreviations are used throughout. In addition, the following abbreviations are used:

Charter	Canadian Charter of Rights and Freedoms, Part I of the Constitution Act, 1982, being Schedule B to the Canada Act 1982 (UK), 1982, c 11
Constitution Act, 1867	Constitution Act, 1867 (UK), 30 & 31 Vict, c 3, reprinted in RSC 1985, App II, No 5. Formerly the British North America Act 1867
Constitution Act, 1982	Constitution Act, 1982, being Schedule B to the Canada Act 1982 (UK), 1982, c 11

Foreword to the first edition

A review of Canadian case law shows that Canadian courts have, in the past, had little occasion to consider points of international law in their judgments. Perhaps for this reason, important concepts that are familiar to international lawyers – the differences between customary laws and conventions, the significance of *jus cogens*, and the role of evolving norms of international law (or "soft law"), to name a few examples – have not always received a sophisticated treatment in our jurisprudence. Yet an understanding of these matters is essential in determining how international norms are incorporated into, or rejected by, our legal system.

It is the thesis of this book that a lack of basic international legal understanding on the part of lawyers and judges is no longer permissible in the integrated world in which we live, and that we must educate ourselves better if we are to manage that integration process in the interests of Canadian society. It is a thesis to which I entirely and enthusiastically subscribe.

It is Canada's good fortune to enjoy a strong reputation on the international scene. As the only G8 country that was never a colonial power, the world perceives Canada to be an honest broker. As a leading member of both the Commonwealth and *la Francophonie*, Canada is looked to by smaller powers as a trusted intermediary. As a peacekeeper, Canada is relied upon by countries in need. As a democracy with a proven commitment to human rights, Canada is regarded as a model for developing legal systems.

Yet while we may justly pride ourselves on our international achievements, we must not ignore that international law is a two-way exchange. The steps we take to shape international affairs also shape us. Developments in international law play themselves out not only internationally, but also here at home. If Canada hopes to continue its prominence in international affairs, its domestic laws must keep faith with its international commitments. It is not enough for Canada, or any country, to sign a solemn treaty or make a grandiloquent declaration. It must carry through with these obligations at the executive, legislative, and judicial levels.

I first met the author in 1998, when he was a parliamentary intern and I was the Chair of the House of Commons Committee on Foreign Affairs and International Trade. He expressed an interest in writing a book on international law in Canada, and I encouraged him to do so. Since then I have often had members of the profession and judiciary remark upon the need for greater attention to this important field. I am delighted to see his very timely work come to fruition.

It goes without saying that this foreword is in no way intended to be an endorsement by myself or the Department of Foreign Affairs and International Trade of the ideas expressed in this book. I hope, however, that it will serve to encourage greater scholarly attention to an area of law that is of increasing importance to Canadians.

Hon. Bill Graham PC, QC, MP
Minister of Foreign Affairs and International Trade
Ottawa, August 2002

Preface to the third edition

The basic principles governing the application and non-application of public international law in the Canadian legal system have not changed in the 16 years since the second edition of this work was published. It would be surprising if they had, for those principles have governed the reception of international law in Westminster-model states such as Canada for longer than there has been a Canada to receive them. The structure of this book is therefore unchanged from the second edition.

Yet much of the book is new. Every chapter has been revised, and most have been considerably expanded. I have made these revisions with three goals.

My first goal was to bring the book up to date. Since the second edition appeared in 2008, the principles it described have been considered, affirmed, and applied by the Supreme Court of Canada in such cases as *Nemeth v Canada (Justice)*, 2010 SCC 56; *Kazemi Estate v Iran*, 2014 SCC 62; *Office of the Children's Lawyer v Balev*, 2018 SCC 16; *Canada (Minister of Citizenship and Immigration) v Vavilov*, 2019 SCC 65; *Nevsun Resources Ltd v Araya*, 2020 SCC 5; and *Quebec (Attorney General) v 9147-0732 Québec inc*, 2020 SCC 32. I have worked these authorities, and many more from the Supreme Court and lower courts across the country, into this new edition – sometimes simply slotting them in where they belong and sometimes rewriting whole sections to account for them.

My second goal has been to move the narrative somewhat away from its previous treatment of English authorities. In the first and second editions, I made a modest effort to address not only the English legal-historical origins of our reception rules but also their continued currency in modern UK law. In this edition I continue to offer an account of the English inheritance upon which Canadian reception law is built. But I make no attempt to describe the reception of public international legal norms in today's United Kingdom. I am not expert enough in the topic to venture into it. And in any case, Canadian reception law is no longer dependent upon UK attitudes and developments, as the Supreme Court of Canada's rejection of the act of state doctrine in *Nevsun* elegantly underscored.

Finally, I have sought in this edition to expand my consideration of topics only touched upon or, in a few cases, not addressed at all in the previous edition. There are new discussions of executive certificates; internationally informed objections to court jurisdiction; non-binding arrangements; statutory versions of the presumption of conformity with international law; the five main treaty implementation techniques; federal jurisdiction to implement Empire treaties; treaty implementation through Parliament's peace, order, and good government power; treaty de-implementation; and the reception of the United Nations Declaration on the Rights of Indigenous Peoples.

I have had help from many people in preparing this new edition. It has been in preparation for so long that I am sure I have forgotten people I should have remembered, and for that I apologize. But I wish to acknowledge the research assistance of Daniel Marin and Simon Domingue, the opportunity that Béatrice Maille and her colleagues at Global Affairs Canada gave me to discuss executive certificates with them in April 2019, the input of Professors Nigel Bankes and Robert Hamilton on my discussion of the UN Declaration on the Rights of Indigenous Peoples, the always helpful staff at the BC Courthouse Library, the attentive and cheerful assistance of Liam Andrews in finalizing the manuscript, the last-minute manuscript help from my talented colleague, Dahlia Shuhaibar, the excellent copy-editing of Leanne Rancourt, and the ongoing support of my publishers – initially Jeffrey Miller and Lesley Steeve at Irwin Law and now the team at University of Toronto Press: Sandra Shaw, Jennifer DiDomenico, Carmen Siu, Josephine Mo, Barbara Porter, Melissa MacAulay, and Ashley Bernicky. All errors and omissions remain, of course, my own.

This work takes account of the law as it stood on 1 June 2024.

Gib van Ert
Ottawa, June 2024

1 Introduction

Canada's achievement of independence in international affairs is a fact to which Canadian law is still reconciling itself. For decades after the inception of Confederation in 1867, and in the centuries of embryonic development before that, foreign relations and the laws that govern them were little concern of ours.

The original inhabitants of these lands were, of course, unaware of European conceptions of the law of nations, though parallels existed in their own legal traditions. The arrival of the colonists did not add much to the stock of international legal thinking here, for the newcomers mostly ignored the precepts of their own international laws or, when they did turn their minds to the matter, invoked international law doctrines to their own advantage. Some recognition of the nation-to-nation context of Indigenous-settlor relations can be seen in the use of the international law term "treaty" to describe agreements between the Indigenous peoples and the newcomers. Yet as British control of these lands solidified, any suggestion of Indigenous sovereignty, as that concept was understood in international law, was loudly denied or quietly ignored.

Also rejected for a time were the occasional colonial claims to self-government, partly for fear that if the imperial authorities ceded control of the colonies' domestic affairs they would eventually have to grant external independence, too. Such fears proved to be well founded. In 1931, Canada finally gained full statehood under international law. Yet centuries of relative isolation from international law left the Canadian bench and bar unprepared for the duties of statehood Canada had now assumed. As late as 1967, one senses incredulity in the banal declaration of the Supreme Court of Canada in the *Offshore Mineral Rights* reference that "There can be no doubt now that Canada has become a sovereign state."[1]

In short, engagement with international law is notably absent in Canada's legal past. It is, however, an undeniable part of Canada's legal present and is likely to be an integral part of our legal future. The period of our external independence has coincided almost perfectly with the most significant era of international legal development in world history. That era is not over yet. Indeed, it may have just begun. The inexorable globalization of our markets, our cultures, and our populations is platitudinous but true. Our laws cannot resist this movement, as Canada's ratification and implementation of multilateral treaties on matters as diverse as human rights, trade, and the environment illustrate. Canadian courts and litigants already look to international law to answer a great range of domestic legal questions. Such references will only grow more frequent. Yet, as I have suggested, for most of Canada's legal history our judges and lawyers have ignored international law. Now that we can no longer do so, where do we begin?

Ill-suited as Canadian history has left us to answer such questions, we have this advantage: the common law. While international law has come to prominence only relatively recently in Canada, the commercial, military, and imperial exploits of Great Britain brought the law of nations to the attention of English jurists as early as the mid-eighteenth century. They received it with enthusiasm, establishing common law doctrines founded on respect for international law and a determination to construe domestic legislation in harmony with it. A body of case law emerged governing the reception of public international law into the law of England. As the common law crossed the Atlantic, its reception rules came with it, lying dormant in Canadian common law for decades or longer. As Canada's international stature and presence grew, especially after the Statute of Westminster 1931,[2] the common law reception system was revived. It could not be applied here without some adjustment, for it was the product of a unitary state with an unwritten constitution, whereas Canada was a federation with entrenched constitutional laws. Reconciling the common law of reception with the con-

1 *Reference re Ownership of Offshore Mineral Rights (British Columbia)*, [1967] SCR 792 at 816.

2 1931 (UK) 22 George V c 4, reprinted in RSC 1985 App II No 27.

stitutional law of Canada became a matter of controversy, as famously exemplified by the *Labour Conventions* case.[3] Nevertheless, the fundamentals of common law reception remained: customary international law was incorporated by the common law of Canada, conventional international law required implementation by legislation before taking direct domestic effect, both these forms of international law were judicially noticed by Canadian courts, and enactments were interpreted as presumptively consistent with international law. Judicial application of these rules has sometimes been tentative and uneven, but the rules themselves remain unchallenged.

The aim of this book is to give a complete account of the reception of international law in Canada. By gathering in one place all the various common law, statutory, constitutional, evidentiary, and interpretive rules governing the reception of public international law into Canadian law, the book seeks to reveal these rules for what they are: not, as they might seem, a haphazard collection of ancient case law overlaid with an equally haphazard modern jurisprudence, but a complete and largely internally consistent system of reception law.

1.1 Monism and dualism: Canada as a hybrid jurisdiction

Discussions of the application of international law in Canada, the United Kingdom, and other Westminster-model countries can bog down in terminology. Monism and dualism, adoption and transformation, incorporation and implementation – the purpose of these various terms is to characterize the constitutional arrangements by which states apply international law domestically.[4]

3 *Attorney General for Canada v Attorney General for Ontario*, [1937] AC 326 (PC).

4 Monism and dualism also represent two sides of a philosophical debate about the relationship of international and domestic law. "For the main part, this discussion [of monism and dualism] is theoretical and lacks practical significance": L Green, "International Law: A Canadian Perspective" in *The Canadian Encyclopedic Digest (Ontario)*, 3d ed, vol 17, title 81 (Agincourt, ON: Carswell, 1984) at 62. "The principal task remains that of creating a sensible working relationship between the two systems [international and domestic law] within the jurisdiction of the particular state, an accommodation between them rather than the attainment of a formal 'harmony,' or the 'primacy' of international law. The problems are obscured if they are placed in the context of the conflict between monists and dualists": I Brownlie, *Principles of Public International Law*, 6th ed (Oxford: Oxford University Press, 2003) at 48.

There are two ways in which international law might enter domestic law. It might apply immediately, without any action by the executive or legislative organs of the state. Or it might apply only upon being confirmed or consented to by one or both of those organs.

In a *monist* jurisdiction, international law applies in the domestic (or "municipal") legal system immediately and directly, without any legislative or executive action. The theory behind this model is that international law and the domestic law of the state in question are one (hence "monism," from the Greek *monos*: single). Where a conflict between the two orders of law arises, monist theory would have international law prevail. Some writers describe the application of international law in monist jurisdictions as proceeding by *adoption*, meaning that the international norm is adopted automatically by domestic law. I dislike this term, for to "adopt" something suggests a positive act of acceptance by someone, whereas the point of the monist/adoptionist model is that no such act is needed. Another term in use is "incorporation": International norms are incorporated ("formed into one body") with domestic norms. Note, however, that incorporation is sometimes used to describe a very different phenomenon, namely the implementation of treaty law by statute. This is particularly true in recent English case law and commentary. In this book I use the term "incorporation" to describe the theory whereby international law enters the Canadian legal order immediately – that is, without legislative or executive action.

In a *dualist* jurisdiction, international law and domestic law are treated as distinct legal systems whose discrepancies can only be cured by positive acts of the legislative or executive organs of the state. The positive act by which an international norm is made part of the domestic legal order in a dualist regime is called "transformation." A common synonym for transformation, particularly in the case of treaty-made international laws requiring legislative enactment, is "implementation." Throughout this book, I describe as implementation the legislative process by which those international laws that do not take immediate effect in Canada are made part of Canadian law.[5]

5 In using the term "implementation" in this way, I am following the practice of legislative drafters across the country who regularly describe the process of

We now have two reception models clearly before us: incorporation (monism/adoption) and implementation (dualism/transformation). Given that there are (at least) six words to describe these two models, it is perhaps surprising that there is none to describe the actual operation of the Anglo-Canadian system. For Canada, like the UK and other Commonwealth jurisdictions, is neither monist nor dualist, adoptionist nor transformationist, incorporationist nor implementationist. Rather, Canada is a hybrid of the two: It allows the incorporation of customary international law but demands the implementation of conventional international law.

1.2 Principles of the reception system

This hybrid approach to the monism/dualism dichotomy is the first of many examples of how the reception system balances two competing principles that may be seen to animate it. I introduce these principles here. They are in some respects a restatement of the monist and dualist positions but refined in the light of the particular characteristics and preoccupations of Westminster-model legal systems such as ours. At various points in the text I refer to these principles as a means of illuminating the values and the tensions behind the reception system's rules. Practitioners using this book as a reference need not trouble themselves with this layer of analysis which, I readily concede, is my own gloss on the law. Readers approaching this book for other purposes will, I hope, find my principled analysis of the reception system explanatory of doctrines and rules that might otherwise appear as inconsistencies in the law.

I call the two principles "respect for international law" and "self-government." They do not sit easily together. Given free rein, either one could consume the other and, in doing so, utterly transform the reception system. Such a transformation might not be objectionable, perhaps, were it not that both principles are compelling descriptions of who we are and who we should be. Thus the rules of reception are not only instantiations of the system's underlying principles, but also the means of balancing them to assure the survival of both.

---

giving domestic legal effect to treaties as implementation. See the discussion at Chapter 7, Section 7.1(a).

(a) Respect for international law

The principle of respect for international law requires that the international laws that regulate the relations of states with each other, with other international entities, and with their own citizens and other persons within their power be observed and applied in domestic law. Why international law merits this respect is an illuminating question. Blackstone considered international law to be a system of rules "deducible by natural reason" resulting from "principles of natural justice." As such, international law was established by and enjoyed "universal consent among the civilized inhabitants of the world."[6] Thus the authority of international law was backed not only by reason and justice but by common consent. Violations of international law were unreasonable, unjust, and had the effect of isolating the offender from the community of civilized states. These reasons for respecting international law derive from an era in which custom was the predominant source of international law. From Blackstone's time to the establishment of the United Nations, developments in international law have increasingly come from posited instruments (treaties), rather than from "the law of nature and reason." For such instruments, respect for international law can be justified on the grounds of international comity, the international law principle of *pacta sunt servanda* (agreements must be kept), and even the honour of the Crown. Today, in the light of the international human rights movement that began with the Universal Declaration of Human Rights 1948,[7] Blackstone's natural law reasoning may be newly compelling. Many of the instruments that constitute this era's greatest international developments take the form of declarations of inherent and universal human rights. Nonetheless, most international agreements concluded by Canada annually are in the nature of state-to-state administrative arrangements rather than grand declarations. The claim of such instruments upon us is *pacta sunt servanda*, which is as much prudential as normative.

Here we are leading into jurisprudential questions about the nature of law's obligatoriness. That is not the subject of this book, but simply raising the question reveals something important about the

---

6 Sir William Blackstone, *Commentaries on the Laws of England*, vol 4 (Chicago: University of Chicago Press, 1979) at 66–7.

7 GA Res 217 A (III), UN Doc A/810.

principle I am considering: Respect for international law requires us to treat international law as just that – law, as deserving of the name as any domestic statute or judgment of the court. The principle requires that international laws that have domestic application be applied and that international laws without domestic application not be violated or frustrated by inconsistent interpretations of domestic law. In short, respect for international law requires that international law be treated as actually or potentially, mediately or immediately, part of Canadian law.

To say that international law should be respected because it is law, and is therefore obligatory for the same reason (whatever it may be) that other forms of law are obligatory, is not as trite as it may seem given the all-too-common attitude that international law is not "real" law. But there is a further reason why the principle of respect for international law is compelling. This reason concerns our identity. The principle depicts those who observe it as members of an international community. Blackstone explained that if we did not respect international law we "must cease to be a part of the civilized world."[8] The language of civilization is tainted with Eurocentrism and has come to be replaced with the language of international community. Thus the single reference to international law in the Canadian Charter of Rights and Freedoms speaks of "the general principles of law recognized by the community of nations."[9] While the language has changed, the opprobrium associated with violations of international law remains. We may now hesitate to use words like barbarous and uncivilized to describe countries that routinely violate international law, but the words we do use – totalitarian, oppressive, renegade, failed – bring the same obloquy. The principle of respect for international law depicts those countries in which it thrives in glowing terms: democratic, rules-based, Western (so much for avoiding Eurocentrism), the leading members of the international community. The force of the principle derives in part from our desire to be so identified, to see ourselves in this light.

Unchecked by other rules of the reception system, respect for international law would remove all legal obstacles between the international legal system and domestic law, thus harmonizing the two legal systems. Since the principle treats international law as law, it characterizes dissent from international norms as unlawful or lawless and

---

8 Blackstone, above note 6 at 67.

9 Part I of the Constitution Act, 1982, being Schedule B to the Canada Act 1982 (UK) 1982, c 11, s 11(g).

therefore to be suppressed. The competing principle of the reception system – self-government – is under constant threat from the principle of respect for international law and might succumb to it were it not for the balance the reception system strikes between the two principles.

(b) Self-government

I call the second principle of the reception system "self-government," by which I mean a community's power and practice of determining its beliefs, status, and future for itself. The opposite of self-government is coercion by any external force. An external force – be it an institution, a people, a legal order, or an idea – is any that does not enjoy the consent of whomever it seeks to control. Submission is not consent. Consent is satisfied only by deliberative, representative, public, and participatory decision-making processes, which are the best means of assuring that what purports to be consent is not merely acquiescence or indifference. Westminster-model constitutions such as Canada's are informed by a commitment to self-government at several points. Examples include the doctrine that the Crown cannot make law outside Parliament, the requirement that legislative initiatives be approved by majority vote, and, in Canadian federalism, the inability of one legislature to make law in another's jurisdiction.

The principle of self-government tends to look on international law, in its current state of development, as a coercive external force in the sense given above. It views methods of international lawmaking as unconsensual as compared to the deliberative, representative, public, and participatory decision-making model that is the parliamentary process. Some may look on this depiction of the parliamentary process with suspicion, given concerns about the deterioration of our parliamentary institutions and the increasingly active role of citizens and non-governmental organizations on the international scene. Rightly or wrongly, however, the reception system does not share this low regard of parliamentary government or this optimism about the developing democratic credentials of the international system.

While the principle of self-government sees no threat in the development of customary international law,[10] it looks suspiciously on

10 As Brudner explains, "A rule of customary law . . . is viewed as the expression not of executive will but of common human reason, the same reason that is

the treaty-making process. Treaty-making in Canada and similarly constituted states remains a prerogative of the Crown. Treaty negotiation frequently takes place behind closed doors (especially in the case of bilateral agreements), and the results of such negotiations are only occasionally brought before Parliament or the provincial legislatures. Even when a treaty is presented to our legislatures, it comes in the form of a "take it or leave it" proposition: Approve or disapprove the treaty (or, more usually, its implementing legislation), but do not seek to amend it. In future, self-government's suspicion of the democratic credentials of conventional international lawmaking may lessen, particularly if the international lawmaking process takes on the qualities of deliberation, representation, and participation, which are the hallmarks of consensual self-government. In the meantime, the reception system reserves to Canadians, through their legislatures, the power to override international law in the name of self-government.

The consequence of self-government's suspicion of international law are reception rules that ensure our power to dissent from international norms. Carried to its logical conclusion, this power to violate international law would circumscribe the place of international law in Canada's domestic law so narrowly as to threaten the existence of the principle of respect for international law. For the parliamentary process, which is self-government's standard of consensual lawmaking, is an impossible ideal for an international legal system predicated on the sovereignty of states. To prevent self-government from utterly marginalizing international law in Canada, the rules of the reception system subject assertions of self-government contrary to international law to strict interpretive requirements.

(c) The balance

The Canadian reception system is based on and committed to both of the principles described above. Each common law and interpretive rule for the application of international law in Canada can be understood to emanate from or embody one of the principles. Yet, as I have suggested,

---

historically embedded in the common law. Hence the automatic incorporation of such a rule is considered to be no more antithetical to the sovereignty of the general will than is the enforceability of judge-made law": A Brudner, "The Domestic Enforcement of International Covenants on Human Rights: A Theoretical Framework" (1985) 35 *University of Toronto Law Journal* 219 at 222.

the two principles are ultimately at odds with each other. A thoroughgoing application of the principle of respect for international law would apply international law in the domestic sphere in spite of inconsistent domestic laws. Similarly, an out-and-out application of the principle of self-government would not trouble itself to ensure respect for international law in the face of seemingly inconsistent domestic provisions. Each principle has in it the seed of the other's undoing. Yet the two principles coexist in Canadian law. They do so by a careful balance that is at once the foundation and the sustenance of the reception system.

This balance is in the form of a series of compromises running through the system. The standard form of this compromise is as follows. Respect for international law is granted the default position in the reception system. It is assumed from the outset and serves as the starting point of every discussion. Yet the system recognizes in our domestic laws an ultimate power, as required by self-government, to dissent from and violate international law. Thus, self-government operates as the exception to the rule of respect for international law. The reception system balances the demands of both principles by granting respect for international law the wider application while granting self-government an ultimate veto. This careful balancing of the principles throughout the reception system is what prevents either from consuming the other, ensuring the survival of both. Judicial decisions that threaten this balance jeopardize the entire system, turning a functioning whole into a muddled assortment of scattered parts. Observance of both principles, and due regard for their balance within the system, are therefore the best criteria for judging the soundness of decisions in this area of the law.

Maintaining the balance between respect for international law and self-government in the reception system requires that the system's institutional actors – principally the legislatures and the courts – play their respective roles. The brute political power to violate international law is associated with our legislatures, as a consequence of the doctrine (however attenuated in this country) of parliamentary sovereignty. That doctrine is only defensible, if it is defensible at all, on the ground that the particular virtues of democratic assemblies – representation, public deliberation, participation, consent – are so great as to justify departures from international norms in extraordinary cases. The role of vindicating the competing principle of respect for international law falls to the courts. By interpreting legislation in conformity with Canada's international obligations wherever possible, and by effecting the incorporation of customary international law by the common law, the courts ensure that respect for international law remains the default position of Canadian law, and that violations of international law in the name of self-government are rare exceptions to the rule.

1.3 Plan of this book

The book can be read cover to cover, but it need not be. Each chapter is written, as far as possible, as a discrete discussion. Chapter 2 gives an introduction to the nature, sources, and forums of international law. Chapter 3 discusses evidentiary, procedural, and jurisdictional issues that may arise when considering international law in Canadian courts. Chapter 4 considers the allocation of foreign affairs powers and responsibilities between the executive, legislative, and judicial elements of the state. Chapter 5 reviews the presumption of conformity with international law. That this single rule of legal interpretation merits an entire chapter is indicative of its significance in the reception system. In Chapter 6, I explain how Canadian common law incorporates rules of customary international law directly into the law of Canada. This is followed, in Chapter 7, by a discussion of the more prevalent form of contemporary international law: treaties. The need for legislative implementation of treaties, the means by which implementation is effected, and the rules of treaty interpretation are the main subjects of this chapter. Chapter 8 considers the reception of other international legal sources in Canada. Chapter 9 examines international law considerations in the judicial review of administrative decisions. Chapter 10 reviews the increasing points of contact between international law and the rights of Indigenous peoples in Canada. Finally, Chapter 11 considers the reception of international human rights law, with special emphasis on the relevance of Canada's international human rights obligations to the interpretation and application of the Canadian Charter of Rights and Freedoms.

2 Definitions, sources, and forums

International law may be defined as the system of law regulating the conduct and relations of states. This definition oversimplifies, as any is bound to do. International law may also regulate relations between states and other entities, such as international organizations or natural or legal persons.[1] To the extent that this is true, however, it is seemingly because states make it true – for example, by creating international organizations and endowing them with legal personality or by declaring and recognizing rights in persons. Though the beneficiaries of such state conduct grow more numerous, the subjects of international law are still, in the main, states.

2.1 The state, state organs, and state responsibility

In considering the domestic reception of rules of public international law one must distinguish the state as it is recognized in international law from the state's organs as established in domestic law. International law regards the state as a unity, consistent with its recognition as a sin-

1 "Nor would it be entirely accurate to define public international law as a system regulating the affairs of nations or States. While this might have been a relatively comprehensive description some decades ago, it fails to take account of the increasingly important fields of international human rights law, international humanitarian law, and international criminal law, which aspire to the establishment of a body of norms applicable to individuals": W Schabas, "Twenty-Five Years of Public International Law at the Supreme Court of Canada" (2000) 79 *Canadian Bar Review* 174 at 176.

gle legal person in international law.[2] International law binds the state as a whole, usually without specifically addressing particular state organs such as its legislature, ministries, regulatory bodies, sub-federal entities, or judiciary.[3] Yet the acts of such organs are attributable to the state as acts of the state itself for the purpose of determining the state's responsibility for breaches of international obligations.[4] Similarly, the conduct of persons or entities that are not state organs but which exercise governmental authority may be attributed to the state.[5] These rules of attribution may sometimes seem to apply international law to particular state organs or entities directly.[6] But they are best understood as applying to the state as a whole.

It is therefore strictly incorrect to say that a given statute, regulation, judicial decision, or other domestic legal norm violates international law. Likewise, it is inaccurate to say that Parliament is competent to violate international law. The act of a state organ cannot itself breach an international obligation, because the organ so acting is not subject to any international obligation it can breach.[7] The obligation is that of the state, of which the organ forms part. This is, of

---

2 J Crawford, *The International Law Commission's Articles on State Responsibility: Introduction, Text and Commentaries* (Cambridge: Cambridge University Press, 2002) [Crawford] at 83; P Saunders & R Currie, *Kindred's International Law: Chiefly as Interpreted in Canada*, 9th ed (Toronto: Emond Montgomery Publications Ltd, 2019) [*Kindred's*] at 442.

3 "In principle, obligations under international law are binding on the State and on all its organs, executive, legislative and judicial": F Vallat, *International Law and the Practitioner* (Manchester: Manchester University Press, 1966) at 4.

4 See Crawford, above note 2, text of and commentary to art 4.

5 *Ibid*, text of and commentary to art 5; see also arts 6–11.

6 See, for example, *LaGrand (Germany v United States of America), Provisional Measures, Order of 3 March 1999*, [1999] ICJ Rep 9 at para 28: "Whereas the international responsibility of a State is engaged by the action of the competent organs and authorities acting in that State, whatever they may be; whereas the United States should take all measures at its disposal to ensure that Walter LaGrand is not executed pending the final decision in these proceedings; whereas, according to the information available to the Court, implementation of the measures indicated in the present Order falls within the jurisdiction of the Governor of Arizona; whereas the Government of the United States is consequently under the obligation to transmit the present Order to the said Governor; whereas *the Governor of Arizona is under the obligation to act in conformity with the international undertakings of the United States. . . .*" [emphasis added].

7 *Ordon Estate v Grail*, [1998] 3 SCR 437 at para 137; *Capital Cities Communications Inc v Canadian Radio-Television Commission*, [1978] 2 SCR 141 at 173.

course, a rather fine distinction, and it can be pedantic to insist upon it. To say "This Act is contrary to international law" is a quite acceptable shorthand in most cases, so long as one does not lose sight of the fact that it is only a shorthand. Similarly, there is no reasonable objection to the statement (often repeated in the case law) that Parliament is sovereign to violate international law, even though what is really meant is that there is no power in the courts to invalidate legislation on the ground that its enactment or enforcement puts the state in breach of an international obligation.

2.2 Public and private international law

Public international law must be distinguished from private international law (also called conflict of laws). The latter consists of rules developed by states as part of their domestic law to resolve problems arising from conflicts between their own laws and the laws of other states.[8] The choice of applicable law and the enforceability of judgments made by foreign courts are typical problems addressed by this area of the law. The preoccupations of private international law are different from those of public international law. Castel and Walker observe:

> Principles and rules of conflict of laws are not international, they are essentially national in character. Since they are part of the local law, they are formulated by the legislative bodies of the different legal units or are to be found in the decisions of their courts. . . . It is traditional to use the expression "conflict of laws" or "private international law" to describe the body of principles and rules applicable to trans-border cases involving private relationships which contain legally relevant foreign elements. The expression "private international law" does not imply that this body of principles and rules is related to public international law as conflicts rules are not international or universal in character.[9]

---

8 Sir Robert Megarry VC has observed: "It may, moreover, be remembered that some say of the two kinds of International Law, Private and Public, that one is not international and the other is not law." He is, with respect, half right. Sir Robert Megarry, *A Second Miscellany-at-Law: A Further Diversion for Lawyers and Others* (London: Stevens, 1973) at 113.

9 J Walker, *Castel & Walker: Canadian Conflict of Laws*, 6th ed (Toronto: LexisNexis Canada, 2005) s 1.3. See also *Dell Computer Corp v Union des consommateurs*, 2007 SCC 34 at para 187.

Thus, private international law is a subset of the domestic laws of states, to be ranged alongside domestic laws of contract, tort, property, and so forth. It is also true, however, that private international law, like other areas of domestic law, is increasingly international in origin and content. For instance, the ongoing work of The Hague Conference on Private International Law has produced numerous treaties in such areas as child protection, family relations, legal cooperation, enforcement of judgments, and commercial law.

2.3 Sources of international law

In any legal system, to know what the law is one must know its sources. Not every rule is law. Some rules are exclusively moral prescriptions. Others are aesthetic propositions. Still others are rules of courtesy. Only those rules promulgated by authorities recognized as possessing lawmaking power, and according to accepted procedures and forms, enjoy the obligatoriness we describe as binding or legal.

Identifying the sources of international law brings special challenges because, unlike domestic legal regimes, the international legal order is not yet endowed with a permanent legislature, recognizable executive, or judiciary of broad compulsory jurisdiction. All of which is not to say that there is no such thing as international law or that it is unenforceable, but only that discerning it requires a different approach than one employs in domestic legal systems. The sources of international law are not to be sought in any authoritative constitution or text. Rather, they are established by the practice of states.[10]

The starting point for all modern considerations of the sources of international law is article 38 of the Statute of the International Court of Justice 1945 (the ICJ Statute).[11] That article is not itself determinative of the sources of international law, but only declaratory of sources firmly established in state practice. It is a direction to the Internation-

10 See, generally, Sir Robert Jennings & Sir Arthur Watts, eds, *Oppenheim's International Law*, 9th ed vol 1 (Harlow, England: Longman, 1992) [*Oppenheim's*] at 23–52; J Crawford, *Brownlie's Principles of Public International Law*, 9th ed (Oxford: Oxford University Press, 2019) [*Brownlie's*] at 18–44; C Emanuelli, *Droit international public : contribution à l'étude du droit international selon une perspective canadienne*, 3rd ed (Montréal: Wilson & Lafleur, 2010) at 44–164; J Currie, *Public International Law*, 2nd ed (Toronto: Irwin Law, 2008) [Currie] at 80–120.

11 [1945] Can TS no 7.

al Court of Justice as to what that court may consider when deciding cases before it and does not necessarily exclude other matters that may give rise to international rights and obligations. Nevertheless, article 38(1) is an important statement of the sources of international law. It provides:

> The Court, whose function is to decide in accordance with international law such disputes as are submitted to it, shall apply:
>
> (a) international conventions, whether general or particular, establishing rules expressly recognized by the contending states;
> (b) international custom, as evidence of a general practice accepted as law;
> (c) the general principles of law recognized by civilized nations;
> (d) subject to the provisions of Article 59, judicial decisions and the teachings of the most highly qualified publicists of the various nations, as subsidiary means for the determination of rules of law.

In short, the main sources of international law are treaties, custom, general principles of law, and, as subsidiary means for determining the law, judicial decisions and the writings of pre-eminent authors. Also to be considered in this discussion are the lawmaking powers of certain international organizations, the legal character of unilateral statements, laws of a peremptory or *erga omnes* character, and so-called soft law.

(a) Treaties

International conventions, or treaties, are now the most significant lawmaking instruments in international law.[12] Treaties are defined in the Vienna Convention on the Law of Treaties 1969 (VCLT),[13] itself a

---

12 On treaties generally, see, e.g., J Hill, *Aust's Modern Treaty Law and Practice*, 4th ed (Cambridge: Cambridge University Press, 2023) [Hill]; I Sinclair, *The Vienna Convention on the Law of Treaties*, 2d ed (Manchester: Manchester University Press, 1984) [Sinclair]; A McNair, *The Law of Treaties: British Practice and Opinions* (Oxford: Clarendon Press, 1938).

13 [1980] Can TS no 37 [VCLT]. Canada ratified the VCLT in 1970. It came into force as against Canada in 1980. This treaty is at least partly declaratory of customary international law: see the *Namibia* case, [1971] ICJ Rep 16 at para 94 and the *Fisheries Jurisdiction* case, [1973] ICJ Rep 3 at para 36.

treaty (and one to which Canada is a party). Article 2(1) of the VCLT defines a treaty as "an international agreement concluded between States in written form and governed by international law, whether embodied in a single instrument or in two or more related instruments and whatever its particular designation."[14] This latter point is important, because treaties go by many names, including convention, agreement, pact, act, charter, statute, declaration, covenant, protocol, and more.[15] As a matter of international law, the actual name of the treaty is of no significance.[16]

The distinguishing characteristic of treaties is that they are agreements that establish binding rights and obligations at international law. This rule-creating aspect of treaties is emphasized in article 38(1) of the ICJ Statute, which provides that the court shall apply "international conventions, whether general or particular, *establishing rules expressly recognized* by the contesting states."[17] Such rules cannot arise, and therefore a treaty cannot be created, unless the parties to the would-be treaty possessed an intent to create legal relations. The requirement of intent to create legal relations is not found explicitly in the VCLT, yet it is undoubtedly part of the definition of a treaty. The International Law Commission considered the requirement of intent to create legal relations to be embraced within the phrase "governed by international law" in article 2(1)(a)'s definition of "treaty."[18]

The requirement of intent to create legal relations means that no state may be bound by a treaty without its consent. The two most usual

---

14 While VCLT, *ibid*, art 2(1) defines treaties as written, unwritten treaties are also possible. Such treaties, while not falling within the VLCT, are nonetheless legally enforceable at international law: see VCLT, art 3.

15 See A Gotlieb, *Canadian Treaty-Making* (Toronto: Butterworths, 1968) at 20–1. Thus, the practice of some judges to speak of "treaties and conventions" is redundant.

16 As a matter of practice, when two (or, rarely, more) states conclude an agreement that is not intended to be a treaty, they may use appellations that, in their view, indicate a lack of intent to create legal relations. The preferred Canadian federal appellation for such instruments is "non-binding arrangements." In Canadian provincial practice, the terms "memorandum" and "memorandum of understanding" are frequently employed to describe intergovernmental agreements between provincial and foreign governments.

17 My emphasis. See *Oppenheim's*, above note 10 at 32.

18 "Reports of the Commission to the General Assembly" (UN Doc A/6309/Rev 1) in *Yearbook of the International Law Commission 1966*, vol 2 (New York: United Nations, 1967) at 189 (UN Doc A/CN.4/SER.A/1966/Add.1).

means of expressing consent are signature and ratification. Where a treaty is to be concluded by signature, the act of signing the treaty represents the state's expression of its consent to be bound by the treaty at international law. Where a treaty is to be concluded by ratification, the process is more formal. The state's consent to be bound is expressed more elaborately, whether through the exchange of instruments of ratification (in the case of a bilateral treaty) or the deposit of an instrument of ratification with some specified depository (in the case of a multilateral treaty). Where treaty-making proceeds by means of ratification, a state's representative may sign the treaty, but that signature will not express the state's consent to be bound. Such a signature is at best a legally unenforceable, but still significant,[19] expression by the signatory state of its intent to bind itself at some later date (for instance, after enacting implementing legislation).[20] In this book, unless otherwise noted, I use the term "ratify" to mean any expression of consent to be bound, whether by signature or ratification.[21]

The VCLT provides that every state possesses the capacity to conclude treaties.[22] The term "state" is not defined. For federations like Canada, this raises the question of whether the governments of constituent units of federations (in Canada's case, the provinces) may

---

19 VCLT, above note 13, art 18(a), provides that a state that has signed a treaty, or has exchanged instruments constituting the treaty subject to ratification, acceptance, or approval, is obliged to refrain from acts that would defeat the treaty's object and purpose. See also art 18(b) in respect of states that have expressed their consent to be bound by the treaty pending its entry into force.

20 "An international instrument is not legally binding on a signatory State until it has also ratified it, unless the instrument provides that it is binding when signed. Signature normally evinces an intention to be bound in the future, although it may also impose an immediate obligation on the signatory not to take measures to undermine the agreement": *De Guzman v Canada (Minister of Citizenship & Immigration)*, 2005 FCA 436 at para 76.

21 For more on treaty-making, see Hill, above note 12, especially at ch 7; P Hogg & W Wright, *Constitutional Law of Canada*, 5th ed Suppl, looseleaf (Toronto: Thomson Reuters, 2021) ch 11; M Copithorne, "Canadian Treaty Law and Practice" (1996) 54 *The Advocate* 35. For a description of Canadian treaty-making practice by the Legal Bureau of the Department of External Affairs, see (1986) 24 *Canadian Yearbook of International Law* 397. For a more recent statement, see Appendix A ("The Treaty-Making Process") of Government of Canada, Treaty Law Division of the Department of Foreign Affairs and International Trade, "Policy on Tabling of Treaties in Parliament" (2008), online: https://www.treaty-accord.gc.ca/procedures.aspx (last visited 1 April 2024).

22 VCLT, above note 13, art 6.

conclude treaties at international law. The question is largely one of domestic constitutional law. At international law, it appears that the term "State" in VCLT article 6 need not necessarily exclude entities, such as provinces, which enjoy something less than full international personality. The authors of *Oppenheim* consider there to be "no justification for the view that [member states of federations] are necessarily deprived of any status whatsoever within the international community: while they are not full subjects of international law, they may be international persons for some purposes."[23] Shaw is of the same view, adding that where member states of a federation have been granted some "restricted international competence," they may be regarded as having "a degree of international personality."[24] But what degree of international personality is needed for the purpose of becoming party to a treaty? In particular, does it suffice that the sub-federal unit enjoys internal competence within the federation to carry out the treaty's obligations? The answer appears to be no: What is also needed is some provision in the federation's constitutional law establishing the capacity of the sub-federal unit to conclude treaties.[25] Whether such a provision may be found in Canadian constitutional law is considered later.[26]

The common law definition of "treaty" is apparently the same as that recognized in international law.[27] I am unaware of any case in Canadian or English law suggesting otherwise. Given that the international law definition of "treaty" was originally customary, the doctrine of incorporation suggests that the international and common law meanings of "treaty" are the same. This eliminates from our law the argu-

---

23 *Oppenheim's*, above note 10 at 249.

24 M Shaw, *International Law*, 8th ed (Cambridge: Cambridge University Press, 2017) [Shaw] at 172.

25 That this is so is suggested by art 5(2) of the International Law Commission's Draft Articles on the Law of Treaties, which provided that "States members of a federal union may possess a capacity to conclude treaties if such capacity is admitted by the federal constitution and within the limits there laid down": quoted in Shaw, *ibid* at 157. This provision was dropped from the VCLT but seems nevertheless to represent the current position. See G van Ert, "The Legal Character of Provincial Agreements with Foreign Governments" (2001) 42 *Les Cahiers de droit* 1093. For a contrary view, see H Cyr, *Canadian Federalism and Treaty Powers: Organic Constitutionalism at Work* (Brussels: P.I.E. Peter Lang, S.A., 2009) at 157–8.

26 See Chapter 4, Section 4.2(c).

27 I speak here of international treaties rather than treaties between the Crown and Indigenous peoples. See the discussion in Chapter 10, Section 10.1(a).

ment that runs, "While this agreement may be a treaty at international law, it is not one for the purposes of domestic law."[28]

States are not the only entities that can make treaties. Non-state entities with international legal personality also have treaty-making capacity.[29]

(b) Custom

In some legal systems, the processes by which new laws are posited are relatively undeveloped or infrequently used. An overt legislature may not exist, or, to the extent that it does, its laws may be considered less significant than legal norms emerging from the traditions and habitual practices of the community. In international law, the primacy of posited law (in the form of treaties) is a relatively recent phenomenon. Thus, custom has been called "the oldest and the original source of international law as well as of law in general."[30]

Customary international law, also known as international custom or (archaically) the law of nations, is revealed by state practice.[31] The physical acts, claims, abstract declarations (such as General Assembly resolutions), national laws, national judgments, and omissions of states are the evidence courts and scholars analyze to determine the existence of customary international law.[32] As La Forest J observed, "To establish custom, an extensive survey of the practices of nations is required."[33] The practice of a single state is insufficient, for no state

---

28 This argument is available to American lawyers. US constitutional law distinguishes between treaties, which are part of "the supreme Law of the Land" under art VI of the constitution, and executive agreements, which are not necessarily self-executing. This distinction has resulted in a rather complex American jurisprudence. Whatever their status in American law, all these instruments are treaties in the contemplation of international law. See, e.g., Hill, above note 12 at 202–6; *Oppenheim's*, above note 10 at 74–7; and J Paust, *International Law as Law of the United States* (Durham, NC: Carolina Academic Press, 1996) at 51–79.

29 See Hill, above note 12 at ch 22.

30 *Oppenheim's*, above note 10 at 25.

31 On custom generally, see *Oppenheim's*, above note 10 at 25–31; *Brownlie's*, above note 10 at 21–8; *Kindred's*, above note 2 at 30–45; Currie, above note 10 at 185–217.

32 M Akenhurst, "Custom as a Source of International Law" (1974–5) 47 *British Yearbook of International Law* 1 at 1–11. See also Shaw, above note 24 at 53–66.

33 *R v Finta*, [1994] 1 SCR 701 [*Finta*] at 773.

can unilaterally make customary international law. What is needed is evidence of general, though not necessarily universal, state practice.[34] The state practice in question need not be unbroken, but breaks with it must be viewed as breaches of the rule rather than as indications of a new rule.[35]

While state practice is a necessary element of custom, it is not sufficient. For not every act, habit, or tradition of states, no matter how generally practised, gives rise to customary international law. What is also needed, if a state's practice is to be indicative of custom, is that the state consider its behaviour to be required by law. As the International Court of Justice explained in *North Sea Continental Shelf*, "Not only must the acts concerned amount to a settled practice, but they must also be such, or be carried out in such a way, as to be evidence of a belief that this practice is rendered obligatory by the existence of a rule of law requiring it."[36] This attitude toward a state's own practices, known as *opinio juris*, serves to differentiate state practices motivated by courtesy or morality (which amount only to international usages) from those motivated by a sense of obligation (which amount to customary international law).[37] Thus, the test for the existence of a rule of customary international law is straightforward: The purported custom must be shown to be supported by consistent state practice motivated by *opinio juris* (that is, the belief that the practice is required by law).[38]

---

34 *North Sea Continental Shelf* cases, [1969] ICJ Rep 3 [*North Sea Continental Shelf*] at para 73; *Fisheries Jurisdiction (United Kingdom v Iceland)*, Merits, [1974] ICJ Rep 3 at 23–6; *Case Concerning Military and Paramilitary Activities in and Against Nicaragua (Nicaragua v United States of America)*, Merits, [1986] ICJ Rep 14 at para 186 [*Military and Paramilitary Activities*].

35 *Military and Paramilitary Activities*, *ibid* at para 186.

36 *North Sea Continental Shelf*, above note 34.

37 International courts and tribunals are sometimes willing to presume that state practice is motivated by *opinio juris* unless proved to the contrary. This approach is advocated in Sir Hersch Lauterpacht, *The Development of International Law by the International Court* (London: Stevens, 1958) at 380. In at least three leading cases, however, the International Court has insisted upon stricter proof: *Lotus* case, [1927] PCIJ (Ser A), No 10 at 33; *North Sea Continental Shelf*, above note 34 at paras 75–81; *Military and Paramilitary Activities*, above note 34 at para 207. See the discussion in *Brownlie's*, above note 10 at 23–5.

38 The Supreme Court of Canada has sometimes failed to recognize and apply the test for customary international law. In *114957 Canada Ltée (Spraytech, Société d'arrosage) v Hudson (Town)*, [2001] 2 SCR 241 [*Spraytech*], the majority effectively declared the precautionary principle to be a rule of customary international

Rules of customary international law are binding upon all states. This includes new states arising after the inception of the rule, and states that did not, by their acts or declarations, participate in the development of the custom. There are two exceptions. First, a custom is not binding on those states that have persistently objected to it from its inception and during its formation. Thus, in the *Anglo-Norwegian Fisheries* case, the International Court of Justice observed that a custom concerning the delimitation of coastline "would appear to be inapplicable as against Norway inasmuch as she had always opposed any attempt to apply it to the Norwegian coast."[39] Proving persistent objection is nearly as difficult as proving custom. Second, it is possible for regional or local custom to develop. Where that is so, only states within the region, and which have not persistently objected to the custom, are bound by it.[40]

A treaty may be declaratory of or come to represent customary international law (including *jus cogens*). In such cases, a Canadian court may look to the treaty, whatever its implementation status in domestic law, to discern customary international law. When a court does so, it is not applying the treaty but the custom the treaty represents.[41]

---

law without considering the requirements of state practice and *opinio juris*. Instead, the majority relied on academic writings and judicial *dicta*. In *Suresh v Canada (Minister of Citizenship and Immigration)*, [2002] 1 SCR 3 [*Suresh*], the Court was asked to consider the status of torture in international law. Here, again, the court neglected state practice and *opinio juris*. This time, however, the court drew on a wider variety of materials, including treaty practice and domestic law. In *Mugesera v Canada (Minister of Citizenship and Immigration)*, [2005] 2 SCR 100, the court made admirable efforts to ensure the conformity of its decision with the international law of incitement to genocide and crimes against humanity as enunciated in the jurisprudence of the International Criminal Tribunals for Rwanda and the former Yugoslavia, yet equated this jurisprudence with customary international law without explaining how it reached that conclusion. More recent cases have adverted to the elements of custom, e.g., *R v Hape*, 2007 SCC 26 at para 46; *Kazemi Estate v Iran*, 2014 SCC 62 [*Kazemi Estate*] at paras 38, 102; *Nevsun Resources Ltd v Araya*, 2020 SCC 5 at paras 77–8.

39 *Anglo-Norwegian Fisheries* case, [1951] ICJ Rep 116 at 131.

40 *Asylum* case, [1950] ICJ Rep 266.

41 An example of this is the use of the Geneva Convention on the High Seas 1958 (1958) 450 UNTS 11 and the United Nations Convention on Law of the Sea 1982 (1982) 21 ILM 126 by Deschênes J in *R v Rumbaut* (1998), 127 CCC (3d) 138 (NBQB). Similarly, in *Suresh*, above note 38, the Supreme Court of Canada referred to numerous treaties in its consideration of whether the

(c) General principles of law

Article 38(1)(c) of the ICJ Statute provides that the court may apply "the general principles of law recognized by civilized nations."[42] It is often said that this provision allows the court to draw on principles of domestic law to decide matters not contemplated in treaty or customary law, thereby avoiding the undesirable result that the court cannot hand down a judgment because of a lacuna in international law.[43] The Supreme Court of Canada noted in *Re Newfoundland Continental Shelf* that article 38(1)(c) "refers to principles of municipal law."[44]

Examples of general principles of law that have been held to constitute international law include the requirement of good faith and the related prohibition on the abuse of rights;[45] the principle that every violation of an engagement involves an obligation to make reparation;[46] the rule that wrongdoers cannot plead their own wrong;[47] the principle that no benefit can be received from an illegal act;[48] the rules of *res judicata*;[49] and considerations of equity.[50]

(d) Subsidiary means: Judicial decisions

Article 38(1)(d) of the ICJ Statute provides that "subject to the provisions of Article 59, judicial decisions and the teachings of the most

---

prohibition on torture was a rule of *jus cogens*. See also *Kazemi Estate*, above note 38 at para 149.

42 See: H Lauterpacht, *Private Law Sources and Analogies of International Law* (London: Longmans, 1927); B Cheng, *General Principles of Law as Applied by International Courts and Tribunals* (London: Stevens, 1953); A McNair, "The General Principles of Law Recognized by Civilised Nations" (1957) 33 *British Yearbook of International Law* 1; *Oppenheim's*, above note 10 at 36–40; *Brownlie's*, above note 10 at 31–4.

43 For more on the problem of *non liquet*, see J Stone, *Of Law and Nations: Between Power Politics and Human Hopes* (Buffalo, NY: W.S. Hein, 1974) at 71–118. In spite of the availability of principles under art 38(1)(c) of the ICJ Statute, above note 11, the court made a finding of *non liquet* in *Legality of the Threat or Use of Nuclear Weapons* (1996), ICJ Rep 226.

44 *Re Newfoundland Continental Shelf*, [1984] 1 SCR 86 at 117.

45 *Trail Smelter Arbitration* (1941), 3 RIAA 1905.

46 *Chorzów Factory* (1928), PCIJ (Ser A) No 17 at 29.

47 *Jurisdiction of the Courts of Danzig* (1928), PCIJ (Ser B) No 15 at 26–7.

48 *Eastern Greenland* case (1933), PCIJ (Ser A/B) No 53 at 94–5.

49 *Administrative Tribunal* case, [1954] ICJ Rep 47 at 53.

50 *Rann of Kutch Arbitration* (1968), 50 ILR 2; *Continental Shelf (Libya v Tunisia)*, [1982] ICJ Rep 18.

highly qualified publicists of the various nations" may be applied by the court "as subsidiary means for the determination of rules of law." Article 59 provides that "The decision of the Court has no binding force except between the parties and in respect of that particular case." The rule is likewise for other international tribunals.[51] In short, international judicial decisions bind their parties but are not themselves sources of law.[52]

In principle, then, there is no doctrine of precedent in international law. Nevertheless, the International Court of Justice and other international adjudicative bodies attach considerable importance to decided cases, making their determinations consistently with prior decisions where possible and carefully distinguishing judgments from which they depart. Like Canadian law, international law has its leading cases.

(e) Subsidiary means: Teachings of publicists

Historically in international law, the writings of publicists (meaning scholarly writers) were formative. When natural law theory was in its ascendancy, such writers as Gentilis, Grotius, Pufendorf, Bynkershoek, and Vattel were looked to as principal authorities rather than subsidiary sources.[53] With the rise of positivism, the role of scholarly exponents of international law diminished. Nevertheless, the writings of leading scholars remain important references for courts and counsel alike. How courts and tribunals use these works was admirably

---

51 Thus, the North American Free Trade Agreement 1992, [1994] Can TS no 2 art 1136(1) provided "An award made by a Tribunal shall have no binding force except between the disputing parties and in respect of the particular case." Similarly, the appellate body of the World Trade Organization (WTO) has described reports of WTO panels as "an important part of the GATT *acquis*" but "not binding, except with respect to resolving the particular dispute between the parties": *Japan – Taxes on Alcoholic Beverages*, WT/DS8/AB/R, WT/DS10/AB/R, WT/DS11/AB/R, Appellate Body Report (AB-1996-2).

52 See, e.g., *Brownlie's*, above note 10 at 35–9.

53 See, e.g., the following passage in Lord Mansfield CJ's judgment in *Triquet v Bath* (1764), 3 Burr 1478 at 1481, 97 ER 936 at 938: "Lord Talbot [in 1737] declared a clear opinion – 'That the law of nations in its full extent was part of the law of England, . . . that the law of nations was to be collected from the practice of different nations and the authority of writers.' Accordingly, he argued and determined from such instances, and the authorities of Grotius, Barbeyrac, Binkershoek, Wiquefort, etc., there being no English writer of eminence on the subject."

explained by Gray J of the US Supreme Court in *The Paquete Habana* (1900):

> where there is no treaty and no controlling executive or legislative act or judicial decision, resort must be had to the customs and usages of civilized nations, and, as evidence of these, to the works of jurists and commentators who by years of labor, research, and experience have made themselves peculiarly well acquainted with the subjects of which they treat. Such works are resorted to by judicial tribunals, not for the speculations of their authors concerning what the law ought to be, but for trustworthy evidence of what the law really is.[54]

Similarly, in *West Rand Central Gold Mining Co v The King* (1905), Lord Alverstone CJ insisted that:

> The mere opinions of jurists, however eminent or learned, that [a doctrine of international law] ought to be so recognized, are not in themselves sufficient. They must have received the express sanction of international agreement or gradually have grown to be part of international law by their frequent practical recognition in dealings between various nations.[55]

This warning about the proper use of publicists in international adjudication did not diminish his lordship's enthusiasm for such works, on which he relied heavily in his reasons.

Similarly, the Supreme Court of Canada has frequently turned to international legal scholarship.[56] In *Finta* (1994), La Forest J described "the views of learned writers" as "extremely useful . . . in bringing before the Court the various relevant sources of law."[57]

---

54 (1900), 175 US 677 at 700. See also *United States v Smith* (1820), 18 US (5 Wheat) 153 at 160–1.

55 *West Rand Central Gold Mining Co v The King*, [1905] 2 KB 391 at 407–8. See also *Trendtex Trading Corp v Central Bank of Nigeria*, [1977] 1 QB 529 at 569 (CA), Stephenson LJ, approving the use of authoritative textbooks and the judicial decisions of foreign courts.

56 See, e.g., *Re Newfoundland Continental Shelf*, above note 44 at 118 (citing decisions of the ICJ and the writings of qualified authors); *Re Foreign Legations*, [1943] SCR 208 at 214–31, Duff CJ (citing such authors as Vattel, Grotius, Oppenheim, and others); and *Spraytech*, above note 38, L'Heureux-Dubé J (citing contemporary authors on the precautionary principle).

57 *Finta*, above note 33 at 761–2, La Forest J (dissenting).

(f) International organizations

Some international organizations have or may have lawmaking power.[58] A body with clear legislative capacity (at least over the member states of the United Nations) is the Security Council. By virtue of article 25 of the United Nations Charter 1945,[59] members agree "to accept and carry out the decisions of the Security Council in accordance with the present Charter." Generally, however, the Security Council refrains from exercising its decision power and instead makes recommendations.

The General Assembly of the United Nations also has some lawmaking powers, though of uncertain extent. It has a limited power to make binding decisions about certain matters,[60] and more general powers to make recommendations and declarations. These latter powers, while not strictly binding, may in some cases combine state practice with *opinio juris* so as to constitute customary international law.[61] For the most part, however, the General Assembly is a deliberative and not a legislative body.

Many other organizations play a role in the development of international law: the United Nations Commission on International Trade Law (UNCITRAL); the United Nations Conference on Trade and Development (UNCTAD); the United Nations Educational, Scientific, and Cultural Organization (UNESCO); the International Labour Organization; the World Trade Organization; the International Law Commission; and more. While it is an overstatement to describe these bodies as sources of international law, their work is frequently of interest to courts and tribunals confronted with international law questions.

(g) Unilateral statements

The ICJ has said it is "well recognized" that unilateral declarations by states may have the effect of creating legal obligations.[62] This will not

58 See, generally, P Sands & P Klein, *Bowett's Law of International Institutions*, 6th ed (London: Sweet & Maxwell, 2009) [Sands & Klein].

59 [1945] Can TS no 7 [UN Charter].

60 *Ibid*, arts 17 & 18.

61 See B Sloan, "General Assembly Resolutions Revisited" (1987) 58 *British Yearbook of International Law* 93 and S Schwebel, *The Legal Effect of Resolutions and Codes of Conduct of the United Nations* (Deventer, The Netherlands: Kluwer, 1985).

62 *Nuclear Test Cases (Australia v France and New Zealand v France)*, Merits, [1974] ICJ Rep 253 at para 43; *Frontier Dispute* case *(Burkina Faso v Mali)*, [1986] ICJ Rep 554 at para 39.

occur, of course, unless it is the intention of the declaring state to be bound by the statement according to its terms. Informing this rule is one of the most fundamental principles of international law, namely the requirement of good faith.[63]

(h) Peremptory norms (*jus cogens*)

VCLT article 53 provides that a treaty will be void "if, at the time of its conclusion, it conflicts with a peremptory norm of general international law." The article goes on to define a peremptory norm of general international law as one "accepted and recognized by the international community of States as a whole as a norm from which no derogation is permitted and which can be modified only by a subsequent norm of general international law having the same character."[64] In this sense, article 53 is a rule against unlawful contracts: States may not make treaties in breach of certain fundamental norms of international law. But the concept may go beyond the law of treaties to control state conduct more broadly. The International Law Commission's Draft Articles on Responsibility of States for Internationally Wrongful Acts affirm the existence of peremptory norms and the possibility of their breach by states without tying such breaches to the law of treaties.[65]

Reference in the VCLT to peremptory norms, also known as rules of *jus cogens* (compelling law), was controversial.[66] Article 53 represents a restraint on the sovereignty of states to conclude certain types of treaties. It declares that some rules of international law may be of such great significance that states cannot contract out of them. This proposition found disfavour with advocates of state sovereignty and with those who worried about which values (or, more to the point, whose values) might be elevated to the status of peremptory norms and thus rendered nearly immune from legal development.

---

63 See M Evans, ed, *International Law*, 5th ed (Oxford: Oxford University Press, 2018) at 100–1.

64 On peremptory norms, see Sinclair, above note 12 at 203–26; *Brownlie's*, above note 10 at 581–8; *Kindred's*, above note 2 at 54–6; Currie, above note 10 at 174–6.

65 See Crawford, above note 2 at arts 40–1 and commentary.

66 Many states withheld their ratification of the VCLT out of disagreement with *jus cogens*. The treaty remains unratified by many states, though significant portions of it are recognized as embodying rules of customary international law.

It would seem to follow from the VCLT's definition of peremptory norms that they are a variety of customary international law. For if state practice motivated by *opinio juris* is lacking, the norm cannot be one "accepted and recognized by the international community" and therefore cannot be peremptory in nature. The test for *jus cogens* must therefore be the same as the test for custom (namely, state practice and *opinio juris*) with the added element that the norm in question is considered by states as non-derogable – that is, impossible to displace by treaty or acquiescence (the development of local custom, for example). Thus, peremptory norms are not an independent source of international law but are instead a sort of entrenched custom.[67]

Which norms qualify as peremptory is a difficult question. Professor Brownlie observed that "more authority exists for the category of *jus cogens* than exists for its particular content."[68] The International Law Commission has identified an "illustrative list" of peremptory norms consisting of the prohibitions of aggression, torture, genocide, crimes against humanity, apartheid and racial discrimination and slavery, as well as the right to self-determination and the basic rules of international humanitarian law.[69]

In *Suresh*, the Supreme Court of Canada suggested the existence of a midway point in international law between customary international law (which is derogable) and *jus cogens* (which is not), describing the international prohibition of torture as a norm that "cannot be easily derogated from."[70] The notion that some rules of customary international law are less easily derogated from than others is wrong. The prohibition on torture is either a *jus cogens* norm or it is not. The ques-

67 Professor Brownlie called *jus cogens* "rules of customary law which cannot be set aside by treaty or acquiescence": I Brownlie, *Principles of Public International Law*, 6th ed (Oxford: Oxford University Press, 2003) [Brownlie] at 515. The Ontario Court of Appeal has called *jus cogens* "a higher form of customary law": *Bouzari v Islamic Republic of Iran* (2004), 71 OR (3d) 675 (CA) at para 86. Similarly, the Federal Court of Appeal has observed, "Before a customary norm of international law can become a peremptory norm there must be a further recognition by the international community, as a whole, that this is a norm from which no derogation is permitted": *Suresh v Canada (Minister of Citizenship and Immigration)*, [2000] 2 FC 592 (CA) at para 31.

68 Brownlie, *ibid* at 490.

69 International Law Commission, *Fourth Report on Peremptory Norms of General International Law (jus cogens)*, (2019) A/CN.4/727.

70 *Suresh*, above note 38 at para 65.

tion may be put as follows: May states or may they not lawfully depart from the international prohibition of torture? The court has since recognized that there may be no derogation from the international prohibition of torture.[71]

(i) *Erga omnes* obligations

An obligation *erga omnes* (for all the world) is one owed to the international community as a whole. Thus, any state may complain of another state's breach of an *erga omnes* obligation, even if, for example, that obligation takes the form of a treaty to which the complaining state is not a party. Like *jus cogens*, the category of obligations *erga omnes* is not a stand-alone source of international law but a description of the character of certain international laws.

There is considerable overlap between the concepts of *jus cogens* and *erga omnes*.[72] In the *Barcelona Traction* case, the ICJ described certain kinds of international obligations, now generally recognized as peremptory, as being obligations *erga omnes*.[73] While all peremptory norms are obligations *erga omnes*, it is not the case that all obligations *erga omnes* are *jus cogens*. Treaties can create legal regimes valid against third parties. Where these third parties are all states, the treaty creates an *erga omnes* regime.[74] The treaty does not necessarily create a *jus cogens* regime, however, because the regime may remain derogable – that is, susceptible to modification or revocation by later state action.

(j) Soft law

Most international activity is not of an explicitly lawmaking nature. The countless ententes, declarations, policy statements, and expressions of intent that characterize contemporary international and dip-

---

71 *Kazemi Estate*, above note 38 at para 47.

72 On obligations *erga omnes*, see M Ragazzi, *The Concept of International Obligations Erga Omnes* (Oxford: Clarendon Press, 2000).

73 *Barcelona Traction, Light and Power Company, Ltd Case (Belgium v Spain) (Second Phase)*, [1970] ICJ Rep 3 at paras 33–4. The examples given by the court included the outlawing of acts of aggression and genocide and rules of basic human rights, such as protection from slavery and racial discrimination.

74 See Hill, above note 12 at 268–9, giving examples of treaties demilitarizing certain territories or establishing free navigation in certain international waterways.

lomatic transactions usually lack the imperative quality of law. It is arguable, however, that while such activity may not represent *lex lata* (the law as it exists), it can nevertheless be looked to as *lex ferenda* (the developing or desirable law). The term "soft law" has come to describe this concept. The term is regrettable in that soft law is really not law at all. Yet it may be used as evidence of new or developing international laws. Thus, soft law may provide the state practice and *opinio juris* needed to support a claim of customary international law, or it may instantiate a general principle of international law.

Commonly cited forms of so-called soft law include resolutions of the UN General Assembly,[75] draft treaties (particularly multilateral conventions drafted by the International Law Commission), certain guides or handbooks created by UN agencies or other international bodies for their own internal use or for the use of states, recommendations and views of treaty-monitoring bodies, and communiqués of international conferences. The Supreme Court of Canada has frequently looked to such materials.[76]

2.4 Forums in which international law is applied

Canadian litigants are increasingly relying on international law in domestic proceedings. The same phenomenon appears to be occurring in other states. But domestic courts and tribunals are not yet the primary forum for the consideration of international law. It is difficult, however, to say what the primary forum of international law is, for there is such a great range of bodies charged with the enforcement, application, and consideration of international law.

(a) Courts of general jurisdiction

The Permanent Court of International Justice was provided for by article 14 of the Covenant of the League of Nations.[77] The court was empowered to render judgments in disputes between states and to give advisory opinions in matters referred to it by the organs of the League. The court sat at The

75 This is not to deny that a General Assembly resolution may represent customary international law. While such resolutions are generally not binding, they may, in some cases, be declaratory of customary international law.

76 For examples, see the discussion in Chapter 8, Section 8.4.

77 The Covenant is articles 1–26 of the Treaty of Versailles 1919, [1919] Can TS no 4.

Hague with a panel of 15 judges. Its operations virtually ceased upon German occupation of the Netherlands in 1940, and the court was dissolved in 1945. Many of its judgments are of lasting influence.

With the replacement of the League of Nations with the United Nations in 1945, the functions of the former court were transferred to the International Court of Justice. That court has sat without interruption ever since. Only states may be parties in cases before the court.[78] Jurisdiction in contentious cases is by consent and proceeds primarily by special agreement (*compromis*) between the disputing states, by treaty provisions granting jurisdiction over matters under the treaty, and by "optional clause" declarations whereby states may recognize the compulsory jurisdiction of the court over matters specified in article 36(2) of the ICJ Statute.[79] Canada has accepted compulsory jurisdiction subject to certain reservations.[80] The court also has an advisory jurisdiction[81] upon request for a legal opinion from the General Assembly, the Security Council, or other UN bodies authorized by the General Assembly to make such requests.[82]

(b) Specialist and regional courts and tribunals

Complementing and sometimes overlapping with the ICJ are several specialist and regional judicial bodies. In criminal law there are (or have been) the International Criminal Tribunals for the Former

---

78 ICJ Statute, above note 11 at art 34(1).

79 These matters are (1) the interpretation of a treaty; (2) any question of international law; (3) the existence of any fact that, if established, would constitute a breach of an international obligation; and (4) the nature or extent of the reparation to be made for the breach of an international obligation.

80 In its Declaration of 10 May 1994, Canada amended its acceptance of the compulsory jurisdiction of the court with the following reservations: (1) disputes in regard to which the parties have agreed or shall agree to have recourse to some other method of peaceful settlement; (2) disputes with the government of any other country which is a member of the Commonwealth, all of which disputes shall be settled in such manner as the parties have agreed or shall agree; (3) disputes with regard to questions that by international law fall exclusively within the jurisdiction of Canada; and (4) disputes arising out of or concerning conservation and management measures taken by Canada with respect to vessels fishing in the NAFO Regulatory Area, as defined in the Convention on Future Multilateral Co-operation in the Northwest Atlantic Fisheries 1978, [1979] Can TS no 11 and the enforcement of such measures.

81 ICJ Statute, above note 11 at art 65(1).

82 UN Charter, above note 59, art 96.

Yugoslavia[83] and Rwanda[84] and the International Criminal Court.[85] In trade and commerce there is the dispute settlement system of the World Trade Organization,[86] which combines ad hoc arbitral panels with a standing appellate body. In human rights there are the European Court of Human Rights[87] and the Inter-American Court of Human Rights.[88] In maritime matters there is the International Tribunal for the Law of the Sea.[89] This is not an exhaustive list.

(c) International arbitral tribunals

The earliest international judicial bodies were arbitral tribunals established on an ad hoc basis to settle particular disputes between states. The arbitrations between the United States and Great Britain conducted under the Jay Treaty 1794[90] and the Treaty of Washington 1871[91] were

---

83 Established in 1993 by the UN Security Council acting under Chapter VII of the UN Charter, *ibid*.

84 Established in 1995 by the UN Security Council acting under Chapter VII of the UN Charter, *ibid*.

85 Established under the Rome Statute of the International Criminal Court 1998, [2002] Can TS no 13. On the ICC and the Yugoslavia and Rwanda tribunals, see Sands & Klein, above note 58 at 383–90.

86 Established under the World Trade Organization Dispute Settlement Understanding, being Annex 2 of the Marrakesh Agreement Establishing the World Trade Organization 1994, (1994) 33 ILM 1144. See Sands & Klein, above note 58 at 379–83.

87 Established under the European Convention on Human Rights, 1950 ETS no 5.

88 Established under the American Convention on Human Rights 1969, (1979) 1144 UNTS 123.

89 Established under Part XV of the United Nations Convention on the Law of the Sea 1982, reprinted in (1982) 21 ILM 1261. As of 6 February 2002, Canada had signed but not yet ratified this treaty. See Sands & Klein, above note 58 at 375–9.

90 1 British and Foreign State Papers 784. The treaty diffused tensions between the United States and Great Britain in the early years of American independence. Article VI of the treaty recognized that "divers British merchants and others His Majesty's subjects" were owed debts by Americans "contracted before the peace" and bound the United States to make "full and complete compensation." "For the purpose of ascertaining the amount of any such losses and damages," art VI provided for the creation of mixed commissions, consisting of two British appointees, two American appointees, and a fifth appointee to be decided by the other four.

91 61 British and Foreign State Papers 40; reprinted in Canada, Department of External Affairs, *Treaties and Agreements Affecting Canada in Force Between His Majesty and the United States of America with Subsidiary Documents 1814–1925* (Ottawa: King's Printer, 1927) at 37. The US government sought reparations from

landmarks. In the late nineteenth century, arbitration came to be seen as a means of securing peaceful resolution of international disputes. A Permanent Court of Arbitration[92] was established at The Hague and a code of procedure drafted.

International arbitration today takes many forms. State-to-state arbitrations similar to those conducted under the Jay Treaty and Treaty of Washington still occur. International commercial disputes are often resolved through mixed arbitrations in which one party is a state and the other a non-state entity, such as a corporate investor. Prominent mixed arbitrations include those under the auspices of the International Centre for the Settlement of Investment Disputes (ICSID),[93] those conducted by the Iran-US Claims Tribunal, and those provided for in bilateral investment treaties. Investor–state arbitrations under chapter 11 of the former North American Free Trade Agreement 1992 are an example.[94] The most pervasive form of international arbitration today is commercial.[95] These arbitrations are established pursuant to concession agreements, private contracts, or bilateral investment treaties and are conducted by tribunals operating under arbitral rules promulgated by the United Nations Commission on International Trade Law

---

Great Britain for alleged violations of British neutrality during the American Civil War. British shipbuilders had built and refitted several Confederate warships, notably the *Alabama*, and these ships went on to inflict losses on northern merchant ships. Under the treaty, a tribunal of five members (one Briton, one American, and three others) met in Geneva to consider what become known as the *Alabama* claims. While the British were absolved of blame in several cases, the United States was nevertheless awarded the sum of $15 million.

92 Established under Chapter II of the Hague Convention for the Pacific Settlement of International Disputes 1899, reprinted in G Martens, *Nouveau Receuil général des traités*, 2d series, vol 26 (Göttingen: Dieterich, 1876–1908) at 920. The Permanent Court of Arbitration was practically defunct from 1932 until the late 1990s but is now active again.

93 The ICSID was established under the Convention on the Settlement of Investment Disputes between States and Nationals of Other States 1966, [2013] Can TS no 24 [ICSID Convention] and exists under the auspices of the World Bank. Arbitrations may be conducted under the ICSID Convention or under the ICSID Additional Facility rules. After a nearly 50-year delay, Canada became a party to the ICSID in late 2013.

94 North American Free Trade Agreement 1992, [1994] Can TS no 2.

95 See generally N Blackaby et al, *Redfern & Hunter on International Arbitration*, 6th ed (Oxford: Oxford University Press, 2019).

(UNCITRAL),[96] the International Chamber of Commerce, the ICSID, or other bodies.

(d) Treaty bodies

Some treaties create bodies charged with the task of monitoring the treaty's implementation and observance. States parties may be required to report on their compliance with the treaty to a committee empowered to hold hearings on the report and question the state's representatives. The composition, powers, and influence of such bodies vary.

Many treaty bodies are products of UN-supported human rights conventions. These include the Committee on Economic, Social, and Cultural Rights;[97] the Committee on the Rights of the Child;[98] the Committee on the Elimination of Racial Discrimination;[99] the Committee on the Elimination of All Forms of Discrimination against Women;[100] the Committee Against Torture;[101] and the Human Rights Committee.[102] The last four of these committees include optional mechanisms, either in their constituting treaties or in protocols to them, by which individuals may petition the committees to hear their claims that the state party has violated a treaty right.[103] Other examples of treaty bodies include the committees of the International Labour Organization (ILO), which have received annual reports from states on their observance of ILO conventions and recommendations since 1926,[104] and the

96 The UNCITRAL Arbitration Rules were adopted by the UN General Assembly on 15 December 1976, GA Res 31/98.

97 Established by the UN Economic and Social Council (ECOSOC) in 1985.

98 Established under art 43 of the Convention on the Rights of the Child 1989, [1992] Can TS no 3.

99 Established under Part II of the Convention on the Elimination of All Forms of Racial Discrimination 1966, [1970] Can TS no 28.

100 Established under art 22 of the Convention on the Elimination of All Forms of Discrimination against Women 1979, [1982] Can TS no 31.

101 Established under Part II of the Convention against Torture and Other Cruel, Inhuman or Degrading Treatment or Punishment 1984, [1987] Can TS no 36.

102 Established under Part IV of the International Covenant on Civil and Political Rights 1966, [1976] Can TS no 47.

103 See M Freeman & G van Ert, *International Human Rights Law* (Toronto: Irwin Law, 2004) at 393–7.

104 These reports are collected pursuant to arts 19 and 22 of the constitution of the International Labour Organization 1946, [1946] Can TS no 48. The ILO was created pursuant to the Labour Part of the Treaty of Versailles, above note 77.

implementation committee created under the Montreal Protocol on Substances that Deplete the Ozone Layer 1989.[105]

The reports, statements, and recommendations of such treaty bodies serve mainly to ensure compliance with their respective instruments. They may also serve, however, to elucidate the content of the international obligations they enforce. In this sense, treaty bodies may not only apply international law but also develop it.

(e) Domestic courts and tribunals

A final forum in which international law has historically been applied is domestic courts and tribunals. Certain areas of international law have fallen to domestic courts for their enforcement for centuries. Examples include the law of sovereign immunity and diplomatic privileges; the law of prize (a branch of maritime law governing the capture and disposition of the vessels and cargo of enemy nations);[106] the law of the sea;[107] and extradition law as established in extradition treaties. In the past, domestic application and enforcement of international law was usually confined to these rather narrow (but important) areas. This began to change in the latter half of the twentieth century, when a sharp increase in international lawmaking activity brought with it an increase in reliance on international law before domestic courts.

There is every reason to believe that this "internationalization" of domestic courts will continue. There is an understandable tendency to view domestic courts as the wrong forum, or at least a lesser forum, in which to bring actions founded in international law. Sometimes this is true, but there are at least two reasons why often it is not. First, it is a common requirement in international law that complainants exhaust their domestic remedies before proceeding before international bodies. In such cases there is no option but to begin one's action domestically. Second, domestic courts are themselves part of the international legal

---

105 [1989] Can TS no 42.

106 See C Colombos, *Treatise on the Law of Prize*, 3d ed (London: Longmans, Green, 1949).

107 See, e.g., *Direct United States Cable Company v Anglo-American Telegraph Company* (1877), 2 App Cas 394 (PC), in which Lord Blackburn found it unnecessary to determine whether, as a matter of international law, Conception Bay was a part of the territory of Newfoundland, but added, "If it were necessary in this case to lay down a rule the difficulty of the task would not deter their Lordships from attempting to fulfil it."

structure. As Brownlie observes, a domestic tribunal applying international law is no longer merely an organ of its national legal system.[108] Instead, it exercises an "international jurisdiction"[109] and thereby becomes an organ of the international judiciary. This point has been made by no less an authority than La Forest J, who has said that "our courts – and many other national courts – are truly becoming international courts in many areas involving the rule of law."[110]

---

108 Brownlie, above note 67 at 708.

109 Brownlie, *ibid* at 584. The existence of this international jurisdiction in domestic courts is why the Supreme Court of Canada was correct, in *Re Secession of Quebec*, [1998] 2 SCR 217 at paras 20–2, to reject the submissions of the *amicus curiae* that the court would exceed its jurisdiction or competence by answering questions on international law.

110 G La Forest, "The Expanding Role of the Supreme Court of Canada in International Law Issues" (1996) 34 *Canadian Yearbook of International Law* 89 at 100. See also *Finta*, above note 33 at 774, where La Forest J observed that a Canadian judge's interpretation of international law "bears some force internationally," citing art 38 of the ICJ Statute.

3 Evidence, pleadings, and jurisdiction

Litigants seeking to rely on or respond to submissions concerning international law must begin by considering how to do so as a matter of evidence and procedure. On their face, questions of evidence and procedure are starkly practical. For instance, if a point of international law requires proof, counsel must consider how to prove it. Conversely, if no proof is required, counsel may wish to object to the admissibility of opinion or other evidence concerning it. Behind these practical matters is a question of principle. How does Canadian law regard international law: as law (as it claims to be) or as fact?

In the previous edition of this work, I noted that the balance of Canadian authority, especially when supplemented with persuasive Commonwealth and foreign sources, indicated that Canadian courts should generally treat international law questions as legal matters to be decided by the courts and not factual matters to be pleaded and proved in evidence. I suggested that what uncertainty surrounded the issue arose mostly from Canadian courts' failing to turn their minds to the question – frequently, it seemed, because they rightly took it for granted that they may have regard to international law in appropriate cases.

Subsequent developments in the case law appear to have settled the issue. Canadian law generally treats international law as a matter of law, not fact, for the purposes of pleading and evidence.

As explained below, however, there are exceptional cases in which points of international law may require proof in evidence. In these rare instances, this may take the form of expert opinion or executive certificates. There are also rare and ill-defined situations in which Canadian courts may decline to consider international legal issues at all on what may loosely be called jurisdictional grounds. All these instances are exceptions to Canadian law's general stance of recognizing a competence in Canadian courts to hear and settle international legal questions that come properly before them as they would other questions of law.

3.1 Judicial notice of international law

By the doctrine of judicial notice, courts and other adjudicating bodies will accept the existence of certain matters without requiring proof.[1] The doctrine is most often invoked in respect of facts, but courts also take judicial notice of law. This form of judicial notice has its origins in the common law but has also been declared in statutes.[2] It is also established in Quebec civil law.[3] The varieties of law that judges are bound to recognize by the doctrine of judicial notice include the principles of equity, common law precedents, and Acts of Parliament. As we will see, judicial notice is also taken of international law, though one evidentiary consequence of this rule – namely, that opinion evidence on international law's requirements is generally inadmissible – has sometimes been neglected.

Judicial notice of international law is to be contrasted with the treatment of foreign law (that is, the domestic law of other states), of which judicial notice is not taken in the common law tradition. Rather, foreign law is treated as a matter of fact to be ascertained by the evidence of experts.[4] An old decision of the US Supreme Court contrasts foreign and international law directly: "Foreign municipal laws must in-

---

1 See S Lederman, A Bryant, & M Fuerst, *Sopinka, Lederman & Bryant: The Law of Evidence*, 5th ed (Markham, ON: LexisNexis, 2018) at § 19:16; S Phipson & H Malek, *Phipson on Evidence*, 19th ed (London: Sweet & Maxwell, 2017) at ch 3; R Sullivan, *Sullivan on the Construction of* Statutes, 6th ed (Markham, ON: LexisNexis, 2014) at § 3.22.

2 The judicial notice of Acts of the federal Parliament is provided for by s 18 of the Canada Evidence Act, RSC 1985, c C-5. The judicial notice of provincial Acts is provided for by provincial legislation; for example, Evidence Act, RSBC 1996, c 124, s 24(2) (British Columbia), Interpretation Act, RSO 1990, c I.11, s 7 (Ontario).

3 Civil Code of Quebec, CQLR c CCQ-1991, art 2807 provides in part, "Judicial notice shall be taken of the law in force in Québec." See generally arts 2806–10.

4 See generally J Walker, *Castel & Walker: Canadian Conflict of Laws*, 6th ed, looseleaf (Markham, ON: LexisNexis Canada, 2005) at ss 7.1–7.5.

deed be proved as facts, but it is not so with the law of nations."[5] Lauterpacht considered that international law need not be proved in the same way as foreign law in common law courts "apparently for the reason that it is not foreign law."[6] The importance of this distinction between international law and foreign law goes beyond the rules of evidence to the foundation of the reception system. While foreign laws generally have no claim to our observance, except insofar as international comity may require in certain cases, international law is binding upon Canada at the international level and may (if incorporated or implemented in domestic law) be binding within Canada. The reception system acknowledges this difference by rules that receive and promote respect for international law within the domestic order – including judicial notice of international law.[7] Anglo-Canadian law is not unusual in this regard. A former president of the International Court of Justice, Dame Rosalyn Higgins, has observed, "There is not a legal system in the world where international law is treated as 'foreign law.' It is everywhere part of the law of the land; as much as contracts, labour law or administrative law."[8]

(a) Case law supporting judicial notice of international law

In 1939, Lauterpacht observed that while English judicial practice supported the proposition that international law is judicially noticed and therefore need not be specifically proved, it was nevertheless difficult "to trace any judicial pronouncement bearing directly on the matter."[9]

5 *The Scotia* 14 Wall 170 (US Sup Ct 1871) [*The Scotia*].

6 H Lauterpacht, "Is International Law a Part of the Law of England?" (1939) 25 *Transactions of the Grotius Society* 51 at 59.

7 One commentator has argued against this approach, suggesting that both international and foreign law are "external sources of law" and that "the blurring of international law into comparative law" allows international lawyers "to develop a more complex and critical model of international law in domestic courts." See K Knop, "Here and There: International Law in Domestic Courts" (2000) 32 *New York Journal of International Law and Politics* 501 at 520, 525. In my view, the differences between foreign and international law are more significant than their similarities. See also S Toope, "The Uses of Metaphor: International Law and the Supreme Court of Canada" (2001) 80 *Canadian Bar Review* 534.

8 R Higgins, "The Relationship Between International and Regional Human Rights Norms and Domestic Law" in *Developing Human Rights Jurisprudence*, vol 5 (London: Commonwealth Secretariat, 1993) at 16. Quoted with approval in *Nevsun Resources Ltd v Araya*, 2020 SCC 5 at para 97 [*Nevsun*].

9 Instead, Lauterpacht relies on *The Scotia*, above note 5 at 188. See also *The New York*, 175 US 187 (1899).

Macdonald made the same observation about Canadian law in 1974.[10] Today, however, there is authority from the Supreme Court of Canada and the Federal Court of Appeal, among others.

For decades, the leading Canadian pronouncement on the judicial notice of international law was *The North*, a 1906 judgment of the Supreme Court of Canada.[11] The question was whether the seizure of an American vessel fishing illegally off the coast of British Columbia was unlawful because the poacher escaped beyond Canada's territorial waters into the high seas before being captured. The poacher relied on a Canadian statute that recognized British waters as extending to only "three marine miles of any coast."[12] Canada relied on the customary international law doctrine of hot pursuit, whereby a state pursuing a vessel within its territorial waters for a suspected violation of its laws may continue that pursuit into international waters. The doctrine is designed to ensure that such vessels do not escape punishment by fleeing to the high seas. In the court below, the admiralty judge took notice of the doctrine of hot pursuit and interpreted the statute in its light. At the Supreme Court of Canada, Davies J (MacLennan J concurring) approved this approach, declaring that "the Admiralty Court when exercising its jurisdiction is bound to take notice of the law of nations" and "The right of hot pursuit . . . being part of the law of nations was properly judicially taken notice of and acted upon by the learned judge."[13]

In *The Cristina* (1938), Lord Macmillan observed that "a doctrine of public international law" is "evidenced by international treaties and conventions, authoritative textbooks, practice and judicial decisions."[14] Notably, Lord Macmillan did not include expert evidence among the means of proving international law. This point was made expressly by

---

10 See R St J Macdonald, "The Relationship Between Domestic Law and International Law in Canada" in R St J Macdonald et al, eds, *Canadian Perspectives on International Law and Organization* (Toronto: University of Toronto Press, 1974) [Macdonald] at 113.

11 *The Ship "North" v The King* (1906), 37 SCR 385 [*The North*].

12 An Act respecting Fishing by Foreign Vessels, RSC 1886, c 94.

13 *The North*, above note 11 at 394. Sedgewick J concurred in the result without giving reasons. Idington J delivered concurring reasons which, while not explicitly affirming that international law was properly noticed in Canadian courts, nevertheless acknowledged and relied upon the doctrine of hot pursuit. Girouard J dissented, finding that the statute excluded reliance on the doctrine. See also *R v Blanco* (1991), 97 Nfld & PEIR 86 at 89 (Nfld SCTD).

14 *Compania Naviera Vascongado v SS Cristina*, [1938] AC 485 (HL) at 497.

Stephenson LJ, considering Lord Macmillan's dictum, in *Trendtex Trading Corp v Bank of Nigeria* (1977):

> [R]ules of international law, whether they be part of our law or a source of our law, must be in some sense "proved," and they are not proved in English courts by expert evidence like foreign law; they are "proved" by taking judicial notice of "international treaties and conventions, authoritative textbooks, practice and judicial decisions" of other courts in other countries which show that they have "attained the position of general acceptance by civilised nations": *The Cristina* . . .[15]

Judicial notice of international law arose in the dissenting reasons of Pigeon J (Beetz and Grandpré JJ concurring) in *Capital Cities Communications Inc v Canadian Radio-Television Commission* (1978).[16] The Canadian Radio-Television Commission (CRTC) permitted a cable company to delete advertisements from US television channels it broadcasted. The American broadcasters challenged this decision, relying in part on the Inter-American Radiocommunications Convention 1937.[17] The majority found that the treaty was unimplemented in Canadian law and drew a distinction between the Canadian government (which was bound by the treaty) and the CRTC (which was not). The dissenting judges rejected the proposition that the CRTC was free to make decisions in violation of Canada's treaty obligations, observing, "It is an oversimplification to say that treaties are of no legal effect unless implemented by legislation."[18] Pigeon J concluded that

> on the appeal from the decision of the Commission, judicial notice ought to be taken that, by virtue of the Convention the appellants had a legal interest entitled to protection in the use of their assigned channels, for broadcasts in an area extending into Canada. Therefore the Commission could not validly authorize an interference with this interest in violation of the convention signed by Canada.[19]

As authority for this proposition, his lordship quoted at some length from *Post Office v Estuary Radio Ltd*,[20] in which Diplock LJ (as he then

---

15 *Trendtex Trading v Bank of Nigeria*, [1977] 1 QB 529 (Eng CA) at 569 [*Trendtex*].
16 [1978] 2 SCR 141 [*Capital Cities*].
17 [1938] Can TS no 18.
18 *Capital Cities*, above note 16 at 188.
19 *Ibid* at 189.
20 [1968] 2 QB 740 (Eng CA) [*Estuary Radio*]. See also *In re Queensland Mercantile and Agency Company*, [1892] 1 Ch 219 at 226 (CA).

was) held that the court must take judicial notice of a treaty concluded by the Crown that extended the UK's internal waters beyond the previous three-mile limit. While Pigeon J spoke in dissent, subsequent Supreme Court of Canada decisions have arguably weakened the authority of the majority judgment.[21] Note that the majority did not refuse to take judicial notice of the Convention itself, but only found that it had no application because it was unimplemented in domestic law.

In *Pan-American World Airways Inc v Department of Trade* (1976), the question was whether the secretary of state had the power to insert a disputed condition into an airline's UK operating permit. The airline challenged the condition as contrary to an agreement between the United Kingdom and the United States. The English Court of Appeal found that the agreement in question was not part of UK law and therefore could not restrict the secretary's powers. Lord Justice Scarman (as he then was) nevertheless made the following observation:

> If statutory words have to be construed or a legal principle formulated in an area of law where Her Majesty has accepted international obligations, our Courts – who, of course, take notice of the acts of Her Majesty done in the exercise of her sovereign power – will have regard to the convention as part of the full content or background of that law . . . even though no statute expressly or impliedly incorporates it into our law.[22]

Judicial notice of international law arose in another case involving Pan-American, this time in Canada. In *Pan-American World Airways Inc v The Queen* (1979),[23] the Federal Court (Trial Division) considered a challenge to federal aeronautics regulations said to be contrary to the terms of the Chicago Convention on International Civil Aviation 1944,[24] to which Canada was a party, as well as being contrary to an alleged "fundamental principle of equity" in international law. The plaintiff tendered expert evidence on Canada's right, as a matter of international law, to levy certain airline charges on the United States

21 I consider this decision more fully in Chapter 9, Section 9.4(a).

22 *Pan-American World Airways Inc v Department of Trade*, [1976] 1 Lloyd's Rep 257 (Eng CA) [*Pan-American*] at 261, Scarman LJ.

23 (1979) 96 DLR (3d) 267 (FCTD), aff'd (1980), 120 DLR (3d) 574 (FCA), aff'd [1981] 2 SCR 565 [*Pan American*].

24 [1944] Can TS no 36.

for air navigation and services it provided over the high seas. In dismissing the plaintiff's arguments, Mahoney J described this evidence as "wholly inadmissible":

> While expert evidence as to foreign law is, of course, admissible, expert evidence as to domestic law is not. It is well established that international law has no force in Canada unless it has been adopted as domestic law. Opinion evidence as to the proper construction to be placed on the Chicago Convention was not admissible and I have not, therefore, considered [the expert's] statement as evidence but, on the assumption that plaintiff's counsel would willingly adopt it as argument, I have considered it such.[25]

The reasoning in this passage is not entirely clear,[26] but the result is clear enough. Justice Mahoney rejected as inadmissible expert evidence as to the meaning and requirements of international law. The decision was upheld on appeal without comment on this point.

In the proceedings against alleged Hungarian war criminal Imre Finta, the testimony of a well-known international criminal law scholar, M. Cherif Bassiouni, was admitted into evidence. Yet in a pre-trial motion, the trial judge observed "It is not necessary to refer to the massive weight of authority produced by the Crown that demonstrates that questions of international law are questions for the judge. That principle is as old as Blackstone."[27] On that reasoning, one would expect the testimony not to be admissible at all, but it appears that the trial judge, like Mahoney J in *Pan-American*, treated the evidence as argument. This supposition is supported by La Forest J's consideration of Bassiouni's testimony on appeal to the Supreme Court of Canada. The learned judge (dissenting) criticized and rejected Bassiouni's testimony, effectively treating it as a question of law (to which no deference was due) rather than a finding of fact. He equated the testimony with scholarly writings, describing "the views of learned writers such as Professor Bassiouni" as "extremely useful" but emphasizing their "subsidiary character in determining what constitutes international law." Justice La Forest concluded that "Bassiouni does not represent

25 *Pan American* (FCTD), above note 23 at 274–5.

26 The case is considered further in G van Ert, "The Admissibility of International Legal Evidence" (2005) 84 *Canadian Bar Review* 31.

27 Quoted in *R v Finta* (1992), 92 DLR (4th) 1 (Ont CA).

the consensus of legal writers" and expressed his "complete agreement with the dissenting judges in the Court of Appeal" on the international legal issue before them.[28] The learned judge also observed that much confusion exists as to the elements of the international offences of war crimes and crimes against humanity and that such legal questions were for the trial judge, not the jury:

> It is, of course, not an answer to this complicated task [of determining the elements of the offences] to say that the contents of international offences are too difficult to distill and, therefore, that the accused cannot be found guilty; the confusion is the reality of the international law which Canada has obliged itself to observe and apply. This abandonment of international obligation, however, is likely to occur where the jury is called upon to determine the contents of the international offences. The necessary confusion could mislead the jury into believing that international norms are not really law and opens the door to manipulative lawyering. The questions of pinpointing international law, therefore, are best left in the hands of the trial judge whose training better equips him or her for the task. Not only is the judge better trained than the jury in evaluating international law, but, in fact, his or her interpretation of international law bears some force internationally (see Art. 38 of the Statute of the International Court of Justice). Again, the inquiries required are not of a kind immediately related to the accused's culpability for the domestic offence; rather, they are more legal and technical. There can, in my view, be no doubt that justice is better served by leaving the question of international law to the trial judge. I can perhaps make the point that the process bears some similarity to that of determining the content and application of common law, except that the latter, fluid and moveable as it may be, is far more precise.[29]

The admissibility of expert evidence on a point of customary international law was considered by the High Court of Justiciary (Scotland's final court of criminal appeal) in *Lord Advocate's Reference No 1 of 2000*.[30] Three anti-nuclear protesters were acquitted of malicious damage to a

---

28 [1994] 1 SCR 701 at 760–4 [*Finta*].

29 *Ibid* at 773–4.

30 2001 SLT 507, [2001] Scot J 84 (HCJ) [*Lord Advocate's Reference*], also known as *HM Advocate v Zelter*.

support vessel for UK Trident submarines (which carry nuclear missiles). At their trial, which occurred before a jury, the accused raised a defence of necessity, arguing that the deployment of nuclear missiles by the UK is contrary to customary international law and therefore criminal in Scots law. Thus, the accused submitted, they were acting to prevent or obstruct a crime. To establish the applicable requirements of customary international law, the accused led expert evidence from international lawyers. The presiding judge (known as the sheriff) admitted this evidence, which was presented before the jury. Upon acquittal, the government referred four legal questions to the High Court of Justiciary, including: "In a trial under Scottish criminal procedure, is it competent to lead evidence as to the content of customary international law as it applies in the United Kingdom?" The joint opinion of Lords Prosser, Kirkwood, and Penrose was that a rule of customary international law is a rule of Scots law and is therefore a matter for the judge and not for the jury. Submissions on questions of international law must be made by counsel, not by expert witnesses. Their lordships conceded, however, "that the question of whether an *opinio juris* has emerged, and won the general acceptance which is necessary to constitute a rule of customary international law, might well make recourse to expertise appropriate," though they nevertheless observed that "having regard to the different skills and expertise of an advocate on the one hand, and some other kind of specialist on the other hand, we find it very hard to imagine any situation in which the appropriate material should be presented to the court in the form of evidence with examination and cross-examination, and perhaps counter-evidence for the other party."[31]

In *Plourde v Service aérien FBO inc (Skyservice)* (2007),[32] an appeal from a decision refusing to certify a class proceeding, the Quebec Court of Appeal noted that, at the hearing of the appeal, it put questions to counsel for the appellant on the meaning of a treaty provision. Counsel declined to answer, saying instead that he intended to call the president of the international conference at which the treaty was negotiated, and that he would answer these questions in evidence. The court rejected this approach, observing that, even without pronouncing on the admissibility of such evidence, it would have no weight.

31 *Ibid* at para 27.

32 2007 QCCA 739 at paras 59–60.

Justice Perram of the Federal Court of Australia considered at length the question of whether international law was properly the subject of expert evidence in *Australian Competition and Consumer Commission v P.T. Garuda Indonesia (No 9)* (2013).[33] The admissibility of a law professor's opinion on matters of international transportation law was challenged on several grounds. His Honour began by observing that "What little authority there is suggests that under Australian law a question of public international law is not one which involves the taking of evidence. On the other hand, under Australian law, foreign law such as Indonesian law is a fact to be proved by evidence."[34] As to why international law, when it comes to the manner of its proof, should be treated as a question of law rather than as one of fact, Perram J made the following observations of note:

> The proliferation of international law concepts throughout modern legal systems, including Australia's, would make it inconvenient to require evidentiary proof each time one arose for consideration. . . . It would add a layer of expense and complexity if that discourse were required to be approached factually.
>
> . . . [D]omestic public law (by which I mean areas such as statutory interpretation, constitutional and administrative law) and international law are intertwined. Whilst it is true that foreign law and domestic law are also intertwined by reason of the principles relating to conflict of laws this does not occur in a way which impacts on the actual content of domestic law. A forum court may apply the law of Malta to a particular contract but this in no way effects the content of Australian law. When, on the other hand, a court construes a statute to comply with a treaty obligation this cannot be said to be so and in such a circumstance, international law then exerts a discernable influence on the content of local law.[35]
>
> . . .
>
> I do not think that the Professor's views are likely to add anything more in the form of evidence than they will add in the form of Mr Leeming's eventual submissions based upon them. Indeed, given the more active role of the Court during submissions it is unlikely that

33 [2013] FCA 323 (Federal Court of Australia) [*P.T. Garuda*].

34 *Ibid* at para 29.

35 *Ibid* at paras 42–3.

> cross-examination of the Professor by counsel is likely to add anything which will not otherwise be obtained by cross-examination of counsel by the Court. In that circumstance, I conclude that the receipt of Professor Dempsey's views . . . would result in a waste of time and resources which is not justified by its likely probative effect.[36]

The admissibility of opinion evidence on international law was commented upon briefly, but importantly, by the Court of Appeal for British Columbia in *R v Appulonappa* (2014).[37] "I agree with the respondents," said Neilson JA, "that, to the extent that both experts strayed into providing opinions on the interpretation and application of international law . . . their testimony was not properly admissible as these were questions of law for the court. I accordingly limit my consideration of their evidence to factual matters."

In *Canadian Planning v Libya* (2015), Braid J rejected the argument that the international law issues raised by Libya ought to be proved by expert evidence. She distinguished authorities requiring foreign law to be proved through experts, observing that in the case before her "the court must interpret Canada's international law obligations – something the Supreme Court has instructed Superior Courts to do," and added that the court "is merely interpreting Canadian law in light of international law, rather than attempting to interpret laws of other states."[38] In a subsequent ruling in the same matter, Braid J admitted (seemingly without opposition) an expert report from Professor Toope on whether international law would preclude third parties from providing information about their financial dealings with Libya for the purpose of determining whether the Libyan bank accounts in issue were immune from enforcement proceedings. Notably, however, Braid J showed no deference to Toope's expertise, and indeed rejected his opinion in favour of her own assessment of the customary international legal position.[39] Rather than treating Toope's views as unrebutted evidence (there being no opposing expert report to counter them), she engaged with them as though they were submissions from a party.

---

36 *Ibid* at para 54.

37 *R v Appulonappa*, 2014 BCCA 163 [*Appulonappa*] at para 62.

38 *Canadian Planning and Design Consultants Inc v Libya*, 2015 ONSC 1638 at para 34 [*Canadian Planning No 1*].

39 *Canadian Planning v Libya*, 2015 ONSC 3386 [*Canadian Planning No 3*] at paras 22–3, 44–9.

In *Boily v La Reine* (2017), a Federal Court prothonotary struck out an expert report as inadmissible for expressing an opinion about international law as it applied in the case, relying in part on a discussion in the second edition of this book on the common law distinction between international law (which is a matter of judicial notice) and foreign law (which is not).[40] On appeal, Gagné J agreed that the report was inadmissible but preferred to base her reasoning on "the inadmissibility of expertise providing legal conclusions on the issue(s) to be decided by the court, whether that law be domestic, foreign or international."[41] On the admissibility of international legal evidence, Gagné J noted that while my book argued for the orthodox view that international legal questions are questions of law, I also presented "several examples of exceptions to this rule where Canadian judges have accepted expert evidence on international law."[42] The learned judge concluded that "there is no authoritative legal position in Canada on whether or not judges are to take judicial notice of international law and consequently, on the admissibility of expertise on international law,"[43] and that there is "clearly no settled position on this point."[44] Justice Gagné went so far as to say that the prothonotary's conclusion that "that expert evidence on international law is inadmissible because judges must take judicial notice of international law could be said to be a legal error" and that "That conclusion is not the law in Canada." Instead,

> Courts' taking judicial notice of international law and their acceptance of expert evidence on international law will continue to be made on a case-by-case basis going forward, until such point as a Canadian court takes a more definitive stance on this practice.[45]

Yet the learned judge went on to make statements and findings very much in keeping with the inadmissibility of expert evidence on international legal issues. She quoted approvingly the Court of Appeal for British Columbia in *Appulonappa* that the experts in that case had "strayed into providing opinions on the interpretation and application of international law

40 *Boily v Her Majesty the Queen*, 2017 FC 396 at paras 12–13.
41 *Boily v Her Majesty the Queen*, 2017 FC 1021 at para 25 [*Boily* appeal].
42 *Ibid* at para 28.
43 *Ibid* at para 27.
44 *Ibid* at para 29.
45 *Ibid* at para 30.

and s. 117 of the IRPA," which testimony was "not properly admissible as these were questions of law for the court."[46] She also expressly declined to rely on Swinton J's use of expert evidence in *Bouzari*, noting trenchantly that "the role of the legal experts in this case seems to go beyond what Justice Swinton presents their role to be at the beginning of her judgment."[47] Ultimately, Gagné J affirmed that "in submitting an expert opinion containing a legal conclusion on international law as it applies to the facts of the case, Mr. Boily submitted inadmissible expert evidence."[48]

As if in response to Gagné J's observation that Canadian law lacks an authoritative statement of whether or not our judges take judicial notice of international law, Nadon JA for the Federal Court of Appeal went a considerable way to supplying it in *Turp v Canada (Foreign Affairs)*. The applicant sought judicial review of the federal government's decision to sell military vehicles to Saudi Arabia. Both sides relied on expert opinion on the international legal issues. In a discussion entitled, "Proof of international law through expertise," Nadon JA observed:

> I think it is useful to remark, without ruling on the question since the parties have not submitted any argument to this effect, that, in my opinion, the parties do not need to file experts' reports to prove international law, because the Court can take judicial notice of said law.[49]

The learned judge proceeded to consider *The North*, *Jose Pereira E Hijos, S.A. v Canada (Attorney General)*,[50] and *Lord Advocate's Reference*, quoting extensively from each. In particular, Nadon JA quoted with emphasis the following passage from *Lord Advocate's Reference*: "we find it very hard to imagine any situation in which the appropriate material should be presented to the court in the form of evidence with examination and cross-examination, and perhaps counter-evidence for the other party." He concluded by expressing his complete agreement with the three decisions and observing:

> Consequently, I think that in a case like the one before us, the parties do not need to rely on expertise in international law. International law, being a question of law, is the prerogative of courts, which can

46 *Ibid* at para 33, quoting *Appulonappa*, above note 37 at para 62.
47 *Ibid* at paras 41–3, considering *Bouzari v Iran*, [2002] OJ No 1624 (Ont SCJ).
48 *Ibid* at para 49.
49 *Turp v Canada (Foreign Affairs)*, 2018 FCA 133 [*Turp* FCA] at para 82.
50 [1997] 2 FC 84 [*Jose Pereira*], considered in Section 3.6(a), below.

> take judicial notice of this law with the help of attorneys arguing the case.[51]

While Nadon JA pointedly left open the possibility of reconsidering this matter in another case (having not heard submissions on the point), this discussion is bound to be significant.

If any controversy remained after *Turp* as to whether courts take judicial notice of international law, it was surely resolved in *Nevsun Resources v Araya* (2020). This was a claim by Eritrean nationals against a BC mining company. They alleged the company was liable to them for its complicity in breaches of customary international law obligations committed against them by Eritrea. On a motion to strike the pleadings, Abella J for the majority of the Supreme Court of Canada quoted Dame Rosalyn Higgins' observation that "there is not 'international law' and the common law. International law is part of that which comprises the common law on any given subject," affirmed that customary international law is incorporated by the common law, approved an observation of mine that Canadian courts are to treat public international law as law not fact, and held that "established norms of customary international law are law, to be judicially noticed."[52]

The question was extensively considered, in the context of treaty interpretation, by De Montigny JA (as he then was) for the Federal Court of Appeal in *International Air Transport Association v Canadian Transportation Agency* (2022).[53] That court was asked to declare invalid certain regulations adopted by the Canadian Transportation Agency. The appellants contended that the regulations violated requirements established in international civil aviation treaties. In support of this position, the appellants submitted two expert reports on the meaning of the Montreal Convention[54] and related treaties. The attorney general of Canada objected that these reports were inadmissible.

Justice De Montigny agreed. He considered there to be "many reasons why Canadian courts should take judicial notice of international

---

51 *Turp* FCA, above note 49 at para 88.

52 *Nevsun*, above note 8 at paras 95–7 (citing to the second edition of this work at 62–9); see also paras 98–100.

53 *International Air Transport Association and others v Canadian Transportation Agency and others*, 2022 FCA 211 [*IATA*].

54 Convention for the Unification of Certain Rules for International Carriage by Air 1999, 2242 UNTS 309 (ratified by Canada 19 November 2002).

law without the need to resort to expert opinion." First, "international law is in many respects domestic law," whether through the incorporation of custom by the common law or the implementation of treaties by statute.[55] Second, the presumption of conformity with international law and the risk that violations of international obligations "will attract international responsibility" favoured judicial notice.[56] A third consideration was the general law on the admissibility of expert evidence, in particular the necessity requirement; the learned judge noted that "expert opinion on a question of law can hardly be necessary, given the Court's expertise on matters of law."[57] Justice De Montigny noted that while the case law has not been consistent, "I think it is fair to say that the jurisprudence has moved towards the exclusion" of expert opinion evidence on points of international law.[58] He concluded:

> Expert evidence on international law, just like expert evidence on any issue of domestic law, should therefore not be countenanced. Counsel should make submissions on international law themselves, without resorting to the added credibility of an expert. Of course, a learned article canvassing some of the legal issues in an expert opinion could, if published, be put before the Court, along with case law and other types of legal sources. But international law should definitely not be pleaded as a fact, to be proven by way of affidavit or testimonial evidence, especially when the objective is to provide legal conclusions on the very issue that is at the core of the dispute between the parties.
>
> . . . The normative content of international law falls within the bailiwick of the court's exclusive jurisdiction.[59]

Justice De Montigny drew a clear distinction between evidence of international law and evidence of foreign law.[60] While international law is not properly the subject of opinion evidence, foreign law is. This distinction mattered in the case before the court, as both parties sought

55 *IATA*, above note 53 at para 48.
56 *Ibid* at para 49.
57 *Ibid* at paras 50–2.
58 *Ibid* at para 54; see also paras 55–8.
59 *Ibid* at paras 65–6.
60 *Ibid* at paras 45, 67–9.

to rely not only on international civil aviation agreements but also on state practice under those agreements. Such practice was properly proved through expert reports. The opinions tendered by the parties were only impermissible to the extent that they crossed the line between describing foreign state practice and opining on the consistency of that practice with treaties to which Canada is a party – the latter being "a matter of legal argument."[61]

The decision in *International Air Transport Association* is a welcome development. Together with *Nevsun*, it ought to settle at long last the principle on which Anglo-Canadian reception law has proceeded, without expressly saying so, for centuries, namely that courts take judicial notice of international law. The one matter De Montigny JA left open, because it was not strictly before him, was whether courts should also take judicial notice of treaties not implemented in federal or provincial statutes.[62] I respectfully suggest that the answer to that question is yes. As noted above, Lord Scarman in *Pan-American World Airways Inc v Department of Trade* was of the view that courts "take notice of the acts of Her Majesty done in the exercise of her sovereign power even though no statute expressly or impliedly incorporates [a given convention] into our law."[63] This approach makes sense for, as De Montigny JA noted, the presumption of conformity with international law serves to avoid attracting international responsibility on the state through non-conformity judicial interpretations of domestic law. That responsibility can arise whether the treaty in issue is implemented or not. Furthermore (and as considered at length in Chapter 7), Canadian treaty implementation practice is far from transparent; legislative provisions that do not appear to be in implementation of Canadian treaty obligations may in fact serve that function. Judicial notice of relevant treaty obligations (without expert evidence) enables courts to interpret statutory provisions in their entire context, including international law.

Alongside the decisions described above must be ranged the untold number of Canadian cases, from the nineteenth century to today, in which our courts have, in effect though without explicitly commenting upon it, taken judicial notice of applicable rules of customary and con-

61 *Ibid* at para 68; see also para 164.

62 *Ibid* at paras 47, 64.

63 *Pan-American*, above note 22.

ventional international law in the course of their decision making.[64] The uncertainty that has for some time clouded the orthodox rule that Canadian courts take judicial notice of international law is regrettable but should not be overstated. The actual practice of Canadian courts in numerous cases, combined with the logical necessity of the rule in order to give effect to such other reception law doctrines as the presumption of conformity, the incorporation of custom by the common law, and even the sovereignty of our legislatures to violate international law, sufficiently establish the judicial notice doctrine in Canada. Those cases that run contrary to the rule (reviewed below) appear to do so out of unfamiliarity with it on the part of counsel and the court rather than out of any principled objection.

(b) Commentators supporting judicial notice of international law

Some of the clearest statements of the rule that courts take judicial notice of international law come not from decided cases but from commentators. Writing in 1965, Castel observed of the Canadian position, "Since international law is part of the law of the land, it need not be proved in court like foreign law. Judicial notice is taken of it as of acts of Parliament or of any branch of the unwritten law."[65] Nine years later, Macdonald con-

---

64 This book is replete with examples, but some notable instances from the Supreme Court of Canada are *Re Foreign Legations*, [1943] SCR 208; *Re Armed Forces*, [1943] SCR 483; *Saint John v Fraser-Brace Overseas Corp*, [1958] SCR 263; *Reference re Ownership of Offshore Mineral Rights of British Columbia*, [1967] SCR 792; *Reference re Newfoundland Continental Shelf*, [1984] 1 SCR 86; *R v Crown Zellerbach Canada Ltd*, [1988] 1 SCR 401; *Slaight Communications v Davidson*, [1989] 1 SCR 1038; *Re Canada Labour Code*, [1992] 2 SCR 50; *Ordon Estate v Grail*, [1998] 3 SCR 437; *United States of America v Burns*, [2001] 1 SCR 283; *Suresh v Canada (Minister of Citizenship and Immigration)*, [2002] 1 SCR 3; *R v Malmo-Levine; R v Caine*, [2003] 3 SCR 571; *GreCon Dimter inc v J.R. Normand inc*, [2005] 2 SCR 401; *R v Hape*, 2007 SCC 26 [*Hape*]; *Health Services and Support – Facilities Subsector Bargaining Ass'n v British Columbia*, 2007 SCC 27; *Yugraneft Corp v Rexx Management Corp*, 2010 SCC 19; *Németh v Canada (Justice)*, 2010 SCC 56; *Ezokola v Canada*, 2013 SCC 40 [*Ezokola*]; *Febles v Canada (Citizenship and Immigration)*, 2014 SCC 68; *Thibodeau v Air Canada*, 2014 SCC 67; *B010 v Canada*, 2015 SCC 58; *R v Appulonappa*, 2015 SCC 59; *World Bank Group v Wallace*, 2016 SCC 15; *Ktunaxa Nation v British Columbia (Forests, Lands and Natural Resource Operations)*, 2017 SCC 54; *Office of the Children's Lawyer v Balev*, 2018 SCC 16 [*Balev*].

65 J-G Castel, *International Law Chiefly as Interpreted and Applied in Canada* (Toronto: University of Toronto Press, 1965) at 44.

cluded that in Canada as in England "the standard practice has been to notice judicially international law, although, as in England, the Canadian courts have not usually seen fit to comment on this point directly."[66] More recent Canadian commentators have also approved the rule.[67]

These conclusions are in keeping with English and US commentary. The fourth edition of *Halsbury's Laws of England* states simply, "The courts take notice of every branch of English law, including the principles of international law."[68] Other English commentary is to the same effect.[69] Similarly, the *Restatement (Third) of the Foreign Relations Law of the United States* observes, "State courts take judicial notice of federal law and will therefore take judicial notice of international law as law of the United States."[70]

(c) Case law against judicial notice of international law

Against the proposition that Canadian courts take judicial notice of international law are cases in which international legal questions were made the subject of expert evidence and thus implicitly treated as questions of fact not law. Given the recent authorities reviewed above, these decisions can no longer be regarded as authoritative on the judicial notice point, assuming they ever were.

The trial judge in *R v Keegstra*[71] rejected as inadmissible evidence submitted by the Crown consisting of a compilation of foreign laws

66 Macdonald, above note 10 at 113; see also 111–13.

67 See G van Ert, "The Admissibility of International Legal Evidence" (2005) 84 *Canadian Bar Review* 31; C-E Côté, "La reception du droit international en droit canadien" (2010) 52 *Supreme Court Law Review* 483 at 560; M Rankin, "The Admissibility of International Legal Opinion Evidence after *R v Appulonappa*" (2015) 93 *Canadian Bar Review* 327. See also F Bachand, "The 'Proof' of Foreign Normative Facts Which Influence Domestic Rules" (2005) 43 *Osgoode Hall Law Journal* 269.

68 *Halsbury's Laws of England*, 4th ed, vol 17 (London: Butterworths, 1973–) at para 100; see also vol 18 at para 1403.

69 See I Hunter, "Proving Foreign and International Law in the Courts of England and Wales" (1978) 19 *Virginia Journal of International Law* 665 at 677–8; F Mann, *Foreign Affairs in English Courts* (Oxford: Clarendon Press, 1986) at 126.

70 American Law Institute, *Restatement (Third) of the Foreign Relations Law of the United States* (St. Paul, MN: The Institute, 1987) § 113 Comment b. (A Fourth Restatement, released in 2018, did not address § 113, so the Third Restatement remains (at the time of writing) the American Law Institute's most recent position on this topic.

71 (1984) 19 CCC (3d) 254 at 275 (Alta QB).

as well as "articles allegedly taken from the European Convention of Human Rights, articles from the alleged International Convention of Civil and Political Rights and art. 4(a) of the alleged United Nations International Convention on the Elimination of All Forms of Racial Discrimination." The court held the foreign laws to be of "no evidentiary value because no proper basis was laid to support their admission. In particular, proof of the existence of legislation from each of the countries named is absent and would require the testimony of an expert from each of those countries as well as proof that any English translation of the legislation was accurate."[72] This finding is consistent with the common law rule that foreign laws are matters of fact not law and must be proved in evidence. The court then added, "For the same reason no conventions or treaties to which Canada may be a signatory were properly before me." This equation of foreign law with international law is mistaken. It is notable that, in its consideration of the same case, the Supreme Court of Canada made extensive use of international legal sources, though again without comment on the propriety of doing so.[73]

International law was treated as a matter for evidence by the Nova Scotia Supreme Court in *Romania v Cheng*.[74] Seven officers of a Taiwanese registered vessel were alleged to have thrown Romanian stowaways overboard at sea during a voyage from Spain to Nova Scotia. The officers were arrested in Halifax Harbour, and Romania sought their extradition. The intervenor, Taiwan, relied on the expert testimony of an international law professor, Stephen Toope, that "the alleged offences according to established principles of international law, were not committed within the territory of Romania" and that "Taiwan, being the flag state of the vessel had a superior jurisdictional claim over the offences than did Romania."[75] Justice MacDonald admitted this testimony, as well as Professor Toope's evidence on the meaning of territorial jurisdiction both in the applicable extradition treaty[76] and the federal Extradition Act. The learned judge observed that he "fully

72 On the admissibility of evidence as to the meaning of foreign language texts of treaties, see Section 3.2(b), below.

73 *R v Keegstra*, [1990] 3 SCR 697.

74 (1997) 158 NSR (2d) 13 (SC), aff'd (1997) 162 NSR (2d) 395 (CA) [*Cheng*].

75 *Ibid* at para 41 (SC).

76 Treaty Between Great Britain and Roumania for the Mutual Surrender of Fugitive Criminals [1894] UKTS no 14.

accept[ed] Professor Toope's conclusions in this regard." Clearly this decision is difficult to reconcile with the orthodox view that international legal questions are questions of law for argument by counsel and decision by the court. To the contrary, MacDonald J and the parties appear to have treated international law as a question of fact to be proved in evidence. Note, however, that there is nothing in the report of this case to indicate that the correctness of this manner of proceeding was considered by the court or that any objection was raised to it.

In *Bouzari v Iran*, an Iranian national sued the government of Iran in the Ontario courts for torture he suffered at the hands of Iranian authorities. Iran did not appear and was noted in default, but the attorney general of Canada intervened to argue that the claim was barred by the State Immunity Act.[77] Both Bouzari and the attorney general called international law professors to give evidence on the international law of state immunity and the meaning of certain Canadian treaty obligations. At first instance,[78] Swinton J clearly preferred the attorney general's expert. While she appears to have relied on his testimony heavily at some points,[79] at others it seems she referred to his evidence only to confirm her own conclusions on the international legal questions before her.[80]

This confusion about the methodological approach to international legal issues continued into the reasons of Goudge JA in the Ontario Court of Appeal.[81] The following passage illustrates:

> [T]he more fundamental question is whether Canada has the international law obligation contended for by the appellant. After careful examination, the motion judge concluded that it does not. She analysed this first as a matter of treaty law and then of customary international law. In both contexts she relied on the expert evidence of Professor Greenwood concerning the scope of Canada's international law obligations. . . . While the motion judge's acceptance of Professor Greenwood's opinion over that of Professor Morgan is not a finding of fact by a trial judge, it is a finding based on the evidence she

---

77 RSC 1985, c S-18.
78 [2002] OTC 297 (SCJ).
79 For example, *ibid* at paras 52–5.
80 For example, *ibid* at paras 72–3. As noted above, Gagné J expressly declined to follow Swinton J's approach to expert evidence in *Boily* (appeal), above note 41.
81 (2004) 71 OR (3d) 675 (CA) [*Bouzari* CA].

> heard and is therefore owed a certain deference in this court. I would depart from it only if there were good reason to do so and, having examined the transcript, I can find none. Indeed, for the reason she gave, I agree with her reliance on Professor Greenwood's evidence.[82]

This is, with respect, an unsatisfactory conclusion. Goudge JA states that Professor Greenwood's evidence, and Swinton J's "findings" based on it, are not matters of fact (which an appellate court will not disturb except in cases of palpable and overriding error).[83] Yet he nevertheless would accord the finding "a certain deference." Elsewhere in his reasons the learned judge observed there was ample evidence to support Swinton J's conclusions on international law, and that he agreed with them.[84] It is hard to know what Goudge JA means by departing only from Swinton J's international legal conclusions if there was good reason to do so. If her conclusions were wrong, would that be a good reason? The way to avoid these difficulties would have been for the motions judge either to affirm the orthodox position that common law courts take judicial notice of international law and therefore rule that the legal opinions of experts were inadmissible or (assuming she was free to do so) reject the orthodoxy and find that the requirements of international law must be proved in evidence and decided by the trier of fact.

Professors of international law gave opinion evidence in a wrongful dismissal claim against the Northwest Atlantic Fisheries Organization on the question of whether that body enjoyed immunity from the Nova Scotia courts at international law. At trial, by agreement of counsel and with the court's approval,[85] both professors were qualified as experts in international law. Both opined not only on the international law issues, but also on the meaning and application of section 3(1) of the order-in-council – a question of domestic law and the very question the court was being asked to determine. No consideration of the admissibility of this supposed evidence appears to have been given. In fact, the Nova Scotia Court of Appeal[86] observed that the "debate was nourished greatly by two eminent international law experts." The ex-

82 *Ibid* at para 68 (CA).

83 *Stein v The Ship "Kathy K"*, [1976] 2 SCR 802 at 808.

84 *Bouzari* CA, above note 81 at paras 79, 83.

85 *Amaratunga v Northwest Atlantic Fisheries Organization*, 2010 NSSC 346 at para 16.

86 *Northwest Atlantic Fisheries Organization v Amaratunga*, 2011 NSCA 73 at para 12.

perts' opinions are not referred to in the reasons of the Supreme Court of Canada.[87]

The cases considered under this heading would tend to undermine the claim that international law is judicially noticed in Canada were the question specifically considered in any of them. As it is, and in light of recent high authority, they must be regarded as *per incuriam*.

(d) Statutory provisions requiring judicial notice of international law

Article 2806 of the Civil Code of Quebec states, "No proof is required of a matter of which judicial notice shall be taken." Article 2807 then provides:

> Judicial notice shall be taken of the law in force in Québec.
>
> However, statutory instruments in force in Québec but not published in the Gazette officielle du Québec or in any other manner prescribed by law, international treaties and agreements applicable to Québec but not contained in a text of law, and customary international law, shall be pleaded.

Emanuelli explains that article 2807 requires Quebec courts to take judicial notice of customary international law[88] and applicable treaties,[89] while nevertheless requiring that these sources of law be pleaded. The justification for this rule is to avoid requiring courts to take judicial notice of sources of law that are not readily available to them unless brought to the court's attention.[90]

There is no statutory parallel to article 2807 in the common law provinces. Federally, however, four statutes provide for judicial notice of certain kinds of treaties, namely extradition agreements, mutual legal assistance agreements, and imperial treaties.

Section 8(3) of the Extradition Act provides, "Agreements and provisions published in the Canada Gazette or the Canada Treaty Series are

---

87 *Amaratunga v Northwest Atlantic Fisheries Organization*, 2013 SCC 66.

88 C Emanuelli, *Droit international public: Contribution à l'étude du droit international selon une perspective canadienne*, 3rd ed (Montreal: Wilson & Lafleur, 2010) [Emanuelli] at 73.

89 *Ibid* at 126–8, 130. This conclusion was approved in *Bertin Mbonjo c Collège des médecins du Québec*, 2016 QCCS 3033 at paras 83–4.

90 Emanuelli, above note 88 at 95.

to be judicially noticed."[91] If one reads only the English version, this may seem to capture more treaties than just extradition agreements. But the French version of section 8 makes clear that the word "agreements" in the English version of section 8(3) is intended to bear the same meaning as the phrase "extradition agreement" (*accord*) in section 2.

Similarly, the Competition Act, in Part III (Mutual Legal Assistance), provides that agreements providing for mutual legal assistance in competition matters and published in the Canada Gazette or the Canada Treaty Series "are to be judicially noticed."[92] Parallel provisions are found in the Mutual Legal Assistance in Criminal Matters Act.[93]

A fourth federal statutory provision of note (though not of much practical importance today) is section 20 of the Canada Evidence Act.[94] It sets out three ways in which imperial treaties (and other imperial instruments) may be proved. The first way is "in the same manner as they may from time to time be provable in any court in England." Since the English position is generally that treaties need not be proved, section 20(a) seemingly imports this rule into Canada – but only for imperial treaties.[95] The two other forms of proof are not onerous: production of a copy of the treaty in the Canada Gazette or a volume of the Acts of Parliament, or production of the treaty itself purporting to the published by the King's Printer.

Given the authorities reviewed earlier in this chapter, these federal statutory provisions must be regarded as declaratory of the common law position rather than introductory of a new rule.

(e) Notice of international law by administrative decision makers

Whether administrative decision makers such as ministers, tribunals, boards, commissions, and the like may or must take notice of inter-

91 SC 1999, c 18. On s 8(3) generally see *Republic of France v Peugnet* (1912), 1 DLR 204 (Sask SC); *Germany v MacKinnon* (1986), 76 NSR (2d) 11 (Co Ct); *R v Waddell*, [1992] BCJ No 2587 (SC); *Air Canada v McDonnell Douglas Corporation et al* (1995), 22 OR (3d) 140 at 147; and *Attorney General of Canada on behalf of the Czech Republic v Ganis*, 2006 BCCA 542 at para 22.

92 RSC 1985, c C-34, s 30.02(3).

93 RSC 1985, c 30 (4th Supp.), s 5(3).

94 RSC 1985, c C-5.

95 The English version of s 20 may seem broader than Empire treaties, but consultation of the French version removes any uncertainty in this regard.

national law is considered in Chapter 9.[96] The question is unlikely to have a single answer, depending necessarily on the nature and powers of the decision maker. It is clear, however, that many administrative decision makers have a power, and even a duty, to consider relevant international legal norms.

3.2 Proof of treaties

Of all international law sources, treaties lend themselves most readily to judicial notice by courts and other adjudicative bodies. As positive statements of the law applicable between their parties, treaties leave less room for uncertainty than unwritten rules of customary international law on such basic questions as the existence, meaning, and scope of a particular international legal obligation. That is not to say that treaties are always easy to understand or interpret. But their content and legal status are readily ascertainable – in most cases without the need of proof.

(a) Proof of treaties generally unnecessary

Judicial notice of international law means that it should not be necessary, in most cases, to lead evidence on the content of a given treaty by means of testimony or affidavit. Courts may ascertain a treaty's content by reference to official publications in which they are reproduced, just as they do with statutes, regulations, judicial decisions, and other sources of law.

Treaties to which Canada is a state party are published in the Canada Treaty Series (Can TS), a publication maintained by the Treaty Section of Global Affairs Canada. Most treaties ratified or acceded to by Canada since 1928 are published in Can TS. This was originally a print volume, but since 1 April 2014 it is available only in electronic format (PDF) from a website maintained by the Treaty Law Division.[97] Can TS and the related website are the best place to determine Canada-specific information about a treaty, such as dates of signature and consent to be bound, in force status, and citation information. If the sought-after information is not available from these sources,

96 See Chapter 9, Section 9.2.

97 www.treaty-accord.gc.ca.

inquiries can be addressed directly to the Treaty Custodian at Global Affairs Canada.[98]

Not all Canada's treaty obligations were assumed by Canada itself. Those dating from the colonial period may be found in the United Kingdom Treaty Series, the British State Papers, and other UK government sources. In many cases these publications will indicate whether the treaty in question binds the UK only or also Canada and its other former dependencies. A tool for finding imperial treaties binding, or formerly binding, on Canada is UK Treaties Online.[99]

Litigants may sometimes wish to rely on treaties to which Canada is not a party. Such treaties are not published in Can TS, of course, yet Canadian courts have frequently taken judicial notice of their content without proof. This is particularly so in the human rights context, where the European Convention on Human Rights 1950[100] (ECHR) has frequently been considered. It seems that another type of judicial notice is at play here, namely judicial notice of notorious facts. The ECHR is a world-renowned human rights instrument. To require a litigant to prove its content in evidence would, in most cases, be pedantic. The same may be said of certain other international instruments, as well as such celebrated foreign laws as the US Bill of Rights. Where a litigant seeks to rely on a less well-known treaty, and cannot rely on judicial notice because Canada is not a party to it, it may be possible to satisfy the court without resort to affidavit evidence or other proof by taking a copy of the treaty from such reliable sources as the United Nations Treaty Series,[101] the European Treaty Series and Council of Europe Treaty Series,[102] leading national treaty series, or eminent publications such as the *Consolidated Treaty Series*.[103]

---

98 Inquiries may be addressed to the Treaty Custodian and Administrator, Global Affairs Canada, Treaty Law Division, 125 Sussex Drive, Ottawa K1A 0G2 or by email to info.jli@international.gc.ca.

99 UK Foreign, Commonwealth, & Development Office, "UK Treaties Online," online: treaties.fco.gov.uk.

100 ETS no 5.

101 Accessible at "United Nations Treaty Collection," online: treaties.un.org.

102 Treaties opened for signature between 1949 and 2003 were published in the European Treaty Series (ETS No 1 to 193 included). Since 2004, this series is continued by the Council of Europe Treaty Series (CETS No. 194 and following). See Council of Europe Treaty Office, online: www.coe.int/en/web/conventions/home.

103 C Parry, ed *Consolidated Treaty Series* (Dobbs Ferry, NY: Oceana, 1969–81).

A litigant may wish to show, or a court may wish to know, whether a state other than Canada is a party to a treaty. This was the case in *Munyaneza v R*, where the trial judge consulted the Red Cross website to determine that Rwanda was a party to the Genocide Convention. On appeal, the appellant invited the Quebec Court of Appeal to criticize the trial judge for having so informed himself. The court wisely declined to do so, saying,

> [I]t is the Court's view that the judge did not err by taking cognizance of the list of State parties to an international treaty to which Canada is also a party. Contrary to the appellant's argument, the Supreme Court did not decide in *Finta*, at 867–868, that a State's signing of a convention has to be established through expert evidence. Rather, that judgment refers solely to the fact that expert evidence and commentary are often necessary in the interpretation of international law, many principles of which remain uncodified.
>
> Certainly, it would have been better for the judge to consult the official source, i.e., the United Nations Treaty Collection, instead of the Red Cross site. Nevertheless, what the judge did was inconsequential.[104]

Official publication of a treaty in Can TS or its UK counterparts suffices to establish the treaty's content. The content is as it appears in the official publication and there should be no need to lead or accept evidence on the point. The treaty's meaning is a question of law and should not usually be the subject of expert evidence. There may nevertheless be exceptional cases where evidence concerning a treaty's content or status is warranted. Potential exceptions are considered below.

(b) Proof of foreign language texts

A partial exception to the principle that the meaning of a treaty is not a matter for evidence seems warranted where the authentic text of a treaty is recorded in a foreign language or (more commonly) where two or more authentic texts of the treaty are prepared, one in the court's own language(s) and the other or others in foreign languages.[105] In such

---

104 *Munyaneza v R*, 2014 QCCA 906 at paras 109–10. This explanation of *Finta*, above note 28, is correct where what is in issue is state practice rather than the content of an international norm.

105 This observation was approved by Brown and Rowe JJ, dissenting (but perhaps not on this point) in *Nevsun*, above note 8 at para 181.

cases, English courts have accepted expert evidence as to the meaning of the foreign language text in an effort to elucidate the treaty's true meaning. In *Fothergill v Monarch Airlines*, the House of Lords was faced with English and French versions of a treaty. The French text was authentic and the English text a translation adopted by Parliament in implementing the treaty. Lord Scarman observed that the court "may receive expert evidence directed not to the questions of law which arise in interpreting the convention, but to the meaning, or possible meanings (for there will often be more than one), of the French. It will be for the court, not the expert, to choose the meaning which it considers should be given to the words in issue."[106]

(c) Proof of recondite expressions within a treaty

The Court of Appeal for England and Wales permitted expert evidence on the meaning of certain treaty provisions, in a qualified way, in *Post Office v Estuary Radio Ltd.*[107] The question was whether a radio tower in the Thames estuary was within UK internal or territorial waters (in which case injunctive relief was available) or was on the high seas (in which case it was not). An order-in-council gave effect to the Convention on the Territorial Sea and Contiguous Zone 1958,[108] in which the expressions "internal waters" and "territorial sea" were defined.

Having observed that the court must take judicial notice of the Convention,[109] Lord Diplock noted a dispute between the parties as to the expression "the natural entrance points" of a coastal indentation, found both in the Convention and the order-in-council implementing it. Expert evidence on the meaning of this phrase had been led by both sides. Lord Diplock explained the conditions on which he was prepared to accede to this way of proceeding:

> Although the ultimate decision upon the meaning of the expressions used in the Order in Council must be one for the court, the subject-matter is sufficiently recondite to render admissible evidence as to what the words used would be understood to mean by persons qualified in this specialised field of claims by states to exercise jurisdiction

---

106 *Fothergill v Monarch Airlines*, [1981] AC 251 (HL) at 293–4.
107 Above note 20.
108 [1965] UKTS no 3.
109 *Estuary Radio*, above note 20 at 756.

> over the coastal sea. The judge preferred on this matter the evidence of the Post Office experts, whose qualifications on this particular aspect of hydrography he considered, with justification, lent greater weight to their opinions as compared with those of the experts called for Estuary Radio Ltd. The Post Office experts were naval officers whose duty it was to advise the Crown not only upon its own claims to internal waters and the territorial sea, but upon the recognition of claims by other states. This court would be chary of differing from the view of the trial judge on a matter of assessing the weight to be given to conflicting evidence of expert witnesses whom he has seen and heard. But in addition, the Post Office experts gave convincing reasons for applying the purely cartographical test, which, according to their evidence, is that adopted by the United Kingdom and other countries in applying the Convention.[110]

While the court here permitted opinion evidence on the meaning of words in a treaty, it did so in a qualified way. First, the court affirmed that it must take judicial notice of the Convention. Second, the opinion evidence was not directed at the meaning of the treaty as a whole but only (it seems) of a particular expression, "the natural entrance points." Third, the subject matter of the treaty was "sufficiently recondite" (i.e., beyond ordinary knowledge or understanding) as to justify evidence as to what specialists understand by the expression at issue. Finally, despite admitting expert evidence on the point, the court affirmed that the ultimate decision as to the treaty's meaning on this point remained with the court.

The rule we can take from *Post Office v Estuary Radio Ltd*, I suggest, is that while a treaty's meaning and interpretation is a matter of law for the court, there may be instances where particular expressions within especially technical treaties may be helpfully elucidated through expert evidence. Taken as a whole, the case law suggests such instances are very rare.

(d) Proof of a treaty's status

Distinct from the questions of a treaty's content and meaning is the question of its legal status. Is the treaty one to which Canada is a party and, if so, is the treaty in force yet, or in force still?

---

110 *Ibid* at 758–9.

When Can TS was only a print publication, it told readers whether Canada had ever been a party to a treaty but not whether Canada remained a party. This is because publication of a treaty in Can TS only occurred once Canada adhered to it. The mere presence of a treaty in that collection established that it was – or at least once was – binding on Canada. But Can TS was not updated to indicate the current status of treaties published in it.

The advent of internet treaty publishing has solved this problem – so long as the Treaty Division is conscientious about keeping its website up to date. That site (treaty-accord.gc.ca) now indicates, for each treaty published there, its "Status for Canada," for example, "In Force" or "Terminated."[111] This important feature should now allow courts to take judicial notice of a treaty's legal status for Canada.

The status of a treaty for Canada has occasionally been considered in Canadian courts. In *Richter Gedeon Vegyészeti Gyar Rt v Merck & Co*,[112] the appellant sought to rely on an old legal assistance treaty between the United Kingdom (for Canada) and Hungary.[113] To prove the treaty was still in force, the appellants tendered in evidence an affidavit from an articling student in their solicitors' firm to the effect that she believed the treaty to be still in force after discussing the matter with a Hungarian lawyer and the registrar of the Treaty Section in the Department of Foreign Affairs. The court described this proof as "sufficient, but barely so" and suggested that the proper thing to do would have been to file affidavits from the department official and the Hungarian lawyer themselves.[114]

The proper course in such cases (prior to the advent of internet treaty publishing, which may render the problem obsolete) is by resort to executive certificates, discussed later in this chapter.[115] In the leading case of *Château-Gai Wines Ltd v Attorney General of Canada*, Jackett P explained that "in case of doubt" about the status of a treaty between Canada and another state, the court treats the executive's word on

---

111 The site also indicates a treaty's status generally, that is, whether it is in force or not for all parties. "Status" and "Status for Canada" must not be confused.

112 [1995] 3 FC 330 (CA) [*Richter Gedeon*].

113 Convention between His Majesty in Respect of the United Kingdom and the Regent of the Kingdom of Hungary Regarding Legal Proceedings in Civil and Commercial Matters 1935 [1939] Can TS no 6.

114 *Richter Gedeon*, above note 112 at 344–5.

115 See the discussion of proof by executive certificates at Section 3.5, below.

the matter "as conclusive that the agreement did come into force as a binding international agreement at that time."[116] The phrase "in case of doubt" serves to emphasize that litigants are not obliged to prove the status of every treaty they rely upon. It is only when the status of a treaty is a matter of dispute or uncertainty that a certificate should be sought.

In *Ganis v Canada (Minister of Justice)*,[117] the Court of Appeal for British Columbia held that whether or not a treaty is in force as against Canada is not a justiciable question and that a determination by the executive concerning the existence of a treaty is not open to judicial review on any standard. Ganis sought judicial review of a surrender order by the minister of justice in favour of the Czech Republic, which sought his extradition. Ganis argued that the extradition treaty between Canada and the Czech Republic was not valid, seeking to exploit a typographical error in certain agreements between the two countries that erroneously referred to a previous extradition treaty between the UK and Czechoslovakia. The minister consulted Foreign Affairs Canada on the point, which advised that a valid extradition treaty was in force between Canada and the Czech Republic and that the error in question was merely typographical. Chief Justice Finch for the court rejected Ganis's attempts to question the validity of the treaty, holding that "the Treaty's existence is not a justiciable issue in our Courts."[118] He observed:

> Matters of foreign affairs, including treaty-making, are part of the Crown's Prerogative powers. While this classification alone will not always put a matter beyond the scope of judicial review there are some powers which, because of their nature and subject matter, will not be amenable to the judicial process: *Black v. Canada (Prime Min-*

116 (1970) 14 DLR (3d) 411 (Exchequer Court of Canada) [*Château-Gai Wines*] at 421–2. Curiously, Vallat contended that the question of whether the United Kingdom or any foreign state is a party to a treaty, or whether a treaty is in force, was not properly a matter for determination by certificate "because questions such as these are mixed ones of fact and law, that is to say, international law, and are not correctly regarded as dependent on recognition by the United Kingdom or the attitude of Her Majesty's Government": Sir F Vallat, *International Law and the Practitioner* (Manchester: Manchester University Press, 1966) [Vallat] at 57. If this is a correct statement of British law, it is clearly not the Canadian approach.

117 2006 BCCA 543 [*Ganis*].

118 *Ibid* at para 26.

> *ister)* 2001 CanLII 8537 (ON C.A.), (2001), 54 O.R. (3d) 215 (C.A.). In *Council of Civil Service Unions v. Minister for the Civil Service,* [1985] 1 A.C. 374, [1984] 3 All E.R. 935 (H.L.) (cited with approval by Laskin J.A. for the Court in *Black, supra,* at para. 36), Lord Roskill identified the Prerogative powers related to treaty-making as falling within that category. Apart from *Charter* issues which might arise on the facts of another case, and apart from the exception below relating to jurisdiction, it appears that the question of a treaty's validity is purely political, and that there is no legal component in these circumstances that would warrant the court's interference.
>
> Our courts are sometimes asked to interpret a treaty's provisions and determine its domestic effect; that task, involving legal questions, is within the judiciary's expertise. A treaty's existence, however, is not an ordinary question of law but a highly political matter as between the executive of two contracting states.[119]

The governmental determination of the treaty's status in *Ganis* took the form of a letter from one ministry to another. This is effectively an executive certificate of the sort contemplated by Jackett P in *Château-Gai Wines*.

Judicial reliance on certificates by the executive to prove the status of uncertain treaty obligations is consistent with the doctrine of judicial notice. It is an instance of courts taking judicial notice of facts after inquiry.[120] The court's deference to the executive on treaty status questions is justified by at least three considerations. First, foreign affairs is a prerogative of the Crown. This does not mean that courts may never form their own opinions about matters of foreign affairs,[121] but it is a factor suggesting deference to the executive. Second, Global Affairs Canada keeps a complete record of treaty matters and is therefore the best source of information on a treaty's status. A third factor is the undesirability, as a matter of public policy, of conflict between the courts and the executive on such an important question as the status of a Canadian treaty obligation. As noted, however, the "Status for Canada"

---

119 *Ibid* at paras 23–4.

120 See Lederman et al, above note 1 at § 19:32.

121 See the discussion at Section 3.5(d), below. See also *Attorney General v Tse Chu-Fai* (1998), 153 ALR 128 (HCA) [*Tse Chu-Fai*], where the High Court of Australia affirmed its right to take the ultimate decision in the matter before it but found the view of the government helpful in determining the question of construction.

information now available online likely obviates the need for executive certificates on the status of Canadian treaty obligations in all but the most unusual cases.

It may be necessary or desirable to refer in court to a treaty signed but not yet ratified by Canada. While some treaties are binding on their parties upon signature, others are not binding until ratified. In such cases, a party's signature to the treaty signals its approval of the text of the treaty and its intention to ratify at a later date but does not bind the party to the treaty.[122]

3.3 Proof of custom

The application of the judicial notice doctrine to treaties is relatively straightforward. Courts and commentators have in the past viewed the judicial notice of custom as equally clear, but one may question that today.

(a) The orthodoxy: Custom is noticed not proved[123]

Courts and commentators in both England and Canada have repeatedly taken the view that customary international law is judicially noticed rather than proved in evidence. Lauterpacht explained that judicial notice is taken of international law (including custom) "as of Acts of Parliament or of any branch of the unwritten law, although having regard to the frequent absence of direct authority the range of judicial inquiry is wider and, on occasions, more laborious than in the case of ordinary rules of municipal law."[124] Speaking of custom, Mann observed:

> Although there is not much judicial authority on the point and the language of judges has not always been precise, it seems to be agreed that international law is never established by evidence in the strict sense. No witness can be examined or cross-examined about the existence of an international rule. No documents can be proved.[125]

---

122 But see the discussion of VCLT art 18 in Chapter 2, Section 2.3(a).

123 This discussion, as found in the second edition of this work, was cited with approval by Abella J in *Nevsun*, above note 8 at para 96.

124 Lauterpacht, above note 6 at 59.

125 F Mann, *Foreign Affairs in English Courts* (Oxford: Clarendon Press, 1986) at 125–6 (footnotes omitted).

Contrasting international law to foreign law (which must, in the common law tradition, be proved in evidence), Macdonald emphasized the practical difficulties to which ordinary evidentiary procedures would give rise if applied to the determination of custom:

> If customary international law were subject to the same requirement for formal proof that foreign law is, grave difficulties would arise. The 'experts' in the *Bremer* case[126] are easy to identify in the case of the law of another state; they are, generally speaking, those who have been licensed to practice law in that state. What would be the equivalent for international law? Those who have argued before the World Court? That would leave out many experts. In addition, international law is a system which relies very heavily on text writers, many of whom are dead or unavailable. Formal proof would require their attendance at court, or else their commentaries would be ignored. Also, much of customary international law derives from matters not susceptible to formal testimony, such as customs, changing world attitudes, and inferences and implications drawn from certain events. These are significant inputs into the process of formulating a customary rule, yet they could only be established in an informal (as with judicial notice of domestic law) rather than a formal (as with foreign law) manner.[127]

Macdonald went on to refer to "several judicial comments [in Canadian cases] which make clear that [customary] international law is judicially noticed in the same way that domestic law is."[128]

The views of these commentators are largely borne out by the cases. The oldest authorities, affirming that the law of nations is the law of the land,[129] were concerned exclusively with customary international law. The courts in these cases determined the law of nations for themselves, relying it seems on submissions, their own knowledge of state practice, and the assistance of scholarly authorities. In *Triquet v Bath*,[130]

126 *Bremer v Freeman* (1857), 10 Moo PC 306, 14 ER 508, establishing that foreign law is a matter of fact to be ascertained by the evidence of experts.

127 Macdonald, above note 10 at 112.

128 *Ibid* at 113.

129 See Chapter 6, Section 6.1.

130 (1764) 3 Burr 1478, 97 ER 936 (KB).

Lord Mansfield CJ described Lord Talbot's method of determining the law of nations in *Buvot v Barbuit*[131] as follows:

> Lord Talbot declared a clear opinion – "That the law of nations in its full extent was part of the law of England, . . . that the law of nations was to be collected from the practice of different nations and the authority of writers." Accordingly, he argued and determined from such instances, and the authorities of Grotius, Barbeyrac, Binkershoek, Wiquefort, etc., there being no English writer of eminence on the subject.[132]

A judgment of the US Supreme Court in 1820 included judicial decisions in the list of means by which the law of nations may be determined but is otherwise consistent with *Triquet v Bath*. Mr. Justice Story explained that the law of nations "may be ascertained by consulting the works of jurists, writing professedly on public law; or by the general usage and practice of nations; or by judicial decisions recognising and enforcing that law."[133] Later cases added treaties to the sources courts may have regard to in determining custom, though in such cases the treaty itself is not the source of the custom but only evidence of it.

Twentieth-century cases continued to affirm that customary international law is judicially noticed by the court rather than being proved in evidence. In *Re Piracy Jure Gentium*, the Privy Council described the process as one of "inductive reasoning":

> In considering such a question [of customary international law], the Board is permitted to consult and act upon a wider range of authority than that which it examines when the question for determination is one of municipal law only. The sources from which international law is derived include treaties between various states, state papers, municipal Acts of Parliament and the decisions of municipal courts and last, but not least, opinions of jurisconsults or text-book writers. It is a process of inductive reasoning. . . .[134]

---

131 (1737) Cas T Talb 281, 25 ER 777 (Ch).

132 Above note 130 at 1481 (Burr), 938 (ER).

133 *United States v Smith* (1820), 18 US (5 Wheat) 153 at 160–1.

134 [1934] AC 586 at 588. Viscount Sankey LC added a comment, the correctness of which may be questioned today: "Speaking generally, in embarking upon international law, their Lordships are to a great extent in the realm of opinion, and

In *The Christina*, Lord Macmillan emphasized the need to establish the alleged custom as one that has "attained the position of general acceptance by civilised nations as a rule of international conduct." This was to be done, in his lordship's view, by means of the traditional method of taking judicial notice of "international treaties and conventions, authoritative textbooks, practice and judicial decisions."[135] In *Chung Chi Cheung v The King*, Lord Atkin explained that "The Courts acknowledge the existence of a body of rules which nations accept amongst themselves. On any judicial issue they seek to ascertain what the relevant rule is, and, having found it, they will treat it as incorporated into the domestic law. . . ."[136] Reflecting on this passage in *Re Armed Forces*, Rand J observed:

> From that language, I do not understand that the ordinary methods of judicial determination are not to be resorted to. To insist upon precise precedent in usage would sterilize judicial action toward changing international relations: and in the reduction of terms of an implied arrangement the court must be free to draw upon all sources of international conventions, including "reason and good sense."[137]

The method employed by the English Court of Appeal in *Trendtex Trading Corp v Bank of Nigeria*,[138] perhaps the most well-known instance of a common law court ascertaining and applying customary international law, is instructive. The report of the case helpfully includes a summary of the parties' submissions, including those of the international law scholar D.P. O'Connell on the ascendancy of the restrictive doctrine of state immunity in customary international law. Thus, the customary position was brought to the court's attention in submissions rather than evidence. Confirming this is the following observation of Stephenson LJ:

> [R]ules of international law, whether they be part of our law or a source of our law, must be in some sense "proved," and they are not

---

in estimating the value of opinion it is permissible not only to seek a consensus of view, but to select what appears to be the better views upon the question."

135 [1938] AC 485 at 497.

136 [1939] AC 160 (PC) at 168.

137 [1943] SCR 483 at 524. The passage is typical of Rand J's unique prose. The phrase "international conventions" must be understood in the sense of laws and practices, not treaties.

138 *Trendtex*, above note 15 at 554.

> proved in English courts by expert evidence like foreign law; they are "proved" by taking judicial notice of "international treaties and conventions, authoritative textbooks, practice and judicial decisions" of other courts in other countries which show that they have "attained the position of general acceptance by civilised nations": *The Christina* [1938] A.C. 485, 497, *per* Lord Macmillan: and those sources seldom if ever come from every civilised nation or agree upon a universal rule; they move from one generally accepted rule towards another.[139]

In this century, the House of Lords in *R v Jones* appears to have found that the crime of aggression was one of customary international law by means of judicial notice. Lord Bingham reviewed several instruments, including a draft treaty, a resolution of an international conference, provisions of the UN Charter and other treaties, General Assembly resolutions, draft codes and accompanying commentary of the International Law Commission, and International Court of Justice (ICJ) jurisprudence.[140]

At the time of writing, the leading Canadian authority on the proof of customary international law is the decision of the Supreme Court of Canada in *Nevsun Resources*. Justice Abella for the majority of the court affirmed that "established norms of customary international law are law, to be judicially noticed" and that taking judicial notice of custom "in the sense of not requiring formal proof by evidence" is appropriate as well as being "an inevitable implication both of the doctrine of adoption."[141] She noted, however, that some commentators "suggest that when recognising new norms of customary international law, allowing evidence of state practice may be appropriate." She preferred to leave that issue for another day, observing that "The questions of whether and what evidence may be used to demonstrate the existence of a new norm are not . . . live issues in this appeal."[142]

(b) Possible scope for expert evidence in custom claims

The authorities reviewed above suggest that it remains methodologically sound for a court to identify the existence of a rule of customary

139 *Ibid* at 569.
140 [2006] UKHL 16 at paras 13–19.
141 *Nevsun*, above note 8 at paras 97–8.
142 *Ibid* at para 99.

international law through judicial notice of publicly available sources such as treaties, resolutions of international organizations, decisions of international tribunals, and commentary by leading scholars.

Yet there may also be scope for expert assistance in determining rules of custom. The decision of the High Court of Justiciary (Scotland's final court of criminal appeal) in *Lord Advocate's Reference No. 1 of 2000*[143] offers some support for this approach, while affirming that the existence of a customary norm remains a question of law. Three anti-nuclear protesters were acquitted of malicious damage to a support vessel for UK Trident submarines (which carry nuclear missiles). At their trial, which occurred before a jury, the accused raised a defence of necessity, arguing that the deployment of nuclear missiles by the UK is contrary to customary international law and therefore criminal in Scots law. Thus, the accused submitted, they were acting to prevent or obstruct a crime. To establish the applicable requirements of customary international law, the accused led expert evidence from international lawyers. The presiding judge (known as the sheriff) admitted this evidence, which was presented before the jury. Upon acquittal, the government referred four legal questions to the High Court of Justiciary, including, "In a trial under Scottish criminal procedure, is it competent to lead evidence as to the content of customary international law as it applies in the United Kingdom?"

The joint opinion of Lords Prosser, Kirkwood, and Penrose was that a rule of customary international law is a rule of Scots law and is therefore a matter for the judge and not for the jury. Likewise, submissions on questions of international law must be made by counsel, not by expert witnesses. Their lordships conceded, however, "that the question of whether an *opinio juris* has emerged, and won the general acceptance which is necessary to constitute a rule of customary international law, might well make recourse to expertise appropriate," though they nevertheless observed that "having regard to the different skills and expertise of an advocate on the one hand, and some other kind of specialist on the other hand, we find it very hard to imagine any situation in which the appropriate material should be presented to the court in the form of evidence with examination and cross-examination, and perhaps counter-evidence for the other party."[144]

143 *Lord Advocate's Reference*, above note 30.

144 *Ibid* at paras 23–7.

A Canadian commentator, Professor Warner La Forest, would go further.[145] She argues that in the past the judicial notice of custom was less problematic because custom was better known or more easily determined than it is today. "It may reasonably be asked, then, whether the assessment of custom appropriately falls within the parameters of judicial notice."[146] While taking this position, Professor Warner La Forest affirms that international law is law not fact and argues that to admit expert evidence on questions of law does not usurp the judicial role of determining the law for itself.[147]

In a less ambitious challenge to the orthodoxy, I have suggested that the judicial notice doctrine is subject to a qualification, of uncertain scope, in respect of custom. While some customary rules are so well established as not to be disputed, other alleged customs may be contested and require proof. State practice, I have suggested, is a matter of fact, while the nature of custom's second element, *opinio juris*, is less clear. Given this uncertainty, I have suggested that some leeway from the court is in order for pleadings or evidence concerning custom.[148] Yet the ultimate issue of the existence of a rule of custom in international and Canadian law should remain a question of law for judicial determination.

Dissenting in part in *Nevsun*, Brown and Rowe JJ proposed a similar approach to proving contested custom allegations. While those judges criticized the majority's approach to custom as "creating an unwieldy hybridization of law and fact," their alternative method may simply be an answer to the question Abella J preferred to leave for another day. The Brown/Rowe approach involves three steps. First, the court must find those elements of custom (i.e., state practice and *opinio juris*) relevant to whatever customary norm is being advanced. In easy cases, this step may be dispensed with through judicial notice – just as the *Nevsun* majority held. Where, however, the existence of the supposed custom is contested, judges should rely on the evidence adduced before them (or, in a summary proceeding, the pleadings). Next, once the necessary facts of state practice and *opinio juris* have been found,

145 A Warner La Forest, "Evidence and International and Comparative Law" in O Fitzgerald, ed, *The Globalized Rule of Law: Relationships Between International and Domestic Law* (Toronto: Irwin Law, 2006) at 367.

146 *Ibid* at 384.

147 *Ibid* at 388.

148 G van Ert, "The Admissibility of International Legal Evidence" (2005) 84 *Canadian Bar Review* 31 at 44–6.

the court passes to the second step, namely "to identify which, if any, norms of customary international law must be recognized to best explain these facts," bearing in mind that "state practice and *opinio juris* may be consistent with more than one possible norm." This is a question of law. The final step is to apply the customary norms, as recognized, to the case at bar.[149]

(c) Some propositions[150]

The question of how properly to establish custom before a domestic court no longer seems as straightforward as it once did. To insist dogmatically on past practice may be inappropriate in some cases. The question is difficult to answer in the abstract and I do not attempt to do so here. I do advance, however, certain propositions which, I hope, may contribute to future consideration of the problem.

First, certain rules of customary international law are so well established in judicial decisions and scholarly works that courts may take judicial notice of them today as they have for centuries. The procedural and evidentiary problems under consideration here arise when litigants allege the existence of customary norms not already well established in international law, or perhaps when litigants seek to apply established customs in novel circumstances.

Second, it is surely right to say, as La Forest J did in *Finta*,[151] the High Court of Justiciary did in *Lord Advocate's Reference No 1 of* 2000,[152] and the Supreme Court of Canada did in *Nevsun*,[153] that questions of international law should be for the judge and not the jury. Whatever approach a court may adopt in adjudicating upon an alleged rule of customary international law, the legal question must be for the judge.

Third, an appellate court should not be bound by the finding of a court of first instance as to the existence or extent of an alleged customary norm. Even where the lower court's determination of that question is founded in part on findings of fact concerning state practice, the question of whether an alleged rule of customary law exists is

---

149 *Nevsun*, above note 8 at paras 178–83.

150 This discussion, as found in the second edition of this work, was cited with approval by Abella J in *Nevsun*, above note 8 at para 96.

151 *Finta*, above note 28 at 773–4.

152 *Lord Advocate's Reference*, above note 30 at para 23.

153 *Nevsun*, above note 8 at paras 95–7, 182.

ultimately a legal one. The appellate court should therefore review the ultimate decision on a correctness standard, even while showing the usual degree of deference to findings of fact in respect of state practice.

Fourth, for one lawyer, as counsel, to examine or cross-examine another lawyer, as expert, on the latter's opinions on a question of law is inconsistent with prevailing conceptions of civil procedure and offers no advantage over the traditional approach of contesting the disputed legal question between counsel in argument. Whatever scope there may be, in particular cases, for expert evidence on the state practice advanced in support of an alleged rule of customary international law, lawyers in the guise of experts should not be asked to swear to the truth of the legal views they hold or to submit to cross-examination on those views by other lawyers.

3.4 Proof of other sources of international law

(a) General principles

General principles of law, as set out in ICJ Statute article 38(1)(c), are rarely invoked in Anglo-Canadian jurisprudence but are, in principle, judicially noticeable as international law to the same extent as treaty and custom.

(b) Subsidiary means: Judicial decisions and scholarly writings

ICJ Statute article 38(1)(d) describes judicial decisions and scholarly writings ("the teachings of the most highly qualified publicists of the various nations") as "subsidiary means for the determination of rules of law." Since these are not in themselves sources of international law, but only subsidiary means for determining international legal rules, it is not quite accurate to say that courts take judicial notice of them. But Canadian courts often have regard to judicial decisions and scholarly works when considering questions of international law.

The Supreme Court of Canada has sometimes used judicial decisions to revisit existing domestic law in light of the international position. In *Mugesera v Canada (Minister of Citizenship and Immigration)*,[154]

154 [2005] 2 SCR 100.

the Supreme Court of Canada went so far as to partially overrule its own decision in *R v Finta*[155] for inconsistency with the jurisprudence of the Yugoslavia and Rwanda international criminal tribunals on the *actus reus* of a crime against humanity. Similarly, in *Ezokola v Canada (Minister of Citizenship and Immigration)*,[156] the court overturned a longstanding Federal Court of Appeal precedent in order to "rein in the Canadian approach to complicity under art. 1F(a)" of the Refugee Convention and "bring Canadian law in line with international criminal law"[157] as found (again) in the jurisprudence of the Rwandan and Yugoslavian tribunals. In *Office of the Children's Lawyer v Balev*,[158] the majority of the Supreme Court of Canada departed from prior Canadian precedents to adopt what is known as the hybrid approach to the determination of a child's habitual residence under article 3 of the Hague Convention on International Child Abduction.[159] In doing so, the majority relied on Hague Convention decisions from the European Union, the United Kingdom, Australia, New Zealand, and the United States, noting that to "avoid frustrating the harmonizing purpose behind the *Hague Convention*, domestic courts should give serious consideration to decisions by the courts of other contracting states on its meaning and application."[160]

As for scholarly writings, Canadian courts sometimes have regard to them to discern applicable international norms. They do so in much the same way they resort to textbooks, monographs, and scholarly articles on matters of domestic law.

3.5 Proof of certain matters by executive certificate

A special evidentiary procedure exists in respect of certain questions touching Canada's external relations. At common law and by statute,

155 *Finta*, above note 28.
156 Above note 64.
157 *Ibid* at paras 30 and 9, respectively.
158 Above note 64.
159 Convention on the Civil Aspects of International Child Abduction 1980, [1983] Can TS no 35.
160 *Balev*, above note 64 at para 33; see also para 49 ("this Court should prefer the interpretation that has gained the most support in other courts and will therefore best ensure uniformity of state practice across *Hague Convention* jurisdictions, unless there are strong reasons not to do so").

such matters may be resolved by a certificate from the appropriate minister of the Crown stating Canada's position. This is in keeping with the constitutional norm that foreign affairs is a prerogative of the Crown.[161]

In the past, executive certificates usually came before the court at the court's own motion.[162] Having identified an issue where executive guidance was desirable, the court would request it. Alternatively, a party to the dispute might obtain a certificate from the government in an effort to advance its case. Today, certificates are often provided by the Department of Foreign Affairs[163] upon request from foreign states that find themselves implicated as parties to Canadian proceedings.

(a) Executive certificates at common law

The common law has long recognized that courts should follow the government's lead in certain narrowly defined foreign relations matters. A certificate from the executive (in any particular form) stating its position on these matters will be noted by the courts and, it seems,[164] treated as conclusive. The recognized areas in which executive certificates have been followed by the courts are (1) the existence or status of a treaty between Canada and another state; (2) the statehood or lack of statehood of a foreign entity; (3) the territorial boundaries of states, including Canada; (4) whether war or armed conflict exists between Canada and another state; (5) whether a person enjoys diplomatic privileges or immunities; and, historically at least,[165] (6) who constitutes the government of a foreign territory.

---

161 "The issue of a certificate is, at common law, in the nature of a prerogative act linked to the functions of the Crown in the realm of foreign affairs": Vallat, above note 116 at 58.

162 See H Kindred, "Foreign Governments Before the Courts" (1980) 58 *Canadian Bar Review* 602 [Kindred] at 610.

163 The statutory name of this department is, at time of writing, the Department of Foreign Affairs, Trade and Development: see s 2(1) of the Department of Foreign Affairs, Trade and Development Act SC 2013 c 33 s 174. However, in late 2015 the federal government changed the department's designation to Global Affairs Canada, without amending the Act. The proper title of the minister leading the department remains the minister of foreign affairs.

164 But see the discussion at Section 3.5(f), below.

165 Canada, like other Commonwealth states, has ceased the practice of recognizing governments (as opposed to states). See E Lee, "Canadian Practice in International Law/La Pratique Canadienne en Matiere de Droit International Public

The leading Canadian authority on executive certificates at common law is *Re Château-Gai Wines Ltd and Attorney General of Canada*.[166] The question was whether a 1933 trade agreement between Canada and France had ever come into force. The attorney general sought to prove that it had by producing two certificates signed by successive secretaries of state for external affairs affirming, in some detail, that the agreement had been signed, ratified, and brought into force. President Jackett accepted these certificates as "conclusive that the agreement did come into force as a binding international agreement at that time."[167] "In principle," he held,

> a question, whether of fact or law or both, as to whether an international agreement between Canada and another country has come into force between Canada and another sovereign power so as to create international rights and obligations, must be determined, in case of doubt, in the same way as
>
> (a) a question as to whether a person is a foreign sovereign power,
> (b) a question as to what persons must be regarded as constituting the effective Government of a foreign territory,
> (c) a question as to whether a particular place must be regarded as being in Canada or as being under the authority of a foreign sovereign authority,
> (d) a question as to whether Canada is at peace or at war with a foreign power, or
> (e) a question as to whether a person in Canada is entitled to diplomatic privileges as being an ambassador of a foreign power or a member of the entourage of such an ambassador.
>
> All such questions are questions within the realm of responsibility of the executive arm of government and, being questions on which the State should speak with one voice, they are questions with regard to

– At the Department of External Affairs in 1987–88/Au Ministere des Affaires Exterieures en 1987–88" (1988) 26 *Canadian Yearbook of International Law* 307 at 324–6. Although the government retains the power to issue an executive certificate on this matter, questions concerning the existence of foreign governments are now usually left to the judiciary to determine on the facts. See C McLachlan, *Foreign Relations Law* (Cambridge: Cambridge University Press, 2014) [McLachlan] at 412–17.

166 *Château-Gai Wines*, above note 116.

167 *Ibid* at 422.

> which the Courts should accept from the appropriate minister of the Crown a certificate as to Canada's position.[168]

In a subsequent decision arising out of related litigation, *Institut National des Appellations d'Origine des Vins et Eaux-de-Vie v Chateau-Gai Wines Ltd*,[169] resort to government certificates to determine the status of a treaty was considered by the Supreme Court of Canada. Again, the question was whether the 1933 Canada–France trade treaty was in force. The appellant argued it was not, due to the parties' failure to exchange instruments of ratification as stipulated by the treaty. The respondents relied on certificates from the secretary of state for external affairs stating that the treaty had been ratified by exchange of notes and was regarded by the parties as in force between them. Justice Pigeon for the majority of the court did not "consider it is necessary to decide whether one should go so far as to say that a certificate from the appropriate Minister is conclusive proof that an agreement exists" but nevertheless expressed the opinion (consistently with Jackett P in *Château-Gai Wines*) "that the question of whether a treaty is in force, as opposed to what its effect should be, is . . . wholly within the province of the public authority."[170]

(b) Statutory provisions for executive certificates

The executive certificate procedure began at common law but is now supplemented, and perhaps displaced,[171] in Canada by a variety of

---

168 *Ibid* at 422. Jackett P cited the following authorities: *Taylor v Barclay*, [1828] 2 Sim 213, 57 ER 762; *Mighell v Sultan of Johore*, [1894] 1 QB 149; *Foster v Globe Venture Syndicate, Ltd*, [1900] 1 Ch 811; *Aksionairnoye Obschestvo A.M. Luther v James Sagor & Co*, [1921] 3 KB 532; *Duff Development Co, Ltd v Government of Kelantan*, [1924] AC 797 (HL) [*Duff Development*]; *The "Fagernes,"* [1927] P 311 (Eng CA); *Engelke v Musmann*, [1928] AC 433 (HL); *Government of the Republic of Spain v SS "Arantzazu Mendi,"* [1939] AC 256 (HL); *Sayce v Ameer Ruler Sadig Mohammad Abbasi Bahawalpur State*, [1952] 2 QB 390; and *Carl Zeiss Stiftung v Rayner & Keeler Ltd (No 2)*, [1966] 3 WLR 125 (HL).

169 [1975] 1 SCR 190 [*Institut National*].

170 *Ibid* at 199. Immediately prior to this, Pigeon J observes (somewhat contradictorily) that "in the interpretation of treaties the approach of the government, though not conclusive, must be given great weight," citing the US case *Charlton v Kelly* (1913), 229 US 447 for this proposition. But the rest of his judgment makes clear that he was in fact referring to the question of a treaty's status and not its meaning.

171 "[S]o far at the power to issue certificates or possibly to provide evidence in other ways is made statutory, it may well be that in accordance with general constitutional principles the prerogative power to issue a certificate is to that

federal statutory provisions.[172] These provisions generally track the common law categories of executive certificate set out in *Château-Gai Wines*. As discussed further below,[173] these provisions are remarkably inconsistent in their wording around the evidentiary effect of the certificates they contemplate.

(c) Rationale for executive certificates

The traditional rationale for judicial reliance on executive certificates is Lord Atkin's dictum that "Our State cannot speak with two voices on such a matter, the judiciary saying one thing, the executive another."[174]

This is, at best, a partial explanation of why judges should cede their usual functions of finding facts and stating the law in respect of a handful of topics involving the foreign affairs prerogative. Considering the question in 1980, Professor Kindred observed:

> [A]lthough their utterances have been persistent and consistent, it is impossible to judge the motivation for the pervading judicial attitude. Whether it be principally out of concern for the constitutional separation of powers between the executive and the judiciary, or from fear of embarrassing the government in the conduct of its foreign policy, or more as a convenient and now hallowed escape for

---

extent absorbed in the statutory power. The statutory power then has to be exercised strictly in accordance with the provisions of the statute": Vallat, above note 116 at 58.

172 See, e.g., Foreign Missions and International Organizations Act, SC 1991, c 41, s 11 (certificates concerning the establishment of diplomatic missions, the privileges and immunities of international organizations, and the privileges and immunities of persons and entities under the Act); Geneva Conventions Act, RSC 1985, c G-3, s 9 (certificate concerning states of war or armed conflict between or in states); State Immunity Act, RSC 1985, c S-18, s 14(1) (certificates concerning the existence of foreign states and heads of government); Criminal Code, RSC 1985, c C-46, s 7(10) and (11) (certificates concerning whether a person is a member of United Nations personnel or otherwise entitled to protection under international law, whether a state is engaged in armed conflict against Canada, and the status of a treaty for Canada); Oceans Act, SC 1996, c 31, s 23 (certificates concerning Canadian maritime zones); Criminal Code, s 477.4(3) (certificate concerning fishing zones of Canada).

173 See Section 3.5(f), below.

174 *The Arantzazu Mendi*, [1939] AC 256 (HL) at 264; see also *Château-Gai Wines*, above note 116 at 422.

> personal misgivings over messing with politics and diplomacy is all speculation.[175]

In other words, to assert that the state cannot speak with two voices on certain foreign affairs matters only provokes the question, "Why not?" Kindred's observation that the answer to that question is speculative holds largely true today, although the separation of powers rationale for executive certificates may now be in the ascendant.[176]

(d) Courts do not take legal direction from the Crown

The common law, and now statutory, practice of issuing executive certificates in respect of certain foreign affairs matters must be understood within the prevailing principle that courts do not take direction from the Crown on questions of international law. Consistently with English and Commonwealth precedents,[177] and the practices of other states,[178] Canadian courts should, and generally do, treat questions of international law as legal questions for determination by them.

In *The Zamora*, Lord Parker for the Privy Council explained:

> If the Court is to decide judicially in accordance with what it conceives to be the law of nations, it cannot, even in doubtful cases, take its directions from the Crown, which is a party to the proceedings. It must itself determine what the law is according to the best of its ability, and its view, whatever hesitation it be arrived at, must prevail over any executive order.[179]

---

175 Kindred, above note 162 at 605.

176 See, e.g., *Tracy v Iran (Information and Security)*, 2016 ONSC 3759 [*Tracy* SC] at paras 145–50 and *Construction Excedra v Saudi Arabia*, 2017 ONSC 105 [*Construction Excedra*] at paras 47–9, 52. Professor McLachlan also favours the separation of powers as justification for judicial reliance on certificates: McLachlan, above note 165 at 243.

177 See McLachlan, above note 165 at 240–8.

178 See, in respect of treaty interpretation, D Sloss, ed, *The Role of Domestic Courts in Treaty Enforcement: A Comparative Study* (Cambridge: Cambridge University Press, 2009). This study finds (at 592–3) that many states' courts do not defer to their governments on the interpretation of treaties: see 363–4 (The Netherlands), 399–400 (Poland), 472–4 (South Africa), and 484 (UK). The exceptions are the United States (523–5) and sometimes Israel (292–5).

179 [1916] 2 AC 77 (PC) at 97. See also, *Carl Zeiss Stiftung v Rayner & Keeler Ltd (No 2)*, [1967] 1 AC 853 (HL) at 950 [*Zeiss Stiftung No 2*]; *Tse Chu-Fai*, above note 121 at para 55.

McPhillips JA applied this passage in *Reference re Japanese Treaty Act*, saying, "Therefore, it is for the Court to say what the state of the law is in respect to the [international legal] questions propounded."[180] Making this same point in the specific context of executive certificates in UK law, Vallat observed, "It is no part of the function of the Foreign Office to try to guide the Court on points of law."[181]

Consistently with this approach, the Supreme Court of Canada has distinguished the narrow Anglo-Canadian practice of executive certificates in certain kinds of foreign affairs matters from the broader American practice of State Department letters of suggestion.[182] In *République démocratique du Congo v Venne*, the question was whether Congo enjoyed state immunity from a civil claim by a Quebec debtor. Justice Ritchie for the majority of the court held that it did, and distinguished recent US decisions adopting a restrictive approach to state immunity on the ground that they "stem[med] from opinions furnished by the State Department" as to the "foreign policy of that country," whereas "no such question arises in this country."[183] In dissent but not on this point, Laskin J noted that there is no practice in Canada of executive suggestion to the courts on matters of foreign policy.[184]

Several recent Canadian appellate decisions are consistent with the principle that international legal questions are for courts to decide, though without extensive consideration of the point. In *Crown Forest Industries Ltd v Canada*, Iacobucci J for the Supreme Court of Canada rejected the respondent's submission that the court should not interfere with the findings, allegedly of fact, made by the trial judge, noting that at issue in the appeal were not factual findings but the trial judge's interpretation of the Canada–United States Income Tax Convention, and that "this being a conclusion as to law or, in the least, mixed law

180 (1922) 29 BCR 136 (BCCA) at 147–78.

181 Vallat, above note 116 at 60; see also 62.

182 See, e.g., J Moore, "The Role of the State Department in Judicial Proceedings" (1962) 31 *Fordham Law Review* 277; I Wuerth, "Foreign Official Immunity Determinations in U.S. Courts: The Case Against the State Department" (2011) 51 *Virginia Journal of International Law* 1.

183 [1971] SCR 997 at 1004–5.

184 *Ibid* at 1013–14. The learned judge rightly added, however, that under the absolute doctrine of state immunity (which he opposed), an executive certificate as to sovereign status "would, in a case like the present one, be sufficient" to determine a claim.

and fact" it was "properly reviewable by an appellate court."[185] In *Ganis*, Finch CJ affirmed that the task of interpreting treaties and determining their domestic effect "is within the judiciary's expertise" as it involves legal questions.[186] In *R v Appulonappa*, Neilson J for the Court of Appeal for British Columbia affirmed, in the context of expert testimony that had "strayed into providing opinions on the interpretation and application of international law," that this testimony was inadmissible "as these were questions of law for the court."[187] Justice Nadon reached the same conclusion, again in the context of expert evidence, in *Turp v Canada (Foreign Affairs)*, observing that international law, "is the prerogative of courts."[188] Beyond these cases are countless instances of Canadian courts rejecting the federal government's submissions on an international law point without any suggestion either from the government or the courts themselves that they should defer to the government or take direction from it due to the international nature of the question.

For Canadian courts to treat international legal issues as matters for government decision by executive certificate, rather than judicial decision by the application of law, would bestow an impermissible power on the Crown, even if only in a narrow range of cases, to determine the legal outcome of domestic judicial proceedings. Recognition of such a power would be inconsistent with English and Commonwealth authorities insisting that, even in executive certificate regimes, legal questions are for the courts. As Lord Cross warned in *The Philippine Admiral*, "if the courts consult the government on [legal] questions what may begin by guidance as to the principles to be applied may end in cases being decided irrespective of any principle in accordance with the view of the executive as to what is politically expedient."[189]

(e) Executive certificates: Fact, law, or position?

The discussion immediately above gives rise to a further question: What is the nature of the information conveyed in executive certificates? President Jackett described certificates as addressing questions

185 [1995] 2 SCR 802 at para 38.
186 *Ganis*, above note 117 at para 24.
187 Above note 37 at para 62.
188 Above note 49 at para 88.
189 [1977] AC 373 (PC) at 399.

"whether of fact or law or both."[190] For this he was criticized by Professor Kindred for endorsing the mistaken notion that courts should follow the government's lead on legal questions.[191]

But Jackett P also observed that, on the matters of foreign relations he identified, "the Courts should *accept* from the appropriate minister of the Crown a certificate *as to Canada's position*."[192] This way of putting it suggests that the courts need not regard executive certificates either as proof of fact or point of law, but instead as a statement of the federal government's position on a matter of foreign relations. This approach is in keeping with the view expressed by Lord Phillimore in *Engelke v Musmann* that

> when a question arises in the Law Courts as to whether a ruler is a Sovereign, and a proper Secretary of State is consulted, the right answer is not "A.B. is a Sovereign," but "A.B. is recognized by His Majesty as a Sovereign," so I think, the exact inquiry in this case is not whether the defendant is a member of the Ambassadorial staff but whether he has been accepted and recognized by the Crown as such a member. . . .[193]

Engelke was cited by Jackett P in *Château-Gai Wines*. Perhaps, then, Jackett P's true meaning was that certificates serve to establish in evidence what Canada's position is on certain matters touching foreign affairs.

A strictly textual analysis of statutory certificate powers does not shed much light on the question. Section 11 of the Foreign Missions and International Organizations Act[194] contemplates certificates containing "statement[s] of fact" ("*les faits en cause*") relevant to the specified issues. Similarly, section 9 of the Geneva Conventions Act[195] provides (in English) for certificates that prove "the facts so stated." The French, however, speaks only of the certificate's "*contenu*." The certificate provisions of section 7(10) and (11) of the Criminal Code[196] speak, in the English version, of "proof of the facts" stated in the cer-

---

190 *Château-Gai Wines*, above note 116 at 422.
191 See Kindred, above note 162 at 613.
192 *Château-Gai Wines*, above note 116 at 422 (emphasis added).
193 [1928] AC 433 at 455. See the discussion in McLachlan, above note 165 at 243.
194 SC 1991, c 41.
195 RSC 1985, c G-3.
196 RSC 1985, c C-46.

tificates, while the French speaks both of the "*faits qu'il énonce*" (in section 7(10)) and the "*contenu*" (in section 7(11)). The certification power in section 14(1) of the State Immunity Act,[197] in its English version, is not limited to proof of facts but extends to "any matter stated in" ("*toute question touchant*") the certificate. The certificate power in section 23 of the Oceans Act[198] is expressed in terms of "the truth of the statement" made therein (the "*renseignements qui y sont énoncés*").

Looking more closely at the statutory provisions, however, one finds support for Jackett P's notion that, at least in some cases, they enunciate Canada's position on a matter of external relations rather than, or more than, a factual or legal determination. Whether a given territory constitutes a state under international law is undoubtedly a legal question, but section 14(1)(a) of the State Immunity Act is directed specifically at the question of "whether a country is a foreign state for the purposes of this Act." Similarly, a certificate under section 11(e) of the Foreign Missions and International Organizations Act concerns not whether a person enjoys diplomatic protection generally but whether that person "has privileges, immunities or benefits under this Act." Certificates under section 9 of the Geneva Conventions Act attesting that a state of armed conflict exists are not at large but for the purpose of "any proceedings for an offence referred to in this Act."

(f) Are executive certificates conclusive?

Closely related to the questions considered immediately above is the issue of a certificate's probative value. Are the positions taken in executive certificates conclusive, in the sense that Canadian courts need not or may not inquire further into the facts or matters stated therein?

In *Château-Gai Wines*, Jackett P observed that the certificate before him "should be accepted by this Court as conclusive that the agreement did come into force as a binding international agreement at that time."[199] Yet Pigeon J pointedly did not consider it "necessary to decide whether one should go so far as to say that a certificate from the appropriate Minister is conclusive proof."[200]

197 RSC 1985, c S-18.
198 SC 1996, c 31.
199 *Château-Gai Wines*, above note 116 at 422.
200 *Institut National*, above note 169 at 199.

The court in *Canadian Planning* regarded the two statutory certificates before it as "conclusive proof that Canada and Libya enjoy diplomatic relations,"[201] but insisted that it was for the court to determine the legal questions of what privileges arise from the existence of that relationship and the immunity afforded to diplomatic bank accounts by customary international law.[202] This is consistent with Vallat's view that "Where the certificate is conclusive, it is conclusive only as regards the facts stated. It is no part of the function of the Foreign Office to try to guide the Court on points of law."[203]

By contrast, the trial judge in *Tracy v Iran (Information and Security)* observed, in a case about the status of diplomatic property, that a section 11 executive certificate is "the most reliable evidence of the Minister's view of the diplomatic status of property" and "should be regarded as conclusive."[204] He specifically declined to follow *Canadian Planning* on this point.[205] Yet the same judge also consulted the Department of Foreign Affairs website and expressly based his conclusion that the assets in question were excluded from diplomatic protection on both the executive certificates and the website.[206] On appeal from that decision, Hourigan JA described executive certificates as "the best evidence of Minister's [sic] communication of diplomatic status," but affirmed that the trial judge had not erred in looking "at the whole context," particularly the government website.[207]

Here again the statutory certificate provisions shed only limited light. The English versions of the certificate provisions of the Foreign Missions and International Organizations Act and Geneva Conventions Act speak of "proof" rather than "conclusive proof." The State Immunity Act speaks of "conclusive proof" in English, but only of "*fait foi*" in French – the same expression found in the French versions of the two previously mentioned statutes. The Oceans Act certificates are

---

201 *Canadian Planning v Libya*, 2015 ONSC 2188 [*Canadian Planning No. 2*] at para 29; see also para 64.

202 *Ibid* at paras 63–4.

203 Vallat, above note 116 at 60.

204 *Tracy* SC, above note 176 at para 151. See also *Construction Excedra*, above note 176 at paras 35, 47, 52.

205 *Tracy* SC, above note 176 at para 156.

206 *Ibid* at para 157.

207 *Tracy v Iran*, 2017 ONCA 549 [*Tracy* CA] at para 119. The phrase "best evidence" was also employed by Lord Sumner in *Duff Development*, above note 168 at 824.

stated to be "conclusive proof of the truth of the statement" ("*preuve concluante des renseignements qui y sont énoncés*"), while a certificate under section 7(10) of the Criminal Code is "in the absence of evidence to the contrary . . . proof of the facts it states" ("*fait foi jusqu'à preuve contraire des faits qu'il énonce*").

The reason to resist the notion that executive certificates are necessarily conclusive of all questions of fact and law they address is to preserve the judicial function from executive incursion. The famous American judicial declaration in *Marbury v Madison* (1803), that it is "emphatically the province and duty of the judicial department to say what the law is,"[208] has been evoked in Commonwealth case law on executive certificates.[209] Commentators have also warned that misuse of executive certificates, whether by the government, the courts, or both, may, in Professor Kindred's phrase, attenuate the judicial function.[210] Professor McLachlan explains:

> Since it lies within the competence of the executive to *conduct* foreign affairs, it must plainly also be competent to inform the court as to steps that it has taken on the international plane to the extent that those steps are relevant to the legal issues before the court. Thus, for example, the recognition of an entity as a state is an act that states are competent to perform on the international plane. Within the domestic polity the act of recognition is plainly within the competence of the executive. Whether a state is, or is not, recognized, is an act that ought to produce consistent effects within the domestic polity. In this context, it is quite understandable that the executive and the judiciary should speak with one voice. . . .
>
> . . . By contrast the executive may not dictate the outcome of a particular decision to the court merely by stating its opinion as policy in the form of a certificate. This would be to usurp the judicial function to determine the case in accordance with the applicable law.[211]

---

208 *Marbury v Madison*, 5 US (1 Cranch) 137 (1803) at 177. Ironically, US courts now grant significant deference to the government on international legal questions, but historically they did not. See D Sloss, "Judicial Deference to Executive Branch Treaty Interpretations: A Historical Perspective" (2007) 62 *New York University Annual Survey of American Law* 497.

209 See *Tse Chu-Fai*, above note 121 at para 55 and *Democratic Republic of the Congo v FG Hemisphere Associates LLC (No 2)* (2011), 14 HKCFAR 395 at 428.

210 Kindred, above note 162 at 612.

211 McLachlan, above note 165 at 243–4.

Similar concerns have been raised, both expressly[212] and implicitly,[213] in English and Commonwealth judicial authority.

In the recent *Canadian Planning* cases, Braid J adopted a respectful yet cautious approach to executive certificates, one that demonstrated a laudable sensitivity for both the judicial function and Canada's compliance with its international obligations. The executive certificate before her opined that certain Libyan embassy bank accounts were protected by diplomatic immunity – thereby purporting to answer the very legal question before the court. The learned judge considered that the answer to that question must come not from the government but from international law. She noted that customary international law "does not leave the immunity of embassy bank accounts wholly in the hands of the host State's executive branch"[214] and that, despite the government's expressed satisfaction that the accounts were being used for diplomatic purposes, "This court, and the Government of Canada, is still bound to follow international law."[215] She concluded:

> I find that the Minister's certificate is conclusive proof that Canada and Libya have a diplomatic relationship. As stated by the Supreme Court of Canada in *Chateau-Gai:* "the question of whether the treaty

---

212 E.g.: *Zeiss Stiftung No 2*, above note 179 at 950, Lord Upjohn ("It has never been the practice of Her Majesty's Secretaries of State to express any views upon the law. While they constantly express views on recognition in answer to questions submitted to them by the courts, the legal consequences that flow from recognition is a matter which is always left to these courts"); *Tse Chu-Fai*, above note 121 at para 55 ("The Executive, a representative of which is a party to a controversy arising under the 1988 Act, cannot, by a certificate furnished by another representative, 'compel the court to an interpretation of statutory words which it believes to be false'").

213 In *The King v Campbell ex p Ahmed Hamid Moussa*, [1921] 2 KB 473, an Egyptian was alleged to have failed to notify the English authorities of his change of address contrary to a regulation applicable to aliens. He admitted to not having done so and to being Egyptian. The magistrate convicted him on the basis of these admissions. He sought to appeal, saying he was entitled to argue, and had intended to argue, that Egyptians were not aliens under the regulation (the British Empire having declared Egypt its protectorate in 1914). Against Moussa's position, the Foreign Office supplied the court with a certificate denying that the existence of the protectorate made Egyptians British subjects. The majority of the court upheld Moussa's right to appeal. None of the judges expressly commented on the certificate, but all three ignored its opinion on the legal issue, leaving it for determination on appeal.

214 *Canadian Planning No 2*, above note 201 at para 55.

215 *Ibid* at para 63.

> is in force, *as opposed to what its effect should be*, is wholly within the province of the public authority." The Minister's certificate can certify the existence of the relationship but it is for the court to determine what privileges arise from the existence of the relationship. As the Minister's certificate itself recognizes, the immunity afforded to diplomatic bank accounts arises out of customary international law.
>
> . . .
>
> The Minister's certificate cannot remove the opportunity for Canadian Planning to allege that the accounts fall into a "commercial purpose" or other exception. To suggest that the Foreign Relations Certificate must end the inquiry would run contrary to international law.[216]

This reasoning is in keeping with those cases and commentators warning against the use of executive certificates to encroach upon the proper role of the judiciary. But Braid J's reasons on this point have been expressly rejected by two of her colleagues on the Superior Court, one of whom was upheld by the Court of Appeal.

In *Tracy v Iran (Information and Security)*, the plaintiffs held judgment in default against Iran and two of its state organs for the enforcement of US judgments under the terrorism exception to the Foreign Sovereign Immunities Act of 1976. Iran moved to set aside the default judgments on grounds including state and diplomatic immunity. One issue was whether two Iranian bank accounts and two real properties were exigible. Iran asserted they were protected by diplomatic immunity. Yet certificates from the minister of foreign affairs indicated these assets were not subject to diplomatic immunity, though others were. Canada argued that it was for the minister alone to determine whether a foreign state's property enjoys diplomatic status, and that the court should accept the minister's certificates as dispositive of the issue. Justice Hainey agreed. Noting that diplomatic relations "fall squarely within the prerogative power of the Minister," he concluded that

> diplomatic immunity cannot be asserted to avoid enforcement in Canadian court proceedings unless the Minister has recognized the diplomatic status of the property sought to be attached. Diplomatic immunity under customary international law should not be accorded

216 *Ibid* at paras 64, 66.

> to property that has not been recognized as having diplomatic status by the Minister on behalf of Canada.[217]

He continued:

> The question of the diplomatic status of a foreign state's mission and property in Canada involves factual issues that are peculiarly within the knowledge of the Minister. Evidence directly from the Minister in the form of a certificate delivered to the court in a legal proceeding is the most reliable evidence of the Minister's view of the diplomatic status of property. In my view it should be regarded as conclusive by the court.
>
> . . .
>
> The Minister's Certificates list all of Iran's property in Canada that Canada recognizes as having diplomatic status. It does not include Iran's Exigible Property. This fact alone, by necessary implication, establishes that this property does not enjoy diplomatic immunity.[218]

This conclusion is in direct conflict with Braid J's decision in *Canadian Planning*. Yet Hainey J made no effort to distinguish that case or explain why he departed from it except to say he was not bound by it and declined to follow it.[219]

The *Tracy* approach to executive certificates relinquishes to the minister what Braid J regarded as the judicial responsibility of deciding international legal questions concerning diplomatic immunity according to international law. The reasons in *Tracy* are, with respect, unsatisfactory as to whether issues of diplomatic status are factual or legal. While the learned judge acknowledges that diplomatic immunity is a matter of conventional and customary international law, he also asserts that questions of diplomatic status involve "*factual* issues that are peculiarly within the knowledge of the Minister." If the diplomatic status of the Iranian property at issue was a question of law (as surely it was), it ought properly to have been decided by the court. The reasoning in *Tracy* risks turning executive certificates into US-style letters of suggestion, contrary to *Congo v Venne*.

---

217 *Tracy* SC, above note 176 at paras 145, 150.
218 *Ibid* at paras 151, 153.
219 *Ibid* at para 156.

The Court of Appeal for Ontario upheld Hainey J's decision. In a brief consideration of the issue, Hourigan JA treated the diplomatic status of the disputed assets as a purely factual matter, framing the issue as "whether on the evidence the Minister had conferred diplomatic status on the Iranian Assets" and concluding that "The evidence, including the fact that the Iranian Assets property was not included in the Minister's certificates," supported the trial judge's finding that the assets were exigible.[220] This way of phrasing the matter is closer to Jackett P's notion of certificates as recognition of the government's position on a matter of foreign affairs. An important difficulty remains, however: It was not for the minister to confer diplomatic status on the assets. They either had that status as a matter of international law or they did not. That was a legal question for the court, not a matter to be determined by the executive.

Justice Braid's more nuanced approach to certificates was also rejected in *Construction Excedra v Saudi Arabia*.[221] The plaintiff contractor claimed to be owed nearly $1 million for construction of a cultural centre that formed part of Saudi Arabia's embassy in Ottawa. It placed a lien against the title and sued to recover the debt. Saudi Arabia pleaded diplomatic immunity. In support it advanced two executive certificates from the minister of foreign affairs. The first certificate asserted that the property was diplomatic premises and enjoyed privileges and immunities under the Foreign Missions and International Organizations Act. The second certificate was blatantly a legal submission in certificate form, quoting extensively from the Vienna Convention on Diplomatic Relations 1961 and concluding that that Convention's effect was that the property "enjoys the privileges and immunities of diplomatic premises." Without considering the abnegation of the judicial function involved in deferring to the government's international legal conclusions as stated in its certificates, Corthorn J expressly deferred to them and granted Saudi Arabia's summary judgment motion.

The deferential approach to government legal positions in *Tracy* and *Construction Excedra* are out of step with traditional concerns for

220 *Tracy* CA, above note 207 at para 118.
221 *Construction Excedra*, above note 176.

the separation of judicial from executive power. In time, Braid J's approach in *Canadian Planning* will, I hope, be favoured.

(g) Executive certificates not the exclusive means of proof

Whatever the probative weight to be given to executive certificates, it seems clear that they are not the only means of proving the facts and matters for which they are used. Certificates are admissible as proof but their absence does not foreclose other means of proof. Where no certificate is in evidence, the court must make the necessary determinations for itself in the usual way. In *Parent v Singapore Airlines*, a passenger suffered an injury at takeoff from Taipei and sued the airline, which blamed the airport and sought indemnity from Taiwan's civil aviation authority. The authority pleaded state immunity, yet the Government of Canada declined to certify Taiwan as a foreign state under the State Immunity Act. This was in keeping with Canada's "One China" policy. Without such a certificate, the Quebec Superior Court was left to determine for itself whether Taiwan was a foreign state at international law and according to the Act.[222] Madam Justice St-Pierre heard evidence, reviewed it against the Montevideo criteria,[223] and concluded that Taiwan was a state and its aviation authority immune from the indemnity claim. The learned judge noted that an executive certificate was not the only means of proving that Taiwan was a foreign state,[224] and that governments may sometimes prefer to leave such sensitive questions to the courts.[225] Similar reasoning would seem to apply to other statutory certificate provisions.[226]

222 Recall that s 3 of the State Immunity Act establishes that foreign states are immune from the jurisdiction of the courts and requires courts to give effect to this immunity even where the state has failed to take any step in the proceeding.

223 Montevideo Convention on Rights and Duties of States 1933, (1936) 165 LNTS 19.

224 *Parent v Singapore Airlines*, 2003 CanLII 7285 (Que Sup Ct) at paras 37–9.

225 *Ibid* at paras 43–50.

226 Note, however, that in criminal proceedings arising from Canadian soldiers' deployment as peacekeepers in Somalia, the Court Martial Appeal Court observed that, in the absence of a s 9 certificate, it was not at liberty to assume the existence of a state of war or of an armed conflict there. *R v Brocklebank*, 1996 CanLII 12045 (CMAC) at footnote 32.

3.6 Pleading international law

In common law jurisdictions, the traditional rule is that law need not be pleaded.[227] This rule has been partially varied by legislation.[228] The current position seems to be that international law ought to be pleaded, though perhaps only to the extent necessary to identify the source of law relied upon. In Quebec, the Civil Code requires pleading of treaties and customs.

(a) In common law jurisdictions

In *Jose Pereira E Hijos, S.A. v Canada (Attorney General)*, MacKay J gave some useful guidance to how international law ought (and ought not) to be pleaded in common law practice.[229] The case arose out of Canada's boarding and seizure of the Spanish fishing vessel *Estai* in 1995. The plaintiffs were the owner and operator of the vessel. Canada moved to strike out parts of the statement of claim because of their reliance on international law, arguing that to plead international law suggested its priority over Canadian law. Justice MacKay rightly rejected that submission but allowed the motion on the altogether different ground that international law need not be specifically pleaded. Justice MacKay observed:

> To the extent that international conventions or treaties are considered authority for international law principles, it is unnecessary to plead them specifically, in the same way that it is unnecessary to plead other authority, e.g., jurisprudence or legislation, and such pleading is not of facts, the essence of pleading, but of law, which is not to be pleaded.[230]

The basic rule is that international law, being law, may be raised without reference in the pleadings. Thus MacKay J struck sentences, phrases, and references to particular treaties from the statement of claim and the

---

227 See, e.g., *North-Western Salt Co Ltd v Electrolytic Alkali Co Ltd*, [1913] 3 KB 422 (CA); *Middlesex County Council v Nathan*, [1937] 2 KB 272 at 276.

228 In British Columbia, see Supreme Court Civil Rules, BC Reg 168/2009, rr 3-7(8) and (9) (permitting pleadings of objections in point of law and conclusions of law supported by material facts). In Ontario, see Rules of Civil Procedure, RRO 1990, Reg 194, r 25.06(2). In the Federal Court Rules, SOR/98-106, see r 175 (permitting a party to raise any point of law in a pleading).

229 *Jose Pereira*, above note 50. The decision was approved on this point by the Federal Court of Appeal in *Turp* FCA, above note 49 at para 85 and again in *IATA*, above note 53 at para 64.

230 *Jose Pereira*, above note 50 at para 22; see also para 25.

reply to the defendants' demand for particulars.[231] However, MacKay J declined to strike out the words "established principles of international law" from the statement of claim, which he considered to be "a part of the factual description of the legal regime here applicable."[232] Similarly, MacKay J allowed certain "general descriptions" of international law and references in the plaintiffs' reply to "International Law giving exclusive jurisdiction to the Flag State" on the ground that these simply elucidated "the plaintiffs' meaning in use of the words 'unlawful' and 'unlawfully' in various paragraphs of the statement of claim" and were merely "general descriptions of sources of law."

In *Mack v Canada (Attorney General)*, the appellants complained that the trial judge had failed to consider customary international law. The court observed that if the trial judge did so, "his oversight is understandable as the term 'customary international law' is not mentioned in the claim and it is questionable whether the pleadings even raise it as supporting the cause of action."[233] The appellants were, however, permitted to make their customary argument with the consent of the respondent. This is a warning to counsel. While judicial notice is taken of international law, counsel should nevertheless plead the general source of the laws upon which they rely, as MacKay J explained in *Jose Pereira*.

(b) In Quebec

The second sentence of article 2807 of the Civil Code of Quebec requires pleading of "international treaties and agreements applicable to Québec but not contained in a text of law, and customary international law," despite the fact that these sources of law are subject to judicial notice.[234]

3.7 Internationally informed objections to court jurisdiction

Public international legal considerations are sometimes invoked to limit courts' jurisdiction or inclination to adjudicate disputes. Such objections, though rare, arise in such a variety of forms and settings that

231 *Ibid* at para 22.

232 *Ibid* at para 26. The "legal regime here applicable" also included Canadian and Spanish law.

233 (2002) 60 OR (3d) 737 (Ont CA) at para 21.

234 See the discussion of art 2807 at Section 3.1(d), above.

categorizing them is difficult. For ease of discussion I classify these objections into three types, without claiming that they are immutable or mutually exclusive. The first class of internationally informed jurisdictional objection concerns state and diplomatic immunity. This is the clearest sort of objection, for they are well established in international law and implemented by federal statutes. The second category of objection may be termed "comity." I include under this heading the foreign act of state doctrine. I am calling the third class of jurisdictional objection "justiciability." I acknowledge, however, that the notion of justiciability overlaps considerably with the notion of comity and is not far removed from immunity-based objections either.

(a) State and diplomatic immunity objections

This work is not the place for an extensive account of the laws of state and diplomatic immunity, whether in international law[235] or in Canada.[236] My limited purpose here is to identify these immunities as the leading class of internationally informed limitation upon adjudicative jurisdiction in Canada.

State immunity is the body of international law governing the extent to which one state's courts may subject other states to their adjudicative and enforcement jurisdiction. The historical position, now subject to some restrictions but still largely prevalent, is that the customary international law principles of sovereign equality and non-interference prohibit states from impleading other states in their domestic courts. State immunity remains largely a rule of customary international law; a comprehensive treaty on the subject was adopted in 2004 but is not yet in force.[237]

---

235 On state immunity, see, e.g., H Fox QC & P Webb, *The Law of State Immunity*, 3d ed (Oxford University Press, 2015). On diplomatic and consular immunities, see I Roberts, ed, *Satow's Diplomatic Practice*, 7th ed (Oxford University Press, 2017) and E Denza, *Diplomatic Law: Commentary on the Vienna Convention on Diplomatic Relations*, 4th ed (Oxford University Press, 2016).

236 A full account of the Canadian law of state immunity has yet to be written. But see J Currie, *Public International Law*, 2d ed (Toronto: Irwin Law, 2008) at 392–403; P Saunders & R Currie, *Kindred's International Law Chiefly as Interpreted and Applied in Canada*, 9th ed (Toronto: Emond Montgomery, 2019) at 384–433. Similarly, there is no complete Canadian study of diplomatic and consular immunity, but see Saunders & Currie, *Kindred's International Law* at 433–9.

237 United Nations Convention on Jurisdictional Immunities of States and Their Property 2004, UNGA Res 59/38. At the time of writing, Canada had not signed this treaty.

Diplomatic and consular immunities are a variety of rules, existing both in customary and conventional international law, to facilitate diplomatic and consular relations between states by delimiting the jurisdiction of host state courts over foreign diplomatic and consular personnel, premises, and property.

Both sorts of immunity have been recognized by Canadian courts as existing in customary international law and incorporated by the common law.[238] Both sorts are also the subject of federal legislation, namely the State Immunity Act and the Foreign Missions and International Organizations Act.

Section 3(1) of the State Immunity Act provides, in English, "Except as provided by this Act, a foreign state is immune from the jurisdiction of any court in Canada." Section 2 defines foreign state to include heads of state, governments, political subdivisions, and state agencies. The general immunity provided by section 3(1) is subject to defined exceptions for waiver (section 4), commercial activities (section 5), death or injury occurring in Canada (section 6(a)), damage to or loss of property occurring in Canada (section 6(b)), support of terrorism (section 6.1), certain maritime claims (section 7), and certain property claims (section 8). Even where these exceptions apply, however, states enjoy immunities from attachment, execution, and certain other remedies as set out in sections 11 to 13.

Parliament has partly curtailed state immunity by means of the Justice for Victims of Terrorism Act.[239] That Act, together with a related amendment to the State Immunity Act, enables domestic proceedings against foreign states listed by the Governor in Council as states for which there are reasonable grounds to believe they support terrorism. The illegality, in international law, of this denial of state immunity is clear.[240] The Justice for Victims of Terrorism Act is a rare instance of Parliament exercising its sovereign power to enact a law that breaches the state's international obligations.

Part I of the Foreign Missions and International Organizations Act serves to implement the Vienna Convention on Diplomatic Relations

---

238 See *Re Canada Labour Code*, [1992] 2 SCR 50 (state immunity) and *Re Regina and Palacios* (1984), 45 OR (2d) 269 (CA) (diplomatic and consular immunities).

239 SC 2012, c 1, s 2.

240 See R Provost, "Canada's Alien Tort Statute" (29 March 2012), online: https://ejiltalk.org/canadas-alien-tort-statute.

1961[241] and the Vienna Convention on Consular Relations 1963[242] in Canadian law. The two conventions govern the establishment, maintenance, and termination of diplomatic and consular relations between states, including provisions on the inviolability of premises, the inviolability of persons, and immunities from civil and criminal jurisdiction. Part II of the Act authorizes the Governor in Council to extend privileges and immunities to international organizations. Part III authorizes the minister of foreign affairs to grant privileges and immunities to the offices and officers of a political subdivision of a foreign state.

(b) Comity objections including act of state

Under the heading of comity I am ranging all arguments to the effect that a court ought not to rule on a question for fear that doing so will adversely affect a foreign state or Canada's relations with it.[243]

The following definition of comity was approved by Estey J in *Spencer v The Queen*:

> "Comity" in the legal sense, is neither a matter of absolute obligation, on the one hand, nor of mere courtesy and good will, upon the other. But it is the recognition which one nation allows within its territory to the legislative, executive or judicial acts of another nation, having due regard both to international duty and convenience and to the rights of its own citizens or of other persons who are under the protection of its laws: *Hilton v. Guyot* (1895) 159 US 113, at pp. 163–64.[244]

Similarly, in *R v Zingre*, Dickson J (as he then was) described comity as proceeding "not as a matter of obligation but out of mutual deference and respect."[245] In *Libman v The Queen*, La Forest J described comity as meaning "no more nor less than 'kindly and considerate behaviour towards others.'"[246]

---

241 [1966] Can TS no 29.

242 [1974] Can TS no 25.

243 Comity is also often given as a reason for courts to take some positive step, such as giving effect to a foreign court's order. But I am considering it here only as a basis for judicial abstention.

244 [1985] 2 SCR 278 at 283. See also *Morguard Investments Ltd v De Savoye*, [1990] 3 SCR 1077 at 1096.

245 [1981] 2 SCR 392 at 401.

246 [1985] 2 SCR 178 at 214 [*Libman*]. See also *Hape*, above note 64 at para 47 ("Comity refers to informal acts performed and rules observed by states in their

Comity considerations are usually invoked by Canadian courts in support of recognizing or giving domestic effect to the laws or acts of foreign states. But comity considerations may also support non-interference or judicial restraint. As La Forest J explained in *Tolofson v Jensen*:

> The underlying postulate of public international law is that generally each state has jurisdiction to make and apply law within its territorial limit. Absent a breach of some overriding norm, other states as a matter of "comity" will ordinarily respect such actions and are hesitant to interfere with what another state chooses to do within those limits. Moreover, to accommodate the movement of people, wealth and skills across state lines, a byproduct of modern civilization, they will in great measure recognize the determination of legal issues in other states. And to promote the same values, they will open their national forums for the resolution of specific legal disputes arising in other jurisdictions consistent with the interests and internal values of the forum state.[247]

As important as comity considerations are, they do not trump all others. As La Forest J noted in the *Tolofson* passage quoted immediately above, domestic courts will resolve disputes before them according both to comity considerations and "the interests and internal values of the forum state." Similarly, in *R v Hape*, LeBel J for the majority observed that the deference comity calls for "ends where clear violations of international law and fundamental human rights begin."[248]

Comity considerations cannot restrain the sovereignty of Parliament or the provincial legislatures to enact laws that violate Canada's international obligations.[249] Yet Parliament is presumed not to legislate in breach of the comity of nations.[250]

---

mutual relations out of politeness, convenience and goodwill, rather than strict legal obligation").

247 [1994] 3 SCR 1022 at 1047.

248 *Hape*, above note 64 at para 52, applied in *Canada (Justice) v Khadr*, 2008 SCC 28 at para 18. Similarly, see La Forest J's observations in *Chan v Canada (Minister of Employment and Immigration)*, [1995] 3 SCR 593 at para 65.

249 *British Columbia Electric Railway Co Ltd v The King*, [1946] AC 527 (PC) at 542, approving Rand J's rejection of the submission that an Act was *ultra vires* for being contrary to international comity.

250 *Daniels v White and the Queen*, [1968] SCR 517 at 541; *Libman*, above note 246 at 195; *Society of Composers, Authors and Music Publishers of Canada v Canadian Assn*

In English law, but not in our own, principles of comity have partially congealed into a doctrine known as "foreign act of state" or often simply "act of state."[251] Considering the doctrine in *Nevsun*, Abella J for the majority quoted Lord Millett's description: "the act of state doctrine is a rule of domestic law which holds the national court incompetent to adjudicate upon the lawfulness of the sovereign acts of a foreign state."[252] Justice Abella also noted that the doctrine has been substantially diluted in the UK by a number of recognized exceptions to it.[253] Asked to give effect to the act of state doctrine in Canada, Abella J declined, saying,

> whereas English jurisprudence continually reaffirmed and reconstructed the foreign act of state doctrine, Canadian law has developed its own approach to addressing the twin principles underlying the doctrine articulated in *Buttes Gas*: conflict of laws and judicial restraint. Both principles have developed separately in Canadian jurisprudence rather than as elements of an all-encompassing "act of state doctrine". As such, in Canada, the principles underlying the act of state doctrine have been completely subsumed within this jurisprudence.
>
> Our courts determine questions dealing with the enforcement of foreign laws according to ordinary private international law principles which generally call for deference, but allow for judicial discretion to decline to enforce foreign laws where such laws are contrary to public policy, including respect for public international law.[254]

Developing this point, Abella J affirmed that there is no jurisdictional bar to a Canadian court dealing with the laws or acts of a foreign state where "the question arises merely incidentally in the course of litigation," and that in certain circumstances the adjudication of international legal questions by Canadian courts will be necessary to determine rights or obligations within our legal system.[255] She reviewed

---

of Internet Providers, 2004 SCC 45 at paras 55 and 150; *Hape*, above note 64 at para 54; see also paras 47–52, 56.

251 See, e.g., *Belhaj v Straw*, [2017] UKSC 3.

252 *Nevsun*, above note 8 at para 29, quoting *R v Bow Street Metropolitan Stipendiary Magistrate, ex parte Pinochet Ugarte (No 3)*, [2000] 1 AC 147 (HL) at 269.

253 *Nevsun*, above note 8 at paras 35–8.

254 *Ibid* at paras 44–5.

255 *Ibid* at paras 48–9, quoting *Hunt v T&N plc*, [1993] 4 SCR 289 at 308–9.

several Supreme Court of Canada authorities in which the human rights practices of foreign states were scrutinized without concern that doing so was impermissible as contrary to the act of state doctrine.[256] She noted, however, that Canadian courts will exercise judicial restraint when considering foreign law questions, and will refrain from making findings that purport to be legally binding on them.[257]

In *Eurobank Ergasias S.A. v Bombardier inc*, Kasirer J for the majority of the Supreme Court of Canada distilled *Nevsun* on comity as follows: "For reasons of comity, Canadian courts should be cautious about criticizing the laws of a foreign state even though, as it is best to acknowledge, Canadian and international law sometimes requires them to do so."[258]

One must take care to distinguish the foreign act of state doctrine (now settled as not forming part of Canadian law) from the notion of Crown act of state. Neither doctrine has made many appearances in Canadian law. Both concern the justiciability of certain governmental acts. In Crown act of state, the state act in question is that of the domestic government – that is, the Crown. In *Rahmatullah (No 2) v Ministry of Defence and another*,[259] Lady Hale hesitated to "attempt a definitive statement" of Crown act of state but depicted it as a defence or objection the Crown could make in respect of

> a very narrow class of acts: in their nature sovereign acts – the sorts of thing that governments properly do; committed abroad; in the conduct of the foreign policy of the state; so closely connected to that policy to be necessary in pursuing it; and at least extending to the conduct of military operations which are themselves lawful in international law (which is not the same as saying that the acts themselves are necessarily authorised in international law).

In Canadian law, Hall J described Crown act of state even more narrowly as a doctrine that "denies a remedy to the citizens of an acquired territory for invasion of their rights which may occur during the change of sovereignty" on the basis that English courts have "no jurisdiction to review the manner in which the Sovereign acquires new

256 *Ibid* at paras 50–4.
257 *Ibid* at paras 47.
258 2024 SCC 11 at para 116.
259 [2017] UKSC 1 at paras 36–7.

territory."[260] This narrower formulation likely represents the Canadian version of Crown act of state – if the doctrine exists in Canadian law at all, which may be doubted.[261]

One must also not confuse the act of state doctrine with the implementation requirement. The Federal Court of Appeal made this mistake – why or how is unclear – in *Queen v Jim Shot Both Sides*, while also wrongly depicting act of state as a principle of international law.[262] Regrettably, the Supreme Court of Canada dismissed the appeal without considering (or correcting) this point.[263]

(c) Justiciability

Sossin describes justiciability as "a set of judge-made rules, norms and principles delineating the scope of judicial intervention in social, pol-

260 *Calder v Attorney General of British Columbia*, [1973] SCR 313 at 404. Hall J found the doctrine to have no application to preclude Aboriginal title claims.

261 A famous Canadian, or proto-Canadian, rejection of Crown act of state came in *Walker v Baird*, [1892] AC 491. The UK and France had concluded a treaty concerning the North Atlantic lobster fishery. One of its provisions was that no new lobster factories should be permitted on the Newfoundland coast after 1 July 1889 without consent of British and French officials. In purported enforcement of British obligations under this treaty, Captain Baird of the HMS *Emerald* entered Mr. Walker's lobster factory and seized his equipment. When Walker sued, Baird tried to plead Crown act of state, that is, that he was acting in performance of his duties under the treaty with France and, as such, the litigation "involved the construction of treaties . . . and other acts of State and were matters which could not be inquired into by the Court." Lord Herschell for an eight-judge panel of the Privy Council called this argument "wholly untenable" and upheld the Supreme Court of Newfoundland's determination that Walker's right to run a lobster fishery could not be affected by a treaty with France that had not been enacted in Newfoundland law. The case is authority that Crown act of state is not a basis for giving direct effect to treaties in domestic law contrary to the implementation requirement. The attorney general, on behalf of Captain Baird, tried to get around the requirement by an argument that the Crown has a power to make treaties of peace, and "there must of necessity also reside in the Crown the power of compelling its subjects to obey the provisions of a [peace] treaty" and even of a treaty aimed at "the preservation of peace." Their Lordships did not find it necessary to consider these issues in Walker's case, there being (it seems) no serious prospect of the French and British empires going to war with each other over Newfoundland lobsters.

262 *Queen v Jim Shot Both Sides*, 2022 FCA 20 at paras 8, 13, 65. See G van Ert, "Act of State and Treaty Implementation in *Jim Shot Both Sides*" (8 October 2023), online: https://gibvanert.com.

263 *Shot Both Sides v Canada*, 2024 SCC 12.

itical and economic life," adding that "if a subject-matter is held not to be suitable for judicial determination, it is said to be non-justiciable."[264] What courts regard as non-justiciable may change over time and depend on the considerations bearing on a particular dispute. We nevertheless have some useful judicial guidance on the justiciability or otherwise of questions touching Canada's external relations.

Historically, the common law position was that exercises of the royal prerogative were not subject to judicial review.[265] The courts could determine whether an alleged prerogative existed and what was its scope.[266] They could also determine whether its use had been restricted by statute.[267] But they could not go on to review the manner in which it was exercised. This deferential approach to the prerogative has since been at least partly abandoned. Judicial encroachment began in earnest with the English case of *R v Criminal Injuries Compensation Board, ex parte Lain*,[268] in which Lord Parker CJ held that the fact that a tribunal was established under the prerogative rather than statute did not insulate it from review. Similarly, in the so-called *GCHQ* case, a majority of law lords held that prerogative acts of the Crown are susceptible to judicial review unless the subject matter of the act is non-justiciable.[269] Lord Roskill placed "the making of treaties" and "the defence of the realm" (both aspects of the foreign affairs prerogative) among those "excluded categories," which "as at present advised I do not think could properly be made the subject of judicial review."[270]

---

264 L Sossin, *Boundaries of Judicial Review: the Law of Justiciability in Canada* (Toronto: Carswell, 2012) at 7, quoted with approval in *Highwood Congregation of Jehovah's Witnesses (Judicial Committee) v Wall*, 2018 SCC 26 at para 33. For a critical review of justiciability in the context of prerogative powers, see J Klinck, "Modernizing Judicial Review of the Exercise of Prerogative Powers in Canada" (2017) 54 *Alberta Law Review* 997–1037.

265 *Rustomjee v The Queen* (1876), 2 QBD 69; *China Navigation Co v Attorney-General*, [1932] 2 KB 197 (CA); *Blackburn v Attorney-General*, [1971] 1 WLR 1037 (CA); *Re Doctors Hospital and Minister of Health* (1976), 12 OR (2d) 164 at 175–6 (Div Ct).

266 *R v Secretary of State for the Home Department, ex p Northumbria Police Authority*, [1989] QB 26 (CA).

267 *Attorney-General v De Keyser's Royal Hotel Ltd*, [1920] AC 508 (HL).

268 [1967] 2 QB 864 (Eng CA).

269 *Council of Civil Service Unions v Minister for the Civil Service*, [1985] 1 AC 374 (HL) [*GCHQ*]. GCHQ stands for Government Communications Headquarters, the employer at issue in the case.

270 *Ibid* at 418.

The Canadian position is stronger. Here it is clear that foreign affairs powers may be judicially reviewed, even to the point of invalidating them, to ensure the supremacy of the constitution of Canada as defined in section 52 of the Constitution Act, 1982. That Act is explicit in stating that the Charter applies to legislatures and governments alike.[271]

In *Operation Dismantle Inc v The Queen*,[272] the appellants challenged a decision of the federal cabinet to permit US cruise missile testing on Canadian territory on the basis of their Charter section 7 right to life. The Supreme Court of Canada affirmed the Federal Court of Appeal's decision to strike the claim and dismiss the cause of action. Importantly, however, the court did not do so based on non-justiciability concerns. Chief Justice Dickson for the majority noted that his approach was "not based on the concept of justiciability" and agreed in substance with Wilson J's discussion of that doctrine. He added that section 52 of the Constitution Act, 1982 is not confined to statutes, regulations, and the common law – leaving open the possibility of constitutional review of prerogative powers.[273] The learned judge expressed "no doubt that the executive branch of the Canadian government is duty bound to act in accordance with the dictates of the Charter."[274] Justice Wilson also affirmed that cabinet decisions made in exercise of the royal prerogative fall within the ambit of the Charter.[275] In her consideration of the availability of constitutional review in this case, Wilson J concluded:

> [I]f we are to look at the Constitution for the answer to the question whether it is appropriate for the courts to "second guess" the executive on matters of defence, we would conclude that it is not appropri-

---

271 Constitution Act, 1982, s 32(1). The pre-1982 constitution is not explicit about its application to executive acts. Yet in *Air Canada v British Columbia (Attorney General)*, [1986] 2 SCR 539, the Supreme Court of Canada held that a prerogative power (the discretion to withhold or grant a fiat to a petition of right) must be exercised in conformity with the constitution (specifically, the division of powers). The court directed an order in the nature of mandamus against the attorney general of British Columbia requiring that he advise the lieutenant governor to grant the fiat.

272 [1985] 1 SCR 441.

273 *Ibid* at 459.

274 *Ibid* at 455.

275 *Ibid* at 464.

> ate. However, if what we are being asked to do is to decide whether any particular act of the executive violates the rights of the citizens, then it is not only appropriate that we answer the question; it is our obligation under the Charter to do so.[276]

The justiciability of executive treaty actions in constitutional cases has been affirmed (if in *obiter*[277]) in subsequent Supreme Court decisions. In *Schmidt v The Queen*, an extradition case, La Forest J for the majority insisted that the "pre-eminence of the Constitution must be recognized; the treaty, the extradition hearing in this country and the exercise of the executive discretion to surrender a fugitive must all conform to the requirements of the Charter, including the principles of fundamental justice."[278] Similarly, in *United States of America v Cotroni* the majority implied that both the Extradition Act and the extradition treaty it implements are subject to Charter scrutiny.[279] In *United States of America v Burns*, the court in an unattributed judgment observed that an extradition treaty that lacked a clause requiring the foreign party to assure Canada that the fugitive would not face capital punishment would arguably violate section 7 of the Charter.[280] In *Kazemi*

---

276 *Ibid* at 472. Justice Wilson's observations here resemble those of Marshall CJ in *Cohens v Virginia* (1821), 6 Wheat 264 at 404: "It is most true that this court will not take jurisdiction if it should not; but it is equally true that it must take jurisdiction if it should! The judiciary cannot, as the legislature may, avoid a measure, because it approaches the confines of the constitution. We cannot pass it by because it is doubtful. With whatever doubts, with whatever difficulties, a case may be attended, we must decide it if it be brought before us. . . . Questions may occur which we would gladly avoid; but we cannot avoid them."

277 A rare case in which a Canadian court actually invalidated a treaty concluded by Canada on the ground of inconsistency with part of the written constitution is *Chua v Minister of National Revenue*, [2001] 1 FC 608 (TD), where McKeown J found a 1995 protocol ([1995] Can TS no 17) to the Canada–US Tax Convention 1980 [1984] Can TS no 15.1 to be contrary to s 15(1) of the Charter. In a separate ruling on remedies ([2001] 1 FC 641 (TD)), McKeown J explained the consequences of his finding on the merits, namely one term of the 1980 Convention was "rendered of no force and effect" and the treaty parties were to renegotiate that part of the agreement. While the domestic effect of the case was to invalidate part of a federal law implementing the protocol, and to effectively order the federal government to withdraw from (and, if desired, renegotiate) the protocol, the international law effect of *Chua* was nil; Canada remained bound by its treaty obligations irrespective of the Federal Court ruling.

278 [1987] 1 SCR 500 at 520–21; see also 533, Wilson J.

279 [1989] 1 SCR 1469 at 1482, La Forest J.

280 [2001] 1 SCR 283 at para 139.

Estate v Islamic Republic of Iran, Lebel J for the majority affirmed that "decisions and laws pertaining to international affairs may be subject to constitutional scrutiny under the Charter. In this sense, there is no Charter free zone and the courts may have to play a part, as they have done in the past," but added, "It is not, however, this Court's task to intervene in delicate international policy making."[281]

Questions touching international law and Canada's external relations are, it seems, justiciable even when they do not implicate the written constitution. In *Re Secession of Quebec*, the *amicus curiae* challenged the Supreme Court of Canada's jurisdiction to answer a question put to it by the Governor in Council as to whether international law gave Quebec the right to secede unilaterally from Canada. He submitted that the question was beyond the competence of the court because it required the court to look to international law. The court rejected that submission as "groundless," noting that the court has frequently had to resort to international law "to determine the rights or obligations of some actor within the Canadian legal system." The court added that the question posed by the Governor in Council was not "an abstract question of 'pure' international law but seeks to determine the legal rights of the National Assembly, legislature or government of Quebec, institutions that clearly exist as part of the Canadian legal order" and that consideration of international law in the circumstances was "not only permissible but unavoidable."[282]

---

281 2014 SCC 62 at para 169. In a similar vein, La Forest J (for himself and two others) in *Kindler v Canada (Minister of Justice)*, [1991] 2 SCR 779 at 837, observed that "the executive has a much greater expertise than the Court in the area of foreign relations, and is in a better position to evaluate many of the considerations which have been set forth above."

282 [1998] 2 SCR 217 at paras 20–3. See also Diplock LJ in *Estuary Radio Ltd*, above note 20 at 761: "This court is not an appropriate tribunal to express opinions on such [international legal] matters, except in so far as it is compelled to decide them in order to determine the legal liability under English law of litigants in English courts." Similarly in *Stoeck v Public Trustee*, [1921] 2 Ch 67, Russell J (as he then was) observed: "A suggestion was made by the Solicitor-General that the Court should be reluctant to construe, and indeed should in the exercise of some discretion refrain from construing, an international document such as the Treaty of Peace, executed between high contracting parties and capable of alteration or interpretation at their hands. I do not appreciate this contention. I apprehend it is the right of a litigant to assert before the Courts of this country, and the duty of those Courts to adjudicate upon, claims founded upon a consideration of the municipal law of this country, and not the less so because the

In *Black v Canada (Prime Minister)*, the Court of Appeal for Ontario considered at length the justiciability of exercises of the royal prerogative, observing that "the expanding scope of judicial review and of Crown liability make it no longer tenable to hold that the exercise of a prerogative power is insulated from judicial review merely because it is a prerogative and not a statutory power" and approving a leading House of Lords decision to this effect.[283] While Laskin JA for the court expressly rested his conclusion in the case on the honours prerogative rather than the foreign affairs power,[284] the decision is nevertheless authority that matters of foreign affairs are not non-justiciable for that reason alone.

In *Veffer v Canada (Foreign Affairs)*, the Federal Court of Appeal rejected the submission that Passport Canada policy with respect to the status of Jerusalem was non-justiciable because that matter was a question of international law. The court was not asked to decide the legal status of Jerusalem nor to interfere with Canadian foreign policy, and Passport Canada policy was subject to Charter scrutiny even though the issuance of passports is a royal prerogative.[285]

In *Hupacasath First Nation v Minister of Foreign Affairs*, the Federal Court of Appeal rejected Canada's submission that its decision to enter into a treaty with China was non-justiciable. Justice Stratas for the court explained:

> In rare cases . . . exercises of executive power are suffused with ideological, political, cultural, social, moral and historical concerns of a sort not at all amenable to the judicial process or suitable for judicial analysis. In those rare cases, assessing whether the executive has acted within a range of acceptability and defensibility is beyond the courts' ken or capability, taking courts beyond their proper role within the separation of powers.[286]

---

law involved has been derived from, and has been enacted for the purpose of giving effect to, certain provisions of a document of an international character."

283 (2001) 54 OR (3d) 215 [*Black*] at para. 47, citing *Council of Civil Service Unions v Minister for the Civil Service*, [1985] 1 AC 374 (HL).

284 *Black*, above note 283 at para 23.

285 2007 FCA 247 at paras 21–3.

286 2015 FCA 4 [*Hucapasath*] at para 66.

The learned judge added that "the category of non-justiciable cases is very small."[287] Among the foreign affairs powers Stratas JA accepted as potentially non-justiciable were the deployment of military forces in a particular way in wartime[288] and the decision, without more, to sign a treaty.[289] To this can be added the decision to expel a diplomat.[290]

---

287 *Ibid* at para 67.

288 See also *Aleksic v Canada (Attorney General)* (2002), 215 DLR (4th) 720 (Ont Div Ct).

289 *Hucapasath*, above note 286 at paras 66, 68. See also *Black*, above note 283 at para 52.

290 *Copello v Canada*, 2003 FCA 295 at paras 21–2.

4 Executive and legislative power in the reception system

Most of this book concerns the judicial branch's powers and duties in the reception of international law in domestic law. But a proper appreciation of the judicial role depends crucially on a proper appreciation of the executive and legislative roles. This chapter describes how Canadian constitutional arrangements allocate the foreign relations power between its executive and legislative elements.

The system governing the reception of international law in Canada is a matter of constitutional law. This is not self-evidently so. There is hardly any reference to international law in those texts described collectively in section 52(2) of the Constitution Act, 1982 as "the Constitution of Canada."[1] But the constitution of Canada "embraces unwritten, as well as written rules."[2] "Unwritten" is something of a misnomer, for unwritten constitutional rules can be found in written texts such as statutes, judgments, and scholarly works. By "unwritten" what is really meant is unentrenched, meaning not to be found among those instruments declared to be "the supreme law of Canada" by section 52 of the

1 But see s 132 of the Constitution Act, 1867 ("The Parliament and Government of Canada shall have all Powers necessary or proper for performing the Obligations of Canada or of any Province thereof, as Part of the British Empire, towards Foreign Countries, arising under Treaties between the Empire and such Foreign Countries") and s 11(g) of the Charter ("Any person charged with an offence has the right . . . not to be found guilty on account of any act or omission unless, at the time of the act or omission, it constituted an offence under Canadian or international law or was criminal according to the general principles of law recognized by the community of nations").

2 *Reference re Remuneration of Judges of the Provincial Court of Prince Edward Island*, [1997] 3 SCR 3 [*Provincial Court Judges*] at para 92.

Constitution Act, 1982. There are numerous statutes, orders, and other texts that, though not referred to in section 52(2), are nonetheless constitutional in nature. Also to be included in a complete account of the Canadian constitution are conventions: non-legal rules of political practice that determine some of the most basic features of Canadian politics and government.[3]

Another part of the unwritten constitution consists of common law rules of a constitutional nature. It is these unwritten laws of the constitution that most significantly determine the place of international law in the Canadian legal order. The common law is the principal author of the reception system. The different rules by which customary and conventional international law enter the Canadian legal system are creations of the common law, not statute. The important role played by interpretive presumptions and rules of judicial notice are features of common law adjudication. Even such central features of the constitution as parliamentary sovereignty and the royal prerogative, both considered in this chapter, arguably exist only on the sufferance of the common law, or are at least heavily dependent on it. Everywhere in these common law rules and structures we find the conflicting principles of respect for international law and self-government identified in Chapter 1. And everywhere we find the conflict diffused by rules that alternatively favour one principle over the other in a manner that ultimately balances the two principles in a stable, if not always harmonious, manner.

It might be thought that the silence of our written constitution on the application of international law leaves a "constitutional vacuum."[4] Yet the rules and principles according to which international law applies in Canadian jurisdictions are no less authoritative – and indeed, no less constitutional – for being unwritten. Those omissions the written constitution has left in respect of international law are supplied by

---

3 See, e.g., *Reference re Amendment of the Constitution of Canada*, [1981] 1 SCR 753 at 876–84 [*Patriation Reference*]; A Heard, *Canadian Constitutional Conventions: The Marriage of Law and Politics* (Toronto: Oxford University Press, 1991); P Hogg & W Wright, *Constitutional Law of Canada*, 5th ed Supp (Toronto: Thomson Reuters, 2021 (updated 2021, release 1)) [Hogg & Wright] § 1:10–1:15.

4 S Toope, "Keynote Address: Canada and International Law" in *The Impact of International Law on the Practice of Law in Canada: Proceedings of the 27th Annual Conference of the Canadian Council on International Law, Ottawa October 15–17, 1998* (The Hague: Kluwer Law International, 1999) 33 at 35.

the unwritten constitution and common law adjudication. That this is so is not simply fortuitous, or a case of necessity being the mother of invention. The written constitution explicitly contemplates that unwritten rules will determine such matters as are not addressed by it. Thus the preamble to the Constitution Act, 1867 provides that Canada will have a constitution "similar in principle to that of the United Kingdom."

Two common law features of Canada's unwritten constitution are considered in this chapter. First is the royal prerogative over foreign affairs, including the Crown's power to conclude treaties on behalf of the state without legislative involvement. Second is the legislative role in Canada's performance, or non-performance, of international obligations.

4.1 The executive power to conduct external affairs

The executive's chief role in the reception system is the conduct of external affairs, and in particular the negotiation and acceptance of legal obligations binding on the state under international conventions. The common law has always regarded the conduct of foreign affairs, including the power to make treaties and (more recently) non-binding international arrangements, as an executive function. The treaty power is anomalous in Westminster-model countries like Canada because it is a power in the executive to make law – albeit international not domestic – without the legislature. This anomaly informs the Canadian approach to international agreements in significant ways.

(a) The royal prerogative over foreign affairs

The royal prerogative, also known as the Crown prerogative or simply the prerogative, has been described as the "residue of discretionary or arbitrary authority, which at any given time is legally left in the hands of the Crown."[5] The prerogative is "a limited source of non-statutory

5 *Reference as to the Effect of the Exercise of the Royal Prerogative of Mercy Upon Deportation Proceedings*, [1933] SCR 269 at 272, quoting A Dicey, *The Law of the Constitution*, 8th ed (London: Macmillan, 1915) at 420; *Canada (Prime Minister) v Khadr*, 2010 SCC 3 [*Khadr*] at para 34. This definition has been criticized for conflating what the Crown is entitled to do by virtue of monarchial power and what it can do by virtue of its powers as a natural person – a mistake that may lead to overly deferential approaches to judicial review. See J Klinck, "Modern-

administrative power accorded by the common law to the Crown."[6] The exercise of prerogative powers for Canada is delegated by the sovereign to the governor general in the Letters Patent Constituting the Office of the Governor General, 1947.[7]

Prerogative acts are those that governments can lawfully do without the authority of the legislatures to which they are responsible. The juridical basis of prerogatives is the common law.[8] Today, most if not all prerogative acts are done on advice rather than being exercised by the governor general or lieutenant governor personally. Continuing prerogative powers of the Crown include granting mercy, bestowing honours, dissolving Parliament or the provincial legislatures and, most importantly for our purposes, conducting external affairs.[9]

The conduct of external affairs includes such elements as sending and receiving diplomats,[10] declaring war and deploying armed forces,[11] issuing and refusing passports,[12] making representations to foreign governments,[13] and negotiating and concluding international agree-

---

izing Judicial Review of the Exercise of Prerogative Powers in Canada" (2017) 54 *Alberta Law Review* 997.

6 *Khadr*, above note 5 at para 34. How limited prerogative powers really are in Canada is illuminatingly scrutinized in P Lagassé, "Parliamentary and Judicial Ambivalence toward Executive Prerogative Powers in Canada" (2012) 55 *Canadian Public Administration* 157.

7 Reproduced in the Revised Statutes of Canada, App II, No 31 (1985).

8 *Prohibitions del Roy* (1608), 12 Co Rep 63, 77 ER 1342 (Eng KB); *Case of Proclamations* (1611), 12 Co Rep 75, 77 ER 1352 (Eng KB); *Patriation Reference*, above note 3 at 876–7; *Council of Civil Service Unions v Minister for the Civil Service*, [1985] 1 AC 374 (HL) at 407, 409.

9 "From matters so relatively minor as the grant of pardons to condemned criminals, of honours to the good and great, of corporate personality to deserving bodies of persons, and of bounty from moneys made available to the executive government by Parliament, they extend to matters so vital to the survival and welfare of the nation as the conduct of relations with foreign states and . . . the defence of the realm against potential enemies": *Council of Civil Service Unions v Minister for the Civil Service*, [1985] 1 AC 374 (HL) at 410, Lord Diplock.

10 E.g., *Copello v Canada (Foreign Affairs)*, 2001 FCT 1350.

11 *Blanco v Canada*, 2003 FCT 263 (FC); *Turp v Chrétien*, 2003 FCT 301 (FC).

12 *Veffer v Canada (Minister of Foreign Affairs)*, 2006 FC 540 at para 8; *Kamel v Canada (Attorney General)*, 2009 FCA 21 at paras 21–4. See also the Canadian Passport Order, SI/81-86, s 4(3) ("Nothing in this Order in any manner limits or affects Her Majesty in right of Canada's royal prerogative over passports").

13 *Khadr*, above note 5 at para 35, citing *Black v Canada (Prime Minister)* (2001), 199 DLR (4th) 228 (Ont CA).

ments with foreign states.[14] The foreign affairs prerogative is, in practice, exercised by ministers and the government departments they lead (chiefly the federal minister of foreign affairs and that department). This means that the power to negotiate, conclude, and ratify treaties on behalf of Canada is vested wholly in the executive. As a matter of law, no involvement by Parliament or the provincial legislatures is required for the federal government to bind Canada by treaty at international law.

Canada did not always possess the power to conduct its own external affairs. For the first half-century or so after Confederation, Canada's international relations were largely conducted by the British imperial government. This was one of the most important ways in which Canada's independence from Britain remained incomplete. The disastrous events of the First World War brought about a desire, both in Canada and in other British dominions, for a greater say in imperial and international affairs. In the years immediately following the war, Canada quickly took its place on the world stage. In 1919, Canada signed the Treaty of Versailles on its own behalf (though as part of the British Empire delegation).[15] Later, Canada became a member of the League of Nations. In 1923, Canada signed a treaty with the United States without British participation.[16] In 1926, the Imperial Conference in London produced the historic Balfour Declaration, in which Britain and the dominions were said to be "in no way subordinate one to another in any aspect of their domestic or external affairs."[17] This equality with and independence from Britain was confirmed with the enactment of the Statute of Westminster in 1931.[18] As the Supreme Court of Canada has

---

14 *Attorney General (Canada) v Attorney General (Ontario)*, [1937] AC 326 (PC) [*Labour Conventions*] at 347 ("the creation of the obligations undertaken in treaties and the assent to their form and quality are the function of the executive alone"); *Hupacasath First Nation v Minister of Foreign Affairs*, 2015 FCA 4 [*Hupacasath*] at para 33. For Canadian law to persist in regarding the negotiation and conclusion of international agreements as an aspect of foreign affairs when so many modern treaties have as much to do with our internal affairs as they do with our external relations may seem discordant. In this respect and others, Anglo-Canadian constitutional arrangements have a high tolerance of anachronism.

15 [1919] Can TS no 4.

16 Halibut Fisheries Convention 1923, (1923) 32 LNTS no 93.

17 *Report of the Inter-Imperial Relations Committee of the Imperial Conference* 1926 at 2, online: https://www.foundingdocs.gov.au/scan-sid-18.html.

18 Statute of Westminster, 1931 (UK), 22 Geo V, c 4. Canada's accession to international sovereignty, including its assumption of the royal prerogative over

observed, Canadian sovereignty "was acquired in the period between its separate signature of the Treaty of Versailles in 1919 and the Statute of Westminster, 1931."[19]

The executive's power to conduct foreign relations, including the conclusion of treaties, without the participation of our legislatures has important consequences for the reception system. As I suggested in Chapter 1, the principle of self-government esteems the parliamentary process as the model of consensual lawmaking. The Crown's prerogative to act without Parliament in the conclusion of treaties is therefore highly suspect from the vantage point of self-government. The federal government's exercise of the treaty power is a leading instance of the external coercion that self-government opposes throughout the reception system. This is in spite of the fact that the government is our own and, in that sense, not external at all. Self-government's suspicion of international law is as much a discomfort with prerogative powers as it is a wariness of the international lawmaking process. Throughout the following discussion we find attempts by Parliament and the provinces to subordinate the treaty power to the mechanisms of self-government.

(b) Treaties and the treaty power

Article 2 of the Vienna Convention on the Law of Treaties 1969[20] defines "treaty" as follows:

> Treaty means an international agreement concluded between States in written form and governed by international law, whether embodied in a single instrument, or in two or more related instruments and whatever its particular designation.

This definition is adopted by the federal Policy on Tabling of Treaties in Parliament,[21] which adds that such instruments "can be called Treaty, Convention, Agreement, Protocol or some similar word" and can also

---

foreign affairs, was a gradual process begun during the First World War and culminating in 1931. For an account, see A Gotlieb, *Canadian Treaty-Making* (Toronto: Butterworths, 1968) [Gotlieb] at 6–10.

19 *Reference re Ownership of Offshore Mineral Rights (British Columbia)*, [1967] SCR 792 [*Re Offshore Mineral Rights*] at 816.

20 [1980] Can TS no 37 at art 2(1)(a).

21 Canada, "Policy on Tabling of Treaties in Parliament" (2008), online: www.treaty-accord.gc.ca/procedures.aspx [Treaty Policy].

occur by exchange of diplomatic notes or letters. The international law concept of treaty also includes international agreements between states and international organizations.[22]

The term "treaty" has a second meaning in Canadian law, namely an agreement between the Crown and Indigenous peoples. The use of "treaty" to describe both international and Indigenous agreements is by no means coincidental. For present purposes, I use "treaty" to mean an international agreement concluded between states or between states and international organizations.

The power to negotiate and conclude treaties (i.e., the treaty power) is not expressly allocated in Canada's written constitution. As the Supreme Court of Canada explained in *Re Newfoundland Continental Shelf*, at the beginning of Canada's constitutional history

> colonies were not competent to sign treaties. They might be consulted about treaties affecting them. They might become involved in negotiations under the aegis of the Imperial authorities, but the ultimate control and responsibility in treaty matters rested with the Imperial government. . . . Treaties were made by the Government of the United Kingdom and not Canada.[23]

The closest thing to an explicit statement about the treaty power in Canada's written constitution is the first paragraph of the preamble to the Constitution Act, 1867, which provides that the founding colonies "have expressed their Desire to be federally united into One Dominion . . . with a Constitution similar in Principle to that of the United Kingdom."[24] The United Kingdom constitution allocates the treaty power to the Crown as a feature of its foreign affairs prerogative. Likewise in Canada, the negotiation and conclusion of treaties is an executive function.[25]

The treaty power remains a prerogative, rather than a statutory power.[26] It is not displaced by section 10 of the Department of Foreign

---

22 There is a treaty on this topic, but it is not yet in force and Canada has not signed it: Vienna Convention on the Law of Treaties Between States and International Organizations or Between International Organizations 1986, (1986) International Legal Materials 543.

23 [1984] 1 SCR 86 at 100 [*Re Newfoundland Continental Shelf*].

24 Constitution Act, 1867 (UK), 30 & 31 Victoria, c 3, preamble.

25 See the authorities cited above note 14.

26 See the discussion in *Hupacasath*, above note 14 at paras 32–4.

Affairs and International Trade Act,[27] which describes the powers, duties, and functions of the minister of foreign affairs relating to the conduct of Canada's external affairs, including the conduct of diplomatic and consular relations, the conduct and management of international negotiations, and the development of international law. The only legislative constraint on the treaty power is section 10(1) of the Official Languages Act, which requires the federal government to "take all possible measures to ensure that any treaty or convention between Canada and one or more other states is authenticated in both official languages."[28] Like other prerogative powers, however, the treaty power is subject to judicial review for conformity with the Charter.[29]

The treaty power is not limited to matters that are properly or historically the subjects of international relations. In particular, there is no prohibition on making treaties concerning matters of domestic law or concern.[30]

In 2008, the federal government adopted the Policy on Tabling of Treaties in Parliament.[31] Annex A to that policy, entitled "The Treaty-Making Process," provides guidance on such matters as the nature and significance of international agreements, the normal procedure for obtaining policy approval prior to entering into international negotiations, the procedure through which binding international agreements are concluded by Canada, and the signature, ratification, coming into force, and publication of such agreements.

The treaty power includes not only the power to negotiate and conclude a treaty, but also to terminate it in accordance with its provisions or general international law.[32]

---

27 RSC 1985, c E-22; *Khadr*, above note 5 at para 35.

28 RSC 1985, c 31 (4th Supp).

29 *Operation Dismantle v The Queen*, [1985] 1 SCR 441 at 459, 463–4. Note, however, that courts interpreting treaties are not to use the Charter to do so: *Office of the Children's Lawyer v Balev*, 2018 SCC 16 at para 35.

30 *Re The Weekly Rest in Industrial Undertakings Act, the Minimum Wages Act, and the Limitation of Hours of Work Act*, [1936] SCR 461 [*Re Weekly Rest*] at 480, 481.

31 Treaty Policy, above note 21.

32 M Copithorne, "National Treaty Law and Practice: Canada" in M Leigh et al, eds, *National Treaty Law and Practice: Canada, Egypt, Israel, Mexico, Russia, South Africa* (Washington, DC: American Society of International Law, 2003) 1 at 11. The denunciation of a treaty by the Government of Canada (in order to subscribe to a successor treaty) was noted by the Supreme Court of Canada in *Johannesson v Municipality of West St. Paul*, [1952] 1 SCR 292 at 302–3, 307. In English law, see *R*

(c) Non-binding arrangements

The defining feature of a treaty, both in international law and in Canada, is that it is an agreement governed by international law. In other words, treaties are legally binding on their parties under international law. In recent years, however, Canada and other states have increasingly resorted to non-binding instruments, known variously as "memoranda of understanding," "non-binding agreements," or (the preferred Canadian term) "non-binding arrangements to conduct foreign policy."[33] The principal reason for doing so seems to be to avoid the complexity of domestic legal requirements around treaty approval. Annex C to the 2008 Policy on Tabling of Treaties in Parliament sets out the steps required for the conclusion of international instruments of a non-binding character. These steps are notably simpler than those applicable to the conclusion of treaties.

The conclusion of non-binding arrangements cannot be regarded as an aspect of the treaty power, for such arrangements are by definition not treaties. The making of non-binding arrangements is, however, an exercise of the foreign affairs prerogative.

(d) Parliament's role in treaty-making

In theory the federal Parliament has no necessary role in the making of either treaties or non-binding arrangements. Yet the Canadian constitution is not exhausted by its legal requirements; constitutional conventions requiring parliamentary involvement in treaty-making might temper the law's rigour. For over 30 years, Canadian commentators declared this to be the case. The works of Gotlieb[34] and Jacomy-Millette,[35]

(Miller) v Secretary of State for Brexit, [2017] UKSC 5 at para 54. See the discussion of treaty de-implementation in Chapter 7, Section 7.5.

33 See C Bradley, J Goldsmith, & O Hathaway, "The Rise of Nonbinding International Agreements: An Empirical, Comparative, and Normative Analysis" (1 February 2022), online: https://www.law.berkeley.edu/wp-content/uploads/2022/02/Hathaway-et-al_Rise-of-Nonbinding-International-Agreements.pdf; A Zimmermann & N Jauer, "Possible Indirect Legal Effects under International Law of Non-Legally Binding Instruments" (May 2021), *KFG Working Paper Series, No 48*, May 2021, Berlin Potsdam Research Group "The International Rule of Law – Rise or Decline?" online: https://ssrn.com/abstract=3840767.

34 Gotlieb, above note 18.

35 A Jacomy-Millette, *Treaty Law in Canada* (Ottawa: University of Ottawa Press, 1975) [Jacomy-Millette]. This is a translation of A Jacomy-Millette,

both writing in the late 1960s, described Canadian constitutional conventions by which Parliament enjoyed some participation, in fact if not in theory, in the treaty-making process. Subsequent authors relied on these works, content to assume that parliamentary practice had not changed with the passage of time.[36] This misconception was kept up with the encouragement of successive Canadian governments, whose policy statements suggested a more active role for Parliament in treaty-making than they have actually allowed.[37] It took a sitting member of Parliament, writing in 1998, to demonstrate that the legislative branch had been almost entirely shut out of the treaty-making process by the end of the twentieth century.[38]

This was not always so. In 1926, Prime Minister Mackenzie King introduced in the Commons a resolution which read in part, "This House . . . considers further that before His Majesty's Canadian Minister advise ratification of a treaty or convention affecting Canada, or signify acceptance of any treaty, convention or agreement involving military or economic sanctions, the approval of the Parliament of Can-

---

L'introduction et l'application des traités internationaux au Canada (Paris: LGDJ, 1971). References in these notes are to the translation.

36 See, e.g., R St J Macdonald, "International Treaty Law and the Domestic Law of Canada" (1975) 2 *Dalhousie Law Journal* 307 at 318; R Rafuse, "Treaty Practice: The Canadian Perspective" in P Alston & M Chiam, eds, *Treaty-Making and Australia: Globalisation versus Sovereignty?* (Annandale, NSW: Federation Press, 1995) 253 at 256; M Copithorne, "Canadian Treaty Law and Practice" (1996) 54 *The Advocate* 35 at 37.

37 In 1980, the Legal Bureau of the Department of External Affairs submitted a paper to the Bellagio Conference on National Treaty Law and Procedure stating that "virtually all international agreements (except those of minor importance) are tabled in the House of Commons and the Senate. This provides members of Parliament with an opportunity to raise questions concerning a particular agreement": (1980) 18 *Canadian Yearbook of International Law* 313. In 1995, a government statement promised "a larger role for Parliament" in foreign policy, with vague references to "informal consultations . . . between Ministers and the relevant Parliamentary Committees" and "holding parliamentary debates on major foreign policy issues": *Canada in the World: Government Statement* (Ottawa: Government of Canada, 1995) at 48–9.

38 D Turp, "Un nouveau défi démocratique: l'accentuation du rôle de parlement dans la conclusion et la mise en oeuvre des traités internationaux" in *The Impact of International Law on the Practice of Law in Canada: Proceedings of the 27th Annual Conference of the Canadian Council on International Law, Ottawa October 15–17, 1998* (The Hague: Kluwer Law International, 1999) [Turp] at 115.

ada should be secured."[39] The resolution was adopted unanimously. It was interpreted as requiring that important treaties be approved by resolution of both Houses of Parliament prior to their ratification by the Crown.[40] As the prime minister explained in the Commons, "The purpose [of the resolution] is to secure in the last analysis the control of Parliament over any agreements of international significance which may bind the people of this Dominion."[41] Mackenzie King affirmed the practice of submitting treaties for parliamentary approval in 1941.[42] In 1962, the leader of the Opposition, Lester Pearson, described the practice of submitting important treaties to Parliament as a "convention of our constitution."[43] Two years later, Mr. Turner, then the parliamentary secretary to the minister of northern affairs, affirmed the practice and described it to the Commons.[44]

As Turp documented, the practice of seeking parliamentary approval of important treaties before ratifying them ended in the late 1960s – too soon for Gotlieb and Jacomy-Millette to notice it had happened. Turp rightly observed that the former practice is not to be

---

39 Canada, Parliament, *House of Commons Debates*, 15th Parl, 1st Sess, Vol 5 (21 June 1926) at 4758–9. It is of some interest that the timing of this resolution coincides with the Balfour Declaration and the inception of Canada's power to conclude treaties on its own behalf. On the Balfour Declaration see Hogg & Wright, above note 3 at § 11:10.

40 On the definition of an "important" treaty, see Jacomy-Millette, above note 35 at 131–75.

41 Canada, Parliament, *House of Commons Debates*, 16th Parl, 2nd Sess, Vol 2 (12 April 1928) at 1955 (Mr. Mackenzie King).

42 Canada, Parliament, *House of Commons Debates*, 19th Parl, 2nd Sess, Vol 4 (5 June 1941) at 3528–9 (Mr. Mackenzie King). In 1937, the famous case of *Attorney General for Canada v Attorney General for Ontario*, [1937] AC 326 (PC) was decided by the Privy Council. In response to a question from Lord Atkin, counsel for Canada explained (at 331), "it is ordinary constitutional practice to ask the approval of the body which will, in the event of the [international treaty] engagement being entered into, have the power to enact the legislation." Lord Atkin (at 347–8) noted this practice but observed that "it has never been suggested, and it is not the law, that such an expression of approval operates as law, or that in law it precludes the assenting Parliament, or any subsequent Parliament, from refusing to give its sanction to any legislative proposals that may subsequently be brought before it."

43 Canada, Parliament, *House of Commons Debates*, 24th Parl, 5th Sess, Vol 3 (9 April 1962) at 2618 (Mr. Pearson).

44 Canada, Parliament, *House of Commons Debates*, 26th Parl, 3rd Sess, Vol 2 (4 June 1964) at 3936 (Mr. Turner).

confused with the practice of inserting provisions in implementing legislation declaring Parliament's approval of the treaty being implemented.[45] For at that point the treaty may have already been ratified and Canada already bound at international law.[46] Turp also reported the decline of the practice of tabling treaties in Parliament. Canadian tabling practice was never as demanding as the Ponsonby Rule, whereby the British government lay unratified treaties before Parliament and will not proceed upon them for 21 sitting days.[47] Yet it was at least an occasional practice of the federal government to table treaties in Parliament, though only after their ratification. That practice disappeared for most of the 1990s; even treaties that were required by law to be tabled in Parliament were not tabled.[48] In 1999, the minister of foreign affairs, Mr. Axworthy, tabled in the Commons dozens of ratified treaties, apparently in response to Turp's concerns. But the minister did not go so far as to support Turp's private member's bill on the participation of the House of Commons in the conclusion of treaties.[49]

Reform finally came in 2008 with the introduction of a federal Policy on Tabling of Treaties in Parliament.[50] The policy provides that

---

45 See the discussion in Chapter 7, Section 7.2(c).

46 Turp, above note 38 at 117–18.

47 See Lord Templeman, "Treaty-Making and the British Parliament" in S Risenfeld & F Abbott, eds, *Parliamentary Participation in the Making and Operation of Treaties: A Comparative Study* (Dordrecht: Martinus Nijhoff, 1994) 153 at 158–9; S Dickson & Sir I Sinclair, "National Treaty Law and Practice: United Kingdom" in M Leigh & M Blakeslee, eds, *National Treaty Law and Practice: France, Germany, India, Switzerland, Thailand, United Kingdom* (Washington, DC: American Society of International Law, 1995) at 234–5.

48 Turp, above note 38 at 120.

49 Bill C-214, An Act to provide for the participation of the House of Commons when treaties are concluded, 2d Sess, 36th Parl, 1999, required, among other things, a resolution of approval by the House of Commons before Canada ratifies important treaties, the tabling of treaties prior to ratification similar to the UK's Ponsonby Rule, the tabling of an explanatory memorandum with each tabled treaty (a practice current in Australia, New Zealand, and the UK at the time and adopted in Canada in 2008), and the publication of treaties in various formats. All these reforms could, of course, be introduced by the government without legislation, but were in this case brought by Turp as a private member's bill. The government opposed the bill and it was defeated. Similar reform proposals were later enacted, however, in Quebec: see An Act respecting the Ministère des Relations internationales, CQLR, c M-25.1.1, ss 22.1–22.7.

50 Treaty Policy, above note 21. See generally T McDorman, "The Tabling of International Treaties in the Parliament of Canada: The First Four Years" (2012)

the minister of foreign affairs will initiate the tabling in the House of Commons of all instruments governed by public international law following their signature or adoption by Canada and prior to Canada becoming bound by them. Each such instrument is tabled together with an explanatory memorandum describing the treaty, how it will be implemented in Canadian law, any reservations or declarations, and what consultations have taken place (including with "self-governing Aboriginal Governments") prior to the treaty's conclusion.

The policy notes that the government "can accept the obligations within many treaties without new legislation" but that "In other cases, Canada must amend its domestic law before undertaking treaty obligations."[51] When treaties do not require implementing legislation, the policy provides for a 21 sitting day waiting period from the time of tabling before taking legal steps to bring the treaty into force for Canada. For treaties that require implementing legislation, the waiting period is 21 sitting days before the introduction of the treaty's implementing legislation, and it is only once the legislation is adopted that the federal government will become a party to the treaty. These waiting periods are clearly modelled on the Ponsonby Rule introduced in British (but not Canadian) practice in 1924. Their purpose is to allow time for parliamentary debate. These tabling practices are subject to an exception "in certain cases, such as where a treaty's ratification is urgently required or where an undue delay in the process would have significant consequences for the national interest."[52]

Once a treaty and its explanatory memorandum have been tabled, and the waiting period has been observed, the policy provides that the government will "consider any concerns raised by the Opposition Parties during the tabling process" but immediately adds that the executive "remains responsible for undertaking any international obligations of Canada"[53] – an affirmation likely added to avoid any suggestion that the policy derogates from or displaces the treaty power. The government

---

35 *Dalhousie Law Journal* 357 [McDorman]; S Danesi, "Tabling and Waiting: A Preliminary Assessment of Canada's Treaty-Tabling Policy" (2014) 20 *Canadian Foreign Policy Journal* 189 [Danesi].

51 Treaty Policy, above note 21 at s 6.2.

52 *Ibid* at s 6.4.

53 *Ibid* at s 6.7(a).

then decides whether to ratify the treaty or to introduce implementing legislation.[54]

The Policy on Tabling of Treaties in Parliament is an improvement in Canadian treaty practice. Before the policy's introduction, Canadian practice was inconsistent and outdated compared to other Westminster-model democracies.[55] The absence of authoritative explanations of proposed government treaty action was particularly regrettable. But it has only been partially corrected: While explanatory memoranda are now tabled in the House of Commons, they are still not published by either Parliament or the government on an easily accessible website, making them hard for courts, academics, and other interested members of the public to find and review.[56]

One must not mistake the parliamentary input now enabled by the tabling policy with parliamentary control over treaty-making. McDorman illustrates this point with the example of a treaty for the amendment of the Northwest Atlantic fisheries regime. The amending treaty was tabled by the federal government in June 2009, together with an explanatory memorandum. In December, the House of Commons approved a motion recommending that Canada not ratify. The federal government proceeded to ratify the treaty the very next day.[57] In short, the 2008 tabling policy does not repeal, or even significantly qualify, the unwritten constitutional principle that treaty-making is a prerogative of the Crown. As Danesi observes, "The policy has not altered the executive preeminence."[58]

It is important to bear in mind that the tabling policy only applies to treaties. Increasing government reliance on non-binding arrangements instead of treaties allows even the modest parliamentary scrutiny introduced by the policy to be avoided altogether.

---

54 *Ibid* at s 6.7(b).

55 See J Harrington, "Redressing the Democratic Deficit in Treaty Law Making: (Re-)Establishing a Role for Parliament" (2005) 50:3 *McGill Law Journal* 465; J Harrington, "Scrutiny and Approval: The Role for Westminster-Style Parliaments in Treaty-Making" (2006) 55 *International and Comparative Law Quarterly* 121.

56 Hard but not impossible. The Supreme Court of Canada quoted from an explanatory memorandum in *Society of Composers, Authors and Music Publishers of Canada v Entertainment Software Association*, 2022 SCC 30 at para 49.

57 McDorman, above note 50 at 371–3.

58 Danesi, above note 50 at 205.

The principle of self-government informs these struggles between Parliament and the executive over the treaty power. The former Canadian practice of seeking parliamentary input in the government's treaty-making process was demonstrably motivated by notions of self-government, for the 1926 resolution that began the practice was passed at a time when the UK was still the only authority competent to conclude treaties on Canada's behalf. In unanimously approving the resolution, the Parliament of Canada called upon the British executive to give it a role in the treaty-making process. The practice was not only about Canadian independence from Britain, for it did not pass away following Canada's realization of full sovereignty with the Statute of Westminster 1931. It continued for 35 years afterwards and was described as a convention of our constitution by no less a figure than Lester Pearson. Turp's attempts to reassert a role for Parliament in treaty-making were unsuccessful at the time but likely influenced the belated introduction of reforms in 2008. Those reforms are now a part of federal practice – except when they are not. An April 2015 question by Marc Garneau (MP for Westmount – Ville Marie) to the minister of foreign affairs, Rob Nicholson, asked how many times the exception to tabling treaties had been invoked and in what circumstances. There had been 19 such instances since the policy was introduced, not all of which were based on urgency.[59]

(e) Is the treaty power exclusively federal?

The treaty power is not only a threat to self-government at the federal level. It may also threaten the self-government of the provinces. Exercise of the treaty-making power by the federal government frequently touches on matters falling within provincial legislative jurisdiction. The great vindication of provincial autonomy in the area of federal treaty-making came in the *Labour Conventions* case, which held that the implementation of treaties concerning matters of provincial jurisdiction must be done by the provincial legislatures, not by Parliament. I consider that case at length in Chapter 7. Another federal–provincial struggle over the treaty power has concerned the federal government's claim to a monopoly on the power to make treaties. This monopoly has been disputed, formerly by Ontario and by Quebec today.

---

59 Order/Address to the House of Commons no Q-1061 (20 April 2015), House of Commons sessional paper 8555-412-1061.

External affairs is ordinarily thought of as a power of the federal government. This is largely accurate. The vast majority of transactions between Canada and foreign states are conducted by federal ministries, principally the Department of Foreign Affairs and International Trade. Yet Canada's provincial governments also make appearances on the international stage.[60] A few have permanent departments dedicated to international affairs.[61] Quebec has many offices abroad, and other provinces have had them in the past.[62] Provinces send ministers and civil servants to meetings with foreign leaders and international organizations from time to time. And all have concluded, and continue to conclude, agreements with the governments of foreign states or (more often) sub-state entities. The subject matters of these agreements have included economic cooperation,[63]

---

60 See, e.g., A de Mestral, "The Provinces and International Relations in Canada" in J-F Gaudreau-Desbiens & F Gélinas, eds, *The States and Moods of Federalism: Governance, Identity and Methodology* (Cowansville: Éditions Yvon Blais, 2005) at 310–25; A Lecours, "Canada" in H Michelmann, ed, *Foreign Relations in Federal Countries* (Montreal: McGill-Queen's University Press, 2009) at 114–35. As Prof. Paquin notes, "L'élargissement des enjeux sur la scène internationale fait en sorte que de nos jours, sur le plan de la prise de décision en matière de politique étrangère, tous les ministères fédéraux et provinciaux, du plus périphérique au plus central, ont une partie de leurs activités qui sont touchées par les négociations internationales": S Paquin, "La réforme inachevée : le fédéralisme canadien et le rôle des provinces dans les négociations internationales" Hors-série (2022) *Revue québécoise de droit international* 73 [Paquin] at 75.

61 The names and structures of government departments often change. At time of writing, however, Quebec has a Ministère des Relations internationales et de la Francophonie and Manitoba has a department of Intergovernmental Affairs and International Relations. New Brunswick, Nova Scotia, Ontario, and Saskatchewan include international relations within their intergovernmental affairs departments without acknowledging international affairs in the department's name. Alberta previously had an International, Intergovernmental, and Aboriginal Relations Department, but now deals with international and intergovernmental matters at the cabinet level, as do British Columbia, Newfoundland and Labrador, and Prince Edward Island.

62 As of 2017, Quebec had 26 offices in 14 countries: Gouvernement du Québec, *Québec on the World Stage: Involved, Engaged, Thriving* (Ministère des Relations internationales et de la Francophonie, 2017) [*Québec on the World Stage*] at vii. Ontario and British Columbia both once had offices in London.

63 See, for example, the Memorandum of Understanding on Economic Cooperation between the Province of Alberta, Canada and the Province of Neuquén, Argentina, 14 November 2000. See also the Memorandum of Understanding on Maritime Commerce between the Province of Ontario and the State of Michigan, 19 April 1988.

cultural relations,[64] family maintenance orders,[65] succession duties,[66] the environment,[67] and more.[68] As Iacobucci J for the Supreme Court of Canada noted in *Global Securities Corp v British Columbia (Securities Commission)*, "administrative arrangements between provinces and foreign authorities are quite common."[69]

Tracking down such arrangements is not easy; what Edward McWhinney said to this effect in 1969 remains largely true today:

> The examples [of interprovincial agreements] are, of course, legion; one of the problems in obtaining detailed records of such transnational agreements entered into by the Canadian provinces is that they have very often been highly informal in their modes of creation, and very often concluded, not by the Prime Minister of the province or his cabinet, but by intermediate-rank civil servants who have acted on a purely functional, utilitarian basis related to the province's needs, and dealt directly with their civil service counterparts in

---

64 See, for example, the Memorandum of Agreement between the Maritime Provinces and the State of Louisiana 1994 and the Entente entre la province du Nouveau-Brunswick et La Commission communautaire française de Belgique 1998.

65 See A Gotlieb, "Canadian Practice in International Law, 1965" (1965) 4 *Canadian Yearbook of International Law* 260.

66 See the reciprocal arrangements between Quebec, Great Britain, Northern Ireland, and Trinidad and Tobago (1932–4) reported in *Canadian Estate and Gift Tax Reports*, vol I, ss 7810, 7825, 7835.

67 Various agreements exist between Canadian provinces and US states touching on shared environmental concerns. Examples include the Great Lakes Charter (11 February 1985) between Ontario, Quebec, and eight US states; Ontario-Michigan Joint Notification Plan of Unanticipated or Accidental Discharges of Pollutants into Shared Waters of the Great Lakes and Interconnecting Channels (19 April 1988); Declaration of Partnership and Memorandum of Understanding on Cooperation Between the Province of Ontario and the State of New York (20 September 1991) (the lengthiest provisions of which concern the environment); the Lake Champlain Management Agreement between Quebec, Vermont, and New York (23 March 2015); the Agreement between the Gouvernement du Québec and the Government of the State of Vermont concerning phosphorus reduction in Missisquoi Bay (26 August 2022).

68 See, for example, Morin's discussion of the 1955 Nova Scotia–Netherlands land settlement agreement, whereby Dutch immigrants could receive loans for farms in the province: J-Y Morin, "La conclusion d'accords internationaux par les provinces canadiennes à la lumière du droit comparé" (1965) 3 *Canadian Yearbook of International Law* 127 at 178.

69 2000 SCC 21 at para 38.

> other countries without apparently being aware that, in doing what comes naturally, they may have created conceptualistic problems for latter-day commentators.[70]

In spite of this evidentiary problem, it is clear that some provinces are more active internationally than others. Quebec is at the forefront.[71] But all Canadian provinces have concluded agreements with foreign governments at one time or another. Most of these agreements are framed in language that makes their non-binding nature plain. Some, however, are not so clear.[72]

Nor is it entirely settled that the treaty-making power is an exclusively federal prerogative. When Canada was formed, the foreign affairs prerogative (and, more to the point, the treaty power) was exercised in practice by the British foreign secretary and his delegates in the Foreign Office. The only mention of international treaties in the Constitution Act, 1867 was section 132, by which the federal Parliament and government were granted competence to perform "the Obligations of Canada or of any Province thereof, as Part of the British Empire, towards Foreign Countries, arising under Treaties between the Empire and such Foreign Countries."[73] When Canada gained full independence from the United Kingdom in 1931, Empire treaties became a thing of

---

70 E McWhinney, "Canadian Federalism and the Foreign Affairs and Treaty Power: The Impact of Quebec's 'Quiet Revolution'" (1969) 7 *Canadian Yearbook of International Law* 3 [McWhinney] at 14, n 18. The notable exception to this rule is Quebec, which (at time of writing) maintains a list of its international arrangements on its website.

71 A 2006 governmental policy statement observed that Quebec has "More than 300 bilateral agreements . . . in effect with national governments and federated states in nearly 80 countries": Ministère des Relations internationales, *Québec's International Policy: Working in Concert* (Québec: Gouvernement du Québec, 2006) [*Québec's International Policy*] at 5. Emanuelli (writing in 2010) states that Quebec has concluded over 550 arrangements with a variety of states, "sans que le gouvernement federal puisse s'y opposer de façon efficace": C Emanuelli, *Droit international public: contribution à l'étude du droit international selon une perspective canadienne*, 3e edition (Montreal: Wilson & Lafleur, 2010) at 92; Côté, in a piece published in 2019, puts the figure at over 700: C-E Côté, "Federalism and Foreign Affairs in Canada" in C Bradley, ed, *The Oxford Handbook of Comparative Foreign Relations Law* (Oxford University Press, 2019) at 285.

72 See G van Ert, "The Legal Character of Provincial Agreements with Foreign Governments" (2001) 42 *Cahiers de droit* 1093.

73 Constitution Act, 1867, s 132. See the discussion in Chapter 7 Section 7.3(a).

the past.[74] No constitutional amendment was made to update section 132 in recognition of Canada's new powers over foreign policy. The assumption, it seems, was that the foreign affairs prerogative passed from the imperial government in Westminster to the federal government in Ottawa. That assumption was quickly challenged and is disputed even today. While it is clear that, practically speaking, the treaty power is exercised principally if not wholly by His Majesty in right of Canada (that is, by the federal government), it is sometimes claimed that the true legal position in Canada is that the treaty power is shared: the federal government is competent to conclude treaties within Parliament's legislative jurisdiction, and the provincial governments may make treaties whose subject matters fall within provincial legislative competence.

(i) *The federal case for an undivided treaty power*

The position of the federal government has always been that the power to conclude treaties with foreign states is exclusive to the federal Crown.[75] At least five considerations support this view – yet none of them is entirely free from doubt.

---

74 In *Thomson v Thomson*, [1994] 3 SCR 551 at para 112, L'Heureux-Dubé J, in a concurring opinion, declared that the federal treaty-making power is found in s 132 of the Constitution Act, 1867. That finding is, with respect, wrong. Section 132 grants the "Parliament and Government of Canada . . . all Powers necessary or proper for performing the Obligations of Canada or of any Province thereof, as Part of the British Empire, towards Foreign Countries, arising under Treaties between the Empire and such Foreign Countries." This section only grants power to perform treaty obligations; it grants no power to incur such obligations. As we have seen, Canada lacked such power for much of its early history. Furthermore, s 132 only grants power respecting Empire treaties. In a letter of 1 February 1985 to the Council of Europe explaining Canadian treaty practice (reprinted in (1986) 24 *Canadian Yearbook of International Law* 397), the Legal Bureau of the Department of External Affairs stated, "The Canadian Constitution contains no provisions regarding treaty-making apart from Section 132 of the Constitution Act, 1867 which has fallen into disuse. . . . Treaty-making in Canada is part of the Royal Prerogative, the residue of authority left in the Crown, and in practice exercised by the Governor General in Council, i.e. the Governor General of Canada acting on the advice of Privy Councillors who are Ministers of the Government."

75 See, for example, P Martin, *Federalism and International Relations* (Ottawa: Queen's Printer for Canada, 1968) at 11–16; M MacGuigan, "Le fédéralisme et les relations internationales du Canada" (1981) 12 *Politique internationale* 189 at

First, the majority of the Supreme Court of Canada supported an exclusively federal treaty power in *Re Weekly Rest* (the Supreme Court of Canada's judgment in *Labour Conventions*[76]). Chief Justice Duff (Davis and Kerwin JJ concurring) held that

> as a result of the constitutional development of the last thirty years (and more particularly of the last twenty years) Canada has acquired the status of an international unit . . . enabling her to enter into, on her own behalf, international arrangements, and to incur obligations under such arrangements . . .

and that "it is now settled that, as regards Canada, it is the Canadian government acting on its own responsibility to the Parliament of Canada which deals with the matter." Furthermore, "the Lieutenant-Governors of the provinces do not in any manner represent His Majesty in external affairs, and . . . the provincial governments are not concerned with such affairs."[77] While Duff CJ spoke only for three of the six judges who heard the case, Crocket J specifically agreed with the chief justice that "the Government of Canada must now be held to be the proper medium for the formal conclusion of international conventions, whether they affect the Dominion as a whole or any of the provinces separately."[78] This view therefore commanded a majority. One might think that enough to resolve the question. Yet the authority of the majority position on this point was put into question by the failure of the Privy Council to endorse it on appeal and, perhaps more importantly, the reliance Duff CJ (quite properly) placed on Privy Council precedents in *Re Aeronautics*[79] and *Re Radio*,[80] both of which the Privy Council arguably departed from in *Labour Conventions*.[81]

A second argument, enjoying the weighty support of Professor Hogg, contends that the exclusive federal power to make treaties is

---

195–6; letter of 1 February 1985 to the Council of Europe from the Legal Bureau of the Department of External Affairs, *ibid*.

76 Above note 14.

77 *Re Weekly Rest*, above note 30 at 496; see also 488–9.

78 *Ibid* at 535.

79 *Reference re: Regulation and Control of Aeronautics in Canada*, [1932] 1 DLR 58 (PC).

80 *Reference re: Regulation and Control of Radio Communication in Canada*, [1932] 2 DLR 81 (PC).

81 See the discussion in Chapter 7, Section 7.3(b).

based on the Letters Patent Constituting the Office of Governor General of Canada 1947,[82] the principal instrument by which the sovereign's powers in respect of Canada are delegated to the governor general.[83] This was also the contention of the prime minister of the day, Louis St-Laurent, who told the House of Commons that "when the letters patent come into force, it will be legally possible for the Governor General, on the advice of the Canadian ministers, to exercise any of these powers and authorities[:] . . . royal full powers for the signing of treaties, ratification of treaties, and the issuance of letters of credence for ambassadors."[84] Yet the Letters Patent argument is open to challenge. Clause II of those Letters reads:

> And We do hereby authorize and empower Our Governor General, with the advice of Our Privy Council for Canada or of any members thereof or individually, as the case requires, to exercise all powers and authorities lawfully belonging to Us in respect of Canada, and for greater certainty but not so as to restrict the generality of the foregoing to do and execute, in the manner aforesaid, all things that may belong to his office and to the trust We have reposed in him according to the several powers and authorities granted or appointed him by virtue of the Constitution Acts, 1867 to 1940 and the powers and authorities hereinafter conferred in these Letters Patent and in such Commission as may be issued to him under Our Great Seal of Canada and under such laws as are or may hereinafter be in force in Canada.[85]

The federal argument is that the treaty power, formerly exercised by the Crown on the advice of British ministers, was passed to the federal government by this clause. But the clause applies only to those powers and authorities lawfully belonging to the sovereign "in respect of Canada." This phrase must be read, it seems, to exclude those powers and authorities lawfully belonging to the sovereign in respect of the provinces, for it is nowhere contended that the Letters Patent 1947 affect the office of lieutenant governor. Thus, if the passage of the treaty power from the

82 RSC 1985 App II No 31 [Letters Patent].

83 P Hogg & W Wright, *Constitutional Law of Canada*, 5th ed Suppl, looseleaf (Toronto: Thomson Reuters, 2021) § 11.2.

84 Canada, Parliament, *House of Commons Debates*, 20th Parl, 4th Sess, Vol 4 (12 February 1948) at 1126 (Mr. St-Laurent).

85 Letters Patent, above note 82. (The original text referred to the British North America Acts 1867 to 1946.)

UK to Canada in 1931 tracked legislative jurisdiction under the Constitution Act, 1867 (which, as we will see, is the provincial argument), nothing in the Letters Patent changed that. To read "in respect of Canada" as meaning "in respect of the federal and provincial governments" only begs the question. A further difficulty in relying on the Letters Patent is that the theory fails to explain where the treaty-making power lay between Canada's acquisition of full sovereignty and 1947.

The third argument for an exclusively federal treaty power draws on Canada's status as a sovereign state at international law. The argument here is that Canada, as a single state for the purpose of international law, must have only one international personality and therefore only one government competent to act on the international scene.[86] This argument often finds support in comparative analyses of the constitutional structures of other federal states, most of which assign treaty-making exclusively to the federal level.[87] There are two points to the contrary. First, the international position is not as straightforward as this argument makes out. International law appears to permit the constituent units of a federal state to enjoy some measure of international personality, including competence to conclude treaties.[88] Second, the comparative approach is not, on its own, conclusive. To say that other

---

86 A typical exposition of this approach is J-Y Grenon, "De la conclusion des traités et de leur mise en oeuvre au Canada" (1962) 40 *Canadian Bar Review* 151. This approach is supported by an American case, *United States v Curtiss-Wright Export Corp* (1936), 299 US 304, in which Sutherland J declared at 318 that "the investment of the federal government with the powers of external sovereignty did not depend upon the affirmative grants of the Constitution. The powers to declare and wage war, to conclude peace, to make treaties, to maintain diplomatic relations with other sovereignties, if they had never been mentioned in the constitution, would have vested in the federal government as necessary concomitants of nationality. . . . Otherwise, the United States is not completely sovereign." Similarly, the external affairs minister of the day, Mr. Martin, argued that "if individual constituent members of a federal state had the right to conclude treaties independently of the central power, it would no longer be a federation but an association of sovereign powers" (quoted in GL Morris, "The Treaty-Making Power: A Canadian Dilemma" (1967) 45 *Canadian Bar Review* 478 [Morris] at 479).

87 For such a comparative approach, see Gotlieb, above note 18 at 25–7, and Morris, *ibid* at 492–7.

88 See the discussion of treaties in Chapter 2, Section 2.3(a). For a comparison of the treaty powers of Quebec and the Belgian communities, see A De Mestral, "Le Québec et les relations internationales" in P Patenaude, ed, *Québec-Communauté Française de Belgique* (Montreal: Wilson & Lafleur, 1991) at 209.

federations do not divide the treaty power between the federal and sub-federal levels suggests certain policy arguments against such a division here in Canada but sheds no light on the actual position of Canadian law.

The fourth argument in support of a federal treaty-making power relies on the constitution's division of legislative powers. The argument is as follows: Matters of provincial legislative jurisdiction can generally be characterized as "merely local or private."[89] By contrast, Parliament's jurisdiction extends to matters of national interest or, in the language of section 91, to matters concerning "the Peace, Order, and good Government of Canada."[90] Executive powers and responsibilities track the legislative division of powers.[91] The obligations of the Canadian state at international law are properly associated with the federal residual power and not with provincial heads of jurisdiction because treaty obligations are not merely local or private but national, and indeed international. There are at least two problems with this argument. First, to found the federal treaty power in Parliament's residual peace, order, and good government power runs contrary to the decision of the Privy Council in *Labour Conventions*[92] that international treaties are not a discrete head of jurisdiction under the Constitution Act, 1867, but fall instead to be implemented by whichever order has jurisdiction over the treaty's subject matter. Historically, *Labour Conventions* has been an unpopular decision among English-Canadian commentators, and has even been questioned by two chief justices of Canada. Nevertheless, it remains the law.[93] A second problem with this argument is its characterization of provincial power as merely local or private and thus inconsistent with treaty-making. Notice first that this is question-begging: Treaties are only necessarily national in scope if the provinces lack the power to bind themselves, and themselves alone, by concluding treaties. That objection aside, it is a mistake to assume that the content of treaty obligations cannot be local or private. States today frequently conclude treaties having to do with their internal af-

---

89 Constitution Act, 1867, s 92(16).

90 *Ibid* preamble to s 91.

91 *Liquidators of Maritime Bank v Receiver General of New Brunswick*, [1892] AC 437 (PC) [*Maritime Bank*].

92 *Labour Conventions*, above note 14.

93 See the discussion of *Labour Conventions* in Chapter 7, Section 7.3(b)(iii).

fairs. There is no shortage of examples of treaties putting into question classical notions of state sovereignty by addressing themselves to their parties' regulation of civil rights, social questions, economic relations, and other matters traditionally seen as the purview of domestic law.

The fifth argument for an undivided federal treaty power is founded on a theory of the development of the unwritten constitution. According to this approach, the treaty-making power has settled exclusively on the federal government by constitutional practice. As Duff CJ explained in *Re Weekly Rest*,

> As a rule, the crystallization of constitutional usage into a rule of constitutional law to which the Courts will give effect is a slow process extending over a long period of time; but the Great War accelerated the pace of development in the region with which we are concerned, and it would seem that the usages to which I have referred, the practice, that is to say, under which Great Britain and the Dominions enter into agreements with foreign countries in the form of agreements between governments and of a still more informal character, must be recognized by the Courts as having the force of law.[94]

The argument here is that the unwritten constitution develops by political and judicial recognition of the legitimacy of adopted practices. In the case of the treaty power, these practices should include not only the assumption of the power by federal officials and the general (though not unanimous) consent of their provincial counterparts, but also the practice of other states in recognizing the federal government, rather than the provinces, as the authority competent to bind Canada at international law. Two problems with this argument can be identified. The first is the concept of crystallization itself, of which the Supreme Court of Canada was critical in *Patriation Reference*.[95] The second is Quebec's persistent objection, which undermines the legitimacy of the practice and thus its suitability to be recognized as unwritten constitutional law.

(ii) The provincial case for a shared treaty power

The argument for the existence of a provincial treaty-making power was first made by Ontario, not Quebec. The attorney general for Ontario made the argument before the Supreme Court of Canada, and

---

94 *Re Weekly Rest*, above note 30 at 477, Duff CJ.

95 *Patriation Reference*, above note 3.

later the Privy Council, in *Labour Conventions*. Before the board, counsel for the attorney general submitted that there were

> no grounds whatever for saying that the parties to advise His Majesty in matters relating to the jurisdiction of the Provinces have in some way come to be the Dominion Ministers. The Province has the right to advise the Crown in matters where its legislative powers apply. Ontario has a right to enter into an agreement with another part of the British Empire or with a foreign State.[96]

This argument had enjoyed limited success before the Supreme Court of Canada. It won some support from Rinfret J in dissent,[97] but it was not supported by Duff CJ (writing for himself and Davis and Kerwin JJ)[98] nor by Crocket J.[99] The remaining judge, Cannon J, dissented without specifically considering the argument. Before the Privy Council, the case was decided on other grounds. Their lordships declined to rule on provincial competence to conclude treaties.

Without a ruling from the Privy Council, the argument persisted, though its champion changed. Ontario has long since abandoned any claim to treaty-making power. As an Ontario government official explained in 1985, "Ontario has no interest whatsoever in a foreign policy which could be described as provincial. There is only one foreign policy and that is that of the federal government."[100] Today, the sole proponent

---

96 *Labour Conventions*, above note 14 at 333.

97 *Re Weekly Rest*, above note 30 at 510–12. At 512, Rinfret J wrote, "In Canada, the practice has grown gradually to enter into international conventions through the medium of the Governor in Council. It does appear that it would be directly against the intendment of the *British North America Act* that the King or the Governor General should enter into an international agreement dealing with matters exclusively assigned to the jurisdiction of the provinces solely upon the advice of the federal Ministers who, either by themselves or even through the instrumentality of the Dominion Parliament are prohibited by the Constitution from assuming jurisdiction over these matters."

98 *Re Weekly Rest*, above note 30 at 496, Duff CJ held that "in no respect does the Lieutenant-Governor of a province represent the Crown in respect of relations with foreign Governments." This statement is clearly *obiter*, and on appeal was explicitly left undecided by the Privy Council. Yet proponents of the undivided treaty power, including the Government of Canada, have made questionable use of this *dictum* as though it were *ratio decidendi*. See McWhinney, above note 70 at 6–7.

99 *Re Weekly Rest*, above note 30 at 535.

100 J Carson, speech at the University of Alberta reprinted in T Keating & D Munton, eds, *The Provinces and Canadian Foreign Policy: Proceedings of a Conference,*

of the argument that provincial governments are competent to conclude treaties binding their provinces at international law is Quebec. Indeed, the argument has come to be known as the Gérin-Lajoie doctrine, after the Quebec minister of education who revived the argument and forcefully asserted Quebec's power to negotiate and conclude, within its legislative jurisdiction, agreements with foreign states.[101] The Gérin-Lajoie thesis is now established Quebec governmental policy, whether the government of the day be federalist or sovereignist. A 2006 policy statement of the Quebec government of Jean Charest declared, "The aim of our policy is to strengthen Québec's international influence. It reaffirms Québec's prerogative to vigorously and independently pursue international initiatives wherever appropriate: whatever falls under Québec's jurisdiction at home falls under its jurisdiction everywhere."[102]

This policy is also enacted in Quebec law. Section 7 of Quebec's so-called Bill 99 (Act respecting the exercise of the Fundamental Rights and Prerogatives of the Québec People and the Québec State) reads as follows:

> The Québec State is free to consent to be bound by any treaty, convention or international agreement in matters under its constitutional jurisdiction.
>
> No treaty, convention or agreement in the areas under its jurisdiction may be binding on the Québec State unless the consent of the

---

University of Alberta, Edmonton, Alberta, 28–30 March 1985 (Toronto: Canadian Institute of International Affairs, 1985) 6 at 6.

101 See, e.g., Paquin, above note 60; C-E Côté, "La doctrine Gérin-Lajoie et le domaine du travail : une relation retrouvée" Hors-série (2016) *Revue québécoise de droit international* 205 [Côté]; S Beaulac, "The Myth of *Jus Tractatus* in *La Belle Province*: Quebec's Gérin-Lajoie Statement" (2012) 35 *Dalhousie Law Journal* 237 [Beaulac]; H Cyr, *Canadian Federalism and Treaty Powers: Organic Constitutionalism at Work* (Bruxelles: Presses interuniversitaires européennes-Peter Lang, 2009); S Paquin, ed, *Les relations internationales du Québec depuis la Doctrine Gérin-Lajoie (1965–2005)* (Lévis: Les Presses de l'Université Laval, 2006); Jacomy-Millette, above note 35 at 78–94.

102 *Québec's International Policy*, above note 71 at 5–6 (preface by Jean Charest). See also *Québec on the World Stage*, above note 62 at 4 ("Québec's international action takes the form of bilateral, regional and multilateral cooperation as well as international missions, the hosting of high-level foreign delegations (e.g., heads of state and government, ministers) and sector-specific interventions to advance Québec government objectives. It can also take the form of agreements with foreign states and international organizations on issues of common interest").

> Québec State to be bound has been formally expressed by the National Assembly or the Government, subject to the applicable legislative provisions.
>
> The Québec State may, in the areas under its jurisdiction, establish and maintain relations with foreign States and international organizations and ensure its representation outside Québec.[103]

Note that section 7 asserts no more than Quebec's right to conclude treaties within its constitutional jurisdiction. No claim is made to conclude treaties touching federal matters. It is, however, the occasional practice of the Quebec government to declare itself bound by treaties concluded by the federal government. This practice is provided for by provincial law.[104] Quebec has made such orders in dozens of instances, including with respect to such leading multilateral treaties as the International Covenant on Civil and Political Rights 1966 and the Convention on the Rights of the Child 1989.[105] The Court of Appeal for Quebec has noted the existence of such decrees.[106]

The legal argument that provinces enjoy a power to make treaties is founded on the decision of the Privy Council in *Liquidators of Maritime Bank v Receiver General of New Brunswick*.[107] The case had nothing to do with treaties. Rather, the question there was whether the government of New Brunswick was entitled to preference over other unsecured

---

103 An Act respecting the exercise of the Fundamental Rights and Prerogatives of the Québec People and the Québec State, SQ 2000, c 46, s 7. This is not the only Quebec law declaring the province's competence to conclude international agreements. The Act respecting the Ministère des Relations internationales, CQLR, c M-25.1.1 provides, at s 19(1), that "The Minister shall see to the negotiation and implementation of international agreements and shall administer the programs created under such agreements."

104 Act respecting the Ministère des Relations internationales, CQLR, c M-25.1.1 at s 22(3). See D Turp, "L'approbation des engagements internationaux importants du Québec: la nouvelle dimension parlementaire à la doctrine Gérin-Lajoie" Hors-série (2016) *Revue québécoise de droit international* 9.

105 "Conventions multilatérales, traités et accords internationaux pour lesquels le Québec s'est déclaré lié" (25 January 2007) [Government of Quebec document on file with the author].

106 *Quebec (Minister of Justice) v Canada (Minister of Justice)*, 2003 CanLII 52182 (Que CA) at para 87.

107 *Maritime Bank*, above note 91. See also *Bonanza Creek Gold Mining Company Ltd v Rex*, [1916] 1 AC 566 (PC) [*Bonanza Creek*], Viscount Haldane at 580: "the distribution under the new grant of executive authority in substance follows the distribution under the new grant of legislative powers."

creditors of an insolvent bank. At common law, the Crown enjoyed preferred creditor status as a matter of prerogative. The liquidators argued that the government of New Brunswick was not entitled to preference because the prerogatives of the Crown could not be invoked by provincial governments. The governor general was the only representative of the Crown in Canada, and the lieutenant governors were mere federal appointees. The Privy Council forcefully rejected this argument, declaring that "a Lieutenant-Governor, when appointed, is as much the representative of Her Majesty for all purposes of provincial government as the Governor-General himself is for all purposes of Dominion government."[108] Thus the prerogative powers of the Crown do not vest wholly in the governor general, but are distributed between the federal and provincial executives.[109]

When *Maritime Bank* was decided, the Crown's prerogative to conclude treaties on behalf of Canada was exercised by the Queen on the advice of her British ministers. Clearly, their lordships did not contemplate that their decision would be used to found the argument for a provincial treaty-making power. Nevertheless, that power follows from the logic of the judgment. If treaty-making is an aspect of the royal prerogative, and the lieutenant governor of a province is "as much the representative of Her Majesty for all purposes of provincial government as the Governor-General himself is for all purposes of Dominion government," then the treaty power must vest in the lieutenant governor and governor general alike, assuming that treaty-making is one of the "purposes of provincial government." Those purposes, it seems, are set out principally in section 92 of the Constitution Act, 1867. They do not exclude the making of treaties with foreign states. Rather, the phrase "provincial purposes" serves only to restrict the subject matters of provincially concluded treaties to those falling within provincial

---

108 *Maritime Bank*, *ibid* at 443. See also *Hodge v The Queen* (1883), 9 AC 117 (PC) [*Hodge*], upon which the board relied, and the later Privy Council decision in *Bonanza Creek*, *ibid*.

109 That prerogatives are divided between the provincial and the federal Crown, within their respective jurisdictions, was affirmed in *British Columbia Power Corp v British Columbia Electric Co*, [1962] SCR 642 at 644–5. This passage was quoted approvingly by La Forest J for the court in *Air Canada v British Columbia (Attorney General)*, [1986] 2 SCR 539 at para 9. Neither case considered the foreign affairs prerogative or the treaty power, however. See also *Breckenridge Speedway Ltd v Alberta* (1967), 61 WWR 257, Porter JA, aff'd [1970] SCR 175.

legislative jurisdiction. In short, this argument proposes that there is no legal bar to the conclusion by provincial ministers, in the name of the lieutenant governor, of legally binding treaties within provincial jurisdiction.

We have already considered the federal arguments for an undivided treaty power, all of which strive to rebut the provincial claim. A further argument against the Gérin-Lajoie thesis might be that it artificially divides the Crown's power to conclude treaties from the general prerogative over foreign affairs of which it forms part. The foreign affairs prerogative includes not only treaty-making but diplomatic relations, the waging of war, and the conclusion of peace. These functions are not divisible from each other but interconnected. Thus, the Crown may declare war pursuant to the terms of an alliance founded upon a treaty and administered in part by the diplomatic corps, and later cease hostilities with the enemy under the terms of a peace treaty negotiated by the Crown's ambassadors. The Quebec position has yet to go so far as to assert a power in the lieutenant governor in council to wage war or to decline to participate in hostilities engaged in by the federal government. How, one might object, can the Crown's power to conclude treaties be so neatly distinguished from its other, seemingly federal, foreign affairs powers?

The Quebec thesis has a strong answer to this challenge. As regards the prerogative power of diplomatic relations, such relations are already engaged in by the provinces. Some provinces have (or have had) permanent offices abroad, not operating under the aegis of Canadian delegations. While the federal government has occasionally grumbled, no serious constitutional challenge has ever been mounted against the power of the provinces to establish such foreign offices. Nor could such challenge be made, for there is nothing in the Constitution Act, 1867 placing diplomacy within exclusive federal jurisdiction. Turning now to the prerogatives of war and peace, *Maritime Bank* supplies the answer: National defence is clearly a matter of federal jurisdiction under section 91(7) of the Constitution Act, 1867. The Quebec position claims no powers of war and peace, nor any other power within federal jurisdiction, as part of the provincial Crown's prerogatives. In sum, the foreign affairs prerogative is indeed susceptible to division: The diplomatic and treaty powers are exercisable by the Crown in the right of Canada and the provinces, while the powers of war and peace are assigned to the federal Crown by section 91(7) and the rule in *Maritime Bank*.

(iii) Case law on the treaty power

As noted, the Supreme Court of Canada in *Re Weekly Rest* considered the capacity of provincial governments to enter into treaties, but on further appeal the Privy Council declined to opine on the issue. No other Canadian court has returned to the question directly, but there is some case law of relevance. First, there is the Supreme Court of Canada's consideration of Canadian legal personality at international law in *Re Offshore Mineral Rights*.[110] Second, there are two judgments in which the capacity of the provinces to conclude treaties was at issue but not decided: *Ontario (Attorney General) v Scott*[111] and *Bazylo v Collins*.[112] Finally, there are certain comments by LeBel J in *GreCon Dimter Inc v J.R. Normand Inc*[113] to be considered.

Re Offshore Mineral Rights held that Canada, and not British Columbia, enjoyed property rights and legislative jurisdiction over the territorial sea and continental shelf adjacent to British Columbia. In determining the territorial sea question, the court placed great emphasis on Canada's achievement of sovereignty at international law. "There can be no doubt now," wrote the court in an unattributed judgment,

> that Canada has become a sovereign state. . . . It is Canada which is recognized by international law as having rights in the territorial sea adjacent to the Province of British Columbia. . . . Canada has now full constitutional capacity to acquire new areas of territory and new jurisdictional rights which may be available under international law. . . . Canada is recognized in international law as having sovereignty over a territorial sea three nautical miles wide. It is part of the territory of Canada.[114]

These observations do not say explicitly that Canada alone has international legal personality. Whether the provinces also have some degree of international personality was not considered by the court. But the thrust of these comments is clear: The achievement of independence from the United Kingdom benefited Canada as a whole more than, or perhaps rather than, its constituent provinces. If the provinces have

110 Above note 19.
111 [1956] SCR 137 [*Scott*].
112 (1984) 11 DLR (4th) 679 (CA Que) [*Bazylo*].
113 [2005] 2 SCR 401 [*GreCon Dimter*].
114 *Re Offshore Mineral Rights*, above note 19 at 816.

no legal personality at international law, their governments may not bind them through treaties, for they have no authority to bind Canada as a whole and the territory for which they do have authority is not a subject of international law and is therefore incapable of being bound.

The court in *Re Offshore Mineral Rights* also noted the role of international recognition in deciding the dispute. They observed that rights in the territorial sea depend on recognition by other sovereign states, and that Canada is recognized as a sovereign state internationally. The implied contrast here is to the unrecognized "state" of British Columbia. The court went on to explain that Canada "is a sovereign state recognized by international law and thus able to enter into arrangements with other states respecting the rights in the territorial sea."[115] The significance of this declaration is perhaps not obvious, but if "treaties" is substituted for "arrangements" – and such arrangements do ordinarily take the form of treaties – the court's meaning is plain: Whatever the merits of the Gérin-Lajoie thesis as a matter of Canadian constitutional law, the recognition requirement in international law makes the federal government Canada's only effective treaty-making power.

I have attempted to demonstrate how the judgment in *Re Offshore Mineral Rights* may be interpreted as relevant to the question of whether provinces enjoy capacity to conclude treaties. Yet I suggest that, on balance, the court's statements about Canada's acquisition of international legal personality ultimately do not address the question in issue here: namely, how is Canada's newly acquired sovereignty distributed between the different levels of government? Notably, the court does not cite its judgment in *Re Weekly Rest* anywhere in this decision.

The only Supreme Court judgment specifically to consider the capacity of provinces to conclude internationally binding agreements is the 1955 case of *Scott*. In point of fact, there was no written agreement before the court in this case. But some sort of agreement clearly existed between Ontario and the United Kingdom, for Ontario's Reciprocal Enforcement of Maintenance Orders Act[116] gave effect to maintenance orders made by English courts, and English law accorded Ontario orders the same recognition. Such an order had been made against Scott in England and was about to be given effect in Ontario, where he now resided, when he challenged the Act as *ultra vires* the legislature. Scott argued,

---

115 *Ibid* at 817.

116 RSO 1950, c 334.

inter alia, that the arrangement between Ontario and the UK was effectively a treaty to which the province had no authority to become a party, because treaty-making power resided exclusively in the federal government. How this argument could be used to invalidate legislation is hard to see; even if the legislature were motivated by an intent to implement a constitutionally improper treaty, the Act would surely remain valid so long as it could be brought under section 92 of the British North America Act, 1867. For, as Lord Atkin held in *Labour Conventions*, "there is no such thing as treaty legislation as such."[117] The judgments in *Scott* did not make this point, however. Justice Rand (for himself and three others) held that the underlying agreement behind the Act was not a treaty but a non-binding agreement between the two jurisdictions: "The enactments of the two legislatures [Queen's Park and Westminster] are complementary but voluntary; the application of each is dependent on that of the other: each is the condition of the other; but that condition possesses nothing binding to its continuance. The essentials of a treaty are absent. . . ."[118] Similarly, Abbott J (for himself and two others) affirmed the view of the court below that there was no "valid legal reason why the Province of Ontario cannot, in relation to a subject-matter within its legislative jurisdiction, make a reciprocal arrangement with another Province or a foreign State in relation to such subject-matter."[119] Ultimately, *Scott* says nothing about provincial capacity to conclude treaties, for it describes the agreement in issue as non-binding. Again, no mention of the court's decision in *Re Weekly Rest* is made. *Scott* is notable, however, as an instance of Supreme Court recognition of the power of provinces to enter into non-binding international agreements.

To my knowledge, the only other case to have considered provincial treaty-making is the judgment of the Quebec Court of Appeal in *Bazylo v Collins*. Like *Scott*, this case concerned the validity of a provincial law giving effect to family law orders from outside the jurisdiction. Unlike *Scott*, however, the Act in question[120] explicitly implemented an entente between the governments of France and Quebec on mutual aid in judi-

117 *Labour Conventions*, above note 14 at 351.
118 *Scott*, above note 111 at 142.
119 *Ibid* at 147. The remaining judge, Locke J, mentioned Scott's treaty argument only briefly (at 153–4).
120 Loi assurant l'application de l'entente sur l'entraide judiciaire entre la France et le Québec, LQ 1978, c 20.

cial matters. The appellant admitted that the subject matter of the Act was within provincial jurisdiction, but contended that Quebec had no power to sign the entente. Justice Rothman for the court noted that the agreement between the two governments "appears to be clothed in the formal dress of something more than a simple administrative arrangement."[121] This treaty-like form is in keeping with Quebec's claim that it is competent to conclude binding treaties at international law. Rather than decide that matter, Rothman J preferred to "read down" the would-be treaty. He found that "whatever the *form* of the Entente, one must look beyond it to its substance" and went on to say that "[i]n spite of its formal appearance, I agree with the trial judge that the Entente was simply an administrative arrangement between the two jurisdictions and not a binding agreement, much less an international treaty."[122]

Here as in *Scott*, the court avoided the question of provincial competence to conclude treaties by holding that the agreements in question were not treaties. It is tempting in both cases to read into their reasons the rule that, had the agreements been treaties, they would have been *ultra vires* the provincial government. But neither case in fact stands for that proposition, and indeed that proposition would not have helped resolve the cases for, as I have argued, an otherwise *intra vires* Act of the legislature could not be made *ultra vires* due simply to the provincial government's unconstitutional attempt to conclude a treaty. In my view, the court in *Bazylo* need not have entertained the appellant's treaty argument. For even if the agreement were intended by the parties to be a binding treaty at international law, that fact alone could not have impugned the Act. The separation of powers doctrine strongly suggests that the validity of legislative Acts does not turn on government intentions in introducing and supporting them. Nor may an Act be *ultra vires* simply because it aims to implement a treaty, for treaty implementation is not a distinct head of power under the Constitution Act, 1867.

Certain comments by LeBel J for the Supreme Court of Canada in *GreCon Dimter Inc v J.R. Normand Inc* might be viewed as suggesting that a Canadian province may hold treaty obligations at international law. I suggest, however, that LeBel J's comments should not be so interpreted. In resorting to the presumption of conformity with international law to resolve a conflict between two Quebec statutory

---

121 *Bazylo*, above note 112 at 270.
122 *Ibid* at 270–1.

provisions, LeBel J referred to the need to interpret those provisions "in a manner consistent with Quebec's international commitments"[123] and harmoniously with "the international commitments of Canada and Quebec."[124] Elsewhere LeBel J described Quebec as a "party" to the treaty in question,[125] namely the New York Convention on the Recognition and Enforcement of Foreign Arbitral Awards 1958.[126] These comments might be regarded as recognition, or at least suggestion, of a provincial power to incur international obligations independently of the federal government. Yet LeBel J's comments must surely not be taken that far. In strictness, neither Quebec nor any other Canadian province is a party to the New York Convention nor has direct international commitments under it. The only Canadian party to the treaty is Canada itself, meaning not the federal government but the state of Canada as recognized by international law. Justice LeBel's use of the terms "party" and "international commitments" are somewhat misleading. Yet the point he was making is sound: A non-conforming interpretation of Quebec law would risk putting the Canadian state in breach of its international obligations. Those obligations rest with Canada as a whole, including its federal and provincial levels. There is therefore a sense in which LeBel J's characterization of the New York Convention as a commitment of both Canada and Quebec is accurate, if unorthodox.[127]

The cases considered above certainly do not decide whether the treaty-making power is undivided (as the federal government claims) or shared (as Quebec claims). If an answer to the question does exist, it is not to be found in the case law – unless *Re Weekly Rest* provides the answer. So far, the case law has assumed that it does not.

(iv) Distribution of the treaty power

Having considered the arguments for and against provincial competence to conclude treaties, one would hope to be in a position to take a side. In the first and second editions of this work, I expressed the view that the debate comes out a draw. The federal arguments from the

123 *GreCon Dimter*, above note 113 at para 45.

124 *Ibid* at para 39.

125 *Ibid* at para 40.

126 [1986] Can TS no 43.

127 See the discussion of state organs and state responsibility in Chapter 2, Section 2.1.

Letters Patent, Canadian statehood, and the division of powers failed, I suggested, to rebut Quebec's position, founded as it is on the strong authority of *Maritime Bank*. As a matter of pure constitutional law, I suggested, the Quebec argument seemed a winner. Yet (I noted) the question of provincial treaty-making is not one of pure constitutional law, for it also involves constitutional practice and international recognition. It is here (I argued) that the Quebec position breaks down, for Canadian practice in treaty-making points clearly toward an undivided federal treaty power, in spite of Quebec's persistent objections. Likewise, international political reality suggests that, with the possible exception of France,[128] no state recognizes Canadian provinces as competent to conclude treaties.[129]

In the present edition of this work, I have come around to the view that the federal claim to an undivided treaty power is stronger than the Quebec position. In a forcefully argued piece[130] with which I do not entirely associate myself, Professor Beaulac convincingly (to my mind) emphasizes the overlooked importance of *Re Weekly Rest*. I am not of his view that the Privy Council's decision in *Labour Conventions* sheds any light on the issue; it seems clear to me that their lordships refrained from expressing any opinion on it. That said, the Supreme Court of Canada did express an opinion, and Professor Beaulac is justified in reminding us of that – even if subsequent cases have treated *Re*

---

128 Controversy around Quebec–France legal relations dates to the 1960s. See, e.g., McWhinney, above note 70 at 10–17 and I Bernier, *International Legal Aspects of Federalism* (London: Longman, 1973) at 60. More recently, see Paquin, *Les relations internationales du Québec depuis la Doctrine Gérin-Lajoie*, above note 101 at ch 8–11; C-E Côté, "Federalism and Foreign Affairs in Canada" in C Bradley, ed, *The Oxford Handbook of Comparative Foreign Relations Law* (Oxford University Press, 2019) at 287.

129 One way the federal government has attempted to manage the issue is through the conclusion of "umbrella agreements" with France and other states that allow Ottawa to assert a supervisory role over Quebec's purported treaty-making. See M Rand, "International Agreements between Canadian Provinces and Foreign States" (1967) 25 *University of Toronto Faculty of Law Review* 75; Bernier, *ibid* at 58–60; Côté, above note 101 at 223–4; and especially C-E Côté, "Le Canada et la capacité des entités infra-étatiques de conclure des traités" in O Fitzgerald, *Reflections on Canada's Past, Present and Future in International Law* (Waterloo: Centre for International Governance Innovation, 2018) [Côté] at 85–104, which explores, and attempts (with some admitted difficulty) to make sense of, Canada's practice with regard to umbrella agreements.

130 Beaulac, above note 101.

Weekly Rest as not determinative. I am also sympathetic to Professor Beaulac's argument against reliance on *Maritime Bank*, given that the treaty power has never been a legislative competence to be divided between the federal and provincial levels but always a matter of Crown prerogative.[131]

The answer to the question of whether the treaty power is distributed between Canada and the provinces or situated exclusively in the federal executive has no bearing on the power of the provinces to conclude non-binding arrangements with foreign states. The treaty power is just that: a power to conclude treaties – that is, international agreements concluded between states and governed by international law. The power and practice of Canadian provinces to conclude non-binding arrangements with foreign governments could only be excluded by a judicial determination that the conduct of external affairs generally is an exclusively federal power – a much broader proposition and one that would be impossible to reconcile with longstanding provincial practice (supported by equally longstanding federal acquiescence) as well as being wholly impractical in a country with an 8,800 kilometre international terrestrial boundary and commercial, social, familial, and cultural connections throughout the world. What Professor Côté persuasively argues in respect of Quebec can be said of all provinces, and indeed all sub-federal entities: Their engagement in legally non-binding international activities appears to have a positive, even necessary, role on the international scene.[132]

4.2 Legislative powers and the state's international obligations

The chief function of legislatures in the reception system is the implementation in domestic law of legal obligations assumed by the Crown in exercise of the treaty power. Laws are made by legislatures and not by the executive. To the extent, therefore, that legal change is needed to perform a treaty, implementing legislation is needed. How treaties are implemented is the subject of Chapter 7. The implementation requirement itself is considered below.

---

131 *Ibid* at 260–1.

132 Côté, "Le Canada et la capacité des entités infra-étatiques de conclure des traités," above note 129 at 104.

A secondary legislative power in respect of the state's international obligations – whether conventional or customary – is also considered here, namely the power to repudiate them. This power can be seen as the obverse of the first: Just as the Crown cannot unilaterally make law by treaty, nor can it circumscribe legislative power by treaty.

(a) The constitutional objection to self-executing treaties

The fundamental rule applicable to treaties in the Canadian reception system is that they do not take direct effect in domestic law. The stipulations of a treaty do not, by virtue of the treaty alone, have the force of law.[133] Rather, Canada is a dualist system in respect of conventional international law.[134]

There is no *prima facie* reason for a state's domestic law to require that international treaty obligations assumed by it be without domestic legal effect until acted upon by the legislature. Indeed, some well-known constitutions explicitly grant the force of law to treaties without legislation.[135] But in Canada and similarly constituted states, treaties are said not to be self-executing, meaning that they are not stand-alone sources of law.[136] Rather, they must be introduced into

133 *Labour Conventions*, above note 14 at 347.

134 *Kazemi Estate v Islamic Republic of Iran*, 2014 SCC 62 [*Kazemi Estate*] at para 149; *Revell v Minister of Citizenship and Immigration*, 2019 FCA 262 at para 131.

135 Article 55 of the French constitution of 4 October 1958 provides that "Les traités ou accords régulièrement ratifiés ou approuvés ont, dès leur publication, une autorité supérieure à celle des lois, sous réserve, pour chaque accord ou traité, de son application par l'autre partie" ("Treaties or agreements duly ratified or approved shall, upon publication, prevail over Acts of Parliament, subject, with respect to each agreement or treaty, to its application by the other party"). Article 25 of the German Basic Law of 23 May 1949 provides that "the general rules of public international law constitute an integral part of federal law. They take precedence over statutes and directly create rights and duties for the inhabitants of the federal territory." Article VI of the US constitution provides that "all Treaties made, or which shall be made, under the Authority of the United States, shall be the supreme Law of the Land." But subsequent US constitutional law has narrowed this provision by drawing a distinction between treaties and executive agreements (both of which constitute treaties for the purposes of international law). For a survey of the practices of these and other states, see J Hill, *Aust's Modern Treaty Law and Practice*, 4th ed (Cambridge: Cambridge University Press, 2023) at 191–206 and D Sloss, ed, *The Role of Domestic Courts in Treaty Enforcement: A Comparative Study* (Cambridge: Cambridge University Press, 2009).

136 However, where a treaty declares or has come to represent customary international law (including *jus cogens*), a Canadian court may look to the treaty,

Canadian law by legislation. Self-executing treaties are objectionable in the Anglo-Canadian tradition because treaty-making is a prerogative of the Crown. For Canadian law to treat international conventions as binding domestic law without legislative action would effectively confer upon the Crown a power to make law. That power was removed from the Crown several hundred years ago and has not been restored.

The rule that the executive lacks power to legislate outside Parliament finds no explicit expression in Canada's written constitutional texts. It is, for the most part, an unwritten law of the constitution. The rule is implicit, however, in the preamble to the Constitution Act, 1867, which endowed Canada with a constitution "similar in Principle to that of the United Kingdom."[137] Centuries ago the sovereign did have a power to legislate, but that power has long since passed to Parliament. In the *Proclamations case* of 1611,[138] Coke CJ held that "the king by his proclamation cannot create any offence which was not an offence before, for then he may alter the law of the land by his proclamation" and "the law of England is divided into three parts, common law, statute law, and custom; but the King's proclamation is none of them." At about the same time it was held in *Archbishop of York and Sedgwick's case*[139] that "the King could not by His grant alter the law of the land." Some 80 years and two revolutions later, a statute confirmed the common law position enunciated in these judgments. Article 1 of the Bill of Rights 1689 declared that "the pretended Power of suspending of Laws, or the Execution of Laws, by regal authority, without Consent of Parliament, is illegal."[140] All these texts refer to the sovereign personally. But the prohibition on regal lawmaking had, by the time of the Constitution Act, 1867, transformed into a broader prohibition on legislation by the executive, meaning not just the sovereign but also cabinet and the executive branch generally.[141]

---

though unimplemented, to discern customary international law as incorporated by the common law. See the discussion in Chapter 2, Section 2.3(b), and *Kazemi Estate*, above note 134 at para 149.

137 Constitution Act, 1867 preamble. On the role of the preamble in importing unwritten constitutional rules, see *Provincial Court Judges*, above note 2 at 68–74, Lamer CJ. The rule that the executive lacks legislative power is also implied by the definitions of the federal and provincial legislatures in the Constitution Act, 1867.

138 (1611) 12 Co Rep 74 at 76, 77 ER 1352 at 1354.

139 (1612) Godbolt 201 at 201, 78 ER 122 at 122.

140 Bill of Rights, 1689 (UK), 1 William & Mary, sess 2, c 2.

141 Of course the executive may exercise lawmaking power where that power is delegated to it by the legislature. Secondary legislation is not a violation of

This broadening of the prohibition, to cover not only the sovereign but all those who govern in the sovereign's name, tells us something about the nature of the objection to regal lawmaking. It was not simply an objection to legislation by a single, hereditary ruler. It was also, and perhaps principally, an objection to legislation by remote, exclusive, and non-participatory means – whether these means be invoked by the monarch alone or by ministers and officials acting in the royal name. The prohibition on executive lawmaking bars both unconstitutional monarchy and cabinet-based oligarchy from our system of government. In their place is posited a parliamentary procedure founded on the values that inform the principle of self-government: representation, deliberation, participation, and consent. The prohibition on executive legislation reveals a subtlety in the self-government principle: Although the executive is drawn from ourselves and responsible to us for its conduct, that does not suffice to satisfy the principle. What is lacking in executive, as opposed to parliamentary, lawmaking is a deliberative, representative, and participatory decision-making process. Likewise, the reception system looks on international law as a coercive external force not simply because international law is in some sense external to the Canadian legal order; the executive is clearly internal to that order, but is treated as objectionably remote nonetheless. It is not externality, but the absence of a deliberative, representative, and participatory legislative process that founds self-government's objection to the direct application of international law in Canada.

While the Crown's legislative prerogative was abolished long ago, other prerogatives remain, chief among them the power to conclude treaties. The Crown's continuing power to conclude treaties without Parliament, combined with the constitutional principle that the Crown has no power unilaterally to make or unmake any law, necessitates the implementation by legislative enactment of treaties that require alteration of domestic law. As Brodeur J explained in *In re Employment of Aliens* (1922), "The bill of rights having declared illegal the suspending or dispensing with the laws without the consent of parliament, the Crown could not in time of peace make a treaty which would restrict the freedom of parliament."[142]

---

the rule that the Crown is not a source of law, because the ultimate source of secondary legislative power is not the Crown but the legislature.

142 (1922) 63 SCR 293 [*In re Employment of Aliens*] at 339. On the "in time of peace" qualification, see the discussion in Chapter 7, Section 7.4(a).

The constitutional inability of the Crown to alter the law by concluding treaties was declared in the famous English case of *The Parlement Belge*. The defendant argued that the plaintiff's right to bring a claim against the owner of the ship was excluded by a treaty between the United Kingdom and Belgium. Rejecting this argument, Sir Robert Phillimore said,

> If the Crown had power without the authority of parliament by this treaty to order that the *Parlement Belge* should be entitled to all the privileges of a ship of war, then the warrant, which is prayed for against the wrong-doer on account of the collision, cannot issue, and the right of the subject, but for this order unquestionable, to recover damages for the injuries done to him by her is extinguished. This is a use of the treaty-making prerogative of the Crown which I believe to be without precedent, and in principle contrary to the laws of the constitution.[143]

Whether Sir Robert's prohibition on giving domestic legal effect to Crown treaty-making has been interpreted too broadly has been a matter of debate.[144] But the orthodox view remains that treaties cannot take direct legal effect in domestic law.

The question of whether the Crown could adversely affect an individual's rights without implementation was considered, in a contemporary context, in *Canada v Miller*.[145] Miller was employed as an interpreter by the International Civil Aviation Organization (ICAO). Pursuant to the Supplementary Agreement between Canada and the International Civil Aviation Organization 1980,[146] the Crown leased premises to ICAO in Montreal to serve as its headquarters. Miller alleged that the building's poor air quality harmed his health and sued Canada for damages. The Crown argued that the effect of the unimplemented treaty was to grant it immunity from Miller's action. Canada lost at first instance and again on appeal, Nuss JA observing (at para 46) that

> If the Crown has committed a fault, in Quebec, which causes a person damages, then, saving a case where domestic law gives the

143 *The Parlement Belge*, [1878–9] 4 PD 129 at 154.
144 See the discussion in Chapter 7, Section 7.4(b).
145 [1999] RJQ 719 (Que CA).
146 [1980] Can TS no 18.

> Crown immunity from suit, it may be sued before the courts having jurisdiction in Canada. There is no principle of law which provides that because the Crown is involved with an International Organization in Canada, it is not subject to the Canadian courts if, because of its extra-contractual acts in Canada, on the occasion of or incidental to such involvement, it causes damages to a person.

The Supreme Court of Canada dismissed Canada's further appeal.[147]

The rule against giving treaties domestic effect without statutory implementation was, in my view, neglected by the Federal Court of Appeal in *Turp v Canada*.[148] Professor Turp sought judicial review of the minister of foreign affairs' decision to licence the export of Canadian-made light armoured vehicles to Saudi Arabia. The court below dismissed the application, and Nadon JA for the Court of Appeal upheld that decision. Part of Nadon JA's rationale for doing so was that only states can complain of violations of the Geneva Conventions (particularly Common Article 1), on which Turp sought to rely. Individuals cannot (in Nadon JA's view) seek remedies in domestic courts for violations of these conventions, which generally express protective obligations on states parties rather than rights conferred on individuals. Not being a state, Turp lacked standing to raise a violation of Common Article 1.[149] Justice Nadon expressly noted the implementation requirement in his reasons. Ironically, however, he proceeded to apply as domestic law the Geneva Conventions' supposed prohibition on individuals invoking those treaties. If there really is such a prohibition in the Geneva Conventions, the rule against self-executing treaties must mean that that prohibition has no direct effect in Canadian law unless implemented by statute. A treaty made by Canada cannot add to or subtract from the rights of Turp (or anyone else) to come to a Canadian court and complain that a government decision or action is unreasonable because it is contrary to international law. For the court to grant direct effect to a treaty-based limit on the rights of individuals to challenge the lawfulness of government action in domestic courts without legislation would recognize in the federal Crown a unilateral power to change the

147 *Miller v Canada*, 2001 SCC 12.
148 2018 FCA 133.
149 *Ibid* at paras 78–81.

law, and in this case to take away people's rights – exactly what the implementation requirement aims to prevent.

(b) Parliamentary sovereignty to violate international law

Canadian legislatures possess a residual sovereignty to legislate in violation of international law. They may do so on purpose, refusing to adopt legislation in implementation of treaty obligations assumed by the executive. They may do so by omission, neglecting to enact implementing legislation due to governmental failure to recognize the need for it. They may even do so by accident, adopting a new law or amending an old one in some way that unintentionally puts the state in breach of an existing obligation. This competence to breach international law, either by act or omission, underscores that Canada's international obligations are just that: international rather than domestic. The fact that Canada is obliged internationally to live up to its promises or conform to certain norms does not, without more, produce obligations that prevail over inconsistent legislation in domestic courts.

A distinction is made in Canada between the terms "Parliament" and "legislature." By Parliament, Canadian courts and writers generally mean the federal (or Dominion) Parliament. By "legislature" they mean any of the 10 provincial legislatures. But all these institutions are, of course, legislatures. One could just as well say they are all parliaments.[150] Each is an institution composed of the sovereign and one or two representative chambers that, with the consent of all their constituent elements, is competent to make law. The Canadian distinction between Parliament and legislature serves only to differentiate the federal institution from its provincial counterparts. It does not denote any important constitutional difference between these institutions other than their separate jurisdictions under Part VI (mainly sections 91 and 92) of the Constitution Act, 1867. For the most part I call the constitutional feature addressed under this heading "Parliament," by which I mean, depending on the context, any parliamentary institution – the federal Parliament, the provincial legislatures, or the Parliament at Westminster.

150 Elected members of the Ontario legislature are called "Members of the Provincial Parliament." The edifice housing Quebec's Assemblée Nationale is the Hôtel du Parlement. The Legislative Assembly of British Columbia meets in Victoria's Parliament Buildings.

(i) The residual sovereignty of Canadian legislatures

At common law, Parliament was sovereign.[151] Sovereignty meant two things: omnipotence and omnicompetence. Omnipotence meant that Parliament was above all other authority. In particular, no power lay in the courts to invalidate Acts of Parliament. Omnicompetence meant that Parliament could legislate on any matter. The omnipotence and omnicompetence of Parliament was described by Dicey thus:

> The principle of Parliamentary sovereignty means neither more nor less than this, namely, that Parliament . . . has, under the English constitution, the right to make or unmake any law whatever; and, further, that no person or body is recognized by the law of England as having a right to override or set aside the legislation of Parliament.[152]

The concepts of omnipotence and omnicompetence are linked. Were a sovereign Parliament to enact a law purporting to repeal the "law" of gravity, that law could not be challenged in court: first, the sovereign Parliament is omnipotent and therefore not subject to review by the courts; second, the sovereign Parliament is omnicompetent and may therefore enact any law, no matter how absurd.[153]

The link between this conception of Parliament as sovereign and the principle of self-government introduced in Chapter 1 goes almost without saying. Parliament is the instrument of consensual self-

151 The literature is immense. A notable work is J Goldsworthy, *The Sovereignty of Parliament: History and Philosophy* (Oxford: Clarendon Press, 1999) [Goldsworthy].

152 A Dicey, *Introduction to the Study of the Law of the Constitution*, 10th ed (London: Macmillan, 1959) at 39–40.

153 An example of this is *British Columbia Electric Railway Co Ltd v The King*, [1946] AC 527 (PC) [*BC Electric Railway*], in which the Privy Council upheld the Supreme Court of Canada's ruling that an Act was not *ultra vires* because it was unenforceable. Viscount Simon, for the board (at 541–2), quoted Rand J's observation that an Act may be futile but is nonetheless the law, adding, "A legislature which passes a law having extraterritorial operation may find that what it has enacted cannot be directly enforced, but the Act is not invalid on that account." Explaining this rule, Sir Ivor Jennings famously gave the example of an Act of the British Parliament forbidding smoking on the streets of Paris, noting that while the law would be ignored in France it would nevertheless be a law under which a Frenchman could be convicted in England: Sir Ivor Jennings, *The Law and the Constitution*, 5th ed (London: University of London Press, 1959) at 170–1.

government. Its claim to sovereignty is nothing more than our own claim to be a self-governing people. It is only as an instrument of our will that Parliament has any legitimate claim to its sovereignty. The sovereignty of Parliament is an institutional arrangement to reflect and promote the self-government of the people it represents.

The juridical basis of parliamentary sovereignty is a controversial question that need not concern us here.[154] Yet parliamentary sovereignty would seem to be amenable to amendment by statute.[155] In Canada, parliamentary sovereignty has been curtailed on at least two occasions. The first time was in 1867, when Canada was formed as a federal state within the British Empire. The constitution of the new state was intended to be "similar in Principle to that of the United Kingdom,"[156] the defining characteristic of which was parliamentary sovereignty. But federalism necessitated written constitutional provisions setting out the jurisdictions of the two orders of government and subjecting legislation to review on *vires* grounds. Furthermore, Empire necessitated (or at least was seen as necessitating) review of legislation on the ground of repugnance with imperial statutes. These demands of federalism and Empire produced Canadian legislatures with important limits to their sovereignty. The limitation for repugnance with imperial statutes was removed by section 2(2) of the Statute of Westminster 1931.[157] But new limits were placed on

154 The controversy can be summarized as a debate between those who consider sovereignty to be a rule of the common law and, therefore, subject to control and abolition by the courts, and those who, following HLA Hart, consider sovereignty to be in the nature of a political fact rather than a legal rule. An excellent summary is Goldsworthy, above note 151 at ch 10.

155 See M Hunt, *Using Human Rights Law in English Courts* (Oxford: Hart, 1997) at 88, 124–5. See also A Bradley, "The Sovereignty of Parliament: In Perpetuity?" in J Jowell & D Oliver, eds, *The Changing Constitution*, 3d ed (Oxford: Clarendon Press, 1994) at 85–9.

156 Constitution Act, 1867, preamble.

157 (UK) 22 George V, c 4, reprinted in RSC 1985, App II, No 27. The repugnancy rule was not entirely repealed by the Statute of Westminster however, for repugnancy with an imperial statute, namely the British North America Act, 1867, formed the juridical basis of federalism review. Thus s 7(1) of the Statute of Westminster provided that invalidity for repugnancy continued to apply to the British North America Act, 1867 and its amendments. When Canada "patriated" its written Constitution in 1982, s 52 of the Constitution Act, 1982 made s 7(1) of the Statute of Westminster 1931 unnecessary; it was repealed by s 53(1) and schedule, item 17.

parliamentary sovereignty in 1982, when Canada adopted a rights-protecting instrument, the Canadian Charter of Rights and Freedoms, and entrenched it, along with several other instruments and provisions, as "the supreme law of Canada."[158]

What is essential about parliamentary sovereignty for our purposes is that those statutory curtailments of it found in the written provisions of the Canadian constitution have not abolished it entirely.[159] There remains vested in all Canadian legislatures a residual sovereignty. The curtailments of parliamentary sovereignty in this country are great in scope, but they are not limitless. A successful challenge to the validity of an Act of Parliament in Canada must demonstrate that the impugned Act is contrary to the supreme law of Canada – usually some matter of legislative jurisdiction or the infringement of a Charter-guaranteed right or freedom. Where an Act is not repugnant to the supreme law of Canada, there is no power in the courts, either by statute or at common law, to invalidate it.[160] The Act is an exercise of the residual sovereignty of the enacting legislature. That legislature remains omnipotent within those areas of competence not excluded by the entrenched provisions of the constitution of Canada.

(ii) Legislative competence to violate international law

International law is one such area of competence. The residual sovereignty of Canadian legislatures extends to the enactment of legislation

---

158 Constitution Act, 1982, s 52(1).

159 See *Reference re Pan-Canadian Securities Regulation*, 2018 SCC 48 at paras 54–8.

160 See, e.g., *Toronto (City) v Ontario (Attorney General)*, 2021 SCC 34 at paras 54, 57–62. This is subject to the rule, now seemingly established in Canadian law, that courts will enforce statutes by which legislatures purport to bind themselves as to the manner and form of future laws. Where an Act purports to bind future legislatures to certain "manner and form" requirements (for example, that statutes must be enacted in both English and French), Canadian courts have allowed such requirements and struck down subsequent legislation that offended them. The leading case is the Supreme Court decision in *R v Mercure*, [1988] 1 SCR 234. See also *Ford c Québec (procureur général)*, [1988] 2 SCR 712 and *Mikisew Cree First Nation v Canada (Governor General in Council)*, 2018 SCC 40 at paras 51, 96. But see also *Reference re Canada Assistance Plan (BC)*, [1991] 2 SCR 525, in which a federal statute declaring that agreements with the provinces would continue subject to provincial consent to their termination was held not to restrain the executive from introducing legislation amending the federal Act. For more on manner and form restrictions, see Hogg & Wright, above note 3 § 12:10.

that is contrary to international law. This claim is supported in both the English and the Canadian authorities, considered below. The claim is also supported by the logic of the self-government principle, which continues to view certain methods of international lawmaking as insufficiently consensual compared to the deliberative, representative, and participatory decision-making model that is the parliamentary process. The sovereignty of our legislatures is what secures our power to break with international law in extraordinary cases.

The doctrine of parliamentary sovereignty only accords legislatures the competence to violate international law. The doctrine does not extend this power to the executive or the judiciary. Whether and to what extent executive acts may be judicially reviewed on the basis of their inconsistency with international law is considered in Chapter 9. The doctrines of judicial notice of international law, the presumption of conformity, and the incorporation of custom all indicate that the judiciary's proper role in the reception system is, in all but exceptional cases, to ensure domestic compliance with international law wherever possible. This scheme is consistent with the principles of the reception system, wherein self-government is associated with representative legislatures and respect for international law is associated with the judiciary.

It is a useful shorthand to speak of a domestic law or legislature violating international law. Courts and commentators have used this expression since the nineteenth century, and I employ it below. I note, however, that the expression is not entirely accurate. Only states – not their constitutive organs – have obligations under international law. Strictly speaking, then, a legislature that enacts a statute the content of which is inconsistent with an applicable rule of international law does not itself violate that law. Rather, it is the state in which the legislature operates that violates the law, by the instrument of its legislature. The same is true of conduct by executive and judicial organs contrary to the state's obligations: Such conduct is attributable to the state itself at international law, and it is the state, rather than its particular organ, that is regarded as having committed the breach.

(iii) The English inheritance

The competence of the UK Parliament to violate international law finds repeated support in older English case law, though decisions holding that it has actually done so are rare.[161] In *Mortensen v Peters*, a Scottish case, Lord Dunedin explained, "Neither are we a tribunal sitting to decide whether an Act of the Legislature is *ultra vires* as in contravention of generally acknowledged principles of International Law. For us an Act of Parliament, duly passed by the Lords and Commons and assented to by the King, is supreme, and we are bound to give effect to its terms."[162] In *Chung Chi Cheung v The King*, a judgment much relied on by Canadian courts, Lord Atkin observed that the courts acknowledge the existence of international law and seek to apply it, but only "so far as is not inconsistent with rules enacted by statutes. . . ."[163] He prefaced this remark by declaring that there is "no external power that imposes its rules upon our own code of substantive law or procedure."[164] In *Collco Dealings Ltd v Inland Revenue Commissioners*, Viscount Simonds approved *Maxwell on the Interpretation of Statutes* to the effect that "if the statute is unambiguous, its provisions must be followed even if they are contrary to international law."[165] In *Salomon v Commissioners of Customs and Excise*, Diplock LJ (as he then was) observed that "the sovereign power of the Queen in Parliament extends to breaking treaties."[166] In *Cheney v Conn (Inspector of Taxes)*, Ungoed-Thomas J recognized that customary international law is incorporated by common law, but noted the inevitable corollary, namely that customary international law, being common law, must yield to statute.[167]

161 I make no effort here to capture the contemporary UK position but focus only on older authorities frequently cited in Canadian decisions.

162 (1906) 8 F (JC) 93 (Scot HCJ) at 100.

163 [1939] AC 160 (PC) at 168. The passage goes on to read, ". . . or finally declared by their tribunals." The suggestion here is that customary international law cannot prevail over the common law rule of *stare decisis*. This question has been the topic of judicial consideration both in Canada and in the UK. The matter is addressed in Chapter 6, Section 6.2(c).

164 This remark may be understood in two ways, quite different but not necessarily contradictory. First, the remark may be seen as a declaration of the independence of English law from the external pressure of international law. This interpretation may seem parochial. Recall, however, that international law at the time (as now) was not the creation of representative legislatures, and therefore lacked, in some respects, the legitimacy of domestic lawmaking procedures. Second, we may interpret the remark as denying that international law is external at all. Upon being accepted and adopted domestically, international law is no longer to be viewed as an external power, but as the law of the land.

165 [1962] AC 1 (HL) at 19.

166 [1967] 2 QB 116 (Eng CA) at 143.

167 [1968] 1 WLR 242 (Ch) at 245.

(iv) Canadian authorities

The competence of Canadian legislatures to violate international law has been affirmed both implicitly and explicitly in the case law. Implicit recognition comes in the form of statements affirming that the legislative competence of the federal and provincial legislatures is, subject to the federalism provisions of the Constitution Act, 1867 (and now the provisions of section 52 of the Constitution Act, 1982), as great as that possessed by the imperial Parliament. Thus, English authorities to the effect that the Parliament at Westminster may legislate contrary to international law apply also to Canadian legislatures. In *Hodge v The Queen*,[168] Lord Fitzgerald famously declared that the authority of provincial legislatures is "as ample within the limits prescribed by section 92 as the imperial Parliament in the plenitude of its power possessed and could bestow." He continued, "Within these limits of subject and area the local legislature is supreme, and has the same authority as the imperial Parliament, or the Parliament of the Dominion. . . ."[169] Following *Hodge*, Lamont J in the Supreme Court of Canada observed in *Arrow River* that the plenary competence of provincial legislatures "has long been well settled."[170] Both these cases concerned the legislative competence of provincial legislatures. It is clear, however, that these decisions apply equally to the federal Parliament.[171]

This implicit recognition of the sovereignty of Canadian legislatures over international law is confirmed by over a century of explicit judicial commentary. In *R v Meikleham* (1906), Meredith CJ, considering a proposal of international law made by counsel, declared, "Although that is, no doubt, a rule of international law, yet, where it is plain that the Legislature has intended to disregard or interfere with that rule, the Courts are bound to give effect to its enactments."[172] Turning again

168 *Hodge*, above note 108.

169 *Ibid* at 132.

170 *Arrow River & Tributaries Slide & Boom Co Ltd v Pigeon Timber Co Ltd*, [1932] SCR 495 [*Arrow River*] at 509–10.

171 In *Croft v Dunphy*, [1933] AC 156 (PC) [*Croft*] at 164, Lord Macmillan found that *Hodge* (above note 108) applied to the federal Parliament *a fortiori*. In *BC Electric Railway*, above note 153 at 541, the Privy Council approved Rand J in the Supreme Court of Canada, who cited *Hodge* as authority that the *federal* Parliament enjoys legislative power as plenary and ample as that of the imperial Parliament.

172 (1906) 11 OLR 366 (Div Ct) at 373. While this remark is forcefully put in the judgment, the headnote prefaces the proposition with "*semble*."

to *Arrow River* (1934), Lamont J, with whom Cannon J concurred, held that a provincial Act that contradicted the Ashburton-Webster Treaty 1842[173] was not invalid for that reason: "The Act must . . . be held to be valid unless the existence of the treaty of itself imposes a limitation upon the provincial legislative power. In my opinion, the treaty alone cannot be considered as having that effect."[174] The form of international law at issue in *Arrow River* was a treaty. That the same rule applies to customary international law was made clear in *Re Foreign Legations* (1943),[175] where the Supreme Court of Canada considered a potential conflict between by-laws of the City of Ottawa and the customary international law of sovereign immunity. The majority held that international law barred the taxation of foreign legations. Yet Duff CJ observed that while this finding meant that courts must construe taxation legislation consistent with the international custom, the ultimate authority of the legislature to violate international law remained.[176] In *British Columbia Electric Railway Co Ltd v The King* (1946), the Privy Council quoted with approval Rand J in the Supreme Court of Canada, who dismissed counsel's contention that an Act was *ultra vires* for being contrary to international comity and impossible to enforce, saying, "Legislation so enacted will be effective in, and must be enforced by, the courts of this country."[177]

Cases in the late twentieth century continued to make the point. In *Swait v Board of Trustees of Maritime Transportation Unions* (1967), Hyde J rejected the argument that the Trustee Act was contrary to Canada's treaty obligations, saying, "the laws of Canada are supreme within the framework of the British North America Act and where Parliament has clearly legislated on some matter within its jurisdiction, the validity of that legislation cannot be affected by external treaties."[178] In *Daniels v White and the Queen* (1968),[179] an Aboriginal man enjoyed a right

173 30 British and Foreign State Papers 360.

174 *Arrow River*, above note 170 at 510. In the result, Lamont and Cannon JJ were in the minority, for the majority found no conflict between the Act and the treaty, so that the issue did not arise. But Lamont and Cannon JJ were uncontradicted on this point.

175 [1943] SCR 208.

176 *Ibid* at 231.

177 *BC Electric Railway*, above note 153 at 542.

178 *Swait v Board of Trustees of Maritime Transportation Unions*, [1967] BR 315 (Que QB) at 319.

179 [1968] SCR 517 [*Daniels*].

to hunt game birds under an agreement between the governments of Canada and Manitoba. That agreement was subsequently constitutionally enshrined in the British North America Act 1930 and declared to have force of law notwithstanding any Act of the Parliament of Canada.[180] Yet the agreement conflicted with an Act implementing the Canada–US Migratory Birds Convention 1916.[181] Justice Hall (dissenting, but not on this point, and with the concurrence of Ritchie and Spence JJ) noted that the presumption that Parliament does not intend to legislate contrary to international law "does not, of course, come into operation if a statute is unambiguous for in that event its provisions must be followed even if they are contrary to the established rules of international law."[182] His lordship paraphrased the speech of Viscount Simonds in *Collco Dealings*, declaring,

> neither comity nor rule of international law can be invoked to prevent a sovereign State (Canada) from taking what steps it thinks fit to protect its own aboriginal population (Indians) from being deprived of their ancient rights to hunt and to fish for food assured to them in Treaties 5 and 6. . . .[183]

In *Capital Cities Communications Inc v Canadian Radio-Television Commission* (1978), Laskin CJ observed that "certainly the convention [the Inter-American Radiocommunications Convention 1937] *per se* cannot prevail against the express stipulations of the Act."[184] The sovereignty of the federal Parliament to violate international law was directly in issue in *Gordon v The Queen in Right of Canada* (1980),[185] in which the petitioner contended that Parliament could not enact legislation that is contrary to customary international law. Justice Meredith held otherwise, saying,

> Where Canada asserts jurisdiction over an area of the sea and purports to limit access thereto, from the standpoint of domestic law the access is in fact limited for a special purpose, and even if the law of Canada contravenes "customary international law," if Parliament, as

180 Constitution Act, 1930 (UK), 20-21 George V, c 26, s 1.
181 [1917] Can TS no 7.
182 *Daniels*, above note 179 at 539.
183 *Ibid* at 540 (emphasis removed).
184 [1978] 2 SCR 141 at 173, referring to [1938] Can TS no 18.
185 [1980] 5 WWR 668 (BCSC).

here, has acted unambiguously, the courts of this country are bound to apply the domestic law.[186]

Justice Meredith went on to approve Lord Atkin's dictum in *Chung Chi Cheung* that no external power imposes its rules upon our own code of substantive law or procedure.[187]

Twenty-first century authorities are, to date, to the same effect. In *Mack v Canada (Attorney General)* (2001), in response to a submission that a head tax against Chinese Canadians was contrary to international law and therefore could not constitute a juristic reason for the enrichment, Cumming J observed that "it is problematic that such norms could supersede the operation of validly enacted, albeit racist, domestic legislation."[188] In *Bouzari v Islamic Republic of Iran* (2004),[189] the appellant argued that international law required Canada to recognize an exception to state immunity in torture cases. Justice Goudge for the Court of Appeal for Ontario observed that it is "open to Canada to legislate contrary to" its international obligations and that "Such legislation would determine Canada's domestic law although it would put Canada in breach of its international obligations."[190] Applying this rule to the State Immunity Act,[191] Goudge JA held that "Canada has clearly legislated so as not to create this exception to state immunity whether it has an international law obligation to do so or not."[192] In *Febles v Canada (Citizenship and Immigration)* (2014), McLachlin CJ observed that "Parliament has the power to pass legislation that complies with Canada's obligations under the *Refugee Convention*, or to pass legislation that either exceeds or falls short of the *Refugee Convention*'s protections."[193] In *Tracy v Iran* (2017), Hourigan JA for the Court of Appeal for Ontario, confronted with a federal law that quite clearly violates the international law of sovereign immunity,[194] found that

---

186 *Ibid* at 670–1.
187 *Ibid* at 671.
188 (2001) 55 OR (3d) 113 (SCJ) at para 50.
189 (2004) 71 OR (3d) 675 (CA) [*Bouzari*].
190 *Ibid* at 690.
191 RSC 1985, c S-18.
192 *Bouzari*, above note 189 at 691.
193 2014 SCC 68 at para 64.
194 Justice for Victims of Terrorism Act, SC 2012, c 1. On the international unlawfulness of this law, see, e.g., R Provost, "Canada's Alien Tort Statute" (29 March 2012), online: https://www.ejiltalk.org/canadas-alien-tort-statute/.

the presumption of conformity with international law is "subject to rebuttal by Parliament through the use of clear statutory language" given that Parliament "has the power to ignore international law" and "Parliamentary sovereignty requires courts to give effect to a statute that demonstrates such an unequivocal legislative intention, absent constitutional concerns." The learned judge later observed, "The recognition of the foreign judgments under the [Act] may violate international law, but Parliament has expressly authorized their recognition."[195]

There is an important qualification to the power of provincial legislatures to enact laws contrary to international law. The territorial jurisdiction of provincial legislatures is limited to the province in which they sit.[196] Parliament, by contrast, may validly enact extraterritorial laws.[197] Thus, if a provincial law is contrary to international law and has extraterritorial effects, it may be challenged as *ultra vires* on the basis of its extraterritoriality – but not on the basis of its conflict with international law.

(v) The argument from **Croft v Dunphy**

Clearly, there is a preponderance of English and Canadian authority supporting the claim that Canadian legislatures are competent to violate international law. Yet two important commentators, Vanek and La Forest, have ventured to disagree. They are inspired by the Privy Council decision of *Croft v Dunphy*. The respondent argued that the federal Parliament, being subordinate to the imperial Parliament, could not have extraterritorial jurisdiction. Lord Macmillan rejected this argument and reaffirmed that Canadian legislatures are not delegates or agents, but have "plenary powers of legislation as large, and of the same nature, as those of [the imperial] Parliament itself."[198] His lordship went on to hold that he need not consider the competence of the federal Parliament to legislate contrary to international law,

195 *Tracy v Iran*, 2017 ONCA 549 at paras 43, 90. See also para 45.

196 *British Columbia v Imperial Tobacco Canada Ltd*, [2005] 2 SCR 473 at paras 26–36.

197 *Re Offshore Mineral Rights*, above note 19 at 816; *Re Newfoundland Continental Shelf*, above note 23 at 103. But see *R v Hape*, 2007 SCC 26.

198 *Croft*, above note 171 at 163–4, quoting Lord Selborne in *The Queen v Burah* (1878), 3 App Cas 889 (PC) at 904, a case concerning the jurisdiction of the Indian legislature.

for the Act in question was not contrary to international law. Yet he observed,

> Legislation of the Imperial Parliament, even in contravention of generally acknowledged principles of international law, is binding upon and must be enforced by the Courts of this country, for in these Courts the legislation of the Imperial Parliament cannot be challenged as ultra vires: per Lord Justice-General Dunedin in *Mortensen v. Peters.* It may be that legislation of the Dominion Parliament may be challenged as ultra vires on the ground that it is contrary to the principles of international law, but that must be because it must be assumed that the British North America Act has not conferred power on the Dominion Parliament to legislate contrary to these principles.[199]

This remark has, understandably, been taken by some as doubting the competence of Canadian legislatures to violate international law. Such a result contradicts much of the board's reasoning in *Croft*, which emphasized the plenary nature of the powers granted to Canadian legislatures. Taken in context, Lord Macmillan seems to say no more than this: A legislature created by the imperial Parliament will be competent to violate international law unless the power to do so has not been conferred on that legislature by the imperial Parliament. If we add to this proposition the confirmation, in the case at bar and others before and since, that Canadian legislatures enjoy powers as ample and plenary as those of the imperial Parliament, we must conclude that Canadian legislatures are indeed competent to legislate in violation of international law.

Lord Macmillan's comments serve to emphasize the important point that, in Westminster-model countries, the only objection one can bring to legislation that violates international law is that it is illegal under domestic law. As Lord Macmillan points out, even that objection could not succeed under the UK constitution, for it was impossible to say that a bill enacted with the assent of the sovereign and the advice and consent of the Lords and Commons was illegal. In Canada, however, it was possible to argue that an Act of Parliament was illegal, for an Act could be found to be *ultra vires* on federalism grounds. In today's Canada, given the entrenchment of further provisions in the Constitu-

199 *Ibid* at 164.

tion Act, 1982, this argument is all the more possible. Yet even today Canadian legislation in violation of international law may only be invalidated for being impermissible in Canadian law; it may not be struck down simply for being illegal at international law.

The first academic to argue against the proposition that Canadian legislatures can violate international law was Vanek in 1960.[200] His argument proceeds on several fronts, some of which are somewhat tenuous.[201] His best argument relies on the presumption of conformity with international law; that is, the rule of statutory construction whereby courts presume that legislatures do not intend to violate international law. Applying this presumption to the British North America Act 1867, Vanek contends that the imperial Parliament could not have intended to create legislatures capable of violating international law. Therefore, Canadian legislatures must lack the power to enact such legislation, and such legislation must be susceptible to *ultra vires* challenges.

The presumption of conformity is just that: a presumption that may be rebutted.[202] There are many reasons to think the presumption is rebutted here. First there are the many judicial affirmations of the plenary and ample powers of Canadian legislatures. One might also argue that even if Canadian legislatures ever did labour under such a disability, that disability was removed by the Statute of Westminster 1931. The strongest argument, however, rests on the consequences of Vanek's argument for Canadian federalism. If it is the case that Canadian legislatures are incompetent to violate international law, what is there to stop the federal government from concluding a treaty touching a matter within provincial jurisdiction, and then challenging provincial legislation on the ground of its inconsistency with the federally concluded treaty? Vanek's argument would force courts to invalidate provincial legislation for being contrary to international law, and therefore *ultra vires* the provincial legislature, where that legislation only became *ultra vires* because the federal government invaded provincial

---

200 D Vanek, "Is International Law Part of the Law of Canada?" (1949–50) 8 *University of Toronto Law Journal* 251.

201 For instance, he seems to confuse a rule of statutory construction (namely the presumption that the legislature did not intend to violate international law) with a law of the Constitution: Vanek, *ibid* at 273–4. He also relies heavily on case law concerning the implementation of British treaties in Canadian law under s 132 of the Constitution Act, 1867; see, for example, Vanek, *ibid* at 273, n 68.

202 See Chapter 5, Section 5.9.

jurisdiction in exercise of its treaty power. It cannot be law that the federal government can effect what are essentially unilateral amendments to section 92 of the Constitution Act, 1867 by concluding treaties with other states. Federalism demands that the presumption of conformity be rebutted in construing the Constitution Act, 1867.

Professor La Forest (as he then was), writing one year after Vanek,[203] concedes from the outset that the federal Parliament can violate international law, citing *British Columbia Electric Railway*[204] and *Japanese Canadians.*[205] He contends only that provincial legislatures cannot do so. La Forest bases much of his argument on what he calls the doctrine of extraterritoriality. While noting that this appellation is a mistaken one, La Forest nonetheless insists that "a colonial or other subordinate legislature" cannot legislate contrary to international law, lest it should legislate contrary to imperial policy or bring international responsibility for the breach upon the imperial government.[206] It is not clear how this argument is intended to apply to provincial legislatures. If La Forest considered provincial legislatures to be colonial or subordinate *vis à vis* the federal Parliament, he did not say so. Nor could he, given *Hodge*. Rather, his argument seems to be more modest, namely that all Canadian legislatures were subject to this disability until the Statute of Westminster, and that this disability has now been lifted from the federal Parliament but not from the provincial legislatures. (He also supports Vanek's "presumption of conformity" argument.)

With respect, La Forest's argument is unconvincing. It neglects *Arrow River*, in which, as we have seen, the minority held, without contradiction by the majority, that the Ontario Legislature can legislate in violation of international law. It is also susceptible to the federalism problems that plague Vanek's argument. Another objection is La Forest's contention that, if Canadian legislatures were incompetent to vio-

---

203 G La Forest, "May the Provinces Legislate in Violation of International Law?" (1961) 39 *Canadian Bar Review* 78 [La Forest].

204 *BC Electric Railway*, above note 153.

205 *Co-operative Committee on Japanese Canadians v Attorney General for Canada*, [1947] AC 87 (PC). It was held here that the presumption of conformity was rebutted by the existence of war. The Privy Council did not explicitly declare that international law had been violated in this case. Yet by concluding that the presumption was rebutted on the facts, their lordships implicitly accepted the competence of the federal Parliament to break international law. See the discussion of this case in Chapter 5, Section 5.3(b).

206 La Forest, above note 203 at 81–2.

late international law before 1931, the Statute of Westminster did not remove this disability from provincial legislatures. La Forest founds this argument on the proposition that "the provinces gained no greater status from the accession of Canada to international stature, and so remained subject to the existing limitations" on their legislative power.[207] This seems circular, asserting in effect that the provinces gained no power to legislate contrary to international law because their powers in respect of international law did not change. The argument also equates the state of Canada with Parliament alone, but why should Canada's achievement of statehood benefit only the federal legislature? Parliament has no more power to conduct external affairs under section 91 of the Constitution Act, 1867 than the provincial legislatures do under section 92 of that Act, for the 1867 constitution envisaged that Canada's external affairs would be conducted by Britain.

I am not the first to disagree with these arguments. Fawcett argued persuasively that Lord Macmillan was wrong to suggest (if this indeed was his suggestion) that the power to enact statutes contrary to international law is one that must be expressly conferred upon Canadian legislatures and is not to be presumed. Fawcett observed, "It is difficult . . . to see what *power* to legislate contrary to international law there was to confer: it is in any case a strange idea that the United Kingdom should openly and deliberately encourage such a course."[208] Macdonald dismisses the arguments of Vanek and La Forest simply by citing the sovereignty of Canadian legislatures and the judgments in *R v Meikleham*, *Arrow River*, *Chung*, and *Swait*.[209] Bayefsky does not address the question, except to say that there is "no doubt" that Canadian legislatures can violate international law.[210] Similarly, Côté declares, without elaboration, that both the federal Parliament and the provincial legislatures may enact statutes in

207 *Ibid* at 88.

208 J Fawcett, *The British Commonwealth in International Law* (London: Stevens & Sons, 1963) at 23–4 (emphasis in original).

209 R St J Macdonald, "The Relationship Between Domestic Law and International Law in Canada" in R St J Macdonald et al, eds, *Canadian Perspectives on International Law and Organization* (Toronto: University of Toronto Press, 1974) at 119.

210 A Bayefsky, "International Human Rights Law in Canadian Courts" in B Conforti & F Francioni, eds, *Enforcing International Human Rights in Domestic Courts* (The Hague: Martinus Nijhoff, 1997) 295 at 313.

violation of Canada's international obligations.[211] Green makes no reference to Vanek and La Forest but simply affirms parliamentary sovereignty to violate international law.[212]

(c) The presumption of conformity with international law

Both the implementation requirement and the residual sovereignty of Canadian legislatures to legislate in violation of international law are qualified, or mitigated, by the rebuttable interpretive presumption that legislation conforms with the state's obligations under international law. That presumption is the subject of Chapter 5.

---

211 P Côté, *The Interpretation of Legislation in Canada*, 3d ed (Scarborough, ON: Carswell, 2000) at 367.

212 L Green, "International Law: A Canadian Perspective" in *The Canadian Encyclopedic Digest (Ontario)*, 3d ed, vol 17, title 81 (Agincourt, ON: Carswell, 1984) at 70. Green intriguingly observes that following *Mortensen v Peters*, above note 162, in which it was held that UK legislation was in violation of international law, the government indemnified the person affected by this judgment.

5 The presumption of conformity with international law

The presumption of conformity with international law is a rule of legal interpretation whereby domestic law is read, wherever possible, consistently with international law and comity. The normative justification for the presumption is respect for international law. To interpret the acts of our legislatures in a way that failed to respect international law or comity would impute to these bodies an unlawful or belligerent intent. Such an imputation is certainly uncharitable and usually wrong. There is also an important prescriptive justification for the presumption. Violations of international law may bring international responsibility upon the state. The judiciary should therefore avoid internationally unlawful constructions of domestic law wherever possible.

5.1 Overview of the presumption

As a matter of statutory interpretation, domestic law is presumed to comply with Canada's international obligations, and courts should avoid interpretations that would violate those obligations.[1] This presumption of conformity with international law has been a feature of

1 See, e.g., *Zingre v The Queen*, [1981] 2 SCR 392 [*Zingre*] at 409–10; *National Corn Growers Association v Canada (Import Tribunal)*, [1990] 2 SCR 1324 [*National Corn Growers*] at 1371; *Ordon Estate v Grail*, [1998] 3 SCR 437 [*Ordon Estate*] at paras 128–31; *R v Hape*, 2007 SCC 26 [*Hape*] at para 53; *Németh v Canada (Justice)*, 2010 SCC 56 [*Németh*] at para 34; *Thibodeau v Air Canada*, 2014 SCC 67 [*Thibodeau*] at para 113; *B010 v Canada (Citizenship and Immigration)*, 2015 SCC 58 [*B010*] at para 48; *Canada (Minister of Citizenship and Immigration) v Vavilov*, 2019 SCC 65 [*Vavilov*] at para 182.

Anglo-Canadian statutory interpretation since the early nineteenth century.

Today the Supreme Court of Canada situates the presumption within the "entire context" aspect of the modern rule of statutory interpretation. The modern rule requires courts to read "the words of an Act . . . in their entire context, in their grammatical and ordinary sense harmoniously with the scheme of the Act, the object of the Act, and the intention of Parliament."[2] The Supreme Court has affirmed that "the values and principles of customary and conventional international law form part of the context in which Canadian laws are enacted,"[3] and that this "follows from the fact that to interpret a Canadian law in a way that conflicts with Canada's international obligations risks incursion by the courts in the executive's conduct of foreign affairs and censure under international law."[4]

The presumption's application is not restricted to primary legislation (i.e., Acts of Parliament or the provincial legislatures) but applies as well to secondary legislation such as regulations. Nor is the presumption restricted to laws expressly or demonstrably intended to implement Canadian obligations under international law. Non-implementing legislation, such as laws that pre-date the international obligation or laws that have no connection to the obligation as a matter of legislative history, have nevertheless been subjected to the presumption. This is consistent with the presumption's nature as a rule of judicial policy rather than a matter of historic legislative intent. The presumption's application does not depend on a preliminary finding of ambiguity on the face of the enactment. The presumption of conformity with international law is rebuttable in principle, although cases where it has been found to be rebutted are few.

5.2 Nature of the presumption

The presumption of conformity is not a conclusion about, or dependent upon, the historical intent of the legislature. Rather, it is an interpretive duty or policy of the judiciary.

---

2 *Bell ExpressVu Limited Partnership v Rex*, 2002 SCC 42 at para 26.

3 *Hape*, above note 1 at para 53.

4 *B010*, above note 1 at para. 47.

As early as 1939, Professor Lauterpacht detected in the English authorities a "duty of Judges to do their utmost to interpret statutes so as not to impute to the Legislature the intention of disregarding International Law."[5] In *Corocraft v Pan American Airways*, Lord Denning MR declared it to be "the duty of these courts to construe our legislation so as to be in conformity with international law and not in conflict with it."[6] Similarly, in *Attorney General v Guardian Newspapers Ltd (No 2)*, Lord Goff of Chieveley said, "I conceive it to be my duty, when I am free to do so, to interpret the law in accordance with the obligations of the Crown" under a treaty to which the United Kingdom was a party, the European Convention on Human Rights 1950.[7]

Turning to Canadian cases, in *Arrow River & Tributaries Slide & Boom Co Ltd v Pigeon Timber Co Ltd*, Riddell JA emphasized the sovereign's "plain duty" under the treaty, saying "The King cannot be thought of as violating his agreement with the other contracting Power; and, if the legislation can fairly be read in such a way as to reject any imputation of breaking faith, it must be so read."[8] In other words, the state's duty to live up to the obligation translates into a judicial duty to interpret laws in conformity with that obligation, where the legislation permits. Similarly in *R v Zingre* (1981), Dickson J (as he then was) described it as "the duty of the Court," in interpreting an extradition treaty and the Canada Evidence Act, to apply "a fair and liberal interpretation with a view to fulfilling Canada's international obligations."[9]

In *R v Hape*, the presumption of conformity was described in terms of judicial policy rather than duty. Justice LeBel explained: "The presumption of conformity is based on the rule of judicial policy that, as a matter of law, courts will strive to avoid constructions of domestic law pursuant to which the state would be in violation of its international obligations, unless the wording of the statute clearly compels that

5 H Lauterpacht, "Is International Law a Part of the Law of England?" [1940] *Transactions of the Grotius Society* 51 [Lauterpacht] at 58.

6 [1968] 3 WLR 1273 (Eng CA) [*Corocraft*] at 1281. See also *Salomon v Commissioners of Customs & Excise*), [1966] 3 All ER 871 (Eng CA) at 874 ("we ought always to interpret our statutes so as to be in conformity with international law").

7 [1990] 1 AC 109 (HL) at 283.

8 *Arrow River & Tributaries Slide & Boom Co Ltd v Pigeon Timber Co Ltd* (1931), 66 OLR 577 (Ont Sup Ct App Div) [*Arrow River* SCAD] at 579.

9 *Zingre*, above note 1 at 409–10; Canada Evidence Act, RSC 1970, c E-10, s 43.

result."[10] This policy-based approach to the presumption suggests that responsibility for discharging Canada's international obligations does not rest uniquely with the Canadian executive or legislative branches, but falls also to the judiciary.[11]

5.3 Case law on the presumption

Common law courts have long used interpretive presumptions "as protection against interference by the state with the liberty or property of the subject."[12] Justice La Forest (then of the New Brunswick Court of Appeal) explained that by insisting on "clear language" in legislation that purports to interfere with rights, "the courts help promote second thought and public debate, a debate that all recognize as an essential safeguard in a parliamentary democracy."[13] By applying such

---

10 *Hape*, above note 1 at para 53. See also F Bennion, *Statutory Interpretation: A Code*, 4th ed (London, Butterworths, 2002) s 270, who describes the presumption as "a principle of legal policy."

11 This point is made expressly in some treaties. In *Office of the Children's Lawyer v Balev*, 2018 SCC 16 [*Balev*] at paras 84–5, McLachlin CJ noted that art 11 of the Hague Convention on the Civil Aspects of International Child Abduction 1980, [1983] Can TS no 35 "specifically requires the contracting states' judicial authorities to 'act expeditiously in proceedings for the return of children,'" and that the responsibility for performing that obligation "falls to judges and court administrators." She called this "unusual, but it is not unheard of," noting that "Canada is a party to other treaties that depend, in part, on judicial action to ensure performance," noting the Vienna Convention on the Law of Treaties 1969, [1980] Can TS no 37, and the extradition treaty at issue in *Zingre* (above note 1), as examples. Other examples include art 4 of the Convention on the Rights of the Child 1989, [1992] Can TS no 3, and art 4(1)(a) of the Convention on the Rights of Persons with Disabilities 2006, [2010] Can TS no 8, both of which require states parties to undertake or adopt "all appropriate legislative, administrative and other measures for the implementation of the rights recognized in the present Convention." Other measures would appear to include judicial measures such as the application of the presumption of conformity to domestic legislation. Article 15(2) of the Disabilities Convention explicitly charges national judiciaries with performance of their state's obligations: "States Parties shall take all effective legislative, administrative, judicial or other measures to prevent persons with disabilities, on an equal basis with others, from being subjected to torture or cruel, inhuman or degrading treatment or punishment."

12 E Driedger, *The Construction of Statutes*, 2d ed (Toronto: Butterworths, 1983) [Driedger] at 183.

13 G La Forest, "The Canadian Charter of Rights and Freedoms: An Overview" (1983) 61 *Canadian Bar Review* 19 at 20.

presumptions, courts engage legislatures in a dialogue about the nature of their acts. In Canada the language of dialogue is usually associated with constitutional, and especially Charter, review.[14] While the Charter changed the terms of this dialogue, the dialogue itself pre-dates the Charter and other entrenched constitutional laws. Even without entrenched provisions, common law courts protected rights by means of interpretive presumptions. This to-ing and fro-ing between courts and legislatures is properly characterized as dialogue, rather than disobedience to the sovereign will of Parliament. In considering an interpretive presumption against expropriation without compensation, Lord Radcliffe described it as "a mistake" to look on the court's vigilance in such matters "as representing any conflict between the legislature and the courts. The principle was, generally speaking, common to both."[15]

It has been observed that little attention has been given to the genesis and historical development of the presumption of conformity.[16] The following survey does not attempt such an analysis but may serve as a starting point for future research. The aim is to show the English history of the presumption and review leading Canadian authorities.

(a) The English inheritance

The origins of the presumption of conformity may be seen in Blackstone's *Commentaries*. Describing "the law of nations," Blackstone explained that

> This general law is founded upon this principle, that different nations ought in time of peace to do one another all the good they can; and in time of war as little harm as possible, without prejudice to their own real interests. And, as none of these states will allow a superiority in the other, therefore neither can dictate or prescribe the rules of this law to the rest. . . .[17]

---

14 *Vriend v Alberta*, [1998] 1 SCR 493 at para 139; *R v Mills*, [1999] 3 SCR 668 at para 57; P Hogg & A Bushell, "The Charter Dialogue Between Courts and Legislatures" (1997) 35 *Osgoode Hall Law Journal* 75.

15 *Belfast Corporation v O.D. Cars Ltd*, [1960] AC 490 (HL) at 523.

16 D Dyzenhaus et al, "The Principle of Legality in Administrative Law: Internationalisation as Constitutionalisation" (2001) 1 *Oxford University Commonwealth Law Journal* 5 [Dyzenhaus et al] at 24.

17 Sir William Blackstone, *Commentaries on the Laws of England*, vol 4 (Chicago: University of Chicago Press, 1979) at 66.

While Blackstone does not enunciate the presumption of conformity here, his concerns for international comity and the sovereignty of states are the basis of the presumption as it developed in later cases.

The first English cases in which the presumption can be discerned arose in the admiralty courts. The earliest case I am aware of is *Le Louis* (1817),[18] a judgment of Sir William Scott (later Lord Stowell) on the legality of the slave trade. A British ship purporting to enforce either French or international law captured a French slave-trading vessel, but not before 12 men died and many more were injured in the struggle. A Vice-Admiralty Court in Sierra Leone condemned the French ship. On appeal, Sir William held that, whatever moral reservations he and most people in Britain had about slavery, the slave trade was not yet abolished at international law and therefore the capture was illegal. His lordship noted that the commission under which the British purported to act "professes . . . to be founded on the Slave Trade Act"[19] but that

> neither this British Act of Parliament, nor any commission founded on it, can affect any right or interest of foreigners, unless they are founded upon principles and impose regulations that are consistent with the law of nations. That is the only law which Great Britain can apply to them; and the generality of any terms employed in an Act of Parliament must be narrowed in construction by a religious adherence thereto.[20]

His lordship went on to say that "no nation can privilege itself to commit a crime against the law of nations by a mere municipal regulation of its own"[21] and that, in construing British law on the matter, Parliament "must be understood to have contemplated all that was within its power, and no more."[22]

18 (1817) 2 Dods 210, 165 ER 1465 [*Le Louis*]. In Sir Peter Benson Maxwell, *On the Interpretation of Statutes*, 1st ed (London: W. Maxwell & Son, 1875) [Maxwell], the case is mistakenly cited as 2 Dods 229. That error was repeated in subsequent editions of the work until 1962 and was only removed when the case was dropped from the work altogether in the twelfth edition (1969). All of which suggests the case has been (unfairly) neglected – except by Prof. Lauterpacht, who discusses it (and cites it correctly): Lauterpacht, above note 5 at 59 n(h).

19 (UK) 51 George III, c 23 (1811).

20 *Le Louis*, above note 18 at 239 (Dods), 1473–74 (ER).

21 *Ibid* at 251 (Dods), 1478 (ER).

22 *Ibid* at 254 (Dods), 1479 (ER).

The significance of these declarations was not lost on Dr. Lushington, who appeared as counsel for the appellants in the case.[23] Sitting as an admiralty judge some 40 years later, he applied and developed the presumption enunciated in *Le Louis*. Thus, in *The Zollverein* (1856), Dr. Lushington declared:

> In endeavouring to put a construction on a statute, it must be borne in mind how far the power of the British legislature extends, for unless the words are so clear that a contrary construction can in no way be avoided, I must presume that the legislature did not intend to go beyond this power. The laws of Great Britain affect her own subjects everywhere – foreigners only when within her jurisdiction.[24]

Similarly, in *The Annapolis – The Johanna Stoll* (1861), Dr. Lushington explained:

> The Parliament of Great Britain, it is true, has not, according to the principles of public law, any authority to legislate for foreign vessels on the high seas, or for foreigners out of the limits of British jurisdiction, though if Parliament thought fit so to do, this Court, in its instance jurisdiction at least, would be bound to obey. In cases admitting of doubt, the presumption would be that Parliament intended to legislate without violating any rule of international law, and the construction accordingly.[25]

By 1875, when Sir Peter Benson Maxwell published the first edition of *On the Interpretation of Statutes*, the presumption of conformity was sufficiently established in English law to merit an entire section in the work. Under the title "Presumption Against a Violation of International Law,"[26] Maxwell gave six pages of case law in support of the proposition that "every statute is to be so interpreted and applied, as far as its

---

23 Interestingly, Lushington was a leading English proponent of abolition in spite of defending the slave traders in *Le Louis*, above note 18. See S Waddams, *Law, Politics and the Church of England: The Career of Stephen Lushington 1782–1873* (Cambridge: Cambridge University Press, 1992).

24 *The Zollverein* (1856), Swab 96 at 98, 166 ER 1038 [*The Zollverein*] at 1040.

25 *The Annapolis – The Johanna Stoll* (1861), Lush 295 [*The Annapolis*] at 306, 167 ER 128 at 134.

26 The running head on the right-hand pages was "Harmony with International Law."

language admits, as not to be inconsistent with the comity of nations, or with the established rules of international law."[27]

If any doubt remained that the presumption was an established rule of statutory interpretation it was dispelled by the English Court of Appeal in *Bloxam v Favre* (1883),[28] in which Sir James Hannen P quoted and approved the passage from Maxwell given above. Similarly in *Colquhoun v Brooks* Lord Escher MR said that

> the English parliament cannot be supposed merely by reason of its having used general words to be intending to do that which is against the comity of nations. It is true that if we came to the conclusion that this had been intentionally done we must carry out the law and leave to the government of the country the task of answering objections, but unless that is perfectly clear we ought to limit the words so as to make them reasonable and proper. . . .[29]

Notable scholarly consideration of the presumption came in 1939 with the publication of Lauterpacht's important essay, "Is International Law a Part of the Law of England?"[30] Lauterpacht commented on the remarkable strength of the presumption as a tool of statutory interpretation:

> The practical effects of this rule of construction have been considerable; it has been applied almost as frequently as the major doctrine of incorporation itself. The absolute superiority of Acts of Parliament, even when they conflict with International Law, has indeed been repeated and emphatically affirmed. But this has been a theoretical affirmation having the probably not unintended effect of stressing the duty of Judges to do their utmost to interpret statutes so as not to impute to the Legislature the intention of disregarding International Law. . . . The presumption that Parliament did not intend to commit a breach of the law of nations has been a powerful weapon wielded with a determination which on occasions has come near to a denial of the supremacy of Parliament.[31]

---

27 Maxwell, above note 18 at 122.
28 (1883) 8 PD 101 (Eng CA) [*Bloxam*] at 107.
29 (1888) 21 QBD 52 [*Colquhoun*] at 57–8.
30 Lauterpacht, above note 5.
31 *Ibid* at 58–9 (footnotes omitted).

This is not the place for an extended treatment of later UK authorities on the presumption.[32] I note only one case of particular interest. In *Collco Dealings Ltd v Inland Revenue Commissioners*, Maxwell was again relied upon as authority for the presumption.[33] This time, however, there was a difference in the phrasing. Viscount Simonds said,

> My Lords, the language that I have used is taken from a passage at p. 148 of the 10th edition of "Maxwell on the Interpretation of Statutes" which ends with the sentence: "But if the statute is unambiguous, its provisions must be followed even if they are contrary to international law."[34]

This ambiguity requirement is not found in Maxwell's original exposition of the presumption, nor in the eight subsequent editions. It was added in the tenth edition (1953), though the case cited in support of it

---

32 But see, for example, *Salomon v Customs and Excise Commissioners*, [1967] 2 QB 116 (Eng CA) [*Salomon*] at 143, Diplock LJ; *Post Office v Estuary Radio*, [1968] 2 QB 740 (Eng CA) [*Estuary Radio*] at 757, Diplock LJ; *Corocraft*, above note 6 at 1281, Lord Denning MR; *Treacy v Director of Public Prosecutions*, [1971] AC 537 (HL) at 561, Lord Diplock; *R v Secretary of State for the Home Department, ex p Bhajan Singh*, [1976] 1 QB 198 (Eng CA) at 207–8, Lord Denning MR; *Ahmad v ILEA*, [1978] 1 QB 36 (Eng CA) [*Ahmad*] at 48, Scarman LJ; *Attorney-General v British Broadcasting Corporation*, [1981] AC 303 (HL) at 352, Lord Fraser of Tullybelton; *R v Secretary of State for the Home Department, ex p Brind*, [1991] 1 AC 696 (Eng CA) [*Brind*] at 717, Lord Donaldson MR, and at 747–8, Lord Bridge; *R v Lyons*, [2002] UKHL 44 [*Lyons*] at para 27, Lord Hoffmann; *Office of the King's Prosecutor, Brussels v Cando Armas*, [2005] UKHL 67 at para 8, Lord Bingham; *Assange v Swedish Prosecution Authority*, [2012] UKSC 22 at paras 10 (Lord Phillips), 98 (Lord Brown), 115–19 (Lord Kerr), 122 (Lord Dyson). For more on the presumption in English law, see generally S Fatima, *Using International Law in Domestic Courts* (Oxford: Hart, 2005) [Fatima].

33 [1962] AC 1 (PC) [*Collco*] at 19.

34 *Ibid*. Viscount Simonds went on (at 19) to find that the Act in question was unambiguous and was not to be read down in the light of "high-sounding phrases" such as "the comity of nations" and "established rules of international law." As Bennion observes, "The concepts of comity and public international law scarcely deserve the dismissive epithet 'high-sounding'": F Bennion, *Statutory Interpretation: A Code*, 4th ed (London, Butterworths, 2002) at s 270. His lordship's rather vociferous rejection of comity and international law is unfortunate in this respect, and also in that it risks detracting from the unanimous affirmation – in five separate speeches – of the presumption of conformity by their lordships in this case. The presumption was approved by Viscount Simonds (at 19), Lord Morton (at 21), Lord Reid (at 22, though he considered that not every infringement of a treaty would necessarily trigger it), Lord Radcliffe (at 23), and Lord Guest (at 24).

dated from 1878.[35] The needless difficulties that this ambiguity requirement has occasioned, and its rejection in Canadian law by the Supreme Court of Canada, are considered later in this chapter.[36]

(b) Canadian authorities

In the past, Canadian case law and commentators cited English authorities on the presumption of conformity. Maxwell's formulation of the presumption was cited in both its ambiguous and unambiguous versions. Commentators agreed that the presumption existed in Canadian law and was to be assiduously applied.[37] Reference to English authorities has now become rare and largely unnecessary as the Supreme Court of Canada has repeatedly endorsed, applied, and explained the presumption.

I discuss only what I regard as leading cases here, in chronological order and with particular attention to Supreme Court jurisprudence. This summary reveals an unfortunate habit in older Canadian cases of acknowledging the existence of the presumption without applying it to the case at bar. In recent years, the Supreme Court of Canada has applied the presumption more vigorously. I leave aside, for the moment, case law on the application of the presumption to the Charter.[38]

The *Arrow River* case (1932) is illustrative of the delicate and sometimes vexed interplay between the presumption of conformity and the sovereignty of Canadian legislatures to violate international law.[39] The question was whether the Ontario Lakes and Rivers Improvement Act[40]

---

35 *Niboyet v Niboyet* (1878), 4 PD 1 (CA).

36 See Section 5.6, below.

37 E.g., "It is not lightly to be assumed that the legislature intends to put the state in default internationally or to enact a statute in contravention of international law. Therefore, if at all possible, and unless the contrary clearly appears, a statute must be interpreted so as to conform with international law . . . The presumption is obviously a necessary and logical consequence of the doctrine of adoption which itself stems from the fact of membership in a community of civilized states": D Vanek, "Is International Law Part of the Law of Canada?" (1949–50) 8 *University of Toronto Law Journal* 251 at 259–60. Driedger (2nd ed) made no comment of his own but quoted from *Salomon*, above note 32: Dreidger, above note 12 at 154–5.

38 See Chapter 11, Section 11.2(c).

39 *Arrow River & Tributaries Slide & Boom Co Ltd v Pigeon Timber Co Ltd*, [1932] SCR 495 [*Arrow River* SCC].

40 RSO 1927, c 43.

was contrary to a treaty[41] between the United States and Great Britain and, if so, whether the Act was invalid for that reason. A five-member panel of the Appellate Division of the Supreme Court of Ontario found that the treaty was "binding in honour upon her Majesty's successor, his present Majesty" and that

> the Sovereign will not be considered as enacting anything that will conflict with his plain duty, unless the language employed in the statute is perfectly clear and explicit, admitting of no other interpretation. . . . The King cannot be thought of as violating his agreement with the other contracting Power; and, if the legislation can fairly be read in such a way as to reject any imputation of breaking faith, it must be so read.[42]

Applying this admirable statement of the presumption, Riddell JA proceeded to construe the impugned Act in such a way as not to violate the treaty.

On appeal to the Supreme Court of Canada, this judgment was unanimously reversed. Justice Smith (with whom Anglin CJ and Rinfret J agreed) held that there was no conflict between the treaty and the Act, because the treaty did not apply to the non-navigable parts of the Pigeon River subject to the Act. Unlike Riddell JA, who narrowed the Act to make it consistent with the treaty, Smith J narrowed the treaty to make it consistent with the Act. In passing, his lordship observed that Riddell JA's reasoning in the court below "is, of course, based on the assumption (unwarranted, as I think) that the construction of these works under legislative authority would be a violation of the treaty."[43] Having concluded that no conflict existed between the Act and the treaty, Smith J made no further comment on the presumption, though he seems at least to have recognized its existence as an interpretive rule.

Justice Lamont (Cannon J concurring) also allowed the appeal, but for a rather different reason. He found that the Act was indeed in violation of the treaty but that it could not be impugned on this ground alone, for the legislature was sovereign to violate international law. In coming to this conclusion, Lamont J turned the presumption on its

---

41 Webster-Ashburton Treaty 1842, 30 British and Foreign State Papers 360.

42 *Arrow River* SCAD, above note 8 at 579.

43 *Arrow River* SCC, above note 39 at 499.

head, saying, "Had the Legislature intended to exclude international boundary rivers from the operation of the Act, I think it would have said so in express terms."[44] Justice Lamont correctly insisted that a treaty cannot alter existing law without implementation, for otherwise the Crown would gain a power to legislate outside of Parliament.[45] His mistake, in my respectful opinion, was to treat this implementation requirement as incompatible with the presumption of conformity. The two rules may harmoniously co-exist in the Canadian reception system, as earlier English cases and later Canadian cases demonstrate. The result of Lamont J's approach was to risk bringing international responsibility upon Canada in the interpretation of a statute which – according to three justices of the Supreme Court of Canada and five of the court below – could fairly be read as consistent with the treaty. Note, however, that while Lamont J declined to apply the presumption to this case, he nevertheless did not reject it as a tool of statutory interpretation.

That the presumption remained a rule of Canadian statutory interpretation after *Arrow River* was affirmed by Duff CJ in *Re Foreign Legations* (1943).[46] Here the international law in issue was not a treaty but the customary law of sovereign immunity, as embodied in the immunity of foreign legations from municipal taxation. All five judges in the case gave reasons, the most extensive and impressive of which are those of Duff CJ. In a remarkable application of the doctrine of incorporation, the chief justice acknowledged the power of the provincial legislature to violate customary international law by granting municipalities the power to levy rates on foreign legations, yet held that the "general language of the enactments imposing the taxation in question must be construed as saving to the privileges of foreign states."[47] As authority for this approach the chief justice looked not to the English authorities but to an American presumption case, *The Schooner "Exchange" v M'Faddon*.[48] Justice Taschereau concurred with Duff CJ in

44 *Ibid* at 509.

45 *Ibid* at 510.

46 *Re Powers of the Corporation of the City of Ottawa and the Corporation of the Village of Rockliffe Park to Levy Rates on Foreign Legations and High Commissioners' Residences*, [1943] SCR 208 [*Re Foreign Legations*].

47 *Ibid* at 231.

48 (1812) 7 Cranch 116 [*The "Exchange"*] at 146.

brief reasons.[49] Two of the remaining three judges agreed with Duff CJ that the customary law of sovereign immunity was part of the law of Canada, but they did not explicitly conclude from this that the presumption applied to the Ontario Act.[50]

A devastating refusal to apply the presumption came in the judgment of the Privy Council in *Co-operative Committee on Japanese Canadians v Attorney General for Canada* (1947),[51] though here again their lordships acknowledged the existence of the rule. The appellants challenged the validity of the War Measures Act,[52] under which three orders in council had been made on 15 December 1945 to transport "persons of Japanese race" to Japan. The appellants argued that the Act

> should be construed as authorizing only such orders as are consistent with the accepted principles of international law, and that the forcible removal to a foreign country of British subjects was contrary to the accepted rules of international law. The Act therefore as a matter of construction did not . . . purport to authorize orders providing for such removal.[53]

In rejecting this argument, Lord Wright for the board conceded that it "may be true that in construing legislation some weight ought, in an appropriate case, to be given to a consideration of the accepted principles

---

49 *Re Foreign Legations*, above note 46 at 249.

50 Rinfret J acknowledged "the legal impossibility of collecting the taxes against foreign states" and observed that it would be "an empty procedure" for the municipal council to enter the taxes on its assessment rolls only to find later that they were uncollectable: *Re Foreign Legations*, above note 46 at 233. All that is missing is for his lordship to say, as Duff CJ did, that the absurdity of this situation means that the legislation ought to be construed as not encompassing foreign legations. A bizarre result, created by failure to apply the presumption, is the conclusion of Hudson J that the municipalities may, under the Act, tax legations but that "assistance of the courts would not be given to enforce payment so long as the diplomatic immunity continued": *Re Foreign Legations*, above note 46 at 247. Similarly, Kerwin J concluded that the municipalities could levy the rates but that the question of whether the foreign states could be sued for them or have their legations sold to pay them off were questions of international law that did not arise here: *ibid* at 238. This is baffling: surely that question was exactly the one posed in this reference.

51 [1947] AC 87 (PC) [*Japanese Canadians*].

52 RSC 1927, c 206.

53 *Japanese Canadians*, above note 51 at 104.

of international law."[54] The preceding survey of English authorities reveals how watered down this description of the presumption is. His lordship went on to say that "those principles find no place in the construction of the War Measures Act" and that the "accepted rules of international law applicable in times of peace can hardly have been in contemplation, and the inference cannot be drawn that the Parliament of the Dominion impliedly imposed the limitation suggested."[55] It is tempting to read this case as authority against the existence or applicability of the presumption. That was not, however, their lordships' finding. The existence of the presumption as a rule of statutory interpretation was not doubted, though Lord Wright's weak description of it flew in the face of over a century of English case law. Rather, the *ratio* of *Japanese Canadians* was that the presumption of conformity was rebutted by wartime conditions, which, in their lordships' view, suggested the legislature's intent to grant the government extraordinary powers. Thus, even such an unpleasant case as this is authority for the presumption.

These early cases are at once authorities for the existence of the presumption in Canadian law and cautionary tales about the consequences of failing to apply it. In *Arrow River*, the *ratio* of the concurring minority of the Supreme Court of Canada would have placed Canada in default of its obligations under an important treaty without any clear signal from the legislature that it intended such a default. In *Re Foreign Legations*, only the judgment of Duff CJ (concurred in by Taschereau J) avoided the absurd result that municipalities could levy internationally unlawful rates but could not actually collect them. Finally, the failure of the Privy Council in *Japanese Canadians* to apply the presumption to the War Measures Act endowed the Canadian government with a shocking power to deport Canadian nationals and residents for no better reason than their ethnic origin.

In 1968 the Supreme Court of Canada had occasion to consider the presumption of conformity in *Daniels v White and the Queen*.[56] This difficult case pitted the presumption against another estimable rule of statutory construction, namely the rule that treaties and statutes relating to Indigenous peoples should be construed liberally and in

54 *Ibid.*
55 *Ibid.*
56 [1968] SCR 517 [*Daniels*].

their favour.[57] Daniels was an Indigenous man accused of possessing game birds contrary to the Migratory Birds Convention Act,[58] a statute implementing the Canada–US Migratory Birds Convention 1916.[59] Daniels claimed a right to hunt game birds under an agreement between the governments of Canada and Manitoba. That agreement had subsequently been made part of Canada's constitution by section 1 of the British North America Act 1930,[60] which declared the agreement to have force of law notwithstanding any Act of the Parliament of Canada – including, Daniels argued, the Migratory Birds Convention Act. A bare majority of the Supreme Court of Canada dismissed Daniels' appeal and affirmed his conviction. Justice Judson for himself and three others made no reference to the presumption. Justice Pigeon agreed with Judson J's reasons but added that "this is a case for the application of the rule of construction that Parliament is not presumed to legislate in breach of a treaty or in any manner inconsistent with the comity of nations and the established rules of international law."[61] His lordship described the presumption as "not often applied" because unambiguous statutes must be followed even if contrary to international law.[62]

57 This has since come to be known as the "Nowegijick principle" after *Nowegijick v R*, [1983] 1 SCR 29.

58 RSC 1952, c 179 (now Migratory Birds Convention Act, 1994, SC 1994, c 22).

59 [1917] Can TS no 7.

60 See Constitution Act, 1930 (UK), 20–21 Geo V, c 26; Manitoba Natural Resources Act, 1930, SC 1930, c 29; and Manitoba Natural Resources Act, 1930, RSM 1954, c 180.

61 *Daniels*, above note 56 at 541.

62 Pigeon J's description of the presumption as "not often applied" is certainly inapplicable today. In the twenty-first century, the Supreme Court of Canada's application or approbation of the presumption of conformity (in its statutory and Charter forms) has been an almost annual phenomenon. See *Society of Composers, Authors and Music Publishers of Canada v Entertainment Software Association*, 2022 SCC 30 [*Entertainment Software*] at para 46; *Quebec (Attorney General) v 9147-0732 Québec inc*, 2020 SCC 32 [*9147-0732 Québec inc*] at para 31; *Vavilov*, above note 1 at paras 114, 182; *Balev*, above note 11 at para 31; *Ktunaxa Nation v British Columbia (Forests, Lands and Natural Resource Operations)*, 2017 SCC 54 [*Ktunaxa*] at para 65; *R v Appulonappa*, 2015 SCC 59 [*Appulonappa*] at para 40; *B010*, above note 1 at para 48; *Saskatchewan Federation of Labour v Saskatchewan*, 2015 SCC 4 at para 64; *Thibodeau*, above note 1 at para 113; *Divito v Canada (Public Safety and Emergency Preparedness)*, 2013 SCC 47 at para 23; *Merck Frosst Canada Ltd v Canada (Health)*, 2012 SCC 3 at para 117; *Németh*, above note 1 at para 34; *United States of America v Anekwu*, 2009 SCC 41 [*Anekwu*] at para 25; *Health Services and Support – Facilities Subsector Bargaining Assn v British Columbia*, 2007 SCC 27 at para 70; *Hape*, above note 1 at paras 53–4; *GreCon Dimter inc v J.R. Normand*

He cited *Collco Dealings* to this effect[63] and concluded that the presumption was nevertheless "recognized as applicable in a proper case."[64] This analysis was opposed in the reasons of two dissenting judges, neither of whom denied the existence of the presumption but only its applicability to the case at bar.[65]

In *Capital Cities Communications Inc v Canadian Radio-Television Commission* (1978),[66] the Supreme Court of Canada considered the application of the presumption to a statutory decision maker, the Canadian Radio-television Commission (CRTC). I consider the case further in Chapter 9.[67] Chief Justice Laskin for the majority declined to apply the presumption to the regulatory activities of the CRTC, saying that the Act under which the commission operated did not implement the treaty at issue and that the ambiguity required to justify resort to the treaty was not present.[68] While the majority in *Capital Cities* rejected the presumption in stark terms, the dissenting judgment of Pigeon J (for himself and Beetz and Grandpré JJ) signalled a new openness to the presumption, and perhaps to international law generally, at the Supreme Court of Canada. Justice Pigeon held that the CRTC had a "duty to implement the policy established by Parliament" and continued, "While this policy makes no reference to Canada's treaty obligations, it is an integral part of the national structure that external affairs are the responsibility of the Federal Government. It is an oversimplification to say that treaties are of no legal effect unless implemented by

---

inc, 2005 SCC 46 [*GreCon Dimter*] at para 39; *Canadian Foundation for Children, Youth and the Law v Canada (Attorney General)*, 2004 SCC 4 [*Canadian Foundation*] at para 31; *114957 Canada Ltée (Spraytech, Société d'arrosage) v Hudson (Town)*, 2001 SCC 40 [*Spraytech*] at para 30.

63 *Collco*, above note 33.

64 *Daniels*, above note 56 at 541.

65 Cartwright CJ did not refer specifically to the presumption relied upon by Pigeon J but declared that it was impossible to uphold the conviction unless an exception for the Migratory Birds Convention Act could be read into s 1 of the British North America Act 1930, and no rule of construction could do that. See *Daniels*, above note 56 at 521–2. In the lengthiest dissent, Hall J (Ritchie and Spence JJ concurring) acknowledged the presumption but declared that it did not come into operation if a statute is unambiguous "for in that event its provisions must be followed even if they are contrary to the established rules of international law." See *Daniels*, *ibid* at 527–41.

66 [1978] 2 SCR 141 [*Capital Cities*].

67 See Section 9.4(a).

68 *Capital Cities*, above note 66 at 172–3.

legislation."[69] Justice Pigeon went on to approve the presumption as it was advanced by Diplock LJ (as he then was) in *Post Office v Estuary Radio*.[70] I argue in Chapter 9 that Pigeon J's dissent is to be preferred over the majority judgment both as a stand-alone proposition and in the light of the Supreme Court of Canada's groundbreaking decision in *Baker v Canada (Minister of Citizenship and Immigration)*.[71] Justice Pigeon's dissent has not, to my knowledge, been subsequently approved in any decided case. Nevertheless, it represents a turning point in the treatment of the presumption of conformity at the Supreme Court of Canada. Though resistance to the presumption still occasionally appears there, the case law after *Capital Cities* has tended to apply the presumption more readily and consistently.

R v Zingre (1981) is a leading example.[72] The question was whether a Manitoba court could properly authorize two Swiss investigating judges under section 43 of the Canada Evidence Act[73] to take testimony in Canada in respect of a prosecution in Switzerland. The accused men argued that the investigating judges were not "any court or judge" for the purpose of section 43 and therefore could not be authorized. The Crown argued that any ambiguity in section 43 should be resolved in the light of a judicial assistance treaty concluded by Great Britain (on behalf of Canada) and Switzerland in 1880.[74] Speaking for the court, Dickson J (as he then was) agreed, saying "I would interpret section 43 in light of Article I of the 1880 Treaty, which recites that the commissions of examination shall be transmitted through the 'proper Diplomatic channel'. . . . I reach this conclusion because the contrary view would result in the purpose of the 1880 Treaty being completely frustrated."[75] His lordship added,

> The argument in favour of granting the order in the case at bar does not rest merely on the notion of "comity." It rests on treaty. In responding affirmatively to the request which has been made the

---

69 *Ibid* at 188.

70 *Estuary Radio*, above note 32 at 757.

71 [1999] 2 SCR 817 [*Baker*].

72 *Zingre*, above note 1.

73 RSC 1970, c E-10.

74 Treaty Between Great Britain and Roumania for the Mutual Surrender of Fugitive Criminals [1894] UKTS no 14.

75 *Zingre*, above note 1 at 406–7.

> Court will be recognizing and giving effect to a duty to which Canada is subject, by treaty, under international law. . . . It is the duty of the Court, in interpreting the 1880 Treaty and s. 43 of the Canada Evidence Act to give them a fair and liberal interpretation with a view to fulfilling Canada's international obligations. . . . The Treaty of 1880 places Canada under a specific obligation to comply with the Swiss request. If Canada denies the Swiss request it will be in breach of its international obligations. . . . As the Canadian Department of External Affairs stated in a note to the Swiss Federal Policy [sic: Police] Department . . . "it is a recognized principle of international customary law that a state may not invoke the provisions of its internal law as justification for its failure to perform its international obligations."[76]

This is a very illuminating passage. Justice Dickson sets the presumption in its full international context: The court's interpretation of the Act as presumptively consistent with the treaty is the means by which the Canadian state will fulfil its obligation to Switzerland under international law. Fulfilment of the international obligation falls, in this case, not on the government or the legislature but on the judiciary, and the judiciary is duty-bound to meet that obligation. Justice Dickson understands the treaty as a responsibility not merely of the Canadian government but of the Canadian state as a whole, including Parliament (which is presumed by the court to have intended the Canada Evidence Act to be interpreted consistently with the treaty) and the courts (which apply the presumption). Justice Dickson is also mindful of the consequence of not applying the presumption: Canada will be responsible at international law to Switzerland for breaching the treaty and will not be permitted to plead the Canada Evidence Act – nor the Supreme Court of Canada's interpretation of it – as an excuse for that breach.

The next major pronouncement on the presumption by the Supreme Court of Canada came in *National Corn Growers Association v Canada (Import Tribunal)* (1990).[77] Acting under section 42 of the Special Import Measures Act (SIMA),[78] the Canadian Import Tribunal conducted an inquiry into US grain corn pricing and concluded that

76 *Ibid* at 409–10.
77 *National Corn Growers*, above note 1.
78 SC 1984 c 25.

American subsidies were injuring Canadian producers. This justified the government's imposition of a countervailing duty on the United States. In construing section 42, the tribunal resorted to article 6(a) of the General Agreement on Tariffs and Trade 1947[79] and article 6 of the GATT Subsidies Code[80] to elucidate the Act's concept of material injury. On judicial review, the Federal Court of Appeal left the tribunal's findings undisturbed, yet the majority held that the tribunal was mistaken to look outside the four corners of the unambiguous Act. The majority of the Supreme Court of Canada disagreed, preferring instead the opinion of MacGuigan J that "it must . . . be presumed that Parliament intended that SIMA should be interpreted in accordance with the Code."[81] Justice Gonthier for the majority rejected the view that resort to international law could only be had upon finding that the legislation under consideration was ambiguous on its face. I consider this aspect of the case below.[82] This rejection of the ambiguity requirement served to restore Canadian jurisprudence on the presumption to the original (and eminently preferable) English position – from which both the English and Canadian jurisprudence had departed by the mid-twentieth century.

The presumption of conformity won the strong support of the Supreme Court of Canada in two 1998 cases. In *Ordon Estate v Grail*,[83] Iacobucci and Major JJ invoked the presumption in support of the construction of a limitation statute:

> Although international law is not binding upon Parliament or the provincial legislatures, a court must presume that legislation is intended to comply with Canada's obligations under international instruments and as a member of the international community. In choosing among possible interpretations of a statute, the court should avoid interpretations that would put Canada in breach of such obligations.[84]

---

79 [1947] Can TS no 27.

80 Agreement on Interpretation and Application of Articles VI, XVI and XXIII of the General Agreement on Tariffs and Trade (the GATT Subsidies Code) 1979, [1980] Can TS no 42.

81 Quoted in *National Corn Growers*, above note 1 at 1366.

82 At Section 5.6.

83 *Ordon Estate*, above note 1.

84 *Ibid* at para 137.

The first phrase of this passage is deceptive in its simplicity. There are two senses in which international law is not binding on Canadian legislatures. First, on the international legal plane, international law addresses itself to the state, not to its composite parts. It is the Canadian state as a whole, and not its various organs, that is a subject of international law.[85] Second, on the domestic legal plane, Canadian legislatures are empowered to enact laws that may bring Canada into violation of its international obligations, and our courts may not strike down such laws solely on the basis of their failure to conform to international law.[86] In this sense, too, it is true to say that international law is not binding upon Parliament or the provincial legislatures. Note that in saying that international law is not binding upon Canadian legislatures, the court in *Ordon Estate* did not deny its bindingness on the Canadian state as a whole. Nor did it (or could it) deny that the conduct of Canadian legislatures is attributable to the Canadian state at international law. Indeed, this consideration was clearly very much on the court's mind, for the rest of the quoted passage goes on to affirm that courts must apply the presumption of conformity and should avoid interpretations that would put Canada in breach of them.

Later in 1998 the court put the presumption admirably to use in *Pushpanathan v Canada (Minister of Citizenship and Immigration)*.[87] Justice Bastarache for the majority of the Supreme Court of Canada held that section 2(1) of the Immigration Act[88] was intended to implement article 1F(c) of the United Nations Convention Relating to the Status of Refugees 1951[89] and therefore must be interpreted consistently with Canada's obligations under that treaty. To that end, Bastarache J applied not only the substantive provisions of the treaty to the Act, but also the international law rules of treaty interpretation, as expressed in articles 31–2 of the Vienna Convention on the Law of Treaties 1969.[90]

---

85 See the discussion in Chapter 2, Section 2.1.

86 See the discussion of parliamentary sovereignty in Chapter 4, Section 4.2(b).

87 [1998] 1 SCR 982 [*Pushpanathan*].

88 RSC 1985 c I-2 (repealed).

89 [1969] Can TS no 6.

90 [1980] Can TS no 37; *Pushpanathan*, above note 87 at paras 51–3. Bastarache J cited *Thomson v Thomson*, [1994] 3 SCR 551 and *Canada (Attorney General) v Ward*, [1993] 2 SCR 689 as authorities for this approach. English authorities include *R v Lambeth Justices ex parte Yusufu*, [1985] Crim LR 110 and *Sidhu v British Airways*, [1997] 1 All ER 193 (HL) at 201–12. See the discussion in Chapter 7, Section 7.6.

Justice Bastarache prefaced his endorsement of the presumption by explaining that the purpose of the Act was to implement the treaty. This should not be taken, in my view, to mean that the presumption does not apply to non-implementing legislation.[91] In dissent, Cory J did not refer to the presumption and yet relied heavily on international law.

In *Baker v Canada (Minister of Citizenship and Immigration)* (1999),[92] an irregular migrant fighting her imminent deportation after residing in Canada since 1981 argued that the minister's decision in her case should be set aside because (among other things) the minister had unreasonably failed to give sufficient weight to the interests of Baker's Canadian-born children as required by the Convention on the Rights of the Child 1989.[93] Justice L'Heureux-Dubé for the majority held that the minister's decision unreasonably neglected international law and was thus "inconsistent with the values underlying the grant of the discretion."[94] These values included children's rights, as revealed in part by international law (particularly the 1989 Convention). This use of a treaty as an element in defining the extent of the discretion granted by the statute amounts to an application of the presumption of conformity: The discretion conferred by the statute is presumed to be consistent with the requirements of international law. While L'Heureux-Dubé J did not expressly describe her invocation of the Convention as an application of the presumption of conformity, she subsequently did so in *R v Sharpe*[95] and *Spraytech v Hudson*.[96] Justice L'Heureux-Dubé's use of international law in *Baker* was the only ground on which Iacobucci and Cory JJ dissented.[97] I suggest in Chapter 9 that this dissent should not be understood as a rejection of the presumption of conformity itself, but only of its application in this instance.[98]

In *Spraytech v Hudson* (2001),[99] the town of Hudson, Quebec, purporting to act under two sections of Quebec's Cities and Towns Act,[100]

---

91 See the discussion at Section 5.5(b), below.
92 *Baker*, above note 71.
93 [1992] Can TS no 3.
94 *Baker*, above note 71 at para 65.
95 2001 SCC 45 at para 175.
96 *Spraytech*, above note 62 at para 30.
97 *Baker*, above note 71 at paras 78–81.
98 See Chapter 9, Section 9.4(b).
99 *Spraytech*, above note 62.
100 Cities and Towns Act, RSQ c C-19.

adopted a by-law restricting the use of pesticides within the town perimeter. The appellants (landscaping and lawn care companies) challenged the validity of the by-law. They were unsuccessful in the lower courts and also in the Supreme Court of Canada. Justice L'Heureux-Dubé for the majority held that the town had the statutory authority to adopt the by-law, noting that her construction of the statute to permit the town to regulate pesticide use was an application of the presumption in that it was consistent with the precautionary principle, which the learned judge suggested may be a rule of customary international law.[101] Justice LeBel concurred in the result but differed from the majority on the relevance of international law to the disposition of the appeal, saying,

> Interesting as they may be, references to international sources have little relevance. They confirm the general importance placed in modern society and shared by most citizens of this country on the environment and the need to protect it. Nevertheless, no matter how laudable the purpose of the by-law may be, and although it may express the will of the members of the community to protect their local environment, the means to do it must be found somewhere in the law.[102]

By "the law," LeBel J apparently did not mean "Canadian and international law" but only the enabling Act under which the town adopted its by-law. In my respectful view, the minority's approach is mistaken. The presumption of conformity applies to all statutes, including those such as the Cities and Towns Act that delegate law- or decision-making power. If one accepts that the precautionary principle is a rule of customary international law (and there is room for disagreement on this point), one must presume that Canadian legislation is consistent with that rule unless that presumption is rebutted by the clear words of the enabling Act or some other convincing indication of the legislature's intent.

In *Canadian Foundation for Children, Youth and the Law v Canada (Attorney General)* (2004), the Supreme Court of Canada considered a

101 *Spraytech*, above note 62 at paras 31–2. The precautionary principle is a concept of international environmental law requiring that lack of full scientific certainty that a given measure is harmful to the environment should not be used as a reason for postponing or rejecting preventative measures.

102 *Ibid* at para 48.

constitutional challenge to section 43 of the Criminal Code,[103] a provision justifying schoolteachers and parents in using reasonable force by way of correction of a child. Chief Justice McLachlin for the majority of the court dismissed the challenge. She began by determining what was meant by the words "reasonable in the circumstances," finding that these words imported certain implicit limitations to the provision's breadth. In particular, she held (citing *Ordon Estate v Grail*) that the phrase should be construed to comply with Canada's international obligations and that "Canada's international commitments confirm that physical correction that either harms or degrades a child is unreasonable."[104] Elaborating on this statement, McLachlin CJ reviewed several articles of the Convention on the Rights of the Child 1989 and article 7 of the International Covenant on Civil and Political Rights 1966.[105] Apart from these treaty considerations, the chief justice also looked to social consensus, expert evidence, and judicial interpretation as guides to the meaning of "reasonable under the circumstances." Taking all these considerations together, McLachlin CJ concluded that section 43 exempted from criminal sanction only minor corrective force of a transitory and trifling nature and that, thus understood, it did not infringe the requirements of fundamental justice of Charter section 7. This application of the presumption of conformity illustrates how powerful an interpretive tool it can be, in spite of the reception system's requirement that treaties be implemented by legislation before taking direct effect in Canadian law. Some might complain that McLachlin CJ's reasons effectively read down section 43, by resort to international law (among other considerations), and thus spared it from a declaration of unconstitutionality. Whether that is so or not, the case stands as a strong and significant application of the presumption of conformity.

A remarkable illustration of the potentially determinative importance of the presumption of conformity is *GreCon Dimter Inc v J.R. Normand Inc* (2005).[106] The case arose from a contract between a German company, G, and a Quebec company, N. When G failed to perform, N became liable to a third party, T, which was also a Quebec company.

103 RSC 1985, c C-46.
104 *Canadian Foundation*, above note 62 at para 31.
105 [1976] Can TS no 47.
106 *GreCon Dimter*, above note 62.

T sued N for damages, and N filed an incidental action in warranty against G. Resisting this action, G challenged the Quebec court's jurisdiction on the basis of a choice of forum clause in its contract with N. That clause directed the parties to a German court. Conflicting provisions of the Civil Code of Quebec applied. Article 3148(2) provided that the Quebec court lost jurisdiction where the parties had agreed to either a choice of forum clause (as here) or an arbitration clause. Yet article 3139 conferred jurisdiction on the Quebec court to hear actions in warranty so long as it had jurisdiction over the principal action, here the action between the two Quebec companies, T and N. Both the Quebec Superior Court and the Court of Appeal held that the Quebec courts had jurisdiction. Justice LeBel for the Supreme Court of Canada reversed this decision, finding that article 3148(2) must take precedence over article 3139. In reaching this result, LeBel J observed, "The interpretation of the provisions in issue, and the resolution of the conflict between them, must necessarily be harmonized with the international commitments of Canada and Quebec,"[107] citing *National Corn Growers*, *Pushpanathan*, *Ordon Estate*, and *Canadian Foundation*, and referring to the presumption "that the legislature is deemed not to intend to legislate in a manner that cannot be reconciled with the state's international obligations."[108] The international obligation in question was that of article II(3) of the New York Convention on the Recognition and Enforcement of Foreign Arbitral Awards 1958,[109] requiring the courts of contracting states to refer disputing parties to arbitration where they have previously so agreed. While this provision concerns arbitration clauses and not choice of forum clauses, LeBel J held that the same position should be adopted in respect of both, and that article 3148(2) must therefore take precedence over article 3139.[110] Much like *Canadian Foundation*, the *GreCon* case reveals the power of the presumption of conformity to tip the scales in cases where the legal issues before the court are otherwise evenly balanced.

The most far-reaching consideration of the presumption of conformity by a Canadian court thus far is found in the judgment of LeBel

107 On the "international commitments of . . . Quebec," see the discussion of this comment in Chapter 4, Section 4.1(e)(iii).

108 *GreCon Dimter*, above note 62 at para 39.

109 [1986] Can TS no 43.

110 *GreCon Dimter*, above note 62 at paras 42–5.

J, for the majority of the Supreme Court of Canada, in *R v Hape* (2007).[111] The question before the court was whether the Charter applied to searches and seizures conducted by RCMP officers abroad. Hape was a Canadian businessman who was suspected of money laundering. With the cooperation of local authorities, the RCMP investigated the offices of Hape's investment company in the Turks and Caicos Islands, where they gathered documents that the Crown later put in evidence at trial. However, no warrants were entered into evidence, and Hape contended that the documents must be excluded on the ground that they were obtained in violation of his right under section 8 of the Charter to be secure against unreasonable search and seizure. Hape argued that the Charter applied to the RCMP's searches and seizures even when those actions took place outside Canada. The majority of the Supreme Court of Canada held that the Charter does not generally apply to searches and seizures in other countries. In reaching that result, LeBel J observed that in interpreting the scope of application of the Charter (section 32(1)), courts should seek to ensure compliance with Canada's binding obligations under international law where the express words are capable of supporting such a construction.[112] On the presumption of conformity with international law, LeBel J made the following comments:

> It is a well-established principle of statutory interpretation that legislation will be presumed to conform to international law. The presumption of conformity is based on the rule of judicial policy that, as a matter of law, courts will strive to avoid constructions of domestic law pursuant to which the state would be in violation of its international obligations, unless the wording of the statute clearly compels that result. R. Sullivan, *Sullivan and Driedger on the Construction of Statutes* (4th ed. 2002), at p. 422, explains that the presumption has two aspects. First, the legislature is presumed to act in compliance with Canada's obligations as a signatory of international treaties and as a member of the international community. In deciding between possible interpretations, courts will avoid a construction that would place Canada in breach of those obligations. The second aspect is that the legislature is presumed to comply with the values and principles of customary and conventional international law. Those values and principles form part of the context in which statutes are enacted,

111 *Hape*, above note 1 at para 53.

112 *Ibid* at para 55.

> and courts will therefore prefer a construction that reflects them. The presumption is rebuttable, however. Parliamentary sovereignty requires courts to give effect to a statute that demonstrates an unequivocal legislative intent to default on an international obligation. See also P.-A. Côté, *The Interpretation of Legislation in Canada* (3rd ed. 2000), at pp. 367–68.
>
> . . . The presumption applies equally to customary international law and treaty obligations.[113]

Four points from this discussion are particularly important.

First, LeBel J describes the presumption as a rule of judicial policy. The presumption is therefore not necessarily rooted in any historical intent of the legislature, and an absence of evidence that the legislature actually considered international law in the course of its deliberations should be no obstacle to its application.[114]

Second, the presumption is rebuttable – but it is not easily rebutted. To the contrary, the party seeking to rebut it must show that "the wording of the statute clearly compels" an internationally unlawful result, or that the statute demonstrates "an unequivocal legislative intent to default" on an international obligation.[115]

Third, LeBel J describes the "values and principles of customary and conventional international law" as forming "part of the context in which statutes are enacted." This *dictum* serves to reconcile (if any reconciliation were needed) the presumption of conformity with the pre-eminent rule of Canadian statutory interpretation, namely that the words of an Act are to be read in their entire context and in their grammatical and ordinary sense harmoniously with the scheme of the Act, the object of the Act, and the intention of Parliament.[116] In the passage quoted above, LeBel J makes clear that the context in which a statute is to be interpreted includes the international obligations of the state.

Fourth, the presumption of conformity applies equally to customary international law and treaty obligations. This was clear from the case law but is put beyond doubt by LeBel J here.[117]

---

113 *Ibid* at paras 53–4.

114 See the discussion at Section 5.2, above.

115 See the discussion at Section 5.9, below.

116 See, e.g., *Rizzo & Rizzo Shoes Ltd (Re)*, [1998] 1 SCR 27 at para 21 and *Bell ExpressVu Limited Partnership v Rex*, 2002 SCC 42 at para 26.

117 See the discussion at Section 5.4, below.

The question in *United States of America v Anekwu* (2009) was the interpretation of section 32(2) of the Extradition Act,[118] which provided that evidence gathered in Canada in support of an extradition request must satisfy the rules of evidence under Canadian law in order to be admitted in an extradition proceeding. The record of the case (prepared by the United States) included a summary of the evidence against Anekwu that involved hearsay in the form of corporate and business records. Hearsay being generally inadmissible under Canadian law, Anekwu challenged the validity of the committal and surrender orders against him as contrary to section 32(2) of the Extradition Act. Justice Charron for the court acknowledged that section 32(2), taken on its own, "reveals no ambiguity" and "mandates compliance with domestic rules of evidence" including the hearsay rule. But she went on to consider the provision in its entire context, particularly section 33(1) (which requires the record of the case to include a summary of the evidence available to the extradition partner for use in the prosecution), and international comity in extradition proceedings generally. The learned judge invoked the "well-established principle of statutory interpretation that in interpreting domestic legislation, courts should strive to arrive at a construction which conforms with Canada's treaty obligations" and observed that adherence to the strictures of the hearsay rule in the extradition context would result in delays and expense that would "disable Canada from complying with its international obligations in a prompt and efficient manner."[119] To avoid such an outcome, Charron J interpreted section 32(2) together with section 33(1) as providing for a modified approach to the hearsay rule unique to the extradition context whereby the Canadian-gathered evidence is admissible when presented in summary form but must then be scrutinized by the court for compliance with Canadian rules of evidence.

In *Németh v Canada (Justice)* (2010), two Hungarian Roma to whom Canada had granted refugee status were sought for extradition by Hungary on a fraud charge. They sought judicial review of the committal and surrender orders made against them on the ground that the principle of *non-refoulement* prevented their extradition to the very country from which they had been granted refuge. Justice Cromwell for the Supreme Court of Canada considered first whether the minister of justice had

118 SC 1999, c 18.

119 *Anekwu*, above note 62 at paras 25–6.

authority to surrender a refugee for extradition to the state from which the refugee had taken refuge, and if so whether that authority had been reasonably exercised in this case. The appellants contended that the prohibition of *refoulement* in section 115 of the Immigration and Refugee Protection Act (IRPA)[120] prevented their extradition to Hungary, and that to interpret section 115 otherwise would breach Canada's international refugee protection obligations. While Cromwell J agreed that international law protects against *refoulement* by extradition, and accepted "of course" that "where possible statutes should be interpreted in a way which makes their provisions consistent with Canada's international treaty obligations and principles of international law,"[121] he held that section 115 concerned removal orders under the IRPA and not surrender orders under the Extradition Act. That provision could not be interpreted as applying to removal by extradition. Furthermore, it need not be so interpreted, for Canada's *non-refoulement* obligation in the extradition context was "fully satisfied by a correct interpretation and application of s. 44" of the Extradition Act.[122] While the IRPA did not constrain the minister from extraditing a refugee, section 44(1)(b) of the Extradition Act potentially did. That provision (which the minister failed to consider) was "Canada's primary legislative vehicle to give effect to Canada's *non-refoulement* obligations when a refugee is sought for extradition"[123] and "must be interpreted in light of [the] human rights object and purpose" of the Refugee Convention.[124] The learned judge allowed the appeal, set aside the judgment of the Court of Appeal and the minster's surrender decisions, and remitted the matter to the minister for reconsideration according to law.[125] The *Németh* case is notable for its nuanced balancing of the presumption of conformity with international law with respect for the means Parliament has chosen to ensure Canada's performance of its obligations.

---

120 SC 2001, c 27.

121 *Németh*, above note 1 at para 26.

122 *Németh*, above note 1 at para 35.

123 *Ibid* at para 77; see also para 102, describing "an important purpose of s. 44(1)(b)" as "to implement Canada's *non-refoulement* obligations in the extradition setting."

124 *Németh*, above note 1 at para 86.

125 A companion case, *Gavrila v Canada (Justice)*, 2010 SCC 57, concerning extradition of a Roma refugee to Romania, was similarly disposed of.

Thibodeau v Air Canada (2014) concerned admitted breaches by Air Canada of the Official Languages Act (OLA).[126] The complainants had been awarded damages against Air Canada pursuant to the OLA's general remedial power despite the limitation on damages liability established by the Convention for the Unification of Certain Rules for International Carriage by Air 1999 (the "Montreal Convention")[127] as implemented by the Carriage by Air Act.[128] Justice Cromwell for the majority of the Supreme Court of Canada agreed with the Federal Court of Appeal that damages were not available. As he put it, the "general remedial power under the *OLA* to award appropriate and just remedies cannot – and should not – be read as authorizing Canadian courts to depart from Canada's international legal obligations under the *Montreal Convention*."[129] While the appellants contended that any conflict between the OLA and the treaty as implemented in federal law should be resolved in favour of the former, Cromwell J found no conflict to resolve, as section 77(4) of the OLA empowers the Federal Court to "grant such remedy as it considers appropriate and just in the circumstances," and an award of damages in breach of Canada's obligations under the Montreal Convention is not appropriate and just.[130] The learned judge explained:

> The appellants' position in effect is that Parliament, through s. 77(4), intended that courts should be able to grant damages even though doing so would be in violation of Canada's international undertakings as incorporated into federal statute law. This proposition runs afoul of the principle of interpretation that Parliament is presumed not to intend to legislate in breach of Canada's international law obligations. . . .
>
> I find it impossible to discern any such intent in the broad and general language of s. 77(4). Instead, this provision should be understood as having been enacted into an existing legal framework which includes statutory limits, procedural requirements and a background of general legal principles – including Canada's international undertakings incorporated into Canadian statute law

126 RSC 1985, c 31 (4th Supp).
127 2242 UNTS 350.
128 RSC 1985, c C-26.
129 *Thibodeau*, above note 1 at para 6.
130 *Ibid* at paras 89, 90, 110.

> – which guide the court in deciding what remedy is "appropriate and just".[131]

Justice Cromwell concluded that there is "no hint in the text, scheme or purpose of the *OLA* that the brief, broad, general and highly discretionary provision in s. 77(4) was intended to permit courts to make orders in breach of Canada's international undertakings which have been incorporated into federal law."[132]

In *B010 v Canada (Citizenship and Immigration)* (2015), five asylum seekers were declared inadmissible on the ground that they had participated in people smuggling contrary to section 37(1)(b) of the IRPA. The question was whether that provision was properly interpreted as rendering inadmissible anyone who assists another to enter the country irregularly, or whether instead its application was limited to those who assist asylum seekers for a financial or other material benefit. Chief Justice McLachlin for the unanimous Supreme Court of Canada concluded that the provision did not make inadmissible to Canada asylum seekers who give mutual assistance to other asylum seekers, nor to persons who act for humanitarian purposes. The chief justice reached that result through an extensive statutory interpretation exercise according to the modern rule of statutory interpretation. After considering the words of the provision in their ordinary and grammatical sense, and its statutory context (including the fact that it was "enacted in anticipation of Canada's obligations under" the Palermo Convention),[133] the learned chief justice turned to the provision's international context, saying,

> This Court has previously explained that the values and principles of customary and conventional international law form part of the context in which Canadian laws are enacted: *R. v. Hape*, 2007 SCC 26, [2007] 2 S.C.R. 292, at para. 53. This follows from the fact that to interpret a Canadian law in a way that conflicts with Canada's international obligations risks incursion by the courts in the executive's conduct of foreign affairs and censure under international law. The contextual significance of international law is all the more clear

---

131 *Ibid* at paras 113–14.

132 *Ibid* at para 117.

133 *B010*, above note 1 at para 43; United Nations Convention against Transnational Organized Crime 2000 (the "Palermo Convention") 2225 UNTS 209.

> where the provision to be construed "has been enacted with a view towards implementing international obligations": *National Corn Growers Assn. v. Canada (Import Tribunal)*, [1990] 2 S.C.R. 1324, at p. 1371. That is the case with the *IRPA*, the refugee protection aspects of which serve principally to discharge Canada's obligations under the 1951 *Convention relating to the Status of Refugees*, 189 U.N.T.S. 150, and its 1967 *Protocol relating to the Status of Refugees*, 606 U.N.T.S. 267 (together the "Refugee Convention"), but also, as explained below, Canada's obligations under the *Smuggling Protocol*.
>
> In keeping with the international context in which Canadian legislation is enacted, this Court has repeatedly endorsed and applied the interpretive presumption that legislation conforms with the state's international obligations. . . . This interpretive presumption is not peculiar to Canada. It is a feature of legal interpretation around the world. See generally A. Nollkaemper, *National Courts and the International Rule of Law* (2011), at ch. 7.
>
> These principles, derived from the case law, direct us to relevant international instruments at the context stage of statutory interpretation. Furthermore, two interpretive provisions from s. 3 of the *IRPA* make Parliament's presumed intent to conform to Canada's international obligations explicit. Section 3(2)(b) expressly identifies one of the statute's objectives as "to fulfil Canada's international legal obligations with respect to refugees and affirm Canada's commitment to international efforts to provide assistance to those in need of resettlement". Similarly, s. 3(3)(f) instructs courts to construe and apply the *IRPA* in a manner that "complies with international human rights instruments to which Canada is signatory" (see *de Guzman v. Canada (Minister of Citizenship and Immigration)*, 2005 FCA 436, [2006] 3 F.C.R. 655, at paras. 82-83 and 87). There can be no doubt that the Refugee Convention is such an instrument, building as it does on the right of persons to seek and to enjoy asylum from persecution in other countries as set out in art. 14 of the *Universal Declaration of Human Rights*, G.A. Res. 217 A (III), U.N. Doc. A/810, at 71 (1948).[134]

The chief justice went on to examine at length the Palmero Convention, the Refugee Convention, and related international instruments to which Canada is a party. Those instruments together

134 *B010*, above note 1 at paras 47–9.

indicated that "people who are not themselves members of criminal organizations, who do not act in knowing furtherance of a criminal aim of such organizations, or who do not organize, abet or counsel serious crimes involving such organizations, do not fall within s. 37(1)(b)."[135]

The companion case to *B010* was *R v Appulonappa* (2015). The appellants were alleged to be the organizers and crew of a human smuggling expedition. They were charged under section 117 of the IRPA of organizing, inducing, aiding, or abetting people coming into Canada in contravention of that Act. The appellants brought a pre-trial challenge to the constitutionality of section 117 on the ground that it criminalized not only people smuggling but also the acts of humanitarian workers, family members, and other asylum seekers, contrary to section 7 of the Charter. Invoking the presumption of conformity with international law and the international legal analysis in *B010*, McLachlin CJ for the Supreme Court of Canada held that Canada's international obligations "shed light on the parliamentary purpose behind s. 117," and that those instruments are not directed at the conduct of asylum seekers helping each other, family members helping asylum seekers, or humanitarians.[136] Adopting "an interpretation which harmonizes obligations in the international instruments to which Canada is a party in a way that avoids conflict and gives expression to each of the various commitments," the chief justice concluded that the purpose of section 117 was "to permit the robust fight against people smuggling in the context of organized crime," thus excluding conduct that "amounts solely to humanitarian, mutual or family aid."[137] While section 117 exceeded its purpose by catching people not intended by Parliament, the section 7 breach could be remedied by reading it down.

In *Office of the Children's Lawyer v Balev* (2018), the Supreme Court of Canada considered the interpretation of Ontario legislation implementing the Hague Child Abduction Convention.[138] The majority invoked the presumption of conformity with international law, while the dissent took no issue with that approach but disagreed with the major-

135 *Ibid* at para 66; see also paras 60–5.

136 *Appulonappa*, above note 62 at paras 40–3.

137 *Ibid* at para 45.

138 Convention on the Civil Aspects of International Child Abduction 1980, [1983] Can TS no 35.

ity's view of the international position.[139] This case – particularly its adoption of the "principle of harmonization" – is considered at length in Chapter 8.[140]

Canada (Minister of Citizenship and Immigration) v Vavilov (2019) was the extraordinary story of a man born in Toronto who, at the age of 16, learned that his parents were not (as he had always believed) Canadians but Russians, and Russian spies at that. After attempting unsuccessfully to renew his Canadian passport, Mr. Vavilov (né Foley) obtained a citizenship certificate – only to be informed that it had been issued in error. The registrar of citizenship cancelled Vavilov's citizenship on the ground that, under section 3(2)(a) of the Citizenship Act,[141] children born in Canada are not Canadian citizens if their parents were employees of a foreign government and not citizens or permanent residents. Since Vavilov's parents were Russian spies, they were (in the registrar's view) Russian government employees such that the general Canadian rule of acquisition of nationality *jus soli*, given effect by section 3(1)(a) of the Act, did not apply.

The majority of the Supreme Court of Canada concluded that the registrar's interpretation of the Act was unreasonable in various respects. These included the registrar's failure to consider the relevant provisions of the Citizenship Act in the rest of their statutory context, being the Foreign Missions and International Organizations Act[142] and the two treaties it implements.[143] After a consideration of the law of diplomatic and consular privileges and immunities and the acquisition of nationality under customary and conventional international law, the majority observed:

> It is well established that domestic legislation is presumed to comply with Canada's international obligations, and that it must be interpreted in a manner that reflects the principles of customary and conventional international law. . . . Yet the analyst did not refer to the

---

139 *Balev*, above note 11 at paras 31 ("Since the purpose of that section is to implement the underlying convention, this Court must adopt an interpretation consistent with Canada's obligations under it").

140 See Chapter 8, Section 8.2(b).

141 RSC 1985, c C-29.

142 SC 1991, c 41.

143 Vienna Convention on Diplomatic Relations 1961, [1966] Can TS no 29; Vienna Convention on Consular Relations 1963, [1974] Can TS no 25.

> relevant international law, did not inquire into Parliament's purpose in enacting s. 3(2) and did not respond to Mr. Vavilov's submissions on this issue. Nor did she advance any alternate explanation for why Parliament would craft such a provision in the first place. In the face of compelling submissions that the underlying rationale of s. 3(2) was to implement a narrow exception to a general rule in a manner that was consistent with established principles of international law, the analyst and the Registrar chose a different interpretation without offering any reasoned explanation for doing so.[144]

Clearly the majority regarded the registrar's failure to consider the international law context of section 3(2)(a) of the Citizenship Act as deeply problematic. Whether that failure alone would have been enough to justify judicial intervention on a reasonableness standard is less certain. But *Vavilov* seems consistent with other authorities in which administrative decision makers who disregard relevant international legal considerations and fail to apply the presumption of conformity have seen their decisions set aside.

In *Society of Composers, Authors and Music Publishers of Canada v Entertainment Software Association* (2022), the court was asked to interpret an amendment to the Copyright Act[145] that expanded the notion of communication of a work to the public by telecommunication to include making it available for download or streaming. The amendment was introduced by the Copyright Modernization Act,[146] a law which, according to the explanatory memorandum tabled by the Government in the House of Commons, was "developed with a view to implementing the rights and protections of the WIPO Copyright Treaty, thereby putting Canada in a position to ratify."[147] Justice Rowe affirmed that, "Where the text permits, legislation should be interpreted so as to comply with Canada's treaty obligations, in accordance with the presumption of conformity."[148] He continued:

> The presumption of conformity is an aid to interpretation. The task remains to give effect to legislative intent. The separation of powers

144 *Vavilov*, above note 1 at para 182; see also para 114.
145 RSC 1985, c C-42.
146 SC 2012, c 20.
147 *Entertainment Software*, above note 62 at para 49.
148 *Ibid* at para 46.

> requires that courts give effect to a statute that demonstrates legislative intent not to comply with treaty obligations: *Hape*, at para. 53. Negotiation, signing, and ratification of treaties are acts of the executive. Once ratified, treaties do not automatically become part of domestic law; rather, they are given effect through domestic legislation. . . .
>
> Accordingly, while a treaty can be highly relevant to statutory interpretation, it cannot overwhelm clear legislative intent. The court's task is to interpret what the legislature (federally and provincially) has enacted and not subordinate this to what the federal executive has agreed to internationally. It is always the domestic statute that governs because "[i]nternational law cannot be used to support an interpretation that is not permitted by the words of the statute": *Kazemi Estate v. Islamic Republic of Iran*, 2014 SCC 62, [2014] 3 S.C.R. 176, at para. 60.[149]

All of which is, with respect, perfectly sound. Having set out these principles, Rowe J went on to conclude that Parliament intended to meet Canada's treaty obligations by means of the amendments, and proceeded to interpret them in a fashion that, in his view, achieved compliance with the WIPO Copyright Treaty 1996[150] while also being consistent with the text, context, and purpose of the Copyright Act.

(c) The presumption in other jurisdictions

A survey of the presumption of conformity in other jurisdictions is beyond the scope of this work. It is worth noting, however, that the presumption has found expression in other Commonwealth jurisdictions,[151]

149 *Ibid* at paras 47–8.

150 [2014] Can TS no 20.

151 In Australian law, the presumption was expressed by Dixon J in *Polites v Commonwealth* (1945), 70 CLR 60 at 67 (HCA) as follows: "It is a rule of construction that unless a contrary intention appears, general words occurring in a statute are to be read subject to the established rules of international law and not as intended to apply to persons or subjects which, according to those rules, a national law of the kind in question ought not to include." See also *Barcelo v Electrolytic Zinc Company of Australasia* (1932), 48 CLR 391 at 423–4 (HCA), and K Ryan, ed, *International Law in Australia*, 2d ed (North Ryde, NSW: Law Book Company, 1984) at 81–2. In New Zealand, the presumption was enunciated in *Tavita v Minister of Immigration*, [1994] 2 NZLR 257 (NZCA) [*Tavita*]. Cooke P (as he then was), for the court, expressed his dissatisfaction with an argument that the minister was entitled to ignore New Zealand's treaty commitments, saying (at 266), "That is an unattractive argument, apparently implying that New Zealand's adherence to the international instruments has been at least partly

in American law,[152] and in other states.[153] As McLachlin CJ once observed, "This interpretive presumption is not peculiar to Canada. It is a feature of legal interpretation around the world."[154]

5.4 The presumption and particular sources of international law

The presumption of conformity with international law applies in respect of both customary and conventional international law.

(a) The presumption and custom

We will see in Chapter 6 that the common law gives direct effect to customary international law where doing so is not precluded by a conflicting statute. This process is known as "incorporation" or "adoption." But it can also be seen as the application of the presumption of conformity

---

window-dressing." In the Caribbean, the Eastern Caribbean Court of Appeal observed in *Spence and Hughes v The Queen*, [2001] ECSC J0402-1 at para 37 that, while the legislature enjoyed sovereign power to violate international law, "it is also well settled law that domestic provisions whether of the Constitution or statute law should as far as possible be interpreted so as to conform to the state's obligations under international law." The decision was upheld on appeal to the Privy Council: [2002] UKPC 12.

152 In US law, the presumption of conformity is known as the Charming Betsy doctrine, after Marshall CJ's statement in *Murray v The Schooner "Charming Betsy"* (1804), 6 US (2 Cranch) 64 at 118 that "an act of Congress ought never to be construed to violate the law of nations if any other possible construction remains." Similarly, in *The "Exchange,"* above note 48 at 146, Marshall CJ, referring to the "implication" that foreign warships in friendly ports enjoy immunity from that country's jurisdiction, observed, "Without doubt, the sovereign of the place is capable of destroying this implication. He may claim and exercise jurisdiction either by employing force, or by subjecting such vessels to the ordinary tribunals. . . . Those general statutory provisions . . . which are descriptive of the ordinary jurisdiction . . . ought not, in the opinion of this Court, to be so construed as to give them jurisdiction in a case, in which the sovereign power has impliedly consented to waive its jurisdiction."

153 See, e.g., H Matusda, "International Law in Japanese Courts" in C Bradley, ed, *The Oxford Handbook of Comparative Foreign Relations Law* (Oxford University Press, 2019) at 543–4; F Casolari, "Giving Indirect Effect to International Law within the EU Legal Order: the Doctrine of Consistent Interpretation" in E Cannizzaro et al, eds, *International Law as the Law of the European Union* (Brill Nijhoff, 2012) at 395–415; A Nollkaemper, *National Courts and the International Rule of Law* (Oxford: Oxford University Press, 2011) at ch 7.

154 *B010*, above note 1 at para 48.

with customary international law to the common law. It is clearer, however, to distinguish the two doctrines.

The incorporation of customary international law by the common law means that the presumption of conformity with customary international law is identical to another established rule of statutory construction: namely, that statutes do not intend to amend or abolish the common law.[155] As Macdonald admirably explains, "Just as, in England, statutes are presumed not to be intended to violate long-standing common law traditions, so too they are presumed not to violate another branch of the common law, international law."[156]

Where the international law in question is customary and the domestic law in question is a statute or regulation, the presumption (unless rebutted) requires that the enactment be read to conform with the custom. Several of the English and Canadian cases reviewed in this chapter involved the interpretation of statutes in the light of customary international law.[157] In *Bouzari v Islamic Republic of Iran*, Goudge JA for the Court of Appeal for Ontario expressly affirmed (albeit in *obiter*) that "so far as possible, courts should interpret domestic legislation consistently with . . . [those] obligations" and that "The same is true where Canada's obligations arise as a matter of customary international law."[158] The Supreme Court of Canada said likewise in *R v Hape*.[159]

---

155 R Sullivan, *The Construction of Statutes*, 7th ed (LexisNexis Canada, 2022) at 531–2. In *Rawluck v Rawluck*, [1990] 1 SCR 70 at 90, Cory J observed, "It is trite but true to state that as a general rule a legislature is presumed not to depart from prevailing law 'without expressing its intentions to do so with irresistible clearness' (*Goodyear Tire & Rubber Co. of Canada v T. Eaton* [1956] SCR 610 at 614)." Note that the phrase "irresistible clearness" is the same employed by Maxwell in describing what is required to rebut the presumption of conformity with international law.

156 R St J Macdonald, "The Relationship Between Domestic Law and International Law in Canada" in R St J Macdonald et al, eds, *Canadian Perspectives on International Law and Organization* (Toronto: University of Toronto Press, 1974) at 99.

157 See, for example, *Le Louis*, above note 18; *The Zollverein*, above note 24; *The Annapolis*, above note 25; *The Ship "North" v The King* (1906), 37 SCR 385; *Re Foreign Legations*, above note 46; *Spraytech*, above note 62.

158 (2004) 71 OR (3d) 675 (Ont CA) at paras 64–5.

159 *Hape*, above note 1 at para 54. See also *B010*, above note 1 at para 48, where the court spoke simply of "the interpretive presumption that legislation conforms with the state's international obligations."

(b) The presumption and treaties

Every time Canada ratifies a treaty it effectively declares to its treaty partners and to the international community generally that its domestic law is consistent with that treaty. For our courts to find otherwise, in a trial or on appeal, runs contrary to the government's own careful assessment of Canadian law upon ratification of the treaty[160] and may place Canada in default of its international obligations under the treaty. Typically, Canadian courts that have made such a finding have justified themselves by resort to the undoubted sovereignty of our legislatures to violate international law. Yet courts must beware of vindicating that notion of sovereignty in cases where the legislature itself has not purported to exercise it.

The presumption of conformity applies to all treaties, whatever their subject matter, for the international law requirements of good faith and *pacta sunt servanda* apply equally to all treaties. The notion of a hierarchy of treaties, with some being more binding than others, is anathema to international law just as the proposition that some statutes are more binding than others is anathema to domestic law. With treaties, as with statutes, the degree of censure arising from breach will vary from treaty to treaty but the fact of censure is constant. The presumption of conformity must therefore apply to all treaties, without distinction. Furthermore, for a court to sit in judgment of which treaties are presumptively respected by our legislatures and which are not would come harrowingly close to judicial review of executive treaty acts, contrary to the orthodoxy (still largely prevalent today) that the Crown's foreign affairs prerogative is not reviewable in His Majesty's courts.[161]

---

160 On governmental review of domestic law prior to treaty ratification in the human rights context, see E Eid & H Hamboyan, "Implementation by Canada of its International Human Rights Treaty Obligations: Making Sense Out of the Nonsensical" in O Fitzgerald, ed, *The Globalized Rule of Law: Relationships Between International and Domestic Law* (Toronto: Irwin Law, 2006) 449 at 455–7.

161 See the discussion in Chapter 3, Section 3.7(c). For these reasons, and given the abundant case law to the contrary, the suggestion by some commentators that the presumption of conformity may only apply in respect of human rights treaties must be rejected. See J Currie, *Public International Law* (Toronto: Irwin Law, 2001) at 226 and Dyzenhaus et al, above note 16 at 32.

(c) The presumption and other international sources

While in principle the presumption of conformity should apply to promote domestic conformity with international law whatever its source, in practice the presumption has so far arisen exclusively from treaty norms and rules of customary international law. The third main source of international law, general principles, is hardly ever invoked before domestic courts, seemingly because "the general principles of law recognized by civilized nations"[162] are already in place in domestic law without the need to refer to whatever international existence they may also have.[163] As for the subsidiary sources of judicial decisions and academic writings, they are not law in themselves but only means for the determination of rules of law. There can therefore be no presumption that a domestic law conforms with a judicial decision or an academic work – though of course the international law described in these sources may be considered in the light of the presumption.

5.5 Particular applications of the presumption

I consider under this heading a variety of particular applications of the presumption of conformity with international law arising from decided cases.

(a) Application to primary and secondary legislation

The presumption of conformity is an interpretive rule applicable both to primary legislation (statutes) and secondary legislation (regulations). Courts have applied the presumption to regulations.[164] The presumption's application to regulations follows logically from its application to the parent statute that creates the regulatory power: If the enabling Act is presumptively consistent with international law, it cannot have empowered anyone acting under it to promulgate secondary legislation

162 Statute of the International Court of Justice 1945, [1945] Can TS no 7, art 38(1)(c).

163 As the court noted in *Re Newfoundland Continental Shelf*, [1984] 1 SCR 86 at 117, the phrase "general principles of law recognized by civilized nations" in art 38(1)(c) of the Statute of the International Court of Justice "refers to principles of municipal law."

164 See, e.g., *Schavernoch v Canada (Foreign Claims Commission)*, [1982] 1 SCR 1092, *International Air Transport Association and others v Canadian Transportation Agency and others*, 2022 FCA 211 at para 87.

in violation of Canada's international obligations. Such a regulation must be *ultra vires* unless it can be shown that the presumption of conformity is rebutted in respect of the enabling Act.

(b) Application to implementing and non-implementing legislation

The presumption of conformity with Canadian treaty obligations applies to all legislation, whether it was historically intended to implement those obligations in domestic law or not. For the presumption to apply both to implemented and unimplemented treaties makes sense, for a primary purpose of the presumption is to prevent breaches of Canada's international obligations. A treaty commitment is no less binding on Canada internationally for being unimplemented in Canadian law. Canada's treaty partners make no distinction between implemented and unimplemented treaties, and, therefore, courts applying the presumption should not do so either. The application of the presumption to implementing and non-implementing legislation is also consistent with the Supreme Court of Canada's treatment of the presumption as a contextual consideration in the modern approach to statutory interpretation, and its depiction of the presumption as a rule of judicial policy.

As we have seen, Maxwell's formulation of the presumption was that "*every* statute is to be interpreted and applied, as far as its language admits, as not to be inconsistent with the comity of nations or with the established rules of international law."[165] This position was adopted by the English Court of Appeal in *Bloxam v Favre* (1883),[166] in which the court approved Maxwell's statement. Similarly, in *Salomon v Customs and Excise Commissioners* (1967), Lord Denning observed, "Our statute does not in terms incorporate the convention, nor refer to it. But that does not matter. We can look at it."[167] Lord Justice Scarman (as he then was) stated in *Ahmad v ILEA* (1978),

> it is no longer possible to argue that because the international treaty obligations of the United Kingdom do not become law unless enacted by Parliament our courts pay no regard to our international

165 Maxwell, above note 18 at 122 (emphasis added).
166 *Bloxam*, above note 28 at 107.
167 *Salomon*, above note 32 at 144.

> obligations. They pay very serious regard to them: in particular, they will interpret statutory language and apply common law principles, wherever possible, so as to reach a conclusion consistent with our international obligations. . . .[168]

One commentator finds support for this approach in no less a figure than A.V. Dicey, whose account of the presumption of conformity included no "restriction of the presumption's applicability to implementing limitation."[169]

The presumption's application to non-implementing legislation has not been the subject of much express consideration in Canada. But the position is nevertheless clear from descriptions of the presumption by the Supreme Court of Canada that pointedly decline to limit its application to international obligations to which express statutory effect has been given in domestic law.[170] In *Hape*, for instance, LeBel J describes the presumption as being one of conformity with international law generally (not just implemented international norms), refers to judicial avoidance of "constructions of domestic law pursuant to which the state would be in violation of its international obligations" (not just those implemented by legislative action), approves Sullivan and Driedger's description of the presumption as one of compliance with "Canada's obligations as a signatory of international treaties" (without reference to their implementation status), and also approves those authors' description of the presumption as concerning the values and principles of international law (again without distinguishing implemented international obligations from non-implemented obligations).[171]

There are some Canadian authorities invoking the presumption in respect of non-implemented treaties. In *Arrow River & Tributaries Slide*

---

168 *Ahmad*, above note 32 at 48.

169 M Hunt, *Using Human Rights Law in English Courts* (Oxford: Oxford University Press, 1998) [Hunt] at 23, citing A Dicey, *Introduction to the Study of the Law of the Constitution*, 10th ed (London: Macmillan, 1960) at 62–3.

170 Professor Sullivan's view was that the presumption of conformity "applies to all legislation – federal, provincial and territorial, both statutes and subordinate legislation – regardless of whether it is implementing legislation": R Sullivan, *The Construction of Statutes*, 7th ed (LexisNexis Canada, 2022) at 560. Professor Schabas also supports the application of the presumption to non-implementing legislation, citing *Zingre*, above note 1: W Schabas, "Twenty-Five Years of Public International Law at the Supreme Court of Canada" (2000) 79 *Canadian Bar Review* 174 at 183.

171 *Hape*, above note 1 at para 53.

& Boom Co Ltd v Pigeon Timber Co Ltd (1932), Riddell JA for the court held that the unimplemented Webster-Ashburton Treaty 1842[172] was "binding in honour upon her Majesty's successor, his present Majesty" and that

> Consequently, the Sovereign will not be considered as enacting anything that will conflict with his plain duty, unless the language employed in the statute is perfectly clear and explicit, admitting of no other interpretation. . . . The King cannot be thought of as violating his agreement with the other contracting Power; and, if the legislation can fairly be read in such a way as to reject any imputation of breaking faith, it must be so read.[173]

In *Re Mitchell and the Queen* (1983), Linden J held that the (not expressly implemented) International Covenant on Civil and Political Rights 1966 "may . . . be used to assist a court to interpret ambiguous provisions of a domestic statute, notwithstanding the fact that the Covenant has not been formally incorporated into the law of Canada, provided that the domestic statute does not contain express provisions contrary to or inconsistent with the Covenant."[174] Similarly, Evans JA in *Rahaman v Canada (Minister of Citizenship and Immigration)* observed, "Nowadays, there is no doubt that, even when not incorporated by Act of Parliament into Canadian law, international norms are part of the context within which domestic statutes are to be interpreted." The learned judge went on to consider a variety of international instruments and authorities that were not alleged to be implemented by the statute at issue in that case.[175]

In *Thibodeau v Air Canada* (2014), Cromwell J applied the presumption of conformity with international law to reject an interpretation of section 77(4) of the Official Languages Act that would authorize awards of damages in violation of the Montreal Convention. That treaty is implemented in federal law by the Carriage by Air Act rather than by the Official Languages Act, yet Cromwell J applied the presumption in respect of the latter enactment, observing that section 77(4) of the Act "should be understood as having been enacted into an existing legal

172 Above note 41.
173 *Arrow River* SCAD, above note 8 at 579.
174 (1983) 42 OR (2d) 481 (Ont HCJ) at 493.
175 2002 FCA 89 at para 35; see also paras 39–50.

framework which includes statutory limits, procedural requirements and a background of general legal principles – including Canada's international undertakings incorporated into Canadian statute."[176]

In *B010 v Canada (Citizenship and Immigration)* (2015), McLachlin CJ observed that Canadian law is interpreted in its international context and that the contextual significance of international law is "all the more clear" where the provision to be construed is implementing legislation – the implication being that the same interpretive approach applies even when the law in question is not implementing legislation. Similarly, McLachlin CJ spoke broadly of "the interpretive presumption that legislation conforms with the state's international obligations" without restricting that presumption to implementing legislation.[177]

(c) Application to prerogative instruments

Post Office v Estuary Radio (1968) is authority that the presumption of conformity is applicable to instruments made under the royal prerogative.[178] Canadian courts have had occasion to consider international legal issues under the Canadian Passport Order (a prerogative instrument)[179] without (to my knowledge) expressly applying the presumption. One reason for applying the presumption to prerogative instruments is that doing so avoids interference with the Crown's conduct of external affairs.[180]

(d) Application to the common law

In considering the presumption of conformity's application to the common law, a clear distinction should be drawn between conventional and customary international law.

Where the international law is conventional and the domestic law is a rule of the common law, the orthodoxy is that the treaty *per se* has no effect on the common law but must be implemented by statute. Thus Megarry VC observed that where Parliament has

176 *Thibodeau*, above note 1 at para 114; see also paras 110–13.

177 *B010*, above note 1 at paras 47–8.

178 *Estuary Radio*, above note 32 at 757 ("there is a presumption that the Crown did not intend to break an international treaty").

179 SI/81-86. See, e.g., *Veffer v Canada (Minister of Foreign Affairs)*, 2007 FCA 247.

180 See, e.g., *Al-Ghamdi v Canada (Foreign Affairs and International Trade)*, 2007 FC 559 at para 76.

refrained from implementing a treaty, the court will not find it easy "to lay down new rules of common law or equity that will carry out the Crown's treaty obligations, or . . . discover for the first time that such rules have always existed."[181] To do otherwise would be inconsistent with the implementation requirement and the constitutional concerns that inform it.[182] Despite these considerations, there is some English and Commonwealth support for developing the common law in the light of the state's treaty obligations.[183] The Canadian position appears to be more in line with Megarry VC's hesitation to bring judge-made law in line with the Crown's exercise of the foreign affairs prerogative.[184]

Where the international law in question is customary in nature, the common law will give effect to the custom – if pertinent to domestic law and not excluded by a conflicting statute – by incorporation.[185] As previously noted, there is a sense in which incorporation can be viewed as an application of the presumption of conformity with customary international law to the common law, but that is not how the case law has approached the matter and it is best to distinguish the incorporation doctrine from the presumption of conformity.

(e) Application to the Charter

A modified version of the presumption of conformity has been adopted by the Supreme Court of Canada as a rule of Charter interpretation. The interpretation of the Charter in the light of international law is considered in Chapter 11.

(f) Application in respect of international law and comity

The presumption of conformity has frequently been expressed as applicable in respect of both the requirements of international law and the

---

181 *Malone v Metropolitan Police Commissioner*, [1979] Ch 344 (Eng CA) at 379.

182 See Chapter 4, Section 4.2(a).

183 E.g., *Tavita*, above note 151 at 266, *Lyons*, above note 32 at para 27 (endorsing "a strong presumption in favour of interpreting English law (whether common law or statute) in a way which does not place the United Kingdom in breach of an international obligation"). See generally Fatima, above note 32 at 342–9.

184 The suggestion to the contrary in *Jose Pereira E Hijos, S.A. v Canada (Attorney General)*, [1997] 2 FC 84 at para 20 must be regarded as an outlier.

185 See Chapter 6.

demands of international comity.[186] Comity "refers to informal acts performed and rules observed by states in their mutual relations out of politeness, convenience and goodwill, rather than strict legal obligation."[187] As ever, this is a rebuttable presumption; international comity considerations cannot restrain the sovereignty of Parliament or the provincial legislatures any more than international legal considerations can.[188]

(g) Application to enactments that pre-date the international obligation

The application of the presumption of conformity in cases where the relevant legislation was enacted prior to the assumption of the international obligation (usually a treaty) raises a deeper question about the nature of the presumption. Is the presumption a conclusion about the legislature's likely historical intent, or is it a free-standing rule of judicial interpretation? If the former, then it is nonsensical to apply the presumption to a statute enacted before the state acquired the relevant treaty obligation. This is especially true where a treaty did not exist at the time of enactment. However, if the presumption of conformity operates independently of legislative intent (except, of course, where that intent is clearly to violate international law), then the presumption applies to all legislation, regardless of its enactment date.

In *Hape*, the Supreme Court of Canada described the presumption of conformity as "based on the rule of judicial policy that, as a matter of law, courts will strive to avoid constructions of domestic law pursuant to which the state would be in violation of its international obligations, unless the wording of the statute clearly compels that result."[189] This affirmation of a judicial policy of avoiding internationally unlawful in-

---

186 *Canadian Pacific Railway Co v The Western Union Telegraph Co* (1889), 17 SCR 151 at 165–8; *Daniels*, above note 56 at 541; *Libman v The Queen*, [1985] 2 SCR 178 at 195; *R v Cook*, [1998] 2 SCR 597 at para 129; *Schreiber v Canada (Attorney General)*, 2002 SCC 62 [*Schreiber*] at para 50; *Society of Composers, Authors and Music Publishers of Canada v Canadian Assn of Internet Providers*, 2004 SCC 45 at paras 55, 150; *Hape*, above note 1 at para 54; see also paras 47–52, 56.

187 *Hape*, above note 1 at para 47. See the discussion of comity in Chapter 3, Section 3.7(b).

188 See, e.g., *British Columbia Electric Railway Co Ltd v The King*, [1946] AC 527 (PC) at 542, approving Rand J's rejection of the submission that an Act was *ultra vires* for being contrary to international comity.

189 *Hape*, above note 1 at para 53. See the discussion of the nature of the presumption of conformity at Section 5.2, above.

terpretations of domestic law strongly suggests that chronology (that is, the fact that the domestic law at issues pre-dates the relevant international obligation) will not be determinative of whether to interpret the domestic law in conformity with the international requirement. But the relevance of chronology to the application of the presumption remains an interesting question to consider.

An extensive – but not wholly satisfying – discussion of the matter is found in *In re Californian Fig Syrup Company's Trade-Mark.*[190] In March 1883, the International Convention for the Protection of Industrial Property 1883[191] was signed by several European states, excluding Great Britain. In August 1883, the UK enacted a statute, seemingly along lines similar to the Convention, whereby foreigners could apply for the protection of their trademarks in Great Britain subject to certain administrative requirements. In March 1884, the UK government acceded to the Convention. In February 1888, the Californian Fig Syrup Company applied to register their trademark in the UK under the provisions of the UK Act and the Convention. The comptroller-general denied registration on the ground that the Act required that such applications be made within four months of registration in their home state; a requirement not found in the Convention. The company argued that the Act should be read "in such a way as to make it harmonize with the provisions of the Convention."[192] Justice Stirling rejected the argument. He said:

> Certainly, according to my construction of the Act, the Act does not afford the means of carrying out the article, and it will be for her Majesty's Government to consider, and seeing the Attorney-General here, I have no doubt that they will consider, what legislative steps ought to be taken to give effect to that article, if necessary. But with that I have nothing to do. I have simply to consider this question; dealing as I am with, and being bound by, a statute of this realm, whether I can give it a different interpretation from that which I should otherwise give it, simply because at the date of the passing of the Act, the Convention had been entered into between certain foreign states, and it was within the bounds of possibility that her

190 (1888) 40 Ch D 620 [*Californian Fig*].
191 74 British and Foreign State Papers 44.
192 *Californian Fig*, above note 190 at 624.

> Majesty might afterwards accede to it, and several years afterward, in point of fact, her Majesty did accede to it. I am of the opinion that I cannot do so.[193]

California Fig is a difficult case. At one extreme there is the unsatisfying result of denying the company registration of its trademark and forcing the legislature to amend an Act that, it would seem, was brought forward in contemplation of recent international activity on the subject. Justice Stirling exaggerates in saying that it was merely "within the bounds of possibility that her Majesty might afterwards accede to [the Convention], and several years afterward, in point of fact, her Majesty did accede to it," for the UK acceded only nine months after passing the Act. At the other extreme, however, is the proposition that the presumption of conformity can in effect "disapply" a statutory requirement that applications be brought within four months of registration in the applicant's home country. This would be a strained construction (indeed, a very strained construction) of the statute. Adding to the difficulty is the chronology of events: while it is arguable that the presumption of conformity should not apply to statutes enacted prior to binding treaty action by the Crown, on the facts of this case it seems entirely possible, and even likely, that Parliament had the recently established Convention in its contemplation. But if that is so, why did it enact a four-month limitation not found in the treaty?

In *Ahmad v ILEA*, Scarman LJ (as he then was) held, in dissent, that section 30 of the Education Act 1944[194] was to be interpreted in the light of international human rights obligations subsequently assumed by the UK: "we have to construe and apply section 30 not against the background of the law and society of 1944 but in a multi-racial society which has accepted international obligations and enacted statutes designed to eliminate discrimination on grounds of race, religion, colour or sex."[195] This approach was implicitly rejected by Lord Lowry in *R v Brown*, who, in discussing the applicability of article 8 of the European Convention on Human Rights, observed that the Convention had not been implemented and that there was no "post-Convention" legislation to be construed according to the presumption.[196] Yet in *Saad & Ors v Sec-*

---

193 *Ibid* at 627–8.
194 (UK) 7 & 8 George 6, c 31.
195 *Ahmad*, above note 32 at 48.
196 [1994] 1 AC 212 (HL) at 256.

retary of State for the Home Department, the Court of Appeal held that a 1993 Act should be construed, so far as possible, on the basis that the United Kingdom intended to comply with its international obligations under a 1967 treaty.[197]

In Canadian law, the majority in *Baker v Canada (Minister of Citizenship and Immigration)* effectively applied the presumption to section 114(2) of the Immigration Act in a case where the treaty, the Convention on the Rights of the Child 1989, was ratified by Canada in 1992 while the Act was enacted in 1977.[198] Justice L'Heureux-Dubé, writing for the majority, did not acknowledge the chronology problem explicitly. Yet she may have done so implicitly by relying on a non-binding, but much earlier, text, namely the preamble to the United Nations Declaration of the Rights of the Child 1959.[199] Similarly, in *Canadian Foundation for Children, Youth and the Law v Attorney General in Right of Canada*, McLachlin CJ for the majority interpreted section 43 of the Criminal Code, a provision first enacted in 1892,[200] as presumptively consistent with human rights treaties ratified by Canada in the late twentieth century.

No definitive rule about chronology and the presumption of conformity arises from these cases, though the Supreme Court of Canada's decisions in *Baker, Canadian Foundation, and Hape* strongly suggest that chronology will not be determinative. The judges in *California Fig* and *Brown* proceeded from the notion that the presumption should be understood strictly as an inference as to the legislature's historical intention. The conception of the judicial role suggested by this approach is the traditional one whereby it is the duty of the court to carry out the legislature's intent. In contrast, the approaches of Scarman LJ, L'Heureux-Dubé J, and McLachlin CJ suggest that the presumption of conformity is a rule of judicial interpretation that "*every* statute is to be interpreted and applied, as far as its language admits, as not to be inconsistent with the comity of nations or the established rules of international law."[201] This approach sets legislative intent partly aside: It does not go so far as to ignore a clear legislative intent to violate

197 [2001] EWCA Civ 2008 at para 72.
198 Immigration Act, above note 88.
199 Declaration of the Rights of the Child, UNGA Res 1386 (XIV), 20 November 1959.
200 SC 1892, c 29.
201 *Bloxam*, above note 28 at 107 (emphasis added).

international law, for legislatures remain sovereign, but it does ignore the absence of legislative intent where that intent was lacking only because the treaty in question was not yet in force.

A proper balancing of the principles underlying Canadian reception law gives this answer to the chronology question: Courts should apply the presumption of conformity without regard to chronology in every case where they can do so without harming the principle of self-government. That principle imposes this limit on the application of the presumption: It must not be applied so as to liberate the executive from the implementation requirement. Legislation that pre-dates newly acquired treaty obligations may be read as consistent with those obligations so long as such an interpretation does not relieve the government of its need to seek implementation of those aspects of the obligation that require significant changes to domestic law. The implementation requirement may be the most important assertion of the principle of self-government in the reception system. So long as treaty-making remains a prerogative of the Crown, treaties cannot be self-executing in Canadian law consistently with self-government, for the Crown is not a fitting source of law. It lacks the features of representation, deliberation, and consent that are the criteria of a self-governing lawmaker. To eliminate the implementation requirement, even if only with respect to treaties touching on matters that are already the subject of existing legislation, would further bolster the already considerable powers of the federal executive at the expense of democratically elected legislatures. In particular, the federal principle might suffer under too rigorous an application of the presumption of conformity to provincial statutes, given that treaties are concluded at the federal level (albeit with varying levels of provincial participation). So long as the presumption is applied in a manner that does not harm the principle of self-government, there should be no objection to applying it irrespective of chronology.

(h) Application in cases of actual or potential conflict with international law

Though it may seem to go without saying, the presumption of conformity has no application where there exists no actual or potential conflict between the domestic law in question and the state's international obligations.

The phrase "actual or potential conflict" is that of Deschamps J in *Quebec (Commission des droits de la personne et des droits de la jeunesse) v Maksteel Québec Inc*,[202] in which the learned judge found the presumption inapplicable because there was no conflict between the statutory provision and the international instruments relied upon by the appellant. Other courts have, at times, declined to apply the presumption (without disputing the presumption itself) for this reason.[203] Similarly, in *Merck Frosst Canada v Canada*,[204] Cromwell J affirmed the presumption of conformity in principle while rejecting the appellant's proposed reliance on the trade secret provision of article 1711 of the North American Free Trade Agreement 1992,[205] observing that Canada was "not necessarily required to adopt the treaty definition of 'trade secrets' into its access to information law in order to fulfill its treaty obligations. These obligations could be fulfilled in other ways." Unlike in *Maksteel*, where Deschamps J was satisfied there was no conflict between domestic law and the state's international obligations, here Cromwell J was not prepared to go that far but was also not prepared to decide whether there was a lack of compliance or not.

The presumption of conformity will also have no bearing where the international sources invoked by the party seeking to rely on it do not express legal obligations of the state. In *Kazemi Estate v Iran*, LeBel J observed that the presumption of conformity could not be invoked where the international considerations relied upon did not amount

---

202 2003 SCC 68 at para 44. Similarly, Bastarache J observed (at para 73), "While international obligations must undeniably be considered in interpreting national human rights legislation . . . in this case the international instruments cited by the Commission do not support its position since the Quebec scheme is broader than international standards in the matter."

203 See, e.g., *Pianka v The Queen*, [1979] AC 107 (PC) at 123, Lord Wilberforce ("Their Lordships agree with the principle of construction, but are of the opinion that there is no principle of international law . . . which impinges on this situation"); *Rahaman v Minister of Citizenship and Immigration*, 2002 FCA 89 at para 50 (unnecessary to consider whether to apply presumption of conformity because there was no conflict between Canadian and international law on the point). See also *Re Canada Labour Code*, [1992] 2 SCR 50 at para 65, where La Forest J observed that while the North Atlantic Treaty Status of Forces Agreement 1951, [1953] Can TS no 13 "might influence the interpretation" of the Act in question, that possibility was excluded by the provisions of a second treaty, the Agreements Concerning Leased Bases in Newfoundland 1941, [1952] Can TS no 14.

204 2012 SCC 3 at para 117.

205 [1994] Can TS no 2.

to binding international norms.[206] Likewise in *Ktunaxa Nation v British Columbia (Forests, Lands and Natural Resource Operations)*, McLachlin CJ and Rowe J noted that international instruments that are not binding on Canada at international law do not attract the presumption of conformity.[207] In *9174 Québec*, Brown and Rowe JJ noted that case law "tie[s] the presumption of conformity to the language of Canada's international *obligations* or *commitments*."[208]

5.6 The presumption and ambiguity

For much of the twentieth century, English and Canadian courts observed a rule that no regard could be had to treaties (or, presumably, other sources of international law) in interpreting legislation unless the relevant legislative text was somehow ambiguous – that is, it could bear two or more meanings. The ambiguity requirement became a prerequisite for the application of the presumption of conformity with international law. This approach is out of step with earlier authorities that favoured a broad application of the presumption. Contemporary Supreme Court of Canada precedents are strongly against requiring ambiguity before applying the presumption of conformity in the interpretation of a domestic enactment. Those precedents are, with respect, right. The ambiguity requirement as formulated in the twentieth-century authorities results in a weak adherence to the principle of respect for international law without any concomitant strengthening of self-government. Thus, the ambiguity requirement is difficult to justify on the reception system's own terms.

The concept of ambiguity is meant to answer the question of whether the court should apply the presumption of conformity. In older cases, the answer to that question tended to be yes. The prevailing judicial approach was to apply the presumption of conformity to avoid internationally unlawful interpretations of domestic laws unless the legislature unambiguously expressed its intention to act contrary to international law. An illustration is Lord Escher MR in *Colquhoun v Brooks* (1888):

> [T]he English parliament cannot be supposed merely by reason of its having used general words to be intending to do that which is against the comity of nations. It is true that if we came to the conclusion that

206 2014 SCC 62 [*Kazemi Estate*] at para 102.
207 *Ktunaxa*, above note 62 at para 66.
208 *9147-0732 Québec inc*, above note 62 at para 33 (emphasis in original).

> this had been intentionally done we must carry out the law and leave to the government of the country the task of answering objections, but unless that is perfectly clear we ought to limit the words so as to make them reasonable and proper. . . .[209]

Similarly, a leading English statutory interpretation text in the late nineteenth century, Maxwell's *Interpretation of Statutes* (1875), insisted that if Parliament intends to violate international law or comity, "it must express its intention with irresistible clearness, to induce a Court to believe that it entertained it; for if any other construction is possible, it would be adopted, in order to avoid imputing such an intention to the Legislature."[210]

This is not to deny that there are old English authorities insisting on Parliament's power to violate international law and the courts' duty to give effect to such exercises of its sovereignty. There are plenty. An example is *R v Keyn* (*The Franconia*) (1876), where Cockburn CJ affirmed that the international legal rule that domestic laws do not apply extraterritorially

> must be taken subject to this qualification – namely, that if the Legislature of a particular country should think fit by express enactment to render foreigners subject to its law with reference to offences committed beyond the limits of its territory, it would be incumbent on the Courts of such country to give effect to such enactment, leaving it to the State to settle the question of International Law with the Governments of other nations.[211]

Note, however, that even this sentiment is qualified by the necessity for an "express enactment."

Under the Maxwell/*Colquhoun* approach, the court will presume legislative provisions were intended to conform to international law and interpret them accordingly, unless the legislature unambiguously expresses its intention to breach the state's international obligations. While these authorities did not speak in terms of the international context in which laws are made, the starting point is nevertheless an awareness of the international legal order and a commitment to reaching internationally compliant results unless Parliament makes "per-

209 *Colquhoun*, above note 29 at 57–8.
210 Maxwell, above note 18 at 122–3.
211 (1876) 2 Ex D 63 (Eng Ct Crown of Cases Reserved) at 160.

fectly clear" that it means to exercise its undoubted power to legislate contrary to international law. If there was a rule about ambiguity in the old presumption cases, it was this: Apply the presumption of conformity unless the legislature has unambiguously signalled its intent to breach international law.

Sometime in the mid-twentieth century, the role of ambiguity in internationally informed statutory interpretation was reversed. The English courts went from requiring unambiguous words to rebut the presumption of conformity to requiring ambiguous words to permit it. In *Salomon v Customs and Excise Commissioners*,[212] Diplock LJ (as he then was) held that no regard could be had to treaty obligations without first demonstrating ambiguity in the text of the statute. Lord Diplock seems to have abandoned this grammatical ambiguity requirement in *Garland v British Rail Engineering*,[213] though the House of Lords held otherwise in *R v Secretary of State for the Home Department, ex parte Brind*.[214] Lord Bingham of Cornhill affirmed the ambiguity requirement in English law in *R v Lyons*.[215]

It is easy to see how this flip could happen. The claim "A statute that is unambiguously contrary to international law must be followed" resembles the claim "A statute that is unambiguous must be given effect even if it is contrary to international law." The first claim can be confused with the second, and vice versa. But the two claims are in fact different.

The first claim recognizes the constitutional orthodoxy, in Westminster-model states, that legislatures are sovereign to violate international law and implies a judicial "no ambiguity" rule: We (judges) will not interpret domestic laws as contrary to international law unless you (Parliament) make yourself perfectly clear. Under this approach, the international law context of the provision at issue is a relevant interpretive consideration from the outset. The second claim, by contrast, sets up ambiguity as a prerequisite to considering the international law context of Parliament's enactment at all. The judicial interpretive

212 *Salomon*, above note 32.

213 [1983] 2 AC 751 (HL). This was a case in European law, but the same principles arguably apply to international law. See Hunt, above note 169 at 17–21.

214 *Brind*, above note 32. Recent UK cases generally continue to require ambiguity: Fatima, above note 32 at § 9.9, § 9.14.

215 *Lyons*, above note 32 at para 13.

strategy, under the second claim, begins by asking: Is this provision unambiguous? If so, the court must give effect to it whatever the international legal context or consequence. The presumption of conformity is ousted by the provision's lack of ambiguity. Indeed, the presumption can only apply if there is some ambiguity in Parliament's expression that permits the courts to resort to international law as an interpretive consideration.

This new approach – ambiguity as a prerequisite to giving interpretive weight to the international legal context of the provision under scrutiny – flips the older "no ambiguity" rule on its head. The old "no ambiguity" rule is a judicial technique promoting the state's compliance with international law. This new ambiguity requirement, by contrast, is a judicial avoidance technique, an excuse not to comply with international law. International law is a mandatory contextual consideration in the one, and an optional extrinsic interpretive aid in the other.

In more extreme expressions of the ambiguity requirement, domestic courts cannot even look at a relevant international norm (usually found in a treaty) if there is not some ambiguity on the face of the enactment to permit resort to it. In its milder form, courts do not forbid regard for international legal considerations entirely but use the supposed lack of ambiguity on a provision's face to rebut the presumption of conformity very readily. Under the new facial ambiguity requirement, "The terms of the treaty only became relevant to the judicial interpretive task once the court had *first* decided that there was an ambiguity or lack of clarity in the statutory language."[216]

The new facial ambiguity requirement had this big problem: Facial ambiguity is often in the eye of the judicial beholder. If judges want to consider international law, they can usually find some ambiguity to permit it. If they don't, they won't.

The new rule had a deeper problem, too. It was methodologically out of step with prevailing ideas about the construction of laws. Professor Côté's *Interpretation of Legislation in Canada* rejects "the idea that interpretation is legitimate or appropriate only when the text is obscure," saying,

> This idea is based on the view, incorrect, that the meaning of a legal rule is identical to its literal legislative wording. The role of the in-

216 Hunt, above note 169 at 19.

> terpreter is to establish the meaning of rules, not texts, with textual meaning at most the starting point of a process which necessarily takes into account extra-textual elements. The *prima facie* meaning of a text must be construed in the light of the other indicia relevant to interpretation. A competent interpreter asks whether the rule so construed can be reconciled with the other rules and principles of the legal system: Is this meaning consistent with the history of the text? Do the consequences of construing the rule solely in terms of the literal rule justify revisiting the interpretation? and so on.[217]

The proper role of ambiguity in the interpretation of laws in the light of international law came up for decision by the Supreme Court of Canada in *National Corn Growers Assn v Canada (Import Tribunal)*.[218] In the Federal Court of Appeal,[219] Iacobucci CJ (as he then was) had declined to resort to the international agreements at issue, applying the dictum of Estey J in *Schavernoch v Foreign Claims Commission*:

> If one could assert an ambiguity, either patent or latent, in the regulations it might be that a court could find support for making reference to matters external to the regulations in order to interpret its terms. Because, however there is in my view no ambiguity arising from the above-quoted excerpt from these regulations, there is no authority and none was drawn to our attention in argument entitling a court to take recourse either to an underlying international agreement or to textbooks on international law with reference to the negotiation of agreements or to take recourse to reports made to the Government of Canada by persons engaged in the negotiation referred to in the regulations.[220]

Here, Iacobucci CJ held that there was no ambiguity. In dissent, MacGuigan JA quoted approvingly Lord Denning MR's statement in *Salomon v Commissioners of Customs & Excise* that "we ought always to interpret our statutes so as to be in conformity with international law. Our statute does not in terms incorporate the convention, nor refer to it; but that does not matter."[221]

---

217 P-A Côté, S Beaulac, & M Devinat, *The Interpretation of Legislation in Canada*, 4th ed (2009) at 268–9.

218 *National Corn Growers*, above note 1.

219 1989 CanLII 5205 [*National Corn* FCA].

220 [1982] 1 SCR 1092 at 1098.

221 *National Corn* FCA, above note 219 at para 10.

At the Supreme Court of Canada, Iacobucci CJ's decision was reversed. Justice Gonthier for the majority of the court explained *Schavernoch* and re-cast the ambiguity requirement as follows:

> The first comment I wish to make is that I share the appellants' view that in circumstances where the domestic legislation is unclear it is reasonable to examine any underlying international agreement. In interpreting legislation which has been enacted with a view towards implementing international obligations, as is the case here, it is reasonable for a tribunal to examine the domestic law in the context of the relevant agreement to clarify any uncertainty. Indeed where the text of the domestic law lends itself to it, one should also strive to expound an interpretation which is consonant with the relevant international obligations.
>
> Second, and more specifically, it is reasonable to make reference to an international agreement at the very outset of the inquiry to determine if there is any ambiguity, even latent, in the domestic legislation. The Court of Appeal's suggestion that recourse to an international treaty is only available where the provision of the domestic legislation is ambiguous on its face is to be rejected. As I. Brownlie has stated at p. 51 of *Principles of Public International Law* (3rd ed. 1979):
>
>> If the convention may be used on the correct principle that the statute is intended to implement the convention then, it follows, the latter becomes a proper aid to interpretation, and, more especially, may reveal a latent ambiguity in the text of the statute even if this was 'clear in itself'. Moreover, the principle or presumption that the Crown does not intend to break an international treaty must have the corollary that the text of the international instrument is a primary source of meaning or 'interpretation'. The courts have lately accepted the need to refer to the relevant treaty even in the absence of ambiguity in the legislative text when taken in isolation.
>
> In *Schavernoch v. Foreign Claims Commission*, [1982] 1 S.C.R. 1092, this Court had occasion to comment upon the circumstances in which it is proper for the courts to consult an underlying international agreement. Though the language used by Estey J. is perhaps not explicit, I do not understand his remarks to mean that consultation of the treaty is proper only where it appears that the text to be interpreted is ambiguous on its face.... The suggestion that recourse can be had to

> an underlying international agreement where a latent ambiguity can be asserted implies that there is no need to find a patent ambiguity before consultation of the agreement is possible. As a latent ambiguity must arise out of matters external to the text to be interpreted, such an international agreement may be used, as I have just suggested, at the preliminary stage of determining if an ambiguity exists.
>
> . . .
>
> Having found that the rules of statutory interpretation allow consideration of an underlying agreement at the preliminary stage of determining if the domestic legislation contains an ambiguity, I do not hesitate to conclude in this case that the Tribunal did not act unreasonably in consulting the *GATT*. The question that remains, therefore, is whether the Tribunal's interpretation of s. 42 in this case, given the relevant *SIMA* and *GATT* provisions, is unreasonable having regard to all the circumstances.[222]

In short, Gonthier J rejected the notion that consultation of a treaty is proper only where it appears that the text to be interpreted is ambiguous on its face and affirmed that there is no need to find a patent ambiguity before such consultation is possible. Rather, an international agreement may be used at the preliminary stage of determining if an ambiguity exists. Ambiguity is not jettisoned here entirely, but it loses its gatekeeper function. The court cannot safely say whether a provision is ambiguous or not until comparing its plain meaning with its international context, such as an underlying treaty. The court reviews the legislative provisions, reviews the relevant international provisions, and decides upon consideration of both whether there is ambiguity in the legislation to be resolved according to the presumption of conformity with international law.

Five years later, the Supreme Court of Canada dropped ambiguity as a precursor to consideration of international law entirely in *Crown Forest Industries Ltd v Canada*. Notably, it was Iacobucci J, now a member of the Supreme Court of Canada, who affirmed that "a court may refer to extrinsic materials [in this case, international agreements] which form part of the legal context . . . without the need first to find an ambiguity before turning to such materials."[223]

---

222 *National Corn Growers*, above note 1 at 1371–2.

223 [1995] 2 SCR 802 at para 44.

Where Gonthier J had seemed to say that ambiguity was still a consideration but could be found by comparing the domestic provision with its international counterpart, Iacobucci J abandoned it. Like Lord Escher in *Colquhoun* and Maxwell in 1875, the court in *Crown Forest* seems, in retrospect, to be espousing the application of the presumption of conformity in all cases save those where Parliament unambiguously exercises its sovereignty to put Canada in breach of its international obligations. The role of ambiguity has shifted back from "A statute that is unambiguous must be given effect even if it is contrary to international law" to "A statute that is unambiguously contrary to international law must be followed."

Since *Crown Forest*, the Supreme Court of Canada's approach to international law considerations in statutory interpretation has been governed not by ambiguity but by context. International law and the state's obligations under it are contextual considerations in the interpretive exercise, and ambiguity is not part of the inquiry.

Justice Linden of the Federal Court of Appeal recognized this change in the law in *Canada v Seaboard Lumber Sales Co.* (1995), saying,

> It is now established that courts will look to relevant international documents to aid interpretation of implementing legislation from the outset of the investigation, and even absent ambiguity on the face of that legislation. Ambiguity may arise out of the consideration of any manner or variety of contextual factors; it should not be taken as a necessary precondition to looking to those factors.[224]

The Supreme Court has kept to this path ever since. In *Baker* (1999), L'Heureux-Dubé J approved Professor Sullivan's statement that "the legislature is presumed to respect the values and principles enshrined in international law, both customary and conventional" as these "constitute a part of the legal context in which legislation is enacted and read."[225] Eight years later, LeBel J in *R v Hape* (2007) approved this passage from *Sullivan and Driedger on the Construction of Statutes* again, observing that the presumption of conformity has two aspects:

> First, the legislature is presumed to act in compliance with Canada's obligations as a signatory of international treaties and as a mem-

224 [1995] 3 FC 113 at 120.

225 *Baker*, above note 71 at para 70.

> ber of the international community. In deciding between possible interpretations, courts will avoid a construction that would place Canada in breach of those obligations. The second aspect is that the legislature is presumed to comply with the values and principles of customary and conventional international law. Those values and principles form part of the context in which statutes are enacted, and courts will therefore prefer a construction that reflects them.[226]

In *USA v Anekwu* (2009), Charron J for the court found that the language of section 32(2) of the Extradition Act "reveals no ambiguity" and "mandates compliance with domestic rules of evidence in respect of evidence gathered on Canadian soil" yet went on to find that, in the context of its related provisions, section 32(2)'s meaning was less clear and that, in the extradition context, insisting that evidence gathered in Canada comply with the Canadian law of hearsay would create "a barrier to the prompt and efficient discharge of our international obligations."[227] In *B010* (2015), in a discussion headed "International Law as Context: General Relevance," McLachlin CJ repeated *Baker* and *Hape*'s affirmation that "the values and principles of customary and conventional international law form part of the context in which Canadian laws are enacted" and noted that this proposition "follows from the fact that to interpret a Canadian law in a way that conflicts with Canada's international obligations risks incursion by the courts in the executive's conduct of foreign affairs and censure under international law." The chief justice added that courts are directed to "relevant international instruments at the context stage of statutory interpretation" – an admonition she followed later in her reasons.[228]

The contextual approach to treaties, and the rejection of ambiguity as a prerequisite to their consideration in the course of statutory interpretation, were expressly affirmed by Rowe J for the majority of the Supreme Court of Canada in *Society of Composers, Authors and Music Publishers of Canada v Entertainment Software Association* (2022), in the following terms:

> A treaty should be considered when interpreting statutes that purport to implement the treaty, in whole or in part. The treaty is rel-

---

226 *Hape*, above note 1 at para 53.

227 *Anekwu*, above note 62 at paras 13, 14, 30.

228 *B010*, above note 1 at paras 47–8; see also paras 51–66.

> evant at the context stage of the statutory interpretation exercise: *Baker v. Canada (Minister of Citizenship and Immigration)*, [1999] 2 S.C.R. 817, at para. 70; *B010 v. Canada (Citizenship and Immigration)*, 2015 SCC 58, [2015] 3 S.C.R. 704, at para. 49; R. Sullivan, *Sullivan on the Construction of Statutes* (6th ed. 2014), at §18.30.
>
> There is no need to find textual ambiguity in a statute before considering the treaty. The modern approach to statutory interpretation requires interpreting the statute's text in its "entire context". The statute's context includes any relevant international legal obligations: *National Corn Growers Assn. v. Canada (Import Tribunal)*, [1990] 2 S.C.R. 1324, at pp. 1371–72; *Crown Forest Industries Ltd. v. Canada*, [1995] 2 S.C.R. 802, at para. 50; Sullivan, at §18.26.[229]

These Supreme Court precedents establish beyond argument that consideration of relevant international legal instruments is part of the modern approach to statutory interpretation. International law enters the analysis at the contextual stage – without depending on a finding of ambiguity at the textual/ordinary meaning stage. This is, with respect, the correct approach. To limit the judicial consideration of international legal obligations to situations where ambiguity appears on the face of the enactment erodes the principle of respect for international law without advancing in any important way the principle of self-government. The current Supreme Court of Canada approach, by contrast, shows respect for international law without compromising the self-government principle.

Despite the voluminous and binding Supreme Court authority against it, lower courts have continued at times to insist on the ambiguity requirement.[230] In one especially striking case, the Federal Court of Appeal went so far as to cite its own overturned decision in *National Corn Growers* as authority for doing so,[231] despite several other Federal

229 *Entertainment Software*, above note 62 at paras 44–5.

230 See, e.g., *Pfizer Canada Inc v Canada (Attorney General)*, 2003 FCA 138 at paras 20–1; *Islamic Republic of Iran v Hashemi*, 2012 QCCA 1449 at paras 40–1; *Gitxaala Nation v Her Majesty The Queen*, 2015 FCA 73 at para 18; *Lum v Alberta Dental Association*, 2016 ABCA 154 at paras 51–4; *Prophet River First Nation v Canada (Attorney General)*, 2016 FCA 120 at para 12; *NV v Nova Scotia (Community Services)*, 2018 NSSC 5 at paras 27, 34.

231 *Tapambwa v Minister of Citizenship and Immigration*, 2019 FCA 34. The appellants argued that s 112(3)(c) of the IRPA had to be interpreted to permit reconsideration of a prior exclusion finding by a pre-removal risk assessment officer. They contended that the international law obligation of *non-refoulement* required

Court of Appeal authorities having recognized and accepted the Supreme Court's rejection of ambiguity.[232] These cases must be regarded as having been decided *per incuriam*.

5.7 Statutory versions of the presumption

Legislatures sometimes enact provisions that resemble or amount to statutory versions of the presumption of conformity with international law.

Section 3(3)(f) of the IRPA provides:

This Act is to be construed and applied in a manner that . . . (f) complies with international human rights instruments to which Canada is a signatory.	L'interprétation et la mise en oeuvre de la présent loi doivent avoir pour effet . . . (f) de se conformer aux instruments internationaux portant sur les droits de l'homme dont le Canada est signataire.

such an interpretation. Rennie JA for the court rejected this argument, noting the presumption of conformity but adding that Parliamentary sovereignty required an unambiguous legislative provision to be given effect even if contrary to the state's international obligations. For this proposition Rennie JA cited, among others, *National Corn Growers Assn v Canada (Canadian Import Tribunal)*, [1989] 2 FC 517 at 530, where (as noted above) Iacobucci JA invoked the ambiguity requirement to reject consideration of a treaty – only to be overturned by the Supreme Court of Canada on this very point. Shortly after the release of *Tapambwa*, the Federal Court of Appeal followed it on this point in *Nova Tube Inc/Nova Steel Inc v Conares Metal Supply Ltd*, 2019 FCA 52 at paras 58–60, with Laskin JA observing at para 60, "I see no ambiguity that would justify resort to Canada's international obligations." The *Tapambwa* saga became even stranger when, on 31 May 2019, the Federal Court of Appeal issued a correction to *Tapambwa* that replaced the citation to Iacabucci JA in *National Corn Growers* (FCA), above note 219 at para 44, to a citation to Gonthier J in *National Corn Growers*, above note 1 at p 1371 – a wholly non-sensical citation in context – without any amendment of Rennie JA's reasoning. No change was made to *Nova Tube*.

232 See, e.g., *Canada v Seaboard Lumber Sales Co*, [1995] 3 FC 113 at 120; *Najafi v Canada (Public Safety and Emergency Preparedness)*, 2014 FCA 262 at para 61; *Pembina County Water Resource District v Manitoba (Government)*, 2017 FCA 92 at para 46 (in which Nadon JA expressly notes that the Supreme Court of Canada overturned the Federal Court of Appeal on this point in *National Corn Growers*, above note 1).

This provision was considered by the Federal Court of Appeal in *De Guzman v Canada (Minister of Citizenship and Immigration)*.[233] The appellant in that case relied on section 3(3)(f) in challenging the validity of a provision in regulations promulgated under the Act[234] that barred her from sponsoring two of her Filipino children for immigration to Canada because she failed to disclose their existence upon landing in Canada herself eight years earlier. Among her arguments, De Guzman alleged that the regulation was inconsistent with various international human rights instruments protecting family rights and the best interests of children, to which Canada was signatory.

Justice Evans for the court rejected De Guzman's argument that section 3(3)(f) requires international instruments to prevail over inconsistent provisions of the Act or its regulations.[235] Considering the meaning of section 3(3)(f) further, the learned judge reviewed several Supreme Court of Canada judgments on the presumption of conformity as well as certain Federal Court judgments interpreting section 3(3)(f). He noted that the words "shall be construed and applied in a manner that complies with . . ." are mandatory and appear to require that courts accord international human rights instruments more than persuasive or contextual significance in interpreting the Act.[236] He observed that the words "instruments to which Canada is a signatory" comprise some instruments that are binding on Canada in international law and some that are not because they are signed but not yet ratified by Canada, and that section 3(3)(f) requires the court to apply it from the date of Canada's signature whether the instrument is binding yet or not.[237] In respect of instruments signed by Canada but not yet binding, Evans JA expressed the view (in *obiter*) that these should be used only as persuasive and contextual factors in interpreting the Act.[238] For binding instruments, however, Evans JA rejected a persuasive or contextual approach in favour of a stronger stance whereby international

---

233 2005 FCA 436 [*De Guzman*]. The decision was cited approvingly by the Supreme Court of Canada in *B010*, above note 1 at para 49.

234 Immigration and Refugee Protection Regulations, SOR/2002-227, s 117(9)(d).

235 *De Guzman*, above note 233 at paras 54–60.

236 *Ibid* at para 75.

237 *Ibid* at paras 76–7, 85.

238 *Ibid* at paras 88–9. This conclusion seems to run contrary to the plain wording of s 3(3)(f), which appears to require internationally compliant construction and application to all instruments to which Canada is signatory, whether they have becoming binding since signature or not.

human rights instruments are determinative of the meaning of the Act (including its regulations) unless, according to the usual rules of statutory interpretation, this conclusion is impossible.[239] Having laid this groundwork, Evans JA reviewed the international instruments on which De Guzman relied and held that the impugned regulation did not conflict with them and therefore could not be challenged on that basis. Generally speaking, Evans JA's analysis of section 3(3)(f) harmonizes its meaning with the common law jurisprudence on the presumption of conformity. This is an eminently desirable result. To have held otherwise would have created two international law interpretive standards – one for the IRPA, and the ordinary presumption of conformity for all other Canadian laws.

Section 3(3)(f) was also considered by the Supreme Court of Canada in *B010 v Canada (Citizenship and Immigration)*, where McLachlin CJ for the court cited *De Guzman* with approval and noted that the provision, together with section 3(2)(b) of the IRPA, "make Parliament's presumed intent to conform to Canada's international obligations explicit."[240]

Several federal laws implementing trade agreements include what amounts to a statutory version of the presumption of conformity with international law. Section 3 of the Canada–Peru Free Trade Agreement Implementation Act provides:

> For greater certainty, this Act and any federal law that implements a provision of the Agreement or a related agreement or fulfils an obligation of the Government of Canada under the Agreement or a related agreement is to be interpreted in a manner consistent with the Agreement or related agreement, as the case may be.[241]

The identical provision, or nearly, is found in trade agreement implementing laws going back to the 1990s.[242]

---

239 *Ibid* at paras 82–3, 87.

240 *B010*, above note 1 at at para 49. See also *Appulonappa*, above note 62 at para 40.

241 Canada–Peru Free Trade Agreement Implementation Act, SC 2009, c 16, s 3.

242 Each time as s 3. See North American Free Trade Agreement Implementation Act, SC 1993, c 44, s 3; Canada–Israel Free Trade Agreement Implementation Act, SC 1996, s 3; Canada–Chile Free Trade Agreement Implementation Act, SC 1997, c 14, s 3; Canada–Costa Rica Free Trade Agreement Implementation Act, SC 2001 c 28, s 3; Canada–EFTA Free Trade Agreement Implementation Act, SC 2009, c 6, s 3; Canada–Colombia Free Trade Agreement Implementation Act, SC 2010, c 4, s 3; Canada–Panama Economic Growth and Prosperity Act, SC 2012, c 26, s 3; Canada–Jordan Economic Growth and Prosperity Act, SC 2012,

The Supreme Court of Canada considered a statutory version of the presumption of conformity in *Canada (Transportation Safety Board) v Carroll-Byrne*. Section 16(a) of the Canadian Transportation Accident Investigation and Safety Board Act[243] provided that the Transportation Safety Board of Canada "shall take all reasonable measures to ensure" that its investigation procedures and practices "are compatible with . . . any international agreements or conventions to which Canada is a party." Justice Kasirer for the court held that this provision "underscores Parliament's intention that the Act conform to Canada's international obligations,"[244] notably under Annex 13 of the Chicago Convention on International Civil Aviation 1944.[245]

Legislatures are free to enact provisions requiring or promoting conformity with international norms other than treaties. Section 8.1(3) of British Columbia's Interpretation Act[246] provides that every Act and regulation must be construed as being consistent with the United Nations Declaration on the Rights of Indigenous Peoples.[247] This provision must be read together with section 2(1), which provides that every provision of the Act applies to every enactment unless a contrary intention appears. In other words, the presumption of consistency between BC laws and the UN Declaration is rebuttable.

5.8 The presumption and indirect treaty effects

As noted in Chapter 4 and considered at length in Chapter 7, treaties require legislative implementation to take direct effect in Canadian law.

---

c 18, s 3; Canada–Korea Economic Growth and Prosperity Act, SC 2014, c 28, s 3; Canada–Honduras Economic Growth and Prosperity Act, SC 2014, c 14, s 3; Canada–European Union Comprehensive Economic and Trade Agreement Implementation Act, SC 2017, c 6, s 3; Canada–Ukraine Free Trade Agreement Implementation Act, SC 2017, c 8, s 3; Comprehensive and Progressive Agreement for Trans-Pacific Partnership Implementation Act, RSC 2018, c 23, s 3; Canada–United States–Mexico Agreement Implementation Act, SC 2020, c 1, s 3; Canada–United Kingdom Trade Continuity Agreement Implementation Act, SC 2021, c 1, s 3.

243 SC 1989, c 3.

244 2022 SCC 48 at para 54.

245 [1944] Can TS no 36.

246 RSBC 1996, c 238.

247 UNGA Res 61/295 (Annex), UNGAOR, 61st Sess, Supp No 49, Vol III, UN Doc A/61/49 (2008) 15.

But what is meant by the qualification "direct effect"? Why should we not simply say (as authorities often do)[248] that a treaty has no effect in domestic law unless implemented by legislation? Why did Pigeon J in *Capital Cities Communications Inc v Canadian Radio-television Commission* describe it (rightly, in my view) as "an oversimplification to say that treaties are of no legal effect unless implemented by legislation"?[249] The answer, in short, is the presumption of conformity with international law. Despite the constitutional objection to self-executing treaties, the presumption of conformity effectively confers some legal weight to the prerogative act of incurring a treaty obligation.

Consider the application of the presumption in the case of a statute enacted after the federal government's ratification of a treaty. A court, confronted with two possible interpretations of the statute, one of which is inconsistent with the treaty, rules out the inconsistent interpretation by applying the presumption. The presumption's portrayal of legislative intent here may be entirely accurate: The legislature may have had the treaty in its actual contemplation and may truly have sought to legislate consistently with it. It is also possible that the legislature did not have the treaty in its actual contemplation, but that it nonetheless had no intent to violate the treaty. In this case, the portrayal of legislative intent demanded by the presumption is slightly further removed from reality: The legislature did not actually intend to legislate consistently with Canada's international obligations, but it did not intend to violate them, either. It simply did not consider the matter. To apply the presumption in both these cases is entirely appropriate. Yet it would be wrong to say that the presumption's application here does not in some sense change the law, for it rules out otherwise viable constructions of the law on the ground that they are inconsistent with a treaty. Thus, the Crown's act of ratifying the treaty is given a certain legal consequence by the application of the presumption. To this extent, minor and indirect though it is, the presumption may be

---

248 But see the more nuanced (and accurate) account in Canada, *Common Core Document Forming Part of the Reports of States Parties: Canada* (2019) UN Doc HRI/CORE/CAN/2019 at para 135: "Treaties, including international human rights instruments, adhered to by Canada are not self-executing and require legislative implementation to be directly applicable in Canadian law. Therefore, the treaties are not subject to direct enforcement in Canadian courts."

249 *Capital Cities*, above note 66 at 188.

said to set aside the implementation requirement and violate the constitutional rule that the Crown is not a source of law.

Now consider the application of the presumption of conformity to a statute enacted before the ratification of a treaty. Once again, a court confronted with various possible interpretations of the Act rules out those that are inconsistent with the supervening treaty. In this situation, the portrayal of legislative intent demanded by the presumption is wholly fictitious: The legislature did not have the treaty in its contemplation because the state was not bound by it at the time of enactment. The application of the presumption here is not based on historical legislative intent but on a policy of the courts to interpret domestic law consistently, where possible, with international law. Here, the argument that the presumption is a violation of the rule against executive legislation and a flouting of the implementation requirement is strong, for the legal effect of the Act in question is being determined by the court's reference to the Crown's subsequent act of treaty ratification. To apply the presumption here results in conferring upon the executive some power unilaterally to make, amend, or at least affect law.

This analysis reveals a conceptual weakness in the statements, found not only in English and Canadian case law but also in this book, that treaties are not self-executing and the Crown is not a source of law. These statements are revealed as simplifications of the effect of treaties, and particularly unimplemented treaties, in domestic law. For most purposes these simplifications are useful and accurate depictions of the law. But they are still simplifications. In more difficult cases, such as the application of the presumption to grants of statutory discretion (considered in Chapter 9), courts may respond by refusing to apply the presumption out of respect for the implementation requirement and the separation of powers that informs it.

Courts and commentators may justify the presumption of conformity as consistent with the rule against executive legislation by saying that it involves no application of treaties in domestic law but serves only as a guide to legislative intent. On those occasions where courts have refused to apply the presumption and insisted that the treaty at issue be implemented by legislation before it can have the desired effect, they declare that the Crown is not a source of law, treaties are not self-executing, and the presumption involves no importation of international law into the domestic field. Yet the critique given above reveals that every application of the presumption involves some breach, however small, of the constitutional prohibition on executive legislation. How then are we to make sense of refusals by courts to apply the presumption in some cases?

The answer, I suggest, is that cases in which courts apply the presumption and cases in which they reject it are not different in nature but only in degree. There is a sense in which all applications of the presumption of conformity amount to recognition of a certain power in the Crown to legislate without Parliament in violation of the implementation requirement. However, these violations of the rule against executive legislation are so minor that we do not complain of them. Courts and commentators have not decried the presumption of conformity as executive legislation, even though it can amount to that, because the legislative effect of applying the presumption is usually minimal. It is only when to apply the presumption would grant significant legal consequence to the Crown's act of ratification that courts and commentators resort to the constitutional prohibition of executive legislation.

But what constitutes a significant legal consequence? How do courts know when to insist upon implementation and when to apply the presumption? The test is not as simple as, "Does this application of the presumption set aside the implementation requirement?" for, as the analysis above shows, the presumption always does that to some extent. I suggest that the problem may be expressed in terms of the principle of self-government: Does this application of the presumption of conformity, consistently with the principle of respect for international law, offend the competing principle of self-government? Where the presumption furthers respect for international law without detriment to self-government, as is most often the case, the courts apply it and do not characterize its application as a breach of the rule against executive legislation. Where, however, the presumption furthers respect for international law at the expense of self-government, the courts insist upon self-government by refusing to apply the presumption and requiring legislative implementation of the treaty.

5.9 Rebutting the presumption

The presumption of conformity is rebuttable. This follows from the constitutional principle, considered in Chapter 4, that Canadian legislatures are competent to violate international law.

What, then, is required to rebut the presumption of conformity with international law? In 1875, Maxwell observed that if a legislature intends to violate international law or comity, "it must express its intention with irresistible clearness, to induce a Court to believe that it entertained it; for if any other construction is possible, it would be adopted, in order to avoid imputing such an intention to the Legislature."[250] The standard to meet in modern-day Canadian law appears to be similarly demanding. In *R v Hape*, the majority held that the presumption is rebuttable where a statute "demonstrates an unequivocal legislative intent to default on an international obligation."[251] In *Németh v Canada (Justice)*, Cromwell J for the court observed, "The presumption that legislation implements Canada's international obligations is rebuttable. If the provisions are unambiguous, they must be given effect."[252] In *Kazemi Estate v Iran*, the majority required "clear words" to rebut the presumption, noting that "International law cannot be used to support an interpretation that is not permitted by the words of the statute."[253]

In the absence of such clear, unequivocal, unambiguous expression of legislative intent to violate international law, the presumption against such a conclusion is not rebutted. The rule, it seems, is that courts will not adopt a legislative interpretation that puts the state in breach of its international legal obligations unless confident that the legislature intended that internationally unlawful result, or at least expressed itself in such terms that the courts are left with no other interpretive option.

As discussed in Section 5.6, above, the Supreme Court of Canada has firmly rejected the requirement that textual ambiguity be found in an enactment before the interpreter may have resort to its international context. While that ambiguity requirement is no longer part of our law, a different "no ambiguity requirement" does seem to exist:

---

250 Maxwell, above note 18 at 122–3.

251 *Hape*, above note 1 at para 53. See also *Tracy v Iran (Information and Security)*, 2017 ONCA 549 at paras 43, 45.

252 *Németh*, above note 1 at para 35, citing *Schreiber*, above note 186 at para 50. See also *Daniels*, above note 56 at 541.

253 *Kazemi Estate*, above note 206 at para 60. In that case, the majority found no conflict between s 3(1) of the State Immunity Act, RSC 1985, c S-18 and Canada's international obligations but affirmed (at para 63) that "the plain language of s. 3(1) read alongside the purpose of the Act eliminates the possibility of relying on the common law or international law to find new exceptions to state immunity."

Courts will decline to interpret a statute as contrary to international law unless it is unambiguously so. In *Daniels v White and the Queen*, Hall J observed:

> It is argued that this is a case for the application of the rule of construction that Parliament is not presumed to legislate in breach of a treaty or in any manner inconsistent with the comity of nations and the established rules of international law. The rule does not, of course, come into operation if a statute is unambiguous for in that event its provisions must be followed even if they are contrary to the established rules of international law.[254]

Justice Hall proceeded to cite similar language from Viscount Simonds in *Collco Dealings v Inland Revenue Commissioners*: "My Lords, the language that I have used is taken from a passage at p. 148 of the 10th edition of 'Maxwell on the Interpretation of Statutes' which ends with the sentence: 'But if the statute is unambiguous, its provisions must be followed even if they are contrary to international law.'"[255] These *dicta* are properly understood as affirmations of the sovereignty of our legislatures to violate international law. They hinge on the finding that a statute is unambiguous, for only unambiguous statutes will rebut the presumption of conformity and allow an internationally unlawful meaning to be accorded to the provision.

That said, a distinction may meaningfully be drawn between a judicial determination that a given legislative provision places the state in contravention of its international obligations and a judicial determination that a given provision does not itself serve to discharge the state's international obligations – but some other provision does. The *Németh* case illustrates this subtle but important point. There, Cromwell J found the presumption of conformity inapplicable to section 115 of the IRPA, which "does not address removal by extradition and so its clear meaning must be given effect,"[256] while also rejecting the notion that this interpretation of section 115 involved a breach of Canada's *non-refoulement* obligations under international refugee law. While the IRPA was the "main legislative vehicle for implementing Canada's international refugee obligations," it was not the only one; section 44 of the

254 *Daniels*, above note 56 at 539.

255 *Collco*, above note 33 at 19.

256 *Németh*, above note 1 at para 35.

Extradition Act also served that function.[257] In short, Cromwell J declined to interpret section 115 in the light of Canada's *non-refoulement* obligations but, in doing so, did not accept that Parliament had intended by section 115 to violate those obligations; rather, Parliament ensured that Canada discharged those obligations through another legislative means. As the learned judge noted, "the IRPA does not and was not intended to implement Canada's international obligations against *refoulement* in the context of expulsion by extradition. That role . . . is assigned to s. 44" of the Extradition Act.[258] The *Németh* case is a wise caution against distorting the legislative scheme adopted by Parliament to discharge the state's international obligations by applying internationally informed interpretations of legislative provisions where they are not needed to ensure internationally conforming results.

257 *Németh*, above note 1 at paras 21, 35, 58.
258 *Ibid* at para 41.

6 The incorporation of custom

By the doctrine of incorporation, rules of customary international law can be recognized and enforced by the judiciary as domestic law without the need for legislative implementation. Eighteenth- and nineteenth-century English authorities frequently depicted the law of nations – meaning customary rather than conventional international law – as forming part of the common law. The Supreme Court of Canada has affirmed the common law's adoption of customary international law in this way, while also recognizing certain limits on the doctrine.

The principle of respect for international law is given its freest reign in this area of the reception system. The incorporation doctrine invites courts not only to adjudicate consistently with international law but to adopt international custom as the rules upon which their adjudication is based. For the reception system so wholly to embrace custom by means of the common law is not only in keeping with the principle of respect for international law but is also consistent with the principle of self-government. For the common law is always susceptible to abolition or curtailment by statute. To permit custom to be incorporated by the common law is to subject it to the exercise of self-government through legislative action. Here is an instance of the reception system balancing its principles: Respect for international law is made the law's default position but subject to rejection or amendment in keeping with self-government.

6.1 Case law on the incorporation doctrine

The incorporation of custom is a theme much less frequently considered by Canadian courts than the other leading features of the reception system, namely the treaty implementation requirement, the presumption of conformity with international law, legislative sovereignty to violate international law, and perhaps even the judicial notice of international norms. The predictable result is that the doctrine's operation, and even its nature, are less developed than they might be. But the doctrine's continued existence in Canadian law is clear.

(a) The English inheritance

The applicability of customary international law in English law was established in the eighteenth century. In *Buvot v Barbuit* (1737), Lord Talbot is said to have declared that "the law of nations, to its full extent, was part of the law of England."[1] Nearly 30 years later, in *Triquet v Bath* (1764),[2] Lord Mansfield CJ (who appeared as counsel before Lord Talbot in *Buvot*) affirmed and relied upon Lord Talbot's *dictum*. Appearing as counsel before Lord Mansfield was William Blackstone, who explained in his *Commentaries* (1765) that "the law of nations . . . is here adopted in it's [*sic*] full extent by the common law, and is held to be a part of the law of the land."[3] Shortly thereafter, in *Heathfield v Chilton* (1767), Lord Mansfield declared that the law of nations is "part of the common law of England" and that "the law of nations will be carried as far in England, as any where."[4]

In *Novello v Toogood* (1823), Abbot CJ held that the Act of Parliament before him "must . . . be construed according to the common law, of which the law of nations must be deemed a part."[5] In *De Wutz v Hendricks* (1824), Best CJ described the law of nations as "in all cases . . . adopted into the municipal code of every civilized country."[6] The unity of customary international law and the common law was affirmed by Lord Langdale MR in *Duke of Brunswick v The King of Hanover* (1844), who declared that "the law of nations . . . when ascertained, is to be deemed part of the common law of England."[7] By 1861, this doctrine

---

1 (1737) Cas T Talb 281, 25 ER 777.

2 (1764) 3 Burr 1478 at 1480–81, 97 ER 936 at 937–8.

3 Sir William Blackstone, *Commentaries on the Laws of England*, vol 4 (Chicago: University of Chicago Press: 1979) [Blackstone] at 67.

4 (1767) 4 Burr 2015 [*Heathfield*] at 2016, 98 ER 50 at 50.

5 *Novello v Toogood* (1823), 1 B & C 554 at 562, 107 ER 204 at 207.

6 *De Wutz v Hendricks* (1824), 2 Bing 314 at 315–16, 130 ER 326 at 326.

7 *Duke of Brunswick v The King of Hanover* (1844), 6 Beav 1 [*Duke of Brunswick*] at 45, 49 ER 724 at 741.

was so well established that Sir John Stuart VC observed that it was supported by "unquestioned authority."[8]

The clarity of the incorporation doctrine in English law was undermined somewhat in the difficult case of *R v Keyn (The Franconia)*.[9] The defendant was charged with manslaughter in the death of a Briton following a collision at sea. He argued that England lacked jurisdiction because at common law the realm ends at low-water mark and all else is high seas. At customary international law, however, the adjacent waters in which the crime took place were recognized as within British territory. The majority held for the defendant. Lord Cockburn CJ rejected the argument that rules of customary international law could entitle or oblige the court to exercise jurisdiction. Nor would unanimous state practice suffice to make such a law binding on England. Only an Act of Parliament would do to indicate the country's assent to be bound by a new international law. For a court to apply such a law without an Act of Parliament would be to usurp the province of the legislature. "The assent of nations is doubtless sufficient to give the power of parliamentary legislation in a matter otherwise within the sphere of international law; but it would be powerless to confer without such legislation a jurisdiction beyond and unknown to the law, such as that now insisted on, a jurisdiction over foreigners in foreign ships on a portion of the high seas."[10] I suggest later that the result in *Keyn* can be explained within the doctrine of incorporation as turning on the distinction between permissive and mandatory customary international law.[11]

The place of customary international law in domestic law arose again in *West Rand Central Gold Mining v The King*.[12] This was a petition of right brought by an English company for recovery from the UK government of an amount of gold taken from it by officials of the South African Republic prior to that state's conquest and annexation by the UK in the Boer War. The suppliants' argument was in three parts: (1) by international law, the sovereign of a conquering state is liable for the obligations of the conquered; (2) international law forms part of the

8 *Emperor of Austria v Day and Kossuth* (1861), 2 Giff 628 [*Emperor of Austria*] at 678, 66 ER 263 at 282.

9 (1876) 2 Ex D 63 (Eng Ct Crown of Cases Reserved) [*Keyn*].

10 *Ibid* at 202–3.

11 See Section 6.3(b), below, in this chapter.

12 [1905] 2 KB 391 (Eng Div Ct).

law of England; and (3) rights and obligations formerly binding on the conquered state must be protected and can be enforced by the courts of the conquering state. On the second proposition, Lord Alverstone CJ observed:

> It is quite true that whatever has received the common consent of civilized nations must have received the assent of our country, and that to which we have assented along with other nations in general may properly be called international law, and as such will be acknowledged and applied by our municipal tribunals when legitimate occasion arises for those tribunals to decide questions to which doctrines of international law may be relevant. But any doctrine so invoked must be one really accepted as binding between nations, and the international law sought to be applied must, like anything else, be proved by satisfactory evidence, which must shew either that the particular proposition put forward has been recognised and acted upon by our own country, or that it is of such a nature, and has been so widely and generally accepted, that it can hardly be supposed that any civilized State would repudiate it. The mere opinions of jurists, however eminent or learned, that it ought to be so recognized, are not in themselves sufficient. They must have received the express sanction of international agreement or gradually have grown to be part of international law by their frequent practical recognition in dealings between various nations. . . . But the expressions used by Lord Mansfield [in *Triquet* and *Heathfield*] . . . ought not to be construed so as to include as part of the law of England opinions of text-writers upon a question as to which there is no evidence that Great Britain has ever assented, and a fortiori if they are contrary to the principles of her laws as declared by her Courts.[13]

Yet Lord Alverstone CJ took issue with the suppliants' first and third contentions. He was not satisfied that international law imposed the obligation contended for, nor was he satisfied that such an obligation (if it did exist) could be enforced by private individuals in domestic courts by way of a petition of right.

In *Chung Chi Cheung v The King*,[14] the appellant was a British subject who had killed another British subject while on board a vessel in

13 *Ibid* at 406–8.
14 [1939] AC 160 (PC) [*Chung*].

the service of the Chinese government. At the time of the offence, the vessel was in the territorial waters of Hong Kong (then a British colony). The appellant was tried by the local British court and sentenced to death. He appealed to the Privy Council, arguing that the local court lacked jurisdiction because the crime occurred on a Chinese ship and China had not waived its right to immunity. The appeal was dismissed on the ground that the immunities accorded to foreign vessels in accordance with international law can be waived by the state to which the vessel belongs, and such a waiver had occurred here. As a preface to his consideration of the immunities of public ships at international law, Lord Atkin declared:

> It must always be remembered that, so far, at any rate, as the Courts of this country are concerned, international law has no validity save in so far as its principles are accepted and adopted by our own domestic law. There is no external power that imposes its rules upon our own code of substantive law or procedure. The Courts acknowledge the existence of a body of rules which nations accept amongst themselves. On any judicial issue they seek to ascertain what the relevant rule is, and, having found it, they will treat it as incorporated into the domestic law, so far as it is not inconsistent with rules enacted by statutes or finally declared by their tribunals.[15]

This passage has been read by some (notably Lord Denning in *Trendtex Trading Corp v Bank of Nigeria*[16]) as a refutation of the incorporation doctrine. Lord Atkin's emphasis on the necessity of accepting and adopting international law can been read as advocating an implementation requirement for customary international law to match that which exists for treaty law. His lordship depicts international law as an imposing external power. Yet Lord Atkin goes on in *Chung* to affirm that rules of customary international law, once discovered, will be incorporated into domestic law subject to existing statute law and finally declared decisions of courts. The argument that ultimately prevailed – that the Chinese government had consented to the British court's jurisdiction – gave effect to the international legal rule as Lord Atkin understood it, namely that the immunities of public vessels may be waived by the nation to which the vessel belongs. In my view, Lord

15 *Ibid* at 167–8.
16 [1977] 1 QB 529 (Eng CA) [*Trendtex*].

Atkin's comments are not a refutation of the incorporation doctrine. Indeed, his declaration that there is no external power imposing its rules upon us is not merely consistent with incorporation, it is the essence of the doctrine. For incorporation operates by automatically assimilating international custom with domestic law, thus internalizing and thereby legitimizing what would otherwise be a coercive external force. As for the acceptance requirement, Lord Atkin makes clear that it is satisfied by judicial incorporation of customary rules into common law jurisprudence, subject always to Parliament's power to alter or abolish the common law by statute.

Any lingering doubt that incorporation is the rule in English law was put to rest in *Trendtex Trading*. The plaintiff company sued the Central Bank of Nigeria for repudiation and breach of contract. The bank had contracted with the company to buy a large quantity of cement to be used to build government barracks. On application by the bank, the plaintiff's action was set aside and further proceedings stayed on the ground that the bank, being a department of the state of Nigeria, was immune from suit in English courts. The Court of Appeal allowed the appeal, finding first that the bank was not in fact an emanation of the state and therefore could not claim immunity, and second that even if the bank were such an emanation it could not claim immunity due to the development, in customary international law, of a restrictive theory of state immunity. Under this theory, states may claim immunity from proceedings in foreign courts where the state acts at issue were of a governmental nature (*jure imperii*) but not where they were of a commercial nature (*jure gestionis*). Though this restrictive theory of state immunity was contrary to binding House of Lords authority pre-dating the development of the theory in international law, the majority of the Court of Appeal held that they could nevertheless incorporate the restrictive theory into English law. In their reasons, Lord Denning MR and Stephenson LJ both identified *Keyn* as the principal departure from the ancient, pro-incorporation authorities, though the latter judge suggested that the difference between *Keyn* and the other authorities is not so great.[17] All three judges held incorporation to be the correct approach, though Shaw LJ felt constrained by precedent not to incorporate the restrictive theory.

---

17 *Ibid* at 568.

Trendtex Trading was not appealed. The House of Lords' first opportunity to consider the matter came in the *I° Congreso del Partido* case.[18] A Chilean company contracted with a Cuban state enterprise to buy sugar. The sugar was dispatched to Chile in two shipments on the vessels *Playa Larga* and *Marble Islands*. Shortly thereafter, the Pinochet regime came to power by force in Chile. Cuba responded by breaking off diplomatic and trading relations. The *Playa Larga* had reached Chile by that point and discharged part of her cargo, while the *Marble Islands* was still at sea. Both ships abandoned their charters. About two years later, the plaintiffs brought an action *in rem* in the UK against the owners of a third vessel, the *Congreso*, claiming for losses occasioned by the disruption of the earlier transactions. The Republic of Cuba moved to set aside the actions on the basis that it owned the *Congreso* and enjoyed state immunity. The motions judge granted this relief. The House of Lords allowed the ensuing appeals. Lord Wilberforce began by explaining that, as these events took place prior to the UK's enactment of the restrictive theory of state immunity in the State Immunity Act 1978, "the law in question is the common law."[19] He noted that England continued to adhere to an absolute doctrine of state immunity long after other states had adopted the more restrictive doctrine but that two landmark 1977 cases – *Trendtex Trading* and the Privy Council decision in *The Philippine Admiral*[20] – had adopted the restrictive doctrine. Lord Wilberforce affirmed the latter decision "unhesitatingly . . . as part of English law." As for *Trendtex Trading*, his lordship hesitated somewhat because the case was not appealed to the House of Lords but nevertheless referred to Lord Denning MR's "admired judgment" and concluded that, on the basis of both cases, the restrictive doctrine of state immunity should be applied.[21] Strictly this may have been *obiter* for, as Lord Wilberforce noted, the application of the restrictive doctrine was not disputed by either party, the real issue being "where the immunity begins and ends."[22] The rest of Lord Wilberforce's decision considered that question, endeavouring to do so "in conformity with accepted international standards."[23] The other judgments in the case agreed with

18 *I° Congreso del Partido*, [1983] 1 AC 244 (HL) [*I° Congreso*].

19 *Ibid* at 257.

20 [1977] AC 373 (PC) [*The Philippine Admiral*].

21 *I° Congreso*, above note 18 at 261.

22 *Ibid* at 262.

23 *Ibid* at 265.

Lord Wilberforce's adoption of the restrictive theory of state immunity but differed, to some extent, on its application to the facts. While none of the judgments in *I° Congreso* expressly affirms the incorporation doctrine, there is seemingly no other way to explain how the English rule of absolute state immunity changed than by incorporation of the restrictive approach established in customary international law and incorporated by the Court of Appeal in *Trendtex*.

(b) Canadian authorities

The incorporation doctrine was approved and applied by the Supreme Court of Canada in the early twentieth century, neglected in the latter part of that century, and reaffirmed in the early part of the twenty-first.

Early Canadian admiralty cases implicitly support the incorporation doctrine by looking to and applying the customary international law of the sea as the law of Canada.[24] Explicit support for the doctrine can be found in *The Ship "North" v The King* (1906),[25] in which Davies J declared that "the right of hot pursuit . . . being part of the law of nations was properly judicially taken notice of *and acted upon* by the learned judge."[26] Similarly, the Exchequer Court in *Dunbar and Sullivan Dredging Co v The Ship Milwaukee*[27] approved Lord Mansfield's classic statement of the incorporation doctrine, in *Triquet v Bath*, that the law of nations is part of the law of England.

Significant though these early cases are, the leading early Canadian authority on the incorporation of customary international law in Canada is the judgment of Duff CJ in *Re Foreign Legations* (1943).[28] The case concerned the susceptibility of foreign and Commonwealth legations to municipal taxation. Concerning the Commonwealth lega-

24 *The Queen v The Ship "Grace"*, [1894] 4 Ex CR 283; *The Ship "North" v The King* (1905), 11 Ex CR 141; *The King v The Schooner "John J. Fallon"* (1917), 55 SCR 348. For the "implicit adoption" approach taken by early Canadian case law, see R St J Macdonald, "The Relationship Between Domestic Law and International Law in Canada" in R St J Macdonald et al, eds, *Canadian Perspectives on International Law and Organization* (Toronto: University of Toronto Press, 1974) [Macdonald] at 99–101.

25 (1906) 37 SCR 385.

26 *Ibid* at 394 (emphasis added).

27 (1907) 11 Ex CR 179 at 188.

28 *Re Powers of the Corporation of the City of Ottawa and the Corporation of the Village of Rockliffe Park to Levy Rates on Foreign Legations and High Commissioners' Residences*, [1943] SCR 209 [*Re Foreign Legations*].

tions (namely the UK and Australia), the matter was settled easily on the ground that Crown property was exempted from assessment under an Ontario statute. As for the foreign legations, the matter fell to be decided according to the customary international law of sovereign immunity.

The principal judgment in the case, that of Duff CJ, has been taken by some as an ambiguous or less-than-wholehearted avowal of the doctrine of incorporation.[29] Yet Duff CJ's judgment affirmed incorporation expressly and by implication. The chief justice began[30] by quoting from Lord Atkin's statement in *Chung*[31] and also Lord Dunedin's observation in *Mortensen v Peters* that

> there is no such thing as a standard of international law extraneous to the domestic law of a kingdom, to which appeal may be made. International law, so far as this Court is concerned, is the body of doctrine regarding the international rights and duties of states which has been adopted and made part of the law of Scotland.[32]

These comments are rightly understood not as rejections of incorporation but as a description of the operation of that doctrine. That this is so is suggested by the terms and methodology of Duff CJ's judgment. Having quoted from these authorities, the chief justice went on to observe that there are "some general principles" of state immunity that have been "accepted and adopted" in Ontario "as part of the law of nations."[33] These principles were not to be found in Ontario statutes; the chief justice's judgment in this matter was based entirely on customary international law. Therefore, Duff CJ's finding that some general principles of state immunity form part of Ontario law was an application of

---

29 See S Toope, "Keynote Address: Canada and International Law" in *The Impact of International Law on the Practice of Law in Canada: Proceedings of the 27th Annual Conference of the Canadian Council on International Law, Ottawa October 15–17, 1998* (The Hague: Kluwer Law International, 1999) 33 [Toope, "Keynote Address"] at 37; A Bayefsky, *International Human Rights Law: Use in Canadian Charter of Rights and Freedoms Litigation* (Toronto: Butterworths, 1992) [Bayefsky] at 6; Macdonald, above note 24 at 101; J Brunnée & S Toope, "A Hesitant Embrace: The Application of International Law by Canadian Courts" (2002) 40 *Canadian Yearbook of International Law* 3 at 42–3.

30 *Re Foreign Legations*, above note 28 at 213–14.

31 *Chung*, above note 14 at 167–8.

32 *Mortensen v Peters* (1906), 8 F (JC) 93 (Scot HCJ) at 101.

33 *Re Foreign Legations*, above note 28 at 214.

the doctrine of incorporation. Furthermore, it was a recognition that the adoption and acceptance required by Lord Atkin in *Chung* need not be by statute but may occur through judicial development of the law in the light of custom. So not only does Duff CJ affirm the incorporation approach, but he understands Lord Atkin's comments in *Chung* to be consistent with it.

The remainder of Duff CJ's judgment is a model of incorporation adjudication. He approves Lord Mansfield's *dictum* in *Heathfield v Chilton* that the law of nations will be carried as far in this country as anywhere,[34] and then makes good on that promise through a wide-ranging survey of leading international law text-writers,[35] celebrated judges,[36] and state practice.[37] What is particularly notable about Duff CJ's reliance on these sources is that he is not at all daunted by the comments of Cockburn CJ in *Keyn*. Nor should he be. For he does not look to these sources as legislators, but as exponents of the existing law. In short, Duff CJ's judgment in *Re Foreign Legations* affirms the incorporation doctrine both explicitly in his *ratio* and implicitly in his methodology.

The concurring judgments in the case tended to support the incorporation doctrine, by inference if not expressly. Justice Rinfret (as he then was) observed that the principle of international law in issue had "acquired validity in the domestic law of England, and, therefore, in the domestic law of Canada" and associated himself with the reasons of Duff CJ.[38] Macdonald[39] and Bayefsky[40] see ambiguity in Rinfret J's reference to the principles of international law that have acquired validity in the domestic law.[41] But Rinfret J's support for the reasons of the chief justice make clear that he was applying the incorporation doctrine, according to which all customary international law has "acquired validity" in domestic law save that which is expressly displaced by statute and that which contradicts the finally declared judgments

---

34 *Ibid* at 214.

35 These include Vattel, Grotius, Hurst, Oppenheim, Hall, Pradier-Fodéré, Pitt, Cobbett, and Calvo: *ibid* at 214–31.

36 These include Marshall CJ, Lord Campbell, and Brett LJ: *ibid* at 214–31.

37 For instance, Duff CJ takes judicial notice of the opinions of Foster, a secretary of state under President Cleveland, and of a circular from the US secretary of state to American diplomats.

38 *Re Foreign Legations*, above note 28 at 232.

39 Macdonald, above note 24 at 101.

40 Bayefsky, above note 29 at 6.

41 *Re Foreign Legations*, above note 28 at 232.

of courts. For his part, Taschereau J (as he then was) was content to "entirely concur" in the reasons of Duff CJ, though he saw fit to observe that "practically in all the leading countries of the world, it is a settled and accepted rule of International Law, that property belonging to a foreign Government, occupied by its accredited representative, cannot be assessed and taxed for state or municipal purposes."[42]

In dissent, Hudson J noted that the privileges attaching to legations are not the subject of Canadian or Ontarian legislation and therefore must derive either from "some general principle of international law" or Imperial legislation.[43] Next his lordship quoted Lord Atkin's *dictum* in *Chung Chi Cheung* that the courts seek to ascertain the applicable international custom and, having found it, "treat it as incorporated into the domestic law."[44] Yet Hudson J preferred to rest his judgment on the finding that an Imperial statute declaring the immunity of foreign sovereigns and diplomats (the Statute of Anne, 7 Anne c 12) was law in Ontario.[45] The remaining dissenting judge, Kerwin J, dispensed with the matter without raising the incorporation point.

Re Foreign Legations is not only a successful application of the incorporation doctrine but a vindication of the principle of respect for international law that informs it. For all the criticism the case has received for its ambiguity as to the operation of the incorporation doctrine, the substantial result of the case was in keeping with the customary law of sovereign immunity. The chief justice's use of sources is liberal and wide-ranging and relies unhesitatingly on scholarly works (the "most highly qualified publicists" of article 38(4) of the Statute of the Permanent Court of International Justice 1920,[46] repeated in article 38(1)(d) of the later International Court of Justice Statute).[47] The clear concern of the chief justice was to ascertain the relevant international rules and apply them as the law of Ontario.

---

42 *Ibid* at 249.

43 *Ibid* at 241.

44 *Ibid* at 243–4, quoting *Chung*, above note 14 at 168.

45 *Re Foreign Legations*, above note 28 at 245. It is helpful here to recall Blackstone's comment on such legislation. He said that it is "not to be considered as introductive of any new rule, but merely declaratory of the old fundamental constitutions of the kingdom; without which it must cease to be a part of the civilized world": Blackstone, above note 3 at 67.

46 [1920] UKTS no 23.

47 Statute of the International Court of Justice 1945 [1945] Can TS no 7.

A more difficult case is *Re Armed Forces* (1943).[48] The Governor in Council referred two questions to the Supreme Court concerning the applicability of Canadian criminal law to US military personnel stationed in Canada during the Second World War. The case was a clash between two rules. The rule of customary international law, supported by the high authority of Marshall CJ in *The Schooner "Exchange" v M'Faddon*,[49] was that sovereign states were immune from the jurisdiction of domestic courts and therefore when a state grants another state's forces the right of free passage through its territory it impliedly waives jurisdiction over those forces during their passage. The competing common law rule was identified by Duff CJ as the "fundamental constitutional principle . . . that the soldiers of the army of all ranks are not, by reason of their military character, exempt from the criminal jurisdiction of the civil (that is to say, non-military) courts of this country."[50] The majority held that the domestic principle trumped the international custom. They did not deny the existence of the customary law principle of sovereign immunity but held that the rule had never been accepted by English and Canadian courts in respect of visiting forces and that, without such acceptance, the international rule contended for did not apply.[51]

The language of acceptance in the majority's reasons may suggest a rejection of the incorporation doctrine in favour of the doctrine of transformation: Rather than apply the customary law automatically, the majority seemingly refused to apply it without some positive act of transformation by the legislature. Yet the majority did not reject incorporation in favour of transformation. Rather, they applied the rule in *Chung* (since departed from in England, as explained below)[52] that incorporation does not permit customary international law to displace finally declared common law decisions.[53] The majority in *Re Armed Forces* con-

48 *Reference as to Whether Members of the Military or Naval Forces of the United States of America Are Exempt from Criminal Proceedings in Canadian Criminal Courts*, [1943] SCR 483 [*Re Armed Forces*].

49 (1812) 7 Cranch 116.

50 *Re Armed Forces*, above note 48 at 490.

51 *Ibid* at 490, Duff CJ (Hudson J concurring) and at 525, Rand J.

52 At Section 6.2(c), below.

53 This explanation of *Re Armed Forces*, above note 48, is consistent with, and draws upon, Macdonald's lucid discussion of that case. See Macdonald, above note 24 at 102–5.

sidered the rule that soldiers are subject to the ordinary criminal courts to be an established feature of the common law; Duff CJ described it as "a well-settled principle which has always been jealously guarded and maintained by the British people as one of the essential foundations of their constitutional liberties."[54] Given Lord Atkin's formulation of the incorporation doctrine in *Chung* – and we have already seen that Duff CJ understood *Chung* as advancing incorporation not transformation – the majority's decision is consistent with that doctrine. Chief Justice Duff did not state explicitly that he was applying *Chung*'s "rules finally declared" proviso, but Rand J did. He explained that the incorporation of international custom was subject to rules and principles "declared or adopted by the courts or Parliament of this country or accepted as embodied in its constitutional practices."[55] The logic of these arguments strongly suggests that, had there been no common law rule opposed to granting immunity to US forces, the majority would have allowed it, without requiring a positive act of transformation before doing so.

The dissenting judges, Kerwin and Taschereau JJ, found no significant inconsistency between sovereign immunity and the constitutional principle described by the majority. They applied the incorporation doctrine without hesitation. Justice Taschereau's reasons are especially clear on this point. He noted the attorney general of Canada's submission that Canada was under an international obligation to accord immunity from jurisdiction to US forces and that "the doctrine of international law involved has become a part of our municipal law."[56] He then put the problem this way:

> In order to reach a proper judicial conclusion it is necessary first to seek if there exists, and if the Court can acknowledge a body of rules accepted by the nations of the world, to the effect that the troops of a foreign sovereign visiting a country, with the consent of the latter's Government, are exempt from criminal proceedings prosecuted in that country. And secondly, having reached on that point an affirmative conclusion, the further question that must be solved is: Are these recognized principles of international law adopted by our domestic law?[57]

54 *Re Armed Forces*, above note 48 at 490.
55 *Ibid* at 524.
56 *Ibid* at 511.
57 *Ibid* at 511–12.

One could hardly ask for a clearer account of the reasoning required by the incorporation doctrine. Applying this method, Taschereau J began with a review of learned authors on the international legal position. He then considered *The Schooner Exchange v M'Faddon* and *Chung* on the point. Having established the rule in customary international law, Taschereau J turned to consider its place in Canada. His lordship affirmed, quoting *Chung*, that "international law has no application in Canada unless incorporated in our own domestic law."[58] Notably, given the reservations some commentators have expressed about *Re Foreign Legations*, Taschereau J then quoted from Duff CJ's reasons in that case. His lordship then again quoted Lord Atkin in *Chung* as follows:

> The Courts acknowledge the existence of a body of rules which nations accept amongst themselves. On any judicial issue they seek to ascertain what the relevant rule is, and, having found it, they will treat it as incorporated into the domestic law, so far as it is not inconsistent with rules enacted by statutes or finally declared by their tribunals.[59]

Applying this statement of the incorporation doctrine almost word for word, Taschereau J declared:

> I have come to the conclusion that there exists such a body of rules adopted by the nations of the world. These rules have been accepted by the highest courts of the United States, and some of them, applicable to the present case, have also been accepted by the Judicial Committee. I have to acknowledge their existence, and treat them as incorporated in our domestic law, following the direction given in the Cheung case. And I see nothing in the laws of the land inconsistent with their application in our territory.[60]

More Supreme Court of Canada support for the doctrine of incorporation came in *Saint John v Fraser-Brace Overseas Corp* (1958).[61] The case was factually similar to *Re Foreign Legations*: The municipality of Saint John, New Brunswick, claimed the right to tax land and personal property owned by the United States. The US had acquired the property

58 *Ibid* at 516.
59 *Chung*, above note 14 at 167–8, quoted in *Re Armed Forces*, *ibid* at 517.
60 *Re Armed Forces*, above note 48 at 517.
61 [1958] SCR 263 [*Fraser-Brace*].

under agreement with Canada for the purpose of building a radar defence system. The finding of the Appeal Division of the Supreme Court of New Brunswick that the property was immune from taxation was upheld unanimously by the Supreme Court of Canada. In his inimitable prose, Rand J (Abbot J concurring) strongly approved the doctrine of incorporation. He gave the following stirring endorsement of *Heathfield v Chilton*:

> It is obvious that the life of every state is, under the swift transformations of these days, becoming deeply implicated with that of the others in a *de facto* society of nations. If in 1767 Lord Mansfield, as in *Heathfield v. Chilton* . . . could say, "The law of nations will be carried as far in England, as any where," in this country, in the 20th century, in the presence of the United Nations and the multiplicity of impacts with which technical developments have entwined the entire globe, we cannot say anything less.[62]

Continuing, he rejected the transformationist view that some judicial precedent or legislative act is required to sanction judicial reliance on customary international law:

> [T]o say that precedent is now required for every proposed application to matter which differs only in accidentals, that new concrete instances must be left to legislation or convention, would be a virtual repudiation of the concept of inherent adaptability which has maintained the life of the common law, and a retrograde step in evolving the rules of international intercourse. However slowly and meticulously they are to be fashioned they must be permitted to meet the necessities of increasing international involvements. It is the essence of the principle of precedent that new applications are to be determined according to their total elements including assumptions and attitudes, and in the international sphere the whole field of the behaviour of states, whether exhibited in actual conduct, conventions, arbitrations or adjudications, is pertinent to the determination of each issue.[63]

62 *Ibid* at 268–9.

63 *Fraser-Brace*, above note 61 at 269. Rand J's language here is reminiscent of his observation in *Re Armed Forces*, above note 48 at 524, that "to insist upon precise precedent in usage would sterilize judicial action toward changing international relations."

Likewise, Locke J (Cartwright J concurring) employed an incorporationist methodology, though without explicitly commenting on it, and approved the judgments of Duff CJ and Rinfret and Taschereau JJ in *Re Foreign Legations*.[64] Justice Fauteux gave no reasons but agreed that the appeal should be dismissed. In sum, *Fraser-Brace* represents the unanimous judgment of the Supreme Court of Canada that customary international law takes direct effect in Canada by virtue of its incorporation by the common law.

There followed, in the later twentieth century, a series of Supreme Court of Canada decisions touching customary international law that were rather less explicit in their support and application of the doctrine of incorporation. This caused some commentators to question whether the doctrine continued to exist in Canada. The Court of Appeal for Ontario nevertheless applied the doctrine in a notable decision.

In *Re Newfoundland Continental Shelf* (1984),[65] the Supreme Court of Canada was asked to determine whether Canada or Newfoundland had the rights to explore, exploit, and legislate in respect of the continental shelf in the area offshore Newfoundland. The court held that continental shelf rights are granted by international law to coastal states as an external manifestation of sovereignty and that Newfoundland, during the relevant period prior to its entry into Confederation, did not have the requisite sovereignty to acquire continental shelf rights. The court's consideration of customary international law, while not inconsistent with incorporation, did not clearly invoke it. This approach constrained the editors of *International Law Chiefly as Interpreted and Applied in Canada* to say only that the case "impliedly confirmed the [incorporation] doctrine."[66]

The incorporation doctrine was affirmed by the Court of Appeal for Ontario in *Re Regina and Palacios* (1984).[67] The case concerned a Nicaraguan national, Palacios, who had been a member of the diplomatic staff at the Nicaraguan Embassy. On 12 July 1983 the embassy advised the Department of External Affairs that Palacios had terminated his duties there. Four days thereafter, Palacios made a week-long trip to the United

---

64 *Fraser-Brace, ibid* at 273–83.

65 [1984] 1 SCR 86.

66 H Kindred & P Saunders, eds, *International Law Chiefly as Interpreted and Applied in Canada*, 7th ed (Toronto: Emond Montgomery, 2006) [Kindred & Saunders] at 192.

67 (1984), 45 OR (2d) 269 (Ont CA) [*Palacios*] at 274.

States. Days later his home was searched and he was charged with several drug and weapons offences. Palacios pleaded diplomatic immunity, relying on the Vienna Convention on Diplomatic Relations 1961[68] as implemented in Canadian law by statute. Article 39(2) provided that "when the functions of a person enjoying privileges and immunities have come to an end, such privileges and immunities shall normally cease at the moment when he leaves the country, or on expiry of a reasonable period in which to do so, but shall subsist until that time." The Crown argued that Palacios lost his immunity upon leaving Canada for the United States. Justice Blair began by finding, on the basis of scholarly authority, that the Vienna Convention codified existing international law on diplomatic immunities. He then observed that the "immunities and privileges of diplomats recognized by customary international law were considered to be incorporated in the domestic law of Canada by the Supreme Court of Canada in the Foreign Legations case."[69] He then considered the customary rules, finding that immunity extended for a reasonable time after the termination of the diplomat's duties, and that the measure of reasonableness was the time required to permit the diplomat to move permanently. Justice Blair added, importantly, that this rule "was recognized as forming part of the common law in two 19th-century cases," namely *Magdalena Steam Navigation Co v Martin*[70] and *Musurus Bey v Gadban*,[71] and that it was "universally recognized by the diplomatic practice of States."[72] The learned judge then noted that the case before him turned on the interpretation of the treaty and that the treaty's provisions prevail over custom wherever they differ from it. Turning to the treaty, Blair JA applied the international law of treaty interpretation, affirming that the treaty must be interpreted so as to give effect to its purpose.[73] He found, however, that the critical words in article 39(2) were ambiguous. He therefore resorted to the customary law rule, described above, to resolve the ambiguity. Blair JA thus upheld Palacios's claim to diplomatic immunity.

In *Re Canada Labour Code* (1992), La Forest J for the majority of the Supreme Court of Canada considered, in *obiter*, the common law

68 [1966] Can TS no 29.

69 *Palacios*, above note 67 at 274.

70 (1859) 2 El & EL 94, 121 ER 36.

71 [1894] 2 QB 352.

72 *Palacios*, above note 67 at 275.

73 *Ibid* at 276–8.

of state immunity as it stood in Canada prior to Parliament's enactment of the State Immunity Act.[74] His view was that Canadian common law conformed with customary international law's restrictive doctrine of state immunity even prior to Parliament's legislative intervention, and that the State Immunity Act was "a codification that is intended to clarify and continue the theory of restrictive immunity, rather than to alter its substance."[75] In reaching this conclusion, La Forest J relied on *I° Congreso*.[76] Justice La Forest's judgment must be viewed as strong authority for the continued presence of the incorporation doctrine in Canadian law. Only incorporation explains how the State Immunity Act can be a codification of, and not an introduction of, the restrictive theory of state immunity in Canadian law. Like *Re Newfoundland Continental Shelf*, however, *Re Canada Labour Code* could have been more explicit on the point.

In *Reference re Secession of Quebec* (1998),[77] the Supreme Court of Canada was called upon to consider the legality, in Canadian and international law, of a unilateral secession from Canada by Quebec. Canada's written constitution makes no provision for the secession of its constituent parts. International law, however, has much to say on the question.[78] In the absence of any domestic constitutional provision, one might have expected customary international law, as incorporated by the common law, to fill the gap. Yet, this was not – explicitly, at least – the court's approach. While the court considered some aspects of the international law of state secession, nowhere did it make clear that those parts of the law that were customary in nature enjoyed direct effect in Canadian law via the doctrine of incorporation.[79] As Toope observes, with palpable frustration, "the Court seems to suggest that customary international law is not part of the law of Canada. . . . Instead, the Court treats inter-

74 RSC 1985, c S-18.

75 *Re Canada Labour Code*, [1992] 2 SCR 50 [*Re Canada Labour Code*] at 73–4.

76 *I° Congreso*, above note 18.

77 *Re Secession of Quebec* [1998] 2 SCR 217.

78 See, e.g., J Crawford, *The Creation of States in International Law*, 2d ed (Oxford: Clarendon Press, 2007) at ch 9.

79 Oddly, the court relied on treaties and ignored customary international law. Toope has called the court's understanding of international law sources in *Re Secession* "impoverished": S Toope, "Self-determination – Canada – Quebec – right to secede under constitutional law and public international law – role of international law in Canadian courts" (1999) 93 *American Journal of International Law* 519 at 523; see also 525.

national law as a 'consideration.'"[80] The only bright spot to be found in *Re Secession* is that the court did not explicitly overrule such incorporation authorities as *Triquet v Bath*, *Heathfield v Chilton*, *Re Foreign Legations*, and *Fraser-Brace*. The doctrine of incorporation was by no means irredeemably rejected in *Re Secession*, only strangely forgotten.

This same oblivion struck the court in *Spraytech v Hudson* (2001)[81] and *Suresh v Canada (Minister of Citizenship and Immigration)* (2001).[82] In *Spraytech*, L'Heureux-Dubé J suggested that the precautionary principle may constitute a rule of customary international law and that her interpretation of the municipal bylaw at issue in the case was thus "consistent with principles of international law and policy"[83] – without reference to the incorporation doctrine, though there was no strict reason to make such reference, as she was not applying a rule of customary international law but only remarking that her result was consistent with the supposed customary rule. In *Suresh*, the Supreme Court of Canada considered the constitutionality of deportation to face torture. The court affirmed the implementation requirement in relation to treaties.[84] But Suresh also relied on peremptory norms of customary international law. On this point the court's conclusion on the status of torture in international law was astonishingly equivocal: The international prohibition on torture was weakly depicted as one that "cannot be easily derogated from."[85] The court thus declined an opportunity to reaffirm its incorporation decisions in *Re Foreign Legations*, *Re Armed Forces*, and *Fraser-Brace*.

---

80 Toope, "Keynote Address," above note 29 at 37.

81 114957 *Canada Ltée (Spraytech, Société d'arrosage) v Hudson (Town)*, [2001] 2 SCR 241 [*Spraytech*].

82 [2002] 1 SCR 3 [*Suresh*].

83 *Spraytech*, above note 81 at paras 30–2.

84 *Suresh*, above note 82 at para 60.

85 *Ibid* at para 65. The actual position of international law is far less subtle: art 2(2) of the Convention Against Torture 1984, [1987] Can TS no 36, to which Canada is a party, declares that "no exceptional circumstances whatsoever . . . may be invoked as a justification of torture," while art 3(1) provides that Canada shall not "expel, return ('*refouler*') or extradite a person to another State where there are substantial grounds for believing that he would be in danger of being subjected to torture." The Supreme Court corrected course in *Kazemi Estate v Iran*, 2014 SCC 62 [*Kazemi Estate*] at para 47, affirming that "our Court cannot entertain any doubt that the prohibition of torture has reached the level of a peremptory norm."

Judicial acknowledgement, and indeed support, of the incorporation doctrine has revived in the first two decades of the twenty-first century. In *Bouzari v Islamic Republic of Iran* (2004),[86] an Iranian national sued Iran in Ontario for torture. Iran did not defend and was deemed to have admitted the truth of Bouzari's allegations. On a motion to determine whether the court had jurisdiction and could proceed to assess damages, the attorney general of Canada (intervening) argued that the action was barred by the State Immunity Act. Bouzari submitted that that Act must be read in conformity with treaties binding on Canada and customary international law, and that these obligations required the court to recognize an exception to state immunity in torture cases. This prompted Goudge JA, for the Court of Appeal for Ontario, to review "the interplay between Canada's obligations at public international law and its domestic legislation." In the course of this discussion, he observed that "customary rules of international law are directly incorporated into Canadian domestic law unless explicitly ousted by contrary legislation" and that the attorney general had acknowledged that rule in this case.[87] The learned judge then reviewed the evidence led in the court below and held that state practice did not support the existence of any customary international obligation to provide a civil remedy for victims of foreign state torture.

In *R v Hape* (2007),[88] LeBel J for the majority of the Supreme Court of Canada affirmed the continued application of the incorporation doctrine in Canada. Using the synonymous term "adoption," LeBel J reviewed the doctrine's application in English law (quoting from *Trendtex Trading*)[89] and its history in Canada. He observed that the Supreme Court of Canada had "implicitly or explicitly applied the doctrine of adoption in several cases," citing *The Ship "North," Re Armed Forces*, *Re Foreign Legations*, and *Fraser-Brace*.[90] While noting that, in some of its decisions, the court had "not applied or discussed the doctrine of adoption of customary international law when it had the opportunity to do so," he observed that "the doctrine of adoption has never been rejected

86 (2004) 71 OR (3d) 675 (Ont CA).
87 *Ibid* at para 65.
88 2007 SCC 26 [*Hape*].
89 *Trendtex*, above note 16.
90 *Hape*, above note 88 at para 37.

in Canada. Indeed, there is a long line of cases in which the Court has either formally accepted it or at least applied it."[91] LeBel J concluded,

> In my view, following the common law tradition, it appears that the doctrine of adoption operates in Canada such that prohibitive rules of customary international law should be incorporated into domestic law in the absence of conflicting legislation. The automatic incorporation of such rules is justified on the basis that international custom, as the law of nations, is also the law of Canada unless, in a valid exercise of its sovereignty, Canada declares that its law is to the contrary. Parliamentary sovereignty dictates that a legislature may violate international law, but that it must do so expressly. Absent an express derogation, the courts may look to prohibitive rules of customary international law to aid in the interpretation of Canadian law and the development of the common law.[92]

Two aspects of this passage are at odds with the English and Canadian authorities reviewed above. First, the application of the incorporation doctrine by courts is not discretionary, as implied by the phrases "customary international law *should* be incorporated into domestic law" and "the courts *may* look to prohibitive rules of customary international law."[93] Second, the final sentence of this paragraph seems to depict incorporation as a doctrine permitting customary international law to be used as an interpretive aid. The incorporation authorities reviewed in this chapter and affirmed by LeBel J in the paragraphs immediately preceding this one in his reasons make clear that the incorporation doctrine is more ambitious than that. These divergences from authority have been rightly criticized.[94] Yet the thrust of LeBel J's observations in *Hape* is that customary international law is part of the common law of Canada unless ousted by contrary legislation.

Justice LeBel for the majority of the Supreme Court of Canada made brief but significant mention of the incorporation doctrine in

---

91 *Ibid* at para 38.

92 *Ibid* at para 39.

93 See the discussion at Section 6.3(d), below.

94 J Currie, "Weaving a Tangled Web: Hape and the Obfuscation of Canadian Reception Law" (2007) 45 *Canadian Yearbook of International Law* 55–96.

Kazemi Estate.[95] I consider those aspects of *Kazemi Estate* elsewhere in this chapter.[96]

The Supreme Court of Canada considered the incorporation doctrine at length, and confirmed its continuing application in Canadian law, in *Nevsun Resources Ltd v Araya* (2020).[97] The case was a claim by Eritrean nationals against a BC mining company. The plaintiffs alleged the company was liable to them for its complicity in breaches of customary international law human rights norms committed against them by the state of Eritrea. The company brought a motion to strike the pleadings, contending that the alleged violations of customary international law were not actionable in BC law. The courts below declined to strike the claim, finding that it was not plain and obvious that claims founded on custom must fail. Justice Abella for the majority of the Supreme Court of Canada agreed. There was no need "to determine definitively whether the Eritrean workers should be awarded damages for the alleged breaches of customary international law" but only whether the plaintiffs' custom-based claims "should be struck at this preliminary stage" as disclosing no reasonable claim.[98] The first question, in the learned judge's view, was whether the customary international law prohibitions relied on by the plaintiffs (forced labour; slavery; cruel, inhuman, or degrading treatment; and crimes against humanity) were part of Canadian law. To do that, said Abella J, "we must first determine whether they are part of customary international law."[99] She proceeded to review the elements of customary international law and the operation of the incorporation doctrine. She approved Professor Koh's statement that "Law-abiding states *internalize* international law by incorporating it into their domestic legal and political structures, through executive action, legislation, and judicial decisions"[100] and noted that while treaties require legislative action to become part of domestic law, "customary international law is automatically adopted into domestic law without any need for legislative action."[101] She noted that the "adoption of customary international law as part of domestic law by way of automatic

95 2014 SCC 62.
96 See the discussions at Sections 6.2(b) and 6.3(b), below.
97 2020 SCC 5 [*Nevsun*].
98 *Ibid* at para 62; see also paras 63–9.
99 *Ibid* at para 73.
100 *Ibid* at para 85 (emphasis in original).
101 *Ibid* at para 86.

judicial incorporation can be traced back to the 18th century,"[102] citing Blackstone, *Triquet v Bath*, and *Chung Chi Cheung*. She noted a scholarly study by Professors Verdier and Versteeg finding that "in virtually all states, [customary international law] rules are in principle directly applicable without legislative implementation."[103] She also cited *The Ship "North"* and Taschereau J's discussion in *Re Armed Forces*. These cases showed that "Canada has long followed the conventional path of automatically incorporating customary international law into domestic law via the doctrine of adoption, making it part of the common law of Canada in the absence of conflicting legislation."[104] Justice Abella concluded that there is "no doubt . . . that customary international law is also the law of Canada," invoking the words of the former president of the International Court of Justice, Dame Rosalyn Higgins, that "there is not 'international law' and the common law. International law is part of that which comprises the common law on any given subject."[105] She went on to conclude that the prohibitions relied upon by the plaintiffs were indeed established in customary international law,[106] and it was not plain and obvious that corporations cannot be liable for their breach. She added, however, that "because some norms of customary international law are of a strictly interstate character, the trial judge will have to determine whether the specific norms relied on in this case are of such a character."[107] As for whether there were any conflicting Canadian laws to prevent the adoption of the customary norms in question, Abella J could not find any.[108] The learned judge went on to consider whether the incorporation doctrine as applied in this case would require a civil remedy for breach of "this part of our common law."[109] She left that point for the trial judge to determine, but noted that since the plaintiffs' claims "are based on norms that already form

---

102 *Ibid* at para 87, citing the discussion of English and Canadian incorporation authorities in the second edition of this work at Section 6.1 (pp 184–208).

103 *Ibid* at para 88, quoting P-H Verdier & M Versteeg, "International Law in National Legal Systems: An Empirical Investigation" (2015) 109 *American Journal of International Law* 514 at 528.

104 *Ibid* at para 90.

105 *Ibid* at para 95; see also para 132 ("Customary international law is part of Canadian law").

106 *Ibid* at paras 100–3.

107 *Ibid* at para 113.

108 *Ibid* at paras 114–16.

109 *Ibid* at para 117; see also paras 118–31.

part of our common law," it may not be necessary to develop new torts to remedy their breach, and indeed doing so "may not only dilute the doctrine of adoption, it could negate its application."[110]

In partial dissent, Brown and Rowe JJ took issue with Abella J's account of the incorporation doctrine in various respects. Their concerns are considered elsewhere in this chapter.

Prior to *Hape* and *Nevsun*, some commentators went so far as to claim that we do not actually know whether customary international law forms part of the law of Canada.[111] That was overstating matters: None of the earlier incorporation cases had been overruled or even doubted by our courts.[112] The Supreme Court of Canada should not be obliged to affirm its own decisions every generation for them to remain binding precedent. That said, one can understand how doubt crept in as the doctrine was neglected in late-twentieth-century Supreme Court decisions. With the affirmations of incorporation in *Hape* and, more importantly, *Nevsun*, there can no longer be any doubt that customary international law is adopted by the common law. Questions about the operation and application of the doctrine remain, however. They are considered in the balance of this chapter.

6.2 Incorporation and domestic law

The Canadian incorporation doctrine sees rules of customary international law adopted by the common law unless ousted by conflicting enactments or, perhaps, contrary precedent.

---

110 *Ibid* at para 128.

111 See, e.g., S Toope, "The Uses of Metaphor: International Law and the Supreme Court of Canada" (2001) 80 *Canadian Bar Review* 534 at 536, and J Currie, *Public International Law* (Toronto: Irwin Law, 2001) at 201. Other commentators considered that incorporation was the Canadian position, e.g., L Green, "International Law: A Canadian Perspective" in *The Canadian Encyclopedic Digest (Ontario)*, 3d ed, vol 17, title 81 (Agincourt, ON: Carswell, 1984) at 64, and W Schabas, "Twenty-Five Years of Public International Law at the Supreme Court of Canada" (2000) 79 *Canadian Bar Review* 174 at 182.

112 Canadian trial and appellate courts continued to treat incorporation as the law in those rare cases in which the matter arose. See, e.g., *R v Sunila* (1986), 26 CCC (3d) 177 (NSCA) at 183; *Jose Pereira E Hijos, S.A. v Canada (Attorney General)*, [1997] 2 FC 84 (FCTD) at para 20; *Suresh v Canada (Minister of Citizenship and Immigration)*, [2000] 2 FC 592 (FCA) [*Suresh* FCA] at para 32.

(a) Incorporation into the common law

Whether customary international law is incorporated into the common law or is instead made part of domestic law in a more general fashion may, in other jurisdictions, be an open question. In Canada, however, it seems settled that rules of customary international law are adopted into the common law.

Old English authorities tend to depict customary international law as part of the common law.[113] Some more recent English authorities do likewise.[114] In the celebrated *Lotus* case, Moore J referred to the "majestic stream of the common law, united with international law."[115] But there are also English authorities that speak instead of customary international law forming part of "domestic" or "English" law.[116]

Canadian authorities have repeatedly depicted the incorporation doctrine as one that recognizes rules of customary international law as part of the common law.[117] In Canada, therefore, the weight of author-

---

113 Blackstone, above note 3 at 67 ("the law of nations . . . is here adopted in it's [sic] full extent by the common law"); *Heathfield*, above note 4, Lord Mansfield (the law of nations is "part of the common law of England"); *Novello v Toogood* (1823), 1 B & C 554 at 562, 107 ER 204 at 207, Abbot CJ ("the common law, of which the law of nations must be deemed a part"); *Duke of Brunswick*, above note 7 at 45 (Beav), 741 (ER), Lord Langdale MR ("the law of nations . . . when ascertained, is to be deemed part of the common law of England"); *Emperor of Austria*, above note 8 at 678 (Giff), 282 (ER), Sir John Stuart VC ("the law of nations is part of the common law of England").

114 See, e.g., *I° Congreso*, above note 18 at 257, Lord Wilberforce (on state immunity, in the absence of statute, "the law in question is the common law"); *Littrel v United States of America (No 2)*, [1995] 1 WLR 82 (Eng CA) at 89, Rose LJ ("in the absence of statutory enactment, it is the common law including the incorporated rules of customary international law, which identifies and defines the extent of sovereign immunity"); *Holland v Lampen-Wolfe* [2000] 1 WLR 1573 (HL) at 1583, Lord Millett (rules of customary international law of state immunity given effect in UK by statute and common law); *R v Bow Street Magistrate, Ex parte Pinochet (No 3)* [2000] 1 AC 147 (HL) at 276, Lord Millett ("Customary international law is part of the common law").

115 *Lotus* case (1927) PCIJ (Ser A) No 10 at 75; see also Lord Finlay at 54.

116 See, e.g., *Trendtex*, above note 16 and *R v Jones*, [2006] UKHL 16 [*Jones*]. See also R O'Keefe, "Customary International Crimes in English Courts" (2001) 72 *British Yearbook of International Law* 293 [O'Keefe], arguing that custom forms part of domestic (English) law as distinct from (English) common law.

117 See, e.g., *Fraser-Brace*, above note 61 at 269, Rand J (to insist on precedent "would be a virtual repudiation of the concept of inherent adaptability which has maintained the life of the common law"); *Palacios*, above note 67 at 275, Blair JA (customary rule "recognized as forming part of the common law in

ity is that custom is incorporated not into domestic law in general but into common law specifically. Certainly, incorporated customs resemble common law rules, for they are adopted by the judiciary and are, in that sense, judge-made law subject to displacement by statute. Indeed, it is unclear that there exists in this country a body of "domestic" law that is distinct from either statute (including regulations made under statute) or common law.

The fact that Quebec is a civil law jurisdiction in private law matters seems to be no impediment to the incorporation of custom into the common law, for common law rules of a public nature (which questions of public international law surely are) apply in Quebec.[118]

(b) Conflict with enactments

Customary international laws are incorporated only so far as they are not inconsistent with rules enacted by statutes.[119] In other words, the incorporation doctrine is pre-empted by contrary statutory provision. This is consistent with the common law character of custom: Custom, like the common law, is subject to being displaced by legislation.

An illustration of this rule is found in the decision of the Supreme Court of Canada in *Kazemi Estate v Iran*. The issue was whether Ms. Kazemi's estate and son could bring legal proceedings in Canada against the state of Iran and its officials for her torture there. Certain parties and interveners tried to rely on alleged customary international legal norms to circumvent or read down the general immunity of states from

---

two 19th-century cases"); *Re Canada Labour Code*, above note 75 at 71, La Forest J (noting that with the rise of restrictive state immunity in customary international law, "The common law responded by developing a new theory of restrictive immunity"); *Hape*, above note 88 at para 36, LeBel J (approving the English tradition of incorporating custom "directly into domestic law through the common law"); *Nevsun*, above note 97, Abella J at para 90 (describing incorporation as making customary international law "part of the common law of Canada in the absence of conflicting legislation"); see also paras 95 and 117.

118 *Prud'homme v Prud'homme*, [2002] 4 SCR 663, especially at para 46.

119 *Chung*, above note 14 at 168; *Re Armed Forces*, above note 48 at 516; *Nevsun* above note 97 at para 86. While this point is not made in the early English incorporation authorities, Prof. Holdsworth considered that "It would, I think, have been admitted that, if a statute or a rule of the common law conflicted with a rule of international law, an English judge must decide in accordance with the statute or the rule of the common law": W Holdsworth, "The Relation of English Law to International Law" (1942) 26 *Minnesota Law Review* 141 at 142.

civil suits in Canada imposed by the State Immunity Act. Justice LeBel for the majority of the court held that the words of section 3(1) of the Act "completely oust the common law and international law as a source of potential exceptions to the immunity which it provides" and that even if customary international law included an exception for torture, "such an exception could not be adopted as a common law exception to s. 3(1) . . . as it would be in clear conflict" with the Act.[120]

A conflict between a customary norm and a rule lawfully made under a regulation would likely also be resolved in favour of the regulation, though I am aware of no authority on the point. Note, however, that a regulation that appeared to conflict with a customary international law norm would have to be considered according to the presumption of conformity with international law to ensure it was *intra vires* the authorizing statute and that its interpretation in context truly gave rise to a non-conforming result.

(c) Conflict with precedent

The incorporation doctrine declares the unity of customary international law and the common law. This unity is achieved by judges who, faced with an international legal question for which the common law gives no answer, apply customary international law. But what if the common law does provide an answer, and that answer differs from that given by custom? Does the doctrine of incorporation go so far as to overturn inconsistent common law authority? Does the common law rule of *stare decisis* give way to international custom?

Conflicts between custom and common law may arise in three ways. First, a change in international custom may give rise to a conflict with the former custom, as incorporated by the common law. An example is the doctrine of state immunity. The old custom granted states absolute immunity from domestic courts. This position became increasingly unworkable as foreign state involvement in commerce and private life increased. Absolute immunity gave way to a restrictive immunity, whereby states could be impleaded in domestic courts when acting otherwise than in their sovereign character (for instance, in a commercial capacity). This development of the law of sovereign immunity left common law courts in England and Canada in a quandary, for the doctrine of incorporation

---

120 *Kazemi Estate*, above note 85 at paras 58, 61.

required application of the new rule but the common law doctrine of *stare decisis* required that cases incorporating the old rule be followed until overruled by a competent court or undone by the legislature.

The second way in which custom and the common law may conflict is quite different. Here, the conflict arises from an expansion of international custom beyond its former bounds and into spheres of law previously reserved to domestic adjudication – for example, the development of customary human rights norms in the latter half of the twentieth century. Any time customary international law ventures into new territory, domestic courts may find its development to be in conflict with established common law rules. Here, too, a court may have to decide between binding precedent and incorporation.

Finally, customary and common law may conflict *ab initio*. Theoretically this should not happen, because common law adjudication should be informed by and incorporate customary rules. For that reason, the most appropriate Latin tag to attach to this sort of conflict may not be *ab initio*, but *per incuriam*.

(i) Strong and weak incorporation

Incorporation authorities of the eighteenth and early nineteenth centuries do not explicitly address the question of a conflict between custom and precedent. Perhaps they assumed that customary international law would remain stable, both in its decided rules and its established scope. But this may be giving the ancient authorities too little credit. Maybe we should read the refrains in these cases – that customary international law will be applied in its full extent, and that civilized countries are bound to see the law of nations carried out – as requiring courts to incorporate custom without regard to precedent. Let us call this approach strong incorporation.

Its rival, weak incorporation, was enunciated in *obiter dicta* by Lord Atkin in *Chung* and applied by the majority of the Supreme Court of Canada in *Re Armed Forces*. Lord Atkin's *dictum* required that precedent be observed even when it conflicts with custom, for common law courts will only treat international law as incorporated "so far as it is not inconsistent with rules enacted by statutes or finally declared by their tribunals."[121] Weak incorporation applies the rule of *stare decisis*

---

121 *Chung*, above note 14 at 168.

as an exception to the general incorporation rule and as a bar to the incorporation of custom where that custom is in conflict with common law decisions. To bring domestic law into harmony with international law in such a case requires, on the weak incorporation view, legislative or appellate court action to sweep away the inconsistent precedent.

(ii) Weak incorporation in Canada

At the time of Lord Atkin's *dictum* in *Chung*, no English court had yet considered a clear conflict between customary international law and common law precedent. Indeed, English judicial consideration of the matter did not come until the 1975 case of *Thai-Europe Tapioca Service v Government of Pakistan*.[122] As we have seen, however, the Supreme Court of Canada struggled with the question much earlier, in the 1943 reference case *Re Armed Forces*. The majority, guided by Lord Atkin's *dictum*, held that the common law rule that soldiers are subject to ordinary criminal courts prevailed over the customary rule that foreign soldiers invited into another state's territory are immune from the jurisdiction of domestic courts. The dissenting justices found no conflict between the two rules, saying that the Canadian rule included a reasonable exemption from it to incorporate the immunity provided at international law. Thus the majority approved *Chung*'s weak incorporation, and the dissent accepted, or at least did not explicitly refute, that same view. Yet, none of the judgments in *Re Armed Forces* gave reasoned consideration to the operation of the incorporation doctrine in the event of conflicting precedent. Their lordships were seemingly satisfied with the *dictum* in *Chung* that conflicting precedent barred the incorporation of customary international law.

The potentially challenging consequences of weak incorporation became clear in Canada in the 1960s and 1970s, when courts wrestled with developments in the customary law of state immunity. The Supreme Court of Canada had authoritatively established the doctrine of absolute state immunity in *Dessaulles v Republic of Poland*.[123] This left lower courts with two options: (1) they could continue to apply the outmoded theory of absolute immunity represented by *Dessaulles* and the cases that followed it, thus conforming to a weak incorporation stance, or (2) they could incorporate the modern theory of restrictive immun-

122 [1975] 1 WLR 1485 (CA) [*Thai-Europe*].

123 [1944] SCR 275.

ity in spite of binding precedent to the contrary, adopting a strong incorporation stance.

In *Congo v Venne*,[124] the Quebec Court of Appeal decided to ignore precedent and apply what they perceived to be the new international law. An architect sought payment for services rendered to the Congo government for its Expo '67 pavilion. Congo pleaded state immunity. The court unanimously rejected the plea, but each judge did so differently. Justice Owen simply declared that absolute immunity should be abandoned, supporting this conclusion with several lengthy passages from scholars of international law and the dissent of Lord Denning in *Rahimtoola v Nizam of Hyderabad*.[125] As for *Dessaulles*, Owen J admitted that it stood for absolute immunity. He considered, however, that certain *dicta* of Ritchie J in *Flota Maritima Browning de Cuba, S.A.*[126] suggested the Supreme Court might be reconsidering the doctrine. Be that as it may, *Flota Maritima* can hardly be said to have overturned *Dessaulles*, as Owen J clearly understood. Yet he nevertheless set *Dessaulles* aside, finding that absolute immunity was "outdated and inapplicable to today's conditions."[127] Justice Brossard went about matters differently. Rather than admit, as Owen J effectively did, that his judgment was contrary to *stare decisis*, Brossard J depicted his reasons as consistent with common law development in this area. Thus, he declared that, "même en appliquant la règle de *stare decisis* au cas sous étude, il n'est plus possible, en l'an de grâce 1968, d'affirmer que la règle de l'immunité demeure absolue au Canada ou dans la Province de Québec."[128] He supported this claim with academic opinions and the comments of Ritchie J in *Flota Maritima* and Jackett P in *Chateau-Gai Wines v Gouvernement de la République Française*.[129] None of this is very convincing, however, for *Dessaulles* was still the law of Canada. Finally, Taschereau J gave a short opinion in which he associated himself with the judgments of

124 *Gouvernement de la République démocratique du Congo v Venne*, [1969] BR 818 (Que) [*Venne*].

125 [1958] AC 379 (HL).

126 *Flota Maritima Browning de Cuba S.A. v Canadian Conquerer (The)*, [1962] SCR 598.

127 *Venne*, above note 124 at 827.

128 *Ibid* at 831. The case is reported in translation in (1969) 5 DLR (3d) 128, where this passage is rendered (at 142) as "But even if the rule of stare decisis is applied to the case at bar, it is no longer possible in 1968 to hold that the rule of immunity based on the sovereignty of a foreign State remains absolute in Canada or in the Province of Quebec. . . ."

129 [1967] 2 Ex CR 252.

both his colleagues and added only a long quotation from a 1968 letter by the US secretary of state to the ambassador of Guinea describing the American policy of restrictive immunity and citing the so-called Tate Letter of 1952, in which that policy was first enunciated. Presumably Taschereau J considered this letter to be evidence of developing state practice in favour of the restrictive approach. But he did not say so.

None of the judgments of the Court of Appeal in *Venne* addressed the fundamental theoretical problem of the case. All three judges acted in accordance with strong incorporation. Yet none of the judges put their judgments on this or any other theoretical footing. This is most evident in the judgment of Taschereau J who, had he explained that incorporation is not frustrated by contradictory precedent, would not have felt obliged to attempt to fit square pegs into round holes – that is, to depict restrictive immunity as consistent with Canadian and English common law that clearly denied it. By failing to enunciate a theory of incorporation to justify their judgments, the Quebec Court of Appeal appeared to refuse to apply *Dessaulles* for no other reason than that they considered it to be wrong.

When *Venne* came to the Supreme Court of Canada,[130] that court did no better in enunciating a theory of incorporation to resolve conflicts between customary and common law. Justice Ritchie for the majority – notably, the same judge whose anti-*Dessaulles* comments were so relied upon in the court below – held that the nature of state immunity, absolute or restrictive, did not arise here because Congo's acts were *iure imperii* not *iure gestionis*, and therefore Congo was immune from Canadian courts even if *Dessaulles* no longer represented the law. Thus, the majority declined to overrule *Dessaulles* but also, in a sense, declined to overrule the Court of Appeal on this point. As for the underlying theoretical issue of whether the doctrine of incorporation is barred by or may surmount inconsistent precedent, the majority was silent. In dissent, Laskin J (Hall J concurring) criticized *Dessaulles* and approved Rand J's pro-incorporation *dicta* in *Fraser-Brace*, quoted above.[131] Those *dicta* suggest, perhaps, a strong incorporation stance.[132] Yet Laskin J was as silent on the point as were the majority and the court below.

130 *République démocratique du Congo v Venne*, [1971] SCR 997.

131 *Fraser-Brace*, above note 61 at 269.

132 Kindred & Saunders, above note 66 at 291.

(iii) *Strong incorporation in England:* Trendtex Trading

Thus, our courts left the theoretical problem underlying *Venne* to be worked out by others. The English Court of Appeal soon obliged in two more cases on state immunity. In *Thai-Europe Tapioca Service* the government of Pakistan pleaded immunity from the claims of German shipowners in a dispute arising under a charterparty.[133] The losses complained of arose from Indian military attacks on Karachi. The Court of Appeal unanimously dismissed the appeal and upheld Pakistan's plea of immunity. Two of the three judges, Lawton and Scarman LJJ, endorsed weak incorporation, holding that the restrictive theory of sovereign immunity was not open to them because it was excluded by the superior authority of decided cases. Lord Justice Lawton considered that a change in the law of sovereign immunity could only be made by the House of Lords.[134] Lord Justice Scarman (as he then was) added that a rule of international law, once incorporated into the common law, becomes part of domestic law and is therefore subject to *stare decisis* like any other rule.[135] The third judge, Lord Denning MR, did not address the point here but gave the leading judgment on the matter in the subsequent case, *Trendtex Trading v Bank of Nigeria.*[136] This, too, was a judgment of the Court of Appeal, yet it went entirely the other way, approving restrictive immunity and explicitly sanctioning strong incorporation.

In *Trendtex*, Lord Denning viewed the matter as a contest between the transformation and incorporation theories. I respectfully disagree with this characterization. The view that customary international law cannot surmount inconsistent precedent still allows for incorporation of custom in cases where no inconsistent precedent exists. Transformation, by contrast, permits no application of international law without some transformative executive or legislative act. That matter aside, Lord Denning's reasoning in *Trendtex* gave the theoretical underpinnings to what I am calling the strong incorporation approach. His lordship explained that incorporation (in my strong sense) must be the correct approach, "otherwise I do not see that our courts could ever

133 *Thai-Europe*, above note 122.
134 *Ibid* at 1493.
135 *Ibid* at 1495.
136 *Trendtex*, above note 16.

recognise a change in the rules of international law."[137] Lord Denning added,

> International law knows no rule of stare decisis. If this court today is satisfied that the rule of international law on a subject has changed from what it was 50 or 60 years ago, it can give effect to that change – and apply the change in our English law – without waiting for the House of Lords to do it.[138]

This final flourish is typical Denning audacity. It may also be seen as a recognition that it is not for the courts to vindicate the principle of self-government by preserving common law decisions in the face of contrary rules of customary international law. Parliament may do that itself by displacing the custom-incorporating judgment by statute. There may be a limited sense in which courts vindicate, or at least affirm, self-government by recognizing Parliament's competence to violate international law. Other than that, however, the role of the courts in the reception system is to defend the principle of respect for international law. To do so in *Trendtex* required setting aside the common law rule in favour of international custom.

Trendtex does much to complete the English theory of incorporation established by eighteenth- and nineteenth-century authorities. Yet *Trendtex* also raises questions about the actual strength of strong incorporation. We have seen that conflicts between custom and common law may arise in at least three ways. Does customary international law displace common law precedent in each instance?

Brownlie took the view that *Trendtex* should be narrowed to cases in which the precedent to be displaced is itself an incorporation of a now-outdated rule of customary international law.[139] So where, as in *Trendtex*, the common law rule at issue is an incorporated rule of customary international law, it should give way to new custom. But where the common law rule is not an incorporated custom (that is, where it is the product of ordinary adjudication), incorporation should not apply and the inconsistent judgment should stand until overturned by a competent court or undone by legislation. This is something of a middle

137 *Ibid* at 554.

138 *Ibid*.

139 I Brownlie, *Principles of Public International Law*, 6th ed (Oxford: Oxford University Press, 2003) at 41–2.

position between weak and strong incorporation. The rationale behind it appears to be the principle of self-government, as expressed in Lord Atkin's *dictum* in *Chung* that there is "no external power that imposes its rules upon our own code of substantive law or procedure."[140] But this *dictum* must not be carried too far. It must be read in the context of Lord Atkin's judgment, which was an affirmation of the incorporation doctrine subject only to the rule, abandoned in *Trendtex*, that incorporation was barred by inconsistent precedent. To say that there is no external power imposing its rules upon us is not to say that international law does not apply to us; it is to say only that international law does not apply directly, but rather as our own common law by means of incorporation. The whole point of the incorporation doctrine is that customary international law is not an "external power," but rather an aspect of the common law.

In my view, the best theory of incorporation is the strong one. If international law is truly to be the law of the land, as the oldest incorporation authorities declare, it must apply even when – perhaps especially when – domestic case law violates it. Strong incorporation requires courts to assure domestic compliance with customary international law in their sphere of influence: adjudication. Unlike conventional international law, where constitutional concerns preclude judges from applying treaties directly in domestic law, there is no reason why judges should not take it upon themselves to assure the compliance of their decisions with custom. It is unbecoming of judges to uphold decisions of their courts that violate international law. Furthermore, it is incongruous for our courts to apply the presumption of conformity, which strives to bring legislation into harmony with international obligations, but not go further and assure that the results of their own adjudication also meet the requirements of international law.

The problem can be framed in terms of the principles of the reception system identified in Chapter 1. Self-government may seem to demand that our judges be free to make and uphold rulings that are inconsistent with international law. But that is not so. The self-government imperative is satisfied by the legislature's power, assured by the doctrine of parliamentary sovereignty, to violate international law. It does not require, nor should it enjoy, the complicity of our courts, which are not the prop-

140 *Chung*, above note 14 at 168.

er vehicle of self-government. Rather, courts must seek to vindicate the competing principle of respect for international law. Only that way can the reception system retain its precarious balance between the two principles. If, in vindicating respect for international law, a court sets aside a desirable precedent in favour of a less desirable custom, our sovereign legislatures can assert our self-government by undoing by statutory action what the court has done by common law adjudication.

(iv) Strong incorporation in Canada

In Canadian law, *Trendtex* provides a much-needed theoretical basis for the Quebec Court of Appeal's abandonment of Supreme Court authority in *Venne*. In the light of *Trendtex*, the Quebec court's judgment is revealed as theoretically sound. The capacity of strong incorporation to explain *Venne*, and to resolve future cases of conflict between custom and precedent, recommends *Trendtex* very highly to Canadian courts. So far, however, no Canadian court has explicitly adopted Lord Denning's reasoning on this point[141] or otherwise ruled on whether the Canadian incorporation doctrine takes a weak or strong form. There is, however, some support for strong incorporation in three Supreme Court of Canada decisions.

In *Re Canada Labour Code*,[142] La Forest J for the majority considered the development of sovereign immunity at common law. Rather than emphasize the inconclusive Canadian case law (as Cory J did in dissent),[143] La Forest J considered at length the reasons of Lord Wilberforce in *I° Congreso del Partido*.[144] That case relied on *Trendtex* and a

---

141 The extent of the sovereign immunity doctrine, the matter that gave rise to these incorporation questions in the first place, was ultimately resolved by Parliament, not the courts: State Immunity Act. See *Athabasca Chipewyan First Nation v Canada (Minister of Indian Affairs and Northern Development)*, [2001] 8 WWR 419 at para 47 (Alta CA). But compare *Re Canada Labour Code*, above note 75 at paras 25–30, in which La Forest J, for the majority, declares the restrictive theory of sovereign immunity to have been common law prior to its "codification" by statute. The dissenting judgment of Cory J in that case (at paras 90–6) depicts the common law development of sovereign immunity in Canada as rather less straightforward, emphasising such cases as *Zodiak International Products Inc v Polish People's Republic*, [1977] CA 366 (Que) and *Amanat Kahn v Fredson Travel (No. 2)* (1982), 36 OR (2d) 17 (Ont HCJ).

142 *Re Canada Labour Code*, above note 75.

143 *Ibid* at 102–5.

144 *I° Congreso*, above note 18.

contemporaneous Privy Council decision[145] for authority that the restrictive doctrine of state immunity represented English common law prior to Parliament's statutory intervention with the State Immunity Act 1978.[146] The *Congreso* case assumed – indeed, it hinged upon – strong incorporation. Justice La Forest did not quote those passages of Lord Wilberforce's judgment approving *Trendtex*. Nevertheless, La Forest J made clear that the common law of Canada conformed with customary international law's restrictive doctrine of state immunity prior to Parliament's enunciation of that position in the State Immunity Act. The learned judge described the Act as "a codification that is intended to clarify and continue the theory of restrictive immunity, rather than to alter its substance."[147] All that is missing from La Forest J's analysis is an explicit statement that the force which brought about this change in the common law was customary international law as incorporated in Canada according to the strong approach set out in *Trendtex*. The fact that he did not go that far is disappointing, but it may be somewhat pedantic to insist on this. What wrought the common law's change in England, as Lord Wilberforce suggested in *I° Congreso*, was strong incorporation. In affirming that case, and finding that the same change occurred in Canadian common law, La Forest J surely threw his support (and that of the majority of the Supreme Court of Canada) behind strong incorporation. *Re Canada Labour Code* is a good indication that Canadian law has embraced strong incorporation.

The Supreme Court of Canada's consideration of incorporation in *R v Hape* may also be seen as support for strong incorporation in Canada. Justice LeBel's discussion of the doctrine relied heavily on *Trendtex*, quoting in particular those passages in which Lord Denning MR held that the Court of Appeal could give effect to new rules of customary international law without waiting for the House of Lords to do so first. Furthermore, LeBel

145 *The Philippine Admiral*, above note 20.

146 (UK) 1978, c 33.

147 *Re Canada Labour Code*, above note 75 at 73–4. La Forest J's use of the word "codification" rather than "implementation," "transformation," or even "enactment" complements his view that the common law had already changed from full to restrictive immunity by the time Parliament acted. See, similarly, *Kazemi Estate*, above note 85 at para 13 (describing how absolute state immunity "was gradually transformed into a more restrictive immunity that forms part of the common law and of public law in England and in Canada, and that the Parliament of Canada incorporated into federal legislation by enacting" the State Immunity Act).

J described the doctrine as requiring customary rules to be "incorporated into domestic law in the absence of conflicting legislation"[148] – without saying that conflicting case law may also pre-empt custom.

Justice Abella's observations about the incorporation doctrine in *Nevsun Resources v Araya* point toward both weak and strong incorporation at points. She relied on Professor Brownlie's account of the doctrine, and also Lord Atkin's formulation in *Chung Chi Cheung*, both of which explain that the courts will treat custom as incorporated into domestic law so far as it is not inconsistent with rules enacted by statutes or finally declared by tribunals.[149] She summarized the doctrine as providing that "norms of customary international law . . . are fully integrated into, and form part of, Canadian domestic common law, absent conflicting law" – a phrase broad enough to capture conflicting statutes and conflicting judicial precedents.[150] Yet elsewhere Abella J seems to point to conflicting legislation as the sole break on judicial incorporation of custom.[151] Given that the strong versus weak incorporation point was not directly before the court in *Nevsun*, the issue must be regarded as still open.

6.3 Application of the incorporation doctrine

The incorporation doctrine applies only in respect of mandatory rules of customary international law, including *jus cogens* norms. The judicial determination of whether to adopt an established rule of custom into Canadian common law is not discretionary.

(a) Incorporation of custom only

Only norms of customary international law are incorporated by the common law. Treaty norms are not incorporated but instead require legislative implementation.[152] Nor are other sources of international law.[153]

148 *Hape*, above note 88 at paras 36 (quoting *Trendtex*, above note 16), 39.
149 *Nevsun*, above note 97 at paras 86, 87.
150 *Ibid* at para 94.
151 See, e.g., *Nevsun*, above note 97 at paras 90 (twice in her own text here and one in her quote of LeBel J in *Hape*), 91 (in the quotation of an article by LeBel J), 128.
152 See the discussions in Chapter 4, Section 4.2(a), and Chapter 7, Section 7.1.
153 See generally Chapter 8.

The ancient authorities speak of "the law of nations," by which was meant what we now call customary international law. "The law of nations" must not be taken as including treaty-made international law and thus denying the implementation requirement. This point is not made explicitly in these early cases, but it is implied – the prohibition on executive lawmaking, which is the source of the implementation requirement, was in place by this time. Furthermore, the authorities sometimes use the phrase *jus gentium* as a synonym for the law of nations, and it is clear that this phrase excludes treaties.

(b) Incorporation of mandatory not permissive customs

Most customary rules prescribe or restrict certain courses of conduct. Some, however, are merely permissive, such as a rule permitting states to exercise jurisdiction over certain people or areas without requiring them to do so. The distinction between mandatory and permissive customary international laws is significant for the doctrine of incorporation in Canada. Mandatory rules of customary international law are incorporated in the manner described previously. But permissive norms are not incorporated; they need legislation to become law. This rule, derived from *R v Keyn*, has been endorsed by the Supreme Court of Canada in twenty-first-century cases.

In *Keyn*,[154] the English Court for Crown Cases Reserved was confronted with two inconsistent legal rules. At customary international law, states enjoyed a three-mile territorial sea. At English common law, however, the realm ended at low-water mark. Thus, the court in *Keyn* was in a position similar to that of the Supreme Court of Canada in *Re Armed Forces* and that of the English Court of Appeal in *Trendtex*: It was forced to choose between custom and the common law. By the narrowest majority (seven to six), the court chose to preserve the common law. The court's hesitance in applying international custom in the face of an established common law rule may be the true explanation of its decision. Yet *Keyn* has been explained by English[155] and Canadian[156]

---

154 *Keyn*, above note 9.

155 See H Lauterpacht, "Is International Law a Part of the Law of England?" (1940) 25 *Transactions of the Grotius Society* 51 at 61; Sir Robert Jennings & Sir Arthur Watts, eds, *Oppenheim's International Law*, 9th ed, vol 1 (London: Longmans, 1992) at 57.

156 See the illuminating discussion in Macdonald, above note 24 at 94–6.

commentators as an application of an exception to the incorporation rule for permissive rules of customary international law. According to this reading, international law as it stood at the time did not require states to extend their jurisdiction to the territorial sea. It simply permitted them to do so, within a three-mile limit. The majority held that where international law gives such an option, the legislature, and not the courts, must exercise it.[157] The doctrine of incorporation did not apply. This reading of *Keyn* reconciles it with the long line of pro-incorporation authorities that precede it while adding a logical, if marginal, refinement of the incorporation doctrine.

The distinction between permissive and mandatory customs was not immediately taken up in Canadian courts, though *Keyn* itself has been frequently applied. In *Gavin v The Queen*,[158] the Supreme Court of Prince Edward Island followed *Keyn* in finding that the realm of Canada, like that of England, extended at common law to the low-water mark and could not be expanded by incorporation of the three-mile limit recognized at international law. The court did not approve, or even mention, the distinction between mandatory and permissive custom. Similarly, in *Re Dominion Coal*,[159] the Nova Scotia Supreme Court cited *Keyn* and *Gavin* as authorities on the point that legislation was necessary to extend territorial boundaries, but did not explain these cases as turning on a rule that only mandatory custom is incorporated by the common law. The Supreme Court of Canada applied *Keyn* in *Re Offshore Mineral Rights*[160] without drawing the mandatory/permissive distinction.[161]

---

157 See also *Ex parte Lo Pak* (1888), 9 NSWLR 221, in which the Crown argued that the New South Wales Government had a prerogative power to prevent foreigners entering the colony. The court rejected that argument. Darley CJ observed (at 237), "It may be that the Sovereign of England may have such a power according to the principles laid down by writers on international law, but so far as I can understand, it has not been a power that has ever been exercised in England. On the contrary . . . it has been considered necessary to pass a statute for the express purpose of enabling that to be done."

158 (1956) 115 CCC 315 at 321–3 (PEISC).

159 *Re Dominion Coal Co Ltd and County of Cape Breton, Re Nova Scotia Steel & Coal Co Ltd and County of Cape Breton* (1963), 40 DLR (2d) 593 at 631 (NSSC).

160 *Reference re Ownership of Offshore Mineral Rights (British Columbia)*, [1967] SCR 792.

161 See also the discussions of *Reference re Ownership of Offshore Mineral Rights (British Columbia)* and *Keyn* in *Re Newfoundland Continental Shelf*, [1984] 1 SCR 86 at 114 and *Re Ownership of the Bed of the Strait of Georgia*, [1984] 1 SCR 388 at 400.

Vanek credits Lauterpacht with first explaining *Keyn* in terms of permissive and mandatory custom.[162] Brun and Tremblay describe two types of custom, "les coutumes internationales prohibitives" and "les coutumes internationales habilitantes." The former are said to be incorporated by the common law, whereas the latter need transformation. As the authors explain, "Il est logique, en effet, que ce qui est permissif ne fasse pas l'objet d'une contrainte."[163]

Justice La Forest drew on the permissive/mandatory distinction in his dissenting judgment in the Supreme Court decision of *R v Finta*.[164] That case concerned the meaning and constitutionality of certain provisions of the Criminal Code concerning war criminals. These provisions were enacted following the report of the Deschênes Commission, one of whose findings was that section 11(g) of the Charter, coupled with the principle of universal jurisdiction recognized at international law over war crimes and crimes against humanity, gave our courts jurisdiction to prosecute war criminals even without statutory authority. Justice La Forest disagreed with the Commission on this point, saying,

> It is not self-evident that these crimes could be prosecuted in Canada in the absence of legislation. On the analogy of other international authority in the area, it is certainly arguable that the international norm regarding universality of jurisdiction is permissive only (see *The Case of the S.S. "Lotus"* (1927). . .), and the language of s. 11(g) of the Charter also appears to be framed in permissive terms. Thus it is by no means clear that prosecution could automatically be pursued for these crimes before the courts of the various states, especially Canada where, barring express exception, crimes must comply with the requirement that they were committed within Canadian territory (s. 6 of the Code).[165]

---

162 D Vanek, "Is International Law Part of the Law of Canada?" (1949–50) 8 *University of Toronto Law Journal* 251 at 262, citing H Lauterpacht, *The Function of Law in the International Community* (Oxford: Clarendon Press, 1933) at 61.

163 H Brun & G Tremblay, *Droit constitutionnel*, 3d ed (Cowansville, QC: Les Éditions Yvon Blais, 1997) [Brun & Tremblay] at 659. Brun & Tremblay's discussion of permissive and mandatory custom was quoted and applied by the Quebec Superior Court in *R v Pezwick* (1987), JE 87-566, a seemingly unreported case concerning the legal status of the Gulf of St. Lawrence, a partial report of which is found in J-Y Morin, F Rigaldies, & D Turp, eds, *Droit international public: notes et documents, tome II*, 3d ed (Montreal: Éditions Thémis, 1997) at 981.

164 [1994] 1 SCR 701 [*Finta*].

165 *Finta*, above note 164 at 734.

In La Forest J's view, international law did not mandate prosecution of war criminals by all states. Rather, international law simply permitted states to assume this jurisdiction. For Canada to do so, in La Forest J's view, it must legislate. The customary law of universal jurisdiction in respect of war crimes was not incorporated by the common law because it was merely permissive in nature.

The House of Lords effectively applied the permissive/mandatory distinction, though not quite in those terms, in *R v Jones*.[166] Lord Bingham agreed with the appellants on the general proposition that a crime recognized in customary international law "may be assimilated into the domestic criminal law of this country" but rejected their submission "that that result follows automatically."[167] His lordship relied on the following passage from Lord Cockburn CJ in *R v Keyn*:

> Nor, in my opinion, would the clearest proof of unanimous assent on the part of other nations be sufficient to authorize the tribunals of this country to apply, without an Act of Parliament, what would practically amount to a new law. In so doing we should be unjustifiably usurping the province of the legislature. The assent of nations is doubtless sufficient to give the power of parliamentary legislation in a manner otherwise within the sphere of international law; but it would be powerless to confer without such legislation a jurisdiction beyond and unknown to the law, such as that now insisted on, a jurisdiction over foreigners in foreign ships on a portion of the high seas.[168]

It seems clear that customary international law does not require states to criminalize and prosecute aggression but only permits them to do so.[169] Lord Bingham did not make this point expressly, but it is implicit in his finding that the international crime of aggression is not incorporated into English criminal law. It is also implicit, of course, in the simple fact that the UK had not criminalized aggression in its domestic law by statute or other positive act. Like *Keyn*, *Jones* can be seen as an application of the principle that common law courts incorporate mandatory customs but defer to the legislature on whether to give effect to permissive customs.

166 *Jones*, above note 116.
167 *Ibid* at para 23.
168 *Keyn*, above note 9 at 203.
169 See O'Keefe, above note 116 at 297.

The distinction between mandatory and permissive rules of customary international law was noted in passing by LeBel J in *R v Hape*. The learned judge described the incorporation doctrine as applying to "prohibitive rules of customary international law."[170] The term "prohibitive" is the one used by Brun and Tremblay in their discussion of *Keyn*, where the authors contrast prohibitive customs (*coutumes prohibitives*) with authorizing or enabling customs (*coutumes habilitantes*).[171] The terms are different, but the meaning is the same.

Justice LeBel returned to the distinction in *Kazemi Estate*, observing that

> the mere existence of a customary rule in international law does not automatically incorporate that rule into the domestic legal order. . . . Should an exception to state immunity for acts of torture have become customary international law, such a rule could likely be permissive – and not mandatory – thereby, requiring legislative action to become Canadian law. . . .[172]

He cited to La Forest J's discussion in *Finta*, considered above, an article he co-authored with his law clerk,[173] and the discussion of permissive and mandatory customs in this section as it occurred in the second edition of this book.[174]

Justice Abella for the majority of the court in *Nevsun* returned to the mandatory/permissive distinction, referring to *Hape*'s "novel use of the word 'prohibitive'" and noting that LeBel J, writing extra-judicially, had clarified (as I argued in the second edition of this book) that "prohibitive" norms are those that are mandatory "in the sense that they

---

170 *Hape*, above note 88 at paras 36, 39.

171 Brun & Tremblay, above note 163 at 659.

172 *Kazemi Estate*, above note 85 at para 61; see also para 107 ("Creating this kind of jurisdiction would have a potentially considerable impact on Canada's international relations. This decision is to be made by Parliament, not the courts").

173 L LeBel and G Chao, "The Rise of International Law in Canadian Constitutional Litigation: Fugue or Fusion? Recent Developments and Challenges in Internalizing International Law" (2002) 16 *Supreme Court Law Review* (2d) 23 at 36, where the authors cite Brun and Tremblay for the proposition that "a prohibitive custom that is universally recognized is akin to a rule of common law in the internal legal order; however, a permissive custom will necessitate legislative incorporation in order to be admitted into the domestic legal order."

174 G van Ert, *Using International Law in Canadian Courts*, 2d ed (Toronto: Irwin Law, 2008) at 218–23.

are obligatory or binding."[175] Yet she also suggested that LeBel J's use of the term "prohibitive" "merely emphasizes the mandatory nature of customary international law."[176] This proposition is, with respect, at odds with LeBel J's further consideration of the permissive/mandatory distinction in *Kazemi Estate* and the authorities cited therein. Curiously, *Kazemi Estate* was not referred to by Abella J on this point.[177]

The best conclusion to be drawn from these authorities is that only mandatory (including prohibitive) rules of customary law become part of Canadian law by incorporation. Customs that require states to do, or prohibit states from doing, certain things are automatically incorporated into Canadian common law. If, however, a custom simply permits states to do something, Canada's decision whether to avail itself of that right or power is not properly made by the judiciary; it must be left to the political elements of the constitution. Merely permissive customs are therefore not incorporated but must be implemented by legislation.

The distinction between mandatory and permissive customs is more evidence of the principles of self-government and respect for international law at work in our reception system. Were the common law to incorporate permissive customary laws, our courts would be forced to make decisions that, in a self-governing regime, ought to be made by parliamentary process, or at least by ministers responsible to such a process.[178] Nor is the principle of respect for international law

---

175 *Nevsun*, above note 97 at para 92.

176 *Ibid* at para 93.

177 In a partial dissent, Brown and Rowe JJ propose an elaborate distinction between mandatory and prohibitive norms inspired by the distinction between *certiorari* and *mandamus* in the law of remedies (*Nevsun*, above note 97 at paras 168–70). However ingenious this may be, it is pure judicial invention with no support in existing law. See the trenchant critique by C-E Côté, "L'Arrêt *Nevsun*, le Capitaine Keyn et les normes prohibitives de droit international coutumier au Canada" Hors-série (janvier 2022) *Revue québécoise de droit international* 51 at 59–62.

178 Similar reasoning was applied by the House of Lords in *Jones*, above note 116. Lord Bingham, at para 29, explained that his reasons reflected "what has become an important democratic principle in this country: that it is for those representing the people of the country in Parliament, not the executive and not the judges, to decide what conduct should be treated as lying so far outside the bounds of what is acceptable in our society as to attract criminal penalties." Similarly, Lord Hoffmann spoke at para 60 of "the democratic principle that it is nowadays for Parliament and Parliament alone to decide whether conduct not previously regarded as criminal should be made an offence."

slighted by the common law's refusal to incorporate permissive customs, for the law in question is *ex hypothesi*, not mandatory. The distinction between mandatory and permissive customs may be helpful in some cases. If it can be shown that the international custom at issue in a given case is merely permissive, that argument will bar the ordinary operation of the incorporation doctrine.

(c) Incorporation of peremptory norms

The Supreme Court of Canada has described peremptory norms of general international law (*jus cogens*) as "a higher form of customary international law"[179] and a non-derogable subset of custom.[180] If peremptory norms are essentially an entrenched variety of customary international law, then the common law seemingly incorporates them just as it incorporates lesser, derogable customs. That conclusion is so far better supported by logic than by precedent, however.[181]

If *jus cogens* norms take direct effect in domestic law through adoption by the common law, one must wonder whether their non-derogable quality survives the transition from international norm to common law rule. As we have seen, ordinary customs are susceptible to displacement by statute just like other common law rules.[182] Is the same true of incorporated peremptory norms?

In *Suresh v Canada (Minister of Citizenship and Immigration)*, the federal government alleged that Suresh, a Convention refugee, was a security risk to Canada due to his involvement with Tamil terrorist organizations. They sought to return him to Sri Lanka. Suresh contended that to do so would be contrary to Canadian and international law because he faced the risk of torture upon his return. At the Federal Court of Appeal,[183] Suresh argued that the prohibition against torture was a peremptory norm of international law and therefore binding on Canada notwithstanding those provisions of the Immigration Act[184] that

179 *Kazemi Estate*, above note 85 at para 151.

180 *Nevsun*, above note 97 at para 83.

181 But see *Kazemi Estate*, above note 85 at para 149 ("unless a treaty provision expresses a rule of customary international law or a peremptory norm, that provision will only be binding in Canadian law if it is given effect through Canada's domestic lawmaking process").

182 See Section 6.2(b), above.

183 *Suresh* FCA, above note 112.

184 Immigration Act, RSC 1985, c I-2 (as amended; now repealed).

permitted his deportation. Justice Robertson for the Federal Court of Appeal appeared at several points to accept the argument that Parliament is incompetent to violate peremptory norms of international law. Yet the judgment ultimately upheld the disputed provision of the Act. Suresh's argument was summarized by Robertson as follows:

> The appellant maintains that customary international law can become part of domestic law by absorption into the common law and that the prohibition against torture is part of customary international law as found in the *Convention Against Torture* and the *International Covenant on Civil and Political Rights*. The appellant also argues that the non-derogable nature of these conventions has achieved the status of *jus cogens* under customary international law.[185]

Justice Robertson then drew this conclusion from the appellant's submission:

> If this argument were accepted then it follows that even if a person were considered a danger to the security of Canada, the Minister is necessarily restrained from "refouling" that person to a country in circumstances where there are substantial grounds for believing that refoulement would expose that person to the risk of torture.[186]

Elsewhere in his reasons, Robertson JA explained that Suresh's submission went not to the constitutional validity of the disputed section of the Immigration Act, "but rather its inapplicability."[187] Having at least entertained the proposition that an incorporated rule of *jus cogens* can be used to "disapply" legislation, Robertson JA held that the "alleged peremptory norm" conflicted with the provisions of the Immigration Act, which itself implemented part of the United Nations Convention Relating to the Status of Refugees 1951,[188] and that the statute prevailed.[189] The suggestion that rules of *jus cogens* may be invoked to invalidate domestic legislation was not considered in the subsequent appeal of the case to the Supreme Court of Canada.[190]

---

185 *Suresh* FCA, above note 112 at para 31.
186 *Ibid*.
187 *Ibid* at para 22.
188 [1969] Can TS no 6.
189 *Suresh* FCA, above note 112 at para 31.
190 *Suresh*, above note 82.

In *Schreiber v Canada (Attorney General),*[191] the appellant had been arrested by Canada for the purpose of extraditing him to Germany. He spent eight days in prison before being granted bail. He sued Germany, seeking damages for personal injuries he allegedly suffered because of his arrest and detention. He had suffered no physical injury but claimed wrongful arrest and imprisonment, along with the attendant mental distress and injury to reputation. Germany resisted on the basis of its state immunity and was successful in the courts below. The Supreme Court of Canada dismissed his appeal, but in doing so made certain observations about peremptory norms in response to arguments advanced by the intervener Amnesty International. Schreiber submitted that Germany lacked immunity from his suit under the personal injury exception in section 6(a) of the State Immunity Act. Effectively supporting Schreiber, Amnesty argued for a broad interpretation of the personal injury exception, submitting (in LeBel J's words) that "the right to the protection of mental integrity and to compensation for its violation has risen to the level of a peremptory norm of international law which prevails over the doctrine of sovereign immunity."[192] In response, LeBel J found that "neither the intervener nor any other party has established that a peremptory norm of international law has now come into existence which would completely oust the doctrine of state immunity and allow domestic courts to entertain claims in the circumstances of this case."[193] In *Schreiber* as in *Suresh*, it is unclear what relevance either the parties or the court contemplated for peremptory norms in this case. The implication of LeBel J's comments is that, had a *jus cogens* exception to the international law of state immunity been proved, the court might have somehow given effect to it despite the express provisions of the State Immunity Act. How this might be done is unclear.

The notion that an incorporated rule of *jus cogens* might prevail over a contrary statute was seemingly rejected in *Kazemi Estate*. At any rate that was how Abella J, considering *Kazemi Estate* in *Nevsun*, saw matters. She summarized *Kazemi Estate* this way:

> The majority did not depart from the position in *Hape* that customary international law, including peremptory norms, are part of

191 *Schreiber v Canada (Attorney General),* [2002] 3 SCR 269 [*Schreiber*].

192 *Schreiber,* above note 191 at para 48.

193 *Ibid* at para 49.

> Canadian common law, absent express legislation to the contrary. However, it concluded that the *State Immunity Act* was the kind of express legislation that prevented a remedy against the State of Iran for the breach of the *jus cogens* prohibition against torture, which it agreed was part of domestic Canadian law. LeBel J. for the majority noted that "[w]hile rights would be illusory if there was never a way to remedy their violation, the reality is that certain rights do exist even though remedies for their violation may be limited by procedural bars" (para. 159). In effect, the majority in *Kazemi* held that the general right to a remedy was overridden by Parliament's enactment of the *State Immunity Act*.[194]

Consistently with *Kazemi Estate*, and despite suggestions to the contrary in *Suresh* and *Schreiber*, peremptory norms of general international law likely cannot be grounds for invalidating or "disapplying" statutes. Such a result is contrary to the incorporation doctrine, the effect of which is to assimilate custom wholly into the common law, meaning that the assimilated custom shares the common law's susceptibility to abolition or curtailment by statute. Such a result is also irreconcilable with the residual sovereignty of Canadian legislatures to legislate contrary to international law – including by displacing common law decisions incorporating rules of customary international law. Finally, to treat the non-derogable nature of *jus cogens* as effective to displace statutes would be at odds with section 52 of the Constitution Act, 1982.[195] That provision requires (and permits) Canadian courts to invalidate legislation only to give effect to the constitution of Canada as supreme law. Peremptory norms are not part of the constitution of Canada as defined in section 52(2) and therefore cannot be the basis for invalidating or declining to enforce enacted laws. For a court to find that peremptory norms were a basis upon which to invalidate a statute would amount to inscribing such norms into section 52(2) as part of the written constitution.

None of which should be taken as contending that our legislatures deserve or need the power to legislate in ways that offend against longstanding and eminently desirable prohibitions of slavery, piracy,

---

194 *Nevsun*, above note 97 at para 121.

195 Constitution Act, 1982, being Schedule B to the Canada Act 1982 (UK), 1982, c 11, s 52.

genocide, and aggression. These and other peremptory norms are already controlled by customary international law (and, in many cases, by treaty). Legislation contrary to peremptory norms would assuredly bring international responsibility on the state. In the very unlikely event that a Canadian law appeared to conflict with a peremptory norm, our courts would be alive to that consequence and would, it seems, apply the presumption of conformity with heightened vigilance.

(d) No judicial discretion not to incorporate

As noted previously in this chapter, LeBel J's discussion of the incorporation doctrine in *R v Hape* can be read to mean that courts enjoy a discretion as to whether or not to adopt a rule of customary international law into the common law.[196] In *Nevsun*, however, Abella J for the majority of the court affirmed that customary international law is "automatically incorporated into Canadian law" and quoted from an article that LeBel J later wrote explaining (in Abella J's words) that "the Court's use of the word 'may' in *Hape* was in no way meant to diverge from the traditional approach of directly incorporating customary norms into Canadian common law."[197]

196 *Hape*, above note 88 at para 39.
197 *Nevsun*, above note 97 at paras 90–1.

7 The implementation and interpretation of treaties

Treaties are the pre-eminent form of international lawmaking. Multilateral treaties of a lawmaking character[1] reshaped international relations in the twentieth century and are likely to continue to do so in the twenty-first. Of particular importance for this book are what might be called inward-looking treaties, by which I mean those in which states parties commit themselves not only to certain courses of conduct on the international plane but also to achieving certain treaty-defined norms and standards in their own jurisdictions. Such treaties, in the Anglo-Canadian tradition, require legislation to give direct effect to them in domestic law.

If the incorporation of custom is primarily informed by the principle of respect for international law, the implementation of treaties is the realm of self-government. The self-government principle structures this area of the law by requiring that government-made treaties be implemented by our legislatures before taking direct effect in domestic law. As described in Chapter 5, however, the implementation requirement is significantly mitigated by the presumption of conformity with international law. The interplay between self-government and respect for international law – the former insisting on treaty implementation and the latter advancing the presumption of conformity – may be seen throughout this chapter.

1 Brownlie succinctly defined lawmaking treaties as treaties that "create legal obligations the observance of which does not dissolve the treaty obligation": I Brownlie, *Principles of Public International Law*, 6th ed (Oxford: Oxford University Press, 2003) [Brownlie] at 12.

7.1 The implementation requirement

As explained in Chapter 4, the fundamental rule applicable to treaties in the Canadian reception system is that they do not take direct effect in domestic law.[2] Rather, treaties require implementation.

(a) "Implementation"

"Implementation" is the technical term long preferred by Canadian legislatures and legislative drafters to describe the domestic performance of a treaty obligation by primary or secondary legislation.[3] It is also the term employed in the federal government's Policy on Tabling of Treaties in Parliament.[4] The term "incorporation" is sometimes used by Canadian judges as a synonym for implementation. Courts sometimes also speak of legislative "ratification" when they mean implementation.[5] Both terms, employed in this context, ignore parliamentary usage and risk confusion with other concepts. Throughout this book I use the term "implementation" as it is used by our legislatures and

2 See Chapter 4, Section 4.2(a).

3 In federal law, see, e.g., Canada–Chile Free Trade Agreement Implementation Act, SC 1997, c 14; Anti-Personnel Mines Convention Implementation Act, SC 1997, c 33; Civil International Space Station Agreement Implementation Act, SC 1999, c 35; Tax Conventions Implementation Act, 2002, SC 2002, c 24; An Act to amend the Criminal Code in order to implement the United Nations Convention against Corruption, SC 2007, c 13; Tax Conventions Implementation Act, 2013, SC 2013 c 27; Canada–United States Enhanced Tax Information Exchange Agreement Implementation Act, SC 2014, c 20, s 99; Port State Measures Agreement Implementation Act, SC 2015, c 18; Canada–European Union Comprehensive Economic and Trade Agreement Implementation Act, SC 2017, c 6. In provincial law, see, e.g., International Conventions Implementation Act, RSA 2000, c I-6; Intercountry Adoption (Hague Convention) Implementation Act, SS 1995, c I-10.01; International Trade and Investment Agreements Implementation Act, RSA 2000, c I-7; North American Environmental and Labour Cooperation Agreements Implementation Act, CCSM, c N95; An Act respecting the implementation of international trade agreements, RSQ, c M-35.2; etc.

4 Government of Canada, "Policy on Tabling of Treaties in Parliament" (2008), online: www. treaty-accord.gc.ca/procedures.aspx.

5 E.g., *Re Canada Labour Code*, [1992] 2 SCR 50 at 90 ("I would note that SOFA has no legal effect in Canada, as it has not been ratified by domestic legislation"); *R v Rumbaut* (1998), 127 CCC (3d) 138 (NBQB) at para 28 ("Neither the 1958 Geneva Convention [on the High Seas, 1958] . . . nor the [United Nations Convention on the Law of the Sea, 1982] . . . have been ratified by the Canadian Parliament and are not, as such, part of Canadian domestic law").

governments, namely as chiefly referring to legislative measures that seek to ensure domestic performance of an obligation assumed by the state under an international agreement.[6]

There is a broader sense in which non-legislative measures, such as the adoption of administrative practices and policies, may also be characterized as implementation. Treaties may positively require states to take measures beyond legislation to implement their provisions.[7] It is not wrong to describe non-legislative measures adopted to perform the state's treaty obligations as implementation, but for clarity when I speak of implementation I refer (unless otherwise indicated) to implementation by law.

We will see that there is no particular form of words required to implement a treaty. Precedents and standard practices have developed, of course, but whether a law implements a treaty or not remains a question of substance rather than an analysis of form. In determining whether a law implements a treaty, the question to be answered comes down to this: Does this enactment perform, in whole or in part, the state's treaty obligations in our law?

(b) Leading cases on the implementation requirement

The constitutional prohibition of Crown lawmaking has long been understood to mean that treaties need legislative implementation to take effect in domestic law. Even once implemented, it is not strictly speaking the treaty that takes effect in domestic law, but the legislative measure that introduces or gives effect to it.

---

6 Legislatures also have the power to implement instruments other than binding international agreements, and they sometimes do. Professor Harrington notes that "nothing bars a domestic legislature from choosing to give a soft law instrument domestic legal effect through the enactment of domestic law": J Harrington, *Halsbury's Laws of Canada – Public International Law* (2023 reissue) at HPI-9. The same is true of non-international instruments, e.g., the Dunsmuir agreement at issue in *Re British Columbia (Attorney General) v Canada (Attorney General); Re An Act Respecting the Vancouver Island Railway*, [1994] 2 SCR 41 [*Re Vancouver Island Railway*].

7 E.g., art 4 of the Convention on the Rights of the Child 1989, [1992] Can TS no 3, which reads in part, "States Parties shall undertake all appropriate legislative, administrative, and other measures for the implementation of the rights recognized in the present Convention."

English and Canadian authorities agree that treaties must be implemented to alter domestic law. A leading authority on the implementation requirement in both jurisdictions is Lord Atkin's decision in *Labour Conventions* (1937), an appeal to the Privy Council from the Supreme Court of Canada. His lordship explained:

> Within the British Empire there is a well-established rule that the making of a treaty is an executive act, while the performance of its obligations, if they entail alteration of the existing domestic law, requires legislative action. Unlike some other countries, the stipulations of a treaty duly ratified do not within the Empire, by virtue of the treaty alone, have the force of law. If the national executive, the government of the day, decide to incur the obligations of a treaty which involve alteration of law they have to run the risk of obtaining the assent of Parliament to the necessary statute or statutes.[8]

The rule was familiar to, and applied by, the Supreme Court of Canada prior to *Labour Conventions*. In *The Ship "North" v The King* (1906), Idington J noted the "general, but not universal, principle that municipal legislation is necessary to give effect to the doctrines of international law," leaving room for the direct application of custom.[9] In *In Re Employment of Aliens* (1922), Duff J explained:

> [T]he Crown, under the British constitution, possesses authority to enter into obligations towards foreign states diplomatically binding and, indirectly, such treaties may obviously very greatly affect the rights of individuals. But it is no part of the prerogative of the Crown by treaty in time of peace to effect directly a change in the law governing the rights of private individuals, nor is it any part of the prerogative of the Crown to grant away, without the consent of parliament, the public monies or to impose a tax or to alter the laws of trade and navigation and it is at least open to the gravest doubt whether the prerogative includes power to control the exercise by a colonial government or legislature of the right of appropriation over

---

8 *Attorney General for Canada v Attorney General for Ontario*, [1937] AC 326 (PC) [*Labour Conventions*] at 347.

9 (1906) 37 SCR 385 at 398. Idington J may have also had in mind the supposed exception to the implementation requirement for treaties of peace and cession (see Section 7.4(a), below).

> public property given by such a statute as the B.N.A. Act. All these require legislation.[10]

Similarly, in *Arrow River* (1932), Lamont J held that the unimplemented Ashburton Treaty[11]

> in itself is not equivalent to an Imperial Act and, without the sanction of Parliament, the Crown cannot alter the existing law by entering into a contract with a foreign power. For a breach of a treaty a nation is responsible only to the other contracting nation and its own sense of right and justice. Where, as here, a treaty provides that certain rights or privileges are to be enjoyed by the subjects of both contracting parties, these rights and privileges are, under our law, enforceable by the courts only where the treaty has been implemented or sanctioned by legislation rendering it binding upon the subject.[12]

The practical effect of the implementation requirement was starkly demonstrated by the judgment of the Supreme Court of Canada in *Francis v The Queen* (1956).[13] An Indigenous man, Francis, brought goods from the United States into Canada without paying any duty. The Crown later confiscated the goods until Francis paid the duty under protest. He then petitioned for the return of the money and a declaration that no duties or taxes were payable by him, relying on article III of the Jay Treaty 1794,[14] which provided in part that the United States and Britain would allow native people to pass across the territories of

---

10 *In re Employment of Aliens* (1922), 63 SCR 293 [*Re Employment of Aliens*] at 329; on Duff J's "in time of peace" qualification, see the discussion at Section 7.4(a), below. See also Brodeur J at 339 (citing *Walker v Baird*, [1892] AC 491, in which a Newfoundland lobster fisher successfully resisted a British sea captain's trespass and seizure on the basis that the treaty between the United Kingdom and France, under which Captain Baird purported to act, had not been enacted in Newfoundland law).

11 Webster-Ashburton Treaty 1842 30 British and Foreign State Papers 360.

12 *Arrow River & Tributaries Slide & Boom Co Ltd v Pigeon Timber Co Ltd*, [1932] SCR 495 [*Arrow River*] at 510. See the helpful discussion of the *Arrow River* litigation in A Daggett, "Treaty Legislation in Canada" (1938) 16 *Canadian Bar Review* 159 at 169–72.

13 [1956] SCR 618 [*Francis*].

14 Treaty of Amity, Commerce and Navigation, between His Britannick Majesty and the United States of America 19 November 1794 (Jay Treaty), 1 British and Foreign State Papers 784.

the two states without paying duty. The difficulty for Francis was that article III was no longer implemented in Canadian law, though (as Rand J explained in his reasons) it had been until the War of 1812. Without legislation implementing his treaty right, Francis argued that the Jay Treaty 1794 and the subsequent Treaty of Ghent 1815[15] were peace treaties and therefore took direct effect in Canadian law without implementation.[16] This argument was rejected, as was Francis's appeal. Chief Justice Kerwin affirmed that "in Canada such rights and privileges as are here advanced of subjects of a contracting party to a treaty are enforceable by the Courts only where the treaty has been implemented or sanctioned by legislation."[17]

A frequently cited affirmation of the implementation requirement in Canada is the observation of L'Heureux-Dubé J in *Baker v Canada* (1999) that "International treaties and conventions are not part of Canadian law unless they have been implemented by statute."[18] As authority for this proposition, L'Heureux-Dubé J cited *Francis* and *Capital Cities Communications Inc* (1978). In that latter case, Laskin CJ held that an international convention could have "no domestic, internal consequences unless they arose from implementing legislation."[19] *Baker, Francis*, and *Capital Cities* are all frequently cited by the Supreme Court of Canada as authorities for the implementation requirement. Yet they are all compromised on this point in different respects, and the court would do better to cite *Labour Conventions* and the other authorities noted above. In *Baker*, the treaty before the court (the Convention on the Rights of the Child 1989) was not expressly implemented, yet to call it unimplemented without consideration of the full context of Canada's adherence to it was, at best, a gross oversimplification, as Martinson J (an expert on children's rights) later had occasion to point out.[20] In *Francis*, the court's finding that an Aboriginal right recognized in an

15 Treaty of Peace and Amity between His Britannic Majesty and the United States of America 24 December 1814 (Treaty of Ghent), 2 British and Foreign State Papers 357.

16 On the supposed direct effect of peace treaties, see Section 7.4(a), below, in this chapter.

17 *Francis*, above note 13 at 621.

18 *Baker v Canada*, [1999] 2 SCR 817 [*Baker*] at para 69.

19 *Capital Cities Communications Inc v Canadian Radio-Television Commission*, [1978] 2 SCR 141 at 173.

20 *BJG v DLG*, 2010 YKSC 44 [*BJG*] at paras 34–6.

international agreement had disappeared from our law when its implementing legislation was repealed is quite consistent with reception law orthodoxy but nevertheless a rather unattractive precedent today. As for *Capital Cities*, the majority's refusal to consider the unimplemented treaty at issue there in the course of judicial review was implicitly rejected by the majority of the court in *Baker*, as the concurring opinion of Iacobucci J rightly noted.[21]

In *Kazemi Estate v Iran* (2014), LeBel J for the majority of the Supreme Court of Canada reaffirmed the implementation requirement in the course of his consideration of the principles of fundamental justice component of section 7 of the Charter. "[I]t must be noted," observed the learned judge,

> that the existence of an article in a treaty ratified by Canada does not automatically transform that article into a principle of fundamental justice. Canada remains a dualist system in respect of treaty and conventional law. . . . This means that, unless a treaty provision expresses a rule of customary international lay or peremptory norm, that provision will only be binding in Canadian law if it is given effect through Canada's domestic law-making process.

He added that while treaties may "assist in establishing the elements of the *MalmoLevine* test for recognition of new principles of fundamental justice . . . not all commitments in international agreements amount to principles of fundamental justice" and that "The interaction between domestic and international law must be managed carefully in light of the principles governing what remains a dualist system of application of international law and a constitutional and parliamentary democracy."[22]

In *Reference Re Pan-Canadian Securities Regulation* (2018), the court touched briefly but notably on the implementation requirement. "As the Privy Council explained in [*Labour Conventions*], the valid exercise of the federal government's treaty-making power is distinct from the legislative enactment of such agreements into domestic law." The court continued: "Though the federal government may have the authority to enter into international agreements upon subjects falling within the

21 See the discussion in Chapter 9, Section 9.4(b).

22 *Kazemi Estate v Iran*, 2014 SCC 62 at paras 149–50.

legislative competence of the provinces, the individual provinces will only be bound by the terms of such an agreement once their respective legislatures enact them into law. . . ."[23]

Many more Canadian authorities on the implementation requirement may be cited.[24]

(c) Indirect effects not excluded

The implementation requirement bars unimplemented treaties from taking direct effect in domestic law. As noted in Chapter 5, however, it goes too far to pretend that an unimplemented treaty cannot have any effect in domestic law.[25] Such a conclusion is impossible to reconcile

---

23 2018 SCC 48 [*Re Pan-Canadian Securities Regulation*] at para 66.

24 See, e.g., *Bitter v Secretary of State of Canada*, [1944] Ex CR 61 at 76–7 ("it has never, so far as I have been able to ascertain, been decided or admitted that the Crown could by its own act in agreeing to the terms of a treaty alter the law of the land or affect the private rights of individuals"); *R v Canada Labour Relations Board ex p Federal Electric Corporation* (1964), 44 DLR (2d) 440 (Man QB) [*Labour Relations Board*] at 454 ("It has been settled law that a treaty binding the Government does not, *ipso facto*, become part of our law and enforceable in the Courts"); *Mastini v Bell Telephone of Canada* (1971), 18 DLR (3d) 215 at 217 (Ex Ct) [*Mastini*] ("In the absence of some . . . legislative act the making of a treaty does not change the domestic law of Canada"); *Operation Dismantle Inc v Canada*, [1985] 1 SCR 441 at 484 ("A treaty . . . may be in full force and effect internationally without any legislative implementation and, absent such legislative implementation, it does not form part of the domestic law of Canada"); *R v Vincent* (1993), 12 OR (3d) 427 at 437–8 (Ont CA) ("According to well-established case law the rights created or conferred by an international treaty belong exclusively to the sovereign countries which are the contracting parties to it. . . . [I]t results from this principle that the provisions of an international treaty confer no right on an individual unless the treaty is implemented by legislation"); *R v Rebmann* (1995), 122 Nfld & PEIR 111 at 121–26 (Nfld SCTD) (a knowledgeable discussion, too long to quote here); *Revell v Minister of Citizenship and Immigration*, 2019 FCA 262 at paras 131 ("Canada is still a dualist system in terms of reception of international law. As such, even those treaties to which Canada is a party will not be binding in Canadian law unless they are given effect through domestic law. For that reason, the mere existence of an international obligation may well bind Canada at international law, but will not be enforceable in a Canadian court of law"); *Society of Composers, Authors and Music Publishers of Canada v Entertainment Software Association*, 2022 SCC 30 [*Entertainment Software*] at para 47 ("Negotiation, signing, and ratification of treaties are acts of the executive. Once ratified, treaties do not automatically become part of domestic law; rather, they are given effect through domestic legislation").

25 See the discussion in Chapter 5, Section 5.8.

with the presumption of conformity with international law and the use our courts sometimes make of unimplemented treaties in judicial review of administrative action. It is more accurate to say that unimplemented treaties do not take direct effect in domestic law, but indirect effects are not excluded.

Justice Duff put it this way in *In re Employment of Aliens*:

> [T]he Crown . . . possesses authority to enter into obligations towards foreign states diplomatically binding and, indirectly, such treaties may obviously very greatly affect the rights of individuals. But it is no part of the prerogative of the Crown by treaty in time of peace to effect directly a change in the law governing the rights of private individuals.[26]

More recently, in *Bhajan v Bhajan* (2010), Weiler JA for the Court of Appeal for Ontario, sitting in a rare five-judge division, observed:

> Under Canadian law, a treaty that has been signed and ratified by the executive still requires incorporation through domestic law to be enforceable. Although the Convention [on the Rights of the Child 1989] has not been specifically incorporated into domestic law *and its provisions therefore have no direct application in Canadian law*, the values reflected in the Convention can help to inform the contextual approach to statutory interpretation and judicial review.[27]

A similar point, though not employing the distinction between direct and indirect effects, was made by the Quebec Court of Appeal when it noted that even though the international treaties before it "were not incorporated into domestic law, that does not necessarily mean that they are of no utility in that area" and that reference to an unimplemented treaty in the preamble of a statute created "a relative interdependence" between the Act and the treaty "of limited impact" but which can "nevertheless guide the courts in interpreting domestic legislation."[28]

In its 2019 common core document for UN treaty bodies, Canada explained that treaties in Canada are "not self-executing and require

---

26 *Re Employment of Aliens*, above note 10 at 329. On the "in time of peace" qualification, see the discussion at Section 7.4(a), below.

27 2010 ONCA 714 at para 14 (emphasis added).

28 *Quebec (Minister of Justice) v Canada (Minister of Justice)*, 2003 CanLII 52182 (Que CA) [*Quebec*] at para 92.

legislative implementation to be directly applicable in Canadian law" and are therefore "not subject to direct enforcement in Canadian courts"[29] – an account that correctly leaves room for indirect effects.

The indirect effect of unimplemented treaties in domestic law has also been recognized in Australia, the United Kingdom, and the Privy Council. The Federal Court of Australia has observed that, despite the implementation requirement, when "a court construes a statute to comply with a treaty obligation . . . international law then exerts a discernible influence on the content of local law."[30] Similarly, in *R (Miller) v Secretary of State for Exiting the European Union*, a Queen's Bench Division composed of the lord chief justice, the master of the rolls, and Sales LJ noted that "treaties can have certain indirect interpretive effects in relation to domestic law" (citing a House of Lords authority on the presumption of conformity[31]), but this does not affect the implementation requirement.[32] Similarly, Lord Hoffman for the majority of the Privy Council in *Higgs v Minister of National Security and Others (Bahamas)* affirmed that treaties have "no effect upon the rights and duties of citizens in common or statute law" but "may have an indirect effect upon the construction of statutes as a result of the presumption that Parliament does not intend to pass legislation which would put the Crown in breach of its international obligations" or "may give rise to a legitimate expectation on the part of citizens that the government, in its acts affecting them, will observe the terms of the treaty."[33]

An unimplemented treaty's indirect effects are interpretive in nature. As explained in Chapter 5, the presumption of conformity with international law applies to implemented and unimplemented treaties alike.[34] This makes sense, for the purpose of the presumption is

---

29 Canada, *Common Core Document Forming Part of the Reports of States Parties: Canada* (2019) UN Doc HRI/CORE/CAN/2019.

30 *Australian Competition and Consumer Commission v P.T. Garuda Indonesia (No 9)*, [2013] FCA 323 (Fed Ct Australia) at para 43; see also para 36 (affirming the implementation requirement).

31 *R v Lyons*, [2002] UKHL 44 at paras 27–8, where Lord Hoffmann spoke of "a strong presumption in favour of interpreting English law (whether common law or statute) in a way which does not place the United Kingdom in breach of an international obligation."

32 *R (Miller) v Secretary of State for Exiting the European Union*, [2016] EWHC 2768 (Admin) at para 33.

33 [1999] UKPC 55 at para 12.

34 See the discussion in Chapter 5, Section 5.5(b).

to prevent breaches of Canada's international obligations. A treaty commitment is no less binding on Canada internationally for being unimplemented in domestic law. Canada's treaty partners make no distinction between implemented and unimplemented treaties, and therefore courts applying the presumption of conformity should not (and do not), either. Ultimately, Canada remains a dualist jurisdiction in respect of treaties, for the presumption is rebuttable. Yet the presumption of conformity operates as a significant qualification of the dualist stance.

The court in *Bhajan v Bhajan* identified judicial review as a distinct means by which unimplemented treaties may have indirect effects, citing *Baker*. I suggest in Chapter 9 that the use of treaties (implemented and otherwise) to review executive action may be regarded as an application of the presumption of conformity to the statutory power under which the decision maker acts, in which case the distinction between indirect interpretive effects and indirect administrative effects collapses. *Baker* itself invoked the presumption of conformity with international law, and two Supreme Court decisions since *Baker* have cited it as an application of the presumption.[35]

(d) Not all treaties need implementation

The implementation requirement is a fundamental feature of the reception system and an important expression of constitutional principle. Yet we must not lose sight of the fact that the great majority of treaties concluded by Canada are in the nature of state-to-state agreements that do not touch upon the internal laws of their parties and need not, therefore, be implemented in domestic law for Canada to perform them.[36] What Vallat observed in respect of the United Kingdom in 1966 remains true for Canada today: "In many cases . . . no legislation is required, because effect can be given to the treaty by purely admin-

35 *Baker*, above note 18 at para 70; *R v Sharpe*, 2001 SCC 2 at para 175; *114957 Canada Ltée (Spraytech, Société d'arrosage) v Hudson (Town)*, 2001 SCC 40 at para 30.

36 This observation, as made in the second edition of this work, was quoted approvingly by Kasirer J for the court in *Canadian Council for Refugees v Canada (MCI)*, 2023 SCC 17 [*Council for Refugees*] at para 154.

istrative action or by refraining from taking action which would be in breach of the treaty."[37]

In a 2002 ruling on a motion concerning ratification of the Kyoto Protocol to the United Nations Framework Convention on Climate Change,[38] the Deputy Speaker of the House of Commons offered the following statistics on the number of Canadian treaties in past years that had required legislative implementation:

> [M]any international agreements do not require enabling legislation. Enabling or implementing legislation is required only when an agreement necessitates amendments to Canadian statute law. Of the more than 1,400 international agreements entered into by Canada from 1928 to 1978, only 111 required enabling legislation and of these 47 dealt with taxation matters. From 1979 to 1986 another 500 agreements were entered into and of these only 33 required legislation.[39]

The deputy speaker did not say where he got these figures, or whether they refer to implementation by Parliament only or Parliament and the provincial legislatures. Nor did he explain what, for the purpose of these figures, constituted implementation. For instance, we cannot know whether a bill bringing amendments to existing law in conformity with an anticipated treaty obligation, but without referring to that treaty in the bill's text, would be regarded as implementing legislation for the purpose of these statistics (though it should be). Nevertheless, these figures illustrate the point that much of Canada's international treaty-making activity does not, and need not, result in implementing legislation.

7.2 How treaties are implemented

Implementation is required to give direct domestic legal effect to treaties. But what constitutes implementation, and how is it done?

---

37 F Vallat, *International Law and the Practitioner* (Manchester: Manchester University Press, 1966) [Vallat, *International Law*] at 10; see also 11–12.

38 (1997) 37 ILM 32 (in force 16 February 2005).

39 Canada, Parliament, *House of Commons Debates (Hansard)*, 37th Parl, 2nd Sess, Vol 138, No 034 (28 November 2002) at 1519 (Deputy Speaker Kilger).

(a) Legislation is needed

Since implementation is about giving legal effect to a treaty, the instrument doing so must be a law. Merely tabling a treaty in the legislature does not constitute implementation,[40] nor will a resolution of the House of Commons approving ratification of the treaty suffice.[41] A treaty probably cannot be implemented merely by referring to it in the Act's preamble.[42] These principles have been enunciated in respect of the federal Parliament, but they undoubtedly apply equally to the provincial legislatures.

Implementing legislation is often primary legislation (that is, an Act of Parliament or a provincial legislature) but it need not be. Delegated legislation, such as regulations promulgated under statutory authority, may also be used to implement a treaty.[43] An example is section 35(1)(d) of the Canada Shipping Act 2001,[44] empowering the Governor in Council on the recommendation of the minister of transport to make regulations implementing, in whole or in part, certain scheduled international conventions.

The procedure for enacting implementing legislation is no different than that of any other bill. It may be introduced by any member, from a government minister to an opposition backbencher.[45] In the federal Par-

---

40 *Labour Relations Board*, above note 24 at 455.

41 See Section 7.2(c), below.

42 *Quebec*, above note 28 at para 91. But reference to a treaty in a law's preamble can assist in determining legislative purpose to implement, e.g., *Entertainment Software*, above note 24 at para 49.

43 See, e.g., *Council for Refugees*, above note 36 at para 31 ("The impugned regulation is part of the legislative scheme that implements a bilateral treaty between Canada and the United States"); *World Bank Group v Wallace*, 2016 SCC 15 [*Wallace*] at para 46 (noting the implementation of the treaties at issue there by several orders-in-council); *Schavernoch v Foreign Claims Commission*, [1982] 1 SCR 1092 (noting regulations implementing a compensation scheme established under an agreement between Canada and Czechoslovakia); *Pan American World Airways v The Queen*, [1981] 2 SCR 565 at 569 (implementation of a civil aviation convention by an Act and regulations under it); *Benin v Whimster*, [1976] 1 QB 297 (Eng CA) (implementation of a compensation fund by regulation); *Stoeck v Public Trustee*, [1921] 2 Ch 67 (implementation of a peace treaty by regulation); etc.

44 SC 2001, c 26. See also Canada Shipping Act, RSC 1985, c S-9, ss 658, 660.9(a).

45 This is subject to the rule, in the federal Parliament, that money bills can only be introduced upon recommendation by the governor general; that is, by

liament (Canada's only bicameral legislature), implementing legislation may be introduced by members of the upper house (senators) or members of the lower house (members of Parliament). The usual practice is for implementing legislation to be drafted by a government department and brought to the floor of the lower house, the House of Commons, by that department's minister. However, opposition MPs will sometimes bring private member's legislation to implement treaties.

A notable example of implementing legislation introduced by an opposition MP, and even enacted against the wishes of the minority government of the day, is the Kyoto Protocol Implementation Act.[46] The bill was introduced in May 2006 by an opposition MP who explained its purpose as "to ensure that Canada meets its climate change obligations under the Kyoto protocol."[47] The bill passed the Commons in February 2007 and the Senate in May, in both cases over government opposition. It received royal assent in June. The Act's implementing purpose was indicated by its short title, its preamble, and section 3, which read "The purpose of this Act is to ensure that Canada takes effective and timely action to meet its obligations under the Kyoto Protocol and help address the problem of global climate change." The Act did not expressly give the Kyoto Protocol the force of law, but that form of implementation was inapt to the protocol's technical nature. When the government failed to abide by the Act's provisions, an environmental group brought judicial review proceedings. In *Friends of the Earth v Canada (Governor in Council)*, Barnes J worried that the Act, lacking the government's support, "embodies a legislative policy which is inconsistent with stated government policy" – surely one of the strangest comments ever found in a judicial review proceeding.[48] Animated, it seems, by this concern, the learned judge went to astonishing lengths to disregard the Act's implementing intent. He was upheld on appeal in a one-paragraph judgment.[49]

---

ministers: Constitution Act, 1867 (UK), 30 & 31 Vict, c 3, reprinted in RSC 1985, Appendix II, No 5, s 54.

46 SC 2007, c 30.

47 Canada, Parliament, *House of Commons Debates (Hansard)*, 39th Parl, 1st Sess, Vol 141, No 025 (17 May 2006) at 1496 (Mr Rodriguez).

48 2008 FC 1183 at para 8.

49 2009 FCA 297. My critique of both decisions is at (2009) 47 *Canadian Yearbook of International Law* 570–81.

(b) Implementation generally precedes the treaty obligation

Implementing legislation is almost always enacted before Canada incurs legal obligations under a treaty whose performance requires changes to domestic law.[50] The almost invariable practice is to review the proposed treaty, review existing law (statutes and regulations, but also policies and practices) and, if potential inconsistencies with the treaty's obligations are identified, consider what legislative, regulatory, or other steps are needed – either federally, provincially, or both – to permit Canadian adherence.[51] In the case of treaties involving signature subject to ratification, the practice is to sign, then implement domestically, then ratify.[52] Lauterpacht noted this practice as long ago as 1939.[53] The Government of Canada confirmed it in its 2013 core docu-

---

50 "Governments have come to take the position that they will normally only ratify a treaty after any necessary enabling legislation has been passed. . . . Today, on only rare occasions does Canada ratify a treaty prior to the enactment of enabling legislation": M Copithorne, "National Treaty Law and Practice: Canada" in M Leigh et al, eds, *National Treaty Law and Practice* (Washington, DC: American Society of International Law, 2003) at 5. See also I Weiser, "Effect in Domestic Law of International Human Rights Treaties Ratified Without Implementing Legislation" in *The Impact of International Law on the Practice of Law in Canada: Proceedings of the 27th Annual Conference of the Canadian Council on International Law* (The Hague: Kluwer Law International, 1999) [Weiser] at 132; "Canada" in C Heyns & F Viljoen, eds, *The Impact of the United Nations Human Rights Treaties on the Domestic Level* (The Hague: Kluwer Law International, 2002) [Heyns & Viljoen] at 118; E Eid & H Hamboyan, "Implementation by Canada of Its International Human Rights Treaty Obligations: Making Sense Out of the Nonsensical" in O Fitzgerald, ed, *The Globalized Rule of Law: Relationships between International and Domestic Law* (Toronto: Irwin Law, 2006) [Eid & Hamboyan] at 449.

51 It may also be possible, in some cases, for Canada to avoid inconsistency between domestic law and the new treaty by entering a reservation to the treaty upon ratification or accession.

52 See, e.g., *X (Re)*, 2009 FC 1058 at paras 68–71 where Mosley J noted that Canada had signed but not yet ratified the Convention on Cybercrime 2001 2296 UNTS 167 "in part because the legislation required for the domestic application of the data preservation and disclosure measures has not been enacted."

53 H Lauterpacht, "Is International Law a Part of the Law of England?" (1939) 25 *Transactions of the Grotius Society* 51 at 74 ("the likelihood of Courts having to refuse to enforce a valid treaty because of the absence of an enabling Act is of a highly theoretical nature owing to the practice of passing the enabling Act *prior* to the ratification of the treaty"). In a footnote to this passage, Lauterpacht

ment for United Nations human rights bodies. What is said here about human rights treaties is true of Canadian treaty practice generally (although provincial involvement is not always required):

> Prior to ratification of a human rights treaty, all jurisdictions in Canada review their legislation for consistency with the treaty. Where existing legislation and policies fulfill the obligations under the treaty, no new measures are required. On occasion, legislation may be amended or new laws enacted to ensure compliance with the treaty. After ratification, these issues are taken into account in drafting future legislation where relevant.[54]

To accept the treaty obligation first and consider what is needed for domestic performance later would risk putting Canada in breach of the new commitment from the moment of adherence, with potential liability in international law to the other party.[55]

The result of this process is that virtually every Canadian treaty is incurred on the strength of a federal government legal determination that existing law suffices to perform the treaty. Often this is because the treaty does not require domestic performance. Many treaties are in the nature of state-to-state agreements that operate exclusively on the international plane and can be performed by Canada without changing (or even engaging) domestic law. If, instead, the treaty does touch on matters of domestic law, the federal government will adhere to the treaty without domestic legislative change where it concludes that existing laws suffice to perform the treaty's obligations. The third possibility is that domestic legislative change is needed, in which case the necessary reforms will be brought prior to Canada's ratification of or accession to the treaty.

It can happen, however, that implementing legislation is brought after Canada's adherence to a treaty. Such delayed implementation is

---

observed that the only case he knew of where a court refused to apply a treaty because of the absence of enabling legislation was *Arrow River*, above note 12.

54 Canada, *Core Document Forming Part of the Reports of States Parties* (28 January 2013) UN Doc HRI/CORE/CAN/2013 [*Core Document* 2013]. Similarly, the Tabling of Treaties Policy (2008) notes (in Annex A), "Some treaties, prior to their ratification, acceptance, approval or accession by Canada, require legislation."

55 J Hill, *Aust's Modern Treaty Law and Practice*, 4th ed (Cambridge: Cambridge University Press, 2023) [Hill] at 189.

rare but may occur if the treaty is unlikely to come into force soon or, if the treaty is already in force, to give further domestic effect to its requirements as its meaning becomes clearer.[56]

(c) Approval is not implementation

Sometimes treaty-related legislation will include a provision indicating the legislature's approval of the treaty.[57] Courts have repeatedly held that such a provision, without more, does not suffice to implement the treaty.[58] This has understandably led courts to wonder what purpose is served by such a provision.[59]

Historically, approval provisions were used by the federal government to satisfy the Canadian constitutional convention, now abandoned, of seeking parliamentary approval of proposed treaty commitments before adhering to them.[60] An example is section 2(1) of the Geneva Conventions Act, which provided that the four Geneva Conventions, set out in schedules to the Act, are approved.[61] Debating the bill in the Senate, Senator Thorvaldson observed:

---

56 An example is Canada's implementation of the Convention on the Elimination of All Forms of Discrimination against Women 1979, [1982] Can TS no 31. In the years following ratification of the treaty, Canada's reports to the CEDAW monitoring committee stated that legislative changes were brought in contemplation of the treaty. See Heyns & Viljoen, above note 50 at 125.

57 See, e.g., Canada–United States Free Trade Agreement Implementation Act, SC 1988, c 65, s 8; North American Free Trade Agreement Implementation Act, SC 1993, c 44, s 10; World Trade Organization Agreement Implementation Act, SC 1994, c 47, s 8; Loi concernant la mise en oeuvre des accords de commerce international, LQ 1996, c 6, s 2; Canada–European Union Comprehensive Economic and Trade Agreement Implementation Act, above note 3, s 9.

58 See, e.g., *Labour Conventions*, above note 8, at 347–8 ("To make themselves as secure as possible they will often in such cases before final ratification seek to obtain from Parliament an expression of approval. But it has never been suggested, and it is not the law, that such an expression of approval operates as law"); *Mastini*, above note 24 at 217; *Re Vancouver Island Railway*, above note 6 at 109; *UL Canada Inc c Québec (Procureur général)*, [1999] RJQ 1720 (Que SC) [*UL Canada*] at para 86; *Council of Canadians v Canada (Attorney General)* (2006), 277 DLR (4th) 527 (Ont CA) at para 25; *Fraser v Janes Family Foods*, 2012 FCA 99 at paras 14, 15, 22; *Turp v Minister of Foreign Affairs*, 2018 FCA 133 at para 28; *Li v British Columbia*, 2021 BCCA 256 at para 107.

59 E.g., *Antonsen v Canada (Attorney General)*, [1995] 2 FC 272 (FCTD) at para 65 [*Antonsen*].

60 See the discussion in Chapter 4, Section 4.1(d).

61 Geneva Conventions Act, 1949, SC 1965, c 44 (now Geneva Conventions Act, RSC 1985, c G-3).

> There are two methods that can be adopted for the ratification of an international convention. The first is by a resolution of the Parliament of Canada, and the second is by approval, as is given in clause 2 of the bill. When that approval is given by both Houses of Parliament, the Government has acquired power to ratify. That, as I understand it, is the procedure being adopted in regard to the ratification of the conventions in this bill.[62]

Today, neither of these methods is regularly employed for the ratification of treaties by Canada. Certainly it is no longer regarded as a convention of the Canadian constitution that the federal government should not ratify a treaty without first seeking parliamentary consent by resolution or approval. The modern practice of inserting approval provisions is, it seems, not legal but political: to deflect (however unconvincingly) the criticism that Canadian treaty-making practice is insufficiently democratic because it is conducted by the executive with little or no role for Parliament or the provinces.

(d) No formal requirements

There are a variety of ways in which legislation can implement treaties.[63] Legislatures are not bound to observe any particular form of implementation, and in fact they employ a variety of methods.[64] The only formal requirement to speak of is not legal but common sense: The legislature must make its intent to implement sufficiently clear so that courts will treat the statute as implementing legislation, or at least

62 Canada, Parliament, *Debates of the Senate (Hansard)*, 26th Parl, 2nd Sess, Vol 1 (26 May 1964) at 556 (Mr. Thorvaldson).

63 See A de Mestral and E Fox-Decent, "Implementation and Reception: The Congeniality of Canada's Legal Order to International Law" in O Fitzgerald, ed, *The Globalized Rule of Law: Relationships Between International and Domestic Law* (Toronto: Irwin Law, 2006) 31 at 42–56; J Keyes & R Sullivan, "A Legislative Perspective on the Interaction of International and Domestic Law" in O Fitzgerald, ed, *The Globalized Rule of Law: Relationships Between International and Domestic Law* (Toronto: Irwin Law, 2006) 277 [Keyes & Sullivan] at 310–29; G van Ert, "What Is Treaty Implementation?" in *Legitimacy and Accountability in International Law: Proceedings of the Canadian Council of International Law 2004* (Ottawa: Canadian Council on International Law, 2005) at 165.

64 A fine illustration of this is the judgment of Lemieux J in *Pfizer Inc v Canada*, [1999] 4 FC 441 (FCTD) at paras 29–31 (aff'd (1999) 250 NR 66 (FCA)) [*Pfizer*], in which the learned judge describes the various ways in which the WTO and TRIPS Agreements were implemented.

reach the treaty-compliant result the legislature intended.[65] The task of determining whether an Act seeks to implement a treaty is no different than that of discerning the legislature's intent more generally. Counsel and courts may determine intent to implement using extrinsic evidence such as legislative history and Hansard.[66]

The primacy of intent over form is illustrated by an old British Columbian case, *In re Nakane and Okazake*.[67] Two Japanese subjects were detained under an Act of the British Columbia legislature. They challenged the Act as invalid because it was inconsistent with a federal Act that, they argued, implemented a treaty between the United Kingdom and Japan. This treaty assured Japanese subjects full liberty to enter, travel, or reside in any part of Canada. The attorney general of British Columbia contended that the federal Act was ineffective to implement the treaty, for it merely declared the treaty to be "hereby sanctioned" and reproduced it in a schedule to the Act. Chief Justice Hunter held that the Act implemented the treaty and thereby invalidated the inconsistent provincial law. Neither the use of the unorthodox term "sanction" nor the placement of the treaty in a schedule to the Act detracted from Parliament's intent, which was to make the provisions of the

---

65 In *Bertin Mbonjo v Collège des médecins du Québec*, 2016 QCCS 3033 at para 81 the court asserted that "Il faut une intention claire et non ambiguë du législateur d'incorporer [une] convention ou [un] traité dans le droit interne." With respect, no such requirement is found in the cases cited by the court as authority for this proposition and it is wrong in principle. While unambiguous implementing legislation would certainly be preferable, the fact is that our legislatures frequently do perform the state's treaty obligations in subtle and perhaps even ambiguous ways.

66 In *Salomon v Commissioners of Customs and Excise*, [1967] 2 QB 116 (Eng CA) [*Salomon*], Lord Diplock observed, "If from extrinsic evidence it is plain that the enactment was intended to fulfil Her Majesty's Government's obligations under a particular convention, it matters not that there is no express reference to the convention in the statute. One must not presume that Parliament intends to break an international convention merely because it does not say expressly that it is intending to observe it." Where a court has difficulty determining whether legislation was intended to implement a treaty, that difficulty should not be used as a reason not to apply the presumption of conformity, for the presumption applies to both implementing and non-implementing Acts. See Chapter 5, Section 5.5(b).

67 (1908) 13 BCR 370 (SC Full Court). Both the decision of Hunter CJ and the appeal are reported in this report.

treaty part of the law of Canada. Chief Justice Hunter was resoundingly upheld on appeal.

It is easy to say that intent should prevail over form. The difficulty, of course, is determining intent where the form is equivocal. A consideration of this problem is found in the Supreme Court of Canada's judgment in *Re Vancouver Island Railway*.[68] The agreement at issue here was not an international treaty but the "Dunsmuir agreement" between the governments of British Columbia and Canada. That agreement was scheduled to an Act of Parliament that declared the agreement "approved and ratified." Justice Iacobucci for eight justices held that these words were insufficient to give the agreement force of law. Relying on a 1945 Supreme Court precedent,[69] the learned judge held that "statutory ratification and confirmation of a scheduled agreement, standing alone, is generally insufficient reason to conclude that such an agreement constitutes a part of the statute itself."[70] He added, "simple 'ratification' or 'confirmation' of a scheduled agreement, without more, is equivocal in terms of the required legislative intention."[71]

The seemingly unlimited variety of forms treaty implementation can take, and the difficulties such variety can cause, are nicely illustrated in *Thomson v Thomson*.[72] This was the first Supreme Court of Canada decision on the Hague Convention on the Civil Aspects of International Child Abduction 1980.[73] Concerning as it did matters of child custody, it fell to be implemented by the provinces. In his reasons, La Forest J described the various ways in which the provinces implemented it:

> The preliminary draft Convention that had been completed by the Hague Conference Special Commission in November 1979 was submitted to the Uniform Law Conference of Canada in August 1980 by its Committee on International Conventions on Private International Law. . . . The Uniform Law Conference agreed upon the text of a "Uniform Act" to implement the Hague Convention. Four provinces (New Brunswick, Nova Scotia, Saskatchewan and Alberta) enacted

68 *Re Vancouver Island Railway*, above note 6.

69 *Ottawa Electric Railway Co v Corporation of the City of Ottawa*, [1945] SCR 105.

70 *Re Vancouver Island Railway*, above note 6 at 109.

71 *Ibid* at 110. For a consideration of Iacobucci J's argument, see *Pfizer*, above note 64.

72 [1994] 3 SCR 551 [*Thomson*].

73 [1983] Can TS no 35.

> legislation that paralleled the Uniform Act, including its provision that, in the event of a conflict between the Convention and any other enactment, the Convention prevailed: *International Child Abduction Act*, S.N.B. 1982, c. I-12.1; *Child Abduction Act*, S.N.S. 1982, c. 4; *The International Child Abduction Act*, S.S. 1986, c. I-10.1; and *International Child Abduction Act*, S.A. 1986, c. I-6.5.
>
> Quebec chose not to enact the Convention at all, but to legislate equivalent provisions: *An Act respecting the civil aspects of international and interprovincial child abduction*, S.Q. 1984, c. 12. The five remaining provinces (Manitoba, Ontario, British Columbia, Prince Edward Island and Newfoundland) adopted the Convention in a more general statute dealing with the civil aspects of child abduction: *The Child Custody Enforcement Act*, S.M. 1982, c. 27 (now R.S.M. 1987, c. C360); *Children's Law Reform Amendment Act, 1982*, S.O. 1982, c. 20; *Family Relations Amendment Act, 1982*, S.B.C. 1982, c. 8, as am. by S.B.C. 1985, c. 72, s. 20; *Custody Jurisdiction and Enforcement Act*, S.P.E.I. 1984, c. 17; and *The Children's Law Act*, S.N. 1988, c. 61. Of these five, Ontario, Prince Edward Island and Newfoundland's enactments all contain the provision that, in the event of a conflict between the Convention and any other legislative scheme, the Convention prevails. Only the British Columbia and Manitoba Acts do not contain such supremacy provisions.[74]

It was the Manitoba implementation scheme that was before the court in *Thomson*. As noted by La Forest J, Manitoba's Child Custody Enforcement Act included both a general scheme for the enforcement of custody orders and an implementing provision (section 17(2)) that read: "On, from and after December 1, 1983, the convention is in force in Manitoba and the provisions thereof are law in Manitoba." Justice La Forest, writing for the majority, considered that the Act created two child enforcement schemes in Manitoba: the Convention scheme adopted in section 17(2) and the general scheme established by the rest of the Act. Justices L'Heureux-Dubé and McLachlin dissented on this point. They preferred to read the entire Act as implementing the Convention and resolve conflicts between the two schemes according to the presumption of conformity.[75]

---

74 *Ibid* at 601–2.

75 *Ibid* at 617–18. The Supreme Court of Canada has since held that the Convention is implemented in every Canadian jurisdiction: *Office of the Children's Lawyer v*

(e) The five main implementing techniques

While there are no formal requirements for implementing treaties in domestic law, there are nevertheless certain identifiable and prevailing techniques. An experienced Department of Justice legislative counsel, John Mark Keyes, has identified five main techniques,[76] which I generally follow in the discussion below.

(i) Force of law and other forms of express implementation

The clearest way for a legislature to indicate its intent to implement a treaty in its jurisdiction is expressly to give it the force of law. Section 3 of the United Nations Foreign Arbitral Awards Convention Act provides that the Convention is "declared to have the force of law in Canada during such period as, by its terms, the Convention is in force."[77] Section 449.1(1) of the Canada Shipping Act reads:

> Subject to such reservations as Canada may make, the International Covenant on Salvage, signed at London on April 28, 1989 and set out in Schedule V, is approved and declared to have the force of law in Canada, from and after the day on which Canada deposits an instrument of ratification with the Secretary General of the International Maritime Organization.[78]

Section 3 of the Multilateral Instrument in Respect of Tax Conventions Act[79] provides that the instrument (which is set out in the Act's schedule) "has the force of law in Canada during the period that the multilateral instrument, by its terms, is in force for Canada." There are many other examples.[80]

Balev, 2018 SCC 16 [*Balev*] at para 22.

76 J Keynes, "Drafting Laws to Implement International Agreements" (January 2011) [Keyes], slide presentation on file with the author. See also Keyes & Sullivan, above note 63.

77 RSC 1985, c 16 (2d supp), s 3.

78 RSC 1985, c S-9, s 449.1(1).

79 SC 2019, c 12.

80 See, e.g., Tax Conventions Implementation Act, 2013, SC 2013, c 27 (implementing six double taxation conventions in federal law); International Sale of Goods Contracts Convention Act, SC 1991, c 13, s 5; Canada–United Kingdom Civil and Commercial Judgments Convention Act, RSC 1985, c C-30, s 2; etc.

Force of law can be given to certain treaty provisions only. Section 3(1) of the Foreign Missions and International Organizations Act provides:

> Articles 1, 22 to 24 and 27 to 40 of the Vienna Convention on Diplomatic Relations, and Articles 1, 5, 15, 17, 31 to 33, 35, 39 and 40, paragraphs 1 and 2 of Article 41, Articles 43 to 45 and 48 to 54, paragraphs 2 and 3 of Article 55, paragraph 2 of Article 57, paragraphs 1 to 3 of Article 58, Articles 59 to 62, 64, 66 and 67, paragraphs 1, 2 and 4 of Article 70 and Article 71 of the Vienna Convention on Consular Relations, have the force of law in Canada in respect of all foreign states, regardless of whether those states are parties to those Conventions.[81]

Similarly, section 26(1) of the Marine Liability Act provides, "Subject to the other provisions of this Part, Articles 1 to 15 and 18 of the Convention and Articles 8 and 9 of the Protocol have the force of law in Canada."[82]

Using the phrase "force of law" is admirably clear, but not necessary.[83] Other statutes use wording which, while perhaps less direct, is nonetheless effective. An old-fashioned form of words is found at section 3 of the International Boundary Waters Treaty Act:

> The laws of Canada and of the provinces are hereby amended and altered so as to permit, authorize and sanction the performance of the obligations undertaken by His Majesty in and under the treaty, and so as to sanction, confer and impose the various rights, duties and disabilities intended by the treaty to be conferred or imposed or to exist within Canada.[84]

British Columbia implemented the United Nations Convention on the Recognition and Enforcement of Foreign Arbitral Awards by an enactment stating, at section 2, "The Convention applies in British Columbia."[85] The Civil International Space Station Agreement Implementation Act[86] declares, at section 3, "The purpose of this Act is to fulfil Canada's obligations under the Agreement," then creates, at sec-

81 SC 1991, c 41, s 3(1).
82 SC 2001, c 6, s 26(1).
83 *Antonsen*, above note 59 at para 64.
84 RSC 1985, c I-17. The Federal Court of Appeal confirmed that these words implemented the treaty in *Pembina County v Manitoba*, 2017 FCA 92 at para 45.
85 Foreign Arbitral Awards Act, RSBC 1996, c 154.
86 SC 1999, c 35.

tion 9, a power in the Governor in Council to make regulations "for carrying out the purposes of this Act and giving effect to the Agreement." Similarly, several federal trade agreement statutes include provisions declaring their purpose to implement the agreement and making consequential amendments.[87]

Statutes giving a treaty the force of law are sometimes supplemented with provisions favouring the treaty, or its implementing legislation, or both, over inconsistent laws. For instance, section 5 of the United Nations Foreign Arbitral Awards Convention Act provides:

> In the event of any inconsistency between the provisions of this Act, or the Convention, and the provisions of any other law, the provisions of this Act and the Convention prevail to the extent of the inconsistency.[88]

Similar wording is used by section 449.1(2) of the Canada Shipping Act. Section 3 of the previous Extradition Act provided that inconsistencies between that Act and an extradition treaty were to be resolved in favour of the treaty.[89] Section 5 of the BC Foreign Arbitral Awards Act[90] provides, "If there is conflict between this Act and any other enactment, this Act prevails." Such provisions underscore the legislature's intent to give the treaty unqualified domestic force.

Implementing laws frequently include the text of the treaty at issue, or its relevant portions, as a schedule. This is convenient but cannot be regarded as necessary to achieve domestic implementation.

(ii) Restatement in law

Another common means of treaty implementation is for the legislature to affect legal changes that, in its estimation, suffice to meet Canada's treaty commitments. Such restatements of the treaty's provisions in domestic law can range from mild paraphrasing to extensive (but consistent) recasting. As an example of the restatement in law technique,

87 See, e.g., Canada–Peru Free Trade Agreement Implementation Act, SC 2009, c 16, s 7; Canada–EFTA Free Trade Agreement Implementation Act, SC 2009, c 6, s 4; Canada–Colombia Free Trade Agreement Implementation Act, SC 2010, c 4, s 7; Canada–Ukraine Free Trade Agreement Implementation Act, SC 2017, c 8, s 7.

88 RSC 1985, c 16 (2nd Supp), s 5. See also the Settlement of International Investment Disputes Act, SC 2008, c 8, s 3.

89 Extradition Act, RSC 1985, c E-23 (repealed).

90 Foreign Arbitral Awards Act, RSBC 1996, c 154.

Keyes[91] points to the Anti-personnel Mines Convention Implementation Act. Compare articles 3 and 4 of the Convention (left) with sections 8-10 of the Act (right):

ARTICLE 3—Exceptions	Transfer for destruction
1 Notwithstanding the general obligations under Article 1, the retention or transfer of a number of anti-personnel mines for the development of and training in mine detection, mine clearance, or mine destruction techniques is permitted. The amount of such mines shall not exceed the minimum number absolutely necessary for the above-mentioned purposes.	8 Every person, other than Her Majesty in right of Canada, who possesses an anti-personnel mine that the person is prohibited by section 6 from possessing shall without delay deliver it, for destruction, to such person as may, by order, be designated by the Minister.
2 The transfer of anti-personnel mines for the purpose of destruction is permitted.	Destruction of mines 9 Subject to section 10, the Minister shall ensure the destruction of all anti-personnel mines stockpiled by Her Majesty in right of Canada or that are delivered under section 8 for destruction.
ARTICLE 4—Destruction of Stockpiled Anti-Personnel Mines	Authorization by Minister
Except as provided for in Article 3, each State Party undertakes to destroy or ensure the destruction of all stockpiled anti-personnel mines it owns or possesses, or that are under its jurisdiction or control, as soon as possible but not later than four years after the entry into force of this Convention for that State Party.	10 The Minister may authorize a number of anti-personnel mines to be placed, acquired, possessed or transferred by any person for the development of, and training in, mine detection, mine clearance or mine destruction techniques, but the number of such mines shall not exceed the minimum number absolutely necessary for the above-mentioned purposes.

91 Keyes, above note 76.

Another example of implementation by restatement is the Quebec *Loi sur les aspects civils de l'enlèvement international et interprovincial d'enfants*,[92] which implements the Hague Child Abduction Convention[93] but does not, in the words of L'Heureux-Dubé J in *W(V) v S(D)*, "adopt the integral wording thereof." Despite the differences in wording, the learned judge held that the "sole purpose of the Act is to give effect to the Convention," pointing to the Act's reference to the Convention in its preamble and in section 1, "which states the common objects of the Act and the Convention."[94]

A leading instance of implementation by restatement is the Crimes Against Humanity and War Crimes Act.[95] That Act is a lengthy and thorough implementation of the Rome Statute of the International Criminal Court[96] in Canadian law,[97] accomplished by restatement of the statute's relevant provisions and requirements in federal law rather than by giving legal force to the text of the statute itself.

The restatement technique runs greater risk of confusion as to a treaty's domestic legal status than the force of law technique. In the absence of an express provision giving the treaty domestic force, litigants and courts are more likely to make the mistake of concluding it is not implemented. An example of this may be the statement of Lemieux J in *Pfizer Inc v Canada* that "it is plain and obvious that Parliament did not legislate into federal domestic law the WTO Agreement"[98] – this despite the fact that the legislation under consideration in that case was the World Trade Organization Agreement Implementation Act[99] and contains, in Part II, over 200 sections amending and repealing federal legislation to bring it into harmony with Canada's WTO obligations. What the learned judge probably meant was that the Act did not expressly give the treaty force of law such that its provisions could be relied upon directly. But that is only one form of implementation. Parliament un-

---

92 RSQ, c A-23.01.
93 Above note 73.
94 [1996] 2 SCR 108 at 133.
95 SC 2000, c 24.
96 [2002] Can TS no 13.
97 *R v Bissonnette*, 2022 SCC 23 at para 101; *Zazai v Canada (Minister of Citizenship and Immigration)*, 2005 FCA 303 at para 2.
98 *Pfizer*, above note 64 at para 44.
99 SC 1994, c 47, s 6.

doubtedly implemented the WTO Agreement in the crucial sense of bringing federal law into conformity with its requirements.

(iii) Administrative action

A less common form of implementation delegates a power, and perhaps a concomitant duty, on some decision maker to perform a treaty in domestic law through administrative action. Statutes granting regulatory power to implement treaties may be included in this category.[100] But this technique need not involve regulation-making power, as illustrated by sections 7 and 9(1) of the Mutual Legal Assistance in Criminal Matters Act.[101] Those provisions make the minister of justice "responsible for the implementation of" every international agreement that contains provisions for mutual legal assistance in criminal matters, require the minister to deal with foreign requests under such agreements in accordance with those agreements, and make fines imposed by foreign courts enforceable by Canadian courts if the minister approves them.

(iv) Reliance on existing law

A frequent, but underappreciated, implementation technique is for the government that contracts the treaty obligation to rely on Canada's existing laws (whether federal, provincial, or both) to discharge the state's new obligations under it. Once Canada has subscribed to the agreement, the existing laws it has relied upon in doing so become, in effect, implementing provisions, despite not having been initially enacted for that purpose.

To understand this form of implementation, one must consider the process the federal government employs before joining a treaty. Where there is reason to consider whether the proposed obligation requires implementation, the federal government conducts an internal review of domestic law to determine what changes, if any, its implementation would require.[102] If the proposed treaty operates purely on

---

100 See the discussion of treaty implementation by regulation at Section 7.2(a), above.

101 RSC 1985, c 30 (4th Supp).

102 A rare judicial decision noting this practice is *BJG*, above note 20 at para 35. In respect of human rights treaties, Heyns & Viljoen, above note 50 at 118, note: "The consultation process . . . prior to ratification of the international human

the international legal plane, without domestic consequences, then no implementing legislation is required.[103] If the treaty does have domestic impacts, new legislation may be needed to implement it. The third possibility, however, is that existing domestic law suffices to discharge Canada's obligations under the proposed treaty. In that case the government may proceed to adhere to it without new implementing laws.[104] The existing laws are co-opted, as it were, to perform the new obligations. This is frequently true of human rights treaties, most of which "are ratified by Canada on the basis that existing domestic laws and programs already conform with a treaty's obligations and no new legislation is required."[105] But it may also be true for other kinds of treaties.

The practice of relying on existing law to discharge new treaty obligations was noted in 1964 by Senator Baird who, in debating the bill that became the Geneva Conventions Act, explained that it made only a few amendments to domestic law, for "[m]ost of the requirements prescribed in the conventions can be satisfied under existing legislation."[106] Similarly, in a case concerning the Convention on the Rights of the Child 1989, Martinson J observed that "Canada has not directly incorporated the Convention into domestic law" and "takes the position that it is not necessary to do because . . . existing domes-

---

rights treaties, includes a thorough review of Canadian legislation to determine its compliance with international human rights treaty obligations and the need to enter reservations, declarations or objections. During this process it has been necessary to amend some legislation and to enact new laws. Provincial and territorial governments also conduct a review of local legislation to determine compliance." See also the federal government's explanation of its process for ratifying human rights treaties in Canada, *Core Document* 2013, above note 54 at paras 121–2.

103 See above at Section 7.1(d). See also *Council for Refugees*, above note 36 at para 154.

104 See Keyes & Sullivan, above note 63, at 322–3.

105 Weiser, above note 50 at 132. See also Eid & Hamboyan, above note 50 at 451–2, 455–7; Government of Canada, "International Human Rights Treaty Adherence Process in Canada" (last modified 5 August 2021), online: https://www.justice.gc.ca/eng/abt-apd/icg-gci/ihrl-didp/ta-pa.html.

106 Canada, Parliament, *Debates of the Senate (Hansard)*, 26th Parl, 2nd Sess, Vol 1 (25 May 1964) at 546 (Mr. Baird). See also Vallat, *International Law*, above note 37 at 12, noting that the UK had not (at the time Vallat wrote) seen the need to implement the European Convention on Human Rights in domestic law because "the ordinary law [was] regarded as being in conformity with all the provisions of the treaty."

tic laws, including provincial and territorial laws, comply with the Convention."[107] Similarly, Canada's 2013 core document for United Nations human rights bodies explained, "Where existing legislation and policies fulfill the obligations under the treaty, no new measures are required."[108]

An illustration of implementation through reliance on existing law is *Canadian Council for Refugees*. Justice Kasirer for the Supreme Court of Canada found that curative provisions in the Immigration and Refugee Protection Act[109] can act as "safety valves" to prevent the risk of *refoulement*. Rejecting the appellants' argument that these safety valves were irrelevant because they were not among the legislative provisions adopted to implement the treaty at issue in that case (the Safe Third Country Agreement 2002[110]), the learned judge affirmed that the "mere fact that these mechanisms predate the treaty does not make them irrelevant" and that since "Canadian domestic law already included provisions that could facilitate individualized consideration of claimants' circumstances . . . [n]ew legislation implementing additional mechanisms was not necessary."[111]

In an English case, Lord Hope of Craighead expressed the view that domestic implementation of article 15 of the Convention Against Torture 1984 (excluding statements obtained by torture from evidence) was unnecessary in UK law because "the same result is reached by an application of common law principles. The rule laid down by article 15 was accepted by the United Kingdom because it was entirely compatible with our own law."[112] Lord Hope's observation makes the point that reliance on existing law to implement a treaty obligation need not be limited to statutes and regulations.

(v) Combination of these methods

Nothing prevents Parliament or a provincial legislature from combining the techniques described here in a single enactment. Keyes[113] points

---

107 *BJG*, above note 20 at para 34.
108 *Core Document* 2013, above note 54 at para 121.
109 SC 2001, c 27.
110 [2004] Can TS no 2.
111 *Council for Refugees*, above note 36 at para 154.
112 *A (FC) and others (FC) v Home Secretary*, [2005] UKHL 71 at para 112.
113 See Keyes, above note 76.

to the implementing legislation for the Canada–Russia Income Tax Agreement,[114] which grants the agreement the force of law (at section 4) and empowers the minister of national revenue to make regulations necessary for carrying out the agreement or giving effect to any of its provisions (at section 6).

(f) Implementation without reference

There is no rule that Parliament or a legislature must expressly refer to a treaty in legislation implementing it, and indeed implementing provisions are sometimes enacted without reference to the treaty that underlies them. The federal government has acknowledged this.[115]

A prominent example of implementation without reference is found in section 269.1 of the Criminal Code. That provision creates an offence of torture that mirrors that found in the Convention Against Torture and Other Cruel, Inhuman or Degrading Treatment or Punishment 1984. But one would not know a treaty was lurking behind this provision just by reading it. Section 269.1 makes no mention of its implementing purpose or the treaty underlying it. There is no doubt, however, that this is implementing legislation. As Canada advised the UN Human Rights Committee in 2002, "Section 269.1 of the Criminal Code was specifically created to fully comply with the requirements of the Convention against Torture."[116]

The possibility that a law discharges a Canadian treaty obligation without reference to that obligation in the law itself complicates treaty implementation in this country. Implementation without reference may happen in two ways. The legislature may enact a new implementing law that omits to mention the treaty to which it gives effect.

---

114 Part I of the Income Tax Conventions Implementation Act, 1996, SC 1997, c 27.

115 The Legal Bureau of the Department of External Affairs affirmed, in a 1985 letter to the Council of Europe, that implementation may occur "by enacting the required legislation without express reference to the treaty": (1986) 24 *Canadian Yearbook of International Law* 397 at 401.

116 Canada, Fourth Report on the United Nations' Convention against Torture and Other Cruel, Inhuman or Degrading Treatment or Punishment (2002) CAT/C/55/Add.8 at para 204. See also the Committee Against Torture's consideration of Canada's third report (1999) CAT/C/34/Add.13 at para 19. See also E Eid, "A Few Treats About Treaties" (paper presented at the British Columbia Continuing Legal Education seminar, "Using International Law in Canada", 8 May 2008, at 2.1.4).

Or (as discussed above[117]) the government may rely on existing legislation to discharge the new international obligation, effectively turning ordinary legislation into implementing legislation after the fact.

The upshot is that legislation may serve to perform Canada's treaty obligations without any indication in the Act, or even in the legislative history, that this is so.[118] To conclude, therefore, that Canadian law does not implement a treaty just because the treaty is not explicitly implemented in any statute risks error.[119] Canadian practice makes it much more likely that the absence of express implementing legislation reflects the federal government's view, upon concluding the treaty, that Canadian law was compliant with the treaty already, and therefore there was no need for new legislation either federally or provincially. Courts can protect themselves from the error of mistaking an absence of explicit implementing legislation for non-implementation by applying the presumption of conformity with international law.

An example of a court mistaking lack of explicit implementing legislation for lack of domestic implementation generally is *Ahani v Canada*.[120] There, both the majority and the dissent in the Court of Appeal for Ontario repeatedly observed that the International Covenant on Civil and Political Rights 1966 (ICCPR)[121] is not implemented in Canadian law.[122] The ICCPR is the twentieth century's leading statement

117 Above at Section 7.2(e)(iv).

118 In the words of Heyns & Viljoen, above note 50 at 157, "It is impossible to determine to what extent proposed laws or regulations have been amended with the treaties in mind."

119 Lord Diplock was alive to this problem in *Salomon*, above note 66. He observed (at 144): "If from extrinsic evidence it is plain that the enactment was intended to fulfil Her Majesty's Government's obligations under a particular convention, it matters not that there is no express reference to the convention in the statute. One must not presume that Parliament intends to break an international convention merely because it does not say expressly that it is intending to observe it."

120 *Ahani v Canada (Minister of Citizenship and Immigration)* (2002), 58 OR (3d) 107 (CA) [*Ahani*]. See also (2002) 155 OAC 1 (CA) and [2002] OTC 18 (SCJ), both of which make the same error. In *Toussaint v Canada*, 2022 ONSC 4747 at para 200, Perell J called it "arguable that the case was wrongly decided."

121 [1976] Can TS no 47.

122 The more immediate question before the court in *Ahani*, above note 120, was whether the Optional Protocol to the ICCPR was implemented, but the court emphasized that neither the protocol nor the treaty enjoyed domestic implementation.

of basic civil and political rights. It is a codification of the Universal Declaration of Human Rights 1948,[123] a resolution of the General Assembly of the United Nations which has largely passed into customary international law. It is true that there is no such thing as the ICCPR Implementation Act. To conclude from this, however, that Canadian law does not implement the ICCPR is, at best, an oversimplification and, at worst, simply wrong. This subtlety was not lost on Dickson CJ, who explained the status of the ICCPR in Canadian law as follows:

> In an effort to make more specific the broad principles agreed to under the United Nations Universal Declaration of Human Rights . . . two human rights covenants were adopted unanimously by the United Nations General Assembly on December 16, 1966: the U.N. International Covenant on Economic, Social and Cultural Rights . . . (1966), and the U.N. International Covenant on Civil and Political Rights . . . (1966). Canada acceded to both Covenants on May 19, 1976 and they came into effect on August 19, 1976. Prior to accession the Federal Government obtained the agreement of the provinces, all of whom undertook to take *measures for implementation* of the Covenants in their respective jurisdictions.[124]

Thus, Canada ratified the ICCPR on the basis that our law satisfied its terms – even though no explicit implementing legislation was ever passed. Governmental satisfaction that our law meets ICCPR requirements is not conclusive of the treaty's status in Canadian law but, inasmuch as it indicates legislative intent, it cannot be ignored. Furthermore, it is well documented that the ICCPR and its companion, the International Covenant on Economic, Social, and Cultural Rights 1966,[125] served as inspiration and models for the drafters of the Canadian Charter of Rights and Freedoms.[126] In spite of all this, Laskin

---

123 GA Res 217 A (III), UN Doc A/810.

124 *Re Public Service Employee Relations Act (Alberta)*, [1987] 1 SCR 313 at 350 (emphasis added).

125 [1976] Can TS no 46.

126 See B Dickson, "The Canadian Charter of Rights and Freedoms: Context and Evolution" in G-A Beaudoin & E Mendes, *The Canadian Charter of Rights and Freedoms*, 3d ed (Scarborough, ON: Carswell, 1996) at 1-4-5; A Bayefsky, *International Human Rights Law: Use in Canadian Charter of Rights and Freedoms Litigation* (Toronto: Butterworths, 1992) [Bayefsky, *International Human Rights Law*] at 33–47;

JA for the majority of the Court of Appeal held that the ICCPR was not implemented in Canadian law.[127] Justice Rothenberg in dissent reached the same conclusion.[128] In fairness to the court, it appears that Ahani conceded – mistakenly, in my view – that the ICCPR was not implemented in Canada.[129] Yet the court ought not to have accepted this submission so readily. That mistake was compounded, I suggest, by the court's failure to apply, or even mention, the presumption of conformity.[130]

It is sometimes possible to determine the implementing intention of a law that does not expressly state that intention by reference to memoranda, press releases, or other materials produced by the federal government to accompany the statute or treaty in question. In *Canadian Generic Pharmaceutical Association v Canada (Minister of Health)* the Federal Court of Appeal noted that a Regulatory Impact Analysis Statement issued by Canada explained certain regulatory amendments as "intended to clarify and effectively implement" Canada's obligations

---

A Bayefsky, *Canada's Constitution Act 1982 and Amendments: A Documentary History* (Toronto: McGraw-Hill Ryerson, 1989) at 150*ff*; D Turp, "Le recours au droit international aux fins de l'interprétation de la Charte canadienne des droits et libertés: un bilan jurisprudential" (1984) 18 *Revue juridique Thémis* 353; G La Forest, "The Canadian Charter of Rights and Freedoms: An Overview" (1983) 61 *Canadian Bar Review* 19 at 25; M Cohen & A Bayefsky, "The Canadian Charter of Rights and Freedoms and Public International Law" (1983) 61 *Canadian Bar Review* 265; R Elliott, "Interpreting the Charter: Use of the Earlier Versions as an Aid" [1982] Charter Edition *University of British Columbia Law Review* 11; WS Tarnopolsky, "A Comparison Between the Canadian Charter of Rights and Freedoms and the International Covenant on Civil and Political Rights" (1982) 8 *Queen's Law Journal* 211; M Freeman & G van Ert, *International Human Rights Law* (Toronto: Irwin Law, 2004) at 187–9.

127 *Ahani*, above note 120 at paras 16, 31.

128 *Ibid* at para 73.

129 *Ibid* at para 31.

130 Blame for this result must also fall on the federal government, which appears to have submitted to the court that Canada ratified the ICCPR on the basis that it created no enforceable obligations and that this country never intended to honour it: *ibid* at paras 102–3. The UN Committee on Economic, Social, and Cultural Rights (responsible for monitoring Canadian compliance with the International Covenant on Economic, Social, and Cultural Rights 1966), has criticized Canada for litigating inconsistently with Canada's human rights obligations. See Committee on Economic, Social, and Cultural Rights, "Concluding Observations of the Committee on Economic, Social, and Cultural Rights: Canada," 4 December 1998, E/C.12/1/Add.31 at para 50.

under two trade treaties.[131] In *Society of Composers, Authors and Music Publishers of Canada v Entertainment Software Association*, Rowe J for the majority of the Supreme Court of Canada noted that the explanatory memorandum tabled in Parliament together with the WIPO Copyright Treaty 1996[132] stated that a recent copyright law "was developed with a view to implementing the rights and protections" of the treaty.[133] When that same case was before the Federal Court of Appeal, Stratas JA noted a statement from the government that the "proposed Bill will implement the associated rights and protections to pave the way for a future decision on ratification."[134]

(g) Effect of non-enforcement provisions

Certain Acts of Parliament implementing Canadian international trade agreements contain specific provisions partly prohibiting any person from gaining a cause of action or taking proceedings under them.[135] For instance, section 6 of the North American Free Trade Agreement Implementation Act reads:

> (1) No person has any cause of action and no proceedings of any kind shall be taken, without the consent of the Attorney General of Canada, to enforce or determine any right or obligation that is claimed or arises solely under or by virtue of Part I or any order or regulation made under Part I.
>
> (2) Subject to Section B of Chapter Eleven of the Agreement, no person has any cause of action and no proceedings of any kind shall be taken, without the consent of the Attorney General of Canada, to

131 2010 FCA 334 at para 22.

132 [2014] Can TS no 20.

133 *Entertainment Software*, above note 24 at para 49.

134 *Entertainment Software Association v Society of Composers, Authors and Music Publishers of Canada*, 2020 FCA 100 at para 55.

135 E.g., Canada–United States Free Trade Agreement Implementation Act, above note 57 at s 5; North American Free Trade Agreement Implementation Act, above note 57 at s 6; World Trade Organization Agreement Implementation Act, above note 57 at s 6; Canada–Israel Free Trade Agreement Implementation Act, SC 1996, c 33, s 6; Canada–Chile Free Trade Agreement Implementation Act, above note 3, s 6; Canada–European Union Comprehensive Economic and Trade Agreement Implementation Act, above note 3, s 8.

> enforce or determine any right or obligation that is claimed or arises solely under or by virtue of the Agreement.

In statutes with provisions such as this, the prohibition on proceedings extends only to Part I of the Act. Part I of each of these statutes is relatively short, containing an approval provision of the sort discussed above, a section empowering the government to make regulations for carrying out the purposes and provisions of the Act, and other administrative and institutional provisions.

Some cases have suggested that the existence of such a non-enforcement provision means that the treaty in question has not been implemented.[136] That is not so. These non-enforcement provisions are narrowly drawn: They apply only to Part I of the Acts and therefore do not affect Part II, which catalogues the many amendments and repeals of federal legislation needed to implement the treaty that is the subject of the legislation. There can be no question that these Acts are precisely what they say they are: implementing Acts. That is not to say that they enact their respective treaties word for word, or that they always do so in a way that is perfectly consistent with their treaties.[137] Nevertheless, these Acts amend domestic law to give effect to Canada's international obligations under the respective treaties.

The effect of non-enforcement provisions was described by Lemieux J as follows: "What Parliament is saying is that these international trade agreements are matters of public law concerning public rights, rights affecting Canada as a sovereign state. They are not matters of private economic or commercial rights giving rise to causes of action and legal proceedings."[138] This description is more accurate but is still, in my view, too broad. Again, Part I of each of the Acts in question here is narrow and does not circumvent or otherwise undermine the actual

---

136 See *Antonsen*, above note 59, and *UL Canada*, above note 58. These two cases contain several errors on implementation and the presumption of conformity and should be used with great care.

137 Thus in *Pfizer*, above note 64, Lemieux J was constrained to find that the World Trade Organization Agreement Implementation Act, above note 57, failed to amend the Patent Act to bring it in line with the requirements of the Agreement on Trade Related Aspects of Intellectual Property Rights (the TRIPS Agreement, being Annex 1C of the Agreement Establishing the World Trade Organization (1994) 33 ILM 1197 (ratified by Canada 31 December 1994)).

138 *Pfizer*, above note 64 at para 55.

legal changes wrought by the rest of the statute. Individuals may gain private economic or commercial rights under these Acts, though not by virtue of sections falling within Part I. Furthermore, non-enforcement provisions do not in any way oust the presumption of conformity with international law. Thus litigants remain free to argue, for example, that a given statutory provision should be read consistently with the Canada–Chile Free Trade Agreement 1996,[139] as implemented in Canadian law by the Canada–Chile Free Trade Agreement Implementation Act, even though section 6 of that Act is a non-enforcement provision.

7.3 Federalism and treaty implementation

Legislative jurisdiction to implement treaties is shared between Parliament and the provincial legislatures. Parliament has jurisdiction to implement Empire treaties and Canadian treaties falling within its legislative jurisdiction as set out in the Constitution Act, 1867. The provinces have jurisdiction to implement treaties within their legislative jurisdiction under that same constitutional instrument. Where, as sometimes happens, a treaty's provisions involve matters of both federal and provincial legislative power, implementing legislation must be brought in every jurisdiction of the country.

(a) Exclusive federal jurisdiction to implement Empire treaties

Section 132 of the Constitution Act, 1867 provides:

> The Parliament and Government of Canada shall have all Powers necessary or proper for performing the Obligations of Canada or of any Province thereof, as Part of the British Empire, towards Foreign Countries, arising under Treaties between the Empire and such Foreign Countries.

The effect of this provision is to confer exclusive legislative jurisdiction on Parliament to implement what are known as Empire treaties (meaning treaties incurred by Imperial rather than Canadian authorities), even where the subject matter of the treaty would otherwise fall

139 (1997) 36 ILM 1067.

within the legislative jurisdiction of the provinces. In this way, section 132 represented a departure from the distribution of legislative powers set out in sections 91 and 92 of the Constitution Act, 1867.[140]

This effect of section 132 was illustrated by *In re Employment of Aliens*,[141] a reference to the Supreme Court of Canada by the federal government challenging the validity of BC legislation authorizing racial discrimination against Japanese and Chinese workers.[142] The BC law was attacked in part for its inconsistency with the Japanese Treaty Act,[143] a federal statute implementing the Treaty of Commerce and Navigation Between the United Kingdom and Japan 1911.[144] This treaty granted Japanese and British subjects "the right, equally with native subjects, to carry on their commerce and manufacture, and to trade in all kinds of merchandise of lawful commerce."[145] The majority of the Supreme Court of Canada held that the Japanese Treaty Act was legislation for performing the obligations of Canada under an Empire treaty and rendered the BC law invalid despite the province's general jurisdiction over property rights and private law.[146] A further appeal to the Privy Council was dismissed.[147]

---

140 For this reason, Rogers described the powers given by s 132 as "tremendous" and warned that they "should never be invoked except for the genuine purpose of making the provisions of a treaty or convention a part of the municipal law of the land, in order to implement international obligations entered into for our national well-being alone": A Rogers, "Some Aspects of Treaty Legislation" (1926) 1 *Canadian Bar Review* 40 [Rogers] at 45.

141 (1922) 63 SCR 293.

142 The BC law was enacted to reverse a decision of the Court of Appeal for British Columbia rejecting earlier discriminatory measures in withering terms. The story is told at greater length in G van Ert, "A Suitable Population: British Columbia's Japanese Treaty Act Litigation, 1920–1923" (2017) 3(1) *Canadian Journal of Comparative and Contemporary Law* 133.

143 1913 SC, c 27 (3 and 4 Geo V).

144 [1911] UKTS No 15.

145 *Ibid* at art I(2).

146 A similar result had been reached by the BC courts several years earlier in *In re Nakane and Okazake* (1908) 13 BCR 370 (SC Full Court). Another illustration of the supremacy of laws enacted under s 132 over provincial enactments – even in matters that would otherwise fall within provincial legislative power – came in *R v Stuart*, [1925] 1 DLR 12 (Man CA) (provincial game law held invalid to the extent of its conflict with a federal law implementing the Migratory Birds Convention 1916, [1917] UKTS no 7 (Cd 8476)).

147 *Attorney-General of British Columbia v Attorney-General of Canada*, [1924] AC 203 (PC).

"With the adoption of the Statute of Westminster," remarked the prime minister, Mr. Bennett, in 1931, "the political Empire disappears."[148] Disappearing along with it, *de facto* if not *de jure*, was section 132. For there was no longer such a thing as an Empire treaty. Yet Parliament's jurisdiction to implement Empire treaties under section 132 would appear to continue to this day. Côté points to the Migratory Birds Convention Act, 1994[149] as "probably the last federal legislation adopted under this power to be still in force."[150] In the unlikely event that some Empire treaty binding on Canada belatedly required implementation today, section 132 would accord legislative jurisdiction to Parliament exclusively, even if the treaty's subject matter might otherwise fall within provincial legislative jurisdiction.

(b) Shared jurisdiction to implement Canadian treaties

The foundation of Canadian federalism is the division of powers set out in the Constitution Act, 1867, formerly known as the British North America Act 1867. The only provision concerning the implementation of treaties in the 1867 constitution is the Empire treaties provision considered immediately above. With no provision made for the implementation of Canadian treaties, it was left to the courts to determine how such treaties would be implemented. The matter was decided – with much controversy – by the Privy Council in the *Labour Conventions* case.[151]

(i) Case law prior to Labour Conventions

The Supreme Court of Canada first considered the question of legislative jurisdiction to implement treaty obligations in *Re Legislative Jurisdiction over Hours of Labour* (1925).[152] The Governor General in Council asked the court four questions arising from the Treaty of Versailles

148 Mr. Bennett's statement was only true for the original dominions, of course. Quoted in J Ewart, *The Independence Papers*, vol 2 (Ottawa: n.p., 1925) at 601.

149 SC 1994, c 22.

150 C-E Côté, "Federalism and Foreign Affairs in Canada" in C Bradley, ed, *The Oxford Handbook of Foreign Relations Law* (Oxford: Oxford University Press, 2019) at 278.

151 *Labour Conventions*, above note 8.

152 [1925] SCR 505 [*Re Legislative Jurisdiction*].

1919.[153] Article 405 of the treaty was an undertaking by members of the Labour Conference of the League of Nations (of which Canada was one) to bring a draft convention limiting the hours of labour in industrial undertakings before "the authority or authorities within whose competence the matter lies for the enactment of legislation or other action." One question referred to the court was whether the provincial legislatures were these authorities. In short, was a treaty concerning working hours to be implemented by Parliament or the provincial legislatures or both? To answer the question, Duff J (as he then was) reviewed the subject matter of the Convention and concluded:

> Under the scheme of distribution of legislative authority in the British North America Act, legislative jurisdiction touching the subject matter of this convention is . . . primarily vested in the provinces. Under the head of jurisdiction numbered 13 in section 92, Property and Civil Rights, or under the sixteenth head, Local and Private Matters Within the Provinces, or under both heads, each of the provinces possesses authority to give the force of law in the province to provisions such as those contained in the draft convention. This general proposition is subject to this qualification, namely, that as a rule a province has no authority to regulate the hours of employment of the servants of the Dominion Government.[154]

In short, legislative jurisdiction to implement the draft treaty was shared by Parliament and the provincial legislatures according to the ordinary division of powers.

This was not the last word on the subject, however. In 1932 the Judicial Committee of the Privy Council heard two appeals touching the issue, both involving technologies unknown at Confederation. In *Re Aeronautics*,[155] the Governor in Council referred questions concerning federal authority to perform the obligations of Canada, or any province thereof, under the Convention Relating to the Regulation of Aerial Navigation 1919.[156] This being an Empire treaty, Canada relied on sec-

153 [1919] UKTS 4 (Cmd 153).

154 *Re Legislative Jurisdiction*, above note 152 at 510.

155 *Reference re: Regulation and Control of Aeronautics in Canada*, [1932] 1 DLR 58 (PC) [*Re Aeronautics*]. The attorney general for Canada was represented by two King's Counsel and a junior by the name of Mr. AT Denning.

156 [1922] UKTS no 2.

tion 132 to found Parliament's jurisdiction. Yet that treaty concerned only civil aviation, while the disputed federal law also extended to military aircraft. The Supreme Court of Canada had ruled that legislative competence was shared, aviation having both federal and provincial aspects.[157] At the Privy Council, Sankey LC held that Parliament's enactment was mostly supported by section 132, also in the light of federal legislative powers under subsections 91(2), (5), and (7) and, if that was not sufficient, under the residual peace, order, and good government power:

> There may be a small portion of the field which is not by virtue of specific words in the B.N.A. Act vested in the Dominion; but neither is it vested by specific words in the Provinces. As to such small portion it appears to the Board that it must necessarily belong to the Dominion under its power to make laws for the peace, order and good government of Canada. Further their Lordships are influenced by the facts that the subject of aerial navigation and the fulfilment of Canadian obligations under s. 132 are matters of national interest and importance; and that aerial navigation is a class of subject which has attained such dimensions as to affect the body politic of the Dominion.[158]

In short, any deficiency in the jurisdiction conferred upon Parliament by means of the civil aviation treaty via section 132 could be made up by Parliament's residual power under section 91 to legislate for the peace, order, and good government of Canada (POGG). This conclusion suggested that, were the treaty not the sort described by section 132, their lordships would have found for the federal power anyway.

The second 1932 decision, *Re Radio*, posed the question of legislative jurisdiction over the regulation and control of radio communication. This time, however, the underlying treaty was not an Empire treaty but a Canadian one, the International Radiotelegraph Convention 1927.[159] There could therefore be no resort to section 132. Viscount Dunedin for a differently constituted Privy Council nevertheless affirmed Parliament's exclusive power to implement the treaty under POGG, for the

157 *Reference re Legislative Powers as to Regulation and Control of Aeronautics in Canada*, [1930] SCR 663.

158 *Re Aeronautics*, above note 155 at 70.

159 [1929] Can TS no 1.

"idea of Canada as a Dominion being bound by a convention equivalent to a treaty with foreign powers was quite unthought-of in 1867" and being therefore "not mentioned explicitly in either s. 91 or s. 92, such legislation falls within the general words at the opening of s. 91."[160] Notably, in light of what came next, Viscount Dunedin specifically rejected the provincial claim to shared treaty implementation jurisdiction according to the ordinary division of powers:

> [T]he argument of the Province comes to this: Go through all the stipulations of the Convention and each one you can pick out which fairly falls within one of the enumerated heads of s. 91, that can be held to be appropriate for Dominion legislation; but the residue belongs to the Province under the head either of heading 13 of s. 92 – Property and Civil Rights, or heading 16 – Matters of a merely local or private nature in the Province. Their Lordships cannot agree that the matter should be so dealt with.[161]

Lord Dunedin went on to emphasize the absurdity of a regime whereby radio transmitters would fall under federal authority and radio receivers under provincial jurisdiction. These comments must have appeared to be *obiter*, in the light of the reasoning quoted above. But Lord Atkin would rely on them effectively to reverse the result of *Re Radio* five years later.

(ii) The decision in **Labour Conventions**

The question of legislative jurisdiction to implement treaty obligations arose a third time in 1935, again concerning the undertaking in article 405 of the Treaty of Versailles that League of Nations members bring certain draft labour conventions before their competent authorities. Canada, being under no strict legal obligation to ratify or enact any of these draft conventions, had declined to do so for years. Then, in the midst of the Great Depression, the Bennett government seized upon them as a means of enacting a "New Deal" program of economic reform resembling that of President Roosevelt's in the United States. Doing so

---

160 *Reference re: Regulation and Control of Radio Communication in Canada*, [1932] 2 DLR 81 (PC) [*Re Radio*] at 83–4.

161 *Ibid.*

in Canada involved Parliament claiming jurisdiction over such plainly provincial matters as working hours and minimum wages.

One can see why the Bennett government felt on solid legal ground. As noted, Viscount Dunedin in *Re Radio* had flatly rejected the province's claim to shared treaty implementation jurisdiction, declining to force courts and governments to comb through treaties article by article to determine which provisions fell to Parliament and which to the provincial legislatures. Yet the controversy split the Supreme Court of Canada evenly.

Chief Justice Duff (Davis and Kerwin JJ concurring) held that legislative authority in respect of international agreements was vested exclusively in the Parliament of Canada. He reached this determination in part through consideration of *Re Aeronautics* and, more particularly, *Re Radio*. But the chief justice also considered that

> as a result of the constitutional development of the last thirty years (and more particularly of the last twenty years) Canada has acquired the status of an international unit . . . recognized by His Majesty the King, by the other nations of the British Commonwealth of Nations, and by the nations of the world, as possessing a status enabling her to enter into, on her own behalf, international arrangements, and to incur obligations under such arrangements. . . . Whatever the form of the agreement, it is now settled that, as regards Canada, it is the Canadian Government acting on its own responsibility to the Parliament of Canada which deals with the matter.[162]

Notably, the chief justice acknowledged the potential of this doctrine to undo the distribution of powers provided for by sections 91 and 92 of the British North America Act, observing that there are "certain fundamental terms of the arrangement upon which the B.N.A. Act was framed which it is difficult to suppose Parliament could in any case disregard." Yet he considered it unnecessary to deal with this contention.[163]

For his part, Rinfret J easily distinguished *Re Aeronautics* (mostly about an Empire treaty) and *Re Radio* (about a technology not contem-

---

162 *Re The Weekly Rest in Industrial Undertakings Act, the Minimum Wages Act, and the Limitation of Hours of Work Act*, [1936] SCR 461 [*Re Weekly Rest*] at 496.

163 *Ibid* at 488.

plated at Confederation). By contrast, the enactments at issue here concerned matters accorded to the provinces at Confederation, namely property and civil rights. Such matters must be the subject of provincial laws unless the federal government first obtained the consent of the provinces to incur the new international obligations in matters of provincial jurisdiction:

> When once [treaty obligations] have been undertaken, Canada is in honour bound to perform them; but there is no necessity, nor even obligation, to undertake them. If the effect of the undertaking is that a subject of legislation within the exclusive jurisdiction of the province will thereby be transferred from that jurisdiction to the jurisdiction of the Dominion Parliament, I consider it to be within the clear spirit of the British North America Act that the obligation should not be created or entered into before the provinces have given their consent thereto.[164]

Justice Rinfret then struck the point Duff CJ sought, rather unconvincingly, to postpone:

> [L]et us assume that the subject matter of the convention was education, a subject in relation to which "in and for each province the legislature may exclusively make laws" (Sec. 93). Can it be said that it would be within the spirit of the Constitution that the Dominion Parliament might acquire exclusive jurisdiction over that very essential subject as a consequence of the fact that the Dominion Government would decide in regard to it to make a convention with a foreign power?
>
> It might be objected that education would not be regarded as the proper subject matter of a treaty or an international convention as these arrangements are generally understood. Until comparatively recently, neither could it be said that questions affecting *The Weekly Rest in Undertakings*, *The Minimum Wages* or *The Limitation of Hours of Work* would be considered as proper subjects for international conventions.[165]

---

164 *Ibid* at 511.
165 *Ibid* at 512.

In separate reasons, Cannon J agreed with Rinfret J, noting that "Respect of their property and civil rights was guaranteed by the British Crown to the inhabitants of the original provinces as far back as the treaty of Paris in 1763" and that it is "not admissible that the Parliament and the Government of Canada could appropriate these powers, exclusively reserved to the provinces, by the simple process of ratifying a labour convention passed at Geneva with representatives of foreign countries." He added, memorably:

> Uniformity is not in the spirit of our constitution. We have not a single community in this country. We have nine commonwealths, several different communities. This is the fact embodied in the law. It may be wise or unwise, according to the preferences and predilection of every one, but this is the basis of our constitution. Diversity is the basis of our constitution. . . .
>
> These are some of the reasons why foreign powers, when dealing with Canada, must always keep in mind that neither the Governor General in Council, nor Parliament, can in any way, and specifically by an agreement with a foreign power, change the constitution of Canada or take away from the provinces their competency to deal exclusively with the enumerated subjects of section 92.[166]

Finally, the reasons of Crocket J should be noted, as his rationale most closely resembles what Lord Atkin concluded when the case went on further appeal to the Privy Council:

> While I agree with the learned Chief Justice that the Government of Canada must now be held to be the proper medium for the formal conclusion of international conventions, whether they affect the Dominion as a whole or any of the provinces separately, I do not think that this fact can be relied on as altering in any way the provisions of the B.N.A. Act as regards the distribution of legislative power as between the Dominion Parliament and the provincial legislatures or as necessarily giving to any matter, which may be made the subject of legislation in Canada, any other meaning or aspect than that which it bears in our original constitution. . . .[167]

---

166 *Ibid* at 520–1.

167 *Ibid* at 535.

The opposite result, said Crocket J, "would strip the legislative charter of the provinces of every vestige of permanency and stability and leave it at all times subject to the will and pleasure of the federal executive."[168]

On final appeal to the Judicial Committee of the Privy Council, counsel for the attorney general of Canada (including the future prime minister, Mr. St Laurent) contended that the Dominion had jurisdiction under section 132 or, in the alternative, under the federal residual power. The attorneys general of British Columbia, New Brunswick, and Ontario all contended that implementing legislation was subject to the division of powers described in sections 91 and 92.

The practice of the Judicial Committee of the Privy Council at this time was not to release dissenting or concurring reasons. In a single set of reasons, therefore, Lord Atkin for the board held that treaty implementation in Canada must take place according to the distribution of powers set out in sections 91 and 92 of the British North America Act 1867. In explaining this conclusion, Lord Atkin made several pronouncements of lasting importance for the reception of treaties in Canadian law.

The learned judge began by calling it "essential to keep in mind the distinction between (1.) the formation, and (2.) the performance, of the obligations constituted by a treaty, using that word as comprising any agreement between two or more sovereign states." He continued:

> Within the British Empire there is a well-established rule that the making of a treaty is an executive act, while the performance of its obligations, if they entail alteration of the existing domestic law, requires legislative action. Unlike some other countries, the stipulations of a treaty duly ratified do not within the Empire, by virtue of the treaty alone, have the force of law. If the national executive, the government of the day, decide to incur the obligations of a treaty which involve alteration of law they have to run the risk of obtaining the assent of Parliament to the necessary statute or statutes.[169]

This passage confirms the dualist approach of Canadian law to conventional international legal obligations; legislation, and not treaty alone, is needed to alter domestic law. Lord Atkin continued:

---

168 *Ibid* at 538.

169 *Labour Conventions*, above note 8 at 347.

> Parliament, no doubt, as the Chief Justice points out, has a constitutional control over the executive: but it cannot be disputed that the creation of the obligations undertaken in treaties and the assent to their form and quality are the function of the executive alone. Once they are created, while they bind the State as against the other contracting parties, Parliament may refuse to perform them and so leave the State in default.[170]

Consistently with his insistence that treaty performance requires legislation, Lord Atkin here points out that while the executive can commit the state to an agreement binding on it under international law, doing so does not compel the legislative branch to enact implementing laws.

Lord Atkin called this scheme "simple" in a unitary state like the United Kingdom, where a single Parliament has power to give domestic effect to any treaty made by the executive. But this same scheme is "complex" in a federal state like Canada because

> The obligations imposed by treaty may have to be performed, if at all, by several Legislatures; and the executive have the task of obtaining the legislative assent not of the one Parliament to whom they may be responsible, but possibly of several Parliaments to whom they stand in no direct relation. The question is not how is the obligation formed, that is the function of the executive; but how is the obligation to be performed, and that depends upon the authority of the competent Legislature or Legislatures.[171]

This complexity is, of course, a key reason why a divided treaty implementation power was rejected by three of the judges in the Supreme Court of Canada. It may have also been what moved the drafters of the 1867 constitution to grant Parliament a unitary power to implement Empire treaties in section 132.

Yet Lord Atkin was undaunted. He went on to reject section 132 as a basis for Parliament's authority and to likewise reject section 91 as such a basis. He distinguished both *Re Aeronautics* and *Re Radio*, concluding that "neither case affords a warrant for holding that legislation to perform a Canadian treaty is exclusively within the Dominion

170 *Ibid* at 348.
171 *Ibid* at 348.

legislative power."[172] He dismissed the suggestions of federal jurisdiction independent of section 132 in *Re Aeronautics* as *obiter* (which they were, but rather influential *obiter*, one might have thought). As for *Re Radio*, he characterized "the true ground of the decision" as an application of the gap theory of the peace, order, and good government power, whereby subject matters such as radio, contemplated neither by section 91 nor section 92, fall to Parliament under its residual POGG power.[173]

The result of this analysis was to leave nothing to support Parliament's jurisdiction over the three New Deal laws and (more importantly) no independent power in Parliament to implement treaty obligations incurred by the federal executive. "For the purposes of ss. 91 and 92," Lord Atkin explained, "there is no such thing as treaty legislation as such. The distribution is based on classes of subjects and as a treaty deals with a particular class of subjects so will the legislative power of performing it be ascertained."[174]

This must be so, in Lord Atkin's view, because the result contended for by the federal government would upset the foundation of the Canadian constitution, namely the distribution of powers under sections 91 and 92. His lordship observed, "No one can doubt that this distribution is one of the most essential conditions, probably the most essential condition, in the inter-provincial compact to which the British North America Act gives effect."[175] He continued:

> If the position of Lower Canada, now Quebec, alone were considered, the existence of her separate jurisprudence as to both property and civil rights might be said to depend upon loyal adherence to her constitutional right to the exclusive competence of her own Legislature in these matters. Nor is it of less importance for the other Provinces, though their law may be based on English jurisprudence, to preserve their own right to legislate for themselves in respect of local conditions which may vary by as great a distance as separates the Atlantic from the Pacific.[176]

---

172 *Ibid* at 349–51.
173 *Ibid* at 351.
174 *Ibid* at 351.
175 *Ibid* at 351.
176 *Ibid* at 351–2.

> . . . In other words, the Dominion cannot, merely by making promises to foreign countries, clothe itself with legislative authority inconsistent with the constitution which gave it birth.[177]

The theme of this passage, and indeed of Lord Atkin's judgment as a whole, is provincial self-government. The provinces' inherent differences demanded a federal arrangement in 1867 and the preservation of that arrangement in 1937. In *Labour Conventions* Lord Atkin treated the federal government, armed with a parliamentary treaty implementation power, as a threat to provincial self-government in much the same way as he depicted international law as a coercive external force inimical to self-government (until incorporated by the common law) in *Chung Chi Cheung*.[178] *Labour Conventions* is an application of the reception system's principle of self-government to Canadian federalism.

Lord Atkin concluded his judgment with the much derided (but, in the context of this decision, very apt) metaphor of Canada's "watertight compartments":

> It must not be thought that the result of this decision is that Canada is incompetent to legislate in performance of treaty obligations. In totality of legislative powers, Dominion and Provincial together, she is fully equipped. But the legislative powers remain distributed, and if in the exercise of her new functions derived from her new international status Canada incurs obligations they must, so far as legislation be concerned, when they deal with Provincial classes of subjects, be dealt with by the totality of powers, in other words by cooperation between the Dominion and the Provinces. While the ship of state now sails on larger ventures and into foreign waters she still retains the watertight compartments which are an essential part of her original structure.[179]

The extent to which this metaphor is now regularly, even unthinkingly, sneered at by Canadian courts and commentators – almost always in contexts having nothing to do with treaty implementation – is indicative of Anglo-Canadian reaction to the decision.

---

177 *Ibid* at 352.
178 [1939] AC 160 (PC) at 167–8.
179 *Labour Conventions*, above note 8 at 353–4.

(iii) *Academic criticism of* **Labour Conventions**

Labour Conventions was received very badly by prominent Anglo-Canadian commentators. Perhaps the most outrageous comments were those of Kennedy, who decried the "bastard loyalty" that gave the BNA Act "the doubtful devotion of primitive ancestor worship" and intoned biblically that "this is the law, and it killeth."[180] Other commentators did not write so vividly but expressed their disapproval clearly nonetheless.[181] Since that time, Anglo-Canadian criticism of the decision has remained constant. Matas, writing in 1945, referred to the result of the case as "this unhappy state of affairs" and bemoaned the Privy Council's overly literal interpretation of section 132.[182] Szablowski, writing in 1956, candidly admitted his bias against the decision in the opening line of his article on the subject, saying "The treatment of the topic of this article is based on the assumption that a modern state, unitary or federal, cannot effectively function in the international forum without possessing full capacity, in law and in fact, to create and to perform binding obligations."[183] McWhinney, who favoured the result in *Labour Conventions*, nonetheless wrote in 1969 that it "has been perhaps the most bitterly-assailed and certainly the most often ridiculed judicial opinion in Canadian constitutional history."[184] A francophone commentator, Professor La Forest (as he then was), observed in 1974 that it had "long been fashionable to predict" that the case would be overruled.[185] Strom and Finkle, writing in 1993, trotted out all the standard objections to *Labour Conventions* and added a castration theme to their analysis. They concluded that the "effect of the judgment was to emas-

180 W Kennedy, "The British North America Act: Past and Future" (1937) 15 *Canadian Bar Review* 393 at 399.

181 An entire issue of the *Canadian Bar Review* was dedicated to the topic, with contributions from FR Scott, Vincent MacDonald, Ivor Jennings, and others. See (1937) 15 *Canadian Bar Review* 393–508.

182 R Matas, "Treaty Making in Canada" (1947) 25 *Canadian Bar Review* 458 at 462, 470.

183 G Szablowski, "Creation and Implementation of Treaties in Canada" (1956) 34 *Canadian Bar Review* 28.

184 E McWhinney, "Canadian Federalism and the Foreign Affairs and Treaty Power: The Impact of Quebec's 'Quiet Revolution'" (1969) 7 *Canadian Yearbook of International Law* 3 [McWhinney] at 4.

185 G La Forest, "The Labour Conventions Case Revisited" (1974) 12 *Canadian Yearbook of International Law* 137 [La Forest] at 147.

culate the federal power."[186] In support, they quoted F.R. Scott's conclusion that "so long as Canada clung to the Imperial apron strings, her Parliament was all powerful . . . once she became a nation in her own right, impotence descended."[187] Finally, they quoted Rand J's view that *Labour Conventions* "besides sterilizing national action would invert the underlying scheme of Dominion and provincial relations."[188] Perhaps the most thorough contemporary critique of *Labour Conventions* is found in Hogg. He questions most every aspect of Lord Atkin's "poorly reasoned decision," in particular his conclusion that section 132 could not have been "strained" to cover Canada's achievement of full statehood, and his statement that "there is no such thing as treaty legislation as such." Yet Hogg acknowledges that the case may be good policy even if it is bad law and accepts that the rule in *Labour Conventions* may be "one of the prices of federalism."[189]

A constant refrain from the critics of *Labour Conventions* has been that it hampers Canada's ability to conduct foreign affairs. Vincent MacDonald, writing in 1937, called the decision "suicidal in point of governmental efficiency."[190] Other early critics agreed, though without illustrating the point with evidence. This lack of evidence led later critics to argue that the efficiency critique was unwarranted. Gotlieb (1968) pointed out that most treaties do not even require implementation, that many of those that do can be implemented under the federal power, and that consultation with the provinces was standard practice even prior to the decision in *Labour Conventions*.[191] McWhinney (1969) went further, saying that "no single example has ever been cited, in the years since 1937 when that decision was first handed down, where its *rationale* has presented any practical difficulties, or even mild in-

186 T Strom & P Finkle, "Treaty Implementation: The Canadian Game Needs Australian Rules" (1993) 25 *Ottawa Law Review* 39 [Storm and Finkle] at 47.

187 FR Scott, "Labour Conventions Case: Lord Wright's Undisclosed Dissent?" (1956) 34 *Canadian Bar Review* 114 at 115, quoted in Strom & Finkle, *ibid* at 57.

188 I Rand, "Some Aspects of Canadian Constitutionalism" (1960) 38 *Canadian Bar Review* 135 at 143, quoted in Strom & Finkle, above note 186 at 57.

189 P Hogg and W Wright, *Constitutional Law of Canada*, 5th ed Suppl, looseleaf (Toronto: Thomson Reuters, 2021) [Hogg & Wright] at § 11.2.

190 V MacDonald, "The Canadian Constitution Seventy Years After" (1937) 15 *Canadian Bar Review* 401 at 419.

191 A Gotlieb, *Canadian Treaty-Making* (Toronto: Butterworths, 1968) at 76–7, 83.

convenience, in the conduct of Canada's foreign relations."[192] If that statement was true at the time, it was not true for long, for Bernier's 1973 monograph included a lengthy illustration of the problems Canada had faced due to the rule in *Labour Conventions*.[193] Nevertheless, La Forest (1974) dismissed such concerns as difficult to take seriously in the light of Canada's major role in international relations.[194] Ziegel (1988) considered McWhinney's statement to have gone too far, but conceded that Canada's record of ratifying conventions, compared to other federal states, is not bad.[195] Howse (1990) argued justifications of the status quo are becoming "less and less satisfactory,"[196] but Rayfuse (1995) shored up the efficiency critique somewhat.[197] Hogg was persuaded by it.[198] Yet Bell[199] and Cameron[200] have separately argued that, in the human rights field at least, *Labour Conventions* has actually encouraged Canadian implementation and compliance with treaty obligations. The argument that *Labour Conventions* hinders Canada's ability to conduct foreign affairs, and the further argument that that hindrance outweighs the benefits of the *Labour Conventions* rule, remain dependant more on anecdote than analysis.

---

192 McWhinney, above note 184 at 5.

193 I Bernier, *International Legal Aspects of Federalism* (London: Longman, 1973) at 152–8.

194 La Forest, above note 185 at 148.

195 J Ziegel, "Treaty Making and Implementing Powers in Canada: The Continuing Dilemma" in B Cheng & E Brown, eds, *Contemporary Problems of International Law: Essays in Honour of Georg Schwarzenberger on His 80th Birthday* (London: Stevens, 1988) 333 [Ziegel] at 339–40, 342.

196 R Howse, "The *Labour Conventions* Doctrine in an Era of Global Interdependence: Rethinking the Constitutional Dimensions of Canada's External Economic Relations" (1990) 16 *Canadian Business Law Journal* 160 [Howse] at 171.

197 R Rayfuse, "Treaty Practice: The Canadian Perspective" in P Alston & M Chiam, eds, *Treaty-Making and Australia: Globalisation versus Sovereignty?* (Sydney: Federation Press, 1995) 253 at 257–9.

198 Hogg & Wright, above note 189 at § 11.12.

199 K Bell, "From Laggard to Leader: Canadian Lessons on a Role for U.S. States in Making and Implementing Human Rights Treaties" (2002) 5 *Yale Human Rights & Development Law Journal* 255.

200 J Cameron, "Federalism, Treaties and International Human Rights under the Canadian Constitution" (2002) 48 *Wayne Law Review* 1.

I have depicted the critics of *Labour Conventions* as Anglo-Canadian. With a few exceptions,[201] English-Canadian commentators have derided the decision and francophone commentators favoured it. As Professor La Forest observed in 1974, "French Canadians overwhelmingly support the decision."[202] This stark division between francophone

201 McWhinney defended the decision in several articles published in the 1960s. In particular, he drew Canadian attention to the fact that the Federal Constitutional Court of West Germany, faced with a problem identical to that in the Canadian case, explicitly preferred Lord Atkin's judgment to the approach taken in American law. See E McWhinney, "Federal Constitutional Law and the Treaty-Making Power – German-Vatican Concordat of 1933 – Decision of West German Federal Constitutional Court" (1957) 35 *Canadian Bar Review* 842; E McWhinney, "The Constitutional Competence within Federal Systems as to International Agreements" (1966) 1 *Canadian Legal Studies* 145 at 146; McWhinney, above note 184 at 5. The German decision is the *Reichskonkordat* case, Decision of the Federal Constitutional Court (Second Senate), 26 March 1957, 6 B Verf GE 309 (1957). Lederman, while not uncritical of the rule in *Labour Conventions*, sympathized with the federalism concerns that supported it and proposed a compromise whereby Parliament would enjoy concurrent but paramount power to implement treaties of national importance. See W Lederman, "Legislative Power to Implement Treaty Obligations in Canada" in J Aitchison, ed, *The Political Process in Canada: Essays in Honour of R. MacGregor Dawson* (Toronto: University of Toronto Press, 1963) 171. Howse's contributions to the *Labour Conventions* debate are notable for their general acceptance of the decision, subject to judicial recognition of federal jurisdiction under the POGG and trade and commerce powers of the Constitution Act, 1867. This argument is similar to the argument I advance below. In his 1990 article, Howse criticized the "watertight compartments" approach to federalism espoused by Lord Atkin, yet demonstrated that critics of the judgment have failed to address his lordship's concern to maintain "the federal balance": see Howse, above note 196, especially at 163–71. Another supportive, or at least less critical, Anglo-Canadian commentator is J Meekison, "Provinces and Foreign Affairs: Provincial Activity Adds New Dimension to Federalism: A Western View" (1977) 2 *International Perspectives* 8. See also M Luz, "NAFTA, Investment and the Constitution of Canada: Will the Watertight Compartments Spring a Leak?" (2001) 32 *Ottawa Law Review* 35 at 60–61 (suggesting that *Labour Conventions* "has prompted 'cooperative federalism'" in Canada and that its reversal "might do Canada more harm than good").

202 La Forest, above note 185 at 137. La Forest cited J-Y Morin "La conclusion d'accords internationaux par les provinces canadiennes à la lumière du droit comparé" (1965) 3 *Canadian Yearbook of International Law* 126 at 137; AM Jacomy-Millette, *L'Introduction et l'Application des Traités Internationaux au Canada* (Paris: Librairie générale de droit et de jurisprudence, 1971) at 75*ff*; A Dufour, "Fédéralisme canadien et droit international" in R St J Macdonald et al, ed, *Canadian Perspectives on International Law and Organization* (Toronto: University of Toronto Press, 1974) at 72. For more recent Quebec support of the decision, see H Cyr, *Canadian Federalism and Treaty Powers: Organic Constitutionalism at Work*

and anglophone commentators on the case is one of its most striking aspects. Also notable is the tacit acceptance of *Labour Conventions* by the federal government, which has never overtly challenged the decision before the courts. Ziegel, writing in 1988, referred to *Labour Conventions* as "a constitutional doctrine that the federal government itself has respected for the past 50 years."[203] Nor was the matter seriously proposed for reform in the Canadian constitutional debates of the 1980s and 1990s. As Struthers notes, for all its wide-ranging proposals the Charlottetown Accord expressly left the matter of treaty implementation off the agenda.[204]

(iv) Judicial criticism of **Labour Conventions**

Criticism of *Labour Conventions* has not been limited to academic writings but has also come from the bench. Lord Simon, speaking for the Privy Council in *Attorney General for Ontario v Canada Temperance Foundation*, suggested that where the subject matter of legislation

> goes beyond local or provincial concern or interests and must from its inherent nature be the concern of the Dominion as a whole (as, for example, in the *Aeronautics* case and the *Radio* case), then it will fall within the competence of the Dominion Parliament as a matter affecting the peace, order and good government of Canada, though it may in another aspect touch on matters specially reserved to the provincial legislatures.[205]

Though *Canada Temperance* was not a case about treaties, Lord Simon's comments were seen as significant. Even more significant were the extrajudicial reflections of Lord Wright in a posthumous tribute to Duff CJ in the 1955 *Canadian Bar Review*. His lordship, who was himself a member of the board that decided *Labour Conventions*, criticized Lord Atkin's judgment and indicated his preference for *Re Aeronautics*,

---

(Brussels: Peter Lang, 2009) at 217–18, and H Brun, G Tremblay, & E Brouillet, *Droit constitutionnel*, 6th ed (Cowansville, QC: Yvon Blais, 2014) at 595–8.

203 Ziegel, above note 195 at 348.

204 *Final Text of the Consensus Report on the Constitution* (Charlottetown, 28 August 1992), quoted in W Struthers, '"Treaty Implementation . . . Australian Rules': A Rejoinder" (1994) 26 *Ottawa Law Review* 305 at 308.

205 [1946] AC 193 (PC) at 205.

Re Radio, and *Canada Temperance*.[206] These comments inspired a correspondent to the *Canadian Bar Review* to speculate that the decision in "one of the most important cases in Canadian constitutional law was determined by the vote of Sir Sidney Rowlatt, a 'taxation judge,' who, I am told, sat throughout the 1937 hearings in his overcoat making neither note nor comment."[207] Emboldened perhaps by the prevailing irreverence, Kerwin CJ indicated one year later, in *Francis v The Queen*, that "it may be necessary . . . to consider in the future the judgment of the Judicial Committee."[208] More suggestion that *Labour Conventions* would not last long came in the unattributed judgment of the Supreme Court in *Re Offshore Mineral Rights*,[209] which was read as implicitly breaching the rule in *Labour Conventions* by finding that Parliament had jurisdiction to implement the Geneva Convention on the Continental Shelf 1958.[210]

By far the most significant judicial doubting of *Labour Conventions* is that of Laskin CJ in *MacDonald v Vapor Canada*.[211] The chief justice began his consideration of *Labour Conventions* by describing the case as "too well-known to require either quotation or statement of its holding." Thus, without quoting from Lord Atkin's judgment, the chief justice proceeded immediately to consider its critics, starting with the *dictum* of Kerwin CJ in *Francis* and Lord Wright's extrajudicial comments in the *Canadian Bar Review*. The chief justice then cited *Re Aeronautics* and quoted at length from *Re Radio*. Following this passage is

---

206 Lord Wright of Durley, "Rt. Hon. Sir Lyman Poore Duff, G.C.M.G." (1955) 33 *Canadian Bar Review* 1123 at 1125–8.

207 B MacKinnon, letter to the editor, (1956) 34 *Canadian Bar Review* 115 at 117. Lord Atkin himself was concerned that the proposed composition of the board that decided *Labour Conventions* would not command sufficient authority in Canada. He expressed this concern to Lord Hailsham LC shortly before the hearings. The Lord Chancellor defended the board, describing the merits of Sidney Rowlatt as "second to none." During the hearings, Lord Hailsham again wrote to Lord Atkin on this matter, expressing his satisfaction that "no less than four of the Canadian Counsel . . . have severally expressed the greatest possible satisfaction at the constitution of the Board": G Lewis, *Lord Atkin* (Oxford: Hart, 1999) at 100–1.

208 *Francis*, above note 13 at 621.

209 *Reference re Ownership of Offshore Mineral Rights (British Columbia)*, [1967] SCR 792.

210 [1970] Can TS no 4.

211 [1977] 2 SCR 134 [*MacDonald*] at 168–9.

a citation of another extrajudicial critique, this time from Rand J.[212] Having thus discredited the rule in *Labour Conventions*, Laskin CJ declined to overrule it, finding instead that the implementing legislation in question was within federal legislative jurisdiction. Yet the chief justice went on to suggest, in especially adventurous *obiter*, a rule by which Parliament could gain jurisdiction to implement treaties whose subject matter falls otherwise within provincial competence:

> In my opinion, assuming Parliament has power to pass legislation implementing a treaty or convention in relation to matters covered by the treaty or convention which would otherwise be for provincial legislation alone, the exercise of that power must be manifested in the implementing legislation and not be left to inference. The Courts should be able to say, on the basis of the expression of the legislation, that it is implementing legislation. Of course, even so, a question may arise whether the legislation does or does not go beyond the obligations of the treaty or convention.[213]

This is a stark denial of Lord Atkin's holding that there is no such thing as treaty legislation as such. What the chief justice is suggesting here, it seems, is that courts may allow treaties to be implemented by Parliament alone where Parliament has explicitly signalled to the courts its implementing intent.[214] To do so, of course, the government (who, in the normal case, will sponsor the implementing bill) must also signal to the opposition, the rest of Parliament, the provinces, and Canadians at large its intent to intrude upon the provincial sphere. The merit of the signal requirement is that it forces a government seeking to breach the established division of powers to pay the political price.

Chief Justice Laskin's comments in *MacDonald v Vapor* were *obiter*. Yet they are a curious sort of *obiter*, for they were seemingly applied as law by Dickson CJ (speaking for himself and seven other justices) in *Schneider v The Queen*. The chief justice questioned the appellant's submissions concerning Parliament's jurisdiction to implement treaties in

---

212 I Rand, "Some Aspects of Canadian Constitutionalism" (1960) 38 *Canadian Bar Review* 135 at 142.

213 *MacDonald*, above note 211 at 171.

214 This "signal requirement" bears a striking resemblance to the dissenting opinion of Beetz J concerning the emergency doctrine of the peace, order, and good government power in *Re Anti-Inflation Act (Canada)*, [1976] 2 SCR 373.

the face of Lord Atkin's famous judgment, from which he quoted. But Dickson CJ went on to describe Laskin CJ's comments in *MacDonald v Vapor* as a holding of the court and applied them to the case at bar, finding that there was nothing in the Act to indicate Parliament's intent to implement Canadian treaty obligations. The chief justice concluded, "The *Heroin Treatment Act* is not legislation falling within the scope of any federal power to legislate for the implementation of international treaties."[215] I have observed elsewhere:

> The constitutional implications of what was contemplated here are enormous. To reverse *Labour Conventions* and bestow upon the federal government a unilateral power to expand Parliament's jurisdiction through international treaty-making would radically reshape the Canadian division of powers. Parliament's powers would increase dramatically, and the provinces' powers would diminish to the same extent.[216]

To date, however, the anti-*Labour Conventions* musings of the Supreme Court of Canada in *Vapor* and *Schneider* have gone nowhere.[217]

---

215 *Schneider v British Columbia*, [1982] 2 SCR 112 at 134–5. For trenchant criticism of this case, see A De Mestral's case note at (1983) 61 *Canadian Bar Review* 856.

216 G van Ert, "POGG and Treaties: The Role of International Agreements in the National Concern Analysis" (2020) 43 *Dalhousie Law Journal* 901 [van Ert] at 911.

217 Another decision that has been seen as detracting from the authority of *Labour Conventions* is *R v Crown Zellerbach Canada Ltd*, [1988] 1 SCR 401 [*Crown Zellerbach*]. A federal law prohibited the dumping of substances at sea, including provincial maritime waters. Large parts of the Act appeared to implement Canada's obligations under the Convention on the Prevention of Marine Pollution 1972, [1979] Can TS no 36, though the Act did not say so explicitly. Le Dain J for the majority of the Supreme Court of Canada accepted Canada's submission that the law was a valid exercise of Parliament's jurisdiction under the national concern branch of POGG, relying on the treatment of marine dumping in the Convention in finding that the subject matter of the legislation met the "singleness, distinctiveness and indivisibility" requirements of the national concern doctrine. Bayefsky, in Bayefsky, *International Human Rights Law*, above note 126 at 30, has argued that this result "clearly contradicted the rule in *Labour Conventions* that Canada's international obligations were irrelevant to determining constitutional validity." With respect, I disagree. Lord Atkin's judgment in *Labour Conventions* was that treaty implementation occurs according to the established jurisdictions of the federal and provincial legislatures, rather than according to some overriding federal power to implement treaties regardless of their subject matter. Federal legislative jurisdiction includes jurisdiction under POGG, including its national concern branch. If it can be shown that legislation

(v) *Labour Conventions* remains good law

The decision of Lord Atkin in *Labour Conventions* continues to govern the legislative implementation of treaties in Canada to this day. In 1994, L'Heureux-Dubé J affirmed the rule in *Labour Conventions* without any mention of *MacDonald v Vapor*.[218] More recently, in the Supreme Court of Canada's unanimous decision in *Re Pan-Canadian Securities Regulation* (2018), Lord Atkin's reasoning was expressly approved in the court's observation that "Though the federal government may have the authority to enter into international agreements upon subjects falling within the legislative competence of the provinces, the individual provinces will only be bound by the terms of such an agreement once their respective legislatures enact them into law."[219] While that statement was strictly *obiter dicta*, Wagner CJ for the majority of the Supreme Court of Canada made a similar affirmation in *ratio* three years later. The question in *Re Greenhouse Gas Pollution Pricing Act* was the constitutionality of a federal law establishing a pricing scheme for greenhouse gas emissions. Several international climate change treaties were relied upon, although none of them specifically required the adoption of a greenhouse gas pricing scheme. In considering the relevance of these agreements, the chief justice cited *Labour Conventions* for the proposition that "the existence of treaty obligations is not determinative of federal jurisdiction: there is no freestanding federal treaty implementation power and Parliament's jurisdiction to implement treaties signed by the federal government depends on the ordinary division of powers."[220]

In the light of these authorities, LeBel J's passing comment in *Kuwait Airways Corp v Iraq* that Parliament enacted the State Immunity Act "pursuant to the federal power in relation to foreign affairs"[221] must

---

in implementation of a treaty amounts to a matter of national concern, federal jurisdiction is established. Lord Atkin's dictum that there is no such thing as treaty legislation as such cuts both ways: the label "treaty legislation" can no more be used to attack an Act as *ultra vires* than it can be used to defend an Act as *intra vires*. See the discussion of Parliament's power to implement treaties through POGG at Section 7.3(c), below.

218 *Thomson*, above note 72 at 611, L'Heureux-Dubé J. See W Schabas, "Twenty-Five Years of Public International Law at the Supreme Court of Canada" (2000) 79 *Canadian Bar Review* 174 [Schabas] at 177 n 16.

219 *Re Pan-Canadian Securities Regulation*, above note 23 at para 66.

220 *Re Greenhouse Gas Pollution Pricing Act*, 2021 SCC 11 [*Re GGPPA*] at para 149.

221 2010 SCC 40 at para 12.

be understood as referring to federal executive power (i.e., the royal prerogative) rather than federal legislative power (i.e., Parliament's jurisdiction).

As the law now stands, no power inheres in Parliament to legislate within provincial jurisdiction simply on the ground that it seeks to implement treaty obligations incurred by the federal government. The validity of treaty-implementing legislation is determined the same way as the validity of any other enactment: by applying sections 91 and 92 of the Constitution Act, 1867. In the normal case, the division of powers described in these sections will require provincial implementation of certain types of treaty obligation. However, if it can be shown that a treaty-implementing enactment is within Parliament's jurisdiction to legislate for the peace, order, and good government of Canada, that enactment will be valid to implement the treaty within what is otherwise the provincial sphere. The fact that such an enactment seeks to implement a treaty is irrelevant to the consideration of validity, for there is no such thing as treaty legislation as such. The federal argument in favour of validity is not strengthened by the claim of implementation. Nor is the provincial argument against validity improved by the fact that the legislation is pursuant to a treaty obligation. In particular, that an Act seeks to implement a treaty is of no assistance to determining whether the Act is of national concern: The implementation of treaties is not a matter of national concern, as that phrase is used in Canadian constitutional discourse. But the fact that the law's subject matter is also a matter of international concern, as evidenced by international activity including treaty obligations, may support the claim to federal jurisdiction under the national concern doctrine.

(vi) In defence of **Labour Conventions**

The rule in *Labour Conventions* is an application of the implementation requirement to Canadian federalism. Lord Atkin's concern – that federalism in Canada would be dangerously undermined by a rule that the federal Parliament can legislate in provincial jurisdiction when implementing treaties – was valid in 1937 and is unanswerable today, for the subject matters of contemporary treaties fall increasingly within provincial jurisdiction. As impractical as some critics say *Labour Conventions* is, the proposed rule in *MacDonald v Vapor* has its own problems. Under that rule, Parliament's jurisdiction would be determined not by section 91 but by the executive in exercise of its treaty power. Where Parliament purported to implement a treaty falling in whole or in part within provincial jurisdiction, that legislation could be challenged by the provinces as overbroad, meaning that the legislation invades the provincial jurisdiction more than the treaty requires (or more accurately, allows). Furthermore, the provinces might seek review of the Crown's exercise of the treaty power on the ground of colourability: The province might argue that the federal government entered the treaty for no better reason than to gain jurisdiction over provincial matters in a manner not contemplated by the Constitution Act, 1867. Both these challenges would involve courts in rather delicate legal and political questions. The rule in *Labour Conventions* has the virtue of sparing courts these difficulties.[222]

Practicalities aside, I suggest that the rule in *Labour Conventions* is the best means of balancing the reception system's principles of self-government and respect for international law. The principle of respect for international law is admittedly hindered by the rule in *Labour Conventions*, for that rule requires that some treaties be implemented by 10 or 11 legislatures instead of one, thus significantly increasing the likelihood that such treaties will not become Canadian law. The rule may force the federal government to delay or even decline ratification of certain treaties for fear of not being able to ensure their implementation in provincial law. Nevertheless, a rule that Parliament can legislate in the provincial jurisdiction to implement treaties would be a greater blow to the reception system. Our federal state combines a federal, pan-Canadian community with 10 provincial communities,[223] a point Lord Atkin's judgment made in his observations on Quebec and "local conditions." For one level of government to violate another's jurisdiction amounts to a non-consensual imposition of law by one community upon another. One might answer that all Canadians elect the federal

222 See Schabas, above note 218 at 177.

223 "We have not a single community in this country. We have nine commonwealths, several different communities. This is the fact embodied in the law. It may be wise or unwise, according to the preferences and predilection of every one, but this is the basis of our constitution. The federative system was adopted in order to give to the provinces their autonomy and to secure, specially in Quebec, the rights to their own customs as crystallized in their civil law": *Re the Weekly Rest*, above note 162 at 521, Cannon J.

Parliament, that it meets the criteria of deliberative, representative, and participatory decision making demanded by self-government, and therefore Parliament cannot be a non-consensual lawmaker. That answer ignores the most basic principle of federalism; namely, that in matters of provincial jurisdiction the proper instruments of our self-government are the provincial legislatures (and likewise in matters of federal jurisdiction, Parliament is the proper site for the exercise of self-government). Elected though the federal Parliament (or at least its lower chamber) is, it is not elected to make law in provincial jurisdiction.

It remains to add that the principle of respect for international law is by no means wholly rejected in *Labour Conventions*. Canadian treaty practice since the decision shows that Canada remains entirely capable of assuming and living up to international obligations in spite of *Labour Conventions*' implementation rules. Furthermore, *Crown Zellerbach* demonstrated that the rule in *Labour Conventions* allows some scope – narrow and extraordinary though it is – for federal implementation of treaties within what would otherwise be provincial jurisdiction where the subject matter of the treaty at issue is a matter of national concern.

(c) Parliament's power to implement through POGG

Labour Conventions established that legislative jurisdiction over treaty implementation is governed by the ordinary distribution of powers between Parliament and the provincial legislatures. Parliament's general power to enact laws for the peace, order, and good government of Canada (POGG) is part of that distribution. Parliament therefore enjoys legislative jurisdiction to implement treaties that fall within POGG – usually its national concern branch but, in principle, its emergency branch, too.

The rule in *Labour Conventions* is not that Parliament can never avail itself of POGG to implement a treaty. But the existence of a treaty obligation is not, in itself, a constitutional basis for Parliament to implement it under POGG. In all cases, the question is whether the federal legislation is within Parliament's jurisdiction – including its POGG power. The treaty-implementing purpose of a federal law is relevant to the question of national concern but does not determine it. As Wagner CJ explained in *Re Greenhouse Gas Pollution Pricing Act*,

> One key consideration for determining whether the matter is qualitatively different from matters of provincial concern is whether it is predominantly extraprovincial and international in character, having regard both to its inherent nature and to its effects. The case law demonstrates that this inquiry is central to the national concern doctrine. . . .
>
> International agreements may in some cases indicate that a matter is qualitatively different from matters of provincial concern. Consideration of international agreements figured into the Court's national concern analysis in *Johannesson* and in *Crown Zellerbach*. . . . Significantly, the existence of treaty obligations is not determinative of federal jurisdiction: there is no freestanding federal treaty implementation power and Parliament's jurisdiction to implement treaties signed by the federal government depends on the ordinary division of powers: *Attorney-General for Canada v. Attorney-General for Ontario*, [1937] A.C. 326 (P.C.). Treaty obligations and international agreements can be relevant to the national concern analysis, however. Depending on their content, they may help to show that a matter has an extraprovincial and international character, thereby supporting a finding that it is qualitatively different from matters of provincial concern.[224]

As the chief justice suggests here, international agreements have figured in many POGG cases.[225]

---

224 *Re GGPPA*, above note 220 at paras 148–9.

225 I reviewed the leading cases (prior to *Re GGPPA*) at length in van Ert, above note 216. Those cases are *Re Aeronautics*, above note 155 (relying in part on POGG to support Parliament's jurisdiction over aeronautics); *Re Radio*, above note 160 (affirming Parliament's jurisdiction to implement a radiotelegraph convention); *Johannesson v Municipality of West St. Paul*, [1952] 1 SCR 292 (relying on Canadian treaties to support Parliament's POGG jurisdiction over aeronautics); *The Queen v Hauser*, [1979] 1 SCR 984 (relying on Canadian narcotics treaties to uphold federal narcotics legislation under POGG); *Crown Zellerbach*, above note 217 (upholding a federal law prohibiting dumping of substances at sea with reference to the marine pollution treaty that the enactment sought to implement and a UN report on the issue); *Ontario Hydro v Ontario (Labour Relations Board)*, [1993] 3 SCR 327 (noting Canada's international obligations in the field of nuclear energy in sustaining Parliament's jurisdiction over labour relations at nuclear

The Supreme Court of Canada's jurisprudence on POGG and treaties establishes, in my view, the following points.[226] First (and as already noted), treaty obligations are relevant to but not determinative of Parliament's jurisdiction under its residual power to legislate for the peace, order, and good government of Canada.

Second, in POGG cases (very much unlike the rest of Canadian reception law[227]), courts look to the state's treaty obligations not for their legal obligatoriness at international law but as judicially noticeable facts that may support a federal claim that the subject of Parliament's enactment is a matter of national concern. The obligatoriness of the treaty as a matter of international law is rightly set aside, for the purpose of POGG analysis, because whether Canada can perform the obligation is not the question; the question is whether Canada can perform the obligation by a single Act of Parliament, or whether it must instead perform the obligation by enactments of the 10 provinces. To be clear, the reviewing court still takes judicial notice of the underlying treaty and still determines its meaning as a question of law; the judicial approach to treaties in POGG cases is not to assimilate them entirely to questions of fact. But the main use the court has made of treaties in POGG cases is as evidence that an issue is one of national concern.

Third, and related to the second point, a treaty may demonstrate the advent of a new matter not in existence at Confederation – that is, a matter that falls within the POGG power because it was not contemplated, and therefore not assigned either to Parliament or to the provincial legislatures, in 1867. This was the case in *Re Aeronautics*, *Re Radio*, and *Hauser*. The point here is not that the treaty is new but that the subject matter addressed by both the treaty and the impugned enactment is.

Fourth, treaties are potentially relevant to the federal claim that a matter originally of a merely local or private nature in the province

---

generating stations). To this list must now be added *Re GGPPA*, above note 220 (holding that international agreements may help to show that a matter has an extraprovincial and international character, thereby supporting a finding of national concern).

226 I consider these points at somewhat greater length in van Ert, above note 216 at 919–22.

227 See the discussions of judicial notice of international law and proof of treaties in Chapter 3, Sections 3.1 and 3.2.

has taken on extraprovincial dimensions and thus become a matter of national concern. *Re Radio*, *Re Aeronautics*, *Johannesson*, and *Crown Zellerbach* are all cases in which treaties were invoked to show that a previously local matter had attained national dimensions – not simply because the federal government had concluded a treaty on the issue but seemingly because other states had also done so.

Fifth, treaties are relevant to the provincial inability analysis. *Re Radio*, *Crown Zellerbach*, *Ontario Hydro*, and *Re GGPPA* are all cases in which treaties were looked to in support of the conclusion that the legislative matter at issue possessed (in Le Dain J's phrase) the "singleness, distinctiveness and indivisibility that clearly distinguishes it from matters of provincial concern."[228] Chief Justice Wagner was explicit on this point in *Re GGPPA*:

> Any province's failure to act threatens Canada's ability to meet its international obligations, which in turn hinders Canada's ability to push for international action to reduce GHG emissions. Therefore, a provincial failure to act directly threatens Canada as a whole. This is not to say that Parliament has jurisdiction to implement Canada's treaty obligations – it does not – but simply that the inherently global nature of GHG emissions and the problem of climate change supports a finding of provincial inability in this case.[229]

Finally, resort to treaties is seemingly permitted at all stages of the POGG analysis. To date, the case law has not identified any part of the POGG analysis to which a treaty obligation of the state might not be considered – so long as the foundational rule in *Labour Conventions* is respected.

7.4 Possible exceptions to the implementation requirement

The requirement that treaties be implemented by legislation before taking direct effect in domestic law is the orthodoxy today. But it has

---

228 *Crown Zellerbach*, above note 217 at 432. See also *Re Radio*, above note 160 at 86 (where Viscount Dunedin observed that, "keeping in view the duties under the Convention," the broadcasting system "could not be divided into two parts [i.e., transmitter and receiver], each independent of the other").

229 *Re GGPPA*, above note 220 at para 190; see also para 151.

not always been settled law, and it may not always remain settled. Four exceptions or potential exceptions to the implementation requirement can be distinguished in the cases.

(a) Peace treaties and treaties of cession

There are suggestions in the English[230] and Canadian[231] literature that treaties of peace (sometimes called treaties of war or treaties affecting belligerent rights) and treaties of cession may be exempt from the implementation requirement. Such treaties, it is contended, have the force of law without legislation. If such an exception to the implementation rule exists, it grants the executive certain legislative powers that, in any other context, would be unconstitutional.

In *Walker v Baird*,[232] an appeal to the Privy Council from the Supreme Court of Newfoundland, Captain Baird of the HMS *Emerald* sought to enforce against Mr. Walker, the proprietor of a lobster factory, the provisions of a UK–France fisheries treaty that had not been implemented in the law of Newfoundland. The Supreme Court of Newfoundland held that Walker's right to run a lobster fishery could not be affected by an unimplemented treaty with France. Lord Herschell for the Privy Council dismissed the attorney general's appeal, rejecting his argument that the litigation involved the construction of treaties and other acts of state that could not be inquired into by the court. But the attorney general also contended that since treaty-making is a power of the Crown, the power to compel subjects to abide by such treaties, at least where made to make or preserve peace between Britain and foreign powers,

230 See, e.g., Sir Robert Jennings & Sir Arthur Watts, eds, *Oppenheim's International Law*, 9th ed vol 1 (London: Longmans, 1992) [Jennings & Watts] at 58 n 23, and Brownlie, above note 1 at 47. Professor Crawford observes that the implementation requirement does not apply "in the very rare cases where the Crown's prerogative can directly extend or contract jurisdiction without the need for legislation": J Crawford, *Brownlie's Principles of Public International Law*, 9th ed (Oxford: Oxford University Press, 2019) at 59.

231 See, e.g., F Vallat, "Treaties" (1933) 6 *Canadian Bar Review* 385 [Vallat, "Treaties"]; J Read, "International Agreements" (1948) 26 *Canadian Bar Review* 520 [Read] at 528; R St J Macdonald, "International Treaty Law and the Domestic Law of Canada" (1975) 2 *Dalhousie Law Journal* 307 at 308–10, 313–14; A Bayefsky, *International Human Rights Law*, above note 126 at 25.

232 [1892] AC 491 (PC).

must also rest with the Crown – without the need for implementing legislation. This point the board explicitly left undecided.

In *Re Employment of Aliens*, Duff J (as he then was) gave an account of the treaty-making power that left room for a peace treaty exception to the implementation requirement, observing that it is "no part of the prerogative of the Crown by treaty in time of peace to effect directly a change in the law governing the rights of private individuals."[233]

In *New Brunswick (Attorney General) v Canadian Pacific Railway*,[234] the appeal division of the Supreme Court of New Brunswick considered an injunction application by the attorney general of New Brunswick for removal of a bridge over the Saint John River. That river forms, for part of its course, the international boundary between Canada (New Brunswick) and the United States (Maine). The Ashburton Treaty 1842 recognized this and other maritime boundaries between the United States and Britain's North American possessions. The defendant contended that Canada, not New Brunswick, had jurisdiction over navigation under the British North America Act 1867 and therefore the province could not properly seek injunctive relief. Justice Barry (as he then was) for himself and his two colleagues affirmed the Dominion's jurisdiction and held that the Ashburton Treaty did not limit or abridge its powers. In reaching this result, Barry J considered whether the Ashburton Treaty was effective in law whether implemented by legislation or not. The court below had affirmed the orthodoxy that "a treaty made by the Crown, and not sanctioned by legislative enactment does not create law by which the Courts are bound."[235] Justice Barry confessed his "inability to follow the reasoning which leads to that conclusion" for he regarded the Crown as "the collective expression used to designate the people" and considered "that where the Crown is a contracting party, the whole body of the people, all the subjects of the sovereign, are intended to be bound by the contract."[236] But the learned judge also relied on various instances of statutory recognition (if perhaps not comprehensive implementation) of the treaty, including an elliptical reference in section 7 of the British North America Act affirming New

233 *Re Employment of Aliens*, above note 10 at 329; see also Brodeur J at 339.
234 (1924) 52 NBR 121 (NB App Div) [*New Brunswick v CPR*].
235 *New Brunswick v CPR*, above note 234 at 144.
236 *Ibid* at 145.

Brunswick's existing boundaries.[237] He added that "the whole geographical structure of the eastern provinces depends upon the boundaries settled by" the Ashburton Treaty and it was therefore "impossible to say that the provisions of the treaty are not to be regarded as the settled and accepted law of this country" enforceable "without further legislative confirmation."[238] Coming to the peace treaty point, Barry J noted partial support for this supposed exception to the implementation requirement in *Halsbury's Laws of England* and in Sir Robert Phillimore's judgment in *The Parliament Belge*.[239] He then concluded that the Ashburton Treaty had "as one of its objects the preservation of peace" between Britain and the United States and picked up the submission made by the attorney general in *Walker v Baird*, calling it "unanswerable" – a curious choice of word given the Privy Council's express refusal to answer it when it came before them.[240]

The rule that treaties of peace do not require implementation was again approved in *obiter* by Duff J (as he then was) in *Secretary of State of Canada v Alien Property Custodian for the United States*.[241] His *dictum* in that case was cited approvingly by Angers J in *Ritcher v The King*.[242] But in *Bitter v Secretary of State for Canada*, Thorson J boldly rejected Duff J's argument:

> What legal effect should be given to the terms of a Treaty of Peace is an interesting question. In *Secretary of State of Canada v. Alien Property Custodian for the United States* . . ., Duff J. made the following striking statement: "The treaty it is to be observed, being a Treaty of Peace, had the effect of law quite independently of legislation." With the utmost respect, I venture the opinion that there is no authority for this statement and that it cannot be accepted without important qualifications. While a Treaty of Peace can be made only by the Crown, it still remains an Act of the Crown. While it is binding upon the subjects of the Crown without legislation in the sense that it terminates the war, it has never, so far as I have been able to ascertain, been decided or admitted that the Crown could by its own act

237 *Ibid* at 146–9.
238 *Ibid* at 149–51.
239 *Ibid* at 152, 154; *The Parlement Belge*, [1878–9] 4 PD 129 [*The Parlement Belge*].
240 *New Brunswick v CPR*, above note 234 at 159.
241 [1931] SCR 169 at 198.
242 [1943] Ex CR 64 at 69.

> in agreeing to the terms of a treaty alter the law of the land or affect the private rights of individuals.[243]

Justice Thorson's strong rejection of a peace treaty exception to the implementation requirement went unconsidered by Kerwin CJ in *Francis v The Queen*. As noted above, *Francis* involved an Indigenous man bringing goods from the United States into Canada without paying duty – something he claimed a right to do pursuant to article III of the Jay Treaty 1794. This provision of the treaty was no longer implemented in legislation. Francis therefore argued that the Jay Treaty, and the subsequent Treaty of Ghent 1815, were peace treaties, which took direct effect in Canadian law without implementation. Chief Justice Kerwin rejected Francis's characterization of the treaties as treaties of peace and insisted on the implementation requirement.[244] In separate reasons, Rand J (Cartwright J concurring), held that implementation was required of all treaties "which purport to change existing law or restrict the future action of the legislation" save those concerning "diplomatic status and certain immunities and to belligerent rights."[245] This is a broad and ill-defined category, one that Rand J seemed to think might extend to peace treaties having fiscal effects upon domestic law.[246] With respect, Rand J's discussion illustrates just how unsatisfying the supposed peace treaty exception is.

In *Mastini v Bell Telephone*,[247] Jackett P mostly ignored *Francis* in holding that the Treaty of Peace with Italy 1947[248] was not law without legislative implementation. He relied instead on Lord Atkin's affirmation in *Labour Conventions* that the performance of a treaty's obligations, if they entail alternation of existing domestic law, requires

243 *Bitter v Secretary of State of Canada*, [1944] Ex CR 61 at 76–7.

244 *Francis*, above note 13 at 621.

245 *Ibid* at 626. See also Rand J's similar observation in *Attorney General for Ontario v Scott*, [1956] SCR 137 at 142: "A treaty is an agreement between states, political in nature, even though it may contain provisions of a legislative character which may, *by themselves* or their subsequent enactment pass into law" (emphasis added). "By themselves" apparently refers to peace treaties.

246 "To the enactment of fiscal provisions, certainly in the case of a treaty not a peace treaty, the prerogative does not extend. . . .": *Francis*, above note 13 at 626, Rand J.

247 *Mastini*, above note 24.

248 [1947] Can TS no 4.

legislative action. He also noted that Rand and Cartwright JJ, concurring in *Francis*, had largely affirmed the implementation requirement.

The law as stated by Thorson J in *Bitter*, and applied by Jackett P in *Mastini*, is more consistent with the constitutional prohibition of executive legislation, and the self-government principle that informs it, than the opposing *dicta* in *Francis* and other cases reviewed here. This is not only my view but also that of Rogers,[249] Read,[250] Fawcett,[251] and Macdonald.[252] There would appear to be no reason to deny the executive lawmaking powers in respect of most treaties while permitting such powers in peace treaties.

Nor should any special rule apply to treaties of cession.[253] The distinction between treaties of peace and treaties of cession is a false one. Where a cession occurs in peacetime, it is inconceivable that it be done on the authority of the executive alone.[254] As Fawcett puts it, "If the Crown cannot, without authority of Parliament, modify private rights within the framework of existing law, it cannot *a fortiori* remove the protection of that law altogether."[255] In the case of cession as provided for by a peace treaty, the same rule should apply, though tempered perhaps by the principle that the safety of the people is the highest law.[256]

249 Rogers, above note 140.

250 Read, above note 231 at 528.

251 J Fawcett, *The British Commonwealth in International Law* (London: Stevens, 1963) [Fawcett] at 58. See also the report of 13 July 1870 by the British Crown Law Officers to the Colonial Office in A McNair, *The Law of Treaties: British Practice and Opinions* (Oxford: Clarendon Press, 1961) at 107–8, who advised the colonial secretary that territory could not be ceded in peacetime by prerogative alone.

252 R St J Macdonald, "The Relationship Between Domestic Law and International Law in Canada" in R St J Macdonald et al, eds, *Canadian Perspectives on International Law and Organization* (Toronto: University of Toronto Press, 1974) at 120.

253 Kerwin CJ noted Indian and New Zealand authorities requiring implementation of treaties of cession in *Francis*, above note 13 at 621. Vallat, "Treaties," above note 231 at 385 notes that cession seems to require legislation except perhaps in India – a proposition that may tell us more about history and politics than law.

254 See *Dunbar and Sullivan Dredging Co v Milwaukee (The)* (1907), 11 Ex CR 179.

255 Fawcett, above note 251 at 59.

256 *Salus populi est suprema lex.*

(b) Rights-granting treaties

The orthodoxy is that the implementation requirement applies equally whether the treaty at issue purports to confer or deprive rights. Sir Hersch Lauterpacht, writing in 1939, observed that treaties require implementation to affect private rights "favourably or adversely." He explained, "it is . . . clearly established that in the absence of express municipal legislation to that effect, subjects cannot, as against the Crown, derive benefits directly under a treaty on the ground that the Crown acts as agent or trustee for the subject."[257] Similarly, Sir Frances Vallat, writing in 1966, explained, "If in the absence of parliamentary authority the Crown cannot deprive a British subject of his rights and remedies under the law, it is also true that an individual cannot claim rights in law solely by virtue of the provisions of a treaty."[258]

But there are commentators, and even judicial authorities, that take issue with the view that the implementation requirement applies equally to rights-granting and rights-depriving treaties. This vein of dissent may be traced to the case most frequently cited as authority against it: *The Parlement Belge*. While Sir Robert Phillimore's decision in that case is routinely cited for the proposition that treaties take no legal effect in domestic law without legislation, Sir Robert himself was not so categorical. In his view there was "a class of treaties the provisions of which were inoperative without the confirmation of the legislature;

---

257 H Lauterpacht, "Is International Law a Part of the Law of England?" (1939) 25 *Transactions of the Grotius Society* 51 at 75 n (c). Lauterpacht cites three authorities: *Civilian War Claimants' Association v The King*, [1932] AC 14 (HL) [*Civilian War Claimants' Association*]; *Rustomjee v The Queen* (1876), 1 QBD 487 (Eng QB), (1876) 2 QBD 69 (CA); and *Baron de Bode v The Queen* (1845), 8 QB 208, "where," says Lauterpacht, "the question seems, in a sense, to have been left open." See also *J.H. Rayner (Mincing Lane) Ltd v Department of Trade and Industry*, [1990] 2 AC 418 (HL) at 500, Lord Oliver ("the royal prerogative, whilst it embraces the making of treaties, does not extend to altering the law or conferring rights on individuals or depriving individuals of rights which they enjoy in domestic law without the intervention of Parliament"); *Higgs v Minister of National Security and Others (Bahamas)*, [1999] UKPC 55 at para 12, Lord Hoffman ("unincorporated treaties cannot change the law of the land" and have "no effect upon the rights and duties of citizens in common or statute law").

258 Vallat, *International Law*, above note 37 at 7–8, citing *Civilian War Claimants Association*, above note 257.

while there were others which operated without such confirmation."[259] This qualification might be taken as a reference to the supposed exception to the implementation requirement for peace treaties. But that is not quite how Sir Robert put it. Rather, he observed that "the question before me is whether this treaty does affect private rights, and therefore required the sanction of the legislature."[260] This seems to leave open the possibility that while the Crown could not affect (i.e., adversely) private rights by treaty without legislation, the rule might be otherwise for a treaty that improves or advances private rights.

No less a commentator than Sir Elihu Lauterpacht (Sir Hersch's son) argued that courts should treat rights-advancing treaties and rights-limiting treaties differently. He suggested that where an obligation entered into by the executive is to the benefit of the public and imposes a burden on itself, courts should hold the executive to that commitment.[261] More recently, Professor Bjorge has attempted to shore up this view with older English and Privy Council authorities.[262]

The argument that rights-granting treaties may be directly effective without legislative implementation was endorsed in dissent by UK Supreme Court justice Lord Kerr in *R (SG & Ors) v Secretary of State for Work and Pensions*.[263] The case was a challenge to UK regulations that were said to discriminate against single parents and domestic violence victims, who tended to be women. The regulations were attacked in part as inconsistent with the best interests of the child principle set out in article 3(1) of the Convention on the Rights of the Child 1989. The majority of the court rejected the challenge, noting in particular that the Convention was unimplemented in UK law. In dissent, Lord Kerr

---

259 *The Parlement Belge*, above note 239 at 150. This passage was quoted by Barry J (as he then was) in *New Brunswick v CPR*, above note 234 at 154. The learned judge also expressed the view (at 146) that "If [a treaty] is susceptible of efficient enforcement without the aid of any auxiliary or enabling municipal legislation, then, I think, as I will endeavor to show later on, that it is enforceable in the municipal courts."

260 *The Parlement Belge*, above note 239 at 150.

261 M Hunt, *Using Human Rights Law in English Courts* (Oxford: Hart, 1997) at 34, citing an unpublished lecture by Sir Elihu Lauterpacht, "International Law and Her Majesty's Judges," F Mann Memorial Lecture 1993; see also 258–9.

262 E Bjorge, "Can Unincorporated Treaty Obligations be Part of English Law?" [2017] *Public Law* 571.

263 [2015] UKSC 1.

noted suggestions by Lords Slynn[264] and Steyn[265] in earlier cases that an exception to the implementation requirement might apply to human rights treaties. He continued:

> I consider that the time has come for the exception to the dualist theory in human rights conventions foreshadowed by Lord Slynn in *Lewis* and rather more firmly expressed by Lord Steyn in *Re McKerr* to be openly recognised. This can properly be done in relation to such conventions without espousing the complete abandonment of the theory advocated by some of the commentators referred to above.
>
> If Lord Steyn is right, as I believe he is, to characterise the rationale for the dualist theory as a form of protection of the citizen from abuses by the executive, the justification for refusing to recognise the rights enshrined in an international convention relating to human rights and to which the UK has subscribed as directly enforceable in domestic law is not easy to find. Why should a convention which expresses the UK's commitment to the protection of a particular human right for its citizens not be given effect as an enforceable right in domestic law?
>
> Standards expressed in international treaties or conventions dealing with human rights to which the UK has subscribed must be presumed to be the product of extensive and enlightened consideration. There is no logical reason to deny to UK citizens domestic law's vindication of the rights that those conventions proclaim. If the government commits itself to a standard of human rights protection, it seems to me entirely logical that it should be held to account in the courts as to its actual compliance with that standard. . . .[266]

In Canada, a somewhat similar view was expressed by Rosenberg JA (dissenting) in *Ahani v Canada (Attorney General)*.[267] The question there was whether Canada could lawfully deport Ahani to Iran despite his outstanding communication with the UN Human Rights Committee and the interim measures request that committee had made to Canada to permit it time to review Ahani's communication. The majority of the

264 See *Lewis v AG of Jamaica*, [2001] 2 AC 50 (PC).

265 See *Re McKerr*, [2004] UKHL 12.

266 *R (SG & Ors) v Secretary of State for Work and Pensions*, [2015] UKSC 1 at paras 254–6.

267 *Ahani*, above note 120.

Court of Appeal for Ontario found that Canada could deport Ahani, concluding that neither the International Covenant on Civil and Political Rights 1966 or its Optional Protocol[268] (under which the Human Rights Committee operates) were implemented in domestic law, and that Ahani had no legitimate expectation of not being deported pending the committee's consideration of his communication.[269] In dissent, Rosenberg JA noted that the implementation requirement serves "to protect Parliament and the people of Canada from executive action," yet here the government invoked it "to shield the executive from the consequences of its voluntary decision to enter into and therefore be bound by the Covenant and the Protocol." In Rosenberg JA's view, the implementation requirement went "only so far as to affirm that the Covenant and the Protocol do not create rights in the appellant that can be enforced in a domestic court" and did not preclude Ahani from advancing "the limited procedural right to reasonable access to the Committee, upon which the federal government has conferred jurisdiction."[270]

In a similar vein are decisions from other Commonwealth jurisdictions that would recognize treaty obligations as founding legitimate expectations of procedural and even substantial rights in administrative decision-making contexts. These authorities, which have yet to attract Canadian support, are considered briefly in Chapter 9.[271]

The cases and commentary briefly surveyed here suggest a path for future development in Anglo-Canadian reception law. In time, the position may come to be that a treaty generally requires implementation to take direct effect in domestic law but may exceptionally apply directly in respect of human rights treaties or rights-granting provisions of treaties generally. There is an obvious attraction to this position, but it would no doubt bring with it new difficulties of application. UK and Canadian courts would find themselves asking for the first time a ques-

---

268 [1976] Can TS no 47 (which includes both the ICCPR and its first Optional Protocol).

269 I have criticized the Court of Appeal's treatment of the ICCPR as unimplemented earlier in this chapter. The court was right, of course, to find that the Optional Protocol is unimplemented.

270 *Ahani*, above note 120 at paras 91–3.

271 At Section 9.5.

tion with which American courts are all too familiar: Is this or is this not the sort of treaty that applies directly as law?

(c) Judicially performed treaties

In *Office of the Children's Lawyer v Balev*,[272] McLachlin CJ for the majority of the Supreme Court of Canada decried the time it took the courts below to bring an application under the Convention on the Civil Aspects of International Child Abduction 1980[273] (the Hague Convention) to a hearing. She noted that article 11 of the Convention "specifically requires the contracting states' judicial authorities to 'act expeditiously in proceedings for the return of children.'" She then observed: "Responsibility for performing Canada's Article 11 obligation falls to judges and court administrators. This is unusual, but it is not unheard of. Canada is a party to other treaties that depend, in part, on judicial action to ensure performance."[274]

The chief justice cited the "performance of Canada's obligation to apply and interpret [treaties] according to the rules of treaty interpretation" as a duty that "falls to Canada's judges." Having considered the Vienna Convention on the Law of Treaties 1969[275] earlier in her reasons,[276] she quoted Lord Diplock's consideration of that treaty in *Fothergill v Monarch Airlines Ltd*:

> By ratifying the Convention, Her Majesty's Government has undertaken an international obligation on behalf of the United Kingdom to interpret future treaties in this manner and since under our constitution the function of interpreting the written law is an exercise of judicial power and rests with the courts of justice, that obligation assumed by the United Kingdom falls to be performed by those courts.[277]

She also relied on Dickson CJ's observation in *R v Zingre* that in responding affirmatively to a request made by Swiss authorities under an extradition agreement, "the Court will be recognizing and giving effect

272 *Balev*, above note 75.
273 [1983] Can TS no 35.
274 *Balev*, above note 75 at para 84.
275 [1980] Can TS no 37.
276 *Balev*, above note 75 at paras 32, 33, 35.
277 [1981] AC 251 (HL) at 283, quoted in *Balev*, above note 75 at para 85.

to a duty to which Canada is subject, by treaty, under international law."[278] The learned chief justice concluded from these authorities that "it was up to the judicial authorities in this case to ensure Canada lived up to its obligation to act expeditiously,"[279] and added that "In light of this appeal, this Court has taken steps to ensure that *Hague Convention* cases are flagged internally and expedited by our registry" and that she hoped other courts would do likewise.[280]

The discussion in *Balev* indicates that where a treaty requires judicial action to ensure the state's performance, the courts may take steps to ensure that performance even in the absence of implementing legislation. In *Balev*, article 11 of the Hague Convention was unimplemented. Likewise in *Fothergill* the Vienna Convention on the Law of Treaties was unimplemented. Yet the courts did not insist on legislative implementation prior to giving effect to these treaties, seemingly because they considered that responsibility for their performance fell to the courts themselves. Clearly there are limits to how far such reasoning can go while still maintaining consistency with the foundational constitutional principle that the Crown is not a source of law. Where that line is to be drawn in particular cases remains to be seen, but it is surely important that the treaties in *Balev* and *Fothergill* both spoke directly to core aspects of the judicial function: the control of their own proceedings and the interpretation of legal instruments.

(d) The rule in *Hape* and *Khadr*

A new exception to the implementation requirement – one of doubtful correctness and longevity – was opened by the Supreme Court of Canada's decision in *R v Hape*[281] and applied shortly thereafter by that same court in *Canada (Justice) v Khadr*.[282] The majority in *Hape* interpreted section 32(1) of the Charter as meaning that criminally accused persons facing trial in Canada are barred from relying on section 8 of the Charter – and seemingly also other Charter rights – to scrutinize the constitutionality of state officials' conduct where that conduct took

278 [1981] 2 SCR 392 at 409, quoted in *Balev*, above note 75 at para 86.
279 *Balev*, above note 75 at para 87.
280 *Ibid* at para 89.
281 2007 SCC 26 [*Hape*].
282 2008 SCC 28 [*Khadr*].

place outside Canadian territory. For courts to give effect to Charter guarantees in such cases was said to be contrary to international law as an impermissible exercise of extraterritorial jurisdiction. This reasoning is flawed, as many Canadian international law scholars and commentators have shown.[283]

In seeming recognition of the danger posed by opening this hole in Charter protection, the majority in *Hape* proposed a possible exception "where the participation of Canadian officers in investigative activities sanctioned by foreign law would place Canada in violation of its international obligations in respect of human rights" and left open "the possibility that, in a future case, participation by Canadian officers in activities in another country that would violate Canada's international

283 I cannot improve on the list of such commentary given by Karakatsanis and Martin JJ in *R v McGregor*, 2023 SCC 4 [*McGregor*] at para 66: K Roach, "*R. v. Hape* Creates Charter-Free Zones for Canadian Officials Abroad" (2007), 53 *Criminal Law Quarterly* 1 at 1; JH Currie, "Weaving a Tangled Web: *Hape* and the Obfuscation of Canadian Reception Law" (2007), 45 *Canadian Yearbook of International Law* 55; G van Ert, "Canadian Cases in Public International Law in 2006–7" (2007), 45 *Canadian Yearbook of International Law* 527 at 544–5; JH Currie, "*Khadr*'s Twist on *Hape*: Tortured Determinations of the Extraterritorial Reach of the Canadian *Charter*" (2008), 46 *Canadian Yearbook of International Law* 307; A Attaran, "Have Charter, Will Travel? Extraterritoriality in Constitutional Law and Canadian Exceptionalism" (2008), 87 *Canadian Bar Review* 515; P-H Verdier, "International Decisions: *R. v. Hape*" (2008), 102 *American Journal of International Law* 143; JH Currie, "International Human Rights Law in the Supreme Court's Charter Jurisprudence: Commitment, Retrenchment *and* Retreat – In No Particular Order" (2010), 50 *Supreme Court Law Review* (2d) 423; ML Banda, "On the Water's Edge? A Comparative Study of the Influence of International Law and the Extraterritorial Reach of Domestic Laws in the War on Terror Jurisprudence" (2010), 41 *Georgetown Journal of International Law* 525; C Sethi, "Does the Charter Follow the Flag? Revisiting Constitutional Extraterritoriality after *R v. Hape*" (2011), 20 *Dalhousie Journal of Legal Studies* 102; M Webb, "The Constitutional Question of Our Time: Extraterritorial Application of the Charter and the Afghan Detainees Case" (2011), 28 *National Journal of Constitutional Law* 235; D Ireland-Piper, "Extraterritorial Criminal Jurisdiction: Does the Long Arm of the Law Undermine the Rule of Law?" (2012), 13 *Melbourne Journal of International Law* 122; C McLachlan, *Foreign Relations Law* (2014), at paras 8.36–8.38, 8.52–8.94; RJ Currie & J Rikhof, *International & Transnational Criminal Law* (3rd ed 2020), at 631–9; L West, "'Within or Outside Canada': The Charter's Application to the Extraterritorial Activities of the Canadian Security Intelligence Service" (2023), 73 *University of Toronto Law Journal* 1; L West, "Canada Stands Alone: A Comparative Analysis of the Extraterritorial Reach of State Human Rights Obligations" (2022) 55 *University of British Columbia Law Review* 845.

human rights obligations might justify a remedy under section 24(1) of the *Charter* because of the impact of those activities on Charter rights in Canada."[284] Justice Binnie considered this proposal in a politely devastating concurrence:

> In an effort to fill the gap created by his rejection of *Charter* applicability, LeBel J. would substitute Canada's "international human rights obligations", as a source of limitation on state power. The content of such obligations is weaker and their scope is more debatable than *Charter* guarantees. Specifically, LeBel J. writes, at para. 101, that relief may be available "where the participation of Canadian officers in investigative activities sanctioned by foreign law would place Canada in violation of its international obligations in respect of human rights". The proposal is that international human rights obligations should become the applicable "extraterritorial" standard in substitution for Charter guarantees even as between the Canadian government and Canadian citizens. . . .
>
> However, the scope of this possible exception is unclear, given the fact that the conduct at issue would necessarily be outside Canada and, according to my colleague, ought not to be judged by the *Charter* standards because "extraterritorial application of the Charter is impossible" (para. 85).[285]

Less than a year later, in *Khadr*, the court availed itself of the safety valve the majority had planted in *Hape*. The case concerned a Canadian citizen detained by the United States at its notorious Guantanamo Bay, Cuba, prison. The detainee, Omar Khadr, sought disclosure from the Government of Canada of documents in its possession relevant to the US charges he faced. Canada refused, arguing that disclosure rights under *R v Stinchcombe*[286] were unavailable to him since *Hape* had held that Canadian agents participating in investigations abroad are not bound by the Charter. In reasons attributed to the court as a whole, the Supreme Court of Canada engaged in the following unprecedented reasoning:

284 *Hape*, above note 281 at para 101.

285 *Ibid* at paras 186, 188.

286 [1991] 3 SCR 326.

> If the Guantanamo Bay process under which Mr. Khadr was being held was in conformity with Canada's international obligations, the *Charter* has no application and Mr. Khadr's application for disclosure cannot succeed: *Hape*. However, if Canada was participating in a process that was violative of Canada's binding obligations under international law, the *Charter* applies to the extent of that participation.
>
> . . . The United States Supreme Court has considered the legality of the conditions under which the Guantanamo detainees were detained and liable to prosecution during the time Canadian officials interviewed Mr. Khadr and gave the information to U.S. authorities, between 2002 and 2004. With the benefit of a full factual record, the United States Supreme Court held that the detainees had illegally been denied access to *habeas corpus* and that the procedures under which they were to be prosecuted violated the *Geneva Conventions*. Those holdings are based on principles consistent with the *Charter* and Canada's international law obligations. In the present appeal, this is sufficient to establish violations of these international law obligations, to which Canada subscribes.
>
> . . . The right to challenge the legality of detention by *habeas corpus* is a fundamental right protected both by the *Charter* and by international treaties. It follows that participation in the Guantanamo Bay process which violates these international instruments would be contrary to Canada's binding international obligations.
>
> We conclude that the principles of international law and comity that might otherwise preclude application of the *Charter* to Canadian officials acting abroad do not apply to the assistance they gave to U.S. authorities at Guantanamo Bay. Given the holdings of the United States Supreme Court, the *Hape* comity concerns that would ordinarily justify deference to foreign law have no application here. . . . Hence no question of deference to foreign law arises. The *Charter* bound Canada to the extent that the conduct of Canadian officials involved it in a process that violated Canada's international obligations.[287]

I characterize this reasoning as a new exception to the implementation requirement because it invites, and indeed requires, courts to go straight to Canada's international obligations, whether implemented

287 *Khadr*, above note 282 at paras 19, 21, 25–6.

in domestic law or not, as a juridical basis for reviewing the conduct of Canadian officials in cases where the Charter's application would otherwise be excluded by the rule in *R v Hape*. Courts are, in effect, required to treat international obligations[288] as immediately and directly enforceable by courts in such cases, without any consideration of their legislative status in domestic law. In authorizing and requiring direct judicial recourse to the state's treaty obligations, not simply for the purposes of applying the interpretive presumption of conformity with international law but as the basis for granting claimants relief against allegedly unlawful government action, the reasoning in *Hape* and *Khadr* is profoundly out of step with Anglo-Canadian reception law.[289]

In *R v McGregor* the majority of the Supreme Court of Canada declined the invitation of several interveners to correct *Hape* on various points, concluding that reconsideration of that decision should await an invitation by a party to the appeal.[290] When a party does eventually put *Hape* in issue, one must hope the court takes the opportunity to make the required international law and reception law corrections to it. The *Hape/Khadr* exception to the implementation requirement must be regarded as *per incuriam*, for it proceeds from *Hape*'s fundamental international legal error, namely its confusion of adjudicative jurisdiction with enforcement jurisdiction.

7.5 Treaty de-implementation

It may become necessary to undo legislative steps previously taken to perform a treaty's obligations in domestic law. This could occur if Canada terminates or withdraws from a treaty that Parliament or the provincial legislatures previously implemented. More likely, perhaps, is that de-implementation is required to reflect a revision or replace-

---

288 The court in *Khadr* spoke in general terms of international human rights law (see paras 1–3, 24, 27, 29, and 31) but spoke specifically of US and Canadian obligations under the four Geneva Conventions of 1949 – instruments that form part of international humanitarian law rather than international human rights law. The court appears not to have appreciated the distinction.

289 The *Khadr* decision is problematic in other respects, too. See my note of the case in G van Ert, "Canadian Cases in Public International Law in 2007–8" in (2007–8) 46 *Canadian Yearbook of International Law* at 647–52.

290 *McGregor*, above note 283 at para 23.

ment by states parties of a previous treaty regime. Keyes and Sullivan point to the shift from the Canada–US Free Trade Agreement 1988[291] to the North American Free Trade Agreement 1992[292] as an example. There, implementing amendments to the Customs Tariff[293] suspended the operation of provisions implementing the early agreement during the pendency of the new one.[294]

The mere Crown act of terminating or withdrawing from a treaty – like the Crown act of acquiring a treaty obligation – has no direct effect in domestic law. An implemented treaty remains implemented even after the federal government, in exercise of the foreign affairs power, withdraws or otherwise departs from the treaty regime. Just as legislation is needed to implement a treaty in domestic law, legislation is needed to de-implement a treaty.

Treaty de-implementation can be harmful to private interests, as the facts of *Francis* demonstrate.[295] It can also cause international concern; Keyes and Sullivan noted that de-implementing provisions "must obviously be used with a great deal of caution" as they "may signal to other parties a lack of commitment to the agreement and perhaps lead to questions about the good faith of a party that uses them."[296]

A notable instance of de-implementation – and yet one so aberrant that little can be learned from it – is the short life of the federal Kyoto Protocol Implementation Act.[297] The Act became law in June 2007 under the first Harper government but very much against its wishes. Mr. Harper's stated policy at the time was that Canada would not comply with its obligations under the Protocol,[298] a treaty obligation his government had inherited from the closing days of the previous government. Despite the new government's objections, the opposition parties, who together controlled both the Senate and the Commons, succeeded in introducing and passing a federal law "intended to meet, in part, Canada's obligations under the [United Nations Framework

291 [1989] Can TS no 3.

292 [1994] Can TS no 2.

293 RSC 1985, c 41 (3d Supp), as amended by SC 1993, c 44, s 117(1).

294 Keyes & Sullivan, above note 63 at 326–7.

295 See the discussion of *Francis*, above note 13, at Section 7.1(b), above.

296 Keyes & Sullivan, above note 63 at 327.

297 SC 2007, c 30 (repealed) [*Kyoto Protocol Implementation Act*].

298 Kyoto Protocol to the United Nations Framework Convention on Climate Change (1997) 2303 UNTS 148; ratified by Canada 17 December 2002.

Convention on Climate Change[299]] and the Kyoto Protocol"[300] and the stated purpose of which was "to ensure that Canada takes effective and timely action to meet its obligations under the Kyoto Protocol and help address the problem of global climate change."[301] The Act imposed a statutory duty on the minister of the environment to prepare an annual climate change plan and to exercise certain regulatory powers, granted by the Act, to ensure that Canada met its obligations under article 3(1) of the Protocol. In judicial review applications brought to sanction the government's failures to comply with the Act, the Federal Court excused the non-compliance in ways that bordered, at times, on flagrant disregard of the plain meaning of an Act of Parliament.[302] The effective result was to de-implement the Kyoto Protocol Implementation Act judicially well before Mr. Harper – returned to government with a majority in the Commons – was able to prevail upon Parliament to de-implement it legislatively.[303]

7.6 Treaty interpretation in Canadian courts

In international law as in domestic law, questions of interpretation can be difficult and contentious. There is a vast literature and jurisprudence on the interpretation of treaties. It is not my purpose here to give an account of the international law of treaty interpretation.[304] My more limited purpose is to review Canadian case law on the proper interpretive approach to treaties. That case law establishes that in construing

299 [1994] Can TS no 7.

300 *Kyoto Protocol Implementation Act*, above note 297, preamble.

301 *Ibid* at s 3.

302 *Friends of the Earth v Canada (Governor in Council)*, 2008 FC 1183; upheld *Friends of the Earth v Canada (Governor in Council)*, 2009 FCA 297. See my consideration of these decisions in G van Ert, "Canadian Cases in Public International Law in 2008–9" (2009) 47 *Canadian Yearbook of International Law* 570.

303 The Act was repealed effective 29 June 2012 by s 699 of the Jobs, Growth and Long-term Prosperity Act, SC 2012, c 19.

304 See, e.g., R Gardiner, *Treaty Interpretation*, 2nd ed (Oxford: Oxford University Press, 2015); Hill, above note 55 at 238–66; I Sinclair, *The Vienna Convention on the Law of Treaties*, 2d ed (Manchester: Manchester University Press, 1984) c 5; Jennings & Watts, above note 230 at 1266–84.

international treaties[305] Canadian courts apply international interpretive rules.

(a) Interpretive rules of the Vienna Convention on the Law of Treaties 1969

The principal source of the international rules of treaty interpretation is the Vienna Convention on the Law of Treaties 1969 (VCLT).[306] Canada acceded to the VCLT in 1970, and the treaty has been binding on Canada since coming into force in 1980.[307] The interpretive provisions of the VCLT are widely regarded as representative of customary international law.[308]

VCLT article 31(1) gives the "General rule of interpretation" that a treaty "shall be interpreted in good faith in accordance with the ordinary meaning to be given to the terms of the treaty in their context and in the light of its object and purpose." The VCLT elaborates on this general rule in articles 31(2) to (4) as follows:

> 2. The context for the purpose of the interpretation of a treaty shall comprise, in addition to the text, including its preamble and annexes:
>
> (a) Any agreement relating to the treaty which was made between all the parties in connexion with the conclusion of the treaty;
>
> (b) Any instrument which was made by one or more parties in connexion with the conclusion of the treaty and accepted by the other parties as an instrument related to the treaty.

---

305 As opposed to Indigenous treaties, to which Canadian courts apply special interpretive rules.

306 [1980] Can TS no 37 [VCLT].

307 VCLT, *ibid*. In *Edwards v The Queen*, [2002] 4 CTC 2202 [*Edwards*] at para 21 n 11, Rip J mistakenly concluded that Canada is not a party to the VCLT. He nevertheless relied on the treaty, noting that Iacobucci J had done so in *Crown Forest Industries Ltd v Canada*, [1995] 2 SCR 802 [*Crown Forest*].

308 A notable illustration of the customary nature of those provisions is found in art 31.13(4) of the United States–Mexico–Canada Agreement (being the annex to the protocol replacing the North American Free Trade Agreement with the Agreement between Canada, the United States of America, and the United Mexican States, Buenos Aires, 30 November 2018, [2020] Can TS no 5), which provides that dispute resolution panels under the agreement shall interpret it "in accordance with customary rules of interpretation of public international law, as reflected in Articles 31 and 32 of the Vienna Convention on the Law of Treaties" – despite the fact that the United States is not a party to that treaty.

> 3. There shall be taken into account, together with the context:
>
> (a) Any subsequent agreement between the parties regarding the interpretation of the treaty or the application of its provisions;
> (b) Any subsequent practice in the application of the treaty which establishes the agreement of the parties regarding its interpretation;
> (c) Any relevant rules of international law applicable in the relations between the parties.
>
> 4. A special meaning shall be given to a term if it is established that the parties so intended.

VCLT article 32, entitled "Supplementary means of interpretation," provides:

> Recourse may be had to supplementary means of interpretation, including the preparatory work of the treaty and the circumstances of its conclusion, in order to confirm the meaning resulting from the application of article 31, or to determine the meaning when the interpretation according to article 31:
>
> (a) Leaves the meaning ambiguous or obscure; or
> (b) Leads to a result which is manifestly absurd or unreasonable.

The concept of "preparatory work of the treaty" is better known, even in English, as the *travaux préparatoires*.

Finally, VCLT article 33 concerns the interpretation of treaties authenticated in more than one language. The basic rule is that the text is equally authoritative in each language, and therefore conflicts between texts that cannot be resolved by applying articles 31 and 32 are to be resolved in favour of the meaning that best reconciles the texts, having regard to the object and purpose of the treaty. Treaty parties may contract out of article 33 by designating one or more languages as authoritative.

(b) VCLT interpretive rules apply in Canada

The authority of the VCLT interpretive rules in Canadian law was recognized in *Pushpanathan v Canada (Minister of Citizenship and*

Immigration),[309] where the court interpreted the term "refugee" in article 1F(c) of the United Nations Convention Relating to the Status of Refugees 1951.[310] Writing for the majority, Bastarache J quoted VCLT articles 31 and 32 in full, observing,

> Since the purpose of the Act incorporating Article 1F(c) is to implement the underlying Convention, the Court must adopt an interpretation consistent with Canada's obligations under the Convention. The wording of the Convention and the rules of treaty interpretation will therefore be applied to determine the meaning of Article 1F(c) in domestic law.[311]

Justice Bastarache added that these interpretive rules had been applied by the Supreme Court of Canada in two previous cases.[312] The authority of the VCLT interpretive rules has been affirmed by the Supreme Court of Canada since.[313]

The treaty provision at issue in *Pushpanathan* was implemented in Canadian law by section 2(1) of the Immigration Act.[314] In a sense, then, Bastarache J was interpreting a federal statute rather than a treaty. Yet he did not see it that way: "Since the purpose of the Act incorporating Article 1F(c) is to implement the underlying Convention, the Court must adopt an interpretation consistent with Canada's obligations under the Convention."[315]

---

309 [1998] 1 SCR 982 [*Pushpanathan*] at para 51.

310 [1969] Can TS no 6.

311 *Pushpanathan*, above note 309 at para 51.

312 *Ibid* at para 53. The cases are *Thomson*, above note 72, and *Canada (Attorney General) v Ward*, [1993] 2 SCR 689. See also *Crown Forest*, above note 307.

313 See, e.g., *Febles v Canada (Citizenship and Immigration)*, 2014 SCC 68 [*Febles*] at para 11 ("the meaning of the incorporated Articles of the Refugee Convention must be determined in accordance with the Vienna Convention"); *Thibodeau v Air Canada*, 2014 SCC 67 [*Thibodeau*] at para 35 (calling VCLT art 31(1) "a fundamental principle of interpretation"); *Wallace*, above note 43 at para 47 (affirming that treaties and implementing legislation "must be interpreted in accordance with the general rules of interpretation set out in the Vienna Convention on the Law of Treaties"); *Canada v Alta Energy Luxembourg SARL*, 2021 SCC 49 [*Alta Energy*] at para 37 (as tax treaties are treaties, their interpretation is governed by the VCLT).

314 RSC 1985, c I-2.

315 *Pushpanathan*, above note 309 at para 51. See also *Re Regina and Palacios* (1984), 45 OR (2d) 269 [*Palacios*] at 277, quoting *Stag Line Ltd v Foscolo, Mango & Co Ltd*, [1932] AC 328 (HL) at 350.

This observation is undoubtedly sound judicial policy. But it does not explain why (or, rather, how) the VCLT's interpretive rules apply in Canadian law. The VCLT is itself a treaty, but not one implemented in Canadian law. Its force, therefore, does not derive from statute. As noted, the VCLT interpretive articles are widely regarded as customary. They might therefore apply in Canada through the incorporation doctrine,[316] but the Supreme Court has never said so. Instead, judicial application of the VCLT rules of treaty interpretation was explained in England by Lord Diplock as the result of the UK's adherence to the VCLT itself. He explained:

> By ratifying that Convention, Her Majesty's Government has undertaken an international obligation on behalf of the United Kingdom to interpret future treaties in this manner and since under our constitution the function of interpreting written law is an exercise of judicial power and rests with the courts of justice, that obligation assumed by the United Kingdom falls to be performed by those courts.[317]

This passage was quoted approvingly by McLachlin CJ in *Balev*, who added, "When international agreements come before the courts, performance of Canada's obligation to apply and interpret them according to the rules of treaty interpretation falls to Canada's judges."[318]

There is some suggestion that VCLT interpretive rules apply even to treaties that pre-date the VCLT.[319] In *R v Parisien*, La Forest J resorted to VCLT article 31 to interpret the terms of an extradition arrangement between Canada and Brazil that was not, on its terms, a treaty, saying, "In interpreting this undertaking [by Canada to Brazil], it must, as in the case of other terms in international agreements, be read in context and in light of its object and purpose as well as in light of the general

---

316 J McIntyre, "Same Pod, Different Peas: The Vienna Convention on the Law of Treaties in Australian and Canadian Courts" (2017) 3:1 *Canadian Journal of Comparative and Contemporary Law* 19 [McIntyre] at 33.

317 *Fothergill v Monarch Airlines*, [1981] AC 251 at 283 (HL).

318 *Balev*, above note 75 at para 85.

319 See *CUDD Pressure Control Inc v Canada*, [1999] 1 CTC 1 at para 18 (invoking the VCLT in respect of a 1942 tax convention). See also the comments on *Febles* in L Katz, "The Use of the Vienna Convention on the Law of Treaties in the Interpretation of the Refugee Convention and the Refugee Protocol" 27 March 2019 *CanLII Connects*, online: https://canliiconnects.org/en/commentaries/66071.

principles of international law."[320] If VCLT interpretive rules apply to treaties that pre-date the VCLT, or to arrangements that are not treaties as a matter of international law, this must be due to the status of the VCLT interpretive rules in customary international law and not the application of the VCLT itself.

(c) VCLT rules prevail over, but resemble, domestic interpretive rules

Where the international law of treaty interpretation conflicts with domestic interpretive rules, the domestic rules give way. This was explained by Blair JA in *Palacios*:

> The principles of public international law and not domestic law govern the interpretation of treaties. I adopt the statement of this rule by O'Connell, *International Law*, 2nd ed. (1970), vol. 1, p. 257, as follows:
>
> > The rules of municipal law for interpretation are not to be utilised unless they can be regarded as "general principles of law recognised by civilised nations." Hence the restrictive rule of common law relating to literal interpretation has no place in international law. The dictionary meaning of words, and the rules of syntax, may be departed from to produce an "effective" result, but only when this is necessary.
>
> These rules of interpretation apply even where, as in this case, a treaty has been incorporated in a statute, as Lord Macmillan stated in *Stag Line, Ltd. v. Foscolo, Mango & Co., Ltd. et al.*, [1932] A.C. 328 at p. 350:
>
> > It is important to remember that the Act of 1924 was the outcome of an International Conference and that the rules in the Schedule have an international currency. As these rules must come under the consideration of foreign Courts it is desirable in the interests of uniformity that their interpretation should not be rigidly controlled by domestic precedents of antecedent date,

320 *R v Parisien*, [1988] 1 SCR 950 [*Parisien*] at 958.

> but rather that the language of the rules should be construed on broad principles of general acceptation.[321]

Justice Blair's approach is implicit in the authorities considered above and is affirmed by Professor Sullivan.[322]

One effect of this rule is seen in the case law surrounding tax treaties. The historic rule of construction for tax statutes was strict interpretation in favour of the taxpayer.[323] Yet in *J.N. Gladden Estate v Canada*, Addy J eschewed that rule when interpreting a tax convention, saying, "Contrary to an ordinary taxing statute a tax treaty or convention must be given a liberal interpretation with a view to implementing the true intentions of the parties. A literal or legalistic interpretation must be avoided when the basic object of the treaty might be defeated or frustrated . . ."[324] Justice Addy's *dictum* was quoted with approval by Iacobucci J in *Crown Forest*.[325]

While the VCLT interpretive rules apply in lieu of domestic rules, courts have noted resemblances between the international and Canadian approaches to interpretation. Justices Moldaver and Côté described the interpretive rules set out in VCLT articles 31 and 32 as "similar to the modern approach to statutory interpretation affirmed by this Court in *Rizzo & Rizzo Shoes Ltd.*"[326] Elsewhere, Côté J described "the methodology prescribed" by the VCLT as "not radically different from the modern principle applicable to domestic statutes in Canada."[327]

---

321 *Palacios*, above note 315 at 277. For more on the desirability of uniform interpretation of treaties from state to state (adverted to in the passage from Lord Macmillan), see Chapter 8, Section 8.2(b).

322 R Sullivan, *The Construction of Statutes*, 7th ed (Toronto: LexisNexis, 2022) at 568–9.

323 The classic text is *Partington v Attorney-General* (1869), LR 4 HL 100 (HL), Lord Cairns. Canadian cases have moved away from strict interpretation. See *Corporation Notre-Dame de Bon-Secours v Québec (Communauté urbaine)*, [1994] 3 SCR 3.

324 [1985] 1 CTC 163 (FCTD) at 166–7. See also *The Queen v Cruickshank*, [1978] 1 FC 256; and DA Ward, "The Principles to Be Applied in Interpreting Tax Treaties" (1977) 25 *Canadian Tax Journal* 263.

325 *Crown Forest*, above note 307 at para 43. See also *Alta Energy*, above note 313 at para 37.

326 *Wallace*, above note 43 at para 47; see also *Febles*, above note 313 at para 12.

327 *Alta Energy*, above note 313 at para 37, Côté J. In that same paragraph, however, the learned judge went on to note this difference: "The national self-interest of

Chief Justice McLachlin observed that article 31(1)'s "principles generally parallel the domestic approach to statutory interpretation."[328] Similarly, La Forest J observed in *Thomson v Thomson* that "By and large, international treaties are interpreted in a manner similar to statutes."[329] As Nadon JA put it, "Whether interpreting a statute or a treaty, the focus is on the text, context and purpose."[330]

(d) VCLT article 31(1): Good faith, ordinary meaning, context, object, and purpose

The VCLT interpretive provisions establish a clear methodology. The interpreter begins with the general rule of good faith interpretation of the text's ordinary meaning in context and in the light of the treaty's object and purpose. The interpreter resorts to supplementary means of interpretation (notably the *travaux préparatoires*) only to confirm or clarify the meaning.

This methodology was endorsed and applied in *Crown Forest Industries Ltd v Canada*.[331] Justice Iacobucci for the court began by emphasizing that in interpreting a treaty, "the paramount goal is to find the meaning of the words in question. This process involves looking to the language used and the intentions of the parties."[332] After reaching a conclusion on the plain language meaning of the treaty, Iacobucci J tested this conclusion against the intentions of the parties, the purpose of the treaty, and its legal context. Here the learned judge considered certain extrinsic materials, citing VCLT articles 31 and 32.[333]

---

each contracting state must be reconciled in the interpretive process in order to give full effect to the bargain codified by the treaty." See also para 50.

328 *Balev*, above note 75 at para 32.

329 *Thomson*, above note 72 at 577. He went on to note, however, there is "a significant difference . . . in the use that may be made of the legislative history and other preparatory material," referring to the supplementary means of interpretation permitted by VCLT art 32.

330 *Pembina County v Manitoba*, 2017 FCA 92 at para 47.

331 *Crown Forest*, above note 307.

332 *Ibid* at para 22.

333 *Ibid* at para 54. Iacobucci J observed that a court may refer to such extrinsic materials without first finding some ambiguity in the text. This is consistent with VCLT art 32, which provides that recourse may be had to supplementary means of interpretation, either to confirm the meaning resulting from the application of art 31 or to resolve some ambiguity, obscurity, absurdity, or unreasonableness in the meaning of the text.

The VCLT interpretive method was considered again by McLachlin CJ in *Febles*. The learned chief justice insisted on a structured approach that begins with the treaty's text:

> Article 31(1) of the Vienna Convention states how interpretation of the Refugee Convention should be approached by considering: (1) the "ordinary meaning" of its terms; (2) the context; and (3) the object and purpose of the Refugee Convention. . . .
>
> As discussed, Article 31(1) of the Vienna Convention provides for interpretation of treaty provisions in accordance with the ordinary meaning of the terms in their context and in light of the treaty's object and purpose. Article 32 only allows for recourse to "supplementary means of interpretation" – including the *Travaux préparatoires* – in order to confirm the meaning resulting from the application of Article 31, or to determine the meaning when the interpretation according to Article 31 leaves the meaning ambiguous or obscure; or leads to a result which is manifestly absurd or unreasonable.[334]

A similar approach was adopted by Cromwell J for the majority of the Supreme Court of Canada in *Thibodeau*. Guided by VCLT article 31(1), the learned judge directed himself to turn first to the text of the disputed treaty provision and afterwards analyze its place within the treaty in light of the treaty's purpose and object.[335]

(e) VCLT article 31(2): Related agreements and instruments

Article 31(2) of the VCLT explains that the context for the purpose of treaty interpretation includes agreements relating to the treaty made by all parties in connection with its conclusion, and any instrument made by one or more parties and accepted by the others as related to the treaty.

In *Coblentz v Canada*, the Federal Court of Appeal considered, but did not decide, whether a Technical Explanation of the Canada–United

334 *Febles*, above note 313 at paras 15, 38 (emphasis in original).

335 *Thibodeau*, above note 313 at para 35; see also paras 36–57. See the discussion in McIntyre, above note 316 at 55–61. Curiously, the same judge proceeded in the reverse order – purpose first, text second – in *Peracomo v Telus*, 2014 SCC 29 at paras 24–6. The learned judge's approach in *Thibodeau* is more in line with the VCLT.

States Income Tax Convention 1980,[336] produced four years after the treaty itself, constituted a related agreement or instrument. The taxpayer argued that the Technical Explanation could not form part of the context for interpretive purposes pursuant to article 31(2)(a), being adopted four years after the Convention, but was only a subsequent agreement "to be taken into account, together with the context" pursuant to article 31(3). Justice Robertson for the court was "certain that the Technical Explanation does not fall within Article 32 of the Vienna Convention" but found it "arguable whether it falls within Article 31(2), or 31(3)." He noted that in *Crown Forest*,[337] Iacobucci J relied upon the Technical Explanation without explaining "which subsection of the Vienna Convention provided him with the basis for doing so."[338]

In *Canada v Alta Energy Luxembourg SARL*, Côté J noted that revisions to the commentaries on the Model Tax Convention on Income and on Capital are not part of the context as defined in VCLT article 31(2) "given that such amendments were not made 'in connexion with the conclusion of the treaty'" but held that they may play an interpretive role under article 31(3).[339]

(f) VCLT article 31(3)(a): Subsequent agreements between the parties

Unlike article 31(2), which develops the concept of a treaty's context, VCLT article 31(3) is concerned with matters that do not form part of a treaty's context but shall nevertheless be taken into account in treaty interpretation. Article 31(3)(a) provides that a "subsequent agreement between the parties regarding the interpretation of the treaty or the application of its provisions" shall be taken into account, together with the context, when interpreting a treaty. The term "agreement" here is broader than the defined term "treaty" and may include formally non-binding instruments and materials, so long as they can properly be characterized as agreements between the parties.[340]

336 [1984] Can TS no 15.

337 *Crown Forest*, above note 307.

338 *Coblentz v Canada*, [1997] 1 FC 368 at paras 12–15 [*Coblentz*].

339 *Alta Energy*, above note 313 at para 41.

340 In *Quebec (Minister of Justice) v Canada (Minister of Justice)* (2003), 228 DLR (4th) 63 (Que CA) at para 185, the attorney general for Canada argued, quite incorrectly, that the Convention on the Rights of the Child 1989 is a subsequent

In *Khan Resources Inc v Atomredmetzoloto JSC*, O'Marra J invoked VCLT article 31(3)(a) to justify reliance on a handbook published by the Permanent Bureau of the Hague Conference on Private International Law describing the operation of the Convention on the Service Abroad of Judicial and Extrajudicial Documents in Civil or Commercial Matters 1965.[341] The learned judge concluded that a conclusion made in the handbook about the exclusive character of the Convention constituted a subsequent agreement between the Convention's parties.

In *Canada v Alta Energy Luxembourg SARL*,[342] the issue was whether the general anti-avoidance rule ("GAAR") in section 245 of the Income Tax Act[343] should apply to a transaction involving a Luxembourg company incorporated for the purpose of effecting a purchase of shares of a Canadian company and benefiting from a Canada–Luxembourg tax treaty.[344] Justice Côté for the majority of the court held that the GAAR should not apply since the impugned transactions were not abusive and were consistent with the treaty. She cautioned against using GAAR "to judicially amend or renegotiate a treaty."[345] In reaching her decision, the learned judge considered reliance on certain OECD commentaries released after the Canada–Luxembourg treaty was concluded, which she suggested may "play a role" either as subsequent agreements between the parties per VCLT article 31(3)(a) or subsequent practice per VCLT article 31(3)(b).[346] But she went on to reject reliance on these later commentaries as not reflecting the intention of the treaty's drafters.[347]

---

agreement between the parties to the International Covenant on Civil and Political Rights 1966. While the 1989 Convention is undoubtedly subsequent to the 1966 Covenant, the former is not an agreement between the parties of the latter.

341 *Khan Resources Inc v Atomredmetzoloto JSC*, 2012 ONSC 1522 at para 73; the Convention is found at [1989] Can TS no 2. The Superior Court's decision was affirmed on appeal, 2013 ONCA 189.

342 *Alta Energy*, above note 313.

343 RSC 1985, c 1 (5th Suppl).

344 Convention between the Government of Canada and the Government of the Grand Duchy of Luxembourg for the Avoidance of Double Taxation and the Prevention of Fiscal Evasion with Respect to Taxes on Income and on Capital 2000, [2000] Can TS no 22.

345 *Alta Energy*, above note 313 at para 30.

346 *Ibid* at para 41.

347 *Ibid* at paras 42–5.

In *Crown Forest*, Iacobucci J had regard to the OECD Model Double Taxation Convention on Income and on Capital in interpreting the Canada–United States Income Tax Convention 1980,[348] noting that reference to such extrinsic material is permitted by the VCLT and that the Model Convention "served as the basis for the [Convention] and also has world-wide recognition as a basic document of reference in the negotiation, application and interpretation of multilateral or bilateral tax conventions."[349] If so, then the Model Convention does not meet article 31(3)(a)'s requirement of a subsequent agreement between the parties. As noted by the Federal Court of Appeal in *Coblentz*, how exactly, in VCLT terms, Iacobucci J justified resort to the Model Convention is unclear.[350]

(g) VCLT article 31(3)(b): Subsequent practice

VCLT article 31(3)(b) provides that "any subsequent practice in the application of the treaty which establishes the agreement of the parties regarding its interpretation" shall be taken into account, together with the context, when interpreting a treaty. Accordingly, courts have looked to subsequent state practice in interpreting treaty provisions.

In *Yugraneft Corp v Rexx Management*,[351] the question was whether an Alberta limitation period applied to the recognition and enforcement of arbitral awards under the New York Convention.[352] Article III of the Convention said only that contracting states "shall recognize arbitral awards as binding and enforce them in accordance with the rules of procedure of the territory where the award is relied upon" – without express indication whether limitation periods came within the notion of "rules of procedure." Justice Rothstein for the court held that the Convention permits local limitation periods to apply. One reason he gave for this conclusion was that it reflects the practice of the contracting states. After quoting VCLT article 31(3), the learned judge noted

348 [1984] Can TS no 15.

349 *Crown Forest*, above note 307 at paras 54–5.

350 *Coblentz*, above note 338 at para 15.

351 2010 SCC 19 [*Yugraneft*].

352 Convention on the Recognition and Enforcement of Foreign Arbitral Awards 1958 [1986] Can TS no 43.

a recent study indicating that at least 53 of the Convention's parties, from both common law and civil law traditions, subject the recognition and enforcement of foreign arbitral awards to time limits.[353]

In *United Mexican States v Cargill*, the Court of Appeal for Ontario considered an application by Mexico to set aside a NAFTA Chapter 11 arbitral award against it. Mexico argued that the state parties to NAFTA had agreed subsequent to its coming into force that an investor could only claim damages suffered in the territory of its investment and not in the territory of its home business operation. Mexico (supported by the United States and Canada, intervening) relied on VCLT article 31(3)(b). Justice Feldman for the court accepted that if the NAFTA parties had come to a clear and agreed-upon position that an investor could not be compensated for damages suffered in the territory of its home business operation, it would have been an error of jurisdiction for the tribunal to make such an award. However, Feldman JA held that no such agreement had been reached.[354]

In *International Air Transport Association v Canadian Transportation Agency*, De Montigny JA (as he then was) considered whether evidence of foreign legislation and decisions was admissible in the interpretation of a treaty to which Canada is a party. He concluded that while such state practice itself is not a source of international law, it can be used as an aid in interpreting treaties pursuant to VCLT article 31(3)(b), so long as the foreign law (a matter of fact to be proved in evidence) can be shown to be consistent with and in application of the treaty in question (a matter of legal argument).[355] The learned judge also noted that "resort to state practice is not contingent on the existence of an ambiguity in the text of a treaty; on the contrary, it is an integral part of the interpretation process and is on a par with the words of the treaty and its context."[356] Justice De Montigny went on to consider expert evidence of state practice

---

353 *Yugraneft*, above note 351 at para 21.

354 *United Mexican States v Cargill, Inc*, 2011 ONCA 622 at para 84.

355 *International Air Transport Association and others v Canadian Transportation Agency and others*, 2022 FCA 211 [*International Air Transport*] at para 68.

356 *Ibid* at para 156.

led by the parties and to make other helpful observations about the use of state practice in treaty interpretation.[357]

The Ontario Superior Court of Justice had occasion to consider what constitutes subsequent practice at length in *United Mexican States v Burr*. Mexico applied to set aside the jurisdictional award of a NAFTA tribunal. One issue was whether legal submissions by the three NAFTA states on the interplay between articles 1119 and 1121 constituted subsequent practice for the purpose of VCLT article 31(3)(b). Justice Dietrich would not exclude the possibility that such submissions, advanced by all three states parties, can constitute subsequent practice, but found that the NAFTA parties' submissions were insufficient to constitute subsequent practice in the case before her.[358]

Subsequent practice was invoked by Rip J in *Edwards v The Queen*[359] to help resolve the question of whether the territory of Hong Kong was covered by a tax treaty concluded by China and Canada prior to Britain's handover of the colony in 1997.[360] Justice Rip noted that the Government of Canada never intended the treaty to apply to Hong Kong. He concluded, in the light of article 31(3)(b), that evidence of the government's administrative practice with respect to the treaty "is admissible and is entitled to great weight."[361] I respectfully agree but would caution that the weight of subsequent practice should be governed by the good faith requirement in article 31(1). If subsequent governmental practice amounts to a bad faith attempt to evade or unilaterally amend the treaty in question, it should be given no weight.[362] Note as well that this case involved a bilateral treaty. The subsequent practice of a single state is likely to be rather less instructive on the meaning of a multilateral treaty.

A leading form of subsequent practice in the application of treaties is their interpretation and application by the courts of their states par-

357 *Ibid* at paras 157–70.

358 *United Mexican States v Burr*, 2020 ONSC 2376, especially at paras 205–17.

359 *Edwards*, above note 307 at para 73.

360 See also *Bouzari v Islamic Republic of Iran* (2004), 71 OR (3d) 675 at paras 77–9 (CA).

361 *Edwards*, above note 307 at para 77.

362 As De Montigny JA observed in *International Air Transport*, above note 355 at para 167, "A manifest misapplication of a treaty, or a practice that is clearly meant to diverge from the accepted interpretation of a treaty, would clearly not amount to state practice in the application of the treaty."

ties. This form of subsequent practice, as approved and relied upon by Canadian courts, is considered in Chapter 8.[363]

(h) VCLT article 31(3)(c): Applicable rules of international law

VCLT article 31(3)(c) identifies "relevant rules of international law applicable in the relations between the parties" as another factor to be taken into account, together with the context, when interpreting a treaty. There are notably few Canadian cases considering article 31(3)(c). But La Forest J appears to have had this provision in mind when he observed, in *R v Parisien*, that international agreements "must be read in context and in light of [their] object and purpose as well as in light of general principles of international law."[364] The Tax Court of Canada has held that relevant rules of international law are those in place at the time the treaty was negotiated.[365]

(i) VCLT article 32: Use of *travaux préparatoires*

VCLT article 32 permits recourse to "supplementary means of interpretation, including the preparatory work of the treaty and the circumstances of its conclusion," in expressly limited circumstances. They may be used either to confirm the meaning resulting from the application of VCLT article 31, or to determine the treaty's meaning when interpretation according to article 31 leaves the meaning ambiguous or obscure or leads to a manifestly absurd or unreasonable result.

These limits on the use of *travaux préparatoires* are not always observed, either in international practice or in Canadian courts. Two leading Supreme Court of Canada authorities approach *travaux* in rather different ways.

In *Pushpanathan v Canada (Minister of Citizenship and Immigration)*, the Supreme Court of Canada had to determine whether a permanent resident of Canada who had been convicted of conspiracy to traffic in narcotics was excluded from refugee status by the Convention Relating to the Status of Refugees 1951, as implemented in federal law. Article

---

363 See Chapter 8, Section 8.2(b).

364 *Parisien*, above note 320 at 958.

365 *MIL (Investments) SA v Canada*, 2006 TCC 460 at para 86.

1F(c) of the Convention provides that it does not apply "to any person with respect to whom there are serious reasons for considering that . . . [h]e has been guilty of acts contrary to the purposes and principles of the United Nations." In the Federal Court of Appeal, Strayer JA considered, at the invitation of counsel for both parties, the Convention's *travaux préparatoires*, which he found "completely unhelpful," finding it "far safer to place the most emphasis on the final text as approved."[366]

Such reasoning would seem eminently supported by VCLT article 31. At the Supreme Court of Canada, however, Bastarache J for the majority found that Strayer JA "erred in dismissing the objects and purposes of the treaty, and in according virtually no weight to the indications provided in the *travaux préparatoires*," adding that the "extremely general words in Article 1F(c) are not so unambiguous as to foreclose examination of other indications of the proper scope of the provision."[367] In his analysis, the learned judge relied on the treaty's *travaux*, particularly debates over the definition of "refugee" before the Social Committee of the UN Economic and Social Council, from which he concluded that article 1F(c) was directed at "non-war-related crimes against humanity."[368] One may wonder whether such liberal resort to *travaux préparatoires* is in keeping with VCLT article 32's depiction of such sources as supplementary means of interpretation.[369]

A more cautious attitude to *travaux* was adopted by McLachlin CJ for the majority of the Supreme Court of Canada in *Febles*. As in *Pushpanathan*, the question here was the ambit of exclusions from refugee status, this time under article 1F(b) of the Refugee Convention, which excludes persons with respect to whom there are serious reasons for considering they have committed a serious non-political crime. The dissenting judges relied on *travaux* to support their view that Febles was not excluded from refugee protection by his US criminal record.

---

366 *Pushpanathan v Canada (Minister of Citizenship and Immigration)*, [1996] 2 FC 49 (FCA) at paras 12–13.

367 *Pushpanathan*, above note 309 at para 55.

368 *Ibid* at paras 58–60.

369 See G van Ert, "Canada" in D Sloss, ed, *The Role of Domestic Courts in Treaty Enforcement: A Comparative Study* (New York: Cambridge University Press, 2009): 166 at 179; McIntyre, above note 316 at 58 (describing *Pushpanathan* as demonstrating overreliance on *travaux*).

Chief Justice McLachlin rejected resort to *travaux* here as inconsistent with the VCLT:

> Article 31(1) of the Vienna Convention provides for interpretation of treaty provisions in accordance with the ordinary meaning of the terms in their context and in light of the treaty's object and purpose. Article 32 only allows for recourse to "supplementary means of interpretation" – including the *Travaux préparatoires* – in order to confirm the meaning resulting from the application of Article 31, or to determine the meaning when the interpretation according to Article 31 leaves the meaning ambiguous or obscure; or leads to a result which is manifestly absurd or unreasonable.
>
> These conditions for use of the *Travaux préparatoires* are not present in this case. With great respect to Justice Abella's contrary view, the meaning of Article 1F(b) is clear, and admits of no ambiguity, obscurity or absurd or unreasonable result. Therefore, the *Travaux préparatoires* should not be considered.[370]

The chief justice went on to find that the *travaux* did not support Mr. Febles' approach in any case.

The *Febles* approach to *travaux préparatoires* is to be preferred to that suggested by *Pushpanathan*. It is more in keeping with the VCLT which, as the chief justice rightly noted, gives precedence to the ordinary meaning of a treaty's terms (interpreted in their context and in the light of the treaty's object and purpose) and permits recourse to supplementary means of interpretation only in narrow circumstances. The *Febles* approach also has the merit of not unduly taxing courts and litigants with the laborious task of tracking down, analyzing, and attempting to make sense of *travaux*.

370 *Febles*, above note 313 at paras 38–9 (emphasis in original).

8 The reception of other sources of international law

Treaty and custom are by far the most significant sources of international law. They are also the only two sources for which the common law has developed clear reception rules. There is, therefore, little case law on the reception of other international legal sources. I briefly consider the reception or non-reception of these other sources here.

8.1 General principles of law (ICJ Statute article 38(1)(c))

As noted in Chapter 2, international tribunals may apply "the general principles of law recognized by civilized nations" (per article 38(1)(c) of the Statute of the International Court of Justice 1945[1]) to resolve controversies for which no applicable treaty or customary rule may exist. The Supreme Court of Canada has noted that this source of international law "refers to principles of municipal law."[2]

This is a pragmatic and potentially useful source of law at the international level, but its relevance to a domestic court is questionable. Domestic legal systems usually do not experience gaps in the law of the sort contemplated by general principles. (Even in international law, cases in which there is a need to supplement treaty and custom by general principles are rare.) Furthermore, to the extent that general principles in international law derive from or are developed from analogies to domestic law, there is seemingly no need for a domestic court to

1 [1945] Can TS no 7.

2 *Re Newfoundland Continental Shelf*, [1984] 1 SCR 86 [*Re Newfoundland Continental Shelf*] at 117.

have regard to them. In short, general principles of law recognized by civilized nations are presumably already established in Canadian law without the need to receive them from international law. There is no established common law rule, analogous to the incorporation doctrine for custom or the implementation requirement for treaties, to explain the interaction of domestic law and general principles. There seems to be no need for such a rule.[3]

8.2 Judicial decisions (ICJ Statute article 38(1)(d))

In the international legal system, judicial decisions are not themselves law. They are only a subsidiary means for the determination of rules of law.[4] Consistently with this subsidiary status, there is no specific common law rule governing or explaining the reception of foreign or international judicial decisions on questions of international law in domestic law. That is not to say, however, that Canadian courts cannot have regard to such decisions. They appear to do so with increasing frequency.

As noted in Chapter 2, judicial decisions in international law are not binding on anyone but the parties. They are likewise not binding on the Canadian courts that have occasion to consider them. In *Mugesera v Canada (Minister of Citizenship and Immigration)*, the Supreme Court of Canada took the unusual step of partially overruling one of its own decisions to accord better with subsequent international jurisprudence on the elements of a crime against humanity. But the court did not take this step out of legal obligation; rather, as it explained,

> These tribunals have generated a unique body of authority which cogently reviews the sources, evolution and application of customary international law. Though the decisions of the ICTY and the ICTR are not binding upon this Court, the expertise of these tribunals and the authority in respect of customary international law with which they are vested suggest that their findings should not be disregarded lightly by Canadian courts applying domestic legislative provisions,

---

3 On "general principles of law recognized by the community of nations" in Charter s 11(g), see M Freeman & G van Ert, *International Human Rights Law* (Toronto: Irwin Law, 2004) at 182.

4 See Chapter 2, Section 2.3(d).

such as ss. 7(3.76) and 7(3.77) of the Criminal Code, which expressly incorporate customary international law.[5]

Mugesera makes clear that the non-binding nature of foreign and international judicial decisions on Canadian courts is no reason to ignore them. To the contrary, it is eminently desirable that Canadian courts make use of relevant decisions of foreign and international courts in determining international legal questions that come before them.

The phrase "judicial decisions" in article 38(1)(d) of the ICJ Statute includes both decisions by international tribunals and decisions of domestic courts on questions of international law. Both must be considered.

(a) Decisions of international courts and tribunals

Canadian courts do not often need to have recourse to decisions of the International Court of Justice (ICJ), its predecessor the Permanent Court of International Justice (PCIJ), or other tribunals established under international law. Where such a need arises, however, Canadian courts are free to consult the decisions of these bodies as subsidiary means for the determination of rules of law.[6] The Supreme Court of Canada has considered ICJ and PCIJ decisions on state jurisdiction,[7] state immunity,[8] and international criminal law,[9] among other subjects. The reception rule governing our courts' consideration of such decisions is, it seems, judicial notice of international law – with the qualification (noted above) that such decisions are not themselves international law but only subsidiary means of determining it.

In *Mugesera*, the government sought to deport a Rwandan national with permanent resident status in Canada. It alleged that Mugesera had committed a crime against humanity and incited other serious of-

---

5 [2005] 2 SCR 100 [*Mugesera*] at para 126.

6 Statute of the International Court of Justice 1945 art 38(1)(d), [1945] Can TS no 7.

7 E.g., *Libman v The Queen*, [1985] 2 SCR 178 at 183–4; *R v Finta*, [1994] 1 SCR 701 [*Finta*] at 805–6; *R v Terry*, [1996] 2 SCR 207 at para 15; *R v Cook*, [1998] 2 SCR 597 [*Cook*] at paras 26–7; *R v Hape*, 2007 SCC 26 [*Hape*] at paras 59–66.

8 E.g., *Amaratunga v Northwest Atlantic Fisheries Organization*, 2013 SCC 66 [*Amaratunga*] at para 27; *Kazemi Estate v Islamic Republic of Iran*, 2014 SCC 62 [*Kazemi Estate*].

9 E.g., *Finta*, above note 7 at 835–6; *Mugesera*, above note 5; *Ezokola v Canada (Citizenship and Immigration)*, 2013 SCC 40 [*Ezokola*].

fences in a violently anti-Tutsi speech over a year before the start of the Rwandan genocide of 1994. The Supreme Court of Canada affirmed the deportation order and, in doing so, partly overruled its decision in *R v Finta* in order to ensure Canadian compliance with subsequent decisions from the International Criminal Tribunal for Rwanda and the International Criminal Tribunal for the Former Yugoslavia on the elements of a crime against humanity.[10] In reasons attributed to the court as whole, the court affirmed that the "interpretation and application of Canadian provisions regarding crimes against humanity must . . . accord with international law."[11] The sentiment is admirable and consistent with the court's approach to foreign jurisprudence on multilateral treaties to which Canada is a party.[12] Yet the court's reasons repeatedly equate the decisions of the two tribunals with customary international law – an oversimplification that risks error. The fact that a decision of an international court or tribunal supports a given interpretation of or approach to a legal doctrine does not, in itself, indicate the position of that doctrine in customary international law. Jurisprudence is only a subsidiary means of determining rules of international law; it is not itself a source of international law. Furthermore, international tribunals are not states and therefore their practices cannot directly contribute to the development of customary international law.

In *Ezokola v Canada*, a former Congolese diplomat was denied refugee protection by the Immigration and Refugee Board on the ground of his supposed complicity in crimes against humanity committed by the Congolese government. The Federal Court quashed that decision, there being no evidence that Ezokola himself had been involved in his state's crimes. The Federal Court of Appeal reversed this decision, relying on a precedent of that court interpreting article 1F(a) of the Convention Relating to the Status of Refugees 1961[13] broadly. The Supreme Court of Canada allowed Ezokola's appeal, calling the Federal Court of Appeal's approach guilt by association and expressly departing from the latter court's precedent in order to "rein in the Canadian approach to complicity under article 1F(a)."[14] In so doing, LeBel and Fish JJ considered,

10 *Mugesera*, above note 5 at paras 143–4.
11 *Ibid* at para 178.
12 See the discussion at Section 8.2(b), below.
13 [1969] Can TS no 6.
14 *Ezokola*, above note 9 at para 30.

among other sources, several decisions of the International Criminal Tribunal for the Former Yugoslavia and the International Criminal Court.[15]

The Supreme Court of Canada and lower courts have frequently considered the decisions of international courts and tribunals for comparative purposes when construing the Canadian Charter of Rights and Freedoms.[16]

(b) Decisions of foreign courts on multilateral treaties

Canadian courts, like their English counterparts,[17] have repeatedly affirmed the importance of considering and, where possible, following decisions from the courts of other states parties when interpreting multilateral treaties. Foreign jurisprudence is helpful in such cases not only in elucidating the meaning of a shared treaty obligation but also in ensuring, wherever possible, that the treaty is accorded the same meaning in each state. Canadian courts have looked to foreign jurisprudence

---

15 *Ibid*, especially at paras 55–67.

16 See Chapter 11, Section 11.2.

17 See, e.g., *Stag Line v Foscolo, Mango and Co*, [1932] AC 328 (HL) at 350 ("It is important to remember that the Act of 1924 was the outcome of an International Conference and that the rules in the Schedule have an international currency. As these rules must come under the consideration of foreign Courts, it is desirable in the interests of uniformity that their interpretation should not be rigidly controlled by domestic precedents of antecedent date, but rather that the language of the rules should be construed on broad principles of general acceptation"); *Scruttons* v *Midland*, 1962 AC 446 (HL) at 471 ("It is (to put it no higher) very desirable that the same conclusions should be reached in whatever jurisdiction the question arises. It would be deplorable if the nations should, after protracted negotiations, reach agreement, as in the matter of the Hague Rules, and that their several Courts should then disagree as to the meaning of what they appeared to agree upon"); *Trendtex Trading Corp v Central Bank of Nigeria*, [1977] 1 QB 529 (Eng CA) at 558 ("The rules applied by each member state on the subject should be the same as the rules applied by the others"); *James Buchanan & Co Ltd v Babco Forwarding & Shipping (UK) Ltd*, [1978] AC 141 (HL) at 152 (multilateral treaties should be interpreted "unconstrained by technical principles of English law, or by English legal precedent, but on broad principles of general acceptation"); *In re H and Others (Minors) (Abduction: Acquiescence)*, [1998] AC 72 at 87 (HL) ("An international Convention, expressed in different languages and intended to apply to a wide range of differing legal systems, cannot be construed differently in different jurisdictions. The Convention must have the same meaning and effect under the laws of all contracting states").

arising from multilateral treaties in such areas as civil aviation,[18] maritime law,[19] copyright,[20] refugee protection,[21] and child abduction.[22] Judicial reliance on foreign decisions in such cases ought not to be limited to these areas. Rather, judicial harmonization of the law consistently with the prevailing interpretation of multilateral treaty provisions is desirable in all cases where such treaties exist, for the essential purpose of multilateral treaty-making is to harmonize the domestic laws of states parties around internationally agreed rules and principles.

An admirable example of a Canadian court striving to interpret a multilateral treaty consistently with judicial decisions of other states parties is the decision of Molloy J in *Connaught Laboratories Ltd v British Airways*.[23] The plaintiff shipped a perishable vaccine from Toronto to Melbourne on the defendant's aircraft. The defendant airline failed to refrigerate the cargo as directed and it was ruined. The plaintiff claimed damages of approximately $75,000. The airline sought to rely on article 22 of the Warsaw Convention 1929 (as amended)[24] which, it argued, limited its liability to roughly $2,500. The plaintiff sought to invoke article 25 of the Convention, which provided an exception to the limits of article 22 in cases where the damage is done recklessly and with knowledge that damage would probably result. The question before the court was whether a subjective or objective test should be applied in determining whether the reckless actor had such knowledge. To decide this point,

---

18 E.g., *Quinn v Canadian Airlines International Ltd* (1994), 18 OR (3d) 326 (Ont Gen Div); *Recchia v KLM lignes aériennes royale néerlandaises*, [1999] RJQ 2024 (Que SC); *Connaught Laboratories Ltd v British Airways* (2002), 61 OR (3d) 204, affirmed (2005) 77 OR (3d) 34 (Ont CA) [*Connaught*]; *Plourde v Service aérien FBO inc (Skyservice)*, 2007 QCCA 739; *Thibodeau v Air Canada*, 2014 SCC 67 [*Thibodeau*]; *International Air Transport Association and others v Canadian Transportation Agency and others*, 2022 FCA 211.

19 E.g., *NV Bocimar SA v Century Insurance Co of Canada*, [1981] FCJ no 1033; *Ordon Estate v Grail*, [1998] 3 SCR 437.

20 E.g., *Society of Composers, Authors and Music Publishers of Canada v Canadian Association of Internet Providers*, 2004 SCC 45.

21 E.g., *Ezokola*, above note 9.

22 E.g., *Office of the Children's Lawyer v Balev*, 2018 SCC 16 [*Balev*].

23 *Connaught*, above note 18.

24 International Convention for the Unification of Certain Rules relating to International Carriage by Air [1947] Can TS no 15 (since amended by several protocols).

Molloy J reviewed several Canadian and foreign authorities. Beginning with the domestic decisions, the learned judge observed:

> As a trial judge in Ontario, it is incumbent upon me to start my analysis with a consideration of the Canadian authorities. If there is binding authority on this point, then of course I must follow it. However, the interpretation of international instruments is not quite the same exercise as the interpretation of domestic statutes. Thus, other Canadian decisions falling short of binding authority are no more likely to be persuasive than decisions from other countries that are also signatories to the Convention, and may even be less so, depending on the level of foreign court and the weight of foreign authorities.[25]

Having concluded that no Canadian decision bound her, she turned to international law. Observing that the Warsaw Convention "is not an ordinary statute" but "an international treaty negotiated by the signatory nations and intended to give rise to the same set of rules to govern liability for damage incurred in the course of international travel,"[26] she quoted with approval the following excerpt from a decision of the Belgian Cour de Cassation:

> The interpretation of an international convention the purpose of which is the unification of the law cannot be done by reference to the domestic law of one of the contracting States. If the treaty text calls for interpretation, this ought to be done on the basis of elements that pertain to the treaty, notably, its object, its purpose and its context, as well as its preparatory work and genesis. The purpose of drawing up an international convention designed to become a species of international legislation would be wholly frustrated if the courts of each State were to interpret it in accordance with concepts that are specific to their own legal system.[27]

---

25 *Connaught*, above note 18 at para 34.

26 *Ibid* at para 44.

27 *Ibid* at para 44, quoting *Tondriau v Air India* (1977), 31 Rev fr dr aérien 193. Molloy J notes that this passage from *Tondriau* was quoted in B Cheng, "Wilful Misconduct: From Warsaw to the Hague and From Brussels to Paris" in *Annals of Air and Space Law*, vol II (Montreal: McGill Institute of Air and Space Law, 1977) 55 and described (at 61) as a "model of how treaties establishing international uniform law should be interpreted and applied."

Justice Molloy also noted the Convention's preamble (which speaks of regulating international carriage by air in a uniform manner) and concluded, "This objective of having uniform regulations limiting the liability of carriers would be seriously weakened if the courts of every country interpreted the Convention without any regard to how it was being interpreted and applied elsewhere. This potential problem supports an approach favouring consistency of interpretation among nations, rather than one in which each country applies its own domestic principles."[28] The learned judge went on to review the text of the Convention, its drafting history and protocols, and the decisions of foreign courts on article 25, all of which led her to conclude that a subjective test must be applied in determining the applicability of article 25.[29]

The Supreme Court of Canada has repeatedly endorsed judicial reliance on foreign judicial decisions in construing multilateral treaties. In *Ezokola v Canada*, LeBel and Fish JJ considered, among other factors in interpreting article 1F(a) of the United Nations Convention Relating to the Status of Refugees 1951, the approach taken by other states parties to that provision.[30] In *Thibodeau v Air Canada*, Cromwell J for the majority of the court relied on judicial decisions from the United Kingdom, the United States, France, Hong Kong, Ireland, New Zealand, Singapore, and South Africa in interpreting a multilateral civil aviation convention. He explained:

> In light of the Montreal Convention's objective of achieving international uniformity, we should pay close attention to the international jurisprudence and be especially reluctant to depart from any strong international consensus that has developed in relation to its interpretation.[31]

In *Office of the Children's Lawyer v Balev*, McLachlin CJ for the majority of the court described the practice of interpreting multilateral treaties in the light of judicial decisions from other states parties as the "principle of harmonization." "A clear purpose of multilateral treaties," she explained, "is to harmonize parties' domestic laws around agreed-upon rules, practices, and principles." To "avoid frustrating the harmonizing

28 *Connaught*, above note 18 at para 46.

29 *Ibid* at paras 52–7.

30 *Ezokola*, above note 9 at paras 30, 42, 69ff.

31 *Thibodeau*, above note 18 at para 50.

purpose . . . domestic courts should give serious consideration to decisions by the courts of other contracting states on [a treaty's] meaning and application."[32] Among the authorities the chief justice cited for this proposition was article 31(3)(b) (subsequent practice in the application of the treaty) of the Vienna Convention on the Law of Treaties 1969.[33] She continued:

> [A] prime consideration in interpreting treaties the principle of harmonization. The aim of treaties like the *Hague Convention* is to establish uniform practices in the adhering countries. This Court has faithfully followed this precept. . . . It follows that this Court should prefer the interpretation that has gained the most support in other courts and will therefore best ensure uniformity of state practice across *Hague Convention* jurisdictions, unless there are strong reasons not to do so.[34]

Applying this approach to the case before her, McLachlin CJ surveyed judicial decisions from the European Union, the United Kingdom, New Zealand, Australia, and the United States on the question of how to determine a child's habitual residence under the Hague Child Abduction Convention.[35] While finding no "Absolute consensus" in state judicial practice, she nevertheless concluded that "the clear trend is to rejection of the parental intention approach and to adoption of the hybrid approach."[36] She added, "The desirability of harmonization weighs heavily in favour of following the dominant thread of *Hague Convention* jurisprudence, unless there are strong reasons to the contrary," of which she found none.[37]

(c) Decisions of foreign courts in other contexts

While Canadian judicial consideration of foreign court decisions on international legal questions usually takes place in the context of multilateral treaties, the decisions of foreign courts on international

---

32 *Balev*, above note 22 at paras 33, 49.

33 [1980] Can TS no 37; *Balev*, above note 22 at para 33.

34 *Ibid* at para 49.

35 Convention on the Civil Aspects of International Child Abduction 1980, [1983] Can TS no 35.

36 *Balev*, above note 22 at para 50.

37 *Ibid* at para 57.

legal questions more generally may be illuminating. In *R v Finta*, La Forest J observed that a Canadian judge's interpretation of international law "bears some force internationally."[38] The same is, of course, potentially true of other national judges.

One way in which the decisions of foreign courts may be relevant internationally is as instances of state practice for the purposes of customary international law. In *Nevsun Resources Ltd v Araya*, Abella J observed:

> The judicial decisions of national courts are also evidence of general practice or *opinio juris* and thus play a crucial role in shaping norms of customary international law. As the Permanent Court of International Justice noted in *Case concerning certain German interests in Polish Upper Silesia (Germany v. Poland)* (1926), P.C.I.J. Ser. A, No. 7, legal decisions are "facts which express the will and constitute the activities of States."[39]

Justice Abella's observation makes clear that foreign court decisions on international legal issues may be relevant, and can be considered, in determining either state practice or *opinio juris* in cases touching customary international law.[40]

8.3 Teachings of publicists (ICJ Statute article 38(1)(d))

Like judicial decisions, the teachings of publicists (that is, scholarly writers), however eminent, are not law but only a subsidiary means for the determination of rules of law. On the role of publicists as a subsidiary source of international law, La Forest J made the following observations in *R v Finta*:

> It is instructive at this point to say something about the utility of the views of learned writers . . . in determining the applicable international law. They are extremely useful, of course, in bringing before the Court the various relevant sources of law, and as Lord Alverstone

38 [1994] 1 SCR 701 at 774.

39 *Nevsun Resources Ltd v Araya*, 2020 SCC 5 [*Nevsun Resources*] at para 79.

40 Similarly, in *R v Parisien*, [1988] 1 SCR 950 at 960, La Forest J noted, in the extradition context but in the absence of an extradition treaty, that the approach he was taking was "consistent with all the cases from different nations that have been brought to our attention."

> observed in *West Rand Central Gold Mining Co. v. The King*... they also render "valuable service in helping to create the opinion by which the range of the consensus of civilized nations is enlarged." But, as he went on to add (at p. 402), "in many instances their pronouncements must be regarded rather as the embodiments of their views as to what ought to be ... the conduct of nations *inter se*, than the enunciation of a rule or practice as universally approved or assented to [by nation states] as to be fairly termed ... 'law'." In a word, international conventions and the practices adopted and approved as law by authoritative decision makers in the world community, along with the general principles of law recognized by civilized countries are what constitute the principal sources of international law. The pronouncements of learned writers on international law are extremely useful in setting forth what these practices and principles are, but the personal views of learned writers in the field, though useful in developing consensus, are of a subsidiary character in determining what constitutes international law.[41]

A similar comment is found in *R v Keyn (The Franconia)*, where Cockburn CJ observed that "no unanimity on the part of theoretical writers would warrant the judicial application of the law on the sole authority of their views or statements."[42]

Such observations are cautions against mistaking scholarly commentary on the law for the law itself. They should not be taken as prohibiting judicial reference to such commentary for the purpose of determining what the law is. Examples of the Supreme Court of Canada relying on leading international jurists are too numerous to mention.[43]

---

41 *Finta*, above note 7 at 761–2.

42 (1876) 2 Ex D 63 (Eng Ct Crown of Cases Reserved) at 203.

43 Some examples include *Arrow River & Tributaries Slide & Boom Co Ltd v Pigeon Timber Co Ltd*, [1932] SCR 495 (referring to the then-current edition of *Oppenheim's International Law*); *Reference as to Powers to Levy Rates on Foreign Legations*, [1943] SCR 208 (*Oppenheim's International Law*, Hall's *International Law*, others); *Reference as to whether members of the Military or Naval Forces of the United States of America are exempt from Criminal Proceedings in Canadian Criminal Courts*, [1943] SCR 483 (*Oppenheim's International Law*); *Flota Maritima Browning de Cuba SA v Republic of Cuba*, [1962] SCR 598 (*Oppenheim's International Law*); *Reference Re: Offshore Mineral Rights*, [1967] SCR 792 (*Oppenheim's International Law*); *Re Newfoundland Continental Shelf*, above note 2 (*Oppenheim's International Law*); *Canada (Attorney General) v Ward* [1993] 2 SCR 689 (Prof. Hathaway); *Cook*, above

8.4 Soft law and international norms not binding on Canada

Since it is not really law at all,[44] so-called "soft law" is not received into Canadian law in any way analogous to the reception of treaties and custom. There do not appear to be reception rules for soft law at all. Certainly there is no presumption that our laws conform to norms that are not binding at the international level. Nor can soft law norms easily be described as the context in which domestic laws are made. And there is no clear basis for our courts to take judicial notice of soft law norms given that they are, by definition, not law.

All of this is not to say that our courts do not look to soft law on occasion. They do. But their basis for doing so is often unclear. The authority of soft law materials is always less than that of a binding legal norm, whether customary or conventional. Such materials are, at best, relevant and persuasive sources for the purposes of domestic adjudication. Their persuasiveness can vary from none to high, depending on the material's provenance and authority.

Similarly, international legal norms by which Canada is not bound – mainly treaties to which Canada is not a party – are not the subject of distinct reception rules but are nevertheless considered by Canadian courts on rare occasions. Such norms are not properly called soft law (since they are "hard" law for those states to whom they apply) but, from Canada's vantage point, they come to much the same thing. Canada, like other states, has no legal obligation under a treaty to which it is not a party.

The international materials most frequently cited by Canadian courts despite their strictly non-binding or soft law character are reso-

---

note 7 (*Oppenheim's International Law*); *Reference re Secession of Quebec*, [1998] 2 SCR 217 (Prof. Cassese); *Schreiber v Canada (Attorney General)*, 2002 SCC 62 (*Oppenheim's International Law*, Prof. Brownlie); *Hape*, above note 7 (Prof. Cassese, Dr. Akehurst, others); *Németh v Canada (Justice)*, 2010 SCC 56 [*Németh*] (Prof. Hathaway, others); *Kazemi Estate*, above note 8 (Prof. Cassese, Prof. Bassiouni, others); *Febles v Canada (Citizenship and Immigration)*, 2014 SCC 68 [*Febles*] (Prof. Hathaway); *Nevsun Resources*, above note 39 (Prof. Crawford, Prof. Cassese, *Oppenheim's International Law*, others); *R v McGregor*, 2023 SCC 4 [*McGregor*] (Prof. Crawford, others); etc.

44 See the discussion of soft law in Chapter 2, Section 2.3(j).

lutions of the UN General Assembly;[45] draft or model treaties;[46] guides, handbooks, reports, and similar explanatory materials produced by UN agencies or other international bodies;[47] and the recommendations and views of UN treaty-monitoring bodies.[48] Another relatively

45 See, e.g., *Pushpanathan v Canada (Minister of Citizenship and Immigration)*, [1998] 1 SCR 982 [*Pushpanathan*] at paras 116–19, Cory J (dissenting; various UNGA resolutions on drug trafficking); *R v Ewanchuk*, [1999] 1 SCR 330 at para 72, L'Heureux-Dubé and Gonthier JJ (concurring; UNGA Declaration on the Elimination of Violence against Women); *R v Sharpe*, 2001 SCC 2 at para 178, L'Heureux-Dubé, Gonthier, and Bastarache JJ (concurring; UNGA Declaration on the Rights of the Child); *R v DB*, 2008 SCC 25 at para 85 (UN Standard Minimum Rules for the Administration of Juvenile Justice); *R v KJM*, 2019 SCC 55 at para 139, Abella and Brown JJ (dissenting; UN Standard Minimum Rules for the Administration of Juvenile Justice); Canadian *Council for Refugees v Canada (Minister of Citizenship and Immigration)*, 2023 SCC 17 [*Canadian Council for Refugees*] at para 144 (UN Standard Minimum Rules for the Treatment of Prisoners, a.k.a. the Mandela Rules).

46 See, e.g., *Pushpanathan, ibid* at para 153, Cory J (dissenting; ILC Draft Articles on the Draft Code of Crimes Against the Peace and Security of Mankind 1996); *Németh*, above note 43 at paras 80–3 (UNGA Model Treaty on Extradition); *Amaratunga*, above note 8 at para 27 (the not-yet-in-force United Nations Convention on Jurisdictional Immunities of States and Their Property 2004); *Uber Technologies Inc v Heller*, 2020 SCC 16 at paras 21–7 (UNCITRAL Model Law on International Commercial Arbitration); *Canada v Alta Energy Luxembourg SARL*, 2021 SCC 49 at paras 5, 35, 38–45 (OECD Model Tax Convention on Income and on Capital).

47 See, e.g., *Canada (Attorney General) v Ward*, [1993] 2 SCR 689 at 713–14 (UNHCR Handbook on Procedures and Criteria for Determining Refugee Status); *Pushpanathan*, above note 45 at para 53 (UNHCR Handbook); *Amaratunga*, above note 8 at paras 27 (ILC report), 62 (UN Human Rights Committee General Comment no 31); *Nevsun Resources*, above note 39 at paras 101 (statement by the UN Office of the High Commissioner for Human Rights on slavery), 102 (report by the International Labour Organization on forced labour), 119 (Human Rights Committee General Comment no 31); *Febles*, above note 43 at paras 92, 97, 99, 101, 127, 131, Abella J (dissenting; UN High Commissioner for Refugees guidelines on the application of the art 1F exclusion clause of the Refugee Convention); *Canadian Council for Refugees*, above note 45 at para 143 (UNHRC Detention Guidelines).

48 See, e.g., *Suresh v Canada (Minister of Citizenship and Immigration)*, 2002 SCC 1 at paras 66 (UN Human Rights Committee General Comment no 20), 73 (recommendations of the UN Committee against Torture); *Canadian Foundation for Children, Youth and the Law v Canada (Attorney General)*, [2004] 1 SCR 76 (where both the majority and dissent had regard to the work of UN treaty monitoring bodies); *Divito v Canada (Public Safety and Emergency Preparedness)*, 2013 SCC

new form of soft law that has yet to be judicially considered in any significant degree consists of the increasing number of non-binding arrangements Canada and other states now conclude in preference to treaty-making.[49]

A good illustration of how Canadian courts may make use of soft law, in contrast to their reception of actual international legal norms, is found in *Dell Computer Corp v Union des consommateurs*.[50] The case arose from a dispute in Quebec over the contractual price for computer equipment sold over the internet. When the seller refused to honour an order for a price erroneously posted on its website, the would-be purchaser and a consumer group filed a motion for authorization to institute a class action. Opposing the motion, the seller sought to rely on an arbitration clause. The lower courts held that the arbitration clause did not apply. Justice Deschamps for the majority of the Supreme Court of Canada allowed the appeal and referred the claim to arbitration. In doing so she interpreted the relevant Quebec legislation, known as Bill 91,[51] in the light of two leading international arbitration instruments, namely the New York Convention on the Recognition and Enforcement of Foreign Arbitral Awards 1958[52] and the UNCITRAL Model Law on International Commercial Arbitration.[53] The New York Convention is a treaty binding on Canada at international law. By contrast, the Model Law is a non-binding instrument prepared by the United Nations Commission on International Trade Law to assist states in implementing international commercial arbitration laws consistently with the New York Convention. Justice Deschamps noted the difference in legal character between these two instruments, observing that the New York Convention attracted the presumption of conformity with international law while the Model Law did not. She observed, "Canada has made no

---

47 at para 26 (UN Human Rights Committee General Comment no 27); *Kazemi Estate*, above note 8 at paras 146–8 (cautioning against giving comments by the UN Committee against Torture greater weight than the pronouncements of state parties and judicial authorities); *McGregor*, above note 43 at para 72, Karakatsanis and Martin JJ (concurring; UN Human Rights Committee General Comment no 31).

49 See the discussion in Chapter 4, Section 4.1(c).

50 2007 SCC 34 [*Dell Computer*].

51 An Act to Amend the Civil Code and the Code of Civil Procedure in Respect of Arbitration, SQ 1986, c 73.

52 [1986] Can TS no 43.

53 UN Doc A/40/17 (1985), Ann I.

commitment to the international community to implement the Model Law as it did in the case of the New York Convention."[54] Yet Deschamps J noted the strong degree of international support for the Model Law, its intentional similarity to the New York Convention, and (most importantly) a provision in Bill 91 expressly requiring the Model Law to be taken into consideration for interpretive purposes.[55] She therefore went on to interpret the relevant provisions of Bill 91 in the light of both the New York Convention and the Model Law.

Dell Computer illustrates two points about soft law. First, since soft law is not strictly law at all it is not subject to the usual reception rules (in this case, the presumption of conformity) that apply to true international law. Second, certain non-binding instruments may nevertheless be relevant for interpretive purposes in some cases.

Three Supreme Court of Canada decisions about freedom of association, as protected by section 2(d) of the Charter, came to split the court profoundly on the relevance and weight of certain international labour law norms, some of which were non-binding on Canada. In *Health Services and Support – Facilities Subsector Bargaining Assn v British Columbia* (2007),[56] McLachlin CJ and LeBel J for what was a unanimous court on this point[57] held that section 2(d) of the Charter protects a procedural right to collective bargaining. In so doing, the majority overruled the so-called Labour Trilogy of cases that had held otherwise.[58] The majority rested its new interpretation of section 2(d) in part on its view that collective bargaining was an integral component of freedom of association in international law. The majority considered three treaties to which Canada is bound, concluding that they all supported a right to collective bargaining in international law: the International Covenant on Economic, Social and Cultural Rights 1966,[59] the International Covenant on Civil and Political Rights 1966,[60] and the International

54 *Dell Computer*, above note 50 at paras 44–6.

55 *Ibid* at paras 40–1, 46.

56 2007 SCC 27 [*Health Services*].

57 Deschamps J's partial dissent generally agreed with the majority's reasons concerning the scope of s 2(d) in the collective bargaining context and gave no consideration to the international labour law issues addressed by the majority.

58 *Re Public Service Employee Relations Act (Alberta)*, [1987] 1 SCR 313; *Public Service Alliance of Canada v Canada*, [1987] 1 SCR 424; *Retail, Wholesale and Department Store Union v Saskatchewan*, [1987] 1 SCR 460.

59 [1976] Can TS no 46.

60 [1976] Can TS no 47.

Labour Organization's (ILO's) Convention (No 87) Concerning Freedom of Association and Protection of the Right to Organize 1948.[61] The majority also noted support for collective bargaining in interpretations of Convention No 87 advanced by the ILO's Committee on Freedom of Association, Committee of Experts, and Commissions of Inquiry, observing that while such interpretations were "not binding, they shed light on the scope of section 2(d) of the Charter as it was intended to apply to collective bargaining."[62] Venturing further into the realm of non-binding materials, the majority briefly turned its attention to the ILO's 1998 Declaration on Fundamental Principles and Rights at Work,[63] a formally non-binding declaration of the ILO which that body regards as obligatory on ILO member states.[64]

While this reliance on non-binding materials elicited no comment in *Health Services* itself, it proved belatedly controversial in *Ontario (Attorney General) v Fraser* (2011).[65] The case was a challenge to Ontario labour legislation relating to agricultural workers. The new Ontario law excluded farm workers from the general labour regime. Eight of nine judges of the Supreme Court of Canada found the regime to be constitutional, but they were split on why. Justice Rothstein (Charron J concurring) attacked *Health Services*, arguing that the court in that case had wrongly conflated ILO Convention No 87 with ILO Convention No 98. The former does not specifically address collective bargaining. The latter does, but Canada is not a party to the latter and it was "therefore inappropriate to interpret the scope of Canada's obligations on the basis of that Convention."[66] Against this, the majority in *Fraser* invoked a decision by the ILO Committee on Freedom of Association, arising from the facts of the *Health Services* case, that concluded the BC government had violated the health service employees' freedom of association rights – while noting that Canada was not a party to Convention No 98.[67] Implicit in the majority's response to Rothstein J is that a decision

61 [1973] Can TS no 14.

62 *Health Services*, above note 56 at para 76.

63 ILO Declaration on Fundamental Principles and Rights at Work, International Labour Conference, 86th Session, Geneva, June 1998, online: https://www.ilo.org/declaration/lang--en/index.htm.

64 *Health Services*, above note 56 at para 78.

65 2011 SCC 20.

66 *Ibid* at para 248.

67 *Ibid* at para 94.

of the Committee on Freedom of Association carries some legal weight – although the majority does not say how much or why.

The controversy continued in *Saskatchewan Federation of Labour v Saskatchewan* (2015).[68] Here Abella J for the majority of the court recognized the right to strike as an aspect of section 2(d) of the Charter's protection of freedom of association. As in *Health Services*, the majority found partial support for this development in Canada's international human rights obligations which, in Abella J's words, "mandate protecting the right to strike as part of a meaningful process of collective bargaining"[69] and "clearly argue for the recognition of a right to strike within s. 2(d)."[70] The obligations included article 8(1) of the International Covenant on Economic, Social and Cultural Rights 1966, article 45(c) of the Charter of the Organization of American States,[71] and ILO Convention (No 87), which, she conceded, "does not explicitly refer to the right to strike."[72] All of these are treaties to which Canada is a party. In addition to these binding authorities, however, Abella J noted the "considerable persuasive weight" of decisions of the ILO Committee on Freedom of Association recognizing the right to strike[73] and pointed to the judicial decisions and constitutional provisions of a variety of mainly European states as signs of "an emerging international consensus that, if it is to be meaningful, collective bargaining requires a right to strike."[74]

Against all this, Rothstein and Wagner JJ (dissenting) emphasized the "unclear" state of international law on the right to strike.[75] They noted in particular that Convention No 87 does not refer to the right to strike, that ILO bodies have disagreed on the interpretation of that Convention, that the right to strike is not expressly protected by the International Covenant on Civil and Political Rights 1966, and that the UN Human Rights Committee has found article 22 of that covenant does not protect the right to strike.[76] The learned judges cautioned against too liberal a use of non-binding international sources:

---

68 2015 SCC 4 [*Saskatchewan Federation*].

69 *Ibid* at para 62.

70 *Ibid* at para 65.

71 [1990] Can TS no 23.

72 *Saskatchewan Federation*, above note 68 at para 67.

73 *Ibid* at para 69.

74 *Ibid* at paras 71, 72–5.

75 *Ibid* at para 150; see also para 156.

76 *Ibid* at paras 151–5.

> [T]his Court has indicated that obligations under international law that are *binding* on Canada are of primary relevance to this Court's interpretation of the *Charter*. . . . While other sources of international law can have some persuasive value in appropriate circumstances, they should be granted much less weight than sources under which Canada is bound. . . .
>
> There is good reason to accord little weight to international instruments to which Canada is not a party. It is the role of the government to accept international obligations on behalf of Canada, not the courts. . . . Judicial review and the use of international law as an interpretive aid should not become a euphemism for this Court interfering in the government's prerogative over foreign affairs.[77]

The concerns raised by Rothstein and Wagner JJ in dissent in *Saskatchewan Federation* were embraced by the majority of the court, outside the context of labour relations, in *Quebec (Attorney General) v 9147-0732 Québec inc* (2020).[78] While that case was strictly concerned with the weight to be given to international sources in Charter interpretation, the majority's insistence on distinguishing between binding and non-binding sources for interpretive purposes is applicable more generally. Justices Brown and Rowe for the majority of the court approved the observation of Professors Brunnée and Toope that there is

> a significant difference between international law that is binding on Canada and other international norms. The former is not only potentially persuasive but also obligatory. This distinction matters – when we fail to uphold our obligations, we undermine the respect for law internationally.[79]

The learned judges also quoted approvingly those authors' call for "greater analytical rigour" and "clarity as to precisely what effect is accorded to international law in a given case and why."[80]

---

77 *Ibid* at paras 157, 159 (emphasis in original).

78 2020 SCC 32.

79 *Ibid* at para 25, quoting J Brunnée & S Toope, "A Hesitant Embrace: The Application of International Law by Canadian Courts" (2002) 40 *Canadian Yearbook of International Law* 3 at 41.

80 *Ibid* at para 26.

9 International law and administrative decisions

Administrative decision makers of all kinds may find themselves involved in matters concerning Canada's treaty commitments or other aspects of international law. Specific reception rules applicable to administrative decision making have not yet developed in Canadian law and may not be necessary. However, the application to administrative decision making of such established doctrines as judicial notice of international law, the implementation requirement, and the presumption of conformity presents particular problems.

In *Canada (Minister of Citizenship and Immigration) v Vavilov*, the Supreme Court of Canada undertook a thoroughgoing renovation of its administrative law jurisprudence, seeking to "chart a new course forward for determining the standard of review that applies when a court reviews the merits of an administrative decision" and to "provide additional guidance for reviewing courts to follow when conducting reasonableness review."[1] The decision under review in *Vavilov* was challenged in significant part for the decision maker's neglect of relevant international legal considerations in her interpretation of the statutory regime she was charged with applying. The *Vavilov* decision is both an illustration of how international law can inform administrative decisions and guidance as to how international law may be used to challenge those decisions on judicial review.

1 2019 SCC 65 [*Vavilov*] at para 2.

9.1 International law as a legal constraint in administrative decision making

In *Vavilov*, the Supreme Court of Canada identified international law as a potential legal constraint on administrative decision makers. One sort of fundamental flaw in an administrative decision, *Vavilov* explains, is "when a decision is in some respect untenable in light of the relevant factual and legal constraints that bear on it."[2] After explaining that "both statutory and common law will impose constraints on how and what an administrative decision-maker can lawfully decide,"[3] the court explained that international law may also impose such constraints:

> We would also note that in some administrative decision making contexts, international law will operate as an important constraint on an administrative decision maker. It is well established that legislation is presumed to operate in conformity with Canada's international obligations, and the legislature is "presumed to comply with . . . the values and principles of customary and conventional international law". . . . Since *Baker*, it has also been clear that international treaties and conventions, even where they have not been implemented domestically by statute, can help to inform whether a decision was a reasonable exercise of administrative power. . . .[4]

The explanation given here of why international law is sometimes an important constraint on administrative decision makers is the presumption of conformity with international law and the related notion that Canada's international obligations are part of the legal context in which Canadian legislation is enacted and read.

This reliance on the presumption of conformity, with its depiction of Canadian law within an international context and its strong preference for internationally compliant interpretations of domestic law, suggests that an administrative decision will not be susceptible to review merely for disregarding some relevant international obligation. A decision maker might ignore the obligation but still reach a result that

---

2 *Ibid* at para 73.

3 *Ibid* at para 111.

4 *Ibid* at para 114. See also *Mason v Canada (Citizenship and Immigration)*, 2023 SCC 21 [*Mason*] at para 72.

conforms with it. Where, however, the decision under review is contrary to or inconsistent with an international obligation of the state, that decision will likely be unreasonable for that reason. Put another way, the presumption that Canadian laws conform to Canada's international obligations means that an administrative decision maker cannot reasonably interpret a domestic provision inconsistently with the state's obligations.[5]

In *Mason v Canada*, Jamal J for the majority of the Supreme Court of Canada noted that the presumption of conformity with international law "assumes additional force" in judicial review when interpreting a law that makes its presumed intent to conform to the state's international obligations explicit on the face of the enactment.[6] The legislation at issue in *Mason* was the Immigration and Refugee Protection Act (IRPA),[7] provisions of which expressly identify the Act's objectives as fulfillment of Canada's international refugee law obligations and compliance with international human rights instruments to which Canada is signatory. While the "interpretative value of international law is especially relevant where a statute is explicitly enacted for the purpose of implementing international obligations,"[8] it remains true that *Vavilov* founds the relevance of international law in administrative decision making not on an international norm's implementation status but instead on the presumption that enactments comply with the state's international obligations – a presumption that applies equally to implemented and unimplemented treaties[9] – and the holding in *Baker* that treaties can inform the reasonableness of an exercise of power even where they have not been implemented domestically by statute.[10]

5 "In other words, in accordance with the presumption of compliance with international law, the decision maker cannot reasonably interpret a Canadian provision in a manner that is incompatible with the obligations imposed on Canada by international law": *Elve v Canada (Citizenship and Immigration)*, 2020 FC 454 [*Elve*] at para 79.

6 *Mason*, above note 4 at para 106.

7 SC 2001 c 27.

8 *Minister of Public Safety and Emergency Preparedness v Verbanov*, 2021 FC 507, Grammond J at para 49.

9 See the discussion in Chapter 5, Section 5.5(b).

10 Even before *Vavilov*, an unimplemented treaty could "help inform the contextual approach to statutory interpretation and judicial review": *Bhajan v Bhajan*, 2010 ONCA 714 at para 14; *Ontario (Children's Lawyer) v Ontario (Information and Privacy Commissioner)*, 2018 ONCA 559 at paras 58–9.

By situating public international legal considerations within the type of legal constraints to which administrative decision makers will be held, *Vavilov* gives public international law a potentially significant place in judicial review. That said, international law remains on the periphery of judicial review, for it will only be relevant in "some administrative decision making contexts."[11] But where it is relevant, it can really matter. The state's international legal obligations are among the legal constraints that, if disregarded, make a decision "untenable."[12] For an administrative decision maker to decide inconsistently with the state's obligations is a "fundamental flaw."[13]

The application of these principles to the facts in *Vavilov* is instructive. Mr. Vavilov was born in Toronto to parents who turned out to be Russian spies. The registrar of citizenship eventually advised Mr. Vavilov he was not a citizen of Canada. She concluded that the effect of section 3(2)(a) of the Citizenship Act[14] was that a child born in Canada is not a Canadian citizen if the parents were employees of a foreign government and not themselves either citizens or permanent residents. Mr. Vavilov did not therefore acquire nationality *jus soli* as generally provided for by section 3(1)(a) of the Act. The majority of the Supreme Court of Canada set aside this decision as unreasonable. The registrar

> failed to justify her interpretation of s. 3(2)(a) of the Citizenship Act in light of the constraints imposed by the text of s. 3 of the Citizenship Act considered as a whole, by other legislation and international

---

11 This qualification appears to be descriptive rather than legal. The point seems to be only that not all Canadian administrative decisions involve matters to which public international law is a potential constraint.

12 *Vavilov*, above note 1 at para 101.

13 *Ibid* at para 101. See *Elve*, above note 5 at para 79 (an erroneous interpretation of international law is a sub-category of fundamental flaw that could cause a reviewing court to lose confidence in the outcome reached). Compare *Thales DIS Canada Inc v Ontario (Transportation)*, 2023 ONCA 866 where the Court of Appeal for Ontario acknowledged (at para 95) *Vavilov*'s affirmation that international law will operate as an important constraint on decision makers in some contexts, but went on to doubt that a World Trade Organization (WTO) decision relied upon by the divisional court in finding the decision under review to be unreasonable truly was a legal constraint on the decision maker, given that "WTO decisions are not binding on either Canadian courts or subsequent WTO panels" and the treaty at issue "does not address what law or rules will govern" dispute resolution.

14 RSC 1985, c 29.

> treaties that inform the purpose of s. 3, by the jurisprudence on the interpretation of s. 3(2)(a), and by the potential consequences of her interpretation.[15]

The relevant provision could not be interpreted as excluding from the general *jus soli* rule children born of foreign spies when read in its entire context, including the Vienna Convention on Diplomatic Relations 1961[16] and the Vienna Convention on Consular Relations 1963[17] as implemented by the Foreign Missions and International Organizations Act.[18] These provisions, and the principles of *jus soli* and *jus sanguinis* acquisition of citizenship in international law, were "a backdrop to s. 3 of the Citizenship Act as a whole."[19] Despite it being "well established that domestic legislation is presumed to comply with Canada's international obligations," the decision maker "did not refer to the relevant international law" and gave no reasoned explanation for choosing an interpretation inconsistent with it.[20]

The post-*Vavilov* decision of the Supreme Court of Canada in *Mason v Canada (Citizenship and Immigration)* confirms the potential significance of international legal considerations in some administrative contexts. Two decisions of the Immigration Appeal Division (IAD) of the Immigration and Refugee Board of Canada interpreted section 34(1)(e) of the IRPA, which provides that permanent residents and foreign nationals are inadmissible to Canada on "security grounds" for "engaging in acts of violence that would or might endanger the lives or safety of persons in Canada." The interpretive question was whether the acts of violence required to make a person inadmissible under this provision had to be linked to national security considerations. Mr. Mason was alleged to have shot two people in a bar fight, while Mr. Dleiow was alleged to have committed intimate partner violence. Neither man was alleged to have threatened national security or the security of Canada by these acts, yet the decision makers found the men inadmissible. Justice Jamal for the majority of the Supreme Court of Canada found the administrative decisions to be unreasonable for their failure to con-

15 *Vavilov*, above note 1 at para 172.
16 [1966] Can TS no 29.
17 [1974] Can TS no 25.
18 SC 1991, c 41.
19 *Vavilov*, above note 1 at para 178; see also paras 177–82.
20 *Ibid* at para 182.

sider three significant legal constraints, one of which was the obligation of *non-refoulement* under article 33 of the Refugee Convention.[21] In an extensive consideration of *Vavilov*'s treatment of international legal considerations and Canada's *non-refoulement* obligations,[22] Jamal J held that the IAD's interpretation of section 34(1)(e) would permit deportation for inadmissibility without a finding that the deportee poses a danger to the security of Canada or has been convicted of a serious offence – a result contrary to the Refugee Convention's prohibition of *refoulement* except in cases where the security or serious criminality exceptions of article 33(2) apply. The way to avoid this potential breach of the Refugee Convention was to interpret IRPA section 34(1)(e) as requiring a nexus with security.[23] The decision makers' failure to consider the relevant interpretive constraints – "especially, the legal constraints imposed by international law" – rendered the decisions unreasonable.[24]

9.2 Notice of international law by administrative decision makers

There is a great deal of international law of potential relevance to Canadian tribunals, boards, commissions, and other administrative decision makers. Labour tribunals may be called upon to consider the many treaties and declarations of the International Labour Organization. Human rights bodies stand to be confronted with a plethora of international human rights instruments.[25] Trade and competition tribunals may need to inform themselves of developments in international economic law. These are some obvious examples. Less obvious, perhaps, are cases where individual government officials exercise discretionary decision-making powers in circumstances falling short of quasi-judicial proceedings. Decision makers and the courts that review them should bear in mind that if an administrative decision places Canada in

---

21 United Nations Convention relating to the Status of Refugees 1951 [1969] Can TS no 6.

22 *Mason*, above note 4 at paras 104–22.

23 *Ibid* at paras 109–11.

24 *Ibid* at para 121.

25 See L Reif, "The Domestic Application of International Human Rights Law in Canada: The Role of Canada's National Human Rights Institutions" in O Fitzgerald, ed, *The Globalized Rule of Law: Relationships Between International and Domestic Law* (Toronto: Irwin Law, 2006) at 467.

default of its international obligations, it will be no excuse for Canada to say, "Our tribunal lacked the power to consider international law."

Vavilov makes clear that, as a general rule, administrative decision makers may, and in some cases must, have regard to relevant international legal considerations in the course of their decision making. Yet whether a particular decision maker or tribunal must have regard to international law and, if so, how that decision maker does so as a matter of procedure and evidence are questions for which there can seemingly be no single answer, for these bodies vary enormously in their powers and purposes. One can imagine instances where regard to international law by a particular administrative body would seem necessary, or at least unobjectionable, while in other cases such considerations might be inappropriate. A workable approach may be that where a decision maker is empowered to decide questions of law, that power should be read to include relevant rules of international law.[26] This approach extrapolates from the presumption of conformity with international law: Since the decision maker's enabling legislation is presumed not to violate international law, it cannot have been given the power to do anything contrary to international law. It must therefore have regard to international law, in proper cases, to understand the ambit of its powers.[27] The specific endorsement and reliance upon the presumption of conformity in *Vavilov* and *Mason* supports such an approach.

Whether or not the Canadian Import Tribunal could take notice of international trade agreements was one of the points of contention in *National Corn Growers Association v Canada (Import Tribunal).*[28]

---

26 A similar approach was adopted by the Supreme Court of Canada in *Nova Scotia (Workers' Compensation Board) v Martin; Nova Scotia (Workers' Compensation Board) v Laseur*, 2003 SCC 54, holding that administrative tribunals that have jurisdiction to decide questions of law arising under a legislative provision are presumed also to have jurisdiction to decide the constitutional validity of that provision.

27 "[I]f Parliament is presumed to intend conformity with Canada's international obligations, it makes little sense to assume that it granted administrative decision-makers discretion to ignore these obligations": J Brunnée & S Toope, "A Hesitant Embrace: The Application of International Law by Canadian Courts" (2002) 40 *Canadian Yearbook of International Law* 3 at 38 n 155.

28 [1990] 2 SCR 1324 [*National Corn Growers*].

Acting under the Special Import Measures Act (SIMA),[29] the tribunal concluded that the federal government could justifiably impose a countervailing duty on American grain corn producers. In construing the SIMA, the tribunal resorted to certain international instruments to elucidate the Act's concept of material injury.[30] On judicial review, the Federal Court of Appeal left the tribunal's findings undisturbed yet held that the tribunal was wrong to consult international sources. On appeal to the Supreme Court of Canada, Gonthier J for the majority disagreed, affirming that Parliament must be presumed to have intended that SIMA be interpreted in accordance with international law. In concurring reasons differing from the majority on this point, Wilson J argued that it was not the court's place to question whether the tribunal had erred by failing to give effect to Canada's international obligations. I do not understand the learned judge to have disapproved of the tribunal taking notice of international law; rather, her concern was that the courts should not review tribunals for failing to do so or doing so incorrectly. Thus, *National Corn Growers* appears to support, in principle at least, the power and even the duty of some administrative tribunals to take notice of international law.[31]

Mason v Canada is further authority for the point. There, Jamal J noted that while an argument founded on article 33 of the Refugee Convention was not presented to the Immigration Appeal Division, that body "was required by its home statute to interpret and apply the *IRPA* in a manner that complies with Canada's international human rights obligations, including Canada's non-refoulement obligation under Article 33 of the *Refugee Convention*."[32]

The power or duty to take notice of international law is not limited to quasi-judicial tribunals but may extend to other types of adminis-

---

29 SC 1984, c 25.

30 General Agreement on Tariffs and Trade 1947, [1947] Can TS no 27 art 6(a); Agreement on Interpretation and Application of Articles VI, XVI, and XXIII of the General Agreement on Tariffs and Trade 1979, [1980] Can TS no 42 [GATT Subsidies Code].

31 See also *Re Canada Labour Code*, [1992] 2 SCR 50 at paras 10–11, where La Forest J describes the consideration of international law made by the Canada Labour Relations Board earlier in the proceedings without any suggestion that the board was wrong to do so.

32 *Mason*, above note 4 at para 104; see also paras 116–17.

trative decision makers. In *Baker v Canada (Minister of Citizenship and Immigration)*,[33] a senior immigration officer decided there were insufficient humanitarian and compassionate reasons to warrant processing Baker's application for permanent residence from within Canada (the usual requirement being that such applications must be made from outside the country). As a basis for her application, Baker relied in part on the effect of her deportation on her Canadian-born children. Baker's application for judicial review of the decision was dismissed, but the court certified the following question pursuant to section 83(1) of the Immigration Act:[34]

> Given that the Immigration Act does not expressly incorporate the language of Canada's international obligations with respect to the International Convention on the Rights of the Child, must federal immigration authorities treat the best interests of the Canadian child as a primary consideration in assessing an applicant under s. 114(2) of the Immigration Act?[35]

Justice L'Heureux-Dubé for the majority of the Supreme Court of Canada reversed the immigration officer's decision as unreasonable, calling it "inconsistent with the values underlying the grant of discretion."[36] To ascertain these underlying values, the learned judge looked in part to "the ratification by Canada of the Convention on the Rights of the Child 1989, and the recognition of the importance of children's rights and the best interests of children in other international instruments ratified by Canada."[37] While the court did not expressly answer the certified question, it affirmed that "for the exercise of the discretion to fall within the standard of reasonableness, the decision-maker should consider children's best interests as an important factor, give them substantial weight, and be alert, alive and sensitive to them."[38]

Likewise, in *Vavilov*, the registrar of citizenship "failed to justify her interpretation of section 3(2)(a) of the Citizenship Act" in the light

33 [1999] 2 SCR 817 [*Baker*].
34 RSC 1985, c I-2.
35 *Baker*, above note 33 at para 9.
36 *Ibid* at para 65.
37 *Ibid* at para 69; see also paras 70–1.
38 *Ibid* at para 75.

of the relevant constraints, including international treaties.[39] She "did not refer to the relevant international law" and gave no reasoned explanation for choosing an interpretation inconsistent with it, despite the interpretive presumption of conformity with international law.[40]

9.3 International law and standards of review

A question that has beset Canadian administrative law for decades, and which the Supreme Court of Canada sought (not for the first time[41]) to settle in *Vavilov*, is what standard of review courts should apply in their exercise of judicial supervision over administrative decision makers.

The central inquiry in determining the standard of review to be applied by a court of law in reviewing an administrative decision has been said to be the legislative intent of the statute creating the decision maker whose decision is being reviewed.[42] The court in *Vavilov* affirmed that legislative intent remains the "polar star" of judicial review.[43] The most notable aspect of the Canadian approach to standards of review, for present purposes, is that it may result in courts deferring to (or at least tolerating) decisions by administrative decision makers on questions of law.[44] Where such legal questions concern the state's obligations under international law, curial restraint on judicial review may put (or leave) Canada out of compliance with those obligations.

The clearest instance of an administrative decision that might place Canada in non-compliance with an international legal obligation is where the administrative decision maker is required to determine a

---

39 *Vavilov*, above note 1 at para 172.

40 *Ibid* at para 182.

41 See, e.g., *Pushpanathan v Canada (Minister of Citizenship and Immigration)*, [1998] 1 SCR 982 [*Pushpanathan*] and *Dunsmuir v New Brunswick*, 2008 SCC 9.

42 *Pushpanathan*, above note 41 at para 26.

43 *Vavilov*, above note 1 at para 33, quoting *CUPE v Ontario (Minister of Labour)*, 2003 SCC 29 at para 149.

44 *Bell Canada v Canada (Canadian Radio-Telecommunications Commission)*, [1989] 1 SCR 1722; *Pezim v British Columbia (Superintendent of Brokers)*, [1994] 2 SCR 557; *Canada (Director of Investigation and Research, Competition Act) v Southam Inc*, [1997] 1 SCR 748; *Pushpanathan*, above note 41. By contrast, English courts have historically applied a standard of correctness to the legal determinations of administrative bodies, e.g. *Anisminic Limited v Foreign Compensation Commission*, [1969] 2 AC 147; *O'Reilly v Mackman*, [1983] 2 AC 237; *R v Hull University Visitor ex parte Page*, [1993] AC 682.

question of international law, such as the meaning of a Canadian treaty obligation, and does so incorrectly. Another possibility is that the decision maker does not have an international legal question directly before them, yet the decision has the effect of placing Canada in international default. In such cases, a deferential or restrained approach to judicial review, upholding the internationally unlawful determination, may create difficulties for Canada as a matter of international law or relations. There is an important difference between legal errors made by tribunals on purely domestic matters and errors implicating Canadian obligations under international law: Legal error on a point of international law may bring international responsibility upon the Canadian state.[45] Curial deference to such errors on review or appeal will serve only to confirm Canada's international default.

Whether that possibility should inform standard of review determinations was, before *Vavilov*, the subject of debate in the Federal Court and Federal Court of Appeal. Before turning to what *Vavilov* says about international law and standards of review, it is helpful to recall that debate.

In *Febles v Canada (Minister of Citizenship and Immigration)*, the majority (Evans JA, Sharlow JA concurring) preferred correctness review over reasonableness, because the question concerned "a provision of an international Convention [article 1F(b) of the United Nations Convention relating to the Status of Refugees 1951] that should be interpreted as uniformly as possible" and correctness review was "more likely than reasonableness review to achieve this goal."[46] The minority view (Stratas JA) was that while "World-wide uniform interpretations of the provisions in international conventions may be desirable," that "depends on the nature of the provision being interpreted and the quality and acceptability of the interpretations adopted by foreign jurisdictions."[47]

This division of opinion in *Febles* recalls a similar disagreement between Gonthier and Wilson JJ in *National Corn Growers*. There, the Canadian Import Tribunal concluded that American subsidies were injuring Canadian grain corn producers, thus justifying the govern-

45 It is not every error of international law that will bring responsibility; for instance, a tribunal may erroneously conclude that Canada's obligations under a given treaty are greater than they really are.

46 2012 FCA 324 at para 24.

47 *Ibid* at para 76.

ment's imposition of a countervailing duty. In reaching this conclusion the tribunal resorted to article 6(a) of the General Agreement on Tariffs and Trade 1947 and article 6 of the GATT Subsidies Code to elucidate the concept of material injury in its constitutive legislation. On judicial review, the Federal Court of Appeal left the tribunal's findings undisturbed but held that it was mistaken to have regard to the international instruments. Justice Gonthier for the majority of the Supreme Court of Canada rejected that view and held that it was not patently unreasonable for the tribunal to consider the GATT provisions. To the contrary, Gonthier J held that "where the text of the domestic law lends itself to it, one should also strive to expound an interpretation which is consonant with the relevant international obligations."[48] Justice Wilson for the minority took issue with Gonthier J on this point, saying that it was not the court's role "to look beyond the Tribunal's statute to determine whether the Tribunal's interpretation of that statute is consistent with Canada's international obligations." She observed that if the tribunal's interpretation was inconsistent with Canada's obligations under the GATT, "then it is for the legislature to address this matter."[49]

Returning to *Febles*, when the case reached the Supreme Court of Canada, that court ignored the standard of review question, although both the majority and the dissent implicitly approached the international legal question as one to be determined on a correctness standard. Despite that approach at the Supreme Court, and Evans JA's majority reasons in the Federal Court of Appeal expressly preferring correctness review, subsequent decisions in the Federal Court[50] and Federal Court of Appeal[51] frequently applied reasonableness review to international legal questions determined by tribunals. When the issue came back before the Supreme Court of Canada in *B010 v Canada (Citizenship and Immigration)*,[52] that court noted the controversy but again declined to resolve it.

---

48 *National Corn Growers*, above note 28 at 1371.

49 *Ibid* at 1349.

50 See, e.g., *Druyan v Canada (Attorney General)*, 2014 FC 705 at para 38; *Haqi v Canada (MCI)*, 2014 FC 1167 at paras 24–6; *Tapambwa v Canada (Citizenship and Immigration)*, 2017 FC 522 at para 20.

51 *Majebi v Canada (Citizenship and Immigration)*, 2016 FCA 274 at para 5; *B010 v Canada (MCI)*, 2013 FCA 87 at para 71.

52 2015 SCC 58.

The Supreme Court of Canada finally addressed the question of standard of review and international law, if somewhat obliquely, in *Vavilov*. The majority's general pronouncements about judicial review are organized around two major discussions, "Determining the Applicable Standard of Review" and "Performing Reasonableness Review." In the first discussion, the court affirms that reasonableness is the presumptive standard of review and sets out how that presumption can be rebutted. Legislative intent, as indicated by legislated standards of review, and statutory appeal mechanisms are two ways in which the reasonableness presumption is rebutted. In addition, correctness review will apply where required by the rule of law. Constitutional questions are an instance of this, as are general questions of law of central importance to the legal system as a whole and questions regarding the jurisdictional boundaries between administrative bodies. These five situations are the ones the majority presently regards as warranting "a derogation from the presumption of reasonableness review."[53] Notably, Canada's obligations under public international law are not specifically considered in this discussion. In particular, they are not treated as necessarily constituting general questions of law of central importance to the legal system as a whole.

Instead, the potential role of international law in judicial review is considered by the court in its discussion of "Performing Reasonableness Review." As explained above,[54] international law is identified as one of the legal constraints that, if not observed, may render an administrative decision unreasonable and therefore invalid. The *Febles* question – Should a reviewing court apply correctness or reasonableness to questions of international law? – is not directly answered because it turns out to have been the wrong question. Even in reasonableness review, the state's international obligations are a potential constraint on administrative decision makers. In the same way that legislation and common law will impose constraints on how and what an administrative decision maker can lawfully decide, Canada's international obliga-

53 *Vavilov*, above note 1 at para 69. See also *Society of Composers, Authors and Music Publishers of Canada v Entertainment Software Association*, 2022 SCC 30 at para 28, recognizing a sixth such situation, namely "when courts and administrative bodies have concurrent first instance jurisdiction over a legal issue in a statute."

54 See Section 9.1.

tions, including unimplemented treaties, are factors in reasonableness review.

In the second edition of this book[55] and elsewhere,[56] I have argued that a deferential standard of review ought not to apply to administrative decisions that conflict with the state's international obligations. My point has been that for courts to tolerate administrative decisions that risk putting Canada offside its international obligations is deferential to one part of the executive (i.e., the tribunal in question), but utterly non-deferential to another part of the executive, namely the federal cabinet members and senior civil servants charged with conducting Canada's foreign relations. A cabinet decision to incur a treaty obligation in exercise of the royal prerogative over foreign affairs is not taken lightly. It is preceded by a complex process including policy formulation, consultations of stakeholders, negotiation with foreign partners, and the weighing of political factors. This is true even of relatively straightforward bilateral agreements between Canada and likeminded states, and all the more so for multilateral treaties, the negotiation and implementation of which can take many years. For the courts to permit administrative decision makers to upset the results of these deliberate, polycentric, and time-consuming processes in the name of deference is faintly absurd. Real deference would see the courts protect the federal government's responsibility for the conduct of foreign relations through intolerance of administrative decisions that disregard Canada's international obligations.

Until *Vavilov*, I had thought only insistence upon correctness review for international legal questions could afford this sort of protection. But the majority in *Vavilov* has reformulated – or perhaps just better explained – the latitude courts have to insist upon certain legal constraints even under a reasonableness standard. By identifying international law as one such constraint and insisting upon the presumption of conformity as an interpretive rule in administrative decision making just as it is in judicial decision making, *Vavilov* shows

55 G van Ert, *Using International Law in Canadian Courts*, 2d ed (Toronto: Irwin Law, 2008) at Section 9.2.

56 G van Ert, "The Reception of International Law in Canada: Three Ways We Might Go Wrong" in O Fitzgerald, *Reflections on Canada's Past, Present and Future in International Law* (Waterloo: Centre for International Governance Innovation, 2018) at 15–30.

deference both to administrative decision makers and those charged with the conduct of Canada's foreign affairs.

Vavilov establishes that international legal questions are reviewed for reasonableness, not correctness. It also establishes that for an administrative decision maker to neglect relevant international legal considerations is unreasonable. In some cases, the weight of an international legal consideration may be such that there is room for only one reasonable interpretation of a decision maker's authority.[57]

9.4 International law and discretionary decisions

One remarkable aspect of the Supreme Court of Canada's decision in *Baker*[58] was its implicit endorsement of the use of international law as a basis for judicial review of administrative decision making, and more particularly its use to control discretionary powers. The implication in *Baker* that international law may serve as a basis for controlling discretionary decisions was made explicit in *Vavilov*. Before turning to *Baker* and *Vavilov*, however, we must consider the case *Baker* arguably departed from, *Capital Cities*.

(a) *Capital Cities Communications Ltd v CRTC*

Baker was not the Supreme Court of Canada's first opportunity to consider the relevance of a Canadian treaty obligation in judicial review of an administrative decision maker's exercise of discretion. In *Capital Cities Communications Ltd v Canadian Radio-Television Commission*,[59] judicial review was sought of a decision of the Canadian Radio-television Commission (CRTC) to alter the licence of Rogers Cable TV Limited to permit that company to delete advertisements from US television channels broadcast on its cable service and replace them with public service announcements. This was an exercise of discretion granted to the CRTC by section 17(1) of the Broadcasting Act.[60] The CRTC's decision was informed by the pro-Canadian broadcasting policy enshrined

---

57 *Mason*, above note 4 at paras 120–2.
58 *Baker*, above note 33.
59 [1978] 2 SCR 141 [*Capital Cities*].
60 SC 1967–68, c 25.

in section 3 of the Broadcasting Act and a non-statutory policy statement published by the CRTC that explicitly permitted "the removal . . . of the commercial value" contained in US television signals.[61] The treaty in issue was the Inter-American Radiocommunications Convention 1937,[62] article 11 of which contained guarantees against interference in the services of another country, and article 21 of which sought to prevent unauthorized retransmissions. The status of the Convention in Canadian law was a matter of dispute. Section 7(1)(d) of the Radio Act[63] provided that the minister may make regulations to carry out such international agreements. One such regulation required licensees, such as Rogers, to observe the provisions of telecommunication agreements in force.[64] Yet Rogers was a licensee under the later Broadcasting Act that, in the majority's opinion, did not implement the Convention.[65]

The appellants argued that the Broadcasting Act should be interpreted in the light of the Convention, or in such a way as not to violate Canada's international obligations thereunder. Chief Justice Laskin for the majority rejected this proposed reliance on the presumption of conformity to control the CRTC's decision. The chief justice first observed that there was no ambiguity in the Broadcasting Act that would require resort to the Convention.[66] This refusal to have regard to a treaty on the ground that the legislation before the court is unambiguous has since been rejected by the Supreme Court of Canada in *National Corn Growers*[67] and later cases.[68] Prompted perhaps by a sense of how intellectually unsatisfying the ambiguity requirement is, the chief justice added that the Convention was nowhere mentioned in the Act, "and certainly the Convention *per se* cannot prevail against the express stipulations of the Act."[69] In this latter observation Laskin CJ appears to reject reliance on the Convention as an implicit limit to the CRTC's discretion – a rejection that is very hard to reconcile with the use of international law by the court in *Baker* some 20 years later.

---

61 *Capital Cities*, above note 59 at 148.

62 [1938] Can TS no 18.

63 RSC 1970, c R-1.

64 General Radio Regulations, Part II, SOR/63/297, s 11.

65 *Capital Cities*, above note 59 at 173–6.

66 *Ibid* at 173.

67 *National Corn Growers*, above note 28.

68 See the discussion in Chapter 5, Section 5.6.

69 *Capital Cities*, above note 59 at 173.

From an international law perspective, the majority's reasons in *Capital Cities* are unsatisfying. Assuming, as appears to have been the case, that the CRTC's decision was inconsistent with a treaty binding on Canada at international law, to affirm the decision serves only to confirm the default. It is clear that Canada could not be heard at international law to plead, in defence of its treaty violation, that the CRTC was not an agent of the federal government or that the treaty was not implemented, or sufficiently implemented, in Canadian law.

The dissenting judgment of Pigeon J (for himself and Beetz and Grandpré JJ) held that the CRTC could not properly issue decisions in violation of Canada's treaty obligations. Upon considering articles 11 and 21 of the Convention, Pigeon J asked whether Rogers' deletion of commercials was an interference with signals and whether its distribution of the programs was a retransmission or rebroadcast, as those concepts are set out in the respective articles of the Convention. On the latter question, Pigeon J held that to find otherwise would "fail to give effect to the true intention" of the Convention.[70] The learned judge was less satisfied that Rogers could be said to be interfering, but expressed the view that "it must be one or the other."[71] He went on to consider whether the Convention remained implemented in Canadian law, finding that, in spite of changes to the regulatory scheme since Canada adhered to the Convention, "Nothing in the legislation enacted in 1968 or in the amendments to the Regulations indicates any intention to free broadcasting undertakings from the obligation of complying with Convention provisions."[72] What is important for our purposes, however, is that Pigeon J did not rest his decision on that finding. He observed that even if the treaty were now unimplemented by the relevant regulations,

> I cannot agree that the Commission may properly issue authorizations in violation of Canada's treaty obligations. Its duty is to implement the policy established by Parliament. While this policy makes no reference to Canada's treaty obligations, it is an integral part of the national structure that external affairs are the responsibility of

---

70 *Ibid* at 183–5.

71 *Ibid* at 186.

72 *Ibid* at 187–8.

the Federal Government. It is an oversimplification to say that treaties are of no legal effect unless implemented by legislation.[73]

Justice Pigeon went on to quote at length from an English decision requiring the court to take judicial notice of a treaty and to apply the presumption of conformity to an order-in-council.[74]

In short, Pigeon J would have applied the presumption of conformity to prevent the CRTC from exercising its statutory discretion inconsistently with Canada's obligations under the Convention. While he spoke in dissent, the majority's reasons in *Baker* suggest that his view may now be the better one.

(b) *Baker v Canada (Minister of Citizenship and Immigration)*

Mavis Baker was a Jamaican citizen who arrived in Canada in 1981 and overstayed her visitor's visa by 11 years. Having been ordered deported, she sought to apply for permanent residence in Canada. Normally these applications must be made from outside the country, but section 114(2) of the Immigration Act granted the minister of immigration a discretion, on "humanitarian and compassionate" grounds, to allow applications from within Canada. The minister refused to exercise her discretion in Baker's favour. Baker sought judicial review of that decision, arguing, *inter alia*, that it unreasonably failed to give sufficient weight to the interests of her Canadian-born children as required by the Convention on the Rights of the Child 1989. Canada is a party to that treaty, but the federal government argued that it was not implemented in Canadian law.[75]

Baker was unsuccessful both in the Trial Division of the Federal Court and in the Federal Court of Appeal. However, the majority of the Supreme Court of Canada allowed the appeal. They found that notes made by the decision maker (formally the minister but in practice an immigration officer under her) gave rise to a reasonable apprehension

73 *Ibid* at 188.

74 *Post Office v Estuary Radio*, [1968] 2 QB 740 (Eng CA), discussed in Chapter 3, Section 3.1.

75 While the treaty was not expressly implemented by the legislation before the court, it goes too far to say that it was unimplemented in Canadian law. See Chapter 7, Sections 7.2 and 7.3(b)(iv).

of bias. Furthermore, the majority held that the decision unreasonably neglected international law and was thus an unlawful exercise of the minister's discretion. The path to this conclusion is clear but winding. First, L'Heureux-Dubé J for the majority declared that "though discretionary decisions will generally be given considerable respect, that discretion must be exercised in accordance with the boundaries imposed in the statute, the principles of the rule of law, the principles of administrative law, the fundamental values of Canadian society, and the principles of the *Charter*."[76] Second, having determined the appropriate standard of review to be reasonableness *simpliciter*, the learned judge held that the decision of the immigration officer was faulty for being "inconsistent with the values underlying the grant of discretion."[77] To determine what those values are, the decision maker was not to look solely to section 114(2), which Strayer JA in the Federal Court of Appeal characterized as conferring upon the minister "a virtually unfettered discretion."[78] Rather, in the third step of her reasoning, L'Heureux-Dubé J held that "Children's rights, and attention to their interests, are central humanitarian and compassionate values in Canadian society."[79] This was revealed by the following "indications" of the importance of children's rights and interests in Canadian society: the objectives of the Act (as set out in section 3), the minister's guidelines, and international law (particularly the Convention on the Rights of the Child 1989).

This use of a supposedly unimplemented treaty as an element in defining the extent of the discretion granted by the statute was, in effect, an application of the presumption of conformity to the enabling provision: the discretion conferred by the statute was presumed to be consistent with the requirements of international law. Justice L'Heureux-Dubé did not describe her invocation of the Convention on the Rights of the Child as an application of the presumption of conformity, though she did refer to the presumption.[80] In subsequent

76 *Baker*, above note 33 at para 56.

77 *Ibid* at para 65.

78 *Baker v Canada (Minister of Citizenship and Immigration)*, [1997] 2 FC 127 at para 20 (CA) [*Baker* FCA].

79 *Baker*, above note 33 at para 67.

80 *Ibid* at para. 70. Why L'Heureux-Dubé J did not invoke the presumption directly is an interesting question. One reason may be that the applicability of the presumption to statutory grants of discretion has been a matter of controversy in other Commonwealth jurisdictions. By not invoking the presumption explicitly,

decisions L'Heureux-Dubé J has cited *Baker* as an example of the application of the presumption.[81] There is no convincing reason to distinguish *Baker*'s use of an unimplemented treaty from the ordinary presumption of conformity.

In arriving at this result, L'Heureux-Dubé J disavowed any intention of upsetting the established rule that treaties are not part of Canadian law unless implemented by statute.[82] Indeed, she affirmed the implementation requirement, citing *Francis v The Queen*[83] and *Capital Cities*.[84] In her view, the use of an unimplemented treaty in this context did not violate or circumvent the implementation requirement. But that is not to say that L'Heureux-Dubé J's use of the Convention on the Rights of the Child did not grant it some legal consequence. While she denied having set aside the implementation requirement, she did not deny having recognized domestic legal consequences arising from the unimplemented treaty. Nor could she plausibly do so, having held that the treaty was an indicator of the fundamental values of Canadian society underlying, and therefore controlling, the grant of discretion.

In separate reasons, Iacobucci J (Cory J concurring) agreed with L'Heureux-Dubé J "except to the extent that my colleague addresses the effect of international law on the exercise of ministerial discretion pursuant to section 114(2) of the Immigration Act." Iacobucci J noted that the Immigration Act did not implement the Convention and observed that "an international convention ratified by the executive branch of government is of no force or effect within the Canadian legal system until such time as its provisions have been incorporated into domestic law by way of implementing legislation."[85] He characterized the result of the majority's reliance on the Convention as being "that

---

L'Heureux-Dubé J may have hoped (in vain) to sidestep the debate. Another possible reason is the chronology problem: The Act in question preceded the Convention on the Rights of the Child by over a decade. On the chronology problem, see the discussion in Chapter 5, Section 5.5(g).

81 See *R v Sharpe*, 2001 SCC 2 at para 175, citing R Sullivan, *Driedger on the Construction of Statutes*, 3d ed (Toronto: Butterworths, 1994) at 330; and *114957 Canada Ltée (Spraytech, Société d'arrosage) v Hudson (Town)*, 2001 SCC 40 at para 30, again citing *Driedger*.

82 *Baker*, above note 33 at para 69.

83 [1956] SCR 618.

84 Above note 59 at 173.

85 *Baker*, above note 33 at para 79.

the appellant is able to achieve indirectly what cannot be achieved directly, namely, to give force and effect within the domestic legal system to international obligations undertaken by the executive alone that have yet to be subject to the democratic will of Parliament."[86] Justice Iacobucci also took the view that the primacy accorded to children's rights under the Convention "is irrelevant unless and until such provisions are the subject of legislation enacted by Parliament."

In these reasons, Iacobucci J appears to reject all reference to an unimplemented treaty during the process of statutory interpretation.[87] But that cannot be his meaning given the weighty Supreme Court of Canada authority in favour of the presumption of conformity. In my view, the key to understanding Iacobucci J's objection to the majority's reliance on international law in *Baker* occurs at the outset of his brief reasons where he refers to "the effect of international law on the exercise of ministerial discretion." What makes *Baker* an unusual case is the majority's application of the presumption of conformity, in effect if not expressly, to a grant of statutory discretion, namely the minister's discretion to exempt persons from regulations on humanitarian and compassionate grounds in section 114(2) of the Immigration Act. To presume that a grant of statutory discretion is subject to conformity with international law introduces international legal norms as controlling factors in the judicial review process. This is the novelty to which Iacobucci J objected.

Justice Iacobucci is not the first judge to express concern about the application of the presumption of conformity to statutory grants of discretion. In *Ashby v Minister of Immigration*,[88] the New Zealand Court of Appeal was asked to declare invalid a decision by the minister of immigration to issue temporary entry permits to apartheid South Africa's Springbok rugby team. The minister's power was a discretionary one under New Zealand's immigration legislation. The appellants argued alternatively that the minister's discretion could only be lawfully exercised in conformity with the Convention on the Elimination of All Forms of Racial Discrimination 1966,[89] or that the minister was bound to take the Convention into account and had failed to do so. The

86 *Ibid* at para 80.

87 See especially *Baker, ibid* at para 79.

88 [1981] 1 NZLR 222 (CA) [*Ashby*].

89 [1970] Can TS no 28.

Convention was implemented in New Zealand by the Race Relations Act 1971, but not by any amendment of the Immigration Act. The court unanimously dismissed the appeal in separate judgments. The decision of Richardson J most resembles that of the dissent in *Baker*, for he held that to limit the minister's discretion by resort to the treaty "would amount to legislating rather than interpreting"[90] and was therefore impermissible. He gave three reasons why this was so. First, he noted that the Immigration Act provided categories of persons to whom the minister may not issue temporary permits and that the rugby team did not fall into any of them. Second, he pointed to a chronology problem: The section in issue was adopted prior to New Zealand's ratification of the treaty.[91] Finally, his lordship observed that when Parliament enacted legislation to implement the Convention it did not amend the Immigration Act to do so.

An English instance of the same problem is *R v Secretary of State for the Home Department, ex parte Brind*.[92] The case concerned a statutory discretion to prohibit the broadcast of certain matters. The UK Home Secretary issued directives, pursuant to a discretion he enjoyed under the Broadcasting Act 1981 and the BBC's licence, prohibiting the broadcast of statements by representatives of proscribed organizations in Northern Ireland (notably the Irish Republican Army and loyalist paramilitaries). Journalists argued that this was a breach of the right to freedom of expression recognized by the European Convention on Human Rights,[93] a treaty to which the UK is a party but which, at the time, had not been implemented into UK law. The journalists admitted that the Convention did not apply directly in the UK. Yet, they argued that courts interpreting the discretion must presume that Parliament intended it to be exercised within the limits of the Convention. The appeal was unanimously dismissed. Lord Bridge of Harwich declared that

> When confronted with a simple choice between two possible interpretations of some specific statutory provision, the presumption

90 *Ashby*, above note 88 at 229.

91 This fact alone should not be dispositive but may support a finding that the presumption is rebutted. See the discussion in Chapter 5, Section 5.5(g).

92 [1991] 1 AC 696 (HL) [*Brind*].

93 1950 ETS no 5.

> whereby the courts prefer that which avoids conflict between our domestic legislation and our international treaty obligations is a mere canon of construction which involves no importation of international law into the domestic field. . . . When Parliament has been content for so long to leave those who complain that their Convention rights have been infringed to seek their remedy in Strasbourg, it would be surprising suddenly to find that the judiciary had, without Parliament's aid, the means to incorporate the Convention into such an important area of domestic law and I cannot escape the conclusion that this would be a judicial usurpation of the legislative function.[94]

(c) Decisions since *Baker*

Decisions since *Baker* have confirmed, if only infrequently, that international legal considerations must inform discretionary decision making in proper cases and may inform subsequent judicial scrutiny of such decisions.

In *Németh v Canada (Justice)*, the Supreme Court of Canada invoked the international law of *non-refoulement* to persecution to control the highly discretionary decision of the minister of justice to surrender persons sought for extradition. The Némeths were Hungarian Roma who had been granted refugee status in Canada in 2001 following racially motivated attacks on them in Hungary. Two years after their recognition as refugees, Hungary issued an international arrest warrant for them on a charge of fraud. Following their committal for extradition by the Quebec Superior Court, the minister ordered their surrender to Hungary. They challenged the minister's decision on the basis that the principle of *non-refoulement* prevented their extradition to the very country from which they were granted refuge.[95]

Justice Cromwell for the court allowed the Némeths' appeal. His judgment turned on the interpretation of section 44(1) of the Extradition Act,[96] which requires the minister to refuse to make a surrender order if satisfied that (1) it would "be unjust or oppressive," or (2) the

---

94 *Brind*, above note 92 at 748.

95 *Németh v Canada (Justice)*, 2010 SCC 56 [*Németh*]. The case was heard and decided together with a companion case, *Gavrila v Canada (Justice)*, 2010 SCC 57, concerning extradition of a Roma refugee to Romania.

96 1999 SC, c 18.

extradition request is "made for the purpose of prosecuting or punishing the person by reason of their race, religion, nationality, ethnic origin, language, colour, political opinion, sex, sexual orientation, age, mental or physical disability or status or that the person's position may be prejudiced for any of those reasons." The minister considered only whether the surrender would be unjust or oppressive in all the circumstances. In doing so, Cromwell J held, the minister erred in law and acted unreasonably in failing to give sufficient weight to the scope of Canada's *non-refoulement* obligations, particularly as they relate to the second ground of impermissible surrender set out in section 44(1)(b).[97] He described this latter provision as "Canada's primary legislative vehicle to give effect to Canada's *non-refoulement* obligations when a refugee is sought for extradition."[98]

In a passage that recalls (without citing) the majority's approach in *Baker*, Cromwell J observed:

> In my view, the Minister applied incorrect legal principles and acted unreasonably in reaching his conclusions. His decision in this case related to the surrender for extradition of refugees to the country they fled. The Minister's approach to the exercise of his powers, in my respectful view, failed to give sufficient weight or scope to Canada's non-refoulement obligations in light of which those powers must be interpreted and applied. While the mandatory grounds for refusal set out in s. 44 must be considered as a whole, the most relevant provision in this case is the second branch of s. 44(1)(b) set out in the closing words of that subsection. This provision was included in the [Extradition Act] in part to give effect to Canada's non-refoulement obligations under the Refugee Convention in the extradition context. While the Minister considered the appellants' status as refugees and examined current conditions in Hungary, his approach in practical terms gave their refugee status no weight and took too narrow a view of Canada's non-refoulement obligations.[99]

97 *Németh*, above note 95 at paras 56–8.

98 *Németh*, *ibid* at para 77; see also para 102 describing "an important purpose of s. 44(1)(b)" as "to implement Canada's non-refoulement obligations in the extradition setting."

99 *Németh*, above note 95 at para 58.

The Federal Court of Appeal has confirmed that international law considerations, including unimplemented treaties, are relevant in judicial review of discretionary decisions, while cautioning that the discretion to be exercised rests with the decision maker and not the reviewing court.

In a decision of Stratas JA in chambers, later seemingly approved by the Federal Court of Appeal, the learned judge explained that, under a given legislative provision,

> an administrative decision-maker might be able to exercise its discretion in more than one way. And it may be that one particular exercise of discretion is more consistent with international law standards than others. When the administrative decision-maker refrains from exercising its discretion in the way that is more consistent with international law standards and instead exercises its discretion in another way, a party can challenge the reasonableness of that exercise of discretion, invoking the decision-maker's failure to follow international law standards. But given the status of international law where domestic law is unambiguous, this is simply an argument that the decision-maker failed to follow a non-binding policy consideration. That failure may or may not render the decision unreasonable. Much will depend on the importance of the international law standard in the context of the particular case and the breadth of the margin of appreciation or range of acceptability and defensibility the decision-maker enjoys in interpreting and applying the legislative provision authorizing its decision.[100]

To similar effect is *Budlakoti v Canada (Minister of Citizenship and Immigration)*, where Stratas JA for the Federal Court of Appeal observed that the appellant may invoke a Canadian treaty obligation "as a matter that the Minister should consider" in a decision under section 5(4) of the Citizenship Act, but it would be for the minister to assess the

---

100 *Gitxaala Nation v Her Majesty the Queen*, 2015 FCA 73 (in chambers) at para 18. For decisions of the Federal Court of Appeal appearing to approve this approach, see, e.g., *Canada (Attorney General) v Kattenburg*, 2020 FCA 164 at para 25 and *Entertainment Software Association v Society of Composers, Authors and Music Publishers of Canada*, 2020 FCA 100 at para 77.

relevance and weight of that consideration and others, subject to potential review by the Federal Court.[101]

In *Turp v Canada (Foreign Affairs)*, Nadon JA for the Federal Court of Appeal rejected the argument that *Baker* required the minister to "give significant, if not decisive, weight to humanitarian considerations" in a decision whether to licence the export of Canadian-made light armoured vehicles to Saudi Arabia. Against this proposition, Nadon JA relied on the authority of *Suresh v Canada (Minister of Citizenship and Immigration)* that it is for the minister to weigh the relevant factors, not the reviewing court.[102]

While the facts of *Vavilov* did not involve a discretionary decision, the depiction of international law there as a legal constraint on administrative decision making, and its express reliance on *Baker* as authority that "international treaties and conventions, even where they have not been implemented domestically by statute, can help to inform whether a decision was a reasonable exercise of administrative power,"[103] affirm that judicial review of discretionary decisions for non-compliance with the state's international legal obligations remains available. What is less clear, however, is how much weight will be given to international legal considerations in a given case.

(d) Statutory discretions and the presumption of conformity

In Chapter 5, I argued that while treaties have no direct effect in domestic law without implementation, the presumption of conformity accords them a degree of indirect effect.[104] In most cases, the degree of effect is modest: In a matter of statutory construction, the presumption permits a treaty to determine the outcome of a contest between two or more interpretive options. But where the provision under consideration is one conferring discretion on a decision maker, as in *Baker*, the effect of applying the presumption of conformity is notably more pronounced. The presumption of conformity, when applied to a grant

101 *Budlakoti v Canada (Minister of Citizenship and Immigration)*, 2015 FCA 139 at para 54 (citing *Baker*, above note 33).

102 *Turp v Canada (Foreign Affairs)*, 2018 FCA 133 at para 56, quoting *Suresh v Canada (Minister of Citizenship and Immigration)*, 2001 SCC 1 at paras 37–8.

103 *Vavilov*, above note 1 at para 114.

104 See Chapter 5, Section 5.8.

of statutory discretion, invites the court to review the discretionary decision not only on the ordinary grounds established in administrative law but also for consistency with international legal norms, whether implemented in the decision maker's enabling legislation or not. For some, this application of the presumption of conformity comes too close to giving direct effect to a treaty in domestic law. Justice Iacobucci's reasons in *Baker*, and the decisions in *Ashby* and *Brind*, are instances of courts declining to construe a statutory discretion in the light of international law on the grounds that doing so conflicts with the implementation requirement and usurps the legislative function.

The methodology in *Ashby*, *Brind*, and Iacobucci J's reasons in *Baker* can be understood as follows. In each case the court began with the rule that statutes be read as presumptively consistent with the state's international obligations. Each judgment appears to accept the existence of the presumption and agree with it in principle. Yet in each case the judge or court declined to apply the presumption for fear of violating the fundamental principle that the Crown concludes treaties, Parliament implements them, and the judiciary looks to the legislature – not the executive – to know what the law is. These judgments indicate that the presumption of conformity is rebutted where its application in the case at bar is inconsistent with the implementation requirement, the separation of powers, and (I would add) the self-government principle that informs these doctrines.

Knowing that the presumption of conformity is rebuttable on these grounds is helpful but hardly dispositive. The majority and dissent in *Baker* were divided on the propriety of applying the presumption in the case before them. The majority found no violation of the implementation requirement or the separation of powers doctrine, or at least no sufficiently important violation to rebut the application of the presumption. By contrast, Iacobucci J viewed this application of the presumption as a threat to the balance of executive and legislative power in Canada's parliamentary tradition. Both sides of the debate agreed upon the importance of the implementation requirement and the separation of powers. The difference of opinion turned not on the significance of these doctrines but on the degree of zeal with which courts should vindicate them. In my view, courts should take the following factors into consideration.

First, a court should consider the extent to which applying the presumption of conformity to the case at bar will relieve the executive of the need to seek implementation of the treaty by Parliament or the provincial legislatures. At the heart of the separation of powers doctrine is the conviction that the only proper way to subject self-governing peoples to law is through the representative, deliberative, participatory, consensual, and public lawmaking procedures of the parliamentary process. The implementation requirement vindicates our commitment to this oldest of constitutional ideals. Yet, as we have seen, there is a sense in which the presumption of conformity inevitably tempers the implementation requirement, if only to a minor extent. A court faced with a contentious application of the presumption, such as its application to a statutory discretion, must balance due awareness of the constitutional importance of the implementation requirement with a realistic assessment of the extent to which the presumption's application in the case at bar would set the requirement aside. A workable rule may be that a court should decline to apply the presumption only where to apply it would wholly or significantly remove the necessity of implementing legislation.

A second consideration should be the content of the treaty obligation in issue. Treaty provisions of a purposive, interpretive, or general nature will often be more susceptible to judicial application by means of the presumption of conformity than specific, particular, or detailed commitments, which will usually require implementing legislation to be given domestic legal effect. The same reasoning suggests that international human rights guarantees, which are frequently drafted as broad statements of principle rather than specific requirements, will generally be more amenable to application through the presumption than more narrowly drawn international commitments.[105] This second point is really an elaboration of the first, namely that courts should refrain from applying the presumption where to do so would make implementation of the treaty significantly unnecessary.

A third consideration, though it did not arise in *Baker*, may be the federalism implications of applying the presumption of conformity to a

105 I offer this as a generalization only. It is clear a human rights instrument may contain specific provisions requiring explicit legislative implementation. Likewise, other international instruments may contain broadly phrased commitments, such as the national treatment obligations found in investment treaties.

statutory discretion conferred by a provincial legislature. As discussed in Chapter 4,[106] treaty-making is regarded in Canada as a prerogative of the federal government. Yet the presumption of conformity applies to all Canadian statutes, whether federal, provincial, or territorial. Applying the presumption to provincial statutes does not violate the federal principle, even though the treaty in question was concluded at the federal level, so long as the presumption involves no significant incursion of federal power into the provincial sphere. That is usually so; I am not aware of any Canadian case in which a court refused to apply the presumption of conformity on federalism grounds, and it seems unlikely that the presumption would normally raise federalism concerns. But where the presumption is invoked to control the ambit of a provincial decision maker's statutory discretion, the objection might arise. A court may particularly hesitate to apply the presumption where doing so would permit a federally concluded treaty, the subject matter of which falls within an area of provincial jurisdiction, to be used to oblige delegates of provincial statutory powers to act consistently with that treaty. This is admittedly speculation on my part as no such case seems to have yet come before a Canadian court.

Finally, courts should be cognizant of the respective roles of legislatures and judges in the Canadian reception system. The system assigns the task of vindicating the principle of self-government to Parliament and the provincial legislatures, in exercise of their sovereignty to legislate in violation of international law and their discretion as to whether, and to what extent, to implement treaty obligations incurred by the executive. In contrast, the role of asserting the principle of respect for international law is confided in the judiciary. It is the judiciary that assures the incorporation of customary international law by the common law. And it is the judiciary that applies the presumption of conformity with international law to Canadian laws. I have suggested that the reception system works by balancing the twin imperatives of self-government and respect for international law.[107] Courts risk upsetting that balance when they take it upon themselves to vindicate self-government rather than leave that responsibility to the legislature. This is not to say that the presumption of conformity is unrebuttable.

---

106 At Sections 4.1(a) and (e).

107 See Chapter 1, Section 1.2(c).

Rather, it is to say that courts should depart from the principle of respect for international law that founds the presumption only where to do otherwise would jeopardize the self-governing character of our parliamentary and constitutional arrangements.

Applying these considerations to *Baker* suggests, in my view, that the case is rightly decided on this point. Justice Iacobucci is correct to notice the separation of powers problems arising from applying the presumption to a grant of statutory discretion. Yet the learned judge gives these problems too much weight in this instance. The presumption clearly gave real legal significance to the Convention on the Rights of the Child 1989 by requiring the minister to exercise her discretion consistently with the values it discloses. Yet it cannot be said that this holding wholly or significantly removed the necessity of implementing legislation to give effect to the treaty in domestic law. At most, the legal effect of the majority's judgment was to render the best interests of the child a mandatory, but not necessarily determinative, consideration for decision makers acting on humanitarian and compassionate grounds under the Immigration Act. The Convention's many other substantive and procedural guarantees, some of which are remarkably far-reaching, are untouched by *Baker*. The majority relied only on the Convention's broad statements of principle, not on its more specific requirements. The limited degree of quasi-implementation effected by the majority in *Baker* demonstrates due respect for Canada's international obligations under the Convention without threatening our self-government.

Looking at the question more broadly, I suggest that to apply the presumption of conformity to provisions granting discretionary decision-making powers will generally be appropriate. The courts presume that legislatures do not intend by their Acts to bring the state into violation of its international obligations. This presumption is not only sound judicial policy but is also an accurate depiction of legislative intent in most cases, for neither our legislatures nor our governments have much to gain from violating international laws, particularly where (as is usually the case) the laws in issue derive from a treaty freely entered into by the state. If the legislature did not intend to violate international law, it surely cannot have intended to delegate the power to do so to administrative decision makers exercising statutory discretions. Conformity with international law is therefore rightly regarded as an implicit limit on the powers of administrative decision makers in most cases.

"The Constitution," said Lord Atkin, "is not to be mocked by substituting executive for legislative interference with freedom."[108] By effectively extending the presumption of conformity from statutory interpretation to judicial review of administrative decisions, the court in *Baker* indicated that delegates of legislative authority, like legislatures themselves, are presumed to observe the requirements of international law. While there may be grounds for finding that presumption to be rebutted in special cases, *Baker* seems to establish that the default position of Canadian administrative law, like that of Canadian law in general, is respect for international law. *Vavilov* appears to confirm this.

9.5 Legitimate expectations

In *Minister for Immigration and Ethnic Affairs v Teoh*,[109] the High Court of Australia held that ratification by Australia of the Convention on the Rights of the Child 1989 gave rise to a legitimate expectation that the minister exercising his discretion would act in conformity with the treaty, in spite of its lack of implementation in Australian law, by regarding the best interests of the applicant's child as a primary consideration in determining whether to grant him a permanent entry permit. Chief Justice Gummow and Deane J observed:

> [R]atification by Australia of an international convention is not to be dismissed as a merely platitudinous or ineffectual act, particularly when the instrument evidences internationally accepted standards to be applied by courts and administrative authorities in dealing with basic human rights affecting the family and children. Rather, ratification of a convention is a positive statement by the executive government of this country to the world and to the Australian people that the executive government and its agencies will act in accordance with the Convention. That positive statement is an adequate foundation for a legitimate expectation, absent statutory or executive indications to the contrary, that administrative decision-makers will act

108 *James v Cowan*, [1932] AC 542 (PC) at 558.

109 (1995) 183 CLR 273 (HCA). See also *Tavita v Minister of Immigration*, [1994] 2 NZLR 257 at 266 (CA).

> in conformity with the Convention and treat the best interests of the children as "a primary consideration." It is not necessary that a person seeking to set up such a legitimate expectation should be aware of the Convention or should personally entertain the expectation; it is enough that the expectation is reasonable in the sense that there are adequate materials to support it.[110]

To allow unimplemented treaties to found legitimate expectations to procedural (and perhaps substantive) rights accords such treaties palpable legal weight. Unsurprisingly, the decision has been controversial.

In England, *Teoh* received initial support from the Court of Appeal in *R v Secretary of State for the Home Department, Ex parte Ahmed*,[111] in which Lord Woolf MR and Hobhouse LJ accepted in principle that the UK's entrance into a treaty could give rise to a legitimate expectation on which the public in general would be entitled to rely. More support came from the Queen's Bench Division in *R v Uxbridge Magistrates' Court, ex parte Adimi*, in which *Teoh* was described as a "seminal judgment."[112] Though it is not strictly an English court, it is notable that *Teoh* was accepted by the Privy Council in *Thomas v Baptiste*.[113]

For all this support, *Teoh* remains controversial. More recent English decisions have expressed reservations about the case,[114] and the High Court of Australia itself has questioned it.[115]

Teoh has made little headway in Canada. The case was not cited by the Supreme Court of Canada in *Baker*. Justice L'Heureux-Dubé for the majority recognized legitimate expectations as a factor affecting the content of the duty of fairness, yet held that, on the facts, the Convention on the Rights of the Child did not give rise to a legitimate ex-

---

110 *Teoh, ibid* at para 34.

111 [1999] Imm LR 22 (Eng CA) at 36.

112 [2000] 3 WLR 434 (Eng QB) at 456.

113 [1999] 3 WLR 249 (PC). This case was considered by the Court of Appeal for Ontario in *Ahani v Canada (Minister of Citizenship and Immigration)* (2002), 58 OR (3d) 107 at paras 50–7, 98.

114 For example, *R (European Roma Rights Centre) v Immigration Officer at Prague Airport*, [2004] QB 811 (Eng CA). See S Fatima, "The Domestic Application of International Law in British Courts" in C Bradley, ed, *The Oxford Handbook of Comparative Foreign Relations Law* (New York: Oxford University Press, 2019) at 497.

115 *Re Minister for Immigration and Multicultural Affairs, ex parte Lam* (2003), 195 CLR 502 (HCA).

pectation to specific procedural rights or the application of particular criteria. No supporting reasons were given for this conclusion, nor was there any discussion of whether Ms. Baker was aware of the Convention or needed to be. Justice L'Heureux-Dubé left the question slightly open by declaring it "unnecessary to decide whether an international instrument ratified by Canada could, in other circumstances, give rise to a legitimate expectation."[116] Advocates of the *Teoh* approach may take some small comfort in that, but they will take little in the judgment of the court below. Justice Strayer for the Federal Court of Appeal observed that, in Canada, the doctrine of legitimate expectations cannot create substantive rights, and that what Ms. Baker sought here was a substantive, not a procedural, matter. Justice Strayer went on explicitly to reject the reasoning of the majority in *Teoh* and adopt the dissent of McHugh J.[117] Justice Strayer did purport to leave open "the interesting question of whether the ratification of multilateral conventions can in any realistic sense be regarded as a meaningful representation to all Canadians that public affairs will thereafter be conducted in accordance with those conventions."[118] Nonetheless, this rejection of *Teoh*, combined with the Supreme Court's tacit approval of this approach, suggest that the doctrine of legitimate expectation will make as few inroads into Canadian reception law as it has in the rest of Canadian law.

---

116 *Baker*, above note 33 at para 29.

117 *Baker* FCA, above note 78 at paras 34–9.

118 *Ibid* at para 31.

10 International law and Indigenous peoples

In the past, the intersection of public international law and the Canadian law of Aboriginal rights has not been very fruitful. Twentieth-century international law and practice had rather little to say on the rights of Indigenous peoples. Few instruments specifically addressed their interests, while general international law neglected their claims to sovereignty and recognition. Though international scrutiny has sometimes played a role in the development of Canadian policy, Canadian Aboriginal law has, to date, developed largely independently from international legal requirements. But Indigenous peoples, particularly from this country, have long pressed their case on the world stage,[1] and the recognition of international norms concerning Indigenous rights is a major feature of international law in the early twenty-first century. Meanwhile, international legal issues are entering the Canadian law of Indigenous rights in new and developing ways.

---

1 The effort famously began with Deskaheh's mission to the League of Nations on behalf of the Six Nations of the Iroquois in 1923–4. See Deskaheh, "The Redman's Appeal for Justice" (6 August 1923), online: http://cendoc.docip.org/collect/deskaheh/index/assoc/HASH0102/5e23c4be.dir/R612-11-28075-30626-8.pdf. On the history of Indigenous international legal activity, see D Sanders, "The Re-Emergence of Indigenous Questions in International Law" [1983] *Canadian Human Rights Yearbook* 3 [Sanders]; I Washinawatok, "International Emergence: Twenty-One Years at the United Nations" (1998) 3:1 *New York City Law Review* 41 [Washinawatok]; SJ Anaya & L Rodriguez-Piñero, "The Making of the UNDRIP" in J Hohmann & M Weller, eds, *The UN Declaration on the Rights of Indigenous Peoples: A Commentary* (Oxford: Oxford University Press, 2018) [Anaya & Rodriguez-Piñero].

Three key issues demand consideration. The first is the significance in Canadian law of international norms concerning Indigenous peoples. By far the most important statement of such norms today is the United Nations Declaration on the Rights of Indigenous Peoples.[2] The Declaration's impact on Canadian law is potentially momentous. The second issue is the constitutional duty of the Crown to consult, and potentially accommodate, Indigenous peoples. Does this duty constrain the foreign affairs prerogative? Finally and relatedly, no contemporary account of international law in Canada is complete without considering the remarkable reception law provisions included in modern treaties between Indigenous peoples and federal, provincial, and territorial governments.

10.1 International legal provisions on Indigenous peoples

This is not the place for anything like a complete account of the international law of Indigenous rights.[3] For present purposes, I briefly review the main instruments, distinguishing formally binding instruments (treaties) from today's leading, if formally non-binding, instrument, the Declaration. First, however, we must consider the legal character of historic and modern treaties between the Crown and Indigenous peoples.

(a) Possible international character of Crown–Indigenous treaties

The fact that Canadian (and indeed Anglo-American) law uses the term "treaty" to describe both agreements governed by international law and agreements between colonial authorities and Indigenous peoples is not mere coincidence. It is evidence of the original, nation-to-nation conception of relations between "Old World" and "New World" powers. Just as British and French kings made agreements with other European princes, so too did they make agreements with the Indigenous

2 GA Res 61/295 (2 October 2007) [UN Declaration].

3 See, e.g., SJ Anaya, *International Human Rights and Indigenous Peoples* (Frederick, MD: Aspen Publishing, 2009); J Hohmann & M Weller, eds, *The UN Declaration on the Rights of Indigenous Peoples: A Commentary* (Oxford: Oxford University Press, 2018); D Newman, ed, *Research Handbook on the International Law of Indigenous Rights* (Cheltenham: Edward Elgar Publishing, 2022).

leaders they encountered in North America. All such agreements were known as treaties because they were fundamentally the same thing: solemn pacts between sovereigns. As Professor Gunn explains,

> [U]ntil relatively recently, European nations took no issue with recognizing the international standing of many Indigenous peoples, engaging consistently in treaties of alliance, cession and protection, which often resulted in benefits for both parties. Europeans regarded Indigenous peoples as sufficiently autonomous to enter into such treaties.[4]

Similarly, Professor Grammond (as he then was) notes that in the earliest era of historic treaties, European powers "recognized that the Indigenous peoples may hold sovereignty over their lands and that treaties were necessary to transfer that sovereignty to colonial powers."[5] Practice was uneven, however, and tended heavily toward European self-interest. As Professor Sanders explains,

> At one end of the spectrum there was recognition of existing property rights and, in time, of the right of the people to regain independence. At the other end of the spectrum, no pre-existing rights were recognized. The indigenous population became a numerical minority and the colonially-established nation state assumed full internal sovereignty over them. The process was always colonial in character.[6]

While initially recognizing Indigenous peoples as sovereigns capable of contracting treaties, international law (as conceived mainly by Europeans) began to insist that treaties must be between states, and that Indigenous communities were, conveniently, not states. As explained in the well-known award in the *Island of Palmas* arbitration (1928), Indigenous peoples were not (now) "recognized as members of the community of nations" with the result that agreements between In-

4 B Gunn, "Exploring the International Character of Treaties 1–11 and the Legal Consequences" in O Fitzgerald, V Hughes, & M Jewett, eds, *Reflections on Canada's Past, Present and Future in International Law* (Waterloo: Centre for International Governance Innovation, 2018) [Gunn] at 117.

5 S Grammond, "Treaties as Constitutional Agreements" in P Oliver, P Macklem, & N Des Rosiers, eds, *The Oxford Handbook of the Canadian Constitution* (New York: Oxford University Press, 2017) at 308.

6 Sanders, above note 1 at 3–4.

digenous peoples and states were "not, in the international law sense, treaties or conventions capable of creating rights and obligations such as may, in international law, arise out of treaties."[7] As international law swung away from recognition of Indigenous sovereignty, Canadian law did likewise. In the succinct words of Professor Imai, "So instead of Indigenous nations capable of making treaties, there was a new legal framework based on 'savages' who were not capable of land ownership and therefore had nothing to give consent to."[8]

Canadian courts have affirmed that "Indian" treaties are not treaties in the international law sense. Justice Riddell made the point starkly in *Sero v Gault* (1922):

> It is well-known that claims have been made from the time of Joseph Brant that the Indians were not in reality subjects of the King but an independent people – allies of His Majesty – and in a measure at least exempt from the civil laws governing the true subject. "Treaties" have been made wherein they are called "faithful allies" and the like, and there is extant an (unofficial) opinion of Mr. (afterwards Chief) Justice Powell that the Indians, so long as they are within their villages, are not subject to the ordinary laws of the Province.
>
> As to the so-called treaties, John Beverley Robinson, Attorney-General for Upper Canada (afterwards Sir John Beverley Robinson, C.J.), in an official letter to Robert Wilmot Horton, Under Secretary of State for War and Colonies, March 14, 1824, said: –
>
> > "To talk of treaties with the Mohawk Indians, residing in the heart of one of the most populous districts of Upper Canada, upon lands purchased for them and given to them by the British Government, is much the same, in my humble opinion, as to

7 *Island of Palmas Case (Netherlands/United States)* (1928), 2 UN RIAA 829 at 858. See also *Cayuga Indians (Great Britain) v United States* (1926), 6 UN RIAA 173 at 176–7 (holding that the Cayuga Nation was "not a legal unit of international law" and that "So far as an Indian tribe exists as a legal unit, it is by virtue of the sovereign nation within whose territory the tribe occupies the land, and so far only as that law recognizes it").

8 S Imai, "Consult, Consent, and Veto: International Norms and Canadian Treaties" in J Borrows & M Coyle, eds, *The Right Relationship: Reimagining the Implementation of Historical Treaties* (Toronto: University of Toronto Press, 2017) at 372.

> talk of making a treaty of alliance with the Jews in Duke street or with the French emigrants who have settled in England. . . ."[9]

Supreme Court of Canada authority on the point is less stridently expressed but reaches the same result: "While it may be helpful in some instances to analogize the principles of international treaty law to Indian treaties, these principles are not determinative. An Indian treaty is unique; it is an agreement *sui generis* which is neither created nor terminated according to the rules of international law."[10] The Supreme Court implicitly affirmed this denial of the international law character of Crown–Indigenous agreements in *Shot Both Sides v Canada*, dismissing an appeal where Rennie JA of the Federal Court of Appeal criticized the trial judge for treating such agreements as international instruments.[11]

One may wonder whether this is correct as a matter of international law. Commenting on the international legal status of the Treaty of Waitangi 1840,[12] no less an authority than Professor Brownlie concluded that Britain "conducted itself on the basis that relations with the Maori tribes were governed by the rules of international law" and that "the fact that *subsequent* developments in international law doctrine denied treaty-making capacity to what were described as 'Native Chiefs and Peoples' is irrelevant."[13] By this same reasoning, many historic treaties between the Crown and Indigenous peoples in British North America could properly be regarded as treaties in the international law sense.

Such reasoning, however, may now be precluded (at least in Canadian courts and tribunals) by *Shot Both Sides*. There, O'Bonsawin J for the Supreme Court of Canada affirmed that Crown–Indigenous treaties are "enforceable from the date of execution" without reference to

---

9 *Sero v Gault* (1922), 64 DLR 327 (Ont SC) at 330.

10 *Simon v The Queen*, [1985] 2 SCR 387 at 404; see also *R v Sioui*, [1990] 1 SCR 1025 at 1038 ("At the time with which we are concerned relations with Indian tribes fell somewhere between the kind of relations conducted between sovereign states and the relations that such states had with their own citizens").

11 2024 SCC 12 [*Shot Both Sides*], affirming *Queen v Jim Shot Both Sides*, 2022 FCA 20.

12 (1840–1841) 29 *British and Foreign State Papers* 1111.

13 I Brownlie, *Treaties and Indigenous Peoples* (Oxford: Clarendon Press, 1992) at 8 (emphasis in original). See also Lord McNair, *The Law of Treaties* (Oxford, UK: Clarendon Press, 1961) at 52–3.

section 35(1) of the Constitution Act, 1982,[14] and seemingly also without the need for implementing legislation. This latter point is not expressly considered by O'Bonsawin J, however. Indeed, a considered authority of the Court of Appeal for Ontario to the effect that Crown–Indigenous treaties do require legislative implementation[15] is neglected in her reasons. So, too, is the practice of both the federal[16] and provincial/territorial[17] legislatures to implement modern treaties by statute. Be that as it may, the result of *Shot Both Sides* is that, from a reception law perspective, Crown–Indigenous agreements differ fundamentally from international treaties in that the former are self-executing while the latter are not.

The present state of Canadian law, therefore, appears to be that treaties between the Crown and Indigenous peoples are not, as a matter of Canadian law, to be regarded as international in character. One consequence of this is that they are not interpreted according to the interpretive rules set out in the Vienna Convention on the Law of Treaties 1969,[18] but according to principles developed in Supreme Court of Canada jurisprudence.[19] A perhaps more important consequence is that treaties are subject to justifiable infringement according to the *R v*

14 *Shot Both Sides*, above note 11 at paras 37–8.

15 *R v Agawa* (1988), 65 OR (2d) 505 (CA), Blair JA at 509 (calling Canadian Indian treaties "not self- executing" and holding that they "can acquire the force of law in Canada only to the extent that they are protected by the Constitution or by statute").

16 E.g., Nisga'a Final Agreement Act, SC 2000, c 7, s 4(1); Tłı̨chǫ Land Claims and Self-Government Act, SC 2005, c 1, s 3(1); Labrador Inuit Land Claims Agreement Act, SC 2005, c 27, s 5(1); Nunavik Inuit Land Claims Agreement Act, SC 2008, c 2, s 5(1); Tsawwassen First Nation Final Agreement Act, SC 2008, c 32, s 4(1); Eeyou Marine Region Land Claims Agreement Act, SC 2011, c 20, s 5(1); Yale First Nation Final Agreement Act, SC 2013, c 25, s 4(1); Tla'amin Final Agreement Act, SC 2014, c 11, s 4(1); Délı̨nę Final Self-Government Agreement Act, SC 2015, c 24, s 4(1); Anishinabek Nation Governance Agreement Act, SC 2022, c 9, s 1; Self-Government Treaty Recognizing the Whitecap Dakota Nation/Wapaha Ska Dakota Oyate Act, SC 2023, c 22, s 4(1).

17 E.g., Nisga'a Final Agreement Act, RSBC 1999, c 2, s 3(1); Tłı̨chǫ Land Claims and Self-government Agreement Act, SNWT 2003, c 28, s 4(1); Labrador Inuit Land Claims Agreement Act, SNL 2004, c L-3.1 s 3(2); Tsawwassen First Nation Final Agreement Act, SBC 2007, c 39, s 3(1); Tla'amin Final Agreement Act, SBC 2013, c 2, s 3(1); Délı̨nę Final Self-Government Agreement Act, SNWT 2015, c 3, s 4(1).

18 See the discussion in Chapter 7, Section 7.6.

19 See the summary of these principles in *R v Marshall*, [1999] 3 SCR 456 at para 78.

Sparrow[20] analysis applicable to Aboriginal rights generally. As Professor Gunn points out, the justifiable infringement scheme of Canadian constitutional law tolerates breaches of treaties in domestic law that international law would not.[21]

(b) Indigenous rights protection in international conventions

The international human rights movement that began after the Second World War has produced treaties directed at the particular conditions of vulnerable groups such as racial and ethnic minorities,[22] women,[23] children,[24] migrants,[25] and the disabled.[26] One group that has yet to be the subject of a major UN human rights treaty is Indigenous peoples. There are, however, two conventions of the International Labour Organization of note,[27] even if Canada is not a party to either of them. They are the Indigenous and Tribal Populations Convention (no 107)

---

20 [1990] 1 SCR 1075.

21 Gunn, above note 4 at 127–8. Article 37(1) of the United Nations Declaration on the Rights of Indigenous Peoples affirms, "Indigenous peoples have the right to the recognition, observance and enforcement of treaties, agreements and other constructive arrangements concluded with States or their successors and to have States honour and respect such treaties, agreements and other constructive arrangements." It is a notion that may prove difficult to reconcile with the model for justifiable infringement of treaty rights propounded in *Sparrow* and later cases. Compare, for instance, the rights limitation provision in art 46(2) (which permits limitation of Indigenous rights to the extent required to protect the human rights of others) with the account of permissible justifications of s 35 rights infringements in *Delgamuukw v British Columbia*, [1997] 3 SCR 1010 at para 165 (which expressly allows infringements of Aboriginal title for "general economic development").

22 For example, International Convention on the Elimination of All Forms of Racial Discrimination 1966, [1970] Can TS no 28.

23 For example, Convention on the Elimination of All Forms of Discrimination against Women 1979, [1982] Can TS no 31.

24 For example, Convention on the Rights of the Child 1989, [1992] Can TS no 3.

25 For example, International Convention on the Protection of the Rights of All Migrant Workers and Members of Their Families 1990, (1991) 30 ILM 1517.

26 For example, Convention on the Rights of Persons with Disabilities 2006 (adopted 13 December 2006), not yet in force. Canada signed the convention on 30 March 2007.

27 For an account of the ILO's early interest in Indigenous peoples, see Sanders, above note 1 at 19–20.

1957[28] and its revision, the Indigenous and Tribal Peoples in Independent Countries Convention (no 169) 1989.[29] Convention 107 came to be regarded as assimilationist, promoting improvements to Indigenous welfare but neglecting Indigenous political and cultural aspirations. Convention 169 is a notable break from its predecessor in this respect, and much closer in vision and approach to the United Nations Declaration on the Rights of Indigenous Peoples (discussed below). Notably, Convention 169 includes, in article 15(2), a duty on governments to consult Indigenous peoples when making decisions pertaining to their lands. Yet Convention 169 initially met with skepticism from Indigenous peoples and organizations due to their lack of participation in its development.[30]

The general lack of formally binding, broadly supported multilateral agreements concerning Indigenous peoples does not mean that Indigenous peoples cannot find support for their rights and aspirations in international law. Indigenous rights are, after all, a type of human rights. The UN Human Rights Committee has found Canada in breach of article 27 of the International Covenant on Civil and Political Rights 1966 (which protects the cultural, religious, and linguistic rights of minorities) in cases brought by Indigenous complainants.[31] Both the Human Rights Committee and the Committee on the Elimination of Racial Discrimination have frequently admonished Canada on its Indigenous rights record.[32] Other UN human rights treaties are

---

28 ILO Convention (No 107) concerning the Protection and Integration of Indigenous and other, Tribal and Semi-Tribal Populations in Independent Countries, (1959) 328 UNTS 247.

29 ILO Convention (No 169) concerning Indigenous and Tribal Peoples in Independent Countries 1989, (1989) 28 ILM 1382.

30 Anaya & Rodriguez-Piñero, above note 1 at 43–5. See also Washinawatok, above note 1 at 48–9.

31 UN Human Rights Committee, Communication No R.6/24, *Lovelace v Canada* (1981), UN Doc Supp No 40 (A/36/40) at 166; UN Human Rights Committee, Communication No 167/1984, *Lubicon Lake Band v Canada* (1990), UN Doc CCPR/C/38/D/167/1984; UN Human Rights Committee, Communication No 2020/2010, *McIvor and Grismer* (2018), UN Doc CCPR/C/124/D/2020/2010.

32 See, e.g., UN Committee on the Elimination of Racial Discrimination, "Concluding Observations on the Combined Twenty-First to Twenty-Third Periodic Reports of Canada," UN Doc CERD/C/CAN/CO/21-23 (13 September 2017) and UN Human Rights Committee, "Concluding Observations on the Sixth Period Report of Canada," UN Doc CCPR/C/CAN/CO/6 (13 August 2015). Topics of continuing concern include violence against Indigenous women and girls, disregard

similarly relevant to Indigenous peoples, though most do not address them explicitly. A limited but notable exception is the Convention on the Rights of the Child 1989, which affirms the right of Indigenous children "in community with other members of his or her group, to enjoy his or her own culture, to profess and practise his or her own religion, or to use his or her own language."[33]

Another avenue, though Canada is at best a reticent participant in it, is the Inter-American Commission on Human Rights. That body is responsible for supervising compliance by members of the Organization of American States (OAS) with the American Declaration on the Rights and Duties of Man 1948.[34] The commission accepts individual petitions alleging violations of the Declaration by OAS states including (since 1990) Canada.[35] A petition by the Hul'qumi'num Treaty Group (representing six Indigenous nations on Vancouver Island) challenging the expropriation of their traditional lands in the late nineteenth century was determined to be admissible in 2009.[36] In 2016, the commission issued a report on murdered and missing Indigenous women and girls in British Columbia.[37]

Yet, for the most part, Indigenous peoples (especially in Canada) still cannot look to international law as a source of indisputably binding, Indigenous-specific limits on state actions affecting them. The paucity of formally binding international norms on Indigenous rights is reflected in Canadian law by a lack of jurisprudence on the reception of international law in matters of Aboriginal rights. There has, quite simply, been little to receive. Apart from occasional cases arising out of the

---

of Indigenous lands and titles, overrepresentation of Indigenous peoples in the criminal justice system, and the welfare of Indigenous children.

33 Above note 24 art 30.

34 OAS res XXX. Reprinted in *Basic Documents Pertaining to Human Rights in the Inter-American System*, OEA/Ser.L.V/II.82 doc 6 rev 1 at 17 (1992).

35 See M Macaulay, "Canada and the Inter-American Human Rights System" (2022) Hors-série (juin 2022) *Revue québécoise de droit international* 15.

36 *Hul'qumi'num Treaty Group v Canada* (2009), Inter-Am Comm HR, No 105/09, Annual Report of the Inter-American Commission: 2009, OEA/Ser.L/V/II/Doc 5, rev 1.

37 OAS, Inter-American Commission on Human Rights, *Missing and Murdered Indigenous Women in British Columbia, Canada*, OR OEA/Ser.L/V/II. Doc.30/14 (2016).

federal Migratory Birds Convention Act[38] and a few other instances,[39] Canadian Aboriginal law and international law have rarely intersected.

(c) The United Nations Declaration on the Rights of Indigenous Peoples

The modern international law of Indigenous rights is dominated by a formally non-binding instrument: the United Nations Declaration on the Rights of Indigenous Peoples.[40] The Declaration is vast, addressing not only civil, political, economic, social, and cultural rights, but also matters of peculiar concern to Indigenous peoples such as rights to lands, territories, and resources; cultural and spiritual traditions; free, prior, and informed consent to measures affecting them; redress for historic wrongs; environmental protection; economic development; and the observance of treaties.

(i) The Declaration's international legal status

The Declaration is the product of decades of efforts by Indigenous peoples. Long delayed by controversy and lack of support by Canada and other colonial states,[41] the Declaration was finally adopted as a resolution of the UN General Assembly in 2007 over the opposition of four states with significant Indigenous populations: Canada, Australia, New Zealand, and the United States. These dissenters have all since changed their position and indicated their support for the Declaration.

Canada's about-face started with a November 2010 "statement of support" from the federal government, which nevertheless emphasized that the Declaration remained "an aspirational document" that is "non-legally binding" and "does not reflect customary international law nor change Canadian laws."[42] The federal government then lifted

38 Notably *R v Sikyea*, [1964] SCR 642 and *Daniels v White and the Queen*, [1968] SCR 517.

39 For example, *Francis v The Queen*, [1956] SCR 618; *Mitchell v Canada (Minister of National Revenue)*, [2001] 1 SCR 911.

40 Above note 2.

41 See Anaya & Rodriguez-Piñero, above note 1 at 38–62.

42 Canada, "Canada's Statement of Support on the United Nations Declaration on the Rights of Indigenous Peoples" (12 November 2010), quoted in *Hupacasath First Nation v Canada*, 2013 FC 900 at para 51.

these qualifications in a May 2016 announcement at the United Nations in New York in which it described Canada as "now a full supporter, without qualification" of the Declaration and affirmed the state's "commitment to adopt and implement the Declaration in accordance with the Canadian Constitution."[43]

While Canada is now a supporter of the Declaration, the instrument's formal international legal status remains as it was in 2007: a non-binding resolution of the UN General Assembly. But we cannot blithely conclude from this that the Declaration is legally ineffective. While the Declaration is not binding on states merely by virtue of its adoption by the General Assembly, it may enjoy legal force by other avenues.

It is clear, for instance, that parts of the Declaration are declaratory of human rights principles binding on states as parties to UN and regional human rights treaties. The Declaration's provisions concerning equality and non-discrimination (article 2); the right to a nationality (article 6); life, liberty, and personal security (article 7(1)); and freedom from genocide (article 7(2)) all overlap with similar requirements of international human rights law.

Other provisions of the Declaration are novel and cannot easily be equated with established international human rights norms. But we cannot safely conclude that such provisions are not binding on states for that reason alone. While they are not binding as conventional international law, they may be (or come to be) declaratory of customary international law. Determining whether that is so requires careful study of contemporary state practice and *opinio juris*. Summarizing the legal status of the Declaration, Anaya and Rodriguez-Piñero conclude:

> Albeit clearly not binding in the same way that a treaty is, the Declaration relates to already existing human rights obligations of States, as demonstrated by the work of UN Treaty Bodies and other human rights mechanisms, and hence can be seen as embodying to some extent general principles of international law. In addition, insofar

---

43 Canada, "Canada Becomes a Full Supporter of the United Nations Declaration on the Rights of Indigenous Peoples" (10 May 2016), online: https://www.canada.ca/en/indigenous-northern-affairs/news/2016/05/canada-becomes-a-full-supporter-of-the-united-nations-declaration-on-the-rights-of-indigenous-peoples.html.

> as they connect with a pattern of consistent international and State practice, some aspects of the provisions of the Declaration can also be considered as a reflection of norms of customary international law.[44]

In short, the Declaration's international legal status is complex and changeable.

(ii) The Declaration's status in Canadian law

The Declaration's status in Canadian law is likewise complicated and evolving. It cannot, at present, be said that the Declaration is fully implemented in Canadian law the way treaty obligations sometimes are. That said, the Legislative Assembly of British Columbia, the federal Parliament, and the Northwest Territories' legislature have each enacted laws specifically aimed at achieving the Declaration's implementation in their respective jurisdictions over time. In addition to these Declaration Acts are other new laws, or amendments to existing laws, that aim to meet the Declaration's requirements in specific areas. Furthermore, the Declaration could have domestic legal consequences through the incorporation doctrine, the presumption of conformity with international law, or both.

BC's main Declaration-related law, and the first such enactment to be adopted in Canada, is the Declaration on the Rights of Indigenous Peoples Act.[45] Section 2 of the Act identifies its purposes as "to affirm the application of the Declaration to the laws of British Columbia," "to contribute to the implementation of the Declaration," and "to support the affirmation of, and develop relationships with, Indigenous governing bodies." Section 3 of the Act provides, "In consultation and cooperation with the Indigenous peoples in British Columbia, the government must take all measures necessary to ensure the laws of British Columbia are consistent with the Declaration." Section 4 concerns an "action plan to achieve the objectives of the Declaration." The government must prepare and implement the action plan in consultation and cooperation with Indigenous peoples. Section 5 provides for annual reporting "on the progress that has been made towards implementing" the section 3 (consistency) measures and "achieving the goals of the ac-

---

44 Anaya & Rodriguez-Piñero, above note 1 at 62.

45 SBC 2019, c 44.

tion plan." Sections 6 and 7 concern decision-making agreements providing for joint Indigenous–government exercise of statutory powers of decision or the consent of Indigenous governing bodies prior to the exercise of such decision powers.

The main federal law is the United Nations Declaration on the Rights of Indigenous Peoples Act.[46] It closely resembles the BC Act, the chief difference being the absence of provisions in respect of statutory powers of decision. Section 4 of the federal Act identifies its twin purposes as to "affirm the Declaration as a universal international human rights instrument with application in Canadian law" and to "provide a framework for the Government of Canada's implementation of the Declaration." Section 5 of the Act is nearly word for word the same as section 3 of the BC Act. It provides, "The Government of Canada must, in consultation and cooperation with Indigenous peoples, take all measures necessary to ensure that the laws of Canada are consistent with the Declaration." Section 6 (like BC's section 4) concerns "an action plan to achieve the objectives of the Declaration," while section 7 provides for reporting to Parliament on the measures taken under sections 5 and 6.

The Northwest Territories legislation is the United Nations Declaration on the Rights of Indigenous Peoples Implementation Act.[47] It resembles the BC and federal enactments in many respects. Like the federal Act, the NWT Act's purposes (stated in section 5) include "affirm[ing] the Declaration as a universal human rights instrument with application to the Indigenous peoples of the Northwest Territories and the laws of the Northwest Territories" and "provid[ing] a framework for the implementation of the Declaration by the Government of the Northwest Territories." Like the BC Act, section 13 of the NWT Act provides for agreements with Indigenous governments for the joint exercise of statutory powers of decision. Like both other Acts, the NWT Act includes action plan and annual reporting provisions (sections 9 to 12). The NWT Act's consistency of laws provision (section 6(1)) is phrased somewhat differently, the government being required to take "all reasonable measures" (rather than all measures necessary) "to ensure that the laws of the Northwest Territories are consistent with the

46 SC 2021, c 14.
47 SNWT 2023, c 36.

Declaration." This may prove a distinction without a difference. These similarities noted, the NWT Act includes innovations of its own. Section 8 requires most bills introduced to the legislative assembly to be accompanied by a statement of consistency with both the Declaration and section 35 of the Constitution Act, 1982.[48] And section 6(2) of the Act requires that the "laws of the Northwest Territories must be interpreted and applied in a manner consistent with the Declaration."

These Declaration Acts are not the only laws referencing the Declaration. The federal Act Respecting First Nations, Inuit and Métis Children, Youth and Families (the "FNIMC Act"),[49] considered at length in a 2024 Supreme Court reference,[50] is (at time of writing) the best-known example of a federal statute serving to partly implement the Declaration. Other federal laws also reference, and may partly implement, the Declaration,[51] including laws enacted prior to the Declaration but since amended to refer to it.[52] In BC the Interpretation Act has been amended to require that "Every Act and regulation must be construed as being consistent with the Declaration."[53] Other BC laws also require interpretation in accordance with the Declaration,[54] or confer responsibilities to implement the Declaration.[55] The Declaration is referred to

48 See also s 16(1), which amends the Statutory Instruments Act, RSNWT 1988, c S-13 to require examination of proposed regulations for consistency with the Declaration and s 35.

49 SC 2019, c 24.

50 *Reference re An Act respecting First Nations, Inuit and Métis children, youth and families*, 2024 SCC 5 [*Re C-92*].

51 E.g., Self-Government Treaty Recognizing the Whitecap Dakota Nation/ Wapaha Ska Dakota Oyate Act, above note 16; Anishinabek Nation Governance Agreement Act, above note 16, s 1; Indigenous Languages Act, SC 2019, c 23; Department for Women and Gender Equality Act, SC 2018, c 27, s 661; Department of Indigenous Services Act, SC 2019, c 29, s 336; Department of Crown-Indigenous Relations and Northern Affairs Act, SC 2019, c 29, s 337; Canadian Energy Regulator Act, SC 2019, c 28, s 10; Impact Assessment Act, SC 2019, c 28, s 1.

52 E.g., First Nations Fiscal Management Act, SC 2005, c 9; First Nations Land Management Act, SC 1999, c 24; Canadian Environmental Protection Act, 1999, SC 1999, c 33; Sechelt Indian Band Self-Government Act, SC 1986, c 27.

53 RSBC 1996, c 238, s 8.1(3).

54 See Adoption Act, RSBC 1996, c 5; Child, Family and Community Service Act, RSBC 1996, c 46 (both to be interpreted in accordance with the self-government and self-determination rights recognized by the Declaration).

55 Poverty Reduction Strategy Act, SBC 2018, c 40 (requiring that the strategy reflect a commitment to the Declaration); Environmental Assessment Act, SBC

in some other provinces' laws as well.[56] The Declaration is a mandatory consideration for decision makers in certain enactments.[57] None of these statutes implements the Declaration in full. But each moves a step toward fully implementing the Declaration's requirements in domestic law.

The Supreme Court of Canada considered the Declaration at length in *Re An Act respecting First Nations, Inuit and Métis children, youth and families*.[58] Quebec challenged the constitutionality of the FNIMC Act, a federal law affirming Indigenous peoples' inherent right of self-government and creating a scheme for exercise of that right in respect of child and family services, which prevailed over provincial laws to the extent of any conflict or inconsistency. The court upheld the law as a valid exercise of Parliament's jurisdiction under section 91(24) of the Constitution Act, 1867. The Declaration featured centrally in the court's reasoning, in part no doubt because Parliament expressly depicted the FNIMC Act's purpose as to "contribute to the implementation of the United Nations Declaration on the Rights of Indigenous Peoples."[59]

The court described the Declaration as having been "incorporated into the country's positive law"[60] by the federal Declaration Act "as a framework for reconciliation."[61] It noted that the FNIMC Act was "a concrete legislative measure to implement the UNDRIP in Canadian law,"[62] that the same Act "was intended to implement certain aspects of the UNDRIP"[63] and "forms part of the implementation of the UN-

---

2018, c 51 (defining the Environmental Assessment Office to include implementation of the Declaration among its responsibilities); Professional Governance Act, SBC 2018, c 47 (charging the superintendent of professional governance with implementation responsibilities).

56 The Path to Reconciliation Act, CCSM, c R30.5, preamble and s 4(a); Child and Youth Advocate Act, RSPEI 1988, c C-4.3, s 12(1)(c); Indigenous Institutes Act, 2017, SO 2017, c 34, sch 20; Child, Youth and Family Services Act, 2017, SO 2017, c 14, sch 1.

57 E.g., Canadian Net-Zero Emissions Accountability Act, SC 2021, c 22, s 9(5); Accessible British Columbia Act, SBC 2021, c 19, s 19(b).

58 *Re C-92*, above note 50.

59 FNIMC Act, above note 49 at s 8(c); see also the first paragraph of the preamble: "Whereas the Government of Canada is committed to implementing the United Nations Declaration on the Rights of Indigenous Peoples."

60 *Re C-92*, above note 50 at para 4; see also para 15.

61 Above note 46.

62 *Re C-92*, above note 50 at para 45.

63 *Ibid* at para 52.

DRIP by Parliament,"[64] and that the federal Declaration Act provides "a framework for the Government of Canada's implementation of the Declaration."[65] Two early commentators have fairly noted that

> it is far from clear what the Court meant when it said that the Declaration was part of "the country's positive law", while at the same time the Court clearly recognized that the Declaration needs implementation not only by the provisions of federal UNDRIP Act itself but by more specialized legislation. . . .[66]

That said, it is notable that the court was careful to speak of the FNIMC Act as a measure for *implementing* the Declaration, while speaking of the Declaration itself as being *incorporated* in the country's positive law by the Declaration Act. If we treat the terms "implementation" and "incorporation" as synonymous – which we should not[67] – then this distinction is meaningless. But the court here appears not to be treating these terms as synonymous. To the contrary, it acknowledges that implementation of the Declaration is an ongoing project, that the FNIMC Act is one step in that process, and that section 5 of the federal Declaration Act anticipates other such steps. Elsewhere in this book I use the term "incorporation" as synonymous with "adoption," meaning the process by which customary international norms may become part of the common law.[68] But the court does not appear to be using "incorporation" in this sense – which is fair, given its recent preference for the term "adoption" to describe the reception of customary international law by the common law.

The Supreme Court of Canada commented on the Declaration's status in federal law again in *Dickson v Vuntut Gwitchin First Nation*.[69] The majority opinion of Kasirer and Jamal JJ observed that the Declaration "has been implemented specifically in respect of the provision

64 *Ibid* at para 134.

65 *Ibid* at para 15.

66 N Bankes & R Hamilton, "What Did the Court Mean When It Said that UNDRIP 'has been incorporated into the country's positive law'? Appellate Guidance or Rhetorical Flourish?" (28 February 2024), online: *ABlawg*, https://ablawg.ca/wp-content/uploads/2024/02/Blog_NB_RH_UNDRIP_Incorporation.pdf at 7.

67 See Chapter 7, Section 7.1(a).

68 See the discussions of *R v Hape*, 2007 SCC 26 and *Nevsun Resources Ltd v Araya*, 2020 SCC 5 in Chapter 6, Section 6.1(b).

69 2024 SCC 10.

of Indigenous child and family services under" the FNIMC Act,[70] and described the Declaration more generally as "brought into Canadian law by the *UNDRIP Act*."[71] Here as in *Re C-92*, the majority acknowledges the Declaration's partial implementation in federal law while being careful not to depict it as wholly implemented. This approach is consistent with section 5 of the federal Declaration Act, which contemplates complete implementation of the Declaration over time and in consultation and cooperation with Indigenous peoples.

The discussion under this heading so far has focused on the Declaration's reception in Canadian law through positive laws – that is, implementation. We cannot, however, preclude the possibility that the Declaration (or parts of it) have become, or will become, recognized as norms of customary international law. If so, such norms may be incorporated by the common law in the way described in Chapter 6. It is also possible that Canadian courts will embrace an interpretive presumption that domestic law conforms to the Declaration's requirements. Whether the Declaration comes to have legal effects in our law through these other reception pathways remains to be seen.

What conclusions can we draw, then, about the legal status of the Declaration in Canada? I suggest two, although the second is perhaps not so much a conclusion as an observation.

First, at present, the Declaration is at best partly implemented in Canadian law. Only three jurisdictions have taken any meaningful steps toward implementation; we cannot yet speak of implementation to any significant extent in most provinces and territories. Even in those jurisdictions that have adopted Declaration Acts, the consistency provisions of those enactments (BC section 3, Canada section 5, NWT section 6(1)) are clear on their face that implementation is to be achieved over time. Consistency, in other words, is not the present state of affairs but a goal to be attained. Initial steps have been taken. More are to come. None of this is meant to downplay the significance of the federal, BC, and NWT legislative measures reviewed above. My point is only that, if thoroughgoing implementation of the Declaration in domestic law is to be achieved, much legislative, regulatory, and policy reform remains to be done.

---

70 *Ibid* at para 47.

71 *Ibid* at para 117.

The court's decision in *Re C-92* is consistent with this first conclusion, despite the fact that some passages of that decision might be understood more broadly. The court recognized the FNIMC Act as partly implementing the Declaration in respect of Indigenous rights concerning the well-being and upbringing of children. The court also recognized the federal Declaration Act as (in Parliament's words) "a framework for reconciliation" that requires "concrete measures" in implementation of the Declaration's requirements.[72] Read as a whole, and in the light of the consistency requirement in section 5 of the federal Declaration Act (of which the court took note[73]), the court in *Re C-92* must be understood as recognizing that implementation of the Declaration is not yet achieved but has now begun.

Second, the precise normative force of the Declaration in our law remains to be worked out. The court in *Re C-92* clearly recognized some normative force in the Declaration, calling it "incorporated into the country's positive law" by the federal Declaration Act and considering the Declaration's provisions at length without any hesitation about its bindingness or otherwise as a matter of international law. Lower courts are implicitly invited to do the same. While the court does not expressly say so, one may wonder whether considerations of the honour of the Crown are not informing this approach. They certainly should. As the court noted, it is always assumed that the Crown intends to fulfil its promises.[74] The Declaration is surely the most important and far-reaching promise the Crown has made to Indigenous peoples since the Royal Proclamation. It is unthinkable that it would not make its way into our law. How that happens may not depend entirely on traditional reception law doctrines. The Declaration's origins are in public international law, but considerations of the honour of the Crown may call for its reception (or, as the court says in *Re C-92*, "incorporation") through different means than apply to other customary and conventional international obligations of the state.[75]

---

72 *Re C-92*, above note 50 at para 4.

73 *Ibid* at paras 4, 15, 85.

74 *Ibid* at para 66, citing *Haida Nation v British Columbia (Minister of Forests)*, [2004] 3 SCR 511 [*Haida Nation*] at para 20, and *R v Badger*, [1996] 1 SCR 771 at para 41.

75 See G van Ert, "Three Good Reasons Why UNDRIP Can't Be Law – and One Good Reason Why It Can" (2017) 75 *The Advocate* 29 at 33–5.

10.2 The duty to consult in matters of external affairs

In the second edition of this work, I suggested that the conduct of Canada's external relations may be a sort of governmental decision making to which the constitutional duty to consult and accommodate Indigenous peoples attaches. I imagined a scenario in which Canada wished to conclude a treaty that, when implemented in domestic law, may infringe some Aboriginal right, and suggested that the prospect of legislative infringement might trigger the duty to consult and possibly to accommodate the affected Aboriginal group.[76]

There remains little case law on this point, but one important decision has emerged. In *Hupacasath First Nation v Minister of Foreign Affairs*,[77] the Hupacasath challenged Canada's decision to enter into an investment treaty with the People's Republic of China on the basis that the agreement had potential effects on their Aboriginal rights under section 35 of the Constitution Act, 1982 such that Canada had a duty to consult with and, if necessary, accommodate them before bringing the agreement into force. The Federal Court of Appeal upheld the lower court's finding that the agreement in question had not been shown to have appreciable effects on the First Nation, such that the duty to consult was not triggered. Importantly, however, the Federal Court of Appeal did not doubt that, on different facts, the constitutional duty to consult recognized in *Haida Nation*[78] and subsequent cases might have applied. In principle, a decision by the federal government in exercise of its foreign affairs prerogative is, it seems, reviewable for compliance with section 35. As Stratas JA for the court observed in rejecting Canada's justiciability objection, "Assessing whether or not legal rights exist on the facts of a case lies at the core of what courts do. Under the constitutional separation of powers, determining this is squarely within our province."[79]

The federal government's 2011 guidelines for federal officials on the duty to consult noted that officials "should assess whether provisions in land claim agreements or self-government agreements require that

---

76 G van Ert, *Using International Law in Canadian Courts*, 2d ed (Toronto: Irwin Law, 2008) at 316–17.

77 2015 FCA 4.

78 *Haida Nation*, above note 74.

79 *Ibid* at para 70.

consultation take place in relation to legally binding international instruments" and also determine whether legislation requires such consultation.[80] What *Hupacasath* contemplates, however, is a free-standing duty to consult, whether or not a consultation requirement has been previously recognized by law or agreement. While *Haida Nation* does not address the duty to consult's application to the foreign affairs prerogative, it is difficult to see how the right to consultation in treaty-making or other matters of external affairs might be confined to those Indigenous peoples who have concluded self-government agreements with the federal government expressly requiring such consultation. Rather, as Professor Côté observes, "An obligation to consult with Aboriginal peoples on foreign affairs is emerging from the constitutional protection of their rights in Canada."[81]

10.3 Reception provisions in modern Crown–Indigenous treaties

In 2003, the governments of Canada and the Northwest Territories concluded a remarkable agreement with the Tłı̨chǫ people.[82] The Tłı̨chǫ Land Claims and Self-Government Agreement was a comprehensive claims agreement (CCA) resembling others the federal and provincial governments have entered into with Indigenous peoples since the 1970s, but with important innovations concerning Canada's international legal obligations. The agreement provided that the Tłı̨chǫ governmental powers it recognized must be exercised in conformity with international law. The agreement also recognized the Tłı̨chǫ's right to consultation in international legal matters affecting them.[83] These ar-

80 Canada, Department of Aboriginal Affairs and Northern Development, *Aboriginal Consultation and Accommodation: Updated Guidelines for Federal Officials to Fulfill the Duty to Consult* (March 2011) at 23, online: https://www.rcaanc-cirnac.gc.ca/eng/1100100014664/1609421824729.

81 C-E Côté, "Federalism and Foreign Affairs in Canada" in C Bradley, ed, *The Oxford Handbook of Comparative Foreign Relations Law* (New York: Oxford University Press, 2019) at 293.

82 Land Claims and Self-Government Agreement among the Tłı̨chǫ and the Government of the Northwest Territories and the Government of Canada, signed 25 August 2003 [Tłı̨chǫ Agreement].

83 For a detailed discussion see G van Ert & S Matiation, "Labour Conventions and Comprehensive Claim Agreements: A New Model for Subfederal Participation in Canadian International Treaty-Making" in O Fitzgerald, ed, *The Globalized Rule*

rangements set out new rules for the interaction of international and domestic law in Canada in matters touching the Tłı̨chǫ people.

The Tłı̨chǫ Agreement was followed by other CCAs and modern treaties in which similar reception law provisions appear. These include the Labrador Inuit Land Claims Agreement,[84] the Tsawwassen First Nation Final Agreement,[85] the Maa-nulth First Nations Final Agreement,[86] the Yale First Nation Final Agreement,[87] the Sioux Valley Dakota Nation Self-Government Agreement,[88] the Tla'amin Final Agreement,[89] the Délı̨nę Final Self-Government Agreement,[90] the Cree Nation Governance Agreement,[91] and the Anishinabek Nation Government Agreement.[92]

The need for reception law provisions in modern Crown–Indigenous treaties is explained by the nature of these agreements, namely that they recognize Indigenous governmental bodies and define those bodies' powers, jurisdiction, and relationship with other Canadian governments. The recognition of these governments raises the prospect of conflict between their laws and actions and Canada's obligations under conventional and customary international law. Just as a provincial, territorial, or even a municipal government may, by its conduct, bring

---

of Law: Relationships Between International and Domestic Law (Toronto: Irwin Law, 2006) [Van Ert & Matiation] at 203.

84 Land Claims Agreement between the Inuit of Labrador and Her Majesty the Queen in Right of Newfoundland and Labrador and Her Majesty the Queen in Right of Canada, signed 22 January 2005 [Labrador Inuit Agreement].

85 Tsawwassen First Nation Final Agreement, initialled by the parties 8 December 2006 and signed 6 December 2007 [Tsawwassen Agreement].

86 Maa-nulth First Nations Final Agreement, initialled 9 December 2006, ratified by Maa-nulth First Nations members in the summer and fall of 2007 [Maa-nulth Agreement].

87 Yale First Nation Final Agreement, initialled 5 February 2010, ratified 11 April 2013 [Yale Agreement].

88 Governance Agreement between Sioux Valley Dakota Nation and Her Majesty the Queen in right of Canada, signed 30 August 2013 [Sioux Valley Dakota Agreement].

89 Tla'amin Final Agreement, effective date 5 April 2016 [Tla'amin Agreement].

90 Délı̨nę Final Self-Government Agreement, signed 18 February 2015 [Délı̨nę Agreement].

91 Agreement on Cree Nation Governance Between the Crees of Eeyou Istchee and the Government of Canada, signed 18 July 2017 [Cree Nation Agreement].

92 Anishinabek Nation Governance Agreement, signed 6 April 2022 [Anishinabek Agreement]. See also c 12 of the Anishinabek Nation Education Agreement, signed 16 August 2017.

Canada into default of its international obligations, so too might an Indigenous government. From Canada's perspective, then, express provisions addressing international law are desirable, perhaps even necessary, in these agreements.

In all these agreements three kinds of reception provision appear: (1) a requirement that Canada consult with or hear from the Indigenous party before consenting to be bound to international agreements that may affect the Indigenous party's rights or when determining Canada's position before international tribunals in cases touching the Indigenous party's laws; (2) a requirement that the Indigenous party take or consider remedial measures where its laws threaten Canada's performance of its international obligations; and (3) dispute resolution mechanisms relating to such international legal concerns.

(a) Consultation provisions

Modern Crown–Indigenous treaties frequently provide a right for the Indigenous party to be consulted, or to make its views known, before Canada consents to an international agreement that may affect that party's interests. Consultation is also contemplated where exercises of Indigenous governmental authority come before international tribunals. These consultation provisions reflect the constitutional requirement, derived from section 35 of the Constitution Act, 1982, that the Crown consult Aboriginal peoples, and in proper cases accommodate their interests, in cases where the Crown contemplates conduct that might adversely affect Aboriginal title or rights.[93]

The Labrador Inuit Agreement provides that Canada shall consult the Nunatsiavut government before consenting to be bound to a treaty that "may affect a right under the Agreement of the Nunatsiavut government, an Inuit community government or Inuit."[94] Similarly, the Tsawwassen Agreement provides:

> After the Effective Date, before consenting to be bound by a new International Treaty that would give rise to a new International Legal Obligation that may adversely affect a right of Tsawwassen First Na-

93 *Haida Nation*, above note 74.

94 Labrador Inuit Agreement, above note 84, s 17.27.3. Note that the agreement creates two levels of government: the Nunatsiavut government and five Inuit community governments.

> tion under this Agreement, Canada will Consult with Tsawwassen First Nation in respect of the International Treaty, either separately or through a forum that Canada determines is appropriate.[95]

Essentially the same provision is found in the Maa-nulth Agreement[96] and the Yale Agreement.[97] Similar rights to consultation are found in the Tla'amin,[98] Délı̨nę,[99] Cree Nation,[100] and Anishinabek[101] agreements.

The Tłı̨chǫ Agreement provides that Canada shall "provide an opportunity for the Tłı̨chǫ Government to make its views known" prior to consenting to be bound by "an international treaty that may affect the rights of the Tłı̨chǫ Government, the Tłı̨chǫ First Nation or a Tłı̨chǫ Citizen, flowing from the Agreement."[102] This formulation is also used in the Sioux Valley Dakota Agreement.[103] While the wording here is in terms of an opportunity to make one's views known, where other agreements refer to the seemingly stronger concept of consultation, in practice it seems likely that all these agreements will be regarded as establishing the same degree of consultation rights for their Indigenous parties.

These agreements also require Canada to consult with Indigenous governments where their exercises of power give rise to concerns before international tribunals about Canada's performance of its treaty obligations. The Tsawwassen Agreement, for instance, provides that Canada will consult with the Tsawwassen First Nation "in respect of the development of positions taken by Canada before an International Tribunal where a Tsawwassen Law or other exercise of power by Tsawwassen First Nation has given rise to an issue concerning the performance of an International Legal Obligation of Canada" and that "Canada's positions before the International Tribunal will take into account the commitment of the Parties to the integrity of this Agreement."[104] The

95 Tsawwassen Agreement, above note 85 at c 2, s 30.
96 Maa-nulth Agreement, above note 86, s 1.7.1.
97 Yale Agreement, above note 87, s 2.8.1.
98 Tla'amin Agreement, above note 89 at c 2, s 24.
99 Délı̨nę Agreement, above note 90 at c 2.13.1.
100 Cree Nation Agreement, above note 91 at c 25.3.
101 Anishinabek Agreement, above note 92, s 11.12.
102 Tłı̨chǫ Agreement, above note 82, s 7.13.2.
103 Sioux Valley Dakota Agreement, above note 88, s 36.03(1).
104 Tsawwassen Agreement, above note 85 at c 2, s 33.

Maa-nulth and Yale Agreements say the same.[105] Similar provisions are found in other agreements.[106] The Cree Nation consultation provision is stated somewhat differently,[107] and the Sioux Valley Dakota Agreement provides that Canada will "involve Sioux Valley Dakota Nation in developing its position" before an international tribunal.[108] Some of these agreements also include a requirement that Canada's position before an international tribunal "take into account the commitment of the Parties to the integrity" of the agreement.[109]

The Labrador Inuit Agreement provides that Canada shall consult the Nunatsiavut government about remedying laws or other exercises of power that cause Canada to be unable to perform its international obligations.[110] The same is true of the Cree Nation Agreement.[111] The Tłı̨chǫ Agreement does not describe this process as consultation, saying only that the Canadian and Tłı̨chǫ governments "shall discuss remedial measures" in such cases.[112] Similar language is employed in the Tsawwassen, Maa-nulth, and Délı̨nę agreements.[113]

---

105 Maa-nulth Agreement, above note 86, s 1.7.4; Yale Agreement, above note 87, s 2.8.5.

106 Tłı̨chǫ Agreement, above note 82, s 7.13.5; Labrador Inuit Agreement, above note 84, s 17.27.4; Tsawwassen Agreement, above note 85, s 33; Tla'amin Agreement, above note 89 at c 28; Délı̨nę Agreement, above note 90 at c 2.13.5; Anishinabek Agreement, above note 92, s 11.14.

107 Cree Nation Agreement, above note 91 at c 25.5: "If requested by Canada, the Cree Nation Government shall contribute to the preparation of Canada's position, including by providing information, evidence and potential witnesses in relation to the law or other exercise of governmental authority under consideration by an International Tribunal or an International Body. Canada shall consider the views expressed by the Cree Nation Government in the elaboration of its position. The specific means of contribution will be discussed by Canada and the Cree Nation Government."

108 Sioux Valley Dakota Agreement, above note 88, s 36.02(1)(a).

109 Tla'amin Agreement, above note 89 at c 2, s 28. See also: Maa-nulth Agreement, above note 86, s 1.7.4; Délı̨nę Agreement, above note 90 at c 2.13.5; Tsawwassen Agreement, above note 85 at c 2, s 33; Sioux Valley Dakota Agreement, above note 88, s 36.02(1)(b).

110 Labrador Inuit Agreement, above note 84, s 17.27.10.

111 Cree Nation Agreement, above note 91 at c 25.6.

112 Tłı̨chǫ Agreement, above note 82, s 7.13.3.

113 Tsawwassen Agreement, above note 85 at c 2, s 31; Maa-nulth Agreement, above note 86, s 1.7.2; Délı̨nę Agreement, above note 90 at c 2.13.6.

(b) Provisions promoting conformity with international obligations

The consultation provisions reviewed above are paired with provisions imposing a duty on the Indigenous party to remedy any law or other exercise of power that, in the opinion of Canada, causes it to be unable to perform an international legal obligation.[114] These provisions apply to Canadian obligations under both custom and treaty. Since Indigenous jurisdiction under the agreements is concurrent,[115] a mere omission by an Indigenous government to implement a treaty will not disable Canadian performance as contemplated by the agreements, for any applicable federal, provincial, or territorial implementing legislation will apply in the absence of Indigenous legislation. Only positive legislative or other acts by Indigenous governments are subject to the duty to conform.

There is likewise a duty on Indigenous parties, where an international tribunal concludes that Canada has failed to perform an international legal obligation as a result of an Indigenous law or other exercise of power, to take the measures needed to enable Canadian performance.[116] This conformity requirement is mandatory and not subject to dispute resolution.

---

114 Tłı̨chǫ Agreement, above note 82, s 7.13.3; Labrador Inuit Agreement, above note 84, s 17.27.5; Tsawwassen Agreement, above note 85 at c 2, s 31; Maa-nulth Agreement, above note 86, s 1.7.2; Yale Agreement, above note 87, s 2.8.3; Sioux Valley Dakota Agreement, above note 88, s 36.01(4); Délı̨nę Agreement, above note 90 at c 2.13.3; Tla'amin Agreement, above note 89 at c 2.26. See also s 36(a) of the Westbank First Nation Self-Government Agreement, ratified 24 May 2003 [Westbank First Nation Agreement]. Notably, s 11.13 of the Anishinabek Agreement, above note 92, provides only that the Indigenous party and Canada "will discuss how the law or other exercise of authority could be modified so that Canada is able to comply."

115 See van Ert & Matiation, above note 83 at 216, 221, 228.

116 Tłı̨chǫ Agreement, above note 82, s 7.13.6; Labrador Inuit Agreement, above note 84, s 17.27.9; Tsawwassen Agreement, above note 85 at c 2, s 34; Maa-nulth Agreement, above note 86, s 1.7.5; Yale Agreement, above note 87, s 2.8.6; Sioux Valley Dakota Agreement, above note 88, s 36.02(4); Délı̨nę Agreement, above note 90 at c 2.13.6; Tla'amin Agreement, above note 89 at c 2.29; Anishinabek Agreement, above note 92, s 11.15. See also s 36(b) of Westbank First Nation Agreement, above note 114.

(c) Dispute resolution provisions

If an Indigenous government disagrees with Canada's assessment of the international consequences of its law or other exercise of power, it may take the matter to dispute resolution. The forms of dispute resolution vary. Under the Tłįchǫ Agreement the process begins with mediation then proceeds to arbitration.[117] The arbitrator is empowered, however, to refer questions of law (which this would be) to the Supreme Court of the Northwest Territories.[118] The dispute resolution provision of the Labrador Inuit Agreement directs these matters to the Federal Court of Canada,[119] while the Sioux Valley Dakota Agreement invokes the Manitoba Court of King's Bench.[120] The Tsawwassen, Maa-nulth, Yale, Tla'amin, and Délı̨nę Agreements refer these disputes to arbitration.[121]

The proceedings contemplated by these provisions are unlike any in Canadian law. They are, in effect, a legal challenge by the federal government to the legality of another government's legislation on the basis of its non-conformity with Canadian legal obligations under international law. If Canada succeeds in the proceeding, the Indigenous government must remedy the breach to enable Canada to perform its international legal obligation. If Canada loses, it is barred from taking any further action aimed at changing the impugned measure for this reason.[122]

(d) Implications of these agreements

These agreements represent something rare in reception law: an innovation. They are an expansion of the Canadian reception system beyond its common law foundations to meet both the needs of the state in

---

117 Tłįchǫ Agreement, above note 82, s 7.13.4.

118 *Ibid*, s 6.5.6(f).

119 Labrador Inuit Agreement, above note 84, s 17.27.6.

120 Sioux Valley Dakota Agreement, above note 88, s 72.01(1).

121 Tsawwassen Agreement, above note 85 at c 2, s 32; Maa-nulth Agreement, above note 86, s 1.7.3; Yale Agreement, above note 87, s 2.8.4; Délı̨nę Agreement, above note 90 at c 2.13.4; Tla'amin Agreement, above note 89 at c 2.27.

122 Tłįchǫ Agreement, above note 82, s 7.13.4; Labrador Inuit Agreement, above note 84, s 17.27.7; Tsawwassen Agreement, above note 85 at c 2, s 32; Maa-nulth Agreement, above note 86, s. 1.7.3; Délı̨nę Agreement, above note 90 at c 2.13.4; Tla'amin Agreement, above note 89 at c 2.27(a).

matters of international law and the obligations of the Crown toward Indigenous peoples. Furthermore, these agreements establish a new model for sub-federal participation in Canada's international treaty-making process. In contrast to the *Labour Conventions*[123] model to which Canada and the provinces are currently subject,[124] this model offers guaranteed consultation rights in exchange for a duty to conform to Canada's international obligations. One wonders what interest, if any, the provinces might have in concluding similar arrangements. At least one provincial leader, former Alberta premier Ralph Klein, has argued that provinces should have "a guaranteed role in negotiating international treaties."[125] The consultation model established in the agreements reviewed above suggests another possible fate for the *Labour Conventions* case: Rather than being overruled by the Supreme Court of Canada (as many have predicted, so far wrongly), the federal government and the provinces might simply contract out of it, adopting in its place the consultation-for-conformity arrangements developed in modern treaties with Indigenous peoples.[126]

123 *Attorney General for Canada v Attorney General for Ontario*, [1937] AC 326 (PC).

124 See Chapter 7, Section 7.4.

125 R Klein, speech to the Canadian Institute of International Affairs' Foreign Policy Conference, Calgary (26 March 2004) [on file with the author].

126 See van Ert & Matiation, above note 83 at 230–2.

11 The reception of international human rights law

The most significant expansion of international law since the close of the Second World War has been in the area of human rights. The second half of the twentieth century saw the proclamation and codification in international law of doctrines once recognized only in the laws of a handful of states and the writings of philosophers. The leading international human rights instruments of the period took the form of multilateral treaties such as the United Nations Convention Relating to the Status of Refugees 1951 and its 1967 Protocol,[1] the many conventions of the International Labour Organization, the International Covenant on Civil and Political Rights 1966 (ICCPR),[2] the International Covenant on Economic, Social and Cultural Rights 1966 (ICESCR),[3] the International Convention on the Elimination of All Forms of Racial Discrimination 1966 (CERD),[4] the Convention on the Elimination of All Forms of Discrimination Against Women 1979 (CEDAW),[5] the Convention Against Torture 1984 (CAT),[6] and the Convention on the Rights of the Child 1989 (CRC).[7] Other significant statements of international human rights took the form of non-binding

1 [1969] Can TS no 29.
2 [1976] Can TS no 47.
3 [1976] Can TS no 46.
4 [1970] Can TS no 28.
5 [1982] Can TS no 31.
6 [1987] Can TS no 36.
7 [1992] Can TS no 3.

instruments, chief among them the Universal Declaration of Human Rights 1948 (UDHR).[8]

The development of international human rights continues in this century with such instruments as the Convention on the Rights of Persons with Disabilities 2006 (CRPD)[9] and the United Nations Declaration on the Rights of Indigenous Peoples 2007 (UNDRIP).[10] Alongside these human rights instruments runs a rich international jurisprudence of human rights, elaborated by regional bodies such as the European Court of Human Rights, the Inter-American Court of Human Rights, the Freedom of Association Committee of the International Labour Organization, the United Nations Human Rights Committee, and other UN treaty bodies.

The human rights movement has legitimized and popularized rights discourse not only in international law but also in domestic legal systems. This phenomenon has been particularly evident in Canada, which, following the constitutional traditions of England, originally possessed no entrenched rights-protecting instrument, but has since adopted one – the Canadian Charter of Rights and Freedoms.[11] In Canada and other Westminster-model constitutions, rights were once thought to be best protected by representative assemblies, ordinary statutes, judge-made law, and ancient notions of the liberties of the subject.[12] The bundle of rights protected by the Westminster model was much smaller than that now recognized at international law. But even if the Westminster model were capable of affording adequate protec-

---

8 GA Res 217 A (III), UN Doc A/810. Judges of the Supreme Court of Canada have frequently referred to the UDHR as a convention or instrument to which Canada is a signatory or party: see *R v Lucas*, [1998] 1 SCR 439 at para 50; *Canadian Egg Marketing Agency v Richardson*, [1998] 3 SCR 157 at para 58; *Delisle v Canada (Deputy Attorney General)*, [1999] 2 SCR 989 at para 71; *R v Advance Cutting & Coring Ltd*, 2001 SCC 70 at paras 10–11. This is mistaken: The UDHR is a non-binding resolution of the General Assembly of the United Nations.

9 [2010] Can TS no 8.

10 GA Res 61/295 (2 October 2007).

11 Part I of the Constitution Act, 1982, being Schedule B to the Canada Act 1982 (UK), 1982, c 11. See B Dickson, "The Canadian Charter of Rights and Freedoms: Context and Evolution" in G-A Beaudoin & E Mendes, *The Canadian Charter of Rights and Freedoms*, 3d ed (Toronto: Carswell, 1996) [Dickson] at 1-4 to 1-5.

12 See J Ajzenstat, "Reconciling Parliament and Rights: A.V. Dicey Reads the Canadian Charter of Rights and Freedoms" (1997) 30:4 *Canadian Journal of Political Science* 645.

tion to its own narrow conception of human rights (and that may be disputed), it is unclear that it was capable, in Canada at least, of affording meaningful protection to the much broader range of human rights established since 1945.

Canadians eventually opted to protect rights by constitutional entrenchment, adopting the Charter in 1982. The Charter is Canada's foremost rights-protecting instrument, but it is not the only one. Before enactment of the Charter, and still today, rights in Canada were also protected by federal, provincial, and territorial statutes.

In this final chapter, I consider the interaction between the international and Canadian laws of human rights. I do not purport to catalogue all instances of Canadian courts using international law in interpreting the Charter or other domestic human rights laws.[13] Instead, I describe the reception rules that have developed around international human rights norms. Inevitably, most of this discussion is devoted to how international human rights law informs Charter interpretation.

11.1 Reception of international human rights law through ordinary laws

The main instrument by which human rights are protected in Canada is the Charter. But human rights are also protected in Canada by a variety of federal, provincial, and territorial bills of rights and human rights codes, and by certain other statutes that, while not expressly addressed at human rights, effectively form part of Canada's overall human rights regime. Before moving on to the Charter (the main focus of this chapter), I offer this brief account of human rights reception through ordinary laws.

---

13 See W Schabas & S Beaulac, *International Human Rights and Canadian Law: Legal Commitment, Implementation and the Charter*, 3d ed (Toronto: Thomson Carswell, 2007) [Schabas & Beaulac]; M Freeman & G van Ert, *International Human Rights Law* (Toronto: Irwin Law, 2004) [Freeman & van Ert] at ch 10; A Bayefsky, *International Human Rights Law: Use in Canadian Charter of Rights and Freedoms Litigation* (Toronto: Butterworths, 1992).

Federal,[14] provincial,[15] and territorial[16] bills of rights and human rights codes play a significant role as implementing legislation for Canadian human rights treaty obligations. In particular, these laws serve to implement Canadian obligations under the ICCPR, the CERD, the CEDAW, and the CRPD to prohibit discrimination and guarantee to all persons equal and effective protection against racial, gender, religious, or other discrimination.[17] In its 2019 common core document for UN treaty bodies, Canada explained:

> All governments in Canada – federal, provincial and territorial – have adopted legislation prohibiting discrimination on various grounds in regard to employment matters, the provision of goods, services and facilities customarily available to the public, and accommodation. This legislation differs in its application from the right to equality in section 15 of the *Canadian Charter of Rights and Freedoms* in that it provides protection against discrimination by individuals in the private sector, as well as by governments.[18]

Given the importance of bills of rights and human rights codes as implementing legislation for the state's international human rights

14 For example, Canadian Bill of Rights, SC 1960, c 44, reprinted in RSC 1985, App III; and Canadian Human Rights Act, RSC 1985, c H-6.

15 Human Rights Code, RSBC 1996, c 210 (British Columbia); Civil Rights Protection Act, RSBC 1996, c 49 (British Columbia); Alberta Bill of Rights, RSA 2000, c A-14; Alberta Human Rights Act, RSA 2000, c A-25.5; Saskatchewan Human Rights Code, 2018, SS 2018, c S-24.2; Human Rights Code, CCSM, c H175 (Manitoba); Human Rights Code, RSO 1990, c H.19 (Ontario); Charter of Human Rights and Freedoms, CQLR, c C-12 (Quebec); Human Rights Act, RSNB 2011, c 171 (New Brunswick); Human Rights Act, RSNS 1989, c 214 (Nova Scotia); Human Rights Act, RSPEI 1988, c H-12 (Prince Edward Island); Human Rights Act, 2010, SNL 2010, c H-13.1 (Newfoundland and Labrador).

16 Human Rights Act, RSY 2002, c 116 (Yukon Territory); Human Rights Act, SNWT 2002, c 18 (Northwest Territories); Human Rights Act, CSNu, c H-70 (Nunavut).

17 Confusingly, in Canadian legal parlance the phrase "human rights law" has come to be equated with what, in international law, is known by the more specific phrase "anti-discrimination law," anti-discrimination being only a subset of international human rights law.

18 Canada, *Common Core Document Forming Part of the Reports of States Parties: Canada* (2019) UN Doc HRI/CORE/CAN/2019 [Canada Core Document] at para 127.

obligations, one might expect Canadian human rights lawyers, commissions, and tribunals to have frequent resort to international law in construing domestic legislation and resolving discrimination claims. And yet Canadian human rights institutions have tended to make little use of international human rights law.[19] Similarly, the jurisprudence of the Supreme Court of Canada on equality matters, whether arising out of human rights legislation or section 15 of the Charter, has largely ignored international anti-discrimination provisions. The exception is Quebec, where the presumption of conformity has frequently been applied and affirmed and international human rights instruments considered by that province's human rights tribunal in its interpretations of the Quebec Charter of Human Rights and Freedoms.[20]

Applying the presumption of conformity to statutory bills of rights and human rights codes is not only good judicial policy but also an accurate depiction of legislative intent, for these instruments (many of which pre-date the Charter) take inspiration from the international human rights movement.[21] To apply the presumption to human rights

---

19 L Reif, "The Domestic Application of International Human Rights Law in Canada: The Role of Canada's National Human Rights Institutions" in O Fitzgerald, ed, *The Globalized Rule of Law: Relationships between International and Domestic Law* (Toronto: Irwin Law, 2006) 467 at 513; Freeman & van Ert, above note 13 at 204.

20 RSQ, c C-12. See, e.g., *Kerdougli v La Vie en Rose inc*, 2018 QCTDP 8 at paras 31–3; *Commission des droits de la personne et des droits de la jeunesse (Pheneus et une autre) v Fornella*, 2018 QCTDP 3 at paras 24–5; *Commission des droits de la personne et des droits de la jeunesse (Saumier) v Les Entreprises Mirabel (RA) inc*, 2017 QCTDP 6 at paras 51–8; *Commission des droits de la personne et des droits de la jeunesse (JS) v Montréal (Communauté urbaine de) (Montréal (Ville de))*, 2014 QCTDP 7 at paras 83–8; *ML et Commission des droits de la personne v Maison des jeunes*, [1998] JTDPQ no 31 (TDPQ); *Roy et Commission des droits de la personne et des droits de la jeunesse du Québec v Maksteel Québec Inc*, [1997] RJQ 2891 (TDPQ) at para 14 (noting that the tribunal has often depicted international law as the "toile de fond [background]" for the interpretation of the Quebec Charter); *Kafé et Commission des droits de la personne du Québec v Commission scolaire Deux-Montagnes*, [1993] RJQ 1297 (TDPQ); *Québec (Commission des droits de la personne) v Immeubles Ni-Dia Inc*, [1992] RJQ 2977 (TDPQ); *Dufour v Centre hospitalier St-Joseph de la Malbaie*, [1992] RJQ 825 (TDPQ) at 835.

21 See, for example, *McKinney v University of Guelph*, [1990] 3 SCR 229 at para 209, in which Wilson J depicts the origins of the Canadian Bill of Rights 1960 as a legislative response to the UDHR, the ECHR, and the ICCPR. See also the

laws is all the more important when one recalls that the prevailing[22] Canadian practice is not to implement human rights treaties explicitly, for "most human rights treaties are ratified by Canada on the basis that existing domestic laws and programs already conform with a treaty's obligations and no new legislation is required."[23] As Canada explained to the United Nations in 2019,

> Prior to becoming a party to an international human rights treaty, all levels of government in Canada review their laws, policies and practices to determine whether they meet the treaty obligations, or whether new measures may be required to ensure full and effective implementation of the treaty. Where existing legislation and policies fulfill the obligations under the treaty, no new measures are required. On occasion, legislation may be amended or new laws enacted to ensure compliance with the treaty. After ratification, these issues are taken into account in drafting future legislation where relevant.[24]

The human rights aspect of other ordinary statutes ought not to be overlooked, though I will not explore the point at any length here. But such laws as the Criminal Code, privacy laws, election laws, laws concerning the UNDRIP, and more have rights-advancing or rights-protecting purposes and features.

---

preambular reference to the UDHR in the Ontario Human Rights Code and the references to the UDHR in the Yukon Human Rights Act, preamble and s 1.

22 Prevailing, but not exclusive. For instance, portions of the Convention Relating to the Status of Refugees 1951, [1969] Can TS no 6, together with its 1967 protocol, [1969] Can TS no 29, are expressly implemented by the Immigration and Refugee Protection Act, SC 2001 c 27. On the implementing role of the previous Immigration Act, see *Pushpanathan v Canada (Minister of Citizenship and Immigration)*, [1998] 1 SCR 982 at para 4.

23 I Weiser, "Effect in Domestic Law of International Human Rights Treaties Ratified Without Implementing Legislation" in *The Impact of International Law on the Practice of Law in Canada: Proceedings of the 27th Annual Conference of the Canadian Council on International Law, Ottawa October 15–17, 1998* (The Hague: Kluwer Law International, 1999) 132 at 132.

24 Canada Core Document, above note 18 at para 136.

11.2 Reception of international human rights law through the Charter

The most obvious portal through which international human rights law might be received in Canadian law is the Charter. In some respects, the Charter has indeed served that function, especially in respect of civil and political rights. The Government of Canada has emphasized this point before United Nations bodies.[25] Yet for much of the Charter's history the Supreme Court of Canada's jurisprudence failed to provide predictable rules for the reception of international human rights law, and international law more broadly, through the Charter's provisions.[26] Whether recent Supreme Court decisions have finally settled on Charter-specific reception rules remains to be seen.

(a) The Charter as implementing legislation

It is a matter of historical record that the drafters of the Charter looked to Canada's international treaty obligations, especially the ICCPR, for inspiration and guidance.[27] The results may be seen on the face of the

---

25 *Ibid* at para 141 ("International treaties that Canada has ratified can inform the interpretation of domestic law. This doctrine is of particular importance in the context of the Canadian Charter of Rights and Freedoms. Human rights treaties are relevant in determining the scope of rights protected by the Charter") and 142 ("Through their relevance to the interpretation of human rights protections in the Charter and under domestic law, these international treaties are considered by the courts when the validity of legislation under the Constitution must be determined").

26 See J Currie, "International Human Rights Law in the Supreme Court's Charter Jurisprudence: Commitment, Retrenchment *and* Retreat – In No Particular Order" (2010) 50 *Supreme Court Law Review* (2d) 423–63.

27 See C Heyns & F Viljoen, eds, *The Impact of the United Nations Human Rights Treaties on the Domestic Level* (The Hague: Kluwer Law International, 2002) at 123, 132; Dickson, above note 11 at 1–4 to 1–5; Bayefsky, above note 13 at 33–47; A Bayefsky, *Canada's Constitution Act 1982 and Amendments: A Documentary History* (Toronto: McGraw-Hill Ryerson, 1989); D Turp, "Le recours au droit international aux fins de l'interprétation de la Charte canadienne des droits et libertés: un bilan jurisprudential" (1984) 18 *Revue Juridique Thèmis* 353; G La Forest, "The Canadian Charter of Rights and Freedoms: An Overview" (1983) 61 *Canadian Bar Review* 19 at 25; M Cohen & A Bayefsky, "The Canadian Charter of Rights and Freedoms and Public International Law" (1983) 61 *Canadian Bar Review* 265; R Elliott, "Interpreting the Charter: Use of the Earlier Versions as an Aid" [1982] *Charter Edition University of British Columbia Law Review* 11; W Tarnopolsky, "A

Charter itself; many of its provisions correspond closely to provisions of the UDHR, ICCPR, and ECHR.[28]

The Charter's international origins have led some courts to observe that the Charter implements some of Canada's international human rights obligations, but that has not been the prevalent view. In the Court of Appeal of Alberta's decision in *R v Big M Drug Mart*, Belzil JA (dissenting) observed that the Charter "was not conceived and born in isolation. It is part of the universal human rights movement" and explained that

> The Charter can be divided into two parts, one dealing with fundamental human rights in harmony with the International Covenant [on Civil and Political Rights 1966], the other dealing with matters peculiar to Canada. . . . That these fundamental freedoms were entrenched in the Charter in conformity with Canada's commitment in the International Covenant cannot be doubted.[29]

These observations were noted, but not much considered, when *Big M Drug Mart* went to the Supreme Court of Canada.[30] Yet Dickson CJ, dissenting in *Re Public Service Employee Relations Act (Alberta)*, made a similar comment, saying that the Charter "conforms to the spirit of [the] contemporary international human rights movement, and it incorporates many of the policies and prescriptions of the various international documents pertaining to human rights."[31] Similarly, Cumming J of the Ontario Superior Court of Justice in *Mack v Canada (Attorney General)* observed, "Undoubtedly, the Charter gives effect to many of Canada's obligations under international law."[32] These views are strongly supported by the Charter's content and drafting history.

The federal government regards the Charter as one means by which Canadian human rights obligations are implemented in domestic law. Canada has explained to UN treaty bodies that "To some extent, hu-

---

Comparison Between the Canadian Charter of Rights and Freedoms and the International Covenant on Civil and Political Rights" (1982) 8 *Queen's Law Journal* 211.

28 Freeman & van Ert, above note 13 at 188, 545–51.

29 [1984] 1 WWR 625 (Alta CA) at 655.

30 *R v Big M Drug Mart*, [1985] 1 SCR 295 [*Big M Drug Mart*].

31 [1987] 1 SCR 313 [*Re PSERA*] at 348.

32 (2001) 55 OR (3d) 113 (SCJ) at para 35.

man rights treaties are implemented by constitutional law, including the Canadian Charter of Rights and Freedoms."[33] Canada relies heavily on Charter provisions in its reports to the Human Rights Committee and other UN treaty bodies.[34]

I argued in Chapter 7[35] that the question of whether a given law implements a treaty should be approached functionally, not formally. If the provision actually serves to give domestic effect to an international requirement, it can usefully and accurately be said to implement that requirement. One can certainly find reasons not to describe the Charter as implementing legislation for Canadian human rights treaties. For starters, it is not quite legislation: It is entrenched constitutional law adopted by a different process than an ordinary Act of Parliament or of a provincial legislature. More significantly, the Charter clearly does not give domestic effect to all human rights treaties to which Canada is a party. A third point is that the Charter contains provisions that have no international origin, such as the language rights guarantees of sections 16 to 23, as well as provisions that depart from international formulations of the right, such as section 7 (whose "principles of fundamental justice" have no international counterpart) and section 12 (which adopts the Anglo-American formulation of "cruel and unusual treatment or punishment" over the international formulation of "cruel, inhuman or degrading treatment or punishment"). All these points must be conceded. But they do not disprove the contention that the Charter does, to some considerable extent, implement Canadian obligations under international human rights law. Viewed in its totality, the Charter undeniably plays a significant role in securing in Canadian law those human rights of a civil and political character declared in the major UN human rights treaties to which Canada is a party.

None of which means that the judiciary (as distinct from the state) is bound to apply norms of international human rights law. As Dick-

---

33 Canada, *Core Document Forming Part of the Reports of States Parties: Canada* (1998) UN Doc HRI/CORE/1/Add.91 at para 137, reproduced in M Freeman & G van Ert, eds, *International Human Rights Law: Texts, Cases and Materials* (Toronto: Irwin Law, 2005) at 641. See also Canada, *Fourth Periodic Report of Canada to the UN Human Rights Committee*, 15 October 1997, UN Doc CCPR/C/103/Add.5 at para 22.

34 For examples of this, see Freeman & van Ert, above note 13 at 631–71.

35 At Sections 7.2(d) and 7.2(e).

son CJ observed in *Re PSERA*, "I do not believe the judiciary is bound by the norms of international law in interpreting the *Charter*."[36] That statement is certainly sound as a matter of Canadian constitutional law. But whether the judiciary is constitutionally bound by the state's international human rights obligations is a distinct question from whether the Charter implements those obligations. The judiciary is not so bound, yet the Charter enables the state (through its judges) to perform those obligations.[37]

(b) Prior approaches to the Charter and international human rights law

In the first and second editions of this book, I tried to explain the Supreme Court of Canada's jurisprudence on international human rights law and the Charter as revealing three interpretive approaches, which I called the relevant and persuasive approach, the presumption of minimum protection, and the context and values approach.[38]

The relevant and persuasive approach treated international human rights obligations as notable extrinsic materials rather than statements of law binding on Canada. The hallmarks of this approach, I suggested, were (1) that it was comparative in outlook, meaning that it treated international human rights law as no more legally significant in Canada than certain persuasive varieties of foreign law; (2) that it allowed, though without reasoned justification, a liberal use of international sources; and (3) that, intentionally or not, it demonstrated a rather weak commitment to the application of international human rights law in Canada.

The presumption of minimum protection, by contrast, treated Canada's international human rights obligations as a (rebuttable) starting point for the content of Charter rights. This approach revealed the following characteristics: (1) it treated international human rights norms as presumptively respected by the Charter; (2) it applied only to international instruments to which Canada is a party; (3) it amounted to the interpretive presumption of conformity with international law

36 *Re PSERA*, above note 31 at 349.

37 The international legal consequences of judicial failure to reach internationally compliant results are noted in Chapter 2, Section 2.1.

38 See G van Ert, *Using International Law in Canadian Courts*, 2d ed (Toronto: Irwin Law, 2008) [van Ert] at 335–51.

while distancing itself from that reception rule;[39] and (4) it required a more serious consideration of international human rights norms, and a greater commitment to assuring their application in Canadian law, than the relevant and persuasive approach.

The context and values approach declined to categorize international human rights law as either persuasive materials or presumptively respected norms, betraying instead an unpredictable, and at times incoherent, flexibility. This approach was less easy to pin down than the first two theories and tended to obscure the legal significance of international human rights obligations by characterizing them as values informing the context of judicial decision making rather than legal norms binding on the state.

The first two approaches originated (I argued) in the dissenting judgment of Dickson CJ (Wilson J concurring) in *Re PSERA*. The third approach could not be clearly associated with a single case, but I pointed in particular to *Suresh v Canada (Minister of Citizenship and Immigration)*, in which the Supreme Court of Canada referred to "Canada's international obligations and values as expressed in '[t]he various sources of international human rights law'"[40] while at the same time opening the door to *refoulement* to torture.[41]

That analysis was, I hope, illuminating at the time. It has become less pertinent, however, with developments in the 2010s and since. I therefore offer the following revised account of the reception of international law, and particularly international human rights law, through the Charter today.

---

39 With one qualification, namely that, when applied to the Charter, the presumption of conformity treats international law as a minimum requirement (or "floor") rather than a constraint (or "ceiling"). See *R v Cook*, [1998] 2 SCR 597 [*Cook*] at para 148, Bastarache J concurring ("I would not be inclined to accept that Canada's international law obligations could truncate rights defined by the Charter"); *R v McGregor*, 2023 SCC 4 at para 68, Karakatsanis and Martin JJ concurring ("Rather than presuming conformity, in the *Charter* context we presume that the *Charter* 'provide[s] protection at least as great as that afforded by similar provisions in international human rights documents which Canada has ratified', creating a floor – but not a ceiling – for Charter protections based on binding international human rights instruments").

40 [2002] 1 SCR 3 [*Suresh*] at para 59.

41 Happily, the Supreme Court appears to have shut that door – for good, one hopes – in *Kazemi Estate v Iran* 2014 SCC 62 [*Kazemi Estate*] at para 47.

(c) Ascent of the presumption of conformity

In the second decade of the twenty-first century, a series of Supreme Court of Canada decisions endorsed what I described in the first two editions of this book as the presumption of minimum protection. In *Re PSERA* (1987), Dickson CJ (dissenting) observed:

> The content of Canada's international human rights obligations is, in my view, an important indicia of the meaning of "the full benefit of the *Charter*'s protection." I believe that the *Charter* should generally be presumed to provide protection at least as great as that afforded by similar provisions in international human rights documents which Canada has ratified.[42]

Rather than positing international human rights law as of comparative interest only, this approach treated the Charter as presumptively (but also rebuttably) consistent with Canada's international human rights obligations. The onus of rebutting the presumption rested, it seemed, on the party seeking to limit the right. The chief justice, writing for the majority two years later, affirmed this approach in *Slaight Communications v Davidson*,[43] yet it did not take hold as the Supreme Court's prevailing interpretive approach to the Charter and international human rights law for another 20 years. Also notable is that while Dickson CJ's presumption strongly resembled the presumption of conformity described in Chapter 5, he specifically refrained from describing it in those terms.[44]

In *Health Services and Support-Facilities Subsector Bargaining Association v British Columbia* (2007),[45] McLachlin CJ and LeBel J for the unanimous Supreme Court of Canada, overruling the so-called Labour

---

42 *Re PSERA*, above note 31 at 349.

43 [1989] 1 SCR 1038 [*Slaight*] at 1056.

44 See W Schabas, *International Human Rights Law and the Canadian Charter*, 2d ed (Scarborough, ON: Carswell, 1996) at 37; Schabas & Beaulac, above note 13 at 86–7; A Bayefsky, "International Human Rights Law in Canadian Courts" in B Conforti & F Francioni, eds, *Enforcing International Human Rights in Domestic Courts* (The Hague: Kluwer Law International, 1997) at 318; M Le Bel, "L'interprétation de la Charte canadienne des droits et libertés au regard du droit international des droits de la personne – Critique de la démarche suivie par la Cour suprême du Canada" (1988) 48 *Revue du Barreau* 743 at 766. See also Bayefsky's criticism of this approach in Bayefsky, above note 13 at 85, 95.

45 2007 SCC 27 [*Health Services*].

Trilogy[46] and invoking Dickson CJ's dissent in *Re PSERA*, affirmed that "the *Charter* should be presumed to provide at least as great a level of protection as is found in the international human rights documents that Canada has ratified."[47] Likewise, in *R v Hape* (released a day before *Health Services*), LeBel J for the majority of the court quoted Dickson CJ on the presumption of minimum protection and went on to say that, in interpreting the scope of application of the Charter (section 32), "the courts should seek to ensure compliance with Canada's binding obligations under international law where the express words are capable of supporting such a construction."[48]

Following these two cases came several more in which the Supreme Court of Canada endorsed Dickson CJ's presumption, either strongly[49] or in a more qualified way.[50] Of particular note is *Ktunaxa Nation* (2017), in which McLachlin CJ and Rowe J for the majority of the court noted that application of the presumption of conformity with international law to the Charter was endorsed by Tarnopolsky JA even before *Re PSERA*, and described Dickson CJ's dissent in that case as "propos[ing], as Tarnopolsky J.A. had done, that the *Charter* be presumed to provide at least as great a level of protection as is found in Canada's international human rights obligations."[51] The learned judges proceeded to affirm that the Supreme Court of Canada "has since adopted this interpretive

46 *Re PSERA*, above note 31; *Public Service Alliance of Canada v Canada*, [1987] 1 SCR 424; and *Retail, Wholesale and Department Store Union v Saskatchewan*, [1987] 1 SCR 460.

47 *Health Services*, above note 45 at para 70.

48 *R. v Hape*, 2007 SCC 26 at paras 55–6.

49 *Divito v Canada*, 2013 SCC 47 at paras 22, 23, and 25; *Saskatchewan Federation of Labour v Saskatchewan*, 2015 SCC 4 at para 64; *India v Badesha*, 2017 SCC 44 at para 38. See also *Loyola High School v Quebec (Attorney General)*, 2015 SCC 12 at para 97, McLachlin CJ, Moldaver J concurring; *Henry v BC (Attorney General)*, 2015 SCC 24 at para 136, McLachlin CJ, Karakatsanis J concurring.

50 *Ontario (Attorney General) v Fraser*, 2011 SCC 20 at para 92 (where the majority insists that Charter rights "*must* be interpreted in light of Canadian values and Canada's international human rights commitments" without repeating Dickson CJ's formulation that the Charter should be presumed to provide at least as great a level of protection as is found in the international human rights documents that Canada has ratified); *Kazemi Estate*, above note 41 at para 150 (where the endorsement seems somewhat less enthusiastic).

51 *Ktunaxa Nation v British Columbia (Forest, Lands and Natural Resource Operations)*, 2017 SCC 54 [*Ktunaxa Nation*] at para 65, citing *R v Videoflicks Ltd* (1984), 48 OR (2d) 395 (CA) at 421.

presumption"[52] and described it as the presumption of conformity.[53] As discussed immediately below, the Supreme Court of Canada's embrace of the presumption of conformity with international law in the Charter context was confirmed in two decisions of the early 2020s.

(d) Reception of international law through the Charter today

In *Quebec (Attorney General) v 9147-0732 Québec inc*,[54] Brown and Rowe JJ for the majority of the Supreme Court of Canada gave a comprehensive and somewhat novel account of the relevance of public international law, particularly international human rights law, in Charter interpretation. That decision, supported by the court's subsequent application of it in *R v Bissonnette*,[55] must now be regarded as the leading authority. While it may be too soon to say that *Quebec Numbered Co.* has settled the issue, that does seem to have been the majority's ambition.

The appeal concerned a Quebec company that sought to avert liability for a regulatory fine on the basis of section 12 of the Charter, "Everyone has the right not to be subjected to any cruel and unusual treatment or punishment." This adventurous argument was, surprisingly, accepted by a majority of the Quebec Court of Appeal. The Supreme Court of Canada unanimously reversed that determination, concluding that "corporations lie beyond section 12's protective scope" and that section 12 is a protection that "only human beings can enjoy."[56] Yet the Supreme Court split deeply on the question of how courts may use international law, and also foreign law, in interpreting the Charter. There were three sets of reasons: Brown and Rowe JJ (Wagner CJ, Moldaver and Côté JJ concurring); Abella J (Karakatsanis and Martin JJ concurring); and Kasirer J (who made no comment on the international legal issues).

While Brown and Rowe JJ gave the majority judgment, it reads as a rebuttal of Abella J's reasons, so it is best to start with her. Justice Abella affirmed the purposive approach to Charter rights set out in *Big M Drug Mart*: "The meaning of a right or freedom guaranteed by the

52 *Ktunaxa Nation*, *ibid*.
53 *Ibid* at para 66.
54 2020 SCC 32 [*Quebec Numbered Co.*].
55 2022 SCC 23 [*Bissonnette*].
56 *Quebec Numbered Co.*, above note 54 at paras 1, 51.

Charter was to be ascertained by an analysis of the purpose of such a guarantee; it was to be understood, in other words, in the light of the interests it was meant to protect."[57] She described "the principles and values underlying the enactment of the *Charter* provision" as "the primary interpretive tools" and the Charter's text as "only the beginning of the interpretive exercise."[58] She described a "complete lack of support in our jurisprudence for an approach to constitutional interpretation focused on the primacy of the text" and observed that the text of Charter provisions may "be of comparatively limited assistance in interpreting their scope."[59] In Abella J's view, the "living tree" approach to the Charter explains Canada's willingness to consider foreign jurisprudence and international instruments in Charter interpretation.[60]

Having laid out these principles, Abella J returned to the case before her. After considering dictionary definitions of cruelty[61] and the origins of section 12 in the English Bill of Rights,[62] the Eighth Amendment of the US Constitution, and section 2(b) of the Canadian Bill of Rights, Abella J turned to consider prohibitions of cruelty in international instruments and the decisions of international and foreign tribunals.[63] From the outset she affirmed that "both those sources which are binding and those which are not have proven to be indispensable in almost all areas of the law."[64] She added:

> This Court has never required that these sources be sorted by weight before being considered; nor has it ever applied the kind of hierarchical sliding scale of persuasiveness proposed by the majority, segmenting non-binding international and comparative sources into categories worthy of more or less influence. This Court has had no difficulty in the past in deciding which sources it finds to be more relevant and persuasive than others without using a confusing multi-category chart.[65]

---

57 *Ibid* at para 68, quoting *Big M Drug Mart*, above note 30 at 344.
58 *Ibid* at paras 70–1.
59 *Ibid* at para 74.
60 *Ibid* at para 79.
61 *Ibid* at paras 82–7.
62 Bill of Rights 1689 (UK), 1 William & Mary, sess 2, c 2, art 10.
63 *Quebec Numbered Co.*, above note 54 at paras 98–117.
64 *Ibid* at para 100.
65 *Ibid* at para 104.

The learned judge went on to review article 5 of the UDHR, article 7 of the ICCPR, article 5(2) of the American Convention on Human Rights 1969,[66] and article 3 of the European Convention on Human Rights 1950.[67] She noted that while the European Convention has been interpreted to include corporate rights, that treaty's prohibition of torture or inhuman or degrading treatment or punishment has been held not to apply to corporations.[68] She also noted that CAT article 16(1) has never been extended to include corporations.[69] She then turned to foreign law, specifically section 12(1)(e) of the South African Constitution and section 9 of the New Zealand Bill of Rights Act 1990.[70] From this review of international and foreign sources, Abella J concluded that it is "widely acknowledged that the right to be free from cruel and unusual punishment is intended to protect human dignity by prohibiting degrading, inhuman, or dehumanizing treatment or punishment that causes physical or mental pain and suffering."[71]

Justice Abella's analysis did not wholly eschew the distinction between binding and non-binding sources of international law. She observed that the latter are "'relevant and persuasive', not obligatory. Simply put, such sources *attract* adherence rather than command it."[72] That said, her approach is clearly ecumenical. Notably, it does not rest either on the presumption of conformity with international law or the presumption of minimum protection enunciated by Dickson CJ in *Re PSERA*.

Returning now to the majority's reasons, Brown and Rowe JJ agreed with Abella J's result but claimed to "differ fundamentally" from her "on the prominence she gives to international and comparative law in the interpretive process."[73] They saw no need "to dispose of this matter by referring extensively to international and comparative

---

66 1144 UNTS 123.

67 213 UNTS 221.

68 *Quebec Numbered Co.*, above note 54 at paras 114–15, citing *Kontakt-Information-Therapie v Austria*, Application No 11921/86, 12 October 1988, DR 57 at 81 and *Identoba v Georgia*, Application No 73235/12, 12 May 2015 (HUDOC) at para 45.

69 *Ibid* at para 117.

70 *Ibid* at paras 118–22.

71 *Ibid* at para 123.

72 *Ibid* at para 102.

73 *Ibid* at para 19.

law."[74] And they disputed Abella J's "claim that all international and comparative sources have been 'indispensable' to Canadian constitutional interpretation."[75] The Charter, according to the majority, was "made in Canada" – a claim that is more rhetorical than it is faithful to the Charter's drafting history – and is "primarily interpreted with regards to Canadian law and history."[76] More substantively, Brown and Rowe JJ insisted that "If [international and comparative] sources are to be accorded a persuasive character, it must be done by way of a coherent and consistent methodology."[77] They criticized Abella J's approach for "indiscriminately drawing from binding instruments *and* non-binding instruments, instruments that pre-date the *Charter and* instruments that post-date it, and decisions of international tribunals and foreign domestic courts."[78]

The learned judges for the majority of the court went on to provide an account of the relevance of international law in Charter interpretation that distinguishes binding from non-binding instruments, affirms the *Re PSERA* presumption (which they describe as the presumption of conformity), and casts international legal considerations in a supporting, rather than starring, role. These features of *Quebec Numbered Co.*, later affirmed in *Bissonnette*, are described in the discussion that follows.

(i) Distinction between binding and non-binding norms

The majority of the court in *Quebec Numbered Co.* insisted that different interpretive value must be accorded to international norms according to their legal status for Canada. Brown and Rowe JJ observed:

> Although this Court has been careful to attach the appropriate weight to international and comparative law in Charter interpretation, it has not always explained how or why different international sources are being discussed or relied on, while others are not. The result has been a want of clarity, even confusion, to which, we say with respect, our colleague Abella J. adds by indiscriminately drawing from binding

74 *Ibid* at para 5.
75 *Ibid* at para 19.
76 *Ibid* at para 20.
77 *Ibid* at para 3.
78 *Ibid* at para 24.

> instruments and non-binding instruments, instruments that pre-date the Charter and instruments that post-date it, and decisions of international tribunals and foreign domestic courts. . . .
>
> . . . [T]he various instruments and case law our colleague Abella J. reviews play different roles in the analysis and receive different weight. Treating them all alike – stating that each is "indispensable" and provides "compelling and relevant interpretive support" (at paras. 100 and 107) – actually risks *undermining* the importance of Canada's international obligations:
>
>> The temptation may be great to treat all international law, whether binding on Canada or not, as "optional information" and to disregard the particular interpretative onus that is placed upon courts by the presumption of conformity with Canada's international obligations. There is a significant difference between international law that is binding on Canada and other international norms. The former is not only potentially persuasive but also obligatory. This distinction matters – when we fail to uphold our obligations, we undermine the respect for law internationally. The distinction also provides the rationale for the traditional common law presumption of conformity with Canada's international obligations as well as for treating differently international norms that do not legally bind Canada.
>
> (J. Brunnée and S. J. Toope, "A Hesitant Embrace: The Application of International Law by Canadian Courts" (2002), 40 *Can. Y.B. Intl Law* 3, at p. 41 (emphasis added); see also J. H. Currie, *Public International Law* (2nd ed. 2008), at p. 260.)[79]

Later in their reasons, the majority affirmed that "binding instruments necessarily carry more weight in the analysis than non-binding instruments."[80]

This approach is broadly similar to, and may indeed be quite directly inspired by, the dissent of Rothstein and Wagner JJ in *Saskatchewan Federation of Labour v Saskatchewan*.[81] There, in refutation of the majority's reliance on international labour law norms that Abella J depicted as mandating recognition of the right to strike as part of a meaningful

79 *Ibid* at paras 24–5 (emphasis in original).
80 *Ibid* at para 38.
81 Above note 49.

process of collective bargaining,[82] the dissenting justices emphasized the unclear state of international law on the right to strike.[83] Turning next to the relative significance of international sources for domestic interpretive purposes, Rothstein and Wagner JJ invoked the court's prior jurisprudence that "obligations under international law that are *binding* on Canada are of primary relevance to this Court's interpretation of the *Charter*" and that "While other sources of international law can have some persuasive value in appropriate circumstances, they should be granted much less weight than sources under which Canada is bound."[84] They added, pointedly, that "Judicial review and the use of international law as an interpretive aid should not become a euphemism for this Court interfering in the government's prerogative over foreign affairs."[85]

Returning to *Quebec Numbered Co.*, the majority's insistence on differentiating binding and non-binding norms in the course of Charter analysis, and giving greater weight to the former, is to be welcomed. It is in keeping with international law's distinction between *lex lata* and *lex ferenda* (the law as it is and the law as it should be), with the common law's distinct approaches to international and foreign law, and with the presumption of conformity with international law as applied by Canadian courts in non-Charter cases. It is, furthermore, an approach long advocated by commentators for these reasons.[86]

(ii) Presumptive conformity with binding norms

Quebec Numbered Co. affirmed the presumptive conformity of the Charter's protections with Canada's international human rights obligations as first enunciated by Dickson CJ in *Re PSERA*. Brown and Rowe JJ noted that Dickson CJ's decision distinguished between non-binding sources and "international human rights documents which Canada has ratified," observing that "This proposition has since become a firmly established interpretive principle in *Charter* interpretation, the presump-

82 *Ibid* at para 62.
83 *Ibid* at paras 150–5.
84 *Ibid* at para 157 (emphasis in original).
85 *Ibid* at para 159, citing *Turp v Canada (Justice)*, 2012 FC 893.
86 See, for example, the discussion in van Ert, above note 38 at 349–51.

tion of conformity."[87] The majority proceeded to emphasize that the presumption applies in respect of binding (i.e., internationally obligatory) instruments only[88] and that it is rebuttable.[89] Similarly in *Bissonnette*, Wagner CJ observed that "Canadian law" (seemingly including the Charter) "is presumed to be in conformity with the commitments set out in" an international treaty ratified by Canada.[90]

(iii) Interpretive relevance of non-binding norms

Relying on *Re PSERA*, the majority in *Quebec Numbered Co.* affirmed that non-binding international human rights sources may be judicially considered in Charter cases as "relevant and persuasive, but not determinative, interpretive tools."[91] Such non-binding instruments are not irrelevant, but their non-binding legal quality must be recognized. The majority pointed to the court's discussion of international legal sources in *Ktunaxa Nation*,[92] noting that the court in that case began with binding instruments, then moved to non-binding ones while "being careful to specify that" the non-binding sources "do not attract the presumption of conformity."[93] Justices Brown and Rowe concluded their discussion of binding and non-binding instruments as follows:

> It follows from all this – and, specifically, from the presumption of conformity – that binding instruments necessarily carry more weight in the analysis than non-binding instruments. While resort may be had to both, courts drawing from a non-binding instrument should be careful to explain why they are drawing on a particular source and how it is being used.[94]

In both *Quebec Numbered Co.* and *Bissonnette*, decisions of international and foreign courts are classified as non-binding sources.[95] This is cer-

---

87 *Quebec Numbered Co.*, above note 54 at para 31, quoting *Re PSERA*, above note 31 at 349.

88 *Ibid* at para 32.

89 *Ibid* at para 34.

90 *Bissonnette*, above note 55 at para 100.

91 *Quebec Numbered Co.*, above note 54 at para 35.

92 Above note 51.

93 *Quebec Numbered Co.*, above note 54 at para 37, quoting *Ktunaxa Nation*, *ibid* at para 66.

94 *Quebec Numbered Co.*, above note 54 at para 38.

95 *Ibid* at para 43; *Bissonnette*, above note 55 at para 103.

tainly accurate in the case of foreign courts; decisions of the domestic courts of foreign states are not in any sense binding on Canadian courts. As for the decisions of international courts, however, more nuance may be called for in particular cases. A decision of an international court or tribunal may indeed be binding on Canada – if it was a party to the dispute.[96] Even when that is not so, the decision of an international court on the meaning of a treaty binding on Canada or a rule of customary international law may be highly authoritative and persuasive. Such a judicial determination ought not to be too readily equated to such non-binding sources as soft law instruments or decisions of foreign courts.

(iv) Use of international law to support or confirm purposive interpretation

Much of the majority's consideration of the reception of international human rights law through the Charter in *Quebec Numbered Co.* drew on principles enunciated in *Re PSERA* and subsequent cases. There was, however, a striking innovation – one that finds no express support in the Supreme Court of Canada's prior jurisprudence. Brown and Rowe JJ observed:

> While this Court has generally accepted that international norms can be considered when interpreting domestic norms, they have typically played a limited role of providing support or confirmation for the result reached by way of purposive interpretation. This makes sense, as Canadian courts interpreting the *Charter* are not bound by the content of international norms. . . .
>
> This Court has recognized a role for international and comparative law in interpreting Charter rights. However, this role has properly been to *support* or *confirm* an interpretation arrived at through the *Big M Drug Mart* approach; the Court has never relied on such tools to define the scope of Charter rights.[97]

It is certainly true that courts interpreting the Charter are not bound (as a matter of domestic law) by Canada's international legal obligations. The state itself is bound, and will be responsible internationally

96 See the discussion in Chapter 2, Section 2.3(d).

97 *Quebec Numbered Co.*, above note 54 at paras 22, 28.

for any breach, including breaches caused by judicial determinations. That reality supports judicial application of the presumption of conformity, but the presumption remains rebuttable. What is less certain in the above-quoted passage is the notion that Supreme Court jurisprudence has limited the interpretive role of international norms in Charter cases to "providing support or confirmation for the result reached by way of purposive interpretation." The court had never enunciated such a limitation before *Quebec Numbered Co.* Neither *Big M Drug Mart* nor *Re PSERA* stated such a rule, and the presumption of conformity as described in other Supreme Court decisions seems at odds with it.

In principle, it is hard to see what is gained by a "support or confirm" limitation on the use of international instruments (particularly binding ones) in Charter interpretation. The whole point of the presumption of conformity is to reach, where possible, interpretations of domestic law that perform and comply with the international obligations freely undertaken by the executive on behalf of the Canadian state in the international legal system. Such compliant results keep Canada onside its international obligations, and thus avoid putting the judiciary at odds with the executive in the conduct of foreign affairs. The presumption is necessarily rebuttable, both in its statutory and constitutional varieties. But there seems no reason in the abstract to insist that the state's international legal obligations may only inform Charter interpretation where they support or confirm reasoning arrived at without consideration of the Charter provision's international context.

The "support or confirm" approach was applied by the Supreme Court of Canada in *Bissonnette*, where it considered the constitutionality of a Criminal Code provision authorizing courts to order that periods of parole ineligibility for murder convictions be served consecutively rather than concurrently.[98] The result in Bissonnette's case (he murdered six people at a mosque in Quebec City) would have been to render him ineligible for parole for 150 years. Chief Justice Wagner for the unanimous Supreme Court of Canada held that a sentence amounting to death in jail was contrary to section 12 of the Charter (freedom from cruel and unusual treatment or punishment). The chief justice reached this conclusion following an analysis of the scope of the impugned provision, Canadian jurisprudence under section 12, and the nature

98 Criminal Code, RSC 1985, c C-46, s 745.51.

of the punishment imposed by the provision. He then found support for it in international and comparative law, "under which a sentence of imprisonment for life without the possibility of parole is generally considered to be incompatible with human dignity."[99] The chief justice's method, it seems, was to reach a conclusion (can we call it preliminary?) about section 12's requirements in the context of the case prior to turning to international and comparative law. He then used these latter sources as support for his conclusion, seeming to give more weight to the binding international sources (the UN Charter 1945,[100] the ICCPR, and the Rome Statute of the International Criminal Court 2000[101]) than the non-binding ones (the European Convention on Human Rights 1950, decisions of international courts, and decisions of foreign courts).[102] International and foreign sources are (rightly) not treated as co-equal, yet both are relegated to a supporting or confirming role.

What, methodologically, is actually happening in *Bissonnette* remains somewhat unclear. The chief justice affirmed the presumption of conformity with international law, but then described that presumption as explaining why the ICCPR is a relevant source for Charter interpretation.[103] This seems at odds with the distinction between the presumption of conformity (applicable to binding international sources) and the weaker relevant and persuasive approach (applicable to non-binding sources). It remains to be seen where the new "support or confirm" approach to international law and Charter interpretation will take us. What *Bissonnette* tells us so far, I suggest, is first that international law is to play a supportive or confirmatory, rather than determinative, role in Charter interpretation, and second that the Supreme Court of Canada remains interested in international norms as factors to consider in Charter interpretation.

(v) Relevance of chronology

The majority in *Quebec Numbered Co.* identified as an "important distinction" whether a given international instrument pre-dates or post-dates the Charter:

---

99 *Bissonnette*, above note 55 at para 98.
100 [1945] Can TS no 7.
101 [2002] Can TS no 13.
102 *Bissonnette*, above note 55 at paras 98–108.
103 *Ibid* at para 100.

> Within the *Big M Drug Mart* approach itself, courts are called on to consider the "historical origins of the concepts enshrined" in the *Charter* when determining the scope of a Charter right: p. 344. International instruments that pre-date the *Charter* can clearly form part of the historical context of a *Charter* right and illuminate the way it was framed. Here, whether Canada is or is not a party to such instruments is less important, as the "drafters of the *Charter* drew on international conventions because they were the best models of rights protection, not because Canada had ratified them" . . . Similarly, it is entirely proper and relevant to consider the *Universal Declaration of Human Rights* . . . which Canada voted to adopt and which inspired the *ICCPR*, the *International Covenant on Economic, Social and Cultural Rights* . . . and related protocols Canada has ratified. . . .
>
> As for instruments that post-date the *Charter*, however, the question becomes once again whether or not they are binding on Canada and, by extension, whether the presumption of conformity is engaged. It can readily be seen that an instrument that post-dates the *Charter* and that does not bind Canada carries much less interpretive weight than one that binds Canada and/or contributed to the development of the *Charter*.[104]

Despite the majority's description of these chronological considerations as important, their practical significance is unclear. For instruments that pre-date the Charter, the majority rightly observes that both binding and non-binding international sources inspired the Charter's drafters. This would seem to negate, or at least temper, the importance of chronological considerations pre-1982. As for post-Charter instruments, the majority's concern appears not to be chronology *per se* but the instrument's legal status for Canada at international law. The clear implication (confirmed in the case law) is that even a post-1982 instrument will attract the presumption of conformity so long as it is binding on Canada and the presumption is not otherwise rebutted. Notably (and commendably), the majority appears to eschew the concern sometimes expressed by commentators that to apply the presumption of conformity in respect of obligations that post-date the Charter permits the federal government effectively to amend the Charter through treaty-making.

---

104 *Quebec Numbered Co.*, above note 54 at paras 41–2.

(e) Merits and problems of the current approach

There is much to be said for the Charter-specific reception rules enunciated in *Quebec Numbered Co.* and *Bissonnette*. The merits of the newly settled scheme include certainty (the absence of which has bedeviled the jurisprudence for decades), a suitable insistence on the greater interpretive weight to be afforded to binding instruments and norms (i.e., Canada's actual legal obligations), and endorsement of the presumption of conformity with international law (properly varied in the Charter context to be a floor for human rights protection but not a ceiling).

Yet there are potential problems in the court's new approach. First, both *Quebec Numbered Co.* and *Bissonnette* appear, in places, to equate the decisions of international courts with those of foreign courts. A Canadian court's interest in foreign jurisprudence on questions of foreign law is necessarily purely comparative. Where, however, an international tribunal or foreign court is considering the requirements of international human rights standards applicable to Canada (for instance under a shared treaty obligation), our courts' interest must be heightened, as explained in *Office of the Children's Lawyer v Balev*[105] and similar authorities.[106] There is room in the *Quebec Numbered Co.* approach for greater attentiveness to international and foreign decisions that consider shared human rights obligations. Future applications of *Quebec Numbered Co.* will, one hopes, allow for this.

A second potential problem lies in the new "support or confirm" limitation on the use of international norms in Charter interpretation. Restricting international norms to the secondary role of supporting or confirming a result already reached without reference to them is at odds with the Supreme Court of Canada's repeated affirmations, in respect of ordinary statutes, that laws are to be interpreted in their entire context including the values and principles of customary and conventional international law. This inconsistency is not necessarily objectionable, for the Charter is no ordinary statute. But an interpretive method that leaves international legal considerations out of the analysis until a (tentative?) interpretive conclusion is reached seems more likely to generate internationally non-compliant results and therefore

---

105 2018 SCC 16, see especially paras 33, 49, 50.

106 See the discussion in Chapter 8, Section 8.2(b).

greater risk of "incursion by the courts in the executive's conduct of foreign affairs and censure under international law."[107]

Whether the new "support or confirm" restraint does in fact produce non-compliant results remains to be seen. The real test will come when the new approach produces an interpretation of the Charter that is at odds with Canada's international obligations. Will a court, in such circumstances, correct course by applying the presumption of conformity with international law? Or will it find the presumption rebutted? This scenario may never arise; it is rare for international human rights law to be ahead of Charter jurisprudence. The "support or confirm" restriction, twinned as it is with the presumption of conformity, may never give rise to the dilemma I am imagining here. But it does seem to open the door to it.

11.3 Reception roles of specific Charter provisions

The Supreme Court of Canada has identified specific roles for international human rights obligations in relation to sections 7 and 1 of the Charter. And the Charter itself speaks of international law in section 11(g).

(a) Section 7

Charter section 7 provides,

Everyone has the right to life, liberty and security of the person and the right not to be deprived thereof except in accordance with the principles of fundamental justice.	Chacun a droit à la vie, à la liberté et à la sécurité de sa personne; il ne peut être porté atteinte à ce droit qu'en conformité avec les principes de justice fondamentale.

Broadly speaking, section 7 has two elements: life, liberty, and security of the person; and the principles of fundamental justice. The first element repeats the wording of UDHR article 3 and resembles other international instruments. By contrast, the phrase "principles of fundamental justice" is not to be found in international instruments; it is

107 *B010 v Canada (Citizenship and Immigration)*, 2015 SCC 58 at para 47.

original to Canadian law.[108] Yet it is this second element of section 7 that the Supreme Court of Canada has explained in part by reference to international law.

In *Re Motor Vehicle Act* (1985), Lamer J (as he then was) observed that the principles of fundamental justice "have found expression in the international conventions on human rights."[109] The Supreme Court of Canada affirmed that "international law and opinion is of use to the courts in elucidating the scope of fundamental justice" in *United States of America v Burns* (2001),[110] relying on *Re Motor Vehicle Act*, *Slaight Communications*, and *Re PSERA*. The court expanded on Lamer J's *dictum* in *Suresh v Canada (Minister of Citizenship and Immigration)* (2002), saying that the inquiry into the principles of fundamental justice is informed "not only by Canadian experience and jurisprudence, but also by international law, including *jus cogens*."[111] Where Lamer J looked only to human rights treaties, the *Suresh* court was now prepared to look to custom as well. The court added the following explanation of the role of international law in elucidating principles of fundamental justice:

> International treaty norms are not, strictly speaking, binding in Canada unless they have been incorporated into Canadian law by enactment. However, in seeking the meaning of the Canadian Constitution, the courts may be informed by international law. Our concern is not with Canada's international obligations *qua* obligations; rather, our concern is with the principles of fundamental justice. We look to international law as evidence of these principles and not as controlling in itself.[112]

In *Canada (Prime Minister) v Khadr* (2010), the Supreme Court of Canada affirmed that the principles of fundamental justice "take into account

108 The phrase seems to have first appeared in s 1(a) of the Canadian Bill of Rights.

109 *Re Motor Vehicle Act (British Columbia) s. 94(2)*, [1985] 2 SCR 486 at 503; see also 512.

110 [2001] 1 SCR 283 [*Burns*] at paras 79–80.

111 *Suresh*, above note 40 at para 46.

112 *Ibid* at para 60.

Canada's obligations and values, as expressed in the various sources of international human rights law by which Canada is bound."[113]

Early in the current century, the Supreme Court of Canada elaborated a test against which to measure novel fundamental justice claims. Principles of fundamental justice have three characteristics: (1) they must be legal principles, (2) there must be significant societal consensus that they are fundamental to the way in which the legal system ought fairly to operate, and (3) they must be sufficiently precise so as to yield a manageable standard against which to measure deprivations of life, liberty, or security of the person.[114] In *Canadian Foundation* (2003), the court rejected the argument that the best interests of the child principle, expressed in CRC article 3(1) and elsewhere, was a principle of fundamental justice. The majority found the rule to be a legal principle capable of sufficiently precise identification and application to be a principle of fundamental justice, but concluded that it lacked the necessary degree of "consensus that the principle is vital or fundamental to our societal notion of justice."[115] Chief Justice McLachlin noted that while the principle is widely supported in legislation and social policy, it may be "subordinated to other concerns in appropriate contexts." The chief justice relied on article 3(1), in which the principle is described as "a primary consideration" rather than "the primary consideration" in all actions concerning children.[116]

In *R v DB* (2008), Abella J for the majority of the Supreme Court of Canada affirmed, as a principle of fundamental justice, a presumption of diminished moral culpability for young persons in sentencing. In reaching this result she relied in part on the principle's expression in CRC article 40 and international practice.[117]

In *Kazemi Estate v Iran* (2014), LeBel J for the majority of the Supreme Court of Canada insisted that international legal requirements

---

113 2010 SCC 3 at para 23. The extent to which the Court in *Khadr* lived up to this statement is rather doubtful. See G van Ert, "Torture and the Supreme Court of Canada" (2014) 65 *University of New Brunswick Law Journal* 21.

114 *R v Malmo-Levine; R v Caine*, [2003] 3 SCR 571 at para 113; *Canada (Attorney General) v Federation of Law Societies of Canada*, 2015 SCC 7 at para 87.

115 *Canadian Foundation for Children, Youth and the Law v Canada (Attorney General)*, 2004 SCC 4 at para 8.

116 *Ibid* at para 10.

117 2008 SCC 25 at paras 60, 67.

do not become principles of fundamental justice by virtue merely of their international obligatoriness:

> When a party points to a provision in an international treaty as evidence of a principle of fundamental justice, a court must determine (a) whether there is significant international consensus regarding the interpretation of the treaty, and (b) whether there is consensus that the particular interpretation is fundamental to the way in which the international legal system ought to fairly operate. . . . The absence of such consensus weighs against finding that the principle is fundamental to the operation of the legal system. . . .
>
> . . . [T]he existence of an article in a treaty ratified by Canada does not automatically transform that article into a principle of fundamental justice.[118]

Notably, however, these words of caution did not discourage the court, in *Canada (Attorney General) v Federation of Law Societies of Canada* (2015), from affirming that an "important indicator that a proposed rule or principle is a legal principle is that it is used as a rule or test in common law, statutory law or international law" and looking to international and comparative norms around state interference with legal representation.[119]

In *India v Badesha* (2017), Moldaver J for the unanimous Supreme Court of Canada affirmed that "In extradition cases, s. 7 of the Charter should be presumed to provide at least as great a level of protection as found in Canada's international commitments regarding non-refoulement to torture or other gross human rights violations." He continued that, given the prohibition on refoulement in CAT article 3(1), "in the extradition context, surrendering a person to face a substantial risk of torture or mistreatment in the requesting state will violate the principles of fundamental justice."[120]

It is difficult to imagine how a person might be deprived of life, liberty, or security of the person contrary to international law but consistently with the principles of fundamental justice. The Supreme Court of Canada's elaboration of a role for international law in the de-

118 Above note 41 at paras 147, 149.

119 Above note 114 at para 91; see also paras 101–2.

120 Above note 49 at para 38.

termination of the principles of fundamental justice is therefore eminently sensible.

(b) Section 11(g)

The only provision of the Charter to make express reference to international law is section 11(g), which provides:

Any person charged with an offence has the right . . . not to be found guilty on account of any act or omission unless, at the time of the act or omission, it constituted an offence under Canadian or international law or was criminal according to the general principles of law recognized by the community of nations;	Tout inculpé a le droit : . . . de ne pas être déclaré coupable en raison d'une action ou d'une omission qui, au moment où elle est survenue, ne constituait pas une infraction d'après le droit interne du Canada ou le droit international et n'avait pas de caractère criminel d'après les principes généraux de droit reconnus par l'ensemble des nations;

This rule against retroactive offences closely resembles prohibitions found in UDHR article 11(2)[121] and ICCPR article 15.[122] One effect of section 11(g) seems to be that if an act is a criminal offence under international law, but not under Canadian law, Parliament may criminalize that offence retroactively.

Unsurprisingly, there is little jurisprudence on section 11(g). In *R v Finta*, Cory J for the majority of the Supreme Court of Canada observed that section 11(g) "allows customary international law to form a basis for the prosecution of war criminals who have violated general principles of law recognized by the community of nations regardless

121 The provision reads in part, "No one shall be held guilty of any penal offence on account of any act or omission which did not constitute a penal offence, under national or international law, at the time when it was committed."

122 The provision reads in part (at para 1), "No one shall be held guilty of any criminal offence on account of any act or omission which did not constitute a criminal offence, under national or international law, at the time when it was committed" and (at para 2), "Nothing in this article shall prejudice the trial and punishment of any person for any act or omission which, at the time when it was committed, was criminal according to the general principles of law recognized by the community of nations."

of when or where the criminal act or omission took place" and that the "use of international legal principles to ground jurisdiction for criminal activity committed outside of Canada has thus been constitutionally permissible since 1982."[123] Justice La Forest (dissenting) found that the Criminal Code provisions challenged by Finta did not violate section 11(g) as being retroactive in part because that provision "specifically refers to the permissibility of conviction on the basis of international law or the general principles of law recognized by the community of nations."[124]

(c) Section 1

Charter section 1 provides:

The Canadian Charter of Rights and Freedoms guarantees the rights and freedoms set out in it subject only to such reasonable limits prescribed by law as can be demonstrably justified in a free and democratic society.	La Charte canadienne des droits et libertés garantit les droits et libertés qui y sont énoncés. Ils ne peuvent être restreints que par une règle de droit, dans des limites qui soient raisonnables et dont la justification puisse se démontrer dans le cadre d'une société libre et démocratique.

The section serves to define acceptable limitations to Charter rights.[125] The test for whether infringement of a Charter right is justified under section 1, known as the *Oakes* test, asks first whether the legislative objective pursued by the impugned provision is pressing and substantial, and second whether there is proportionality between that objective and the means used to achieve it. This proportionality analysis is in three branches. First, there must be a rational connection between the limit on the Charter right and the legislative objective. Second, the limit must impair the right or freedom only minimally, that is, no more than reasonably necessary to accomplish the objective. Third, at the

123 *R v Finta*, [1994] 1 SCR 701 at 807.

124 *Ibid* at 784 (emphasis removed).

125 On similarities between Charter s 1 and leading international instruments, see Schabas & Beaulac, above note 13 at 255–91.

final balancing stage, there must be proportionality between the deleterious and salutary effects of the law.[126]

It is clear that international law can be invoked to justify limitations of Charter rights in accordance with section 1. In the leading case, *R v Oakes* (1986), Dickson CJ invoked two treaties on the international drugs trade[127] to support the view that Parliament's objective in legislating a "reverse onus" provision in anti-narcotics legislation was pressing and substantial, as required by the first branch of what is now known as the *Oakes* test.[128] Thus a party seeking to justify the infringement of a Charter right may do so by resort to international law. The international law invoked need not necessarily be a human rights treaty, as *Oakes* demonstrates.[129]

In *Slaight Communications v Davidson* (1989), Dickson CJ again observed that international law may be used to justify limitations of Charter rights under section 1. Here, however, the chief justice spoke specifically of international human rights:

> Given the dual function of s. 1 identified in *Oakes*, Canada's international human rights obligations should inform not only the interpretation of the content of the rights guaranteed by the Charter but also the interpretation of what can constitute pressing and substantial s. 1 objectives which may justify restrictions upon those rights. Furthermore, for the purposes of this stage of the proportionality

126 See, e.g., *Canada (Attorney General) v Hislop*, 2007 SCC 10 at para 44; *Carter v Canada (Attorney General)*, 2015 SCC 5 at para 94; *Conseil scolaire francophone de la Colombie-Britannique v British Columbia*, 2020 SCC 13 at paras 145–6; etc.

127 Protocol for Limiting and Regulating the Cultivation of the Poppy Plant, the Production of, International and Wholesale Trade in, and Use of Opium 1953, (1963) 456 UNTS 56, and the Single Convention on Narcotic Drugs 1961, [1964] Can TS no 30.

128 *R v Oakes*, [1986] 1 SCR 103 at 140–1. The chief justice went on to find that the impugned provision did not survive the rational connection test.

129 This was disputed by Bastarache J (Gonthier J concurring) in *Cook*, above note 39. At para 147, the learned judge opposed the use of international law of a non-human rights character to limit Charter rights, arguing that "using international law as an interpretative aid in defining the content of the various rights in the *Charter* is an entirely different exercise from using non-human rights aspects of international law to circumscribe the *Charter* as a whole." With respect, the position enunciated in *Oakes* is generally to be preferred, for the *Cook* argument would tolerate interpretations of the Charter that violate general international law.

> inquiry, the fact that a value has the status of an international human right, either in customary international law or under a treaty to which Canada is a state party, should generally be indicative of a high degree of importance attached to that objective.[130]

Applying this *dictum*, Dickson CJ considered international instruments at length in his section 1 analysis for the majority in *R v Keegstra* (1990), concluding,

> Canada, along with other members of the international community, has indicated a commitment to prohibiting hate propaganda, and in my opinion this Court must have regard to that commitment in investigating the nature of the government objective behind s. 319(2) of the Criminal Code. That the international community has collectively acted to condemn hate propaganda, and to oblige State Parties to CERD and ICCPR to prohibit such expression, thus emphasizes the importance of the objective behind s. 319(2) and the principles of equality and the inherent dignity of all persons that infuse both international human rights and the Charter.[131]

Similarly, in the companion case of *Canada (Human Rights Commission) v Taylor* (1990), Dickson CJ observed:

> The stance taken by the international community in protecting human rights is relevant in reviewing legislation under s. 1, and especially in assessing the significance of a government objective. . . . Both Article 4 of the International Convention on the Elimination of All Forms of Racial Discrimination . . . and Article 20 of the International Covenant on Civil and Political Rights . . . as well as the jurisprudence of the European Convention for the Protection of Human Rights and Fundamental Freedoms . . . demonstrate that the commitment of the international community to eradicate discrimination extends to the prohibition of the dissemination of ideas based on racial or religious superiority.[132]

---

130 *Slaight*, above note 43 at 1056–7.

131 *R v Keegstra*, [1990] 3 SCR 697 at 754–5; see also 749–55.

132 [1990] 3 SCR 892 at 919–20. See also *Ross v New Brunswick School District No 15*, [1996] 1 SCR 825, La Forest J at paras 97–8 and *Saskatchewan (Human Rights Commission) v Whatcott*, 2013 SCC 11, Rothstein J at para 67, both relying on *Taylor* on this point.

The role of international human rights laws in justifying Charter breaches was recognized again, by the majority and dissent, in *R v Zundel* (1992).[133] The majority held that the false news provision of the Criminal Code[134] was an unconstitutional violation of the freedom of expression guarantee in Charter section 2(b). In coming to this finding, McLachlin J (as she then was) noted that

> no suggestion has been made before this Court that Canada's obligations under the international human rights conventions to which it is a signatory require the enactment of any provision(s) other than that section which was under review in *Keegstra*: s. 319. The retention of s. 181 is not therefore necessary to fulfil any international obligation undertaken by Parliament.[135]

The dissent would have upheld section 181 as justifiable in the light of Canada's commitments under the ICCPR and the CERD.[136]

In *R v Lucas* (1998), Cory J for the majority of the Supreme Court of Canada upheld defamatory libel provisions of the Criminal Code as justifiable limits on free expression. Among the considerations supporting these provisions' pressing and substantial objective was the fact that "a number of international conventions . . . contain explicit limitations of freedom of expression in order to protect the rights and reputations of individuals." After citing such instruments, Cory J observed that the "existence of these provisions reflects a consensus within the international community that the protection of reputation is an objective sufficiently important to warrant placing some restrictions upon freedom of expression."[137]

In *Lavoie v Canada* (2002) the Supreme Court divided deeply on the constitutionality of preferential treatment of Canadian citizens by the federal Public Service Employment Act.[138] Justice Bastarache for the plurality of the court (four of nine judges) concluded that the impugned provision infringed the equality guarantee of section 15(1) of the Charter but was a reasonable limit on equality demonstrably justi-

---

133 [1992] 2 SCR 731 [*Zundel*].

134 Above note 98, s 181, repealed by 2019, c 25, s 62.

135 *Zundel*, above note 133 at 764.

136 *Ibid* at 811.

137 *R v Lucas*, [1998] 1 SCR 439 at para 50.

138 SC 2003, c 22.

fied in a free and democratic society under section 1. The learned judge observed that a law is not non-discriminatory "because it reflects an international consensus as to the appropriate limits on equality rights" – yet such a consensus was a "highly relevant" consideration at the section 1 stage of the analysis. Justice Bastarache went on to observe that Parliament's approach was supported by "widespread international practice" of imposing citizenship-based restrictions on access to the public service.[139]

Just as international law may be invoked to justify limitations on Charter rights, there is also authority that considerations of international comity may be used in section 1 analyses. In *United States of America v Burns* (2001), the Supreme Court of Canada, in considering whether extradition of two Canadians to the United States to face the death penalty was justifiable under section 1, observed that "there is no doubt that it is important for Canada to maintain good relations with other states."[140] Yet the court held that the means employed in the case at bar (namely, extradition without assurances from the United States that the death penalty would not be sought) were not necessary to further the objective of comity.[141] Similarly, Jamal J for the court in *Canadian Council for Refugees* (2023) observed that, had a section 7 breach been made out in that case, a contextual approach to section 1 "would likely consider international comity and the sovereignty of foreign states."[142]

11.4 Human rights as public policy

International human rights instruments and norms are sometimes looked to by courts as evidence of Canadian public policy. In *Re Drummond Wren*,[143] a covenant in a deed of land required that it not be "sold to Jews or persons of objectionable nationality." A motion was brought

139 *Lavoie v Canada*, 2002 SCC 23 at paras 48, 56.

140 *Burns*, above note 110 at para 136; see also para 134.

141 Comity was rejected as a ground for justifying Charter violations by Wilson J, dissenting, in *United States of America v Cotroni*, [1989] 1 SCR 1469 at para 96; see also para 85.

142 *Canadian Council for Refugees v Canada (Minister of Citizenship and Immigration)*, 2023 SCC 17 at para 125.

143 [1945] OR 778 (HCJ).

to declare the covenant invalid as contrary to public policy. In granting the motion, Mackay J looked to the recently signed United Nations Charter[144] and the Atlantic Charter (a 1941 joint declaration by the United States and the United Kingdom) as indications of Canada's public policy against racial discrimination. The learned judge wrote:

> That the restrictive covenant in this case is directed in the first place against Jews lends poignancy to the matter when one considers that anti-semitism has been a weapon in the hands of our recently-defeated enemies, and the scourge of the world. But this feature of the case does not require innovation in legal principle to strike down the covenant; it merely makes it more appropriate to apply existing principles.[145]

Doubt was cast on *Re Drummond Wren* in *Re Noble and Wolf,*[146] where a covenant against selling, renting, or otherwise assigning land to "any person of the Jewish, Hebrew, Semitic, Negro or coloured race or blood" was upheld despite its validity being attacked by both the vendor and the purchaser. "It is the province of the statesman," opined Schroeder J, "and not the lawyer, to discuss, and of the Legislature to determine, what is best for the public good."[147] The case went on to the Supreme Court of Canada, where it was disposed of without comment on the public policy argument.[148] Yet in *Bhadauria v Seneca College,*[149] Wilson JA (as she then was) relied on *Re Drummond Wren* without mentioning the contrary authority.[150] On appeal to the Supreme Court of Canada, Laskin CJ declared that "I do not myself quarrel with the approach taken in *Re Drummond Wren,*" yet noted there was authority against it.[151] One

---

144 [1945] Can TS no 7.

145 *Re Drummond Wren*, above note 154 at 783.

146 [1948] OR 579.

147 *Ibid* at 594.

148 *Noble and Wolf v Alley*, [1951] SCR 64.

149 (1980) 27 OR (2d) 142 (CA).

150 *Ibid* at 147–9.

151 *Seneca College v Bhadauria*, [1981] 2 SCR 181 at 192. For a New Zealand authority consistent with *Re Drummond Wren*, see *Van Gorkom v Attorney-General*, [1977] 1 NZLR 535 (Sup Ct) at 542–3.

can hardly doubt today that *Re Drummond Wren* is sound despite *Re Noble and Wolf*.

In *Nevsun Resources Ltd v Araya*, Abella J for the majority of the Supreme Court of Canada considered the English case of *Oppenheimer v Cattermole*, in which the House of Lords refused to recognize and apply a Nazi decree depriving Jews of their citizenship and property. Justice Abella quoted with approval Lord Cross's observation that the Nazi law "constitutes so grave an infringement of human rights that the courts of this country ought to refuse to recognise it as a law at all" and that it is "part of the public policy of this country that our courts should give effect to clearly established rules of international law."[152] The learned judge went on to affirm, in the context of conflict of laws, that there exists "judicial discretion to decline to enforce foreign laws where such laws are contrary to public policy, including respect for public international law."[153] In the light of *Re Drummond Wren*, one may doubt that resort to international human rights law as public policy is limited to private international law cases.

The general proposition that treaties concluded by Canada may be relied upon as statements of Canadian public policy may be questioned so long as treaty-making remains an executive rather than a legislative function. Courts should not, as a rule, look to the executive's prerogative acts as indicators of the values held by Canadian society, for prerogatives have much weaker representative and democratic credentials than legislation and are therefore less likely to reflect Canadian values. There is surely an exception to this rule, however, for human rights treaties. These treaties not only reflect Canadian public policy, as evidenced by our constitutional and statutory human rights guarantees, but are also attempts to depict the legal significance of being human. Canadian public policy must surely encompass conceptions of humanity recognized in international law.

---

152 *Nevsun Resources Ltd v Araya*, 2020 SCC 5 [*Nevsun*] at para 34, quoting *Oppenheimer v Cattermole*, [1976] AC 249 [HL] at 248.

153 *Nevsun*, *ibid* at para 45.

Table of international instruments

Treaties

Other instruments

Table of statutes

Table of cases

International and regional decisions

Canada (including Privy Council appeals from Canada)

United Kingdom (including Privy Council appeals other than from Canada)

Other jurisdictions

Index

About the author

Gib van Ert practises public law and civil litigation in Ottawa and Vancouver. He is a former Executive Legal Officer at the Supreme Court of Canada, where he served as principal advisor to two chief justices, and a former president of the Canadian Council on International Law. He regularly acts in cases involving the reception of public international legal norms in Canadian law.

Printed and bound by CPI Group (UK) Ltd, Croydon, CR0 4YY

15/09/2026

14962403-0003